Withdrawn from
Dublin City Public Libraries

D1434005

# Afghan Crucible

Leabharlanna Poiblí Chathair Baile Átha Cliath
Dublin City Public Libraries

# Afghan Crucible

*The Soviet Invasion and the Making
of Modern Afghanistan*

Elisabeth Leake

OXFORD
UNIVERSITY PRESS

# OXFORD
UNIVERSITY PRESS

Great Clarendon Street, Oxford, OX2 6DP,
United Kingdom

Oxford University Press is a department of the University of Oxford.
It furthers the University's objective of excellence in research, scholarship,
and education by publishing worldwide. Oxford is a registered trade mark of
Oxford University Press in the UK and in certain other countries

© Elisabeth Leake 2022

The moral rights of the author have been asserted

First Edition published in 2022
Impression: 1

All rights reserved. No part of this publication may be reproduced, stored in
a retrieval system, or transmitted, in any form or by any means, without the
prior permission in writing of Oxford University Press, or as expressly permitted
by law, by licence or under terms agreed with the appropriate reprographics
rights organization. Enquiries concerning reproduction outside the scope of the
above should be sent to the Rights Department, Oxford University Press, at the
address above

You must not circulate this work in any other form
and you must impose this same condition on any acquirer

Published in the United States of America by Oxford University Press
198 Madison Avenue, New York, NY 10016, United States of America

British Library Cataloguing in Publication Data
Data available

Library of Congress Control Number: 2021948706

ISBN 978-0-19-884601-7

DOI: 10.1093/oso/9780198846017.001.0001

Printed and bound in Great Britain by
Clays Ltd, Elcograf S.p.A.

Links to third party websites are provided by Oxford in good faith and
for information only. Oxford disclaims any responsibility for the materials
contained in any third party website referenced in this work.

# Acknowledgements

Researching and writing a work of history can at times feel like a solitary process, but bringing this project to fruition has truly been a collective effort, one that has been made even more meaningful after eighteen months of working from home during a pandemic. This book would not have been possible without the generosity and support of many friends and colleagues.

The seeds of this project were sown as I was finishing my Ph.D. at Cambridge, when my supervisor, Christopher Bayly, suggested that a study of the Soviet invasion of Afghanistan was the logical sequel to my research on the Afghan–Pakistan borderlands in the mid-twentieth century. While Chris's passing meant that he never saw any parts of this project, I am forever indebted to his support and I returned frequently to Chris's own writing as I completed the manuscript.

The majority of this project was researched while I was a Leverhulme Early Career Fellow at Royal Holloway, University of London. The Leverhulme Trust's generous funding made much of this book's research possible, while the project's intellectual questions began developing with the support of Sarah Ansari and Francis Robinson. Sarah, in particular, has been a model academic mentor, and I strive to live up to her wise, kind, and generous standards. I completed the book after taking up a permanent position at the University of Leeds. I am grateful to the School of History and Faculty of Arts, Humanities, and Cultures for supporting a year of research leave, in which I drafted the manuscript, and special thanks must go to Simon Ball, then our Director of Research, who helped me scrape together the funding for a final research trip to Moscow. At Leeds, I also teach a final-year, year-long seminar on the histories of Afghanistan and Pakistan, and my students' enthusiasm for the topic has kept my own interests kindled.

I have benefited from Odd Arne Westad's wise counsel since the inception of this project, and his support throughout has been instrumental. Usually during long, wet walks along the Norfolk coastline, accompanied by Tiggy the corgi, Arne pushed me to be ambitious and thorough in my research and writing while also helping me to temper my expectations. He generously read and commented on the entire manuscript and helped me thrash out the broader implications. To say this project would have not come to fruition without Arne's support would be an understatement, and thanks as well to Ingunn Bjornson for her hospitality and patience as Arne and I talked all things Afghanistan and the Cold War.

Special thanks must go to Artemy Kalinovsky, Timothy Nunan, and Benjamin Hopkins. Artemy helped me to navigate the Russian archives (and assuaged my fears about my language skills), provided additional materials and further reading suggestions, and commented on large parts of the manuscript. In conversations over the years, his friendship and own expertise on the Soviet presence in Afghanistan have greatly informed my work. Tim likewise has served as a key interlocutor throughout this project's development. Whether he was inviting me to workshops in Berlin, taking the time to discuss sources and advise on archives, or providing detailed and thoughtful feedback on the manuscript, I have benefited throughout from his generosity and insight. Ben also has been a long-time supporter of this project. Our discussions of Afghan history and ethical research processes have been hugely important, and he, too, read and commented on much of the manuscript.

In August 2020, Cemil Aydin, Jeffrey Byrne, Robert Crews, Daniel Haines, Alessandro Iandolo, and Lydia Walker all kindly took part in a virtual workshop for the project. They offered indispensable feedback on the manuscript, and I was awed and humbled by their generosity of time and thought. I am truly grateful to them and hope I have managed to make the best use of their advice! Other friends and colleagues also have been liberal with their feedback on parts of the manuscript, including Martin Bayly, Amanda Behm, Mark Condos, Sean Fear, Bérénice Guyot-Réchard, Will Jackson, Ria Kapoor, Sarah Miller-Davenport, and Robert Rakove. Thanks as well to Simon Fuchs for his suggestions and help with transliterations. So many other friends and colleagues have provided emotional and intellectual support throughout the entirety of this project that it is impossible to name them all: you know who you are, and thank you! Of course, all errors and shortcomings remain my own.

My particular thanks go to the patient and hard-working librarians and archivists at the Afghanistan Center at Kabul University, the Carter and Reagan Presidential Libraries, US, UK, and Indian National Archives, UN and UNHCR archives, and Russian state archives. Thanks as well to my Leeds colleague Robert Hornsby for generously sharing his research from the Russian State Archive of Socio-Political History and to Hayatullah Beyan for his translation work on several *mujahidin* publications. Finally, special thanks to the Centre of South Asian Studies at the University of Cambridge, where I spent much of my leave writing the book, and particularly to Barbara Roe, Kevin Greenbank, and Rachel Rowe.

Since my undergraduate days, Paul Kennedy has been an unceasing supporter of my work, and it is thanks to him that Andrew Gordon agreed to represent me. Andrew and the David Higham Associates team have been crucial advocates for this project, and Andrew not only provided feedback as the project developed but also pushed me to write in a more accessible way. That this book has found a receptive home at Oxford University Press is due to Andrew and my editor, Luciana O'Flaherty. Many thanks to Luciana for her careful reading of the manuscript, as well as to Kizzy Taylor-Richelieu, Nico Parfitt, and the rest of the OUP team.

Finally, this project would have been unthinkable without the love and support of my family. Since my schooldays, my father, Ray, has read multiple drafts of my work, and *Afghan Crucible* has been no different. His love of history has fueled mine. While my mother, Julie Shimada, prefers to read fiction and says history is 'too dense', it is her passion for social justice and racial equality that has infused my work.

Given the time in which I was writing and the questions of belonging, citizenship, and nationhood that became central to this book, my mind often turned to the experiences of my mother's Japanese American family, who were interned during the Second World War. While their experiences are not comparable with those in and of Afghanistan, reflecting on my family's own history of forced migration, displacement, and discrimination has nevertheless given a greater sense of urgency and compassion to this book.

Throughout this entire process, my partner, Harry, has been my rock. His support, patience, and love have been unceasing, while his now-casual discussions of diasporas and frontiers show that, willingly or not, he has perhaps absorbed a little too much of my work. Harry's faith in the project and in my ambitions has made the difference in this book coming to fruition.

# Contents

# List of Figures

# List of Maps

# List of Abbreviations

| | |
|---|---|
| CENTO | Central Treaty Organization |
| CIA | Central Intelligence Agency |
| CPSU | Communist Party of the Soviet Union |
| DOAW | Democratic Organization of Afghan Women |
| DRA | Democratic Republic of Afghanistan |
| DOMA | Democratic Youth Organization of Afghanistan |
| EEC | European Economic Community |
| GMD | Guomindang |
| IIG | Interim Islamic Government |
| ILO | International Labour Organization |
| ISI | Inter-Services Intelligence, Pakistan |
| KGB | *Komitet Gosudarstvennoy Bezopasnosti* (Committee for State Security) |
| KhAD | *Khadimat-i Atal'at-i Dowlati* (State Information Services) |
| KOAW | Khalqi Organization of Afghan Women |
| NAM | Non-Aligned Movement |
| NFF | National Fatherland Front |
| NGO | non-governmental organization |
| NSC | National Security Council |
| NSDD | National Security Decision Directive |
| NWFP | North-West Frontier Province |
| OIC | Organization of the Islamic Conference |
| PDPA | People's Democratic Party of Afghanistan |
| PLO | Palestine Liberation Organization |
| PRC | People's Republic of China |
| PYO | Progressive Youth Organization |
| RAWA | Revolutionary Association of the Women of Afghanistan |
| RTV | Refugee Tentage Village |
| SWAPO | South West Africa People's Organization |
| UN | United Nations |
| UNGA | UN General Assembly |
| UNGOMAP | UN Good Offices Mission in Afghanistan and Pakistan |
| UNHCR | United Nations High Commissioner for Refugees |
| UNICEF | United Nations International Children's Emergency Fund |
| USIS | US Information Service |
| WFP | World Food Programme |

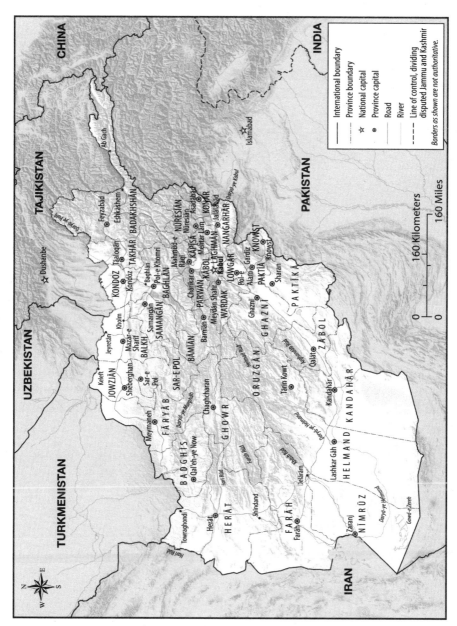

**Map 1.** Map of Afghanistan

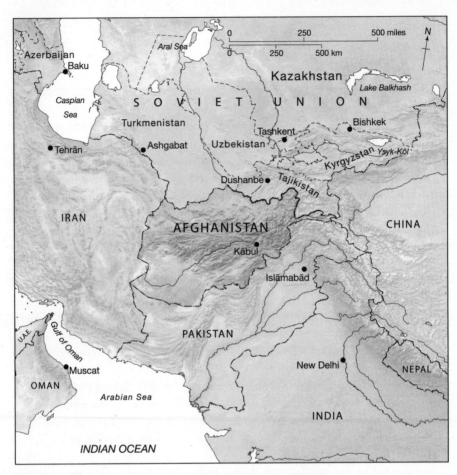

**Map 2.** Map of Afghanistan and neighbouring countries, c.1979

# Prologue

Leabharlann Peambróg
Pembroke Library
01-2228450

The evening of 6 Jaddi 1358 (27 December 1979 in the Gregorian calendar) was dark and harshly cold. For Fatima, a teacher, it was remarkable as a Thursday: in her Kabul neighbourhood, Thursdays meant access to hot water. As she washed her two-month-old daughter's clothes that evening, waiting for her husband, a lieutenant in the Afghan army, to return home for dinner, she became aware of the sound of aircraft and tanks. 'The radio and television stopped broadcasting normal programmes.' Meanwhile, Abdul Ghafoor, a government employee at home in Khair Khana, an area just north of Kabul, 'heard the sound of gunfire and heavy weapons' around 8 p.m., and his cousin stopped by to let him know 'something strange is going on in the city'. That same night, in Kunduz, a city in northern Afghanistan, schoolteacher Abdullah observed 'aircraft passing by in the sky and a white line of their smoke'. Back in Kabul, 22-year-old Laila gave birth to a daughter in a hospital as Soviet tanks and soldiers streamed past: 'People in the hospital, especially the doctors, tried to keep us calm and assured us that it was not a war, but that foreigners had come to Kabul.'[1]

The doctors were both right and wrong; foreigners had indeed come to Kabul. Fifty thousand Soviet troops had poured into the country, beginning on the 24th. Their intention was a quick regime change—the replacement of one leader, Hafizullah Amin, with another, Babrak Karmal. However, they entered a country already at war with itself.

A coup led by the People's Democratic Party of Afghanistan (PDPA), eighteen months before, had created an unexpected but seismic shift in Afghanistan. Upon coming to power, the leaders of the PDPA had announced: 'The last remnants of imperialist tyranny and despotism have been put to an end.'[2] This pronouncement hinted at the aspirations of the PDPA, whose socialist intentions soon became apparent. Afghanistan's new rulers sought the total reshaping of Afghan society and politics: the creation of a new, modern, socialist Afghanistan. However, what might have been just one in a series of twentieth-century coups turned into a civil war. The PDPA disastrously failed to implement its ideas, and armed insurgency broke out almost immediately. A competing set of Afghan leaders emerged who, just like the PDPA, sought to institute their own political systems in Afghanistan. Afghan political parties in exile around Peshawar, Pakistan, decried the socialist takeover and called for *jihad*, holy war. Among these parties were several groups who saw the fight against the PDPA not merely as a chance to prevent the spread of socialism but also as an opportunity to replace it, and Afghanistan's older governing structures, with an Islamist model that was just as radically modern as the PDPA's. What quickly emerged in Afghanistan and its surroundings was not just a fight for control of the

Afghan government. It was a battle between competing political and social aspirations, a battle over the very nature and meaning of Afghan modernity.

The rise of either the PDPA or the Afghan Islamists was not preordained, and indeed both of these groups, in previous decades, had lived at the margins of Afghan politics. Earlier Afghan campaigners from within the government and outside it also had sought to modernize Afghan politics and society, and constitutionalists, parliamentarians, and royalists had led earlier charges to create a more representative and extensive government. But circumstances converged to quash more moderate reformers and bring these two more radical visions of Afghanistan's future to the fore in the 1980s. Local alliances, regional partnerships, international attention, and pure chance helped create a battle between a PDPA state and its Islamist antagonists. The Islamists found supportive allies in Pakistan, Iran, and the Muslim world, while the PDPA's Soviet allies chose to take extreme action to maintain Afghan socialism, launching their invasion in December 1979. The Soviet intervention would explode an already violent conflict into a decades-long war whose ramifications continue to be felt across the world.

The civil war of the 1980s in Afghanistan was an event of not just national or regional but global significance. The quickly shifting international sands in which the PDPA's coup and the subsequent Soviet invasion occurred ensured this. The late 1970s were a unique moment when Cold-War detente was evaporating, political Islam was emerging as a potent force, and crises of state leadership were rampant. An uneasy status quo existed in international relations that quickly tipped into chaos thanks to events in Afghanistan, Iran, and elsewhere. The Afghan civil war attracted interest and actors from across the world. Soviet and American policymakers, officials from the UN and other international organizations, leaders from states such as Pakistan, Iran, India, and China, NGOs from across Europe and North America, and resistance fighters from across the Muslim world converged in Afghanistan because the conflict posed a litmus test for the international order, not just for Afghanistan.

War in Afghanistan raised a fundamental question about the nature of modern statehood and sovereignty. Creating a modern nation state had defined much of Afghanistan's twentieth-century domestic and foreign affairs, but the country succumbed to a horrifically violent war where different Afghans' visions of the world, and Afghanistan's place in it, grew increasingly incompatible. Not only that, but the same international system that required an Afghan nation state to exist allowed the Soviet Union to stage an invasion contrary to international law. But, despite both Soviet intervention and American covert aid, neither Cold-War superpower proved capable of steering Afghanistan's national project and instead only exacerbated the crisis. The war additionally revealed the limitations of international institutions such as the United Nations, which managed to negotiate a Soviet withdrawal but not end the raging war. For both Afghan and international actors, the fight taking place in Afghanistan was about not just the country's own future but the way that international politics could, or should, function at the end of the twentieth century.

Events in Afghanistan signalled broader failings in an international order based on a system of nation states.

What became clear in the days and months following the Soviet invasion was that the civil war had irrevocably transformed the nature of Afghan politics, the future of the Afghan state, and the daily lives of many Afghans. Afghan civilians became increasingly divided, forced to choose between supporting pro- or anti-government forces. 'The major change', Abdullah recalled, 'was a split between family members and relatives. Some of our relatives followed the government, while others either remained neutral or followed the mujahedin.' For his part, he lost his teaching job and was forced to join the government security service and combat the resistance. After eighteen months on a battlefront in Kandahar, Abdullah finally managed to escape to Pakistan, to be joined two years later by his family.

Violence became a part of daily life. Fatima's husband never came home. A week after the Soviets entered the capital, his body was found in a local hospital; he 'had been shot from behind by a Kalashnikov in his office…with one bullet. His name had been registered as the first martyr in the hospital registry.' As conflict raged, families were torn apart, and, increasingly, Afghans had to seek refuge abroad. Laila's husband, a political activist, was imprisoned and disappeared. 'We still have no clue what happened to him.' In the coming years, her father, father-in-law, and two brothers-in-law were also killed. Laila and her children would walk twelve days to a refugee camp in Pakistan before later returning to Afghanistan. Only Abdul Ghafoor's daily life remained largely unchanged, as he continued working for the government: 'There was no degrading or humiliating treatment towards us.' 'Of course,' he reflected, 'if I look at the country, we suffered and we suffered tremendously'.

The individual stories of Fatima, Abdul Ghafoor, Abdullah, and Laila are real, though their names are not. These are names I have assigned to several Afghans interviewed by the research organization, Afghanistan Analysts Network, on the fortieth anniversary of the Soviet invasion.[3] In their own ways, these Afghans contributed to the creation of a modern Afghan state—through working for the government, teaching, or raising the next generation of Afghan citizens. But their stories of everyday, individual strivings to change Afghan society and politics were swept away by the currents of history, overcome by a much larger, more violent struggle, one headed by competing Afghan elites and intellectuals who had very different visions of what a future Afghanistan should look like, as well as the means, military and political, to enact them. Their stories, as well as their anonymity, speak to one of the real tragedies of the Soviet–Afghan war and the decades of conflict that have persisted in Afghanistan since. While Afghan elites across the political spectrum fought for, and tried to implement, their visions of Afghan modernism, millions of Afghans were caught in the crossfire. The Afghan civil war of the late 1970s and 1980s created a refugee crisis of apocalyptical proportions.

This book seeks to reshape how we understand the local and global significance of Afghanistan's civil war. It demonstrates that what occurred in Afghanistan was, in many ways, not exceptional, and it thus questions the idea of Afghanistan as the 'graveyard of empires'.[4] Rather than thinking of Afghanistan in isolation or as a powerless, peripheral state in twentieth-century world politics, this book centres events and actors in Afghanistan within a global history of empire and anti-colonialism, Cold War and regional calculations, and international institutions and politics.

In so doing, it reveals that Afghan intellectuals' competing visions of socialism and Islamism (and constitutional monarchism and parliamentarianism) were rooted in broader twentieth-century movements that saw these socio-religious–political models as alternatives to the European empires that had dominated the globe in the nineteenth and early twentieth centuries and whose effects lingered in the form of Cold-War competition between the United States and the Soviet Union. Afghan elites formed their own notions of political and social modernity that, while informed by global circumstances, sought to rectify local inequalities. It reveals the ways these Afghan aspirations came up against each other, as well as the ways they clashed with American and Soviet realpolitik and the liberal international order, as overseen by the United Nations. In the halls of the UN General Assembly and among Afghan refugees, leaders of the international system tried to instil their own ideas of Afghan statehood and citizenship. The war that accompanied the Soviet occupation of Afghanistan, then, was a battle for control of Afghanistan, a conflict about the nature of Afghan politics, a debate on the role of the Afghan citizen, and a struggle for the supremacy of state sovereignty in the international political system. It was a clash between different Afghan visions of the future, though one in which foreign actors took active part.

Thus, this book is simultaneously a history of ideas—specifically competing ideas of modernity—and of implementation. Afghan socialists and Islamists, Soviets and Americans, all defined modernity in different ways. They were informed by developments within Afghanistan and networks expanding across the world. While the PDPA firmly believed that it could create socialist structures within Afghanistan, Islamists debated modes of organization that applied the lessons of the Quran to the politics of the twentieth century. Soviet officials felt obligated to support their PDPA allies but increasingly wondered whether socialism aligned well with Afghanistan's existing social and political networks. US leaders remained attached to British colonial-era tropes that deemed Afghanistan 'backward', 'feudal', and 'tribal'—in essence, fundamentally un-modern. Meanwhile, workers with the United Nations High Commissioner for Refugees (UNHCR) tried to infuse displaced Afghans with Western notions of citizenship and social responsibility, reshaping Afghan livelihoods against the backdrop of a refugee crisis. Each of these conceptualizations, as the American case particularly shows, had roots in longer historical trajectories. And key in all of this were the many generations of Afghans who sought to create a modern Afghanistan. Afghans envisioned and made Afghanistan the crucible for new and competing visions of modernity, the potential archetype for a truly postcolonial state.

But it is not enough to acknowledge that Afghan Islamists, socialists, and other reformers *thought* about transforming Afghan politics and society. Their shortcomings in putting these ideas into *practice* were key to Afghanistan's descent into civil war. The fact that Soviet officials proved no more successful than their Afghan compatriots in implementing socialism, while Americans focused on a divided, leaderless resistance, not a singular, unified movement, only exacerbated matters. Exploring how different historical actors tried to enact modernity reveals the uncertainties of events during this time period and the consequences—intended and unintended—of decision-making in Kabul, Islamabad, Peshawar, Moscow, Washington, and Geneva. This nuances narratives that focus on Afghanistan as a 'fragmented' or 'failed' state.[5] That such tropes have come to dominate discussions of Afghanistan in the media and policy circles today is a direct result of the very complicated, intricate, and interwoven historical events of the 1980s.

This book covers the period between the April 1978 PDPA coup and the Soviet withdrawal in February 1989 as simultaneously a moment of continuity and a moment of rupture. Rather than offering a military history, it focuses on ideas and implementations, understandings and misunderstandings, and practices of statebuilding and nation-building. It shows how the war in Afghanistan ultimately became a global one where worldwide attention focused on Afghanistan, and many Afghans, themselves, had to reconceptualize their place in the national, and international, order.

# Introduction

Afghanistan in the 1980s was one of the Cold War's killing fields.[1] It was a battlefield in the worldwide superpower competition between the United States and Soviet Union that devolved into widespread, life-shattering violence. From this vantage, the Soviet invasion was not atypical and sat alongside superpower interventions and proxy wars across the world, running from Guatemala and the Dominican Republic through the Congo to Hungary and Czechoslovakia, Iran and Lebanon, the Philippines, Indonesia, Korea, and, of course, Vietnam. The Afghan civil war demonstrated how the Cold War shaped the Third World, not only as an event co-opted by the superpowers (however reluctantly) but as a development that influenced the United States' and the Soviet Union's own trajectories and had lingering effects across Asia and the Middle East.[2]

While scholars have compared the Soviet invasion of Afghanistan with other Cold-War crises to demonstrate the conflict's global (and violent) nature, *Afghan Crucible* takes a different approach. Instead I examine a *single* conflict—effectively a single decade—through the multiple perspectives of many of the local, regional, and international actors who took part. Each chapter offers a different lens of analysis, examining a particular group of historical actors, often based in a specific geographical location, and the ways they approached the war.* This alternative form of comparison likewise demonstrates the pervasiveness of the Cold War and the ways it intersected with that other worldwide phenomenon of the twentieth century, decolonization. But it also allows us to peel back the layers of global, regional, and local engagement with Afghan politics and society and reveal with far greater nuance the numerous, frequently competing, and often interconnected motives that drove different actors who became involved in the crisis.

The Afghan crisis was deeply messy. While the superpower-led Cold War was pervasive, it was also entangled with regional power competitions, including the Sino-Soviet split and Indo-Pakistani hostilities. It spurred on alternative visions of internationalism that rejected US or Soviet domination but drew on a shared tactical playbook. It forced Afghan actors into competition with international organizations, while Afghans' daily lives were under scrutiny by local Afghan and global forces alike. The war was as much about territory, ethnicity, and community as it was about global alliances, political aspirations, and the nature of state power. In other words, we cannot understand the Afghan crisis of the 1980s or its global moment without putting together these diverse perspectives. To do otherwise masks its sheer complexity.

---

* To understand how this structure derived from the available historical material, see 'Note on Sources'.

Exploring the Afghan civil war from the perspective of the Cold-War superpowers, diplomats and officials from the United Nations, Afghanistan's neighbours, as well as competing Afghan interest groups themselves, demonstrates that, while US and Soviet decision-making towards Afghanistan followed the same fundamental logic as other Third World interventions, the Cold War provides only one lens through which to understand the conflict.[3] Empire continued to cast a long shadow, in terms of the borders drawn by European powers in the nineteenth and early twentieth centuries and the (often racialized and ethnicized) assumptions that foreign observers brought into their dealings with non-Western states and populations. Regional players like Pakistan saw the war as an opportunity to expand their own influence and rejig local power dynamics. Meanwhile, for many Afghans, the war involved the experience of exile, debates about homeland, belonging, and citizenship, and tussles between different political futures that had their roots in neither international nor indigenous visions of statehood but were an uneasy marriage between the two.

Much of Afghan history (up to and during the war) was driven by global forces— but not in a way that excluded Afghans or Afghanistan. Afghanistan's economy was rooted in trade links expanding north, south, east, and west. Its intelligentsia shared histories and practices of poetry, literature, and language spanning South Asia and the Middle East. Afghan leaders participated in pan-Asian and pan-Islamic movements in the twentieth century, framing their own experience of informal British rule as a model for anti-colonial solidarity, joining the 1955 Afro-Asia Conference in Bandung to express racial solidarity and reject Cold-War binaries, and helping found the Non-Aligned Movement in 1961. Afghan intellectuals received educations across South Asia, the Middle East, and further abroad in Europe, North America, and the Soviet Union. Like their counterparts across the decolonizing world, they turned to the promises of liberalism, constitutionalism, socialism, and Islamism as modes of shaping their country's future and the international system.[†]

Educated Afghans, both within and outside the ruling elite, drove the conversations about Afghanistan's political future *because* they positioned themselves as global actors taking part in universalist debates about politics, the social contract, and international relations. Afghan elites' visions of modernity emerged in part from exchanges with external sources but also looked to develop models that fit Afghanistan's local circumstances and that could be exported abroad (indeed, this was one reason that combatants from across the Muslim world flocked to Afghanistan's battlefields). Afghanistan thus was not merely the site of international intervention either before or during the Soviet invasion. Instead, the dynamics that emerged after 1978 resulted from the intricate entanglements between Afghans and foreigners as well as between Afghanistan's past and its (then) present.

Afghanistan's experiences of empire were key. Empires, or 'imperial formations', have functioned in different forms across time and space, but they have effectively

---

[†] For more on Afghanistan's global history, as well as alternative histories of the Soviet invasion, see 'Further Reading'.

served to undermine the sovereignty and autonomy of subject populations and promote inequality in the international system.[4] The British and Russians in the nineteenth century, and later the Soviets and Americans, all attempted to understand Afghanistan and, to an extent, remake it in their own image. In the context of the Cold War, both Soviet and American officials sought to use their financial and political influence to develop Afghanistan's infrastructures along socialist and capitalist lines, respectively. In this regard, the Soviet intervention can be seen as the apex of Cold-War imperialism, with Soviet officials entering Afghanistan to take control of state-building and force through an Afghan socialism that conformed to Soviet-led models.[5]

While Afghanistan was ostensibly politically independent after 1919, many Afghan intellectuals saw the remnants of empire in the stagnation of the Afghan economy, the state's ongoing political tensions with its neighbours, particularly Pakistan after 1947, and its limited government, which continued to exclude all but a handful of elite Durrani Pashtuns, members of a single 'tribe' and ethnicity in a country with numerous groups. The central state's reach into many of Afghanistan's provinces remained uneven and limited, and local community, or *qawm*, leaders still wielded huge influence.[6] In turn, convinced of the need fundamentally to reshape Afghan politics and society and free the country of its reliance on foreign aid, educated Afghans debated a host of ideas for changing Afghanistan's political trajectory, for making it more independent and more representative of the Afghan people. Two strains of more radical political thought ultimately came to the fore in competition with the moderate Westernizing tendencies of Afghanistan's earlier rulers: Marxism-Leninism and political Islam. Both of these concepts, as articulated by Afghan ideologues, drew their power from their anti-imperial force and the ways they provided alternatives to the status quo.

Tracing the networks that linked Afghans' aspirations to a broader global context sheds light onto some of the myriad ways that educated Afghans (and intellectuals across the world) understood and aspired to certain forms of national and international politics, as well as providing a corrective to the idea put forward by the political scientist Barnett Rubin that 'the "traditionalism" and "localism" of Afghanistan are not survivals of ancient traditions but rather the results of the country's forced integration into the contemporary state system'.[7] Afghan intellectuals and leaders did not see themselves as citizens of a state forced unwillingly and inappropriately into an international states system. Instead, for Afghans and many of their allies across South Asia and the Middle East, Afghanistan was, according to the historian Faiz Ahmed, 'an ideal conduit through which an assortment of radical political coalitions could take shape—and did take shape'.[8] Afghanistan, by shedding imperial oversight in 1919, taking the lead in pan-Asian and pan-Islamic anti-colonial networks, and working to establish a stable government rooted in constitutionalism (even while retaining its monarchy), offered the prototype for the postcolonial state. Afghan elites and intellectuals sought to reaffirm and reform a form of statehood that married aspects of Western liberalism with Islamic and indigenous practices, while embracing participation in global governance. In this regard, Afghanistan's exceptionalism derived from the possibilities it presented as a model, not from the West's limited circumscription of what a state should look like.[9]

As such, Afghan reformers (constitutionalists, monarchists, socialists, Islamists) sought the vague but potent promise of 'modernity'. Modernity is, itself, a claims-making project: to be or become 'modern', to transition from a past to a different future, to change the individual's, the community's, and, ultimately, the nation's practices and understandings of their role in politics and society. Modernization constitutes the processes or movements through which modernity is achieved, the social and political evolutions necessary to create a rupture with the past. Development often provides the key practices of modernization, focusing on the active changing of social, economic, and political structures, attitudes, and relationships. Many Afghans aspired to a modernity of their own definition, but difficulties emerged in implementing their interpretations of modern statehood.[10]

Twentieth-century conflicts over modernity, and the ways they played out in Afghanistan, had many roots in nineteenth-century imperialism, but the modernity sought by Afghan reformers did not merely derive from foreign models.[11] Certainly, Afghan leaders ruminated over the promises and pitfalls of the US-backed modernization theory and Soviet economic and social models and ideas of *kul'turnost'*, or culturedness.[12] Likewise they engaged with anti-colonial ideas, such as Jawaharlal Nehru's non-aligned India underpinned by democratic representation and socialist economic planning, Julius Nyerere and Kwame Nkrumah's competing aspirations for a federated Africa, or Mao's militant interpretation of communism, Maoism, as a force for global revolution. These anti-colonial visions of modernity questioned and fought against Western articulations of statehood and citizenship, though they also frequently adopted some of the same practices and structures that had been used by imperial powers.

Afghan intellectuals were co-producers of these new visions of a postcolonial future. With an eye on both local and international developments, they drew on and created their own different models of modernity, sometimes in competing ways.[13] Much like Afghanistan's constitutionalists, Afghan socialists and Islamists took inspiration from anti-colonial attempts to wrest control of modernization and framed themselves as anti-colonial leaders. They sought to revolutionize Afghan politics, economics, and society, to overcome ethnic and tribal divides, and to create a state that touched the lives of all Afghanistan's citizens. The People's Democratic Party of Afghanistan also saw the Soviet Union as its aspirational model and sought to use socialism to provide political, economic, and social uplift. Equally, its members looked to communist parties across the non-Western world to find parallels and root themselves in a global struggle against Western (now American-led) imperialism. Afghan Islamists also responded to what they saw as the moral and political decay resulting from the forced implementation of Western models of governance in the eras of empire and Cold War. They rejected both Soviet and American models, rooting their conception of modernity in the belief that Islam and its tenets provided a means to create new alternative national and state (and global community, or *ummah*) structures. (Notably, Maoist theories on guerrilla warfare would also underpin the Islamist resistance movement.) Afghan intellectuals and activists tailored these universalist ideas to the circumstances they saw most in need of change within Afghanistan: a clientele state, an economy reliant on foreign aid, prejudicial social and regional divisions, and a lacking sense of nationalism.

Exploring how different actors inside and outside Afghanistan responded to the Saur Revolution, as the PDPA called their 1978 coup, and the subsequent Soviet invasion reveals why none of these visions of Afghan modernity ultimately came to pass. The Afghan crisis of the 1980s derived from politics and interests born in multiple locations, which collectively were irreconcilable. Not only did the war bring together the Cold-War superpowers on opposing sides, but interference from Afghanistan's neighbours narrowed the window of possibility for more moderate Afghan modernizers, as Pakistan and Iran supported revolutionary Islamist groups. Meanwhile the Afghan government's ready turn to violence and the civil war between government and resistance forces laid waste to pastures, fields, and villages. Close to one million Afghans were internally displaced, while millions more fled to neighbouring Pakistan and Iran, only to find themselves the subjects of both Afghan resistance party and UNHCR modernizing efforts. In turn, many Afghan refugees reconfigured their ideas of community and nation based on their experiences abroad. In the 1980s, Afghan refugees were the targets, the victims, *and* the agents of the war for Afghanistan's future.

Examining the different interest groups that became involved in the Afghan civil war provides an opportunity to reflect on the global moment of the late 1970s and 1980s. This was a time when a socialist state seemed like a viable option in Afghanistan, following on from successes elsewhere in the Third World. It was a time, too, where political Islam seemed to offer a very real alternative to a Cold-War world divided between two superpower spheres. It was also a time when global governance was simultaneously expanding and constricting. No one doubted the UNHCR's worldwide remit to alleviate the suffering of refugees, and the UN General Assembly represented a key arena of international affairs. But the United Nations also wrestled with the contradiction of trying to uphold an international states system whose members overwhelmingly rejected the legitimacy of one state's leaders, the PDPA, while refusing to extend recognition to any alternative state claimants, the Islamists or other resistance parties. It was a moment that revealed the limitations of the international system, not just of Afghan visionaries.

The Afghanistan of the 1980s was a place of potentials. Afghan modernizers' ideas and aspirations mattered and reflected a time and place where it seemed possible that either side could succeed in fundamentally reshaping Afghanistan. Of course, the civil war between the two sides did change Afghanistan, but not in the ways that either group hoped. Aspirations for a reinvigorated modern Afghanistan crumbled under the weight of a war that killed hundreds of thousands and displaced millions.

Instead, what was left in 1989 when the Soviets finally withdrew their troops was ruin and ruination: the ruins of an Afghan state fashioned by Afghan socialists and buttressed by their Soviet supporters, the ruins of an Islamist resistance movement that had devolved into factional in-fighting, the ruins of an Afghan society that had fled conflict and dispersed across the world.

# 1
# Afghanistan's Many Pasts

Late on an afternoon in October 1965, groups of students congregated on the leafy boulevards of Kabul University. Against the backdrop of low-lying mountains and large, modern brick buildings filled with lecture halls and laboratories, Afghanistan's future leaders spilled out into the sunshine. The students were a study in diversity. Some of the male students wore Western-style suits, while others wore the traditional *salwar kameez* (a flowing pyjama top and loose trousers). Some had the full beards and kufi caps of the devout Muslim, while others were clean shaven with oil-slicked hair. Dotted around could be seen women, also in different stages of traditional and foreign dress, some with their heads covered, others with carefully styled updos. As they stood in clusters, holding textbooks, what stood out most among the students was a sense of energy, youth, and potential.

As they left their classrooms and emerged into the autumnal sunshine, students excitedly discussed the nationwide elections that had recently taken place and the opening of Afghanistan's first elected assembly. Kabul University had closed its doors in early September to allow students to go home and vote, the first time they and most other Afghans had ever had a chance to do so. Now, they compared notes, discussing the polling process, what it had felt like to cast their vote, and finally their political choices. While officially no political parties existed, newly elected politicians ranged from staunch supporters of King Zahir Shah, the architect of Afghanistan's new constitution and this era of reform, to supporters of the king's cousin, Mohammad Daoud Khan, languishing in exile since almost destroying Afghanistan's economy through a years-long stand-off with Pakistan, to more radical ideologues who advocated turning Afghanistan socialist or Islamist.

Afghan politics in the 1960s was diverse yet fundamentally forward-looking. Perspectives covered a vast political spectrum, yet collectively they sought to advance Afghanistan and Afghan citizens alongside the rest of the world. Discussions took place across the country, in cities such as Kandahar and Jalalabad, in provinces from Badakshan to Helmand, in villages bordering Pakistan, Iran, and Soviet Tajikistan. Increasing numbers of Afghans attended local *madrassas* and state-run colleges and universities, as well as schools beyond Afghanistan's borders, in Pakistan, Iran, Egypt, the Soviet Union, and the United States. Centres of education also became centres of debate about Afghanistan's past, present, and future. At the heart of Afghan higher education, Kabul University, the ideas and individuals that would come to define debate, and ultimately war, in the late 1970s and 1980s converged.

Kabul University, the country's pre-eminent higher-education institution, was established in 1932. It grew from one faculty for the study of medicine to twelve scattered across the city. Its expansion and consolidation were underpinned by the United States' Cold-War ambitions and US policymakers' intention to develop educated citizens who sympathized with capitalism and Western values across the world. The US Agency for International Development, in the early 1960s, paid for the establishment of a modern university campus, built by the West German company Hochtief in Aliabad district, west of the city centre. It was replete with laboratories, dormitories, and classroom buildings, and by 1961 it was co-educational. The US government also provided grants for teaching staff to be educated in the United States—and encouraged the learning of English.[1]

Student development followed apace. As early as 1950, the university's first Student Union was established, though its political activities were quashed by the government within months. During Afghanistan's constitutional period, 1964–73, student activism again came into prominence. Almost half the student body, comprised of individuals from across Afghanistan, lived on campus but had little recourse to extracurricular activities, such as sports or social clubs, which largely did not exist. At the same time, they were exposed to a host of new ideas and experiences, interacting with classmates from across the country and teachers who frequently had trained abroad. Students were also encouraged to take active part in state politics. Political discussions, and increasingly protests, were a hallmark of Kabul University throughout the 1960s. The university became a hotbed for a range of political opinions, some of which advocated working with the monarchy to pursue modernization and liberalization, others of which rejected this notion and sought alternative forms for a modern Afghan state.[2]

In the mid-1960s, Kabul, and specifically Kabul University, were home to a number of men who would change the course of Afghan history. At the time, they belonged on the political fringes. Some were students: Gulbuddin Hekmatyar, one of the leaders of the student Muslim Youth organization; Ahmad Shah Massoud, also a member of Muslim Youth studying in the Faculty of Engineering; Mohammad Najibullah, a member of the socialist People's Democratic Party of Afghanistan (PDPA), completing a degree at the College of Medicine. Babrak Karmal and Hafizullah Amin, two of the founders of the PDPA, were graduates, while Nur Mohammad Taraki, who would become the first leader of the socialist Democratic Republic of Afghanistan (DRA), lived nearby, and at least one biography had him taking classes at the university. All three were active in Kabul and nationwide politics after the founding of the PDPA in early 1965. Finally, there was Burhanuddin Rabbani, a lecturer in the Faculty of Theology who, alongside Hekmatyar and Massoud, would go on to be one of the leading Islamist intellectuals of the Afghan resistance.

In one time and place—Kabul in the mid-1960s—many of the key political actors who would go on fundamentally to shape Afghanistan's trajectory in the 1980s and beyond were active and probably interacting. Thinking about this moment also demonstrates the deeper historical roots of Afghan socialist (both pro-Soviet and Maoist) and Islamist thought and the essential differences that emerged between the two. Neither the PDPA nor the Muslim Youth had a clear prerogative, nor was either a clear front runner in the milieu of Afghan political mobilization. Indeed, the rise of both groups in the 1970s was contingent—not only on domestic circumstances but, equally importantly, on each group's international ties. Rooting Afghan socialism and Islamism in this political environment further shows that, while neither coup nor civil war was preordained, the circumstances were already in place for a clash between different Afghan thinkers and activists. It is remarkable to think that, if something had happened on or near Kabul University's campuses in the 1960s, the leaders of the PDPA, *Jam'iyyat-i Islami-yi Afghanistan*, and *Hizb-i Islami-yi Afghanistan* could have been destroyed, and Afghanistan's history might have been very different. Rarely can we identify such a time and place that have been so important for so many actors who would have such a vital impact on history—and it is a moment that is frequently given short shrift in studies of the Soviet invasion of Afghanistan.

It is impossible to come to grips with the Soviet invasion of Afghanistan without considering its pre-history. By this I mean more than just beginning with the coup—the 'Saur Revolution'—that brought the PDPA to power in April 1978. Events between April 1978 and February 1989 were the culmination of numerous parallel and interweaving historical forces, all of which had embedded Afghanistan into global networks in different ways. Years before Soviet soldiers crossed the Amu Darya river and entered Afghanistan on Christmas Eve 1979, Afghanistan was already the site of three other wars. The first was a war of ideas. As exemplified by the rise of different political groups at Kabul University, Afghans across the political spectrum debated and discussed Afghanistan's future, the way its politics and society should develop along certain ideological lines. In this battle, ultimately Afghan pro-Soviet socialists and Islamists rose to the fore, even as their ideas remained vague and contested by other modernizing advocates. The second was a regional conflict that had significance for Afghanistan's relations with its neighbours, as well as its own ethnic balance and sense of statehood. Afghan leaders' overwhelming focus on their state's ethnic Pashtuns not only increased tensions with Afghanistan's other ethnic groups but also brought the country into tension with its neighbours, particularly Pakistan. Finally, Afghanistan was a battleground in the Cold War, the global fight for supremacy between the United States and Soviet Union and their respective ideological and political models. Events in the 1980s represented the collision of these three conflicts, with widespread consequences not only for Afghans but also for their neighbours and the international community.

In 1905, a group of educated Afghans came together to create a secret organization, *Mashruta-khwahan*, or constitutionalists. As the name indicated, this cohort sought the creation of a codified government, a constitutional monarchy and parliament that would support Afghanistan's political, social, and economic development. In many ways, Mashruta's timing seemed auspicious: Afghanistan's amir, Habibullah, had come peacefully to power in 1901, the first transfer of power in years unaccompanied by a war of succession. Among his advisors was Mahmud Tarzi, an ambitious modernizer who had spent time in exile in Karachi and Damascus and became the chief of the Bureau of Translation of the Royal Court. Habibullah's government, drawing on cosmopolitan advisors from within Afghanistan and India and the Ottoman Empire, pursued reforms such as the establishment of a department of education and the illustrious Habibia College, the first Afghan school with a modern curriculum. Meanwhile abroad, the Japanese had emerged exultant in the 1905 Russo-Japanese war, highlighting the growing weaknesses of Afghanistan's northern neighbour and opportunities for Afghans to test the informal imperial controls that had been placed upon them by the Russians to the north and the British to the south in colonial India. What better time not only to assert Afghanistan's independence but also to reform its political system?

Mashruta-khwahan was short-lived. Government agents caught wind of the group and in 1909 arrested and executed many of its participants on charges of planning to overthrow the monarchy. Nevertheless, its ethos of political modernization lived on in the form of the Young Afghans, a movement of students and teachers from Habibia and the accompanying Harbiya, a military school established by Turkish officers, some of whom had ties with Mashruta and many of whom found inspiration in the Young Turk movement seeking constitutional reform in the Ottoman Empire. Habibullah's advisor Tarzi sympathized and, using *Siraj al-Akhbar-i Afghaniyyah* (*Lamp of the News of Afghanistan*), Afghanistan's first regularly published newspaper, advocated political and social progress for the nation. Tarzi used articles in the paper to articulate an Afghan nation state, defining 'Afghan' in geographical and religious terms, trying to avoid the ethnic and tribal factionalism that had riven countrywide politics throughout the nineteenth century and beyond. He also celebrated the modernism of central authority and claimed that Afghanistan had the opportunity to become 'a mighty and powerful state, with all the aptitude and potential to establish and build a great Islamic state in Asia'. Tarzi and many of his contemporaries embraced the potentials of pan-Islamism and unity across political boundaries, while vociferously critiquing British imperialism with its continued hold over Afghanistan's foreign (and sometimes domestic) policy.[3]

Habibullah never fully embraced the vision of Afghanistan put forth by Tarzi and other Young Afghans. While he pursued minor reforms, he largely focused on maintaining his own power, sensitive to the pressures placed on him by British imperialists intent on retaining Afghanistan as a buffer to their rule in colonial India and wary of both modernists and Islamic revivalists who demanded changes to governance. To the frustration of both pan-Islamists and nationalists, Habibullah opted to keep Afghanistan neutral during the First World War. Nevertheless, the efforts of Tarzi and others to give both voice and action to their visions of a modern Afghanistan are revealing. They demonstrate that, from the beginning of the twentieth century, educated Afghans actively discussed and debated what a modern Afghan polity was and should look like. Many Afghans in Kabul, in other centres of learning within Afghanistan, and abroad, envisioned and aspired to new political structures. In other words, the conflicts that broke out later in the twentieth century about the nature and future of Afghan politics had their roots in earlier reform movements.

The rise and fall of Mashruta-khwahan, taken alongside the more moderate but equally ambitious Young Afghans, demonstrates the multiple forms that Afghan modernity might take. These groups turned to various political projects—constitutionalism, pan-Islamism, monarchism, parliamentarianism—as modes of advancing Afghan politics and society, and frequently these movements, as demonstrated by Tarzi's writings, overlapped. Afghanistan, in many modernizers' eyes, could have a monarchy and parliament while embracing Islam as a social and political factor internally and in foreign relations. In the early twentieth century, a strong monarchy underpinned by a national council provided a clear means of leading Afghanistan into the future. Indeed, even by the late twentieth century, the monarchy's popularity had not faded. A survey taken among Afghan refugees based in Pakistan in 1987 indicated that the majority of respondents preferred the return of Afghanistan's exiled king, Zahir Shah, to the governance of either Afghan socialists or Islamists.[4]

Perhaps most emblematic of the promises and pitfalls of pursuing modernization was the rise and fall of King Amanullah, who replaced Habibullah, his father, upon his assassination in 1919. Amanullah's reign, though brief, deserves special mention for several reasons. First, his victory in the Third Anglo-Afghan War in 1919 signalled to the world, and is frequently remembered as the moment, that Afghanistan had become truly politically independent. Amanullah wrestled back control of Afghanistan's foreign policy from the British. Independence gave Afghanistan the means to pursue bilateral treaties with countries across the world and served as an impetus for joining the League of Nations in 1934.

Amanullah is also remembered for his ambitious programme of political, economic, and social reform, which, in many ways, created a template for future movements to modernize Afghanistan. He and his wife, Queen Soraya Tarzi (daughter of Mahmud Tarzi), focused on gender norms and the place of women, land reform, education, and the somewhat ambiguous role of religion in Afghan politics. In power, the PDPA would draw parallels between Amanullah's reform efforts and its own. Amanullah embraced the top-down modernization of Afghan state and society, in part along Western lines, inspired by visits to Europe, and in part drawing on the appeal of pan-Islamism. Most significantly, Amanullah passed the constitution of 1923, whose authors included legal jurists from Afghanistan, Turkey, and India and which created the infrastructures of state power. The creation of a state-wide legal code meant that 'the Afghan government shared in global processes of state formation, but in a language and genealogy of its own'.[5] The constitution established the amir as the supreme executive and legal authority of the state, supported by a council of ministers and state council, and tried to instil the idea of the individual citizen, rather than the *qawm* or community, as the key unit of Afghan political participation. Alongside this, Amanullah tried to curtail the power of *qawm* leaders, whose alternative source of leadership had helped restrict locals' ties with the central government in Kabul throughout earlier decades.

Amanullah looked not only to the rule of law but to the institutionalization of other reforms. He revised Afghanistan's tax system, increasing levies to pay for expanded education and marriage reforms. With the help of the German and French governments, he set up new foreign-language high schools in Kabul. He tried (and ultimately failed) to build a new capital on the outskirts of Kabul, and he enraged more conservative elements of Afghan society by encouraging co-education, the lifting of *purdah* (women's seclusion) and unveiling of women, and the widespread adoption of Western dress. Alongside him, Queen Soraya famously went unveiled in public in Afghanistan and also founded a women's magazine, *Ershad-i Niswan* (*Guidance for Women*). But the speed and ferocity of Amanullah's reform programme, which lacked both infrastructural and popular foundations, led to countrywide revolts, and he was forced into exile in 1929. Particularly striking about Amanullah's fall was that it demonstrated the continued force of local leaders, whether religious, ethnic, or tribal, who mobilized against his proposed reforms. (It is no coincidence that subsequent leaders did not push to embed the state's reach across Afghan territory in the same way.) The strength of feeling outside Afghanistan's cities also drew attention to Afghanistan's ongoing urban–rural divides.[6]

In the aftermath of Amanullah's meteoric rise and fall, the Musahiban family wrested power. While the dynasty's founder, Nadir Shah (1929–33), was assassinated within years of assuming the throne, his offspring and family members would continue to charge forward—albeit more slowly and cautiously than Amanullah—with modernizing Afghanistan. The reign of the Musahiban family can be roughly divided into three stages: its ascendancy and coalescence of power, roughly 1933 until the mid-1960s; the constitutional period under King Zahir Shah, 1964–73; and the coup and rule by Mohammad Daoud Khan, 1973–8.

During this time, several periods of limited government liberalization provided opportunities for the growth of an Afghan intellectual elite who aspired to move beyond the slow reform efforts undertaken by the government. The end of the Second World War coincided with a new prime minister who initiated a number of short-lived reforms to present a positive image, including free(er) press, the establishment of political parties, and parliamentary elections. As in the era of Mashruta and the Young Afghans, new groups emerged advocating different aspirations for Afghanistan's future. The *Wish Zalmayan* (Awakened Youth) was the most well-known organization to emerge at this time, alongside *Hizb-i Vatan* (Party of the Homeland), both of which demanded progressive reform.[7] Notably, Wish Zalmayan formed in Kandahar, highlighting that debates about Afghan modernity extended beyond Afghanistan's capital. The state soon cracked down on dissent, however, particularly after the resignation and replacement of the prime minister with Mohammad Daoud, the king's cousin. Daoud's autocratic regime clamped down on any criticism, and not until he, too, was forced to resign did reforms again progress. In 1963, Prime Minister Daoud was ousted after a series of foreign and domestic policy blunders. A rumbling dispute with Pakistan over their shared Pashtun community and Daoud's support for an independent 'Pashtunistan' had damaged the Afghan economy, as the prime minister chose to close Afghanistan's eastern border with Pakistan, through which most imports and exports travelled. Within Afghanistan he had tried to promote social change, returning to the issue of getting rid of *purdah*, which met with outcry and was largely unsuccessful.[8]

The period 1964–73 was marked by a new constitution drafted at King Zahir Shah's behest, passed by legislatures in 1964. The new constitution provided opportunities for parliamentary democracy, which led to another spate of political organization. The PDPA was formed in 1965. Alongside this was the *Shu'lah-i Javid* (Eternal Flame), another leftist party that took its inspiration from Mao Zedong's revolutionary thought rather than the Soviet model, as well as Islamist organizations such as the *Sazman-i Javanan-i Musalman* (Organization of the Islamic Youths) and *Jam'iyyat-i Islami-yi Afghanistan* (Islamic Society of Afghanistan).[9] Despite the rhetoric of openness and liberalization, in fact the royal family kept a tight rein on the country's politics, and these parties were allowed to have little national political influence. Indeed, the passing of the 1964 constitution was accompanied by the political reorganization of Afghanistan from twenty-nine provinces into eighteen as a means of increasing the central government's hold across the country. After the 1973 coup that brought Daoud back into power, yet another crackdown on dissidents occurred, as the new president consolidated his rule.

Alongside these domestic reforms, which, as we shall see, were underpinned by foreign aid, Afghan leaders also exerted their right to govern and projected the legitimacy of the Afghan nation state to an international audience. Afghanistan not only joined the United Nations shortly after its founding—it was prevented from being an original member owing to its neutrality in the Second World War—but also used its dispute with Pakistan over the Durand Line to draw both national and international attention to Afghanistan's territorial boundaries. For the Musahiban dynasty, asserting Afghan modernity and legitimacy was an international, as well as a domestic, priority.[10]

Yet the Musahiban increasingly held a difficult position. While Zahir Shah framed his rule as constitutionally based, the fact remained that Afghanistan continued to be governed (often unilaterally) by a monarchy in an era when democratically elected leaders, assemblies, and parliaments were increasingly becoming the norm across much of the world. Where Afghanistan in the early twentieth century had seemed ahead of the curve in terms of achieving political independence from the European imperial powers who ruled most of the globe, by the 1960s its leaders looked increasingly out of step with Afghanistan's collaborators at the 1955 Afro-Asian Conference at Bandung or in the Non-Aligned Movement, which demanded increased representation and political participation for the non-Western world (even while an autocratic strain remained in many newly independent regimes). The government still exerted only limited controls across the country, while its overweening focus on the border dispute with Pakistan seemed outdated. While Afghan leaders asserted Afghanistan's modern nation statehood by participating in such international conferences and the UN and pursuing reforms like the creation of a constitution, these did not make up for a lack of widespread influence or participation in Afghan politics. Who and what constituted an Afghan nation state remained up for debate.

Throughout all of this, Kabul University was a key centre of political mobilization. At an early stage, student activists worked together across the political spectrum, but increasingly ideological (and personal) divides put a halt to such cooperation. Nevertheless, the prominence of Kabul University signalled the rise of an enlarged educated class with certain expectations of the Afghan state. A dangerous flaw emerged in official Afghan focus on expanding education: additional job opportunities simply did not follow. Educated Afghans were largely employed by the state, but they struggled against an entrenched bureaucracy that still used familial, ethnic, and tribal patronage networks to fill important posts. As such, expectations developed in university settings and expanded by political reforms such as the 1964 constitution were frequently left unfulfilled. Increasingly disenchanted with the Musahiban ruling family and existing state systems, many Afghan intelligentsia were subsequently ambivalent to the 1973 coup that overthrew the king and replaced him with Daoud and increasingly receptive to political organizations, including leftists and Islamists, that coalesced in the late 1960s and 1970s. The hopes and frustrations expressed by politicized students were symptomatic of a broader issue in Afghanistan—the unmatched ambitions of Afghanistan's educated youths and the political stagnation of a system that still relied on one-family rule—that would lead in part to the state's undoing.[11]

At Kabul University and across Afghanistan, young idealists, teachers, clerics, and government officials debated their country's future and the political forms that would best serve the country and its citizens. While various proposed forms of Afghan modernism each had their own merits, shifts in the 1970s would ultimately bring two groups to the forefront of Afghan anti-monarchical politics: the socialists and the Islamists. Other groups persisted, and their remnants could be seen in some of the resistance parties that formed in 1979, but both regional and international circumstances conspired to give the Islamists and pro-Soviet socialists particular sway. This is not to say that Afghan politics functioned as a binary between the two—parties and organizations across the political spectrum continued—but these two political factions ultimately would take the leading role in the civil war that wracked Afghanistan in the 1980s. Neither the socialists nor Islamists represented singular, unified movements, and each suffered from massive infighting. Nevertheless, they coalesced around two competing visions of what Afghanistan might become, and during the course of the late 1970s and 1980s, they each tried to put these ideas into practice.

When political parties were allowed to form in 1965, one of these was the PDPA. From the very beginning, the PDPA was a party of contradictions—contradictions that would ultimately lead to its fracture and disintegration into warring factions. Ideologically speaking, the PDPA presented two faces. To the outside world, the PDPA did not look all that exceptional—another group demanding representation and political reform. But, internally, the messages given to party members were radical.

The PDPA turned to the Soviet Union as a model for drastic social and political change. It followed in a longer line of Third World reformers and activists who identified Marxism-Leninism as the key to overcoming the social and political stagnancy caused by colonial rule and to modernizing their societies. After all, Lenin had identified imperialism as the highest stage of capitalism—the unapologetic exploitation of a country and its inhabitants for the capitalist gains of its colonial rulers. The 1917 Bolshevik Revolution demonstrated that Marxism could topple an ancient, powerful regime. It provided a source of inspiration to anti-colonial activists across the world, ranging from Jawaharlal Nehru in India, to Ho Chi Minh in Vietnam, to, later, Che Guevara and Fidel Castro in Cuba.[12] Although Afghanistan had never officially been colonized by Great Britain, there was little question that Afghanistan's trajectory had been moulded directly and indirectly by the British presence in South Asia and ongoing British attempts to control Afghanistan's foreign policy until (and even after) 1919. Marxism offered an opportunity to overthrow the political systems in Afghanistan that had been allowed to develop under British officials' watchful eyes.

While Marxism provided the ideology, the Soviet Union provided the necessary backing. The founding of the PDPA coincided with the height of the Sino-Soviet split. Between 1963 and 1965, Soviet leaders reinvigorated their quest for influence in the Third World, fearful of being outmanoeuvred by the Chinese and their message of revolutionary anti-imperialism. Soviet efforts took the form of economic aid as well as embracing militant anti-imperialism. Between this Soviet move, which successfully undermined the international messaging of the People's Republic of China (PRC), and long-standing ties between Afghanistan and the Soviet Union, the PDPA emerged as a pro-Soviet Marxist force. The Afghan Maoist movement, lacking support from the PRC and refusing to take part in Afghan elections, never managed to gain the same traction and instead found itself at odds with not just the PDPA but other Afghan reformist groups.[13]

Ironically, most PDPA members' grasp of Marxist ideology was actually quite weak. They relied on second-hand education materials—Persian-language versions of Soviet texts translated by the Tudeh communist party in Iran.[14] Rather, it was the model of statehood that the Soviet Union presented that appealed to these educated Afghans. The Soviet Union had managed completely to transform its economy from one of agrarianism to one of industrialism. Its populace was apparently widely educated and politically engaged (at least according to Soviet propaganda). It was highly secular and centralized, not riven by the factionalism that inevitably emerged in Afghanistan as the state vied with local religious, ethnic, and tribal leaders for influence. And, in all, the state and government played a key role, handing out dictates and making sure everything ran smoothly. It was this model, vaguely embodied for Afghans by the concept of 'socialism', that appealed to urban, educated Afghans and became the motivating force behind the establishment of the PDPA.[15]

Four men would ultimately determine the trajectory of the PDPA and its impact on Afghanistan. Nur Mohammad Taraki and Babrak Karmal were both members of the party's central committee from its inception, while Hafizullah Amin was an alternate. Mohammad Najibullah was a party member who would rise to prominence in the late 1970s.

Nur Mohammad Taraki was born in the village of Sor Qala in Ghazni province in 1917—the same year as the Bolshevik Revolution, as he liked to remind people. He was a Ghilzai Pashtun, which placed him among Afghanistan's powerful Pashtun ethnic group but historically in tension with the ruling Durrani Pashtuns. In contrast to his PDPA compatriots, he came from humble beginnings. His family was poor and semi-nomadic and sent Taraki at a young age to work as a servant for a widow. However, his father determined that he should receive an education, and Taraki subsequently attended schools in Afghanistan and nearby colonial India (in what would become Pakistan). At the age of 15, he found work with a trading company in Kandahar, where his efforts led his bosses to send him to clerk in their Bombay office in colonial India.[16]

Taraki returned to Afghanistan, moving to Kabul in 1937 at the age of 20. The details of his young adult life in Afghan politics remain unclear. According to one account, Taraki began working for the government's Department of Press; another placed him at the University of Kabul, attending the Faculty of Law and Political Science, obtaining a diploma from the Faculty of Economics, and beginning work at the Ministry of National Economy.[17] His official biography, reprinted in the *Kabul Times* several months after the April 1978 coup, skips over this time almost entirely, instead vaguely painting him as a reluctant low-level official and a journalist whose writings increasingly critiqued the Afghan government. Accounts largely agree that Taraki was at least nominally involved with Wish Zalmayan, as it emerged. In the 1950s, he worked a brief stint in the Afghan embassy in Washington, during which he openly criticized the government under Zahir Shah and Prime Minister Daoud. Afterwards, he worked independently as a translator for the subsequent decade. The year 1965 marked a turning point in Taraki's career, with the foundation of the PDPA on 1 January at his home in Kart-i Char, a residential neighbourhood in western Kabul, near Kabul University. Taraki was subsequently named secretary-general of the party.

Even at this early stage, one of Taraki's closest confidants and protégés was Hafizullah Amin. Like Taraki, Amin was a Ghilzai Pashtun, though he came from less humble beginnings. He was born in 1929 in Paghman, near Kabul. Raised by his elder brother, a schoolteacher and company secretary, Amin also trained as an educator, attending a teachers' college in Kabul before receiving a BS in Physics and Mathematics from Kabul University. He subsequently earned an MA in Educational Administration and Organization at Columbia University in the United States in 1957. Upon returning to Afghanistan, he first lectured at Kabul University before being appointed Principal of the Teachers' College of Kabul and subsequently working with the Ministry of Education. He dabbled in leftist politics, also coming into contact with Wish Zalmayan before helping to establish the PDPA. By winning a parliament seat in 1969, Amin gained increasing political clout within the PDPA, and by 1978 Amin was effectively Taraki's second-in-command.[18]

Born in the same year as Amin, Babrak Karmal came from a well-to-do background, the son of a major-general in the Afghan army who had also served as governor of Paktia province. He became politically active from an early age. After graduating from a German-speaking high school in 1948, he was initially barred from entering the College of Law and Political Science at Kabul University, owing to his political activities with the Student Union during its brief run. He finally matriculated in 1951, before being imprisoned in 1953 for his anti-government politics. He did not graduate with a degree until 1960, after which he began working for the state, first in the Ministry of Education and later in the Ministry of Planning. Questions persist as to Karmal's ethnic background. While he would declare in 1986 that he was ethnic-ally Pashtun on his mother's side, others claimed he was Tajik or descended from Hindu migrants from Kashmir.[19] Such debates mattered, because they placed Karmal apart from the majority of Afghans who used ethnonyms or tribal and ethnic affiliations to demonstrate their position and links within their communities and broader Afghan society.

Najibullah would not come to the fore of the PDPA until the 1980s, but he, too, was a member of the PDPA from the beginning. Known as 'Dr Najib' in the early years—before becoming the leader of the DRA in 1986, he frequently dropped the 'ullah' that gave his name its religious meaning, 'Honoured of God'—he was a Ghilzai Pashtun born in Kabul in 1947 to a government official. Thanks to his father's posting to Peshawar, Najibullah had strong links with Pashtun nationalists in Pakistan, something that probably drove his later promotion of Pashtun ethnonationalism (to the dismay of Afghanistan's other ethnic groups). Like his compatriots, Najibullah also was highly educated, having graduated from Habibia College and the College of Medicine at Kabul University in 1975, where he was known as 'Najib the Bull' for his athletic prowess and his tall, burly stature. His political activities slowed his studies. He joined the PDPA in 1965 and faced prison in 1969 and again in 1970. He would join the PDPA's central committee in 1977 and its Revolutionary Council in 1978. Much as Amin was close to Taraki, Najibullah was firmly allied with Karmal, whom he would ultimately replace. Najibullah was known to be 'hard-working, self-assertive and intensely involved' in the Parcham faction of PDPA, but he also later helped friends escape PDPA repression because of 'the bonds of friendship established during these student days'.[20]

The PDPA platform, published in Taraki's *Khalq* newsletter on 11 April 1966, outlined a vision for sweeping political and economic change. In demanding a 'national democratic state', the PDPA condemned Afghanistan's limited economic growth and 'the pathetic condition of [the] peoples of Afghanistan who are engulfed in poverty, ignorance, and disease'. It blamed 'feudalists, the big businessmen and the corrupt businessmen and the imperialistic monopolizing companies' for these unbearable circumstances. To overcome these limitations, the party called for a total overhaul of the state's economy, overseen and run by the government. The two key economic recommendations involved the expansion of heavy industry—'the means towards rapid economic development'—and agricultural reform, including the establishment of cooperatives and improved infrastructures. Workers—both men and women—would be protected, with regulated salaries and working hours and the provision of state-built housing. The platform also made much of the need to 'solve the urgent problems of the nomads and tribal life in a democratic and humane way and to guide and direct them towards agricultural and industrial activities'.

Politically speaking, the PDPA emphasized the importance of a parliament as the 'best organ for making laws and administrating people' and as the key form of 'national democracy'. The platform also included a protracted list of necessary personal freedoms:

> freedom of thought and belief; freedom of speech; freedom of pen and press; social freedom; freedom of forming political parties; freedom of organizing unions; freedom to strike; freedom to demonstrate; freedom to travel; freedom to choose one's work or occupation; protection of the rights of the individual; freedom to establish residence; freedom to communicate and the right to defend oneself in court; the right to vote...the right to be elected...equality before the law...

It concluded: 'the entire protection of all of the democratic rights and freedoms, political and social, of the individuals is a duty without any discrimination without [sic] sex, male or female, race, tribe, region, religion and degree of culture, occupation or wealth.'[21]

Notably, the PDPA made much of the idea of an Afghan 'nation'. It wrestled with Afghanistan's ethnic diversity—ethnic groups such as Tajiks, Hazara, Uzbeks, and Turkmens had historically fraught ties with the Pashtuns, who overwhelmingly dominated state politics—but fundamentally argued that unity would prevail. 'When the actual pattern of the country is taken into consideration', the platform declared,

> it is found that Afghanistan is a country composed of hard-working people who are endowed with different regional cultures which have together over the centuries resulted in giving the country its national character and which have united the people because of common griefs in their struggles against feudalism and colonialism.

The experience of labouring under the Musahiban family's rule, the PDPA argued, united all Afghans regardless of ethnic, tribal, or locational differences. Echoing Tarzi fifty years before, 'Afghan' was an identity above all else, and the PDPA would strive to uphold this. The PDPA's pledge was 'the fight of all sections of the population against national oppression and the removal of the causes of ethnic, racial, tribal and local differences which result in national disaffections'. Afghan-ness would be promulgated through compulsory, free education conducted in local languages, not just Dari or Pashto, and the party promised 'to develop the languages and the cultures of the various people and tribes of the country and the national cultural heritage of Afghanistan'. In this reading, the PDPA put forward the argument that it could and would embrace differences between communities across Afghanistan, but, ultimately, they would overcome any divisions by promoting a conception of national unity that was rooted in a shared experience of working for national progress.[22]

In outward-facing declarations, like the published platform, the party's stance was fairly moderate. While it paid homage to 'the Great Socialist Revolution of October', it made no mention of Marxism-Leninism and largely spoke of alternatives to capitalism, rather than articulating a clear definition of socialism. Instead, as noted, the political emphasis was on representational government and human rights. This was necessary to prevent a harsh reaction from the state as well as Afghans who associated communism with the Soviet Union's violent campaigns against Central Asian Muslims in the 1920s.[23] But it probably also helped frame many of the PDPA's aspirations in terms recognizable (and appealing) to a wide berth of educated Afghans. Political and economic reform and the promotion of individual rights were hardly issues of contention for Afghans aware of their country's stagnancy.

However, in internal documents, the PDPA articulated a more radical vision. The party's constitution, which was kept secret until it was leaked in 1978, explicitly embraced Marxism-Leninism as the future of Afghanistan. The constitution tasked the party member with, among other duties, 'raising his own ideological awareness and learning the political theories of Marxism-Leninism', 'propagating the thoughts of scientific socialism, the ideas of proletarian rationalism and internationalism among the masses', and 'expanding and strengthening the friendly relations between Afghans and the Soviets'. In language similar to that found in early Bolshevik and Chinese communist declarations, members were encouraged towards developing and expanding 'criticism (in general) and self-criticism and correcting and pursuing mistakes that veer from the path of true criticism'.[24] The PDPA also clearly modelled its structures on the Soviet Union's. The constitution made the party congress the highest authority, followed by the central committee, which ran day-to-day operations. A number of subcommittees and conferences reported to the central committee.[25] The constitution revealed the PDPA's aspirations fundamentally to alter Afghanistan and establish a regime, inspired by the Soviet Union, that openly embraced socialism.

But in the space intervening between the party's formation and its ultimate rise to power, the PDPA ran into a number of problems. First, while the party tried to make its message universal, in reality it represented a finite few, not the Afghan masses, despite later claims. The PDPA focused on recruiting elites. These included Afghans educated abroad, intellectuals sent West to complete their studies, military officers sent to the Soviet Union for training, as well as students at Kabul University.[26] While these groups were exposed to differing models of modernization, they all agreed on one thing: the centrality of the state in ruling Afghanistan and the need to eliminate older social and political structures ('family, clientism or tribalism').[27] However, they did not take into account how Afghans outside Kabul's elite circles might react to these issues. How would they sell this message of progress to the country?

Secondly, the PDPA's political aspirations fell immediately short. The 1965 parliamentary elections, which had helped precipitate the PDPA's formation, were not intended to induce broad political change. Taraki and many other PDPA members faced defeat in the elections, which were largely rigged in favour of government stalwarts. Only three PDPA members succeeded, including Dr Anahita Ratebzad, one of the only women voted into office. As such, the PDPA remained very much a party on the outskirts of power. Instead, Taraki's influence largely continued to develop via his publication, the leftist paper, *Khalq* (*The Masses,* or *The People*), though even this was shut down within six weeks of beginning printing owing to its anti-government message.

Finally, and ultimately most importantly, the PDPA almost immediately succumbed to infighting, which led to its division into two different factions. In July 1967, only two and a half years after its inception, a split occurred between followers of Nur Mohammad Taraki and Babrak Karmal. These two groups became known by their affiliated publications—the erstwhile *Khalq* and Karmal's *Parcham* (*Banner*), which began printing in 1968 and managed to evade government closure. The split resulted from both personality clashes and ideological differences. Both factions claimed to represent a singular PDPA, but, in practice, they each had separate secretary-generals and central committees.[28] Taraki's Khalq promoted a workers-led revolution along Leninist lines. Karmal's Parcham was more moderate, advocating a broader national-democratic front, which would include Afghans from across the economic and political spectrum, to spark political change. The two groups were also divided in their ethnic make-up. While Khalq was more reflective of Afghanistan's ethnic diversity, including other groups alongside the Pashtun political majority, Parcham, in contrast, was dominated by Kabuli (urban, educated, fairly well-to-do) Pashtuns.

Even at this early stage, personalities were also an issue. Both Taraki and Amin clashed with Karmal.[29] One contemporary told the anthropologist David Edwards:

When Hafizullah Amin would come in [to the parliamentary chamber], he would go and sit down with some mulla, and talk and joke. Then he would sit with some elder or some khan or some other deputy or with some educated person...He would talk and joke with everyone...Everyone rejected his political connections, but all of the deputies had social and personal relations with him...

In contrast, Karmal 'wouldn't socialize with the deputies. He would come in, looking very serious. He would always go to the left and sit down in a chair in his customary and permanent place. That wretched man would just sit there, quietly, not saying anything. This was his character...'.[30]

Over the subsequent decade, the Khalq and Parcham factions lived uneasily side by side. The Parcham faction supported Daoud in his 1973 coup, while Khalq did not. However, any hopes that Karmal and his allies might have had that they would be given a seat at the governing table were quickly dashed. Daoud and his cronies almost immediately sidelined Parcham members. After being effectively shut out of the government, the Parcham faction reunited with their Khalq counterparts in 1977, thanks to Soviet pressures on both to cooperate. While the two sides presented a united front, in fact ongoing feuding between them persisted, as did mutual suspicion. It is thus unsurprising that the united front would break down within months of the April 1978 coup. By September 1978, leading Parcham members of the new PDPA government would be effectively banished and would return to power only on the heels of the Soviet invasion.

Much as Kabul University served as the crucible for emergent leftist politics among educated Afghans, so did it serve an even greater role for Afghan Islamism. In the mid-1960s, the Organization of Muslim Youth, or Sazman-i Javanan-i Musalman, emerged as an important body on campus. Much like the PDPA, Muslim Youth's message was not inward-looking. It was directly informed by external developments—the religious–political thought and political changes emerging across the Muslim and decolonizing worlds. Where PDPA leaders drew inspiration from Marxism-Leninism and tenets advocated by the Soviet Union, Islamists were informed by a network of thinkers and organizations firmly rooted in the non-European, anti-colonial international sphere.

In the early to mid-twentieth century, a number of individuals and groups turned to Islam as a source of political mobilization and anti-imperial inspiration. They sought to justify resistance against and expulsion of imperial forces, chief among them Great Britain, using the rationale of religion and to assert that Muslims sat on the same civilizational plane as Europeans. Islam provided a means for articulating a new political life for former colonial subjects. This political vision drew cohesion from its members' shared religion and guidance provided by the Quran.[31] Particularly crucial in many of the demands for politicized Islam that coalesced during this time was that they were forward-looking. While they drew on the past, they reconceptualized the future.

The early decades of the twentieth century saw an explosion in pan-Islamist activity and the politicization of Islam. Ottoman intellectuals revived the idea of an 'Islamic civilization' that rivalled Europe and advocated an intellectual and political renaissance among Muslim populations, something that spoke to Afghan Islamic revivalists. The Khilafat Movement that emerged in colonial India at the end of the First World War over concerns about the Ottoman caliph—seen by many Sunni Muslims as the human representative of God—protested against the interference of British officials in colonial subjects' religious lives and more broadly resisted imperial governance. In Egypt, in 1928, the Society of Muslim Brothers, or Muslim Brotherhood, was formed in response to frustrations with infighting among other (mainly secular) Egyptian nationalist groups, as well as recurrent British interventions (in the interest of maintaining access to the Suez Canal). The Brotherhood developed cells across Egypt that advocated individual, private re-adherence to Islam as well as a 'comprehensive system of values and governance intrinsically different from—and superior to—the secular political systems of the West'. By the mid-twentieth century, the Muslim Brotherhood had become 'the flagship organization of Sunni revivalist Islam'.[32]

Islam had previously served as a key influence within Afghan society and politics. The slogan 'Islam in danger' was used as a rallying call by Afghan rulers during the First, Second, and Third Anglo-Afghan wars. It created a clear point of opposition to British imperialism and the threat of foreign rule and consequently an easy source of countrywide mobilization. Amanullah used Afghanistan's Islamic past to demonstrate its independence from British rule shortly after the Third Anglo-Afghan War, inviting Indian Muslims to participate in *hijrat*, or religious migration, to Afghanistan in support of the Khilafat movement and to escape religious persecution under British rule. Equally notably, however, Afghan *ulama* also used the call of Islam in danger to encourage widespread uprisings against Amanullah's own secularist reforms later in the 1920s. Islam provided a double-edged sword, but it tended to be politicized only in times of conflict, whether in terms of external aggression or of internal discord.[33] In 1951, Sayyid Ismail Balkhi, a Shi'a cleric, formed a secret political organization to oppose the Afghan government, advocating an Islamic republic to resolve Afghanistan's outstanding sociopolitical issues and to repulse discrimination against Afghanistan's Hazara community. He was arrested and imprisoned but served as an inspiration for religiously informed revolutionary politics, particularly to Shi'ite Afghan Islamists in the 1980s.[34]

Afghans thus were active in these early pan-Islamic networks, which would help underpin some of the linkages and political ideas in Afghanistan later in the twentieth century. Many local clerics had ties with the Deoband school of thought and its associated *madrassas* in colonial India, even as the Afghan state increasingly constructed its own centres of both religious and secular learning. From the 1950s, Afghan students also were sent to universities abroad, such as al-Azhar in Cairo, where they encountered and became involved with the Muslim Brotherhood.[35]

Against this backdrop, three religious intellectuals informed Afghan Sunni Islamist thought: Sayyid Abu'l-A'la Mawdudi (1903–79), Abul Hasan 'Ali Nadwi (1913–99), and Sayyid Qutb (1906–66). Parallel to this was the emergence of revolutionary political Shi'ism in Iran under the leadership of Ayatollah Khomeini.[36] Mawdudi and Nadwi both emerged in colonial South Asia—Nadwi remained in India after 1947, while Mawdudi settled in newly established Pakistan, where he formed the *Jama'at-i Islami*. Qutb, a leading member of the Muslim Brotherhood, grew up, and was later executed, in Egypt.

The politico-religious thought of Mawdudi and Qutb was particularly evident in later Afghan Islamist rhetoric. (Nadwi's writings increasingly focused on the role and opportunities for a Muslim minority in independent India, a situation that clearly differed from Muslim-majority Pakistan, Egypt, and Afghanistan. However, he was also responsible for first introducing Mawdudi's writings into Egypt in 1951, which shaped Qutb's own thinking.[37]) Mawdudi and Qutb, if in slightly different ways, argued that religion and politics were fundamentally connected. Islam was neither merely the realm of religious scholarship nor that of individual worship. It was a universalist system that provided guidance for all aspects of life, not only for individuals but for society among the *ummah*. In the words of Qutb: 'Religion in the Islamic understanding is synonymous with the term nizam [order] as found in modern usage, with the complete meaning of a creed in the heart, ethics in behavior, and law in society.'[38] Mawdudi explicated:

> Our way is quite different both from the Muslim scholar of the recent past and modern Europeanized stock. On the one hand we have to imbibe exactly the Qur'an spirit and identify our outlook with the Islamic tenets while, on the other, we have to assess thoroughly the developments in the field of knowledge and changes in condition in life that have been brought during the last eight hundred years; and third, we have to arrange these ideas and laws of life on genuine Islamic lines so that Islam should once again become a dynamic force; the leader of the world rather than its follower.[39]

Mawdudi's writings point to an important issue. The interpretation of Islam advocated by both Mawdudi and Qutb was modern. In this it sharply contrasted with Salafism, another Sunni religious movement that looked to emulate early Muslim legal and theological practices.[40] While Mawdudi and Qutb looked to the past and the Quran to guide political structures and relationships, their interpretations resulted directly from these thinkers' encounters with their own times. Mawdudi and Qutb sought alternatives to the imperial structures that had shaped their upbringings, as well as the continued pervasive power of foreign countries in the era of decolonization and Cold War. Neo-colonialism, whether in the form of economic pressure, development aid with political strings attached, covert intervention, or political interference, continued to shape politics in the non-Western world and left not just former imperial powers but countries such as the United States and Soviet Union with outstanding influence in other countries' domestic affairs. Equally, Mawdudi's and Qutb's political Islam critiqued postcolonial leaders' ready adoption of Western models of statehood and development. Indeed, Qutb was executed for coming up against Nasser's avidly secular nationalism, while Mawdudi interrogated the potential of Pakistan as an *Islamic* state, not just a state *for* Muslims.

Intellectuals across the political and religious spectrum sought alternatives to continued systems of inequality—hence the continued spread of Marxism-Leninism, Maoism, socialism, Afro-Asian solidarity networks, and politicized religion. 'Mawdudi's ideal was in the *image* of the past but in the *nature* of the modern world.'[41] In effect, Mawdudi wanted to use the Quran, the very basis and root of Islam, to create a new, alternative political order, to fuse religion and the state. Qutb similarly sought a 'powerful social movement' that would 'repair the ruptures in society that had resulted in apostasy, alienation, and decadence, and to establish a balanced and cohesive system based on the universal principles of Islam'.[42] With Islamism, in the words of the historian Faisal Devji, 'a global history of the West is matched at every point by its effects upon the Muslim world, which is seen as being co-extensive with it and forming a mirror history of the West itself'.[43]

This new generation of Islamic thinkers, through the democratization of religious knowledge, aspired 'to develop a modern political ideology based on Islam, which they see as the only way to come to terms with the modern world and the best means of confronting foreign imperialism'.[44] But *how*, exactly, such ideas were to be put into practice was unclear. Mawdudi was vague on this—for example, envisioning a state anchored in democracy but also relying on *imamat-i salihah* (virtuous leadership) of a caliph or amir, appointed through indeterminate means. He envisioned rule of Islamic law (*shari'a*), a consultative assembly (*shura*), and a judicial system—but how these various branches would work together and alongside an amir was never clear.[45] Qutb similarly argued that state sovereignty rested in the 'supreme authority of God, *hakimiyya*, and His message as revealed in the Qur'an'.[46] Like Mawdudi, Qutb identified a caliph as God's representative on earth and emphasized the primary role of *shari'a* in dictating social expectations and participation. *Shari'a* would ensure legal justice, security, material sustenance, social equilibrium. He also indicated that the *shura* would play a crucial role. But, again, Qutb did not identify specific mechanisms for putting such a system into place. He 'seemed more interested in the spirit of Islam that holds the government together in its unity than in its actual structure'.[47] One point that was clear, however, was *jihad* was meant to eliminate *jahiliyya*, or religious ignorance, and establish *hakimiyya*.[48] In Mawdudi's reading, *jihad* provided the means of obtaining political power rather than constituting a militarized 'holy war'.[49] However, Afghans across the spectrum later used both rationales to justify both a military and a political *jihad* against the Soviets and PDPA.

Thus, Afghan Islamism—alternatively referred to by various scholars and contemporaries as 'radical', 'militant', and 'fundamentalist' Islam—did not emerge in a vacuum.[50] Instead it paralleled and was entangled with the ongoing discussions of what an Islamic state looked like. It emerged at a moment when splits were emerging in many Muslim-majority states in the decolonizing world about what constituted a modern future: the Western model of secular, development-oriented statehood or an alternative that embraced the overlap between the political and the religious and sought guidance in Islam. This was apparent in Nasser's clashes with the Muslim Brotherhood and equally in Ayatollah Khomeini's critiques of both the Shah and clerics within Iran whom he accused of being reactionary. Afghan intellectuals came into contact with these currents.[51]

The Islamist movement that emerged at Kabul University was more informed by the Muslim Brotherhood in Egypt than the Islamic traditions and schools of South Asia affiliated with Mawdudi and Nadwi. There are two key reasons for this. First, the history of relations between Afghanistan and Pakistan after 1947, as we shall see shortly, meant that the government did not encourage Afghans to go to Pakistan to study in *madrassas* or other institutions. (Moreover, Mawdudi and his political organization, Jamaʿat-i Islami, were also preoccupied with domestic politics in Pakistan.) Instead, the Afghan government funded the study of Afghan educators at al-Azhar University in Cairo, whence many returned to teach in Kabul. Thus, Qutb's teachings took root among faculty members at Kabul University who not only came into direct contact with the Muslim Brotherhood but subsequently had the opportunity further to disseminate these ideas to their students in Kabul. Indeed, the term *ikhwan* (Arabic for 'brother') was frequently used by Afghans, both as a source of pride and as an insult, to indicate those who engaged with a politicized Islam. In contrast, Mawdudi's teachings arrived in Afghanistan more circuitously in the ways they informed Qutb's, and thereby the Brotherhood's, own thought, and via illicit trans-frontier movement in the Afghan–Pakistan borderlands, which Afghan state leaders actively tried to curb.[52] Nevertheless, Mawdudi's presence would continue to be felt even after his death in September 1979, as the Afghan resistance coalesced around Peshawar, Pakistan.

The Organization of Muslim Youth was founded by Kabul University students but inspired by faculty members from the Faculty of Theology who had studied in Cairo, particularly the charismatic Ghulam Mohammad Niazi. Professors like Niazi 'did not take a direct role in student activities', but 'they informed the students of movements going on in other parts of the Muslim world and provided them with a sense of how Islam could be made relevant to the social and political transformations everywhere apparent in the latter half of the twentieth century'.[53] The Muslim Youth encouraged its members and potential recruits to look to God and the Quran, not godless Marxism-Leninism, to provide a plan for future development that would bring equality and prosperity to all Afghans. It is thus of little surprise that the grounds of Kabul University became a war zone, increasingly replete with violence, between young Islamists and Marxists, as they, and their competing visions of Afghan and global modernity, came into conflict. Indeed, in 1972, a number of Muslim Youth leaders, including Gulbuddin Hekmatyar, the future leader of Hizb-i Islami, were arrested after protests led to the death of a young Afghan Maoist.[54]

However, much like the PDPA, Afghan Islamists faced internal divisions during the 1970s as different interest groups emerged. They lacked clear leadership, thanks to internal divides and organization. The movement's student founder died in 1970, leaving a power void. A generational divide also became increasingly apparent between older members of the faculty and younger student firebrands who made up some factions of the Muslim Youth more inclined to militancy. In parallel to the Muslim Youth, faculty members at Kabul University organized themselves secretly, something that few students knew. A council comprised of university faculty members, known as Jamʿiyyat-i Islami-yi Afghanistan, was established in 1973 and would serve as the basis for the political party of the same name that took a lead in the anti-socialist resistance.[55]

How the Islamist message should be disseminated was disputed. Some students saw the organization as one rooted in campus politics, while others advocated for the movement to go national. Additional groups emerged alongside the Muslim Youth promoting Islam to resolve Afghanistan's future, such as *Hizb-i Tauhid*, the Monotheism Party. As factions of the Muslim Youth began to assert their influence beyond Kabul, members were mobilized into small cells, based on their location. They were deliberately kept in the dark about the organization's broader membership to prevent infiltration by government agents.[56] Islamists had the most success in recruiting members among educated Afghans, ranging across state-run *madrassas*, higher-education faculties, and secondary schools. They were particularly successful around the city of Herat and in the eastern provinces of Baghlan, Takhar, Mazar, Panjshir, Ghorband, Laghman, Kunar, and Nangarhar among Afghans who had been taught in the state system. Notably, these areas would later correspond with some of the major areas of early resistance to the PDPA. In contrast, Islamists had far less impact in areas of Afghanistan where state systems were less embedded and where tribal politics and local religious leaders held greater sway.[57] Like socialism, Islamism in the 1960s and 1970s remained largely a phenomenon among educated Afghans.

In contrast to the PDPA, which had a party manifesto and specific structures (even after the Khalq–Parcham split), Afghan Islamists remained dispersed without a clear organizational platform. While Islamists aspired to 'the overthrow of the ruling order, its replacement by the Islamic order [*nizam*], and the application of Islam in political, economic, and social spheres', in the words of Hizb-i Islami's Gulbuddin Hekmatyar, they had no clear plans for implementation, nor did they have a strong centre to lead such a process.[58] Given the lack of direction provided by Qutb, Mawdudi, or other Islamist thinkers, this is hardly surprising, but few among the Afghan Islamists seemed to have come up with very specific plans either. The Islamists also lacked a clear leader of the likes of Taraki, Amin, or Karmal, instead relying on a broad base of organizers.[59] Events like the campus killing in 1972 forced the Muslim Youth and other Islamist organizations to go largely underground, as they were seen as an anti-government body.

Circumstances did not improve after the 1973 coup that brought Daoud to power. Instead, his alliance with the PDPA's Parcham faction further threatened Islamists and led to a new wave of repression. As Mohammad Es'haq, a member of Jam'iyyat, later recalled:

> The little political freedom which was granted by the monarchy ended with the coup. The Communists got a free hand to propagate their ideology under the guise of supporting the new republic. Daud was a prince, with no party and no direct contact with the people. The communists provided him with party and supporters. Because of the above developments the Islamic movement lost hope in a peaceful way of struggle and resorted to secret means of opposing Daud and his communist colleagues.[60]

Es'haq's memoir, published in a Jam'iyyat newsletter in 1989, gives an indication of what was to come. A number of Islamist leaders fled to Pakistan within a year of Daoud's rise to power, otherwise facing the threat of imprisonment. Peshawar subsequently became the centre of Afghan Islamist organization and mobilization. Those Islamists who remained within the country made various secret plans for attempting to overthrow Daoud's regime, in coordination with the exiles in Peshawar.

The year 1975 was crucial. In late July, coordinated Islamist attacks took place on government structures in Badakhshan, Laghman, Logar, and Panjshir. The attacks failed totally and completely. They were poorly planned, uncoordinated, and run by small groups of dissidents. They did not attract local support and were all immediately defeated by government forces, with the brief exception of Panjshir, where rebel forces held out for most of a day. In the aftermath, more Islamists were rounded up, imprisoned, executed by government forces, or forced to flee for their lives.[61] Es'haq, who took part in the Panjshir revolt remembered: 'For six days we were wandering in the mountains with no food, no warm clothes and being followed by the enemy. This was a testing time.' He and his brother managed to flee first to their home village before travelling on to Kabul and then to Peshawar (his brother was subsequently killed in fighting in 1979). Es'haq made an important point in his reflections. 'In isolation, we started to look at the problem from a critical angle. Why was such action taken? Was it an independent action or part of [a] bigger plan? I knew that everything had gone wrong.'[62]

Es'haq was not alone in this judgement. The failure of the 1975 revolts not only led to the destruction of the Islamist movement within Afghanistan—any remnants were in prison or in hiding—but also led to infighting among exiled Islamists. Factions accused each other of formulating the doomed rebellion and not providing adequate support for Islamist forces that had remained in Afghanistan. The accusations and tensions boiled down to two key groups: the supporters of Rabbani and the supporters of Hekmatyar.

Burhanuddin Rabbani represented an older generation of Afghan Islamists. He had been a professor at Kabul University, where he taught in the Faculty of Islamic Law. He had received a master's degree in Islamic philosophy at al-Azhar University in the mid-1960s, and had also begun the task of translating Sayyid Qutb's written works into Persian. He was a close friend and ally of Ghulam Mohammad Niazi and chairman of Jam'iyyat, the secret faculty council. He managed to flee to Pakistan when Niazi was imprisoned in 1974. (Rabbani was also part of Afghanistan's ethnic Tajik community, a point to which we will return.) In contrast, Gulbuddin Hekmatyar represented the younger generation. He had become involved in Islamist politics as a student in Kabul University's School of Engineering and played a key role in the Muslim Youth Organization's founding. There is little doubt that Hekmatyar was more militant in his pursuit of Islamist politics: he indicated keen willingness to use violence, as demonstrated in the 1972 events that led to his brief imprisonment, as well as his later tactics during the war.[63]

Rabbani's and Hekmatyar's followers blamed each other for the failings of 1975. While Rabbani had been in Saudi Arabia at the time of the revolts, seeking regional support for Afghanistan's Islamist exiles, Hekmatyar's advocates claimed, without any clear evidence, that Rabbani, in fact, sympathized with and had warned the Afghan government about the rebellions. In turn, Rabbani's followers accused

Hekmatyar of disastrously poor planning and falsely promising local Islamist groups that government troops in Kabul were ready and eager to mobilize in their support. The divide on this issue, no doubt aggravated by the fact that blame could not be easily pinned on any single individual, led to a rupture in exile Islamist politics. Rabbani remained the head of Jam'iyyat-i Islami-yi Afghanistan, now effectively a political association, but Hekmatyar and his followers left to create their own, more militant party, Hizb-i Islami-yi Afghanistan. Hizb-i Islami, in turn, would undergo a second split in 1979, owing to clashes between Hekmatyar and Yunis Khalis, an older cleric who, along with other *ulama*, accused Hekmatyar of lacking the religious understanding to lead a truly Islamist revolution.[64] Much like the PDPA, this only complicated matters, since both parties continued to call themselves Hizb-i Islami.

Thus, the events of 1975 crucially shaped the Islamist resistance that emerged in the wake of the 1978 coup. Not only did they result in these two parties, Jam'iyyat and Hizb-i Islami, which would become two of the most prominent and influential Islamist parties of the 1980s. They also point to a critical issue. The resistance to the Soviets that grew in leaps and bounds from 1978–9 had a much longer history. The pre-coup experiences of these Afghan Islamists had significant consequences. As one observer noted in 1984, the Islamists' struggle against the Daoud regime meant 'they had acquired legitimacy by the Soviet intervention. They could tell the refugees that they had started the armed struggle in 1975, predicting that "godless communism" was Afghanistan's main enemy.'[65] Additionally, the Islamists' earlier activities, and exile in Peshawar, meant they already boasted organizational structures, including trained, armed cadres and ties with the sympathetic government of Pakistan, even if they lacked a clear vision for an Islamist Afghanistan. In this sense, once conflict had erupted, Afghan Islamists were well placed to combat the PDPA, based on their past experiences, and could use this history to appeal to new followers.

While the PDPA, Jam'iyyat, and Hizb-i Islami sought alternatives to a system that they viewed as stale and elitist, chafing at the slow pace of modernization and the fact that power remained overwhelmingly in the hands of a dynastic ruling family, Afghan state leaders had more strategic concerns. They could focus on internal reform only against the backdrop of their regional relationships. For a landlocked state like Afghanistan, this was particularly the case. Good neighbourly relations meant the easy transit of goods and people, as well as ideas, in and out of the country. Bad dealings could obstruct this, halting Afghan exports and barring the entry of necessary supplies. As such, Afghanistan's domestic and foreign policies could not help but be interlinked, and, for much of the twentieth century, tense regional relations undermined, rather than benefited, Afghan progress.

The fact that relations between Afghanistan and Pakistan soured almost from the moment of Pakistan's independence in August 1947 fundamentally shaped both states' trajectory as well as that of the greater South Asian region. Afghan leaders had seen the partition of the subcontinent into the states of India and Pakistan as the opportunity to undo colonial wrongdoings and, more specifically, to reunite the

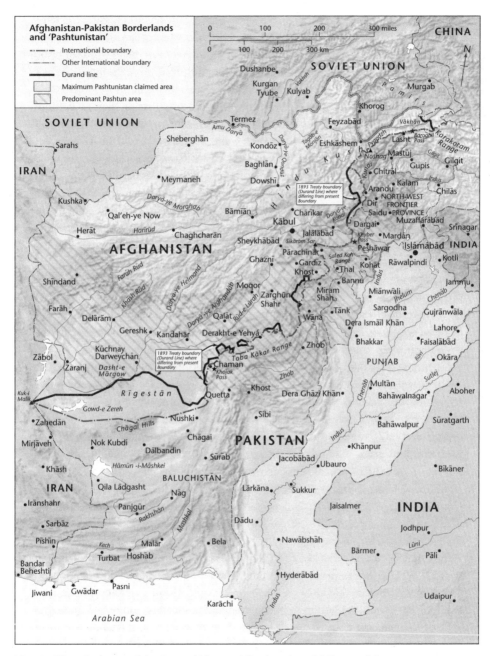

**Map 3.** Historical map of the Durand Line and 'Pashtunistan' (Library of Congress, Geography and Map Division)

Pashtun populations that had been bifurcated by the drawing of the Durand Line in 1893. Pakistani leaders maintained that the Durand Line represented an international border, citing treaty precedent; Afghans insisted it was a colonial relic that had been unfairly imposed by British imperialists and did not match the region's history or ethnic composition. Afghan leaders, particularly Mohammad Daoud Khan, advocated the creation of an autonomous 'Pashtunistan' carved out of Pakistan's provinces, Balochistan and the North-West Frontier Province (NWFP) (what is now Khyber Pakhtunkhwa), and comprising Pakistan's ethnic Pashtun minority (see Map 3).

The Afghan government's emphasis on ethnic Pashtuns and Afghanistan's supposedly Pashtun national identity helped neither its foreign nor its domestic affairs. The overwhelming focus on Pashtunistan created hostility with Afghanistan's neighbours and also alienated Afghanistan's other ethnic groups (see Map 4), who already resented Afghan Pashtuns' preferential treatment. This was exacerbated by leaders like Daoud who actively promoted the 'Pashtunization' of Afghanistan. Afghanistan's leaders eliminated non-Pashtun ethnic patronyms and limited support for non-Pashto and non-Dari language broadcasts, effectively excluding Afghans who spoke Turkic languages or other Persian-language offshoots like Hazaragi. They also celebrated an annual Pashtunistan Day and renamed a major square in Kabul as Pashtunistan Square.[66] Such policies did little to endear the ruling elite to Afghanistan's diverse population, nor did they give many Afghans an active stake in the government's survival. Unsurprisingly, then, educated reformist groups like the PDPA began to criticize the persisting divisions of tribe and ethnicity within Afghanistan as a critical weakness in the state's national identity and structure.

Afghan officials never made clear whether they meant Pashtunistan to be truly independent or a subsidiary of Afghanistan. Nevertheless, the conflict between Afghanistan and Pakistan resulted in a series of almost-wars. The Pashtunistan issue reared its ugly head in the mid-1950s, early 1960s, and again in the mid-1970s, as tensions emerged between Daoud and Pakistan's Zulfikar Ali Bhutto. Indeed, it was against the backdrop of the Pashtunistan dispute that Bhutto welcomed fleeing Afghan Islamists and allowed them to settle around Peshawar. They offered a potential future tool in the Pakistani state's attempts to undermine Afghan demands and move bilateral relations away from the two countries' shared Pashtun population. Conflict was avoided, as both leaders concluded they would benefit from friendlier relations. A series of official state visits in 1976 led to the tacit agreement not to let the Pashtunistan dispute again become the centre of attention, a policy that was reaffirmed during Daoud's final visit to Pakistan, a little more than a month before his death.[67] Yet the Pashtunistan issue was unlikely to go away, given its links to the Durand Line dispute and thus the sanctity of Afghanistan and Pakistan's borders. Even the PDPA, while advocating trans-tribal and trans-ethnic unity in Afghanistan, decried the Durand Line as 'the colonialists' borderline', and elements within the party continued to advocate a specifically Pashtun nationalism.[68]

The dispute between Afghanistan and Pakistan inevitably spilled into their relations with their other neighbours and blended with Cold-War considerations. Iran, for example, refused to support Afghanistan's rulers in their dispute with Pakistan. The Shah feared that Afghanistan might be tempted to make similar claims to Iran's and Afghanistan's shared ethnic groups, such as the Baloch, or that cross-border populations might try to make their own independence claims, as occurred in Pakistani Balochistan in the mid-1970s. And, as a staunch ally of the United States,

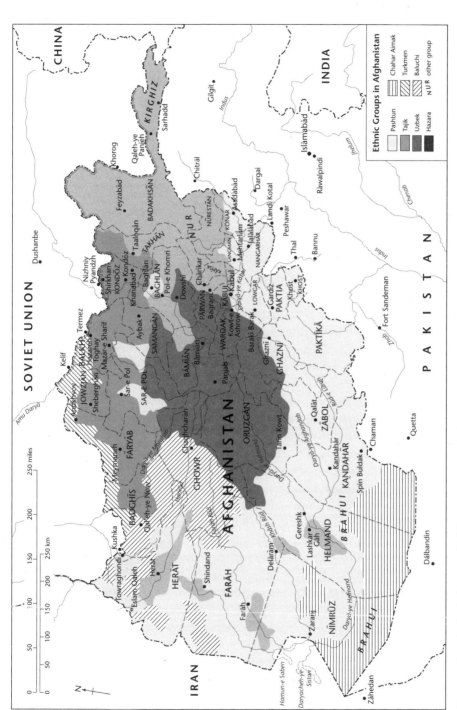

**Map 4.** Historical ethnic map of Afghanistan, c.1979 (Library of Congress, Geography and Map Division)

**Ethnic Groups in Afghanistan**

- Pashtun
- Tajik
- Uzbek
- Hazara
- Chahar Aimak
- Turkmen
- Baluchi
- N U R other group

the Shah evinced suspicion of President Daoud for his seemingly pro-Soviet leanings, a circumstance not helped by Daoud's initial alliance with the PDPA. Daoud's
decision to remain visibly neutral in the Cold War, as well as his active efforts to
improve relations with Iran, helped to normalize relations. By the mid-1970s, Iran
had agreed to a ten-year deal to provide $2 billion in economic aid to the Afghan
state, among other development support programmes.[69]

China, sharing a short, 76-kilometre border with Afghanistan, also kept a wary
eye on South/Central Asia, though this had more to do with Sino-Soviet relations
than local affairs. By 1978, the Sino-Soviet split that had ruptured the communist world
still lingered, dividing countries and leaders between those supporting the moderate
Soviet paths of Nikita Khrushchev and Leonid Brezhnev and those embracing the
more militant Mao Zedong thought.[70] This ideological split had real, practical implications. A border dispute erupted between the Soviet Union and China, while countries emerging from empire had carefully to navigate choosing one side or the other
in a quest for economic and political aid. In decolonizing countries, communist
movements were forced to pick either the Soviet Union or China. Other independent states had to walk a fine line between the two. In South Asia, India was more
sympathetic to the Soviet Union—driven in part by the Sino-Indian border dispute
that broke out in war in 1962—while Pakistan actively fostered good ties with China.
Afghanistan tended towards the Soviets, though this did not stop Chinese efforts to
seek good relations. China continued to provide foreign aid to the Afghan government, including $33.6 million for irrigation projects and a textile factory and tech-
nical expertise to explore riverine fishery and tea plantation development.[71]

Fears of a Soviet plot, real or imagined, to encircle China with Soviet allies led
Chinese leaders to link their thinking on Afghanistan to events in South-East Asia.
Sino-North Vietnamese relations had been ruptured by Hanoi's decision in 1968 to
enter negotiations with Washington at a time when US–China relations were hostile.
They became even worse in the 1970s, ironically because Vietnamese leaders who
sympathized with Maoism became alienated by US-Sino rapprochement from 1971.
Chinese leaders, fearing a Soviet–Vietnam axis, attempted to develop local allies but
with disastrous results. China supported the Communist Party of Kampuchea, or
Khmer Rouge, as it pursued a radical, violent policy of modernization, as well as a
genocide against ethnic minorities. The Khmer Rouge's policies sparked a border
dispute and refugee crisis that inundated Vietnam. Vietnam subsequently invaded
Cambodia in late December 1978 and established the People's Republic of Kampuchea.
In retaliation for this attack on its ally, the PRC invaded Vietnam in mid-February
1979 in an effort to force a Vietnamese withdrawal from Cambodia. Chinese forces
failed and withdrew ignominiously back into China by mid-March.[72] In this context,
the PDPA's successes would gain significance in Chinese eyes. In December 1978,
the *Beijing Review*, one of the government's international mouthpieces, decried
Vietnam's decision to sign 'with the Soviet Union a "treaty of friendship and cooperation" which is actually a military alliance'.[73] Chinese officials could not, and did not,
separate concerns about Soviet policy in South-East Asia from that in South-West

Asia. Increased Soviet–Afghan cooperation threatened to create a debacle like that in South-East Asia and the total encirclement of China.

Finally, while sharing no direct borders with Afghanistan, India nevertheless remained interested in Afghan affairs. The two countries found common ground in their tense relations with Pakistan, the country that now stood between the two. Not only were relations frequently dictated by the fate of Kashmir, a former princely state in the border regions that both countries claimed as their own, but India and Pakistan competed in their military, economic, and social development. The presence of Afghanistan as another South Asian neighbouring state meant, then, that it potentially served as a fulcrum in the regional power balance.

Playing on Afghan antagonism towards Pakistan, Indian leaders pledged their friendship, quietly backing Afghanistan's stance on the Pashtunistan dispute and providing economic aid. India even openly declared support for Pashtunistan during the 1965 Indo-Pakistan war, trying to get Afghanistan on side, though with little success. The Afghan regime remained mutedly neutral in the conflict, as it occurred at a time when Afghan–Pakistan relations were actually improving.[74] Despite both states' professed non-alignment in the Cold War, something Jawaharlal Nehru had touted in the mid-1950s, both countries' pursuit of foreign development aid also brought them into increased contact with the Soviet Union, serving as an additional point of synergy. Unlike their shared neighbour, Pakistan, which publicly broadcast its relationship with the United States in the late 1950s and early 1970s (the 1965 war led to a brief cooling in relations), both India and Afghanistan continued to maintain active ties with the Soviet Union.[75]

At the moment that the reign of Mohammad Daoud Khan ended in April 1978, the entire region, not just Afghanistan, was in flux. This contingency, perhaps more than anything else, reshaped what would begin as a domestic coup into a region-engulfing civil war. Pakistan, India, China, and most notably Iran had all recently emerged from, or were undergoing, domestic turmoil. In Pakistan, President Bhutto, the charismatic leader of the Pakistan People's Party, languished in prison in April 1978, having been overthrown by the Pakistan army under its chief of army staff, Mohammad Zia-ul-Haq.[76] Zia had been an outsider before Bhutto made him head of Pakistan's army. Born into a humble family in 1924 in Jalandhar, in what became Indian Punjab, he had not gone straight into the army. He first attended St Stephens College in Delhi before joining the British Indian Army. Unlike many of Pakistan's army leaders, he never attended Sandhurst. A devout Muslim, he opted to move to Pakistan at the time of partition in August 1947. He would later say: 'I will tell you what Islam and Pakistan means to me. It is a vision of my mother struggling on, tired, with all her worldly possessions in her hands, when she crossed the border into Pakistan.'[77] Zia, a sombre, stern-looking man, eschewed the lifestyle embraced by many army leaders: 'Drinking, gambling, dancing, and music were the way the officers spent their free time. I said prayers, instead.'[78] Bhutto probably chose him to lead the Pakistan army because he seemed largely isolated from his peers—and thus less likely to overthrow a civilian regime. In fact, Zia proved far wilier. Within a year of coming to power, Zia had executed Bhutto, abandoned a plan for a new national government, and appointed a federal cabinet under his own leadership.[79] Zia would go on to be one of the longest-serving leaders of Pakistan until his death in a mysterious plane crash in 1988.[80]

India, meanwhile, had just come through its own test of democracy. In June 1975, Prime Minister Indira Gandhi had declared a state of emergency, effectively halting democracy. During the emergency, Gandhi's government locked away many of her political opponents in prisons, and undertook mass social change, including programmes for slum clearance and forced sterilization. When, in January 1977, Gandhi announced that fresh elections would take place, a coalition of politicians created the Janata Party to oppose Gandhi's re-election. The Janata coalition soundly defeated Gandhi's regime, but it soon discovered that remaining in power was more difficult than winning it. Infighting left the party largely helpless, and Gandhi would return to power in January 1980 after the Indian National Congress emerged victorious in the next election.[81]

For the People's Republic of China, the death of Mao Zedong in 1976 had brought a new coterie of leaders into power and an end to the hugely traumatic Cultural Revolution, which had overturned almost every aspect of Chinese society. Deng Xiaoping ultimately emerged as the country's new leader. Deng was a political reformer who had taken a leading role in helping China recover from the disastrous Great Leap Forward but had been denounced as a reactionary during the Cultural Revolution. He represented a new, more pragmatic strain of Chinese politics that recognized the potential benefits of engaging with non-communist countries like the United States and limited privatization to encourage economic growth. He assumed leadership at the Central Party Work Conference, held in Beijing from 10 November to 15 December 1978, and from there moved forward with widespread development, as well as managerial improvements that would increase China's productivity and profitability.[82]

Finally, Iran's Shah, Mohammad Reza Pahlavi, faced one of the most famous revolutions of the twentieth century. Demonstrations against his regime had commenced in October 1977 and grew in intensity from January 1978. Iranians from across the social and political spectrum protested the Shah's authoritarianism, driven by demands for political liberalization and representative government, the devastating economic consequences of the global oil crisis earlier in the 1970s, and discontent with government interference in social, cultural, and religious practices. This coincided with the mobilization of Shi'ite religious–political thought, spearheaded by Ayatollah Ruhullah al-Musavi Khomeini, an Iranian cleric who had lived in exile for fourteen years following his arrest for criticizing the Shah in earlier decades. Protests grew into frequent clashes with state forces, and violence only spurred on further agitation. Despite powerful Cold-War allies like the United States, the Shah lost his footing. By September 1978, he had declared martial law, but the death of thousands of protestors and strikes and protests effectively brought the country to a standstill. On 16 January 1979, the Shah would leave Iran one final time, spending the rest of his life in exile. Khomeini returned to Iran on 1 February to massive fanfare and set to work creating a new religio-political state based on a radical interpretation of Shi'ism.[83]

Afghanistan thus was clearly not alone in facing a crisis of political leadership in the mid- to late 1970s. Different factions vied for power in all of its neighbours. Leaders in China, India, and Pakistan proved more adept at using existing political structures to hold onto power, while, in Iran, Khomeini proved a better revolutionary. Regional developments reveal why the 1978 coup, unlike those before it, turned into a decades-long war. Circumstances were already in place for the war in Afghanistan to spread into the neighbouring states. National, regional, and international dynamics underpinned the reactions of Pakistan, Iran, China, and India to the PDPA's April 1978 coup and the following December 1979 Soviet invasion. A complicated web of alliances entangled these states and their reactions to events unfolding in Afghanistan. Pakistan and Iran shared relations not only as neighbouring states but also as joint participants in US-backed Cold-War alliances. Pakistan and China, meanwhile, had developed political ties in the early 1960s, largely thanks to both countries' hostilities with India, which were further strengthened by Sino-American rapprochement in the 1970s, which Pakistan's leaders helped broker. India, despite its poor relations with Pakistan and China, saw itself as the key regional power, and it reached out to Afghanistan throughout the twentieth century to serve as a counterpoint to Pakistani machinations. As such, in thinking about the regional response to the Soviet invasion of Afghanistan, it is necessary to acknowledge the interplay of Afghanistan's neighbours—both with each other and with Afghanistan. They, as much as Afghan leaders, helped create the opportunities for civil war.

When Afghanistan is discussed in relation to the Cold War, focus tends to be on the Soviet invasion and occupation as one of the final battlefields of a global conflict that all too often manifested in violence outside of Europe. In reality, it had been a site of Cold-War competition, albeit of a perhaps milder nature, for far longer. Afghanistan became embroiled in the Cold-War competition between the United States and the Soviet Union from the mid-1950s. This was due, in part, to the Musahiban family's quest for foreign aid to shore up its development plans and, in part, to the ongoing Pashtunistan dispute with Pakistan. The division of this part of South-Central Asia along Cold-War lines—a US–Pakistan alliance on one side, a Soviet–Afghan friendship on the other—would have long-term consequences.

Afghanistan's leaders had engaged with Soviet and American representatives for decades. Indeed, Russia had been one of the first countries to recognize Afghanistan's independence in the aftermath of Amanullah's victory in the 1919 Third Anglo-Afghan War. Afghanistan had reciprocated, recognizing the Bolsheviks. Lenin wrote encouragingly to Amanullah: 'May the desire of the Afghan people to follow the Russian example be the best guarantee of the strength and independence of the Afghan state.' Of course, Amanullah, while interested in reform, had little desire for a political revolution. Yet both states' coinciding change in political trajectory seemed auspicious. The two sides signed a treaty of friendship in 1921.[84] Amanullah and his successors, however, still had to balance relations with the Soviets to the north and the British to the south. British colonial officials in India remained convinced that the Bolsheviks, like their czarist predecessors, aspired to extend their power and influence south into India. In reality, Stalin was preoccupied with domestic policies, including the pursuit of land reform, a series of five-year plans, and pacifying Soviet Central Asia. Soviet–Afghan relations really began to flower in the mid-1950s, following the Second World War, the hardening of the Cold War, the death of Stalin, and the rise of Khrushchev.

American approaches to Afghanistan and Afghans, for their part, were hugely shaped by their reliance on British colonial precedent. The United States first officially encountered Afghanistan around the time of the Third Anglo-Afghan War. Nevertheless, until 1947, American officials largely left Afghanistan alone, relying on their British allies to monitor the region and prevent it from influencing international politics. American officials began to take a growing interest in South and Central Asia as a consequence of the British withdrawal from the subcontinent, but, even then, relations between the United States and Afghanistan remained limited.

Soviet and American attention to Afghanistan sharpened as the Cold War went global in the 1950s. American focus on containing Soviet influence meant that, in South Asia, officials opted to ally with Pakistan. Jawaharlal Nehru's India, a seemingly natural ally as the region's largest democracy, had rebuffed American overtures. In contrast, Pakistan's civilian and military leaders actively sought US support, aware of their state's weaknesses in the aftermath of partition, and US leaders warmed to their wooing. Pakistan became a member of the Baghdad Pact, later Central Treaty Organization, in 1955 and a recipient of extensive economic and military aid. In turn, its leaders supported the United States' foreign policies, such as its intervention in the Suez Canal crisis.

The United States' alliance with Pakistan seesawed throughout the twentieth century, ranging from the very close—President Nixon's obvious support and overt sympathy for General Yahya Khan even as hundreds of thousands were killed in east Bengal in 1971 (what became Bangladesh)—to the icy cold—President Johnson's decision to cut aid after the 1965 Indo-Pakistan war, due to the humiliation of Cold-War supplies provided to two countries being used against each other and with absolutely no relation to the Cold War.[85] Notoriously, the US–Pakistan alliance came into the international spotlight in the aftermath of the 1960 U-2 spy plane incident. The plane flown by Gary Powers and shot down over the Soviet Union had taken off from Peshawar. The relationship again came under scrutiny a decade later when Yahya Khan brokered a thaw in US–China relations, facilitating Nixon's famous visit to China in 1972.

American leaders avoided similar political entanglement with Afghanistan. This, in large part, resulted from officials' inability to reconcile Afghanistan's and Pakistan's conflicting views on the legality of the Durand Line and the Pashtunistan question. On the one hand, American leaders wanted to support their Pakistani allies. On the other, they worried about driving Afghan leaders into waiting Soviet arms. The United States' Pakistani allies rejected the Afghan position in the mid- to late twentieth century that an autonomous Pashtun state would serve as the ideal buffer to Soviet expansionism, a line of argument touted by Afghan officials. As a consequence, American officials rebuffed Afghan requests to be involved in regional defence agreements. This did not entirely eliminate engagement between US and Afghan officials. Trade and economic agreements between the United States and Afghanistan continued throughout the second half of the twentieth century, though they did not always amount to much. While Kabul University and the Kandahar Airport provided successes, the creation of the Helmand Valley Authority, modelled after the Depression-era Tennessee Valley Authority, was notorious for failing in its endeavours to create new tracts of arable land where social and political development could flourish.[86]

By the late 1970s, Afghanistan was not an immediate source of either fascination or concern in the United States' global Cold-War strategy. US interest in Afghanistan largely focused on its proximity to other potentially important powers. The fact that it bordered the Soviet Union could not be overlooked, even while there seemed little reason to provide expansive aid to the state's regimes. Similarly, Afghanistan's significance lay in its nearness to the oilfields of the Persian Gulf. While little oil had been discovered in Afghanistan itself, its neighbour, Iran, accounted for a huge proportion of the world's oil. And oil, in the 1970s, was a crucial commodity. The 1973 global oil crisis, precipitated by the Arab–Israeli conflict and US support for the Israelis, had demonstrated to foreign powers, especially the United States, how reliant their economies and societies had become on this commodity. OPEC's decision to place an oil embargo had global consequences.[87] This crisis had little to do with Afghanistan or Pakistan, but there always remained the possibility that US officials could use these countries as a back door into their oil-producing neighbours. This certainly had been a possibility envisioned by British imperialists before South Asian independence, and it was an idea that had not fully disappeared.[88] Thus, Afghanistan's part in a broader South-West Asia and a corridor to the Gulf meant that US policymakers could never fully discount it.

Unlike the United States' presidents, Soviet Premier Nikita Khrushchev and his successors had no qualms about openly embracing Afghanistan's stance on the Durand Line and decrying Pakistan for its westward tilt. Khrushchev, who unexpectedly succeeded Stalin, turned the Soviet establishment on its head. He openly criticized his predecessor's policies and questioned his legacy. He called for peaceful coexistence with the United States, while simultaneously arming communist and anti-Western forces across the globe and using force to crush dissidence. He also embraced the globalization of the Soviet message, arguing that the Soviet Union had a duty to spread communism across the world and to support sympathetic liberation movements. Importantly, he revised the logic of socialist revolution, arguing that Third World countries could jump straight from colonial holding to state of the proletariat, and dismissed the need for states to undergo the intervening stages of capitalist development.[89] The PDPA's rhetoric at its first party congress in 1965 echoed Khrushchev's rationales.[90]

The Pashtunistan dispute provided the Kremlin with new opportunities to reach out to its Afghan neighbours. A serious consequence of the ongoing conflict between Afghanistan and Pakistan was the temporary but frequent closure of transborder trade routes between the two states. Afghanistan relied heavily on imported goods to power the economy and state (and, at times of drought, to feed its population). Its economy was predominantly export based. Historically, Afghanistan's main trade routes had run south through what had been colonial India and became Pakistan. The closure of these routes, then, created a huge problem for the Afghan government. If these roads were barred, Afghan goods could not leave, nor could necessary supplies come in. Indeed, the border blockade instituted by Daoud in 1961 had such severe consequences that it forced the prime minister to resign in 1963. The Soviet Union, also sharing a long border with Afghanistan, provided an alternative route for Afghan imports and exports, an opportunity that Soviet leaders were quick to exploit.

Khrushchev visited Afghanistan during his first tour of South Asia in 1955. He presented the Afghan government with a pledge of an annual 150 million roubles in aid and a trade agreement that opened Soviet transit systems to Afghan goods. Additionally, and equally precious, Khrushchev made an open declaration of support on the Pashtunistan dispute. Nikolai Bulganin, who would succeed Khrushchev as premier and accompanied him on his trip, subsequently reported:

> We regard as justified and well-founded the demand of Afghanistan that the inhabitants of the bordering region of Pushtunistan should be given the opportunity for a free expression of their will. The people of this area have as much right to national self-determination as any other people. No justification can be found for those who refuse to reckon, and do not reckon, with the lawful national interests of the people of Pushtunistan.[91]

Five years later, after shooting down Gary Powers' spy plane, Khrushchev furiously told Pakistan's ambassador in Moscow to inform his government that the Soviet Union saw the plane as having taken off from 'occupied Pashtunistan', not Pakistan. This must have delighted his Afghan counterpart, who witnessed the exchange.[92]

There was little question that the Soviet Union far outstripped the United States in providing Afghanistan with economic and political support. In a precursor to what was to come during the Soviet occupation, support for state infrastructure and economic modernization was a top priority. Soviet advisors were the driving force behind Afghanistan's first Five Year Plan, announced in March 1956, and Moscow signed a $25 million contract in the same year to develop the Afghan armed forces. Soviet engineers paved roads across Jalalabad, helped plan and construct the Salang Tunnel under the Hindu Kush mountain range, and developed state-run farms. They erected hydroelectric dams to generate power and energy. Soviet officials built a military base at Bagram, which would become a centre of Soviet (and later American) military activity. By 1970, some seven thousand junior officers in the Afghan army had trained in either the Soviet Union or its ally and eastern-bloc member, Czechoslovakia. In contrast, only about six hundred had received training in the United States. The presence of Soviet officials and engineers and their families across Afghanistan, their work building industry and modern agriculture, created 'a material world in which Afghans could imagine themselves as "proletarians"'.[93] Soviet leaders also made use of the Soviet Central Asian nations to extend cultural and ideological ties. For example, the Tajik Council of Ministers organized an exhibit on 'People's Education in Soviet Tajikistan' in Kabul in late 1965, where one Tajik representative reported: 'Very often the space of our exhibition became a sight of lively discussions and arguments among the visitors.'[94]

Nevertheless, Soviets' interest in developing Afghan communism was limited. While officials took note of the formation of the PDPA, they did nothing to push it to the forefront of Afghan politics. Karen Brutents, a Deputy Head in the International Department of the Communist Party of the Soviet Union (CPSU), recollected that the party 'wasn't doing a bad job in learning the "technique" and "technology" of the activity of a Communist Party', but he maintained that Taraki, Amin, and Karmal pursued 'a strange mixture of nationalism with some elements of Marxism, of Communist ideology'. The PDPA, in his eyes, was just one of many elements of Afghan society discontented with the lack of progress under first Zahir Shah and then Daoud.[95]

Soviet leaders welcomed the 1973 coup that returned Daoud to power, particularly as his partnership with the PDPA seemed to indicate a leftward tilt. Following his successful coup, Daoud visited Moscow to meet Brezhnev, the Soviet leader who had come to power in 1964. Both men emphasized their common views on domestic planning and international relations, and it was against this background that the KGB representative in Kabul was instructed to encourage the Parcham and Khalq factions of the PDPA to reunite 'in order to defend the interests of workers, peasants, and all the working sections of Afghan society based on cooperation with…the government of the Republic headed by Mohammed Daud'.[96] Any Soviet expectations that Daoud's reign might further strengthen ties with the Soviet Union, however, were disappointed by the same corruption and indolence that had defined earlier Afghan regimes. Daoud proved no more successful in major reforms than his predecessors. Nevertheless, Soviet leadership did little to help build up the PDPA, and the PDPA, in turn, did not inform the Soviets of its 1978 coup plans.

A brief point should be made about the ways that both Soviet and American officials understood Afghan history and structures, as these would shape both superpowers' approaches to the conflict in the 1980s. Soviet and American views, to some extent, overlapped. Both placed huge emphasis on Afghanistan's Pashtun population, conflating the structures that existed among different Pashtun groups with political supremacy. In this regard, both drew on earlier British representations of Afghanistan, particularly Mountstuart Elphinstone's 1815 text *An Account of a Kingdom of Caubul*.

Both American and Soviet leaders relied on British colonial tropes that regarded Afghanistan as fundamentally 'tribal' and therefore backward. British officials equated tribe with nation in conceptualizing Afghanistan. They also conflated Pashtun and Afghan identity, which helped accelerate the Pashtunization of Afghanistan to the detriment of its other ethnic and tribal communities, a point to which we will frequently return. The focus on Afghanistan as tribal resulted from early British encounters with Durrani Pashtun elites and their attempts to understand the social and political dynamics at work in Afghanistan (and why the state's power seemed to be so limited to cities such as Kabul, Kandahar, or Herat). However, the idea of a tribal society took on increasingly negative implications, owing in part to the igno- minious British defeat during the First Anglo-Afghan War (1839–42), in part to British experiences skirmishing with populations along the Indo-Afghan frontier as they attempted to extend their rule, and in part to the European rage for classifying societies on a sliding scale of progress and modernity. By the mid-nineteenth century, foreign officials had cemented the Western conception of Afghanistan as 'a particular "violent geography" and a people who frequently fell under the rubric of "tribals", "fanatics", "intrigues", and "militants"'.[97]

By the middle of the Cold War, Soviet and American perspectives began to show an important divergence. While Soviet leaders continued to conflate Pashtun and Afghan identities, they also cautioned their Afghan counterparts about the potential dangers of alienating the state's other ethnic groups. Reflecting broader shifts in the Soviet world, particularly Khrushchev's embrace of global revolution, Soviet thinkers and scholars also refocused on the question of postcolonial states' ability to embrace socialism. 'By the 1960s, the [Soviet] orthodoxy held that Asian and African societies were indeed subject to the same transitions as European societies, but that the shift from stage to stage was not uniform, even within a single country.'[98] The significance of this viewpoint was that it led Soviet scholars to reconsider Afghanistan's historical progression. They emphasized that an Afghan state had emerged from a system of loosely connected tribal confederations. Not only that but, basing their thoughts on close scrutiny of Afghanistan's historical economic structures, they argued that Afghans had developed a national market incorporating local markets, a sure sign that Afghanistan had passed through the necessary feudal stages of economic devel- opment to become, arguably, capitalist. This framing of Afghanistan's structures and history created the foundation to posit that Afghanistan had reached the appropriate stage of development where it was ripe for revolution—and to turn socialist. This would provide a key rationale for the Politburo's acceptance of the PDPA's 1978 rise to power and their willingness to frame it as more than a mere coup.[99]

American officials, for their part, struggled to comprehend Afghanistan and its political and social dynamics. American reliance on British conceptions of Afghan statehood provided an easy, if inaccurate, way for officials to understand competition between different Afghan interest groups and place emphasis on ethnic, familial, and linguistic ties within subgroups of Afghans and particular practices, such as the *jirga*, or council, and *lashkar*, or war party.[100] Ambassador Theodore Eliot, who was in office at the time of the April 1978 coup and whose tenure corresponded with the rise and fall of Mohammad Daoud Khan, likened Daoud to Sitting Bull, the famous Lakota chieftain who had resisted American westward expansion. 'He was a powerful chief, devoted to his larger tribe, namely the country of Afghanistan, but naive about the power he faced north of the border.'[101] Another career diplomat, James W. Spain, similarly compared Pashtun tribal *lashkars* to the 'American Indian "war party"', while John Harrod, an officer with the United States Information Services, noted: 'You had this definite feeling that it was Indian Country out there.'[102] Given the frequent comparisons between Afghans and American Indians, it was hardly surprising that the tribe and tribal politics became an important conceptual framework for Americans, like their British counterparts, to describe what was going on within Afghanistan. The American scholar Louis Dupree, who also was rumoured to work for the Central Intelligence Agency (CIA) in Afghanistan, argued in the 1970s that Afghanistan was 'attempting to create a nation-state out of a hodgepodge of ethnic and linguistic groups'.[103] But understanding Afghanistan as a largely divided or tribal nation did not prepare American observers for the PDPA's coup and the sudden death of Daoud. The consequence of this emphasis on tribal politics was the pervasive assumption that Afghan politics were less functional, less advanced, than those in Western states such as Great Britain, France, the United States, or even the Soviet Union.

Thus, tensions existed within Soviet and American perspectives on the nature of Afghan statehood and nationhood. While Soviet leaders insisted that Afghanistan should be considered a modern state with a functioning state-wide economy, whose circumstances made it ready to embrace socialism, American leaders placed greater emphasis on the Afghan state's limitations and supposed backwardness, pointing to its reliance on tribal structures. These differing views would fundamentally shape both powers' reaction to the PDPA coup. While for Afghanistan's northern neighbours the 'Saur Revolution' became the opportunity for the Soviets to encourage and support Afghanistan's turn to communism, American officials would mobilize a resistance based on tribal factionalism and resistance to state oversight. As we shall see, both interpretations had acute limitations and unintended consequences.

Early 1978 in Afghanistan, then, was the calm before the storm. President Daoud was neither popular nor totally reviled. Instead, his regime had assumed the same patterns as those before it. Despite pledges for radical reform and modernization, his government had failed to make any sweeping changes, and instead, he seemed more interested in just remaining in power.

However, a sweeping range of forces were ominously, if clandestinely, ranged against Daoud. Tensions persisted between Pashtuns and other ethnic groups; urban intellectuals in cities like Kabul and labourers and low-level bureaucrats in the provinces; state leaders and *qawm* leaders. Despite numerous setbacks, both the PDPA and Afghan Islamists had continued to recruit and mobilize their power, envisioning a future Afghanistan that bore little resemblance to the status quo. Regional relations were ambivalent, yet the fact that Afghanistan's neighbours, too, were embroiled in domestic crises only added to the sense that change might be coming. Questions swirled across China, India, Pakistan, and Iran about political systems, representation, and reform. And, from afar, the Cold War loomed. While the 1970s signalled a period of detente between the United States and Soviet Union, a time of relative cooperation and coexistence, it was not bound to last. Afghanistan's uncomfortable regional relations and its somewhat ambiguous place in the global Cold War thus meant that, when conflict erupted, it would not, could not, remain contained within the state of Afghanistan. Instead, the war in Afghanistan would come to embroil political actors from across the globe, and it would leave almost no Afghan life untouched.

A desire for progress and change had united many Afghan elites across the political spectrum who sought to reform Afghanistan. Yet two sets of circumstances would ultimately force back more moderate reformers and constitutionalists and bring the PDPA and the Islamists to the fore. The first of these was the PDPA's unexpected success in coming to power. The second was the way in which regional and international actors would respond to this event. While the 'communism' of the PDPA was middling, even in Soviet eyes, the PDPA's rise to power nevertheless came to be framed by outside observers as a leftist threat to the regional and international status quo. In turn, Afghan Islamists' own search for power and influence would coincide with and find key allies within the Islamization of politics in both Pakistan and Iran.

What differentiated the Afghanistan of 1978 from the Afghanistan of 1919 or 1964–5 was the range of competing forces at play. Where, earlier in the twentieth century, Amanullah or Zahir Shah could assert a singular vision of an independent Afghan state that contrasted itself with colonial subjugation and drew on parallels from European modernization, by the late twentieth century, conceptions of modernity had multiplied, fanned by anti-colonial movements sweeping the globe as well as the Cold War. A 'modern' Afghanistan could mean a number of things: a liberalizing monarchy that continued to reform slowly off the back of both American and Soviet aid, a socialist state that rejected capitalist models, an Islamic state that rebuilt politics and society completely independent of Western (American, European, or Soviet) influence. Given Afghanistan's interconnectedness in regional and world affairs, however, no state-builder would be able to pursue changes within Afghanistan alone and uninterrupted. Regional and international stakes meant that neighbouring powers would be eager to create new alliances or strengthen older ones, while foreign observers would be wary of how any changes within Afghanistan might shift the global balance of power. Thus, only the smallest flame was needed to ignite a fire that would sweep across Afghanistan and engulf the Afghan state, millions of Afghans, and bring in regional and global forces. And that flame was lit at the end of April 1978 by a political assassination, a coup, and a revolution.

# 2
# Kabul

On 27 April 1978, a 15-year-old boy cycled his usual half-hour route to school in Rustaq district, Takhar, a north-eastern province of Afghanistan bordering Tajikistan. Forty years later, he recalled: 'we all stood in line as usual, but neither national anthem was sung, or register taken. Instead, the school [principal]...and the other teachers stood in front of us, delivering propaganda: "Today is the revolution," he said, "The dictatorial regime of Daud Khan had been overthrown".' He further recollected:

> We could hear Radio Afghanistan from a window in the school playing revolutionary songs and a repeated statement...'The Revolution of 7th Saur has been victorious and the armed forces of the country are in control. We congratulate the people of Afghanistan.' The teachers told us to clap and then go into class. We didn't learn anything that day. After only a few hours, we went home. My father asked why I'd come home early and I explained it all to him. 'God bless us,' he said. 'The future is not good.'

Meanwhile, a civil servant, and PDPA activist, in Kabul, penned the following poem:

> These are republican days, full of happiness
> I cannot sleep because of happiness and delight
> Everywhere, there is dance and music
> What beautiful nights they are when you see others free
> Young people are making efforts for the wellbeing of the country
> They are dancing and laughing, delighting in their happiness
> Wake up...and burn down the house of ignorance
> See! Every youth competes with the other.[1]

What was clear was that something momentous had happened on 27 April, what became known as the date of the 'Saur Revolution' to PDPA acolytes. But how momentous, or what it meant, remained to be unseen. Was this 1973 all over again? Or something different?

Ten days earlier, Mir Akbar Khyber, one of the leaders of the outlawed People's Democratic Party of Afghanistan, had been assassinated, leading to a mass demonstration on 19 April at his funeral. Afghanistan's President, Mohammad Daoud Khan, had reacted to the unrest by arresting seven of the PDPA's top leaders.

Circumstances, however, conspired against him. The PDPA used the president's actions as the premise to fight back and assert its political influence. Daoud's reign had been one of disappointment for the PDPA. His Parchamite allies had found themselves sidelined from the government, and persecution against socialists, like the Islamists, had continued. But, in contrast to the Islamist revolt of 1975, launched by small, uncoordinated groups across the country and directed vaguely by leaders in exile, the PDPA, in 1978, was more prepared, even if many had not anticipated a sudden rise to power.

Not only had the Khalq and Parcham factions reunited in 1977, however reluctantly, thanks to pressure and power-broking by Soviet officials, but PDPA leaders remained active within Afghanistan and had managed to infiltrate key state institutions. Colonel Qadir, a PDPA member, had established the United Front of Afghan Communists within the army in 1974, and this, in 1978, gave the party the necessary armed support to challenge Daoud's government.[2] Perhaps most significantly, the arrests took place against a backdrop of widespread ambivalence, even hostility, to Daoud's regime, which had failed, to any obvious extent, to improve economic or social circumstances across the country.

Daoud catastrophically erred in his handling of the PDPA arrests. While Nur Mohammad Taraki and Babrak Karmal were thrown in prison, government forces left Hafizullah Amin under house arrest. This gave Amin an opportunity to change Afghanistan's political narrative. In haste, he alerted the PDPA's allies within the armed forces and put a government overthrow in motion. On the 27th, tanks poured into the city, positioning themselves in strategic installations and at street intersections, while jet fighters targeted the presidential palace.[3] A gruesome shootout led to the deaths of President Daoud, his family, and senior advisors, and the PDPA went from being an illegal party to the new head of state. In the immediate aftermath, PDPA-controlled radio proclaimed: 'The time of fraternity and equality has begun. The national revolutionary council', it promised, 'is looking after your rights.'[4]

Three days after the 27 April 1978 coup, a new Revolutionary Council, under the leadership of Taraki, was announced. The PDPA initially trod carefully in its public pronouncements, but Western commentators were quick to identify Taraki as an avowed communist, whose pro-Moscow leanings were 'ominous for this region'.[5] By the end of 1978, these fears seemed to have been realized. Taraki's second-in-command, Amin, declared the coup—by then known, at least to the PDPA, as 'The Glorious Saur Revolution'—as the 'continuation of [the] Great October Revolution'.[6] By drawing a direct connection between Russia's 1917 Bolshevik Revolution and events in Afghanistan, the PDPA left no doubts that the new regime was intent on making Afghanistan a socialist state.

In practice, however, the PDPA was a party of contradictions. It claimed to be steering Afghanistan on a new course towards becoming a modern state. But, in many aspects, its aims differed little from the regimes it succeeded. Its leaders issued a series of decrees that promised to transform Afghan politics, economics, and society. Yet the government lacked mechanisms for pushing through said reforms. It claimed to represent all Afghans but quickly succumbed to infighting between squabbling factions and resorted to violence against the broader populace. Indeed, the regime's ready turn to cruelty—to arrests, tortures, disappearances, displacements, and executions—served to distinguish the regime from others in twentieth-century Afghanistan more than anything else.[7]

So, was the PDPA revolutionary? In some ways, decidedly yes, but in others less so. The party's plans for modernization might not have differed drastically from earlier regimes, despite their socialist dressing, but the PDPA's ready use of violence ensured that its governing efforts were widely felt. Moreover, what has so often been overlooked is that PDPA leaders, at least initially, firmly believed that their vision for a modern Afghanistan *could* work. Not only that, but the PDPA, in evolving form, managed to cling on to power for fourteen years, outlasting not only the Soviet occupation of Afghanistan but the Soviet Union, itself. The ultimate shortcomings of the regime should not lead to a total dismissal of the PDPA as a party of failure. The breadth of PDPA reforms—and the extent of countrywide resistance—fundamentally altered Afghanistan's trajectory.[8]

Looking at the rise and fall of the PDPA between 1978 and 1992, three distinct phases of rule emerge. The first, under Taraki and Amin, was the most critical in terms of the articulation and imposition of the party's socialist goals. From April 1978 to December 1979, the most sweeping, radical changes were pushed forward, with corresponding backlash from many Afghans. The next phase occurred under Babrak Karmal, who was carried into power on the backs of the Soviet armed forces and never recovered from this association with a foreign power. From January 1980 to May 1986, Karmal focused far more on staying in power and asserting his regime's legitimacy than in instituting broad political change. Under his governance, Afghanistan stagnated, wrought by the civil war and neglected by a regime that spent time and money on building the state's armed forces while relying on the Soviets to state-build. The final period, under Mohammad Najibullah, from 1986 to 1992, which we will explore in more depth in later chapters, saw the almost total rollback of the PDPA's earlier policies and the return to earlier political, economic, and social practices.

Ambitious plans are always far easier to articulate than to implement, and the PDPA soon found itself in the uncomfortable position of trying to push through sweeping political, social, and economic changes among a resistant and increasingly restive population. The rise and ultimate fall of the DRA, as promoted by the PDPA, demonstrated not merely the shortcomings of PDPA thinking but its inability to follow through its pledges to revolutionize Afghanistan for the benefit of the people. Instead, PDPA action remained largely confined to Kabul, dotted around Afghanistan's other urban centres, and underpinned by violence. As a party that emerged in the political and intellectual melting pot of Afghanistan's capital, it failed to break out of this comfort zone and become a truly national organ and government.

On 10 May, less than two weeks after the April 1978 coup, Taraki broadcast a statement over Radio Afghanistan, which was also printed in the English-language *Kabul*

*Times* and distributed to foreign embassies (see Figure 2.1). In it, he explained why the overthrow of Daoud had been necessary. Daoud was 'anti-democratic and anti-national', 'despotic and demagogic'. 'He suspended the political freedoms of the people. He deprived them of their democratic rights and shamelessly insulted and belittled all the free people of Afghanistan.' Daoud's 'regime of suffocation and terror', Taraki explained, was little better than colonialism, recalling the decades of informal British rule that had limited Afghan independence in domestic and foreign policy. His death had 'ended the black talisman of [a] terroristic and fascist regime'.

Thus, it had been necessary for the PDPA to lead what Taraki asserted was 'a triumphant revolution of the people of Afghanistan and not a coup d'etat'. Afghanistan's new prime minister pledged that his regime, 'with the support and participation of the broad masses of the people, [would] consolidate and complete the democratic and national revolution which has started lawfully and triumphantly in Afghanistan and lead it towards ultimate success'. In effect, the DRA would be a state formed by the people, for the people. Its leaders promised they would do what those before them had not—secure the democratic rights of all Afghans and introduce them to a new era of modernity.

What was particularly interesting in Taraki's statement was its subsequent articulation of the PDPA's governing intent. While briefly promising respect for the 'principles of the Holy Islamic religion', Taraki focused on thirty key policies. Nearly one-third concentrated on economic reform, including fixed prices, land reform and reclamation, a revitalized taxation system, expanded foreign and domestic trade, and state control of natural resources. Another significant portion pledged huge political and social changes, such as the 'democratisation of social life', the creation of new laws, equal rights for women, universal education, a 'progressive national, cultural system', free health services, and punitive measures against prostitution, gambling, alcoholism, and drug addiction. Seven points were more outward-looking, articulating the new regime's approach to foreign policy. In rather grandiose terms, Taraki assured listeners that Afghanistan would play its part in pursuing world peace and upholding the Universal Declaration of Human Rights and the Charter of the United Nations. It would continue to pursue non-alignment and 'positive and active neutrality', but also would support national liberation in Asia, Africa, and Latin America, resist Israeli aggression towards Palestine, and combat South African apartheid. Finally, more ominously, Taraki warned that the new government would 'weed out' all 'anti-revolutionary, anti-democratic elements and elements opposed to the interest of the people' of Afghanistan.[9]

As a statement of intent, Taraki's speech was wide-ranging and ambitious. It demonstrated a clear desire to change the status quo and disrupt almost every aspect of Afghan life. But certain tensions existed. First, Taraki's pledges were not all that different from those made by Daoud when he came to power in 1973. Then, Daoud similarly had promised a 'revolution solely for the prosperity and happiness of our people', though with little material success.[10] Would Taraki be any more victorious?

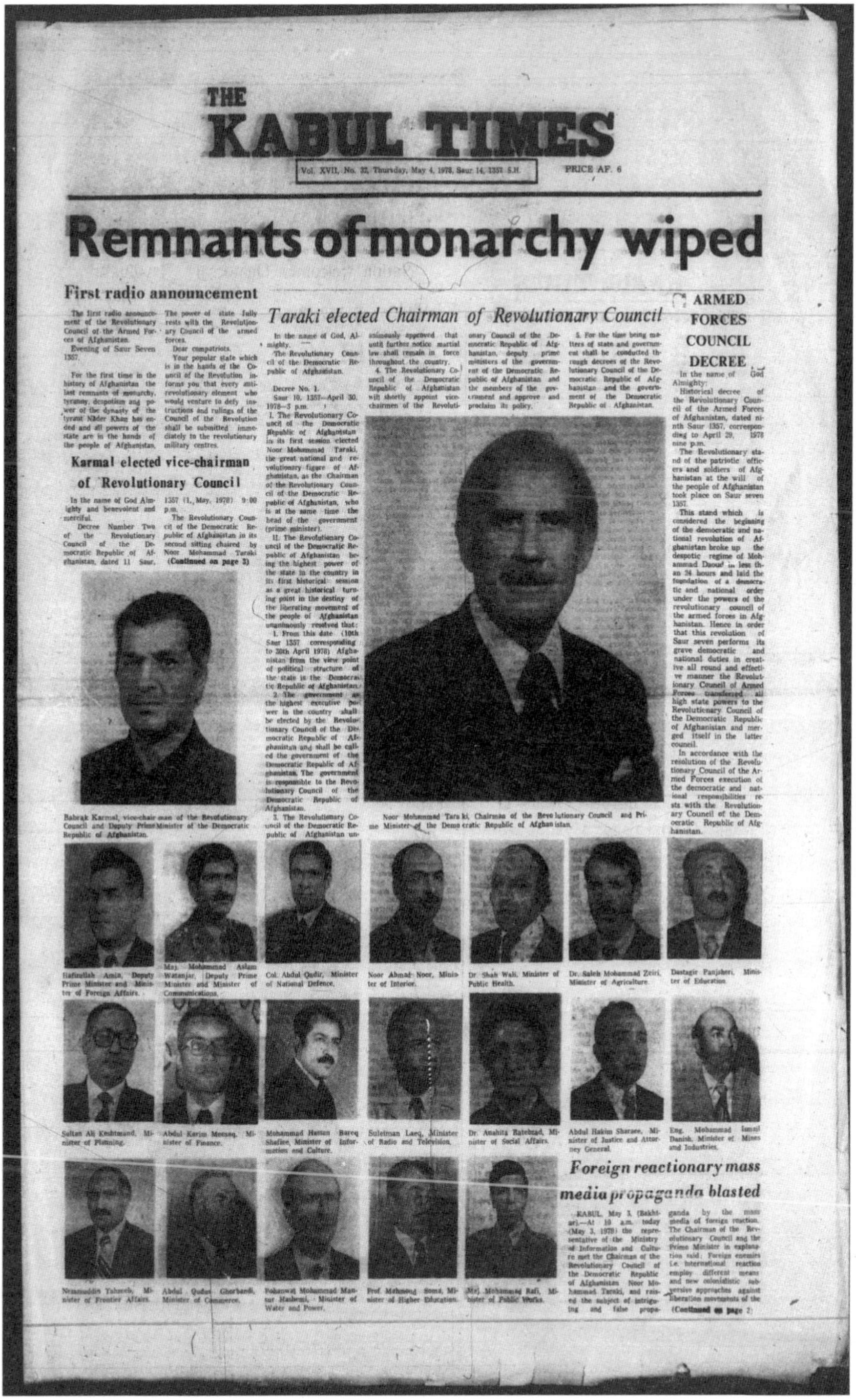

THE KABUL TIMES

Vol. XVII, No. 32, Thursday, May 4, 1978, Saur 14, 1357 S.H. PRICE AF. 6

# Remnants of monarchy wiped

## First radio announcement

The first radio announcement of the Revolutionary Council of the Armed Forces of Afghanistan.

Evening of Saur Seven 1357.

For the first time in the history of Afghanistan the last remnants of monarchy, tyranny, despotism and power of the dynasty of the tyrant Nader Khan has ended and all powers of the state are in the hands of the people of Afghanistan. The power of state fully rests with the Revolutionary Council of the armed forces.

Dear compatriots.

Your popular state which is in the hands of the Council of the Revolution informs you that every anti-revolutionary element who would venture to defy instructions and rulings of the Council of the Revolution shall be submitted immediately to the revolutionary military centres.

## Karmal elected vice-chairman of Revolutionary Council

In the name of God Almighty and benevolent and merciful.

Decree Number Two of the Revolutionary Council of the Democratic Republic of Afghanistan, dated 11 Saur, 1357 (1, May, 1978) 9:00 p.m.

The Revolutionary Council of the Democratic Republic of Afghanistan in its second sitting chaired by Noor Mohammad Taraki

(Continued on page 3)

Babrak Karmal, vice-chairman of the Revolutionary Council and Deputy Prime Minister of the Democratic Republic of Afghanistan.

## Taraki elected Chairman of Revolutionary Council

In the name of God, Almighty.

The Revolutionary Council of the Democratic Republic of Afghanistan.

Decree No. 1.

Saur 10, 1357—April 30, 1978—3 p.m.

I. The Revolutionary Council of the Democratic Republic of Afghanistan in its first session elected Noor Mohammad Taraki, the great national and revolutionary figure of Afghanistan, as the Chairman of the Revolutionary Council of the Democratic Republic of Afghanistan, who is at the same time the head of the government (prime minister).

II. The Revolutionary Council of the Democratic Republic of Afghanistan being the highest power of the state in the country in its first historical session as a great historical turning point in the destiny of the liberating movement of the people of Afghanistan unanimously resolved that:

1. From this date (10th Saur 1357 corresponding to 30th April 1978) Afghanistan from the view point of political structure of the state is the Democratic Republic of Afghanistan.

2. The government as the highest executive power in the country shall be elected by the Revolutionary Council of the Democratic Republic of Afghanistan and shall be called the government of the Democratic Republic of Afghanistan. The government is responsible to the Revolutionary Council of the Democratic Republic of Afghanistan.

3. The Revolutionary Council of the Democratic Republic of Afghanistan unanimously approved that until further notice martial law shall remain in force throughout the country.

4. The Revolutionary Council of the Democratic Republic of Afghanistan will shortly appoint vice-chairmen of the Revolutionary Council of the Democratic Republic of Afghanistan, deputy prime ministers of the government of the Democratic Republic of Afghanistan and the members of the government and approve and proclaim its policy.

5. For the time being matters of state and government shall be conducted through decrees of the Revolutionary Council of the Democratic Republic of Afghanistan and the government of the Democratic Republic of Afghanistan.

Noor Mohammad Taraki, Chairman of the Revolutionary Council and Prime Minister of the Democratic Republic of Afghanistan.

## ARMED FORCES COUNCIL DECREE

In the name of God Almighty:

Historical decree of the Revolutionary Council of the Armed Forces of Afghanistan, dated ninth Saur 1357, corresponding to April 29, 1978 nine p.m.

The Revolutionary stand of the patriotic officers and soldiers of Afghanistan at the will of the people of Afghanistan took place on Saur seven 1357.

This stand which is considered the beginning of the democratic and national revolution of Afghanistan broke up the despotic regime of Mohammad Daoud in less than 24 hours and laid the foundation of a democratic and national order under the powers of the revolutionary council of the armed forces in Afghanistan. Hence in order that this revolution of Saur seven performs its grave democratic and national duties in creative all round and effective manner the Revolutionary Council of Armed Forces transferred all high state powers to the Revolutionary Council of the Democratic Republic of Afghanistan and merged itself in the latter council.

In accordance with the resolution of the Revolutionary Council of the Armed Forces execution of the democratic and national responsibilities rests with the Revolutionary Council of the Democratic Republic of Afghanistan.

Hafizullah Amin, Deputy Prime Minister and Minister of Foreign Affairs.

Maj. Mohammad Aslam Watanjar, Deputy Prime Minister and Minister of Communications.

Col. Abdul Qadir, Minister of National Defence.

Noor Ahmad Noor, Minister of Interior.

Dr. Shah Wali, Minister of Public Health.

Dr. Saleh Mohammad Zeiri, Minister of Agriculture.

Dastagir Panjsheri, Minister of Education.

Sultan Ali Keshtmand, Minister of Planning.

Abdul Karim Meesaq, Minister of Finance.

Mohammad Hassan Bareq Shafiee, Minister of Information and Culture.

Suleiman Laeq, Minister of Radio and Television.

Dr. Anahita Ratebzad, Minister of Social Affairs.

Abdul Hakim Sharaee, Minister of Justice and Attorney General.

Eng. Mohammad Ismail Danish, Minister of Mines and Industries.

Nezamuddin Tahzeeb, Minister of Frontier Affairs.

Abdul Qudus Ghorbandi, Minister of Commerce.

Pohanwal Mohammad Mansur Hashemi, Minister of Water and Power.

Prof. Mahmoud Soma, Minister of Higher Education.

Maj. Mohammad Rafi, Minister of Public Works.

## Foreign reactionary mass media propaganda blasted

KABUL, May 3, (Bakhtar).—At 10 a.m. today (May 3, 1978) the representative of the Ministry of Information and Culture met the Chairman of the Revolutionary Council of the Democratic Republic of Afghanistan Noor Mohammad Taraki, and raised the subject of intriguing and false propaganda by the mass media of foreign reaction. The Chairman of the Revolutionary Council and the Prime Minister in explanation said: Foreign enemies i.e. international reaction employ different means and new colonialistic subversive approaches against liberation movements of the

(Continued on page 2)

**Figure 2.1.** Front page of *Kabul Times*, 4 May 1978 (University of Arizona Libraries, Special Collections)

Secondly, one has to wonder how appealing or persuasive most Afghans listening in would have found Taraki's language (and how many Afghans were, in fact, listening?). Time and again, Taraki accused previous regimes of being 'anti-democratic' and 'anti-national' and emphasized the need to destroy 'old feudal and pre-feudal relations' and to unite 'all democratic, progressive, patriotic, and national forces'. But was this really how most Afghans saw their government or themselves? Did most Afghans self-identify with Taraki's clarion call to 'workers, peasants, officers and soldiers, craftsmen, intelligentsia, patriotic clergy, toiling nomads, small and medium classes and strata ie., businessmen and national entrepreneurs'?[11]

The short answer is, no. Taraki could have been speaking a foreign language, as far as many Afghans were concerned. The disconnect between what the PDPA hoped to achieve and what most Afghans expected or wanted was vast. Two key issues ultimately hampered the PDPA. The first was the regime's decision hastily to push forward reforms while dismissing, even attacking, the role of Islam and readily turning to violence. The second was, from December 1979, the regime's clear association with and reliance on the Soviet Union. Rather than representing Afghanistan, the PDPA increasingly appeared the puppet of a foreign power that had no business in internal Afghan affairs. Despite its aspirations to create a modern, unified Afghanistan, the regime increasingly struggled even to be labelled 'Afghan'.

The 10 May announcement laying out the PDPA's intentions made no mention of socialism, communism, or Marxism-Leninism, instead promising a 'democratic' and 'national' government. Initially, as with leaders' previous public statements, the party tried to skirt the issue of political ideology. But its leanings quickly became clear. In private conversation, Taraki had already told the Soviet ambassador that 'Afghanistan, following Marxism-Leninism, will set off on the path of building socialism and will belong to the socialist camp.'[12] He admitted that he needed to tread 'carefully' and not inform the public yet, though Amin's November speech likening the Saur Revolution to events in Russia in 1917 made very clear the regime's predilections.[13]

Yet, almost immediately, the PDPA's intention to overturn longer-standing Afghan political practices became clear. By December 1979, the PDPA had issued a wealth of decrees that dealt with all matters of Afghan life. They focused not only on creating new government structures but also on reforming the Afghan nation. This involved wide-ranging reforms that not only affected existing leadership structures but touched the lives of Afghan citizens across the country. The PDPA's efforts continued to echo earlier generations of Afghan modernizers, who had also focused on issues of education, gender, agriculture, and industry, but the socialist camp gained importance, as it provided various models for the PDPA to emulate, particularly in the realm of economics. Yet these policies also threatened to completely reshape social, political, and economic structures within Afghanistan without providing adequate compensation. The PDPA's initiatives, with some overlap, can be broken down into political, economic, social, and religious interventions.

The PDPA's first area of reform focused on creating new government structures and cementing the party's vision for the Afghan nation and citizen. This became apparent through government policies and propaganda campaigns. The first three decrees, passed within days of the April coup, sought to eliminate the remnants of the Daoud regime. The first two decrees established the thirty-five-member Revolutionary Council, with Taraki at its head, and an accompanying twenty-one-person cabinet. The third, on 14 May, abrogated Daoud's 1977 constitution. Amin became deputy prime minister and foreign minister, while Karmal was named vice president. Of the cabinet members, thirteen had been members of the PDPA since its inception. Eleven represented the Khalq faction, and ten belonged to Parcham. Collectively, they were highly educated, with eleven former government employees, three journalists, two doctors, two lawyers, two academics, and a landlord, or *khan*. They too were ethnically diverse: eleven were Pashtun, six were Tajik, two Hazara, and two Uzbek. As such, this body, at least initially, seemed to support PDPA pledges to create a government that more authentically represented Afghans. It acknowledged Afghanistan's diverse ethnic make-up and balanced Khalq and Parcham interests. This would change almost immediately, however, when Taraki and Amin sought to oust the Parcham faction.[14] What would be left would be a predominantly Khalq, Ghilzai Pashtun leadership committee—a much less diverse regime, in terms of both politics and ethnicity, and one that more closely resembled pre-revolutionary governments.

Decree four of 12 June provided the DRA with fresh cultural representation in the form of a new national flag and anthem. The flag was a deep, blood red, with 'the people' (خلق) printed on the top right corner. According to an official press release, published to coincide with the flag's first hoisting outside the House of the People in Kabul, the flag was the 'reflector of the revolutionary thoughts of our people, symbol of work and revolutionary struggle'. Taraki called it the 'grand and glorious red flag…the prideful and great symbol of the people, the toiling people under the leadership of their grand party'. Outside observers, in contrast, noted that the flag bore a marked resemblance to flags from the Soviet Central Asian Republics, sparking uneasy rumours about the PDPA–Soviet relationship. The PDPA's leftist leanings were made even more evident by the new national anthem, which spoke of 'the red road to victory, the pure path of brotherhood', how 'our revolutionary homeland is now in the hands of the workers', and encouraged singers with the chorus to 'be ardent, be more ardent'.[15]

Decree five, passed on 12 June, withdrew Afghan citizenship from twenty-three members of the royal family. The decision to declare the royal family persona non grata was not merely a matter of political manoeuvring and reaffirming the Musahiban as the historic oppressors of the Afghan people. The PDPA also surreptitiously embedded in the fifth decree a litmus test of what the regime saw as the key tenets of Afghan citizenship. The royal family was accused of 'grave and open treasons against national independence, national sovereignty and national interests'. They had undermined countrywide unity and autonomy through policies focused on preserving their own power. In effect, they had put themselves before the nation.

'Every citizen', the decree explained, 'is obliged to defend and support [the] independence, territorial integrity and national sovereignty of the people of Afghanistan'. The remnants of the royal family—those who had fled the 1973 coup and survived in

1978—lived in exile thousands of miles away. They could not speak to Afghanistan's territorial integrity: they simply lacked proximity. Instead, the PDPA rooted Afghanistan's independence and national sovereignty in public property and the PDPA's oversight of it. This point—the sanctity of public property—was key. 'Protect the property of the people', the decree demanded, 'and [do] not…accord the right and permission to [your]self or anyone else to misuse public property'.[16] The Musahiban family's misappropriation of public property was a key reason it was named an enemy of the state (this was ironic, given that the PDPA leaders soon engaged in similar practices of acquiring and bequeathing state properties and funds to family members and supporters).[17] These political decrees thus refocused attention on the government's responsibilities to the Afghan people—and every Afghan's own responsibilities to Afghanistan.

Alongside this political wrangling, the PDPA also pursued a propaganda campaign to emphasize further synergies between regime and citizen. In particular, the PDPA developed a cult of personality around Nur Mohammad Taraki. The official biography of Taraki, published in the *Kabul Times* on 30 October, subtly undermined longer-standing conceptions of Afghan leadership. The biography blatantly contrasted Taraki with the Musahiban dynasty that he had helped oust. Where they ruled for generations, as part of the Durrani Pashtun elite that had overseen Afghanistan since 1747 (with a year-long, aberrant interlude in the late 1920s), Taraki was poor, a nobody. He belonged to the masses and was, according to his biography, the 'true son of the people'. While the Musahiban had cited divine authority and a clear right and mandate to rule—a mandate won over time, owing in part to their Durrani lineage and in part to the wider-held belief that each Afghan's place in life had been predetermined by God—Taraki had gained legitimacy as an 'active and struggling young man fond of hard work'. 'Far from affirming the notion that "anyone can be president" or that "right ultimately wins out over might," Taraki's biography—read through the lens of traditional Afghan political principles—proposes the altogether novel and heretical notion that God erred in allocating his blessings and that human action can correct that mistake.'[18]

The story that the PDPA tried to promote was that 'Comrade Taraki', through his history of political activism, 'had appraised the Afghan society on a scientific basis and had intimated…that it was possible in Afghanistan for the people to wrest the power'. The biography's author concluded: 'The true son of the people, Comrade Noor Mohammad Taraki, has spent a life-time in close contact with workers, peasants and the patriotic and hard-working intelligentsia, sharing their pains and aspirations, listening to their problems and not sparing them any moral cooperations.' Moreover, 'he has also imported political and social consciousness among them'.[19]

In this telling, Afghanistan was ripe for revolution, thanks to the work of Taraki and his comrades in spreading the revolutionary message throughout the country and preparing Afghans for massive political change. This, of course, diverged from the truth. Before the coup, the PDPA claimed to have 50,000 members, but, in reality, observers estimated a number between 3,000 and 10,000.[20] Indeed, it was almost immediately apparent that PDPA leaders were sensitive to their limits, even if they did not want to acknowledge them. The biography of Taraki, like his 10 May broadcast, emphasized widespread support from 'peasants' and 'patriots', 'small and medium classes and strata' and 'toiling workers', while the *Kabul Times* in the immediate aftermath of the coup carried countless stories of 'tribal elders', 'noble clergy', and ethnic Pashtuns pledging their allegiance to the new regime and delighting in its success. In fact, widespread support was not so forthcoming. The PDPA clearly felt the need publicly to assert its right to rule and supposed popularity, but ironically it did so by citing the support of many of the same groups or institutions it had previously described as being 'feudal' or 'semi-feudal'. Some articles claimed the support of whole tribes for the PDPA without critiquing unequal political and social relations prevalent within some tribal structures—the very definition of feudalism, for many observers. Others reasserted the regime's affinity with Islam and claimed that Afghans across the country were praying for its success. Already, at a very early stage, dissonance emerged in the messages that the PDPA sought to put forward. These messages halted in July, about the same time as the Khalq–Parcham split, but resumed again in early 1979.[21]

In the realm of economics, the PDPA intended decrees six and eight to induce a total overhaul of Afghan agricultural production and rectify the plight of workers long dependent on *khans* for tracts of land and loans to pursue farming. Given Afghanistan's largely rural, agrarian population and its industrialization, which remained limited and urban, this focus followed a clear logic. And while, with retrospect, land reform signalled a key failure of the PDPA's governance, the party cannot be entirely faulted for its single-minded focus on this policy.

The new Afghan government took early steps toward land reform within months of coming to power. Decree six, published on 12 June, outlawed the practice of usury, or the provision of unfair loans by landowners to those farming their land, and excused small landowners and landless farmers from paying back loans and mortgages. The Revolutionary Council lauded the decree as 'a giant step along the path of overthrowing the feudalist system in the country and a bold revolutionary move in the interest of peasants with little or no land'.[22] The *Kabul Times*, effectively serving as a government mouthpiece, published an article two days later touting the benefits of 'integrated farming', where farmers tended small plots of land, rotated crop rotation, and raised livestock to be self-sufficient. 'Crop livestock systems for small holdings are a far cry from the specialized large scale operations common to many countries. The fact remains that in Asia the small farm is an integral part of the over all [*sic*] agricultural system. With a reasonable amount of technical advice and support', the article concluded, 'it can be made more productive, more efficient, and more beneficial to the national economy'.[23] Already PDPA leaders hinted that the small farmer, not the large landowner, would produce a more efficient economic system.

Such statements and editorials gave some indication of what the PDPA wanted to undertake, and additional interviews by Taraki provided further confirmation. As early as 9 June, Taraki told a reporter from *Die Zeit*, a West German newspaper from Hamburg: 'We want to put effective land reforms into force, give peasants land of their own, set up agricultural cooperatives and put an end to feudal dependence.' However, at the time, he admitted: 'I believe it will be a year or two before we can go through with our plans.'[24] Taraki similarly told a Pakistani journalist that land reform was crucial but gave no indication that it was imminent, instead noting that 'the setting up of cooperatives…is being studied.'[25] Yet, on 12 August, mere weeks after these interviews, the government gave 158 families in Helmand 10 acres of land each (to whom it had previously belonged was not mentioned in the publicity).[26] At least on a small scale, the government had already begun land redistribution.

Just months later, on 2 December, decree eight was published outlining the government's plans for land reform. It targeted the 85 per cent of Afghanistan's population engaged in cultivation or nomadic pastoralism, intending to turn them into sedentary, land-bound agriculturalists.[27] The government identified three categories of land, from the most arable to the least. A family could own no more than 30 *jiribs* (about 15 acres) of the best land, with a sliding scale of larger plots of less productive land, and could not mortgage, rent, or sell land above these limits. Any land that exceeded size limits would be redistributed to landless labourers, sharecroppers, and nomads, who were to be (forcibly) settled. The government further promised to provide fertilizers, seeds, and machinery 'under easy terms', and took control of water supply and irrigation.[28] This decree, at least in rhetoric, made good on the government's promises to provide Afghanistan's 'working class' with further opportunities for self-improvement, under the guiding hand of a benign government.

Put in a global context, the PDPA's pursuit of land reform was not all that revolutionary. It was neither a totally impossible goal nor an entirely novel idea. The PDPA formulated its ideas at a time when decolonization swept the globe and informed critical international movements. Governments in newly independent states across Asia and Africa, as well as Latin America, sought to develop their economic independence and self-sufficiency. Across the political spectrum, land reform was seen as a key way of achieving this. In the Democratic Republic of Vietnam (North Vietnam), state leaders pursued widespread land redistribution from large landholders to peasant agriculturalists from 1953 to 1956. Land reform played a key role in the Cuban Revolution and swept through Latin America in the 1960s on the back of a glut of labour and the need for agrarian reform. In Ghana (the former Gold Coast), socialist-leaning Kwame Nkrumah pursued land reform in the late 1950s for economic development and to undermine tribal politics and strengthen the state's central hold. A military junta in Nigeria promulgated the Land Use Decree in 1978 to induce new economic productivity and equability. The Communist Party of India advocated land reform in West Bengal as part of its political platforms. In 1962, the Nepalese government passed the Land Reorganization Act in response to widespread discontent with landed elites. Much like the PDPA in Afghanistan, Nepal limited landowner's holdings to a certain size, 16.4 hectares, and tried to oversee and moderate agricultural loans.[29] Even Daoud's government in Afghanistan had briefly toyed with land reform in 1976, though his government's programmes were never fully enacted.

The People's Democratic Party of Afghanistan, thus, was only one of many parties that emerged across the non-Western world in the mid-twentieth century that embraced tenets of socialism and Marxism-Leninism as the best means to induce statewide (and worldwide) modernization. Indeed, in December 1978, Soviet observers approvingly noted, 'these reforms will help abolish any remains of feudalism and semi-feudal social relations...and the building up of a society free from exploitation', though they remained divided on how, exactly, the PDPA should proceed.[30] That the PDPA should follow the widely pursued model of land reform as the path to social and economic modernization made sense.

The PDPA was clearly aware of these global dynamics and did not pursue land reform as a specifically Afghan concern. Indeed, the PDPA's eighth decree, which enacted land reform, was accompanied by a celebration of Ethiopian Solidarity Week. The revolutionary socialist regime that replaced Emperor Haile Selassie in Ethiopia had passed the Nationalization of Rural Lands Proclamation on 4 March 1975, declaring

> a person's right, honour, status and standard of living is determined by his relation to the land...it is essential to fundamentally alter the existing agrarian relations so that the Ethiopian peasant masses...may be liberated from age-old feudal oppression, injustice, poverty and disease, and in order to lay the basis upon which all Ethiopians may henceforth live in equality, freedom, and fraternity...[31]

This sounded decidedly similar to PDPA rhetoric, such as a 2 December *Kabul Times* editorial, which claimed:

> The sons and daughters of our downtrodden will have the chance to enjoy a humanely life [*sic*] under protection of laws and regulations of their own Khalqi order. They will be furnished with assistance and economic facilities to be able to cultivate the land they will have in possessions and produce for themselves.[32]

The PDPA clearly saw itself belonging to the same league as other worldwide regimes that identified a need for agrarian change and better lives for poor, rural citizens and acted upon it. As such, the PDPA should not be seen as an outlier because of its pursuit of land reform, even as it clearly failed in Afghanistan.

The problems in the Afghan case lay in the speed and manner of implementation. It is not entirely clear why the PDPA chose to move forward so quickly with land reform, though there seem to be two potential reasons. The first is that Taraki, Amin, and the rest of the Revolutionary Council were aware of the growing resistance within Afghanistan and saw land reform as a means of accruing popular support. Reports were already flourishing internationally of Afghans fleeing across the border into Pakistan and of clashes between government forces and resistance groups.[33] Kabul had been under a curfew since late July, and anyone living within the city was forbidden from carrying firearms, under threat of 'military regulations'.[34] All was not well.

Moreover, the PDPA was in the throes of an internal split. In July 1978, Amin and Taraki pursued a purge of Parcham members from the Revolutionary Council. Babrak Karmal was sent as ambassador to Prague, isolating him from decision-making in Kabul. His allies were similarly exiled. Additionally, in August, Khalq officials claimed to have discovered a plot through which Colonel Abdul Qadir (who had helped stage the April coup) planned to overthrow the government alongside Parcham members. Taraki and Amin used this as an excuse to complete their purge of Parcham members and imprison many of them.[35] Karmal was removed from post and sought asylum in Czechoslovakia, and recently released documents show that the Afghan government tried to have him assassinated.[36] Soviet observers expressed growing exasperation with the PDPA's penchant for in-fighting. Boris Ponomarev, representing the Kremlin during a visit to Kabul in October 1978, listened with polite scepticism as Taraki claimed that Parcham had threatened to start an uprising against the government before issuing a stern warning against 'unjustified repressions', cautioning that such action 'undermines the authority of the revolutionary government'.[37] Taraki and Amin disregarded this advice. From then until December 1979, Khalq ran the DRA. With this in mind, land reform potentially served as a means of shoring up popular support for the Khalqis and distracting Afghans, especially those outside Kabul, from the problems within the PDPA.

Alternatively—or perhaps additionally—the PDPA had potentially entered a dangerous zone in which its leaders believed their own propaganda and genuinely felt that Afghans across the country wanted and were ready for land reform. Karen Brutents, from the Soviet International Department, later recalled that Taraki 'was in some sort of self-aggrandising trance. I had this strong feeling that the man was just drowning in ecstasy from the successes already achieved'.[38] Reading through the *Kabul Times*, one could be led to believe that the DRA was a clear success, that Afghans across the country joyfully embraced the government's decrees, and that the PDPA was revolutionizing Afghan society in a way no regime had ever done. One headline, for example, read: 'Peasants Hailed Decree no. 6'.[39] It is impossible to know how, exactly, decision-making took place within the Revolutionary Council. But clearly the government was taking the line professed by Taraki shortly after the coup: 'Amanullah failed because he was too weak. He did not develop an effective or a strong central government. He did not have enough power.' In contrast, Taraki claimed: 'We [the PDPA] are strong enough to keep all antidemocratic and antinational forces…under control. We shall defeat them and silence them. The people will follow us out of conviction or out of fear of punishment.'[40] Where this government strength derived from was unclear—it controlled the army, yes, but not perhaps the public—yet Khalq leaders expressed confidence they possessed it.

**Figure 2.2.** Leonid Brezhnev (left) meets Nur Mohammad Taraki in Vnukovo airport, Moscow (ITAR-TASS News Agency/Alamy Stock Photo)

In practice, land reform failed abysmally. While decrees six and eight might have freed peasants from debt to landlords, they also disrupted broader economic systems. The same *khans* and landowners whom the PDPA blamed for creating historical inequality had provided tenants with lines of credit to buy seed and equipment. Such loans were no longer possible under the PDPA's decrees—instead, the government pledged to take over this role.[41] Moreover, decree six raised broader concerns about buying–selling relationships and the issue of ownership. The elimination of farming tenants' debts and loans turned what had been the lenders' money into the borrowers'. With one fell swoop, money and tools had changed ownership, thanks to government intervention. What did this mean for others? Could the same thing happen to people who, say, loaned money for purchasing building materials? Or sold goods on credit? Fears that the government would take the same heavy-handed approach to other facets of Afghan economic life became palpable, to the extent that, on 30 July, the government felt impelled to publicize 'the profound respect that it observes for private ownership' and to request 'all owners of shops, houses, apartments, inns and patriotic businessmen to proceed with their transactions with full confidence in the principle of respect for private ownership'.[42] A contradiction emerged that would be difficult for the government to overcome, as it intervened in some economic aspects of Afghans' lives while pledging not to touch others.

Land reform alienated many of the families who might otherwise have served as the regime's political base outside of Kabul. It not only undermined local leaders whose power had derived from landownership but also placed labourers in the precarious position of having to farm with potentially little recourse to needed equipment and goods. The decrees disrupted social and economic balances and instead threatened to make both workers and landlords reliant on the government. Most problematically, what was never clear from the PDPA's pronouncements was *how* its officials planned to enact and enforce land reform. The decrees were not accompanied by an explanation of policy mechanisms, nor was it apparent whether the PDPA had considered the long-term aspects of the process. The PDPA's Soviet allies bewailed the government's inability to recognize 'the importance of the consecutive implementation of the planned reforms'.[43]

Instead, as one contemporary Pakistani journalist noted in 1980:

> When land reforms were announced and implemented, it was mainly by city people: party cadres, government functionaries, youth organization people. They were going out in the countryside and demarcating the lands, telling people this land belongs to you. They had a lot difficulty. The masses didn't know them. What would happen after they left to go back to the cities? A feudal system is very entrenched, and is all-encompassing. It is not just a question of ownership, it's a whole system in which credit, patronage, all these things are tied up. If you break one major link, then the whole chain gets upset, and you must be ready to handle all the problems arising out of the disturbances you have made.[44]

Redistribution officially began on 1 January 1979 and continued for six months, at which point the government claimed to have met with complete success. But few means existed actually to measure this success, and, as the country increasingly devolved into civil war, the PDPA's claims seemed increasingly dubious. Lack of infrastructure meant that the PDPA had little means to ensure that long-term change accompanied its decrees.[45]

In the realm of Afghan social dynamics, the PDPA again sought fundamental change and fell short. This was particularly apparent in the regime's approach to gender and the role of women. The PDPA's seventh decree on women's rights has received exceptional attention for its role in antagonizing many rural and conservative elements of Afghan society. On 17 October, the decree was issued for 'ensuring of equal rights of women with men and in the field of civil law and for removing the unjust patriarchal feudalistic relations between husband and wife and for consolidation of further sincere family ties'.[46] In a series of six articles, the PDPA eliminated forced marriages and bride price, limited dowry size, and raised engagement and marriage ages to 16 and 18 for women and men, respectively.

At face value, decree seven appears unexceptional. The 1970s had witnessed an upsurge in global discourse about human and women's rights, with the United Nations declaring 1975 International Women's Year and subsequently passing (in 1979) the Convention on the Elimination of All Forms of Discrimination against Women.[47]

Liberal Afghan intellectuals in the 1970s had critiqued how 'excessive expenditure in marriage undermines the human dignity of women as it tends to render them into a kind of property of the husband or his family'.[48] Against this backdrop, the PDPA seemed to conform to international norms and align with broader conversations about rights and eliminating discriminatory practices. Moreover, the PDPA's decree built on earlier reform movements. Policies aimed at modernizing Afghan society, and women's roles within it, had begun developing as early as the reign of Abdur Rahman in the late nineteenth century. Amanullah Khan passed the Family Code of 1921, which outlawed child marriage and marriage between closely related family members, placed restrictions on dowries, and gave wives legal rights in line with the Quran and Islamic law. Under Zahir Shah, the Marriage Law of 1971 similarly sought to limit costs associated with marriage.[49]

However, a number of problems quickly emerged with the PDPA's decree. Much as with land reform, decree seven on marriage and bride price lacked any discussion of mechanisms. How would the state actually ensure that the changes detailed in the decree were implemented? While state-run offices existed where new couples were supposed to register their nuptials, it was unclear, beyond questioning at these offices, how marriage practices would actually be policed.

From the perspective of (Western-)educated intellectuals who had trained in Kabul or abroad, existing systems appeared to treat women as second-class citizens. Given the PDPA's message of egalitarianism, of course the Revolutionary Council would call for reform to align with the regime's goals of Afghan modernization, much like those before it. But decree seven was no panacea.[50] The decree did not acknowledge how marriage practices served a broader function in social and political relations, especially in rural Afghanistan. As Nancy Tapper, an anthropologist who completed fieldwork in Afghanistan in the late 1970s, noted, marriage in twentieth-century Afghanistan played a distinctly different role from what it did in Europe or North America, especially following the First World War, when women's suffrage was largely legalized and women increasingly entered the workforce. In Afghanistan, 'the making of marriages is the central focus of most economic and political activity and the principal means by which status is expressed and validated'.[51] She explained: 'the choice of spouse, the character and amount of the prestations [dowry and brideprice], and the manipulation of ritual symbols [and] marriage arrangements communicates the real and potential strengths and weaknesses of a household'.[52]

Marriage and its associated rituals provided an opportunity for the exchange of valuable resources (including women's bodies and reproductive abilities), as well as assertions of a household's honour, through providing or receiving adequate dowries. The size of the brideprice and dowry also became associated with the value and status of the bride in her new household. As such, according to Tapper, many women embraced these practices because they gave them more influence in their new homes. Tapper consequently predicted the decree was 'likely to alter the whole system of economic goals and values throughout much of rural Afghanistan and perhaps in addition lead to fundamental changes in the nature of ethnic relations in the countryside'.[53]

In consequence, decree seven left women more poorly off in some respects. The abolition of brideprice ironically benefited men, not women. It eliminated a key source of rural women's honour and influence in the houses into which they married, putting them at further risk of ill-treatment, while instead giving men easier opportunities to find brides, since they did not need to accrue funds. Similarly, by limiting dowry, the decree 'deprive[d] women of the principal buffer in case of divorce, separation or abandonment as there is no alimony in Islam'.[54] Moreover, the decree did not propose any alternatives to make up for the potential economic and social disruptions caused by outlawing brideprice and arranged marriages. It did not provide financial support to brides-to-be, nor did it offer alternative means for families to gain additional income. Families could also get around decree seven by avoiding civil registration and instead having marriages performed in mosques.[55] Ultimately, decree seven did not give adequate consideration to the social context in which marriages took place in much of Afghanistan.

One area where the PDPA did move Afghanistan forward, albeit in a limited way, was in the increased representation of women in the higher echelons of government. A key example of this was Dr Anahita Ratebzad. Born Naheda Ratebzad in the village of Gulnara in Kabul province in 1931, Ratebzad was the daughter of a journalist who fell out of favour with the ruling family and died either in exile or in prison. Her mother was the half-sister of Mahmud Tarzi, the leading reformer discussed in Chapter 1, but was outside elite circles and ended up supporting her daughter by serving as nursemaid to one of the princes of the Musahiban family. This tie to the royal family allowed Ratebzad access to a girls' school, the Francophone Malalai Lycée. She subsequently trained as a nurse in the United States at the Chicago School of Nursing before returning to Kabul as Director of Nursing at Kabul's Women's Hospital, where she taught. She later received her MD from Kabul University in 1963. She was an early member of the PDPA and, as previously mentioned, one of the few PDPA candidates to win a seat in the 1965 elections.[56] As a party member, she was responsible for establishing the Democratic Organization of Afghan Women (DOAW). Ratebzad belonged to the Parcham wing of the PDPA and was reputed to be the lover of Babrak Karmal (she was rumoured to be estranged from her doctor husband, with whom she had several children, but who reportedly disapproved of her involvement with the PDPA).[57]

Dr Ratebzad's rise, rather ironically, was the product of earlier regimes' modernizing efforts. She was highly educated, thanks in part to earlier government decisions to allow women into Afghan higher-education institutions and to send promising students abroad for additional training. When the PDPA came into power, Ratebzad was at the forefront of party politics. A member of the Revolutionary Council, she was also appointed Minister of Social Affairs. In this capacity, before the party split that led to her political exile alongside other Parcham members, Ratebzad played a key role in articulating the PDPA's vision for women.

Rhetorically, the PDPA placed women at the forefront of the revolutionary struggle, but in fact it took less concrete action to turn speeches into practice. Women underwent little political transformation. The fight for women's equality remained secondary to the PDPA's propaganda campaigns, and DOAW and Soviet activities included convening seminars, handing out pamphlets and educational supplies, and organizing local celebrations.[58] The number of women who rose through the ranks of the PDPA remained few. Early pronouncements by Ratebzad and others largely praised women as the mothers of the revolution. Soraya, president of the DOAW, declared: 'Now, all injustices and slavery have been eliminated, and Afghan mothers can rear heroes and heroines.' In the scholar Nancy Hatch Dupree's opinion, 'it was disappointing to note that women were still being assigned primarily culture-bound stereotyped roles as mothers duty-bound to fulfill supportive roles for family and nation.'[59]

Bold rhetoric in articles across the *Kabul Times* argued, 'women have always been prominent in political and social struggles', citing Afghan heroines such as Aisha Durrani, a poet, and Malalay, who rallied Afghan troops against the British during the Second Anglo-Afghan War. But, in fact, women seemed to remain secondary. While the PDPA alluded vaguely to the establishment of new primary schools to expand women's education, job security, and access to healthcare (the *Kabul Times* ran a full-page debate about the merits and limitations of abortion), little real headway was made.[60] Dupree points to the ousting of Ratebzad as one of the key reasons women's advancement stalled: 'Those who knew Dr Anahita in those days had confidence in her leadership and great hopes that the Ministry of Social Affairs would provide means to implement positive programs.'[61] Instead, as part of the purge of Parcham supporters, Dr Ratebzad was sent as ambassador to Yugoslavia, effectively halting her participation in social reforms within Afghanistan until after the Soviet invasion, when she returned as Minister for Education under Karmal.

Decree seven came into force after the exile of Ratebzad. It would be too speculative to say whether the discussion of marriage, dowry, and brideprice might have been more thoughtful and careful if she had had any influence—after all, she, too, was a firm believer in the need for social change. For the remainder of the Khalq's time in power, the DOAW (which became the Khalqi Organization of Afghan Women, or KOAW) continued to advocate educational reform. When, on 1 October 1979, the Constitution Drafting Committee was appointed, four women were included—out of a total of fifty-eight members.[62] This goes to show that, despite claims and some limited reforms and decrees, the role of women did not change that drastically under the PDPA. Yes, exceptional women like Dr Ratebzad acquired new publicity, but, for the vast majority, little difference emerged in terms of political participation.

One of the reasons that the PDPA increasingly looked away from women's rights was probably the growing tensions the party faced in its approach to Islam—perhaps the single most inflammatory issue that helped spark civil war in Afghanistan. Islam infused many daily aspects of Afghan life, particularly outside of major urban centres. Islamic law, as indicated, informed marriage practices, brideprices, and dowries. Green, one of the on the original Afghanistan flag, was closely associated with Islam.

Additionally, religious figures tended to have important social and political positions and mediated disputes, especially in times of crisis. Throughout Afghan history, *mullahs* and *pirs* (Sufi saints) had frequently played critical roles in mobilizing locals against perceived threats to their autonomy and rights. Religious leaders, for example, had been key in the overthrow of King Amanullah in 1929.[63] Given the PDPA's attempts to institute widespread change, much of which clashed with long-standing practices or threatened to undermine local political and social relations, *mullahs* and *pirs* unsurprisingly once again played a crucial role in critiquing the new regime and, ultimately, leading an open rebellion against the government.[64]

From the outset, the PDPA's messages regarding Islam were mixed. In some ways, this was of little surprise, given the PDPA's reliance on the Soviet model. Soviet policy towards Islam had been middling. In Soviet Central Asia, Khrushchev had undertaken an anti-religious campaign, closing shrines and Muslim pilgrimage sites and narrowing opportunities for religious study to *madrassas* run by the state-sanctioned Religious Board of the Muslims of Central Asia and Kazakhstan. At the same time, Soviet scholars and leaders assured potential allies in Algeria and the United Arab Republic that Marxism and Islam could be unified in a national liberation movement and that Marxism did not seek to overturn Islam. To this end, while asserting itself in the Central Asian Republics, the Kremlin also sought to deploy Central Asian representatives abroad to demonstrate Soviet respect and support for Islam. By the mid-1970s, the Religious Board was hosting diplomatic visitors from Indonesia and Turkey. For Soviet leaders, the relationship between Marxism and Islam was tangled.[65]

Taraki knew that religion could pose a threat to the new regime, even as he tried to limit its influence. In his 9 June interview with *Die Zeit*, he declared: 'We are strong enough to keep all antidemocratic and antinational forces, who could turn against our revolution in the name of religion…under control.'[66] Still the PDPA initially took an ambivalent approach to Islam. In some announcements and publication headlines, the regime allied itself with Islam. 'We are sons of Muslims and respect principles of Holy Islam: Taraki', read a 13 June headline in the *Kabul Times*.[67] In other instances, PDPA members held religion at a clear distance. In a public address on Eid al-Fitr on 4 September, the holiday marking the end of Ramadan, Taraki barely mentioned Islam, instead focusing on 'our toiling people [who] once again have the opportunity to prepare themselves for the construction of their homeland with great strength…and resume their work and business with a new determination and high spirit'. This was a potentially controversial statement, as he seemed to imply that Ramadan, in fact, had disrupted the revolution because labourers could not work as effectively while fasting. For a speech meant to mark an important religious holiday, Islam was remarkable for its absence.[68]

Government rhetoric also became increasingly inflammatory. By the summer of 1978, the PDPA had stopped using the traditional Islamic invocation 'In the name of God, the Merciful, the Compassionate' at the beginning of government decrees.[69] Taraki's religious critiques also became more vehement, as news reports increasingly appeared in international media outlets about Afghan clerics and refugees fleeing to Pakistan and as domestic resistance also began to build. Speaking to the Khalqi Organization of Afghan Youth on 25 November, Taraki told his audience: 'we respectfully look at those Muslims who offer prayers well and perform their ablution. You should also respect them and we also pay respect to them.' But then he went on to warn: 'we will not allow any person to act against our society and the people of Afghanistan in the guise of religion and faith.'[70]

A further *Kabul Times* editorial cautioned against *ikhwanis*, a term associated with the Muslim Brotherhood and Afghan Islamists. It quoted Taraki as declaring: 'Ikhwanis are not those who perform ablution and offer prayer. However, Ikhwanis are those who with white turbans perform ablution and offer prayers to the benefits of the imperialists and under the cover of religion.'[71] Such statements made increasingly clear how the regime wrestled with Islam. On the one hand, the PDPA at least grudgingly recognized that practising Islam played a large part in daily life for many Afghans—thus praying and ceremonial bathing were praised. On the other hand, certain religious practices, in the PDPA's eyes, signified being un-Afghan or anti-Afghan, as they demonstrated clear affiliations between Muslims within Afghanistan and those in the country's increasingly hostile neighbours, Pakistan and Iran. These two arguments were difficult to reconcile.

Hafizullah Amin's 8 November speech commemorating the Soviet Union's 1917 October Revolution further inflamed social relations within Afghanistan. In this speech, Amin made clear that the Khalq saw themselves as the successors of Lenin and the Saur Revolution akin to the October Revolution. Much as the Soviet Union 'became the…attraction for all the forces fighting against capitalism', so too was the Saur Revolution 'an inspiration of freedom movement for the peoples of countries [whose] conditions are similar to Afghanistan'. Amin's only mention of Islam was to link it directly with the evils of imperialism, in which he accused 'the so-called Moslem "Farangis" [foreigners]' of falsely 'arous[ing] the feelings of the toilers'.[72] This speech, taken alongside other PDPA statements and decrees, indicated the regime's suspicion of Islam. But Khalq's choice to present a hostile front towards Islam was a mistake. Taken alongside its poorly planned economic and social changes, and its turn to violence, the PDPA antagonized millions of Afghans on many fronts.

The fundamental problem for the PDPA was that its leaders associated Islam with feudalism and thus held the clergy, alongside tribal and *qawm* leaders, responsible for Afghanistan's social and political divisions and the absence of a strong state. By this reckoning, the power of religious leaders had to be restricted, even eliminated, in order to free Afghan peasants from local power hierarchies and to make them active, equal citizens in a new Afghanistan. To this end, Soviet advisors urged the PDPA to 'fractionalize' the clergy and 'reduce the influence of reactionary Muslim leaders', while emphasizing the need to demonstrate that 'the new power does not persecute the clergy as a class, but only punishes those who act against the revolutionary system'.[73]

The PDPA interpreted such advice liberally. The new government dispatched 'security groups' from provincial hubs out into the countryside to round up potential opposition leaders, *mullahs* and *pirs* chief among them. Some clerics and their families were massacred on the spot, while many more were arrested and taken away to state-run prisons whence they disappeared, never to be heard from again. In January 1979, for example, the Mujaddidi family, a hereditary family of *pirs* with long-standing political and social influence, were arrested in Kabul, and all male family members executed at the infamous Pul-i Charkhi prison.[74] (Sighbatullah Mujaddidi, a member of the family who had been in exile since 1973, would go on to use his family's standing and historical influence to launch one of the main nationalist resistance parties, the National Liberation Front (*Jabhah-i Nijat-i Milli-yi Afghanistan*) in Peshawar.)

The PDPA's ready use of violence in eliminating its perceived enemies, taken alongside its determined push to reform, spurred a major backlash, not only fomenting resistance among Afghans across the country but creating an obvious space in which Afghan Islamists could position themselves as the saviours of Afghan society and politics. Islam, because of the PDPA's focus on it, became a crucial shared arena of contestation between the PDPA, on the one hand, and the growing Afghan resistance, on the other. In particular, the PDPA's attacks on Islam provided an opportunity for Afghan Islamist groups to rise to the fore of insurgency movements. Where the PDPA vowed not to let Islamic practices sway Afghans from the path to social and political modernity, parties such as Jam'iyyat and Hizb-i Islami argued that Islam, in fact, played an essential role in Afghan modernization. Islam became a source of violence, not only in the PDPA's approaches to Afghanistan's civilians but in the way that the civil war increasingly became framed by some party leaders as a conflict between socialism and Islamism.

Taken as a whole, the PDPA's policies indicated a host of ideas about how to govern Afghanistan. But, in power, the PDPA suffered from a lack of planning, which meant that, once the government's policies had been decreed, officials could not adequately enact them. No clear contingencies existed to replace economic losses consequent on land or marriage reform. Who would implement policies and how remained unclear. Reports emerged of PDPA cadres arriving in Afghan villages, staying to begin processes of reform, then leaving, declaring success without waiting to see how reform took root. Alongside this, PDPA leaders seemed to have given inadequate thought to how non-party members might react to their policies, or how best to tailor universal issues—political, economic, and social rights—to a local setting that existed beyond Kabul's intellectual milieu. As one observer remarked: 'What went wrong was the failure of the Party to comprehend the contradictions in the rural sector, to understand their own social structure in order to mobilize the masses and contain the counterrevolution.'[75] Failure, then, lay in both thought and implementation, with dire consequences—for the PDPA, for Taraki and Amin, and for Afghanistan as a whole.

The eruption of resistance clearly proved the weaknesses in PDPA tactics. The PDPA increasingly had to compete to represent Afghanistan to the Afghan people.

Anti-regime groups aroused Afghans' wrath towards the Khalq, alleging in radio broadcasts that government forces burned Qurans and destroyed mosques.[76] The outbreak of an armed uprising in Herat, in western Afghanistan, in March 1979 provided a clear example of the growing unpopularity of the regime. 'The destabilizing activities of the enemy of the new system, including the reactionary clergy, are much more active and widespread than the work of the party,' worried the PDPA's Soviet allies.[77] While Radio Kabul initially accused Iran of having deployed 4,000 soldiers disguised as Afghan civilians to stir trouble, in fact the revolt was comprised of civilians and Islamist groups working with sympathetic Afghan army personnel.[78] One estimate had 200,000 people protesting against the reign of the PDPA. 'For two days, anticommunist protesters stalked the street looking for Khalqis and Soviet advisors.' Some were armed, and fifty Soviet advisors were reportedly killed. Afghan air force pilots refused government orders to strafe the protesting crowds, risking insubordination. Eventually, Khalqi forces brought in from elsewhere in the country crushed the rebellion, but further armed protests emerged in Jalalabad in April and even in Kabul from June.[79]

The government's brutal reaction to the insurrection in Herat highlighted another, perhaps the most fundamental, flaw in the PDPA's governance: its reliance on violence. The PDPA's early decrees ostensibly had given the government total control of Afghanistan, and the regime quickly proved merciless in its efforts to shore up its rule. Twenty-five thousand people were killed when the government took back control of Herat.[80] 'In pursuit of a plan to eliminate opposition, Khalq used mass arrests, torture, and secret executions on a scale Afghanistan had not seen since the time of Abdul Rahman Khan, and probably not even then.'[81] The PDPA, and their Soviet backers, placed great emphasis on building up secret government forces to terrorize Afghans into submitting to the regime. Midnight arrests became increasingly commonplace, and those taken away rarely returned.

The threat of violence overhung the regime. A woman who was a schoolgirl in Kabul at the time of the coup later remembered:

After the coup, the communists named the Arg 'Khana-ye-Khalq' (the House of the People) and opened it up for visits. Daud Khan's family and many others had been killed there during the coup... After a couple of weeks, I went, along with my sisters and other relatives. We didn't see any dead bodies, but we could see signs of blood in various places... On most of the walls, I could see bullet holes... There was a smell in the Arg, a smell of blood or... I cannot name it specifically. The atmosphere was silent and everyone was terrified. Some people were crying. I was scared because I'd never witnessed such destruction in my life before.

Even Afghanistan's presidential palace was weaponized against Afghans. 'Anyone could go and look around'—and see what would happen to those who resisted the PDPA.[82] They, too, could end up like Daoud and his family.

The PDPA under Taraki and Amin targeted groups that posed any potential threat: Parchamites, Maoists, Islamists, army officers, bureaucrats, ethnic leaders, teachers, clerics, and students. In rural areas, where anti-government leaders were less easily identified, the government resorted to the practice of collective punishment. In April 1979, the government reportedly massacred a thousand unarmed men in the village of Kerala in Kunar Valley in retribution for resistance. They also resorted to burning crops to deny any local rebels food. Such events clearly undermined the regime's claims to represent the Afghan people and to provide them with new rights and opportunities. 'If the people needed evidence that the Saur Revolution had introduced not needed reform but an era of irreligious disorder, then mass arrests and incidents like the massacre at Kerala provided it and eroded the little store of credibility the regime had built up with the people.'[83]

The Herat rebellion and growing countrywide resistance had two immediate consequences. First, the government attempted to backtrack. Kabul broadcast a message immediately after Herat was quelled from the 'loving people of the Soviet Union in name of the toiling Muslims of Afghanistan' that asserted land reform was 'in conformity with the principles of the holy Koran, which says that the land belongs to those persons who work on it'. The broadcast exhorted: 'Support your government because it protects your interests and is seriously trying to strengthen brotherhood among the Muslims of your country.'[84] In a speech in early May 1979, Amin claimed: 'The toiling Muslims here are proud to engage in their religious rights and high hopes in complete freedom. Infidelity is not at all an issue.'[85] He similarly told a Polish reporter in June: 'we respect our customs, traditions and religion.'[86] The PDPA also organized highly publicized meetings with loyal clerics and tribal leaders, where these Afghans would make declarations such as 'the enemies of the Great Sawr Revolution...accuse our Khalqi state—God forbid—of being infidels while they themselves are infidels and exploiting faith and religion' and

> we, the meeting of the General Jirga of Islamic Ulemas of Afghanistan, who have been witnessing the actions, behavior, the deeds and accomplishments of our state since the success of the Great Sawr Revolution, have realized with all certainty that the present state of the Democratic Republic of Afghanistan is the servant of God and the people of God and the servant of the poor and destitute, savior and protector of the sacred religion of Islam and the Mohammadan Shari'at.[87]

The PDPA tried to refashion its anti-religious image into one that fused socialism and Islam.

The second consequence was political. Almost immediately after fighting in Herat had ceased, a reshuffle took place within the PDPA. While Taraki remained secretary-general of the PDPA, Amin replaced him as prime minister. Amin's political influence throughout the government was on the rise, and this caused increased tensions within Khalq between Taraki's followers and Amin's. Taraki and Amin also came into direct competition with each other, and the division between the two came into the open in July 1979, when Amin charged Taraki with causing the PDPA's reforms to fail. Taraki, in turn, accused Amin of nepotism. On 14 September, following Taraki's return from a visit to Cuba (for a Non-Aligned Movement conference) and Moscow, he attempted to trap, and probably kill, Amin at a meeting at the presidential palace. Amin evaded capture but used events as an excuse to have his own followers arrest Taraki. On 16 September, Amin became secretary-general, while Taraki was murdered by several of Amin's followers, ignominiously suffocated with a pillow.[88]

Suffice to say that Amin did not ascend to a position of strength. He assumed control of an Afghanistan that had decidedly devolved into civil war, where civilians increasingly resisted the PDPA's reforms and chose violent revolt or exile over accepting the status quo (if a status quo could even be said to exist). State propaganda continued to assert that the PDPA was in control and accruing more and more followers. Amnesty was offered to those who had fled, and a PDPA membership drive, replete with membership cards, was promoted. Aware that international news outlets reported with increasing interest on Afghan rebels, Amin launched a campaign for the National Organization for Defence of the Revolution, a move intended to build support and create additional political units to back the government across the country. But this was to little avail. Amin soon met with his own end at the hands of Parcham and their invading Soviet allies.[89]

Babrak Karmal returned triumphantly from exile at the end of December 1979. In a radio address on 1 January 1980, he greeted his fellow 'suffering Muslim compatriots of Afghanistan', invoking the traditional opening 'In the Name of God, the Compassionate and merciful'. He further tried to prove his religious credentials by calling Amin 'that treacherous foe of God and Honesty, the rogue who savagely fought in the name of God, Islam, humanity and nationality'. He claimed that his return to power was 'based on the will of the great majority of the masses and with the help of the national liberation army of Afghanistan' and pledged to 'safeguard the gains of the great and glorious Saur Revolution'. Of course, Karmal's 'national liberation army' was hardly Afghan. The Soviet troops who had flooded into the country that December were largely responsible for Karmal's return to power.

Karmal tried to present a more moderate face. He argued: 'While under the circumstances it is not our direct duty to practice socialism, the new government of the DRA deems it its historic national duty to expand and consolidate the progressive social and political pillars of [the] DRA.' He pledged to release those imprisoned by the Khalq regime, to 'abolish all anti-democratic and anti-human regulations', eliminate arbitrary arrests, and 'respect the sacred principles of Islam'.[90]

In reality, Babrak Karmal's policies largely failed. Soviet advisors and officials, not Parcham, were increasingly responsible for political developments within the country. Moreover, much of the PDPA's focus became staying in power, not instituting political change. Karmal rolled back a number of Khalqi reforms, reversing land reform and trying to make new, more conciliatory deals with rural leaders. Yet Parcham also focused on strengthening its military and security forces, the arms of the government most capable of keeping it in power, and its use of violence remained

**Figure 2.3.** Soviet poster: 'People of Afghanistan will destroy the international imperialist mercenary gangs' (Album/Alamy Stock Photo)

rampant. Not only did the PDPA introduce compulsory universal military service in January 1981 for all men over the age of 18; it also reorganized governing structures to put the Ministry of Defence, Ministry of the Interior, and *Khadimat-i Atal'at-i Dowlati* (KhAD), the state's security service, under control of the party's general secretary (Karmal).[91]

Even these moves were inadequate, as young men evaded the draft, frequently by fleeing to Pakistan or Iran, where many also joined the resistance. KhAD, under the leadership of Najibullah, inspired terror, not loyalty, among those Afghans who remained, as arrests and torture continued despite Karmal's pledges. By 1985, while the PDPA retained control of many of Afghanistan's major cities and communication routes, its grasp on the countryside was weak. In all, it governed barely one-third of the state.[92] This again proved that the PDPA remained a product largely of Kabul, not Afghanistan, highlighting persistent internal divides. Only in Kabul did the PDPA remain securely in power, and even this was tested, as guerrilla fighting continued to rock the city, and thousands of Afghans, displaced from their homes because of fighting, swelled its neighbourhoods and strained its infrastructures.

Karmal's failure to extend support for the PDPA, as well as the entrenched civil war, eventually led to his replacement in May 1986 by Najibullah. Najibullah would serve as PDPA general secretary and president of the Revolutionary Council until the PDPA totally collapsed in April 1992. As we shall see, by the time of the Soviet withdrawal, the PDPA under Najibullah bore little resemblance to that under Taraki and Amin. The early reforms had been largely swept aside, and any semblance of revolution was gone.

The 'Saur Revolution' effectively lasted only from April 1978 to December 1979. From that point on, the PDPA's ambitions for sweeping political and social change were benched in favour of the far more practical but less venerable aim of merely staying in power. Even as visions of socialist modernism in Afghanistan slowly faded, the PDPA retained its grip on power. In some ways, the party's long-standing ideological ambiguities served leaders well, as they continued to reinterpret what they meant by a 'socialist' Afghanistan to their own benefit. While ideological vacillating, accompanied as it was by only limited successes in implementation, did not endear the government to Afghans, it did keep them in power. The reign of the PDPA notably lasted more than twice as long as those of Amanullah or Daoud.

The PDPA did not emerge in a vacuum. Its rise mirrored and arose from political changes taking place in Afghanistan throughout the mid-twentieth century, especially in major urban centres like Kabul. Moreover, it paralleled political movements across the non-Western world, where socialism was frequently idealized in countries emerging from colonialism as the best way of introducing equality and opportunities. The major problem the PDPA ran into was its inability to introduce effective measures to accompany the reforms it pursued. Alongside this, the government's hostile approach to Islam, its refusal to recognize how religion infused many aspects of Afghans' daily lives, and its widespread use of violence also restricted its success and created opportunities for the regime's enemies to claim their own legitimacy. Thus, by January 1980, the whole of Afghanistan, much like the PDPA itself, was falling into disarray. It was into this chaos that Soviet policymakers chose to intervene, trying to find a way to support a neighbouring socialist regime and keep it in power. But whether they would have better luck remained to be seen.

# 3
# Moscow

K. Rashidov, a reporter with *Izvestia*, one of the Soviet Union's state-sponsored newspapers, paid a visit to Afghanistan in April 1980, mere months after Soviet troops had crossed the Soviet–Afghan border, ostensibly in accordance with the two countries' 1978 Treaty of Friendship. Rashidov sought to turn Soviet readers' attention to the lofty work being carried out by Soviet troops, their contributions to building infrastructures and supporting local Afghan communities, rather than any military manoeuvres. He reported local praise: 'Villagers talked with a great sense of gratitude about the peace-loving missions of the limited contingent of Soviet troops that is temporarily stationed on the territory of sovereign and independent Afghanistan.' According to one interviewed village elder: 'A brother came to a brother's aid, to make it easier for him to work and struggle.' This same elder noted that, nearby, Soviet soldiers had built a new bridge over a deep gorge, which eliminated the need for villagers to take a 10-kilometre detour to reach the other side.

Rashidov's article pointedly focused on Soviet soldiers' civic, rather than martial, duties. He wrote: 'The people with whom I talked cited cases in which firewood was brought in on army trucks, electric power lines were built to some villages and aid was provided during spring floods.' He cited an emotional Afghan mother who proclaimed 'the Russian military doctor not only saved my youngest, who was burning up with fever, but left us free medicine', and a teacher in Kabul who declared 'the Afghans clearly see and understand the main thing: the inner need for kindness that is inherent to Soviet people, their unselfishness, and the profound internationalism that the socialist system has instilled in them'. Rashidov reflected: 'In the village elder's words, one hears something more than ordinary gratitude. One clearly detects something else: admiration for the unselfishness, kindness and—most important— unaffectedness of the "strong people".'[1]

The purpose of accounts like those written by Rashidov and dozens of other Soviet reporters and printed in *Izvestia*, *Pravda*, and further state-sanctioned newspapers and journals was obvious: to justify the presence of Soviet troops in Afghanistan and to show that they were welcomed with open arms by Afghans across the country. Such reports emphasized that Soviet soldiers had entered Afghanistan only at the DRA's request, and that their activities were merely the manifestation of friendly political relations between two sovereign, independent (and socialist) states. They portrayed the soldiers' activities as largely peaceful and humanitarian—building roads, schools, and hospitals, delivering food and medical supplies, protecting villages from attack. These troops were helping the DRA to transition into a strong, modern state. Only in the later years of the occupation, as Mikhail Gorbachev made clear that a troop withdrawal was necessary and imminent, did the Soviet press begin reflecting on the bitter fighting, violence, and fear that defined many Soviet soldiers' experience of Afghanistan.

The Soviet invasion took place to reinforce the faltering socialist state in Afghanistan. It was not meant to be a drawn-out military encounter, nor was its initial focus on making war. Soviet troops entered Afghanistan to assist the processes of Afghan state-building, to provide Babrak Karmal with the necessary support to remain in power, to reinvigorate the Afghan socialist project, and to make up for the failures of government reform under the Khalq faction. Rooting out the resistance was part of a broader agenda to make Afghanistan's political, economic, and social structures functional and independent. For Soviet officials in Moscow and on the ground in Afghanistan, pursuing Soviet-style modernization schemes, with their emphasis on state-led agriculture, industrialization, and infrastructure-building, offered obvious ways of helping their PDPA allies. Even while many officials through-out the Soviet communist party remained sceptical as to whether the Soviet socialist model offered the best fit for Afghanistan, most nevertheless worked to replicate it, bereft of alternatives. That both the Soviet and Afghan armed forces failed to elimin-ate armed insurgency, and that Soviet state-building initiatives within Afghanistan collapsed, were the unintended consequences of Soviet decision-making in Moscow, the continued PDPA *and* Soviet struggles to implement reforms across Afghanistan, and the growing violence, which, of course, was only exacerbated by the entry of Soviet troops and the explosion of further conflict.

Moscow's focus on Afghan state-building and its attempts to foster socialist rule within that country despite uncertainties about the PDPA's aspirations remain largely overlooked by academics and the general public alike in favour of a morbid fascination with the Soviet army's military defeat. But 'parallel to the military effort of the 40th army, there was also a smaller "army" of Soviet advisers working to rebuild state institutions, improve the party's internal cohesiveness and relationship with the population, and carry out agricultural reform'.[2] While the Soviets may ultimately have placed more people in the field in combat roles, the men and women sent to Kabul and into Afghanistan's provinces in civilian occupations played an equally important role.

Indeed, collectively Soviet civilian and combatant forces supported and enabled Afghanistan's attempt at socialist transformation and helped to keep the PDPA in power even beyond the Soviet withdrawal. Focusing on these non-combatant personnel, rather than on military operations, demonstrates that the joint Soviet–Afghan effort left virtually no aspect of Afghan life untouched. This reinforces a key point that is easy to overlook with hindsight: the Soviets entering Afghanistan did not foresee an ignominious withdrawal. As such, we need to take seriously their attempts to create a stable, functioning Afghan state, even if this failed to materialize. Not only that, but Soviet involvement offers one reason why the PDPA managed to stay in power for so long. Afghan leaders had active Soviet partners who worked to build up the state. Soviet visions of Afghan modernity—or Moscow's decision to support and continue many of the PDPA's efforts to assert Afghan socialism—fundamentally shaped Afghanistan's trajectory, and many Afghans' lives, for the rest of the 1980s and beyond. Their failings equally informed Afghanistan's future, as well as the thousands of Soviet veterans who returned, traumatized and bitter, to their homes.

The Soviet Union's decision to send troops into Afghanistan was a political gamble—one that clearly did not pay off. Once troops had arrived, the USSR's leaders could not easily withdraw them without huge political embarrassment. Thus, both leaders in Moscow and troops on the ground had a clear mandate. They had to establish the legitimacy of Babrak Karmal and help solidify his rule. This meant not just clearing out local resistance but creating the means by which the PDPA could govern. Thousands of officials, technical experts, engineers, and advisors joined the Soviet military presence in Afghanistan in an effort to create functioning departments and establish nationwide infrastructures that would help the DRA on a path towards a more fully realized political system.

This was no mere military occupation. It was an attempt to reinforce the socialist vision first espoused by Nur Mohammad Taraki, even as both Soviet and Afghan leaders increasingly admitted that perhaps some intermediary steps were needed. Soviet support for Afghan socialism, in some ways forced upon Soviet policymakers who did not want to see a neighbouring socialist country fail, began to shift only as politics within the Soviet Union also started changing. Gorbachev, much as he saw the need to reform Soviet politics and society and improve relations with the United States, also concluded that the Soviet relationship with Afghanistan needed amendment. Socialism, or the PDPA's vision of it, had largely disappeared, as the government of Kabul backtracked and backtracked. So, what was the point of Soviets dying for a project that, in many ways, had already begun to fail?

The April 1978 coup that brought the PDPA into power had come as a surprise, but the Soviet Union's leaders had little choice but to embrace the PDPA when Taraki sought support and recognition. In an era of global Cold War, and in the decades since Khrushchev had pledged the USSR's support for worldwide socialist revolution, Premier Brezhnev and his Politburo could not turn their backs on a fledgling socialist state—not only a socialist state, but one sharing a border with the Soviet Union, itself. Moreover, Soviet policy of the previous decade towards the Third World seemed to signal the boundless possibilities of helping local Marxist parties to build class consciousness and foment top-down revolution.

Soviet foreign policy in the 1970s was often stagnant and risk adverse. The Politburo, comprised of seasoned politicians such as Brezhnev, Foreign Minister Andrei Gromyko, and head of the Committee for State Security (KGB) Yuri Andropov, reacted against the more vigorous policies pursued in the 1950s and 1960s by Khrushchev, including the terrifying, near disastrous brinkmanship of the 1962 Cuban Missile Crisis. Instead, these veterans of the Soviet system saw detente and peaceful coexistence with the United States as a means of consolidating and perhaps broadening Soviet influence, ideally at the expense of China, which the

Politburo continued to see as a major threat. Detente did not stop the Soviet Union from interfering in subordinate countries' affairs or from continuing to develop its massive military–industrial complex. During the 1968 Soviet invasion of Czechoslovakia, Brezhnev rejected the idea that socialism could be rolled back, dramatically declaring that socialist leaders' decision-making 'must damage neither socialism in their country nor the fundamental interests of the other socialist countries nor the worldwide workers' movement'.[3] Fortunately, the parallel desire of the United States to avoid conflict while bogged down in Vietnam helped stymie international tensions. Both the US and USSR sought stability at home and in international relations. In turn, Brezhnev avoided domestic reform or ideological revisions.

A fundamental tension arose, however, in Brezhnev's personal vision of detente, which, in turn, became the Politburo's vision of detente. While he, Gromyko, Andropov, and Minister of Defence Dmitry Ustinov upheld and promoted detente in Europe, they maintained the Soviet Union was responsible for 'proletarian internationalism' in the Third World. Events in the late 1960s, such as the 1967 Arab–Israeli War and the coup in Nigeria where Soviet allies had suffered defeats, had persuaded Soviet leaders to shift their focus and alliances away from nationalist non-communist leaders, who could be swayed by local political issues, to more orthodox communist parties. By the 1970s, the Soviets sought to back 'countries of socialist orientation' under leaders who had a clearer pro-Soviet ideological orientation.[4]

Gromyko, who took a lead in formulating Soviet foreign policy, prioritized Europe and left non-Western affairs largely in the hands of the International Department and KGB, both of which would play key roles in Afghanistan. Notably among younger officials in the International Department and KGB, debates emerged about the nature of revolution and Soviet intervention in the Third World. One key argument would also be used by the PDPA: that a state's weakness could be turned to the advantage of socialist revolution with the creation of strong top-down structures, and this could replace the slower social progression that underpinned orthodox Marxism. In this reading, 'vanguard parties', 'who could make the right tactical decisions and steer the complicated processes of building alliances, instituting social reform, and furthering socialist education', were key.[5] Such parties, ideologues like Karen Brutents of the International Department argued, could help guide decolonizing countries by providing a means of tackling internal divisions between different interest groups and combating foreign, particularly American, imperialism. The PDPA certainly saw itself as such a vanguard, though its leaders, particularly Taraki and Amin, clearly did not see the benefits of Leninist models of alliance-building that Brutents advocated.

Younger Soviet views on vanguard parties received further impetus on the ground as the United States withdrew from Vietnam, leaving the communist North Vietnamese forces victorious, and as the Soviet Union backed the winning side in Angola. With encouragement from the International Department and KGB, the Soviet government continued to provide support for Marxist parties across Africa, as local struggles for political independence persisted. Alongside their Cuban and

East German allies, the Soviets gave financial and technical backing to the socialist Movimento Popular de Libertação de Angola, the Partido Africano de Independência da Guine e Cabo Verde, and the African National Congress in South Africa. In Angola in the mid-1970s, the Soviets took advantage of and fostered the ongoing civil war to bring the MPLA to power, aware that the United States' Central Intelligence Agency was providing parallel support to the MPLA's main rival, the Frente Nacional de Libertação de Angola, and basking in the knowledge that China had lost favour in Africa by allying with the South African apartheid regime in supporting the MPLA's enemies. The Soviets and Cubans managed to overcome the difficulties of creating supply lines running through the Congo, as well as Chinese, South African, and American involvement. As Cuban soldiers successfully participated in the MPLA's armed struggle, the US Senate chose to halt covert operations in Angola, leaving an open playing field to the MPLA. The MPLA victory indicated to Soviet policymakers that, by working with local Marxist parties, they could thwart American (and Chinese) designs abroad and develop vanguard parties to embed newly independent states' political and social transformation in an international revolutionary movement headed by Moscow.

Ethiopia in 1974 seemed to offer further proof of the power of Marxist leadership, as the country's armed forces led a revolt against the monarchy of Haile Selassie and declared by early 1975 the victory of Ethiopian socialism. We have already seen how the PDPA clearly found inspiration in Ethiopian pursuit of land reform (and probably the National Democratic Revolution Programme of Ethiopia's reliance on political purges, executions, and violent quashing of dissent). After some hemming and hawing, but with heavy encouragement from the Soviet embassy in Addis Ababa, the Kremlin entered an alliance with Mengistu Haile Mariam's regime, providing extensive military aid during Ethiopia's 1977 war with Somalia over the contested Ogaden desert. Alongside this, Soviet leadership sent experts to help 'further the mobilization of the masses to defend revolutionary conquests'. This met, however, with limited success. The Soviet argument that Ethiopia still required a vanguard party to develop social consciousness and wider-spread political participation fell on deaf ears. Moreover, the war in Ethiopia also helped to rupture the uneasy peace with the United States. Zbigniew Brzezinski, President Jimmy Carter's national security advisor, concluded in his memoir: 'detente lies buried in the sands of the Ogaden.'[6]

Even as members of the Politburo gloated at socialist success in places like Ethiopia and Angola, seeing this as evidence of the Soviet Union's superpower status, tensions were emerging. By the end of the 1970s, Politburo membership had not changed, and thus overall foreign policy also remained largely the same. Politburo members continued to support the idea of supporting foreign socialist revolutions, with intervention if necessary, even as reports began trickling in from Soviet experts on the ground that state and party leaders in newly independent states were not necessarily interested in, or successful at, replicating Soviet models. Brutents presciently argued in early 1979 that creating socialist states in the non-Western world had largely become a Soviet, rather than a local, endeavour. The stagnancy at the top of the Soviet hierarchy meant that few foreign-policy changes had occurred by the time the PDPA suddenly came to power, and, ironically and tragically, what would play out on the ground in Afghanistan ultimately became, indeed, a Soviet, rather than a local, project to build socialism.[7]

The first two years of relations between the nascent DRA and the Soviet Union were marked by frustration for the Soviet embassy in Kabul and the CPSU's International Department back in Moscow. While the Daoud regime had disappointed hopes of a clear leftist turn, it had not threatened Soviet regional aims, and the Kremlin had been happy to leave it largely alone. With the 1978 coup, Ambassador Aleksandr Mikhailovich Puzanov expressed welcome to a regime that was 'more sympathetic towards the Soviet Union, further consolidating and strengthening our position in Afghanistan', but he had limited faith in the new government's actual abilities to establish a socialist system in Afghanistan. He sceptically noted that Taraki's and Amin's obsession with far-left rhetoric outshone any policies meant to ameliorate the position of the toiling masses.[8] For his part, Taraki evidently gloated not only at the coup's success but at the Soviets' surprise. Brutents recalled in the 1990s a conversation with Taraki in September 1978, where Taraki boasted: 'Tell Ulyanovsky [deputy head of the International Department] that he always used to tell me that we were a backward country that was not ready for a revolution yet; but, you see, now I am sitting in the Presidential Palace and receiving you here.'[9] While the PDPA claimed to embrace the ideas of socialist modernity and made them their own, the question remained how they would put them into practice. As we have seen, not well.

Not only that, the ambassador and his Soviet compatriots almost immediately became embroiled in the PDPA's infighting. Representatives from both the ruling Khalq and the subordinated Parcham factions sought Soviet support, vying for control within the DRA and trying to undercut the other. In one particularly dramatic scene between Puzanov, Taraki, and Karmal in June 1978, Karmal declared: 'they have isolated me, I am not engaged in either domestic or foreign policy issues, I live as if in a gilded cage.' He went on: 'For me, as a communist, this is a heavy tragedy.' Taraki vigorously refuted this assertion, claiming (disingenuously) 'there is no split in the Party, unity is being strengthened', before threatening: 'If someone moves against the revolution and the unity of the Party, then there will be a purge of the Party.' Taraki then refused point blank to talk any further with Karmal, forcing the Parcham leader to leave the room before he would resume discussions with Puzanov.[10]

Taraki's subsequent purge of all Parchamites from his government belied his claims of party unity and frustrated Soviet observers, who wished that the government would focus on developing policies for the uplift of Afghanistan's citizens, not political backstabbing. Taraki's and Amin's preoccupation with ridding their regime of Parchamites seemed to indicate limited foresight regarding the practicalities of ruling and the need to make Afghanistan socialist in more than just name. Puzanov expressed doubts, observing that Taraki did not seem to understand how to calculate an accurate amount of economic aid that Afghanistan needed from the Soviet Union. Other Soviet observers also noted the regime's failings in establishing a power base outside of Kabul and its only limited attempts to gain local allies, what had been identified as a key vanguard party activity. These concerns, however, were brushed aside by a more sympathetic Kremlin, where the Politburo saw the PDPA as a potentially important regional ally, particularly in the face of instability emanating from Iran. Taraki's and Amin's quest for Soviet aid coincided with the roiling Iranian revolution, whose leader, Ayatollah Khomeini, expressed hostility towards both the United States and the Soviet Union. Iranian unrest could not be allowed to spill over into the Soviet Central Asian republics.[11] Brezhnev, the feeble general secretary whose failing health, by this time, limited his role in decision-making taking place in the Politburo, emerged from a drug-induced haze long enough to declare 'we are sincerely happy that the Afghan people have succeeded in defending the revolution and the revolutionary achievements from all internal and international predators within such a short period' and to pledge, 'all activity towards the revolutionary transformation of the Afghan society will be backed up'.[12]

The March 1979 uprising in Herat came as an unpleasant wake-up call to the PDPA and a confirmation of the Soviet embassy's uncertainties about the government's abilities. The fact that a number of Soviet advisors (and, rumour had it, their families) were killed in the fighting added urgency for Soviet observers. It did not, however, convince Taraki that perhaps he needed to rethink his political strategy and how he implemented, and not just visualized, his concept of modernity. Instead, Taraki flew to Moscow to meet Prime Minister Alexei Kosygin, Foreign Minister Gromyko, Defence Minister Ustinov, and the International Department's Boris Ponomarev to beg for military assistance. They flatly refused. In a Cold-War atmosphere, Kosygin pointedly observed: 'The Vietnamese people withstood a difficult war with the USA and are now fighting against Chinese aggression, but no one can accuse the Vietnamese of using foreign troops.'[13]

Taraki did not leave chastened and repentant. While he accepted, however reluctantly, the Soviet refusal to send troops in to defend his regime, this did not stop him from making additional demands. When Kosygin tried to soften the blow of rebuttal by pointing to the military equipment, helicopters, anti-aircraft units, and the 100,000 tons of wheat that had been approved for shipment to Kabul, Taraki sulkily stated that 100,000 tons were not enough. He had to admit his regime's shortcomings: 'we will not be able to reap the entire harvest because the landlords whose land was confiscated [as part of land reform] did not sow it, and in a few places the crops were destroyed.' He also admitted Afghanistan could not pay for an additional 100,000 tons of wheat and demanded Soviet aid, which Kosygin agreed to consider. Nevertheless, the Soviet premier warned Taraki: 'We think it important within your country you should work to widen the social support of your regime, draw people over to your side, insure that nothing will alienate the people from the government.' For state-building to succeed, the PDPA needed the acceptance, or least the submission, of the Afghan people. This might take, Kosygin hinted, more intermediary steps than the Khalq anticipated. He also made a point of observing: 'One should take care of one's staff and have an individual approach towards it. Have a thorough and good understanding with each person before hanging any labels on them.'[14]

Clearly Taraki did not heed these warnings. His government failed to halt spreading disunity within his party and across the whole of Afghanistan, as resistance to the PDPA grew and became increasingly violent. But the explosion of anti-regime activity and its clear links to external forces created an additional source of concern to Soviet observers. Soon after the Herat rebellion, the Soviet government made accusations, both in internal documents and in the press, against Pakistan, Iran, China, and the United States, claiming (not inaccurately) that these foreign powers were providing support to Afghan insurgents.[15] Indeed, Afghanistan's neighbours, Pakistan chief among them, had begun arming the resistance, and President Carter would authorize covert aid by the beginning of July. Events in Afghanistan were gaining regional and global momentum. On 28 June 1979, Gromyko, Andropov, Ustinov, and Ponomarev softened their stance on moving Soviet troops into Afghanistan, proposing to send one group of officers to help train Afghan troops (adding to the three thousand or so Soviet military advisors already in place), as well as detailing a battalion to Bagram airfield and a detachment to Kabul to protect the Soviet embassy—and 'in the event of a sharp aggravation of the situation for the security and defense of particularly important government installations'.[16]

As the infighting within the PDPA only grew worse, leading ultimately to Taraki's own death, Amin rejected Soviet suggestions for a new coalition government that would bring back in some Parchamites. Soviet observers were further dismayed by rumours that Amin sought other foreign allies. While the Politburo initially indicated its willingness to recognize Amin as the new head of the PDPA, Soviet leaders' faith quickly declined as allegations emerged that Amin had sought an understanding with the Soviet Union's Cold-War enemy, something the CIA denied. Gromyko, Ustinov, Ponomarev, and Andropov reported to the Politburo: 'Amin's conduct in the area of relations with the USSR ever more distinctly exposes his insincerity and duplicity.' They continued: 'in the person of Amin we have to deal with a power-hungry leader who is distinguished by brutality and treachery. In conditions of organizational weakness of the PDPA and the ideological immaturity of its members the danger is not precluded that, thanks to the preservation of his personal power, Amin might change the political orientation of the regime.'[17] Not only was Afghanistan's socialist orientation under threat, but Amin appeared more invested in his own power than in the stability of the Afghan state or his allies.

Thus, a variety of factors led Soviet officials to contemplate the removal of Amin as the head of the DRA and consequently the use of the Soviet armed forces to achieve this end. Amin's commitment to socialism and the socialist side appeared up for debate, and Soviet leaders increasingly believed that he would choose whichever ally (and ideology) would keep him in power. Amin's turn to the US had the potential to embarrass the Soviets, particularly as it would contrast with Soviet successes in Africa. Instead, as Czechoslovakia had shown a decade earlier, socialism could not retrench. Amin's continuing attempts to purge any and all suspected enemies meant that any hopes of some sort of cross-party government, supported by the Soviets, was out of the question. Amin clearly had no wish to share power.

Amin's coup, furthermore, had done nothing to halt the Afghan resistance. If anything, violence had only grown worse, and the DRA's ability to deal effectively with rebel fighters had declined. The PDPA looked less and less like a potential vanguard party. The Afghan army was increasingly divided into two halves. Some men and units would readily use violence to suppress any real or perceived defiance across Afghanistan's provinces, antagonizing local populations and thereby increasing support for the resistance to the detriment of the government. Other factions, in contrast, increasingly questioned government oversight, because of either its policies or Amin's continued attempts to weed out enemies, and simply deserted. It was not an effective fighting machine and no longer served the government's purposes, as highlighted by a failed campaign in Paktia province and Amin's requests to the Soviet Union in early December 1979 for Soviet personnel to serve alongside Afghan troops.[18]

At the beginning of December, Andropov confided to Brezhnev that he had been contacted by Babrak Karmal and his Parcham allies abroad. Karmal proposed the creation of a new regime in Afghanistan and sought Soviet aid, armed if necessary. 'We have two battalions stationed in Kabul', Andropov mused, 'and there is the capability of rendering such assistance. It appears that this is entirely sufficient for a successful operation. But, as a precautionary measure in the event of unforeseen complications, it would be wise to have a military group close to the border. In case of the deployment of military forces', he added, 'we could at the same time decide various questions pertaining to the liquidation of gangs [resistance groups].' Andropov went on to conclude suggestively: 'The implementation of the given operation would allow us to decide the question of defending the gains of the April revolution, establishing Leninist principals [sic] in the party and state leadership of Afghanistan, and securing our positions in this country.'[19]

A week later, on 8 December, a meeting took place in Brezhnev's office, including Andropov, Gromyko, Ustinov, and Mikhail Suslov, Brezhnev's second-in-command. Kosygin, who was known to be against a possible military intervention, was excluded. The meeting took place against the backdrop of cooling US–Soviet relations. While the first Strategic Arms Limitation Treaty had been signed in June 1979, relations had quickly soured, thanks in part to the NATO decision to deploy long-range nuclear weapons in Western Europe, which the Soviets saw as a clear threat.[20] American weapons, Ustinov and Andropov hinted, might also be deployed in Afghanistan. At the meeting, participants unanimously agreed on the need to remove Amin, replace him with Karmal, and send in Soviet troops to support these moves and reinvigorate Afghan socialism. In many ways, these decisions paralleled previous Soviet choices to send armed support to allied parties and groups in decolonizing Africa. But the problem was that, in Afghanistan, Soviet policy required an accompanying regime change, not just supporting the PDPA. Thus, this decision was resisted two days later by the chief of the general staff, Nikolai Ogarkov, who argued that 75,000 to 85,000 Soviet troops were inadequate to stabilize the country. He was flatly told he had no choice and to accept the directive.

On 12 December, the Politburo unanimously agreed to the measures decided upon on the 8th, and further agreed to leave Soviet operations in Afghanistan under the purview of Andropov, Ustinov, and Gromyko. A task force was formed by the Soviet Ministry of Defence to oversee military operations of the 40th Army and to report to S. L. Sokolov, marshal of the Soviet Union. Ustinov and Ogarkov prepared a directive for issue on 24 December, the same day that thousands of Soviet troops swept across the border:

> Considering the military–political situation in the Middle East, the latest appeal of the government of Afghanistan has been favorably considered. The decision has been made to introduce several contingents of Soviet troops deployed in southern regions of the country to the territory of the Democratic Republic of Afghanistan in order to give international aid to the friendly Afghan people and also to create favorable conditions to interdict possible anti-Afghan actions from neighboring countries.[21]

On Christmas Eve 1979, the Soviet minister of defence ordered an offensive. Airborne troops landed at Kabul airport and a military airbase at Bagram, north of the city. The next day, four motorized rifle divisions crossed into Afghanistan, the 357th and 66th from Kushka in Turkmenistan, the 360th and 201st from Termez, Uzbekistan. En route from Uzbekistan, the 360th secured the Salang Tunnel before arriving in Kabul, while the 201st spread east through Kunduz, Badakshan, and Baghlan (see Map 5). Further airborne troops were deposited near Herat, Kandahar, and Jalalabad, Afghanistan's other major cities. By the 27th, fifty thousand Soviet troops were on the ground. Paratroops quickly disrupted Kabul's lines of communication and took control of government buildings. That evening, they attacked the palace and killed Hafizullah Amin.[22]

With that, the invasion was underway, and Soviet–Afghan relations entered a new stage. An irony emerged that would never fully be eliminated. As the Cold-War historian Odd Arne Westad observed, 'in spite of the Soviet preponderance of military power, international standing, and technical prowess, Moscow did not succeed in forcing the *Khalqis* to revise their notions of Communism, short of armed intervention'.[23] The Soviets, under the guidance of Andropov, Ustinov, and Gromyko, concluded that the only way to establish a proper socialist regime in Afghanistan was through the use of violence—by ending Amin's life and by providing Karmal with the weaponized support of the Soviet army. Soviet decision-making had some precedent. After all, Brezhnev's decision to send troops into Czechoslovakia during the Prague Spring of 1968 had followed a similar rationale. There, Soviet concerns had also revolved around the twin questions of the security and stability of an allied (and neighbouring) state and its approach to communism. But whereas, in the Czech

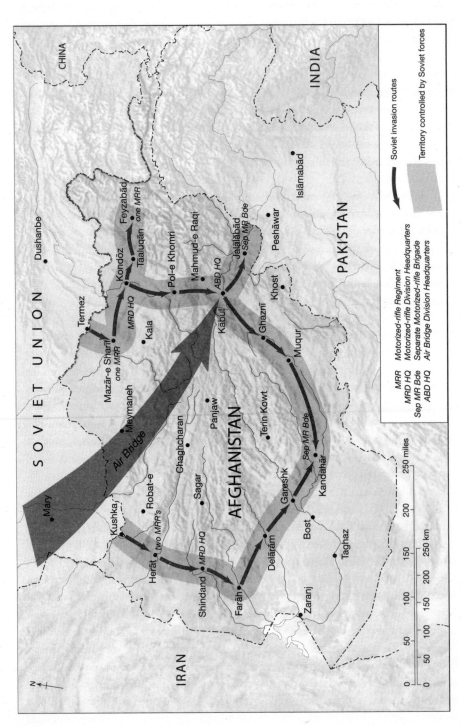

**Map 5.** Map of Soviet military movements

case, Soviet forces swept in and effected a quick regime change, replacing the moderate reformist Alexander Dubček with the more hard-line Gustav Husak, in Afghanistan they encountered an explosive war already underway between the PDPA and resistance forces.[24]

What was to take place after regime change in Afghanistan? Karmal's government needed to be made more secure and, following the standards of Soviet engagement with the Third World in the 1970s, more ideologically pliable. It needed to become embedded in Afghan society and politics, and the Soviets needed to help, firm in their belief that they were the revolutionary leaders of the Third World.[25] Brutents pointed retrospectively to the belief that, 'even though neither our top leaders nor our middle-level officials knew the Afghan situation and its background very well, they were still capable of making better, more reasonable recommendations and plans than the Afghan leaders themselves'.[26] Soviet hubris—the belief that the Soviets, rather than the Afghans, would have to pursue socialism—would play out on the ground, creating a fundamental tension. Who was responsible for Afghanistan's future development? The PDPA or the Soviets? What would become clear was that, as in earlier interventions, the Politburo would focus on Soviet, not locally led, modernizing efforts to the detriment of Afghan socialism, which would not be accepted as organic and indigenous.

We can briefly return to a point made by the sidelined Kosygin, who presciently had warned in March after the siege of Herat:

> Our mutual enemies are just waiting for the moment when Soviet forces appear on Afghan territory. This would give them an excuse to deploy on Afghan territory military formations hostile to you ... One cannot deny that our troops would have to fight not only with foreign aggressors, but also with a certain number of your people. And people do not forgive such things.[27]

Kosygin's warning proved entirely accurate.

The Politburo's first goal was easily, if bloodily, attained: within forty-five minutes of launching an attack on Amin's headquarters at Taj Bek Palace, a heavily fortified structure in the south-western outskirts of Kabul, the president was dead, either assassinated or caught in crossfire shooting.[28] There was nothing to stop Babrak Karmal from assuming power, with the full support of the Soviet army and the Kremlin. But the Soviets also needed to ensure that Karmal remained in power longer than his two predecessors—and that he embraced, and implemented, an appropriate ideological and political line. We have already seen that Karmal and Parcham were more ideologically moderate and politically pragmatic than their Khalqi counterparts (and, the Soviets hoped, more compliant to Soviet advice), but what this meant in practice was unclear. Statements by Karmal and members of the Soviet Politburo accusing Amin of betraying the revolution and the Afghan people gave only limited insight. They did not present a clear alternative vision for Afghanistan. Karmal's initial programme and slogan were vague. While 'forward toward peace, freedom, national independence, democracy, progress and social justice' might sound inspiring, what this actually entailed was debatable.[29] Karmal and his Soviet allies thus needed to make up for lost time, and the earlier regimes' missteps, if they wanted to save the revolutionary gains of April 1978—or save the revolution, full stop.

Thus, the main goal of Karmal's Soviet backers was to uphold and prove the legitimacy of the new government of the DRA to both national and international audiences. This involved installing Karmal as a figurehead, returning government focus to thoughtful political and social reform, rooting out pockets of armed resistance across the country, and making pitches abroad that Karmal represented the will of the Afghan people. Gromyko and Ustinov recognized at an early stage that withdrawing Soviet troops prematurely would be disastrous, even as they underestimated the size and resilience of resistance. They calculated that Soviet and Afghan armed forces needed at least a year to eliminate the insurgency.[30] These military predictions proved far from realistic.

The Soviet invasion acted like lighter fluid on the already smouldering civil war. Within days of entering, for example, Soviet forces had set up a base of operations in Kandahar. Given its location near Pakistan, its road links to Kabul and Herat, and its nearby airport, Kandahar was clearly a strategic target for the Soviets. But, as quickly as Soviet troops arrived in Kandahar, local resistance mounted. According to newspaper reports gleefully emerging in America, Soviet forces entering the city at the end of December had been met by 'several hundred farmers and herdsmen armed with shovels and clubs' marching through the streets and shouting, 'Death to the Russian invaders!' The Soviets responded by sending in two Soviet MIG fighter planes, which broke up the protest but did not end resistance. 'Another report current in Kandahar', noted the New York Times, 'is that a Soviet soldier wandering through town a few days ago had his throat cut. Whether the report is true or not, and again it impossible to be sure, it is certainly true that Russians do not wander here any more.'[31]

On the military side, the Soviet war in Afghanistan was hard fought and, despite the technical superiority of the Soviets, ended in impasse. It consisted of four main phases. The first, from December 1979 to February 1980, involved direct conflict as Soviet forces took a leading role in installing Karmal in Kabul and extending the PDPA's influence across the country. The second phase, lasting from March 1980 to April 1985, focused on consolidating Soviet and PDPA rule and gaining strategic superiority across the country through the control of key cities and roads. The next stage, from April 1985 to January 1987, was generally more scaled back, despite a brief surge in 1986, with Soviet forces trying to turn over responsibility to the Afghan soldiers they had trained. The final stage, January 1987 to February 1989, was defined by the staged Soviet withdrawal of troops, during which the army largely turned to defensive tactics.

The Soviet armed forces that entered Afghanistan had orders to secure infrastructures and bases. They hoped to avoid confrontation and were ill-prepared for the type of combat that emerged in the Afghan war. The army had training to fight a large land war, the sort of traditional combat that had defined conflicts in Europe in the nineteenth and twentieth centuries. Instead, they faced a disparate Afghan resistance that largely relied on small-scale skirmishing, guerrilla tactics, sabotage, and mining. Soviet strategic planning simply did not correlate. While Soviet forces initially succeeded in securing PDPA strongholds across the country and throughout the war largely managed to retain control of countrywide *zastavy*, or guard posts, they lacked the manoeuvres to uproot or eliminate insurgents, a problem exacerbated by the tactical brilliance of some resistance leaders.

Afghan resistance fighters did their best to avoid terrain where Soviet forces could use their superior technology to inflict casualties, including artillery and missiles, instead taking advantage of craggy hills and mountains, building a series of tunnels to ensure easier mobility, and swooping in to engage Soviet troops in close combat. According to a retrospective by the Russian general staff: 'The peculiarities of counter-guerilla war and the rugged terrain determined the Soviet tactics in Afghanistan, where it was impossible to conduct classic offensive and defensive warfare.' The army was forced to adopt new tactics, such as the 'block and sweep', the cordoning-off of a region and then methodical elimination of enemies within it (see Figure 3.1).[32] The war kept most of the Soviets stationed in Afghanistan busy, either participating in combat or supporting combat activities.

But upholding the Karmal regime required more than a militarily active Soviet army. For the Soviet intervention to be deemed a real success, Afghanistan needed the infrastructures and willing citizens that could embed the PDPA and its socialist practices in Afghan society and politics. After all, why else were Soviet troops even

**Figure 3.1.** Soviet mine searchers on the road in Panjshir, August 1988 (Internet Archive, The Afghan Media Resource Center/Kushdil)

in Afghanistan? An Afghan state, presumably built along socialist lines, had to emerge, or at least survive. A 10 March 1980 memorandum discussed by the Politburo effectively spelled out Soviet concerns and aims. 'The situation in Afghanistan and around it continues to remain complicated,' its authors acknowledged. 'Although the new measures which have been undertaken by the Afghan leadership inside the country and in the international arena are facilitating the stabilization of the situation in the country and the consolidation of the international position of the DRA, this process is going slowly.' They recommended:

> Judging by everything, a successful resolution of the internal problems and the consolidation of the new structure in Afghanistan will demand not a small amount of effort and time, for the length of which the Soviet forces there will remain the basic stabilizing factor standing in opposition to the further expansion of the activity of domestic and foreign counter-revolutionary forces.[33]

Soviet armed forces, therefore, were in Afghanistan to create the circumstances through which Afghan state-building could resume.

Soviet leadership thus set itself a daunting three-part programme: ensuring Karmal established a functioning socialist Afghan regime; eliminating, or at least limiting, internal resistance; and upholding Afghanistan's (and the Soviet Union's) international reputation and standing. From the very beginning, both Brezhnev's and Karmal's governments understood they required a political settlement involving Afghanistan and its immediate neighbours, Pakistan and Iran, to end regional and international support for the Afghan resistance groups and to create the circumstances under which Soviet troops could exit Afghanistan and leave behind a fairly secure, self-sufficient state.

Soviet state-builders who entered Afghanistan to support Karmal did not start from scratch in December 1979. Not only could they build on the longer history of twentieth-century Soviet–Afghan cooperation, but some initial steps had been taken following the April 1978 coup, even if Taraki and Amin had largely ignored Soviet suggestions about the economic and political development of Afghanistan.[34] To re-emphasize the primacy of state-building in Soviet endeavours, it is important to recognize that, in 1978 and 1979, Soviet leaders initially believed their support for the PDPA would almost entirely take the form of technical assistance.[35] The new treaty of friendship signed between Brezhnev and Taraki in December 1978 had two articles related to economic, scientific, and technical cooperation, and the two countries pledged to 'develop and deepen co-operation in the fields of industry, transport and communications, agriculture, the use of natural resources, development of the power-generating industry and in other branches of the economy'. The Soviets promised 'assistance in the training of national personnel and in planning the development of the national economy' and the 'exchange of experience in the fields of science, culture, art, literature, education, health services, the press, radio, television, cinema, tourism, sports, and other fields'.[36]

The fruits of this treaty had begun emerging in early 1979, with agreements for the Soviet Union to extend lines of credit to support numerous Afghan development projects. These included the rebuilding of Kabul airport, exploration and exploitation of oil deposits, creation of electric transmission lines, and the provision of equipment and specialists for the building of seven machine-tractor stations to help with the industrialization of Afghan agriculture.[37] The Soviets had pledged themselves to the PDPA's vision for Afghanistan, even as they questioned Taraki's and Amin's implementation, and, as these early works show, both Soviet and Afghan leaders adopted a common model of modernization.

Soviet advisors, however, were trapped by a fundamental conundrum. On the Afghan side, the PDPA was unquestionably eager to follow what it perceived to be a socialist model and was zealous in putting changes like land reform into progress. If questioned by Soviet observers like Ambassador Puzanov about the speed or level of reform, Taraki and his comrades pointed to the Soviet precedent and the rapid changes that had taken place in the Soviet Union after the 1917 October Revolution. Words of caution from the likes of Kosygin—who reminded Taraki that many of the Soviet officials who had suffered Stalin's accompanying purges had subsequently risen to high ranks in the CPSU after his death—fell on deaf ears.[38] Indeed, Soviet cautions that land reform should take place gradually met with direct challenges from the Khalq, who argued quick land reform was necessary to revolutionize class relations.[39] Soviet officials thus had to walk a careful balance, encouraging first Khalqi and then Parchamite socialist fervour while also trying to temper their policies and expectations, given that Afghanistan, in many Soviet eyes, remained under-equipped for mass modernization and industrialization.

Nevertheless, the Soviet occupation meant that the time for doubts or questions about the PDPA's aspirations had passed. Karmal needed to demonstrate that the PDPA's brand of socialism worked, that it could better the lives of Afghans across the country. The Soviets had to help reinvent the PDPA as a vanguard party that could lead the country's unification and turn to socialism. The Soviet advisers who flooded into Afghanistan to support and direct Karmal's state-building efforts shared this burden. In some ways, they did not lack experience. The sending of advisors and technocrats had become standard Soviet (and American) practice in the Cold War, as countries emerged from decolonization. These specialists were trained to apply their experiences working in the Soviet Union within Third World countries.[40] In other words, their job was to export Soviet models abroad. This duty extended into Afghanistan, even while some Soviet economists warned that the blind application of Soviet practices would lead only to failure (land reform was a case in point).[41]

However, at the same time, Soviet officers entered Afghanistan largely unprepared. The scale of the invasion—the sheer number of Soviets who entered the country to bolster Afghan socialist modernism—knew no equal in the Soviet Union's other international forays. While a few cadre members had some knowledge of Afghanistan and its political and social dynamics, most did not. Gone were the days when ethnographers, working with local elites, informed Soviet socialist state-building practices, as had been the case throughout Central Asia in the interwar years. Gone, too, were many of the older generations of Soviets who had experienced the high modernism of early Soviet consolidation efforts and had participated in the central-ization and strict organization of party structures, the Red Army, and state appar-atuses. Experts on Afghanistan, or even officials who spoke Afghan languages, were few and far between. Central Asian interpreters ended up playing a key role as inter-mediaries between Soviet and Afghan officials. The young Soviet state-builders who entered Afghanistan, then, knew the models of Soviet socialism they should be imple-menting, but they did not necessarily know how, particularly in a foreign (and increasingly hostile) context.[42]

Karmal faced the difficult position of divorcing himself from the Khalqi precedent while also claiming to represent authentic PDPA socialism. He and his allies needed to acknowledge the mistakes made by Taraki and Amin in pushing forward too hastily with policies such as land reform and gender equality. At the same time, he could not stray too far from the ordained socialist path (as Amin's gruesome end had shown). In a joint statement following Karmal's visit to Moscow in October 1980, he and Brezhnev pledged to 'promote the expansion of bilateral cooperation and contacts between party, state and public organizations and cultural and scientific institutions, with a view to using available opportunities for more thorough famil-iarization with the life, work, revolutionary experience and achievements of the two countries' peoples'. They 'called for further expansion and improvment [sic] of the forms of [technical, economic, and trade] cooperation, with due regard for the top-priority and long-term objectives of the rehabilitation, progress and further development of Afghanistan's economy'.[43]

One quick remedy was to decelerate the speed of change. The other was to take a more conciliatory stance regarding the place of Islam in Afghan society. Karmal resumed the traditional incantations praising God in political speeches, and intro-duced a new flag that reinserted green, the colour of Islam, alongside communist red.[44] Like his predecessors, his regime also publicized statements by sympathetic clergy who affirmed the DRA's adherence to Islam. Karmal received help in his efforts by statements like that made by Brezhnev at the 26th Congress of the CPSU in March 1981. The Soviet general secretary emphasized that countries that had 'chosen the path of socialist development' needed the 'gradual elimination' of 'imper-ial monopolies', the 'transition to the planned development of productive forces', the 'encouragement of the cooperation movement in the countryside', the 'heightening of the role of the working masses', and the 'gradual strengthening of the government apparatus with national cadres loyal to the people'. Brezhnev also assured audiences: 'We Communists respect the religious conviction of the people who profess Islam, or any other religion.' He explained: 'The main thing is the aims that are pursued by the forces that proclaim one slogan or another. The liberation struggle may develop under the banner of Islam.'[45] Brezhnev thereby reminded the world of the Soviet Union's earlier claims that religion, particularly Islam, was not contrary to socialist practice and instead could parallel and overlap in the pursuit of social, political,

**Figure 3.2.** Leonid Brezhnev and Babrak Karmal (ITAR-TASS News Agency/Alamy Stock Photo)

and economic uplift. Islam, in other words, could play an active role in moving Afghanistan towards its (socialist) future.

Brezhnev's speech not only attempted to integrate Islam into socialist modernism but also indicated that the Soviet Union welcomed the gradual, rather than immediate, acceptance of socialism within the country, a point somewhat at odds with earlier Soviet policy in the Third World, as well as the Soviet troop presence in Afghanistan. He emphasized communism's space for religion, so long as it complemented the work of socialism and did not work against it, while suggesting areas for development—a planned economy, agricultural cooperatives, the creation of party cadres, and increased democratic representation. Karmal thus had room for manoeuvre while pursuing the establishment of a socialist state in Afghanistan, and he had extensive support from the Soviet advisors sent to Kabul, as well as from policymakers back in Moscow. Karmal's government thus undertook numerous reforms and policies aimed at creating a functioning, productive economy, a unified, dynamic party, and a civilian population that not only accepted but even embraced his regime.

Speaking about the Afghan economy at the PDPA's national conference in mid-March 1982, Karmal outlined his views on Afghanistan's present and future. 'Profound changes', he noted, had taken place since April 1978. He pointed to the 'elimination' of the 'political, social and economic supremacy of the feudal lords and big moneylenders' and praised the progress of land reform. He touted the growing strength and role of the state sector in industry and transportation. All this led, he argued, to the 'gradual establishment of new relations of respect, trust, cooperation and brotherhood among all of Afghanistan's national patriotic forces' while taking into account 'the national distinctiveness of the peoples inhabiting Afghanistan'.[46] Karmal's speech emphasized his government's work to create a unified Afghan nation and a sense of countrywide patriotism underpinned by state infrastructures to create egalitarian opportunity and participation.

A key question that persisted was the balance between private and public ownership in Afghanistan, particularly in the agriculture sector. This was something Karmal tried to tackle almost immediately in the context of land reform. Within months of coming to power, Karmal's government took steps to return state-seized land to mid-level *khans*, arguing that they should not have been affected by land reform in 1978–9, given the size of their holdings (and hoping to regain their loyalty to the state). Amendment no. 1 to decree no. 8 in August 1981 further authorized a host of groups to own plots larger than the original legislation allowed. This revision targeted *mullahs*, tribal leaders, officials, and 'modern-minded owners', indicating the political nature of this act and Parcham's move to divorce land from class reform. It intended to increase the regime's allies, rather than improving land usage. Thus, Karmal's regime had acknowledged that the PDPA's land policies, as implemented, had failed because they antagonized so many rural Afghans, and introduced new reforms.[47]

What would happen in the realm of industry remained less clear. Karmal and his government sought the primacy of state-run development, but, in a country with almost no pre-existing statewide economies, businesses, or systems, this was almost impossible.[48] Most Afghans relied on local businesses, partnerships, and economic structures and informal trade networks. The state had interrupted these practices and struggled to absorb them. In March 1982, Karmal could only pledge 'to make full use of the possibilities of all structures in the interests of the development of the country's productive forces'.[49] This did not mean Karmal and his Soviet advisors halted their focus on economic change, but the infrastructures that would support a countrywide economy needed firmer establishment before the balance between private and public business ownership could truly shift in favour of the state.

Karmal and his ministers relied heavily on Soviet advisors. Soviet officials and workers, in turn, filled the gap between public and private sectors. They were uniquely placed to do so, given they were not Afghan. Ponomarev's claims in March 1980 that 'only Afghan citizens are working throughout the structure of the state and administrative agencies', a statement made to reassert the legitimacy and authority of Karmal's regime, thus rang false.[50] In reality, Soviet advisors were everywhere.

Instead, the question was the extent to which Karmal controlled policy, and thereby Afghan state-building, versus his Soviet advisors. Journalists in the West reported that 'every Afghan minister has Soviet advisors who attend all important meetings and give him orders as to how he should run his ministry'. Karmal, in one speech, acknowledged Soviet 'experts and advisers for nearly all areas of government and for the ministries and administration of government'.[51] Sultan Ali Keshtmand, the Chairman of the DRA's Council of Ministers, typically met Soviet advisors every week before assembling the council's executive committee, and frequently adopted advisors' proposals.[52] By the time that Najibullah came to power in 1986, a typical council meeting, he would later recall, involved each minister bringing his own Soviet advisor. 'We sit down at the table…The meeting begins, the discussion becomes heated, and gradually the [Soviet] advisers come closer and closer to the table. So accordingly our people move away, and eventually only the advisers are left at the table.'[53]

Soviet advisors wielded huge power and influence in the DRA, shaping the regime's policies in almost all fields. The former diplomat and author Rodric Braithwaite claimed: 'The plethora of Soviet advisors, their micromanagement of everyday business, robbed their Afghan opposite numbers of any sense of responsibility and initiative. Why take risks, if the Soviet comrades were willing to take risks for you?'[54] Yet scholars Paul Robinson and Jay Dixon have argued that Afghans 'were less subordinate to the Soviets than is commonly assumed', citing Valerii Ivanov, the secretary for the Permanent Intergovernmental Commission on Economic Cooperation, who claimed that it was 'the Soviets [who] accepted "eighty-five to ninety [per cent]" of Afghan proposals'.[55] Given that much of the archive for Soviet decision-making, particularly for the International Department or Politburo, remains classified, gauging the extent of Soviet control within the Karmal regime remains up for debate. But what is clear is that Karmal's policies resulted from a joint Soviet–Afghan effort. Not only that, but the shortcomings of Soviet policy highlighted by Karen Brutents in 1979 remained: where Soviet policy stopped and local policy started was ambiguous. The fact that many Afghan government decisions continued to follow Soviet modernization planning indicates the extent of foreign influence and the Soviet imprint on 1980s Afghanistan. As *Izvestia* reported in mid-1984: 'In 1982–1983 alone, with the Soviet Union's assistance, the DRA erected and commissioned 16 major enterprises that are playing an important role in the country's economy. At present, facilities built through Soviet–Afghan cooperation are producing approximately 70% of industrial output in the DRA's state sector.'[56]

Given the huge publicity and international outcry that accompanied the sending of Soviet troops into Afghanistan and the monumental growth in foreign funding to the enemies of the PDPA, Soviet prestige was at stake. Withdrawing from Afghanistan before the country became relatively stable politically and socially would signal a defeat of the Soviet Union as a superpower, demonstrate its weakness in comparison with the United States, and damage its reputation worldwide but especially in the non-Western world. In contrast, supporting the PDPA in creating a functional socialist state—or a functional state led by a vanguard party on its way towards socialism—would make the Soviet foray in Afghanistan a success. The Politburo could dimly cite Soviet efforts in Africa as a sign that they could succeed in Afghanistan. But regional and international activities would ultimately conspire against a socialist Afghanistan. Nevertheless, in the early years of the occupation, Soviet officials on the ground in Afghanistan and their counterparts in Moscow worked to create the opportunities for the PDPA to implement its socialist visions. But, as mission creep set in, and as Soviet soldiers and civilians became enmeshed in all aspects of Afghan daily life, increasingly the focus turned to survival and maintenance.

The activities of the Permanent Intergovernmental Commission on Economic Cooperation give some indication of the extent of Soviet involvement in attempts to revive and direct Afghanistan's economic progress—and thus to mould the Afghan state. The commission's activities highlighted the premium placed by both Soviet and Afghan leaders on state-led economic development, and it also demonstrated the fundamental role played by Soviet workers and ministries in building Afghanistan. The commission coordinated work between the two states, beginning in December 1978 and continuing through the early 1990s. It made recommendations and facilitated arrangements across a host of economic fields, ranging from automobile transport to gas exploration, energy-industry development, technical developments, the building of transport facilities, and the creation of light industry and riverine ports.

Soviet advisors working for the commission did not merely make sweeping recommendations for economic change in Afghanistan. In stark contrast to the bold statements made by the PDPA, which had limited follow-through, their work focused on the minutiae, the details that would make economic practices more effective in Afghanistan. Looking to rural Afghans and the further development of farming, for example, the Soviet Ministry of Agriculture provided materials via the Commission in 1983 for constructing laboratories in Kabul to measure chemicals in Afghan soil and grow specialized seeds, cotton among them, as well as the specialists to run the labs. It also provided the materials to construct a hatchery and poultry farm.[57] A protocol signed between Afghan and Soviet ministers for 1984 further pledged to work on disease control and veterinary medicine for farm animals, while noting the agricultural successes that had resulted from the creation of machine and tractor stations. Both sides agreed to explore further mechanization of agriculture, as 'the activities of machine and tractor stations have a certain positive impact on the process of social and economic transformations in the Afghan village.'[58]

Agriculture was just the tip of the iceberg. Soviet workers and their Afghan counterparts also tackled transportation infrastructures and the development of new economies. They constructed telephone lines and a central telegraph office in Kabul. They built—and rebuilt, owing to the war—roads, bridges, and tunnels.[59] The commission organized workers from the Soviet Ministries of Transport Construction and Automobile Transport to reinforce Afghan roads, notably the Salang Tunnel passing under the Hindu Kush mountain range. They were also charged with constructing facilities for the upkeep of government vehicles and conducting other activities to strengthen Afghanistan's transport systems and infrastructures.[60] These projects provided the DRA with small victories in its ongoing war with both Afghan resistance fighters and sceptical international audiences. Upon the completion in June

1982 of a new motor vehicle and train bridge over the Amu Darya river, separating Afghanistan from Soviet Uzbekistan, Karmal not only declared that 'its significance for the development of our economy is enormous', but described it as 'a symbol of our friendship, intimacy, comradeship and brotherhood' with the Soviets.[61]

The Commission also turned its attention to the energy sector, working to extend Afghanistan's power lines into the provinces (presumably, in part, to help power those beneficial tractor and machine stations) and to develop the state's fuel industry, encouraging oil exploration and the construction of gas-filling stations. The Commission coordinated efforts of the Soviet Ministries of Construction of Gas and Oil Industries, the Gas Industry, and Geology to identify potential gas fields, build drilling sites, and establish the pipelines and other means for the movement and export of gas.[62]

Creating a functioning gas industry in Afghanistan was important for numerous reasons. It provided a necessary resource for the development of Afghanistan's internal economy. Workers from the Soviet Ministry of Construction of Gas and Oil Industries built a unit for processing gas and turning it into motor fuel, which, in turn, could be used to power the vehicles needed not only for productive agriculture but for the movement of people and goods across Afghanistan's growing road network.[63] Even more importantly, gas represented one of Afghanistan's key export commodities—one that went overwhelmingly to the Soviet Union.

In comparison to Afghanistan's other main exports—wool, citrus and dried fruits, olives, cotton fibre—gas had particular value. The DRA provided gas to the Soviet Union as a means of paying off its financial debts to the Soviet Union. As this took the form of a 'sale', it created the equally beneficial appearance to foreign observers that the relationship between Afghanistan and the Soviet Union was based on economic transactions, not one-way giving, and Afghanistan's economy was breaking even.[64] As such, this exchange gave Afghanistan the facade of stability, independence, and successful state-led development. By 1984, a DRA spokesman reported that gas sales to the Soviets accounted for almost half of the state's income. Much of Afghanistan's gas was piped directly across the border into Soviet Uzbekistan and Turkmenistan, using pipelines built in the country by Soviet workers.[65] Still, in practice, Afghanistan struggled to fulfil its side of the bargain. In 1982, H. Mangal, Afghanistan's ambassador to the Soviet Union, admitted that his country could not supply its full quota of natural gas, owing to 'sabotage on Afghan territory'. He requested additional Soviet aid to increase extraction so the Afghans could meet their target, to which the Soviet Union's deputy minister of foreign trade agreed, pointing out that Soviet organizations were already hard at work 'taking measures to maximize gas extraction'.[66]

Soviet and Afghan officials also attempted to use the intergovernmental commission and the Ministry of Foreign Trade to facilitate the DRA's economic presence abroad and shore up its legitimacy to international audiences. Alongside the numerous infrastructure projects taking place within Afghanistan, the Kremlin provided PDPA leaders with lines of credit to make foreign purchases for goods like wheat.

Soviet officials and funding enabled the DRA to purchase rice from India and Sri Lanka, soap and other household goods from the GDR, batteries from Japan, oil and grease from Great Britain and the Netherlands, and dishware from France.[67] Creating trade agreements between the DRA and other states provided a means of demonstrating Afghanistan's status as an independent state and presented a key opportunity for normalizing the country's relations with foreign powers. Soviet officials particularly emphasized potential partnerships with India, which was ideally placed as a regional player and a non-aligned country sympathetic to the Soviet Union but independent of the eastern bloc. The Ministry of Foreign Trade in 1982 proposed a tripartite trade deal between the Soviet Union, the DRA, and India, through which the DRA would purchase goods from India that the Soviet Union could not provide. While DRA representatives were enthusiastic, it is unclear whether the agreement ever got off the ground.[68] Afghan trade representatives also pushed for a permanent exhibition hall in Moscow that would include not only a store selling Afghan-made handicrafts but also a restaurant serving 'Afghan national food'.[69] The exhibition would showcase Afghanistan's exports and culture to international audiences and extend Afghanistan's reputation abroad.

Yet, for new economic practices to take root, Karmal and his allies needed a receptive domestic audience more than an international one. Afghanistan's citizens had to be willing to take part in the state's development. A modern economy relied on an engaged civilian population willing to accept and participate in reform efforts. Thus, equally key to efforts to build a legitimate Afghan state were practices to extend and deepen PDPA party membership and increase Afghans' participation in politics. The PDPA would always struggle if it did not gain an adequate support base. As members of the Politburo observed in April 1980, Karmal needed to pursue 'consistent and purposeful measures for achieving a genuine ideological, political, and organizational unity in the ranks of the PDPA, and for strengthening its influence in the country, for unifying all national–patriotic forces, for creating an effective apparatus of local government'.[70]

Karmal and his Soviet allies undertook a host of activities to gain followers. His government pursued a recruitment drive for the PDPA and expanded party structures beyond Afghanistan's urban centres and through the provinces. By the time Karmal fell from power in early 1986, his office would claim that party membership had exploded from around 22,000 members to close to 150,000, and the party would boast of committees in 205 districts and subdistricts by mid-1984. Village-based party organizations grew from 277 in 1983–4 to 1,160 in 1987.[71] Soviet observers lauded these steps and made sure to publicize the PDPA's efforts. One commentator wrote in *Voprosy Istorii* that the PDPA had nearly doubled the number of card-carrying party members. 'The working people's endeavor to link their destiny with that of the party', the author claimed, 'is eloquent testimony to its growing prestige and to the masses' confidence in it'. The report also made a point of noting that 40 per cent of new recruits were 'workers or peasants'.[72] The PDPA was no longer the party of the intelligentsia; it belonged to the people.

Afghan leaders needed to strengthen the PDPA to reinforce the government. The DRA followed the Soviet model, whereby party and state leadership were largely one and the same. Thus, more party followers meant more state adherents.[73] By overcoming the Khalq–Parcham split and recruiting new members, the government would achieve a number of objectives. It would legitimize the coup by broadening Karmal's base of support, it would provide the manpower to run the government across the country, and it would embed Soviet-backed Afghan visions of socialism in society. Karmal ultimately failed in this. Not only did numerous hurdles exist, but the fact that the PDPA never fully resolved the Khalq–Parcham divide, and that corruption and nepotism ran rampant from the highest levels of government to provincial cells of the PDPA, constantly undermined both the party's and the state's position.

The government's Soviet advisors undertook additional steps to turn the PDPA's new recruits and committees into functioning elements of the party. By July 1980, the Soviets had built a satellite ground station to broadcast Soviet television programmes in Kabul and monitored Afghan radio and TV broadcasting, ensuring that regularly broadcast religious sermons included appeals for cooperation with the DRA. They organized annual festivities to celebrate Afghan–Soviet Friendship Week. The Soviet and DRA Ministries of Education worked together, alongside Soviet teachers seconded to Afghan universities and local editors, to translate hundreds of Russian textbooks into Dari and Pashto. The Soviet Ministry of Education, working with the Ministry of Industry, also sent specialists to create boarding schools in Kabul, Jalalabad, and Mazar-e Sharif to educate younger pupils. Alongside this, the Soviet Union's State Committee on Vocational Technical Education undertook the building of vocational institutions in these same cities, where Soviet specialists trained young Afghans to become electricians, mechanics, and welders, to repair cars and industrial parts, and to operate agricultural machines.[74] The goal was not only to indoctrinate the next generation of party members but also to teach them useful skills necessary to keep the government and its initiatives functioning.

Alongside these attempts to gestate future generations of party leaders and workers, Karmal, with Soviet encouragement, tried to build alliances between the PDPA and other sectors of Afghan society. We have already seen this in Karmal's attempts to reach out to clergy and tribal leaders through his amendments to the regime's land reforms and his reinsertion of Islamic language into official pronouncements. Like Taraki before him, he publicized the opinions of sympathetic groups of clerics. He also continued to reach out to Afghanistan's ethnic groups. He reconstituted his cabinet to include, for the first time, a Hazara prime minister, Sultan Ali Keshtmand (though the region of Hazarajat remained outside government control throughout the 1980s), and prioritized Kabul-educated Dari-speakers, rather than ethnic Pashtuns (though they still remained in the majority).[75] In a nod to Afghanistan's Pashtuns, and particularly those living along the border with Pakistan, he extended the powers of the Ministry for Tribal and Frontier Affairs, establishing local *jirgas* to bring in the voices of tribal leaders who were not necessarily PDPA members.[76]

The most famous of Karmal's initiatives, along these lines, was his announcement in June 1981 of the National Fatherland Front (NFF). The NFF was intended to represent all Afghans sympathetic to, or willing to cooperate with, the PDPA. A reporter from *Pravda* claimed it involved 'millions of Afghan patriots' and described it as a sign that 'the popular government is doing everything it can to enlist patriotic-minded representatives of national commercial and industrial capital, the clergy and other strata of the population in the building of a new life'.[77] The front had the ability to appoint local administrators and *imams*, as well as to distribute aid from the Soviets. According to its first vice-chairman, Barek Shafii, the front involved itself in every aspect of Afghan life. It was 'taking part in implementing land, water and public education reform, setting up reading and writing courses, organizing cooperatives and holding volunteer workdays'. Shafii took particular pains to note that the Supreme Council of Ulamas and Clergy of the DRA was a key partner organization.[78] The NFF served as another way for the DRA to shape the lives of Afghans under the premise that it was not a purely PDPA initiative. It aligned with Soviet officials' focus on vanguard-led alliance-building in the 1970s, as well as earlier pleas to Taraki and Amin to work with non-Marxist social groups to enable Afghans' transformation into socialists.

To ensure that Afghans across the country heard of these developments, the DRA's Soviet allies developed the broadcasting infrastructures—print, audio, and visual—to promote the Front's activities and launched additional propaganda campaigns. The CPSU Central Committee ordered prominent Soviet newspapers, such as *Pravda*, *Izvestia*, and *Komsomol'skaia Pravda*, to send advisors to develop Afghanistan's print publications, and also directed Soviet instructors to Kabul University to teach journalism. It authorized an annual 50,000 roubles to print Dari- and Pashto-language posters and illustrated leaflets, and directed Novosti, the Soviet news agency, to develop and publish brochures 'explaining the basic principles of domestic and foreign policy of the DRA and aimed at the general Afghan reader'. The Central Committee also ordered the Soviet Ministry of Communication to aid the PDPA in developing systems for distributing newspapers and journals in Kabul and the provinces. It similarly decreed Soviet ministries should explore opportunities for television and film. These included the transmission of Tajik television broadcasts across the border into ethnic Tajik-majority areas of Afghanistan, as well as the translation of a propaganda film, 'Conspiracy against the Republic', which documented the 1978 Saur Revolution and its struggle against counter-revolutionary forces, into Dari and Pashto (it also had English narration for foreign audiences). Soviet officials further agreed to supply the equipment necessary to set up transceiver radio stations and went so far as to order the Soviet armed forces to consider, alongside the Ministry of Culture, ways to provide additional 'cultural services' while occupying Afghanistan.[79] Such efforts, Soviet officials hoped, would bring home the benefits of PDPA rule and the Soviet alliance, highlighting the ways in which the Soviet Union contributed to the PDPA's lofty aspirations.

The Komsomol proved another of the Soviet Union's forces for modernizing Afghan society. The Komsomol had formed an integral part of the Soviet party-state apparatus since its founding in 1918. Its mandate was clear—to use Soviet youth organizations to develop model citizens and spread the Soviet message abroad through its cadres (and thereby internationalize Soviet young adults' own perspectives).[80] Soviet leaders had already dispatched one group of Komsomol workers following the 1978 coup to work with the Democratic Youth Organization of Afghanistan (DOMA). Their presence only grew after the December 1979 invasion, with a clear agenda: to win the hearts and minds of young Afghans and steer them in the direction of Soviet-style socialism.[81]

Komsomol workers had a number of responsibilities. They comprised the men and women on the ground responsible for putting into practice much of the propaganda churned out by Soviet and Afghan press agencies. They distributed state-sanctioned books and organized the showing of Soviet films, translated or dubbed in Dari and Pashto, at subsidized prices. They had orders to create youth newspapers. They established orchestras and organized musical performances. They set up youth clubs and sports groups, arranging for the import of equipment such as tennis balls and rackets. They identified promising young writers and students who could be sent to parts of the Soviet Union for additional training. In a protocol on cooperation between the Komsomol and DOMA for 1981–2, both sides pledged to boost friendship and solidarity between the youth of their countries through activities like exchange programmes for DOMA members to learn about Soviet culture, the sending of Soviet art collections and performers to entertain Afghan audiences, and the provision of additional sports equipment and cultural goods for young Afghans.[82]

Komsomol workers also provided a clear link between the Soviets' civilian and military activities. Thousands served as soldiers in the Soviet armed forces stationed across Afghanistan, while others worked as teachers or in hospitals. Another important group advised on expanding DOMA's membership and creating local structures. And many Komsomol workers served in more menial ways, building irrigation ditches and roads and overseeing the mechanization of Afghan agriculture that the intergovernmental commission organized and funded.[83]

But Komsomol workers, like their advisor comrades, increasingly found themselves straining to complete their missions. More and more, Soviets struggled to move not only around Afghanistan but even within the cities and villages in which they were stationed. They were hemmed in and targeted by resistance forces. They also lacked faith in their local allies. One Komsomol report as early as September 1981 indicated that DOMA groups fought badly, bitterly noting, 'we don't see this with the rebels!' Afghan students also did not readily respond to Komsomol–DOMA efforts, as demonstrated by the strings of protests that continued to sweep through Kabul University and other institutions throughout the 1980s. Soviet observers complained about a 'low level of consciousness' among Afghan students whom they did try to sway.[84]

Komsomol and DOMA workers' target audiences exhibited the same fundamental problem that hampered all the PDPA and Soviet attempts to legitimize the DRA. Despite the huge efforts put in by Soviet and Afghan officials and labourers, they could not paper over the fact that few Afghans bought into the PDPA's promises of socialism, particularly a form of socialism that was increasingly kept in place by the use of armed force. Indeed, the heavy emphasis that Afghan and Soviet leaders placed on developing Afghanistan's army and intelligence operators and using them to enforce the government's writ, particularly KhAD, did little to endear the regime. Efforts to turn the Afghan army into an effective fighting force floundered, as recruits—most of whom had been conscripted—showed little enthusiasm for combat, and desertions were frequent.

Among government departments, KhAD flourished, owing, no doubt, to organizational support from the KGB. The KGB had taken a leading role in the Soviet Union's earlier Third World interventions, and many of its younger members, in parallel to Brutents in the International Department, had recognized the need for cooperation across party lines and anti-colonial movements in the pursuit of a Marxist state. From September 1979, the KGB advocated that the PDPA take a more flexible approach to tribal and clergy leaders. KGB officers helped KhAD to infiltrate tribal groups and refugee camps in Pakistan and to bribe tribal leaders within Afghanistan to cooperate with the regime. Referred to as the 'revolution's sharp sword', the information services had extensive powers, including establishing irregular militias to counter insurgents, policing the country (including within the PDPA and the government's ministries), and interrogating and torturing potential enemies of the state, or making them disappear. Thanks to KGB training, Karmal once asserted: 'Khad has become a real fighting force against the enemies of the Revolution.'[85] KhAD was a force intended to inspire loyalty to the regime through fear, force, and coercion, not by encouraging an embrace of the PDPA's political aspirations.

Karmal and his top-level Soviet advisors ultimately failed to develop the millions of patriotic, loyal citizens they claimed would emerge from the state's endeavours. Despite the huge number of new party recruits reported by the PDPA, these members' ideological fervour was frequently debatable. PDPA recruiters appeared to have prioritized numbers over political persuasion. Pakistani and American estimates of 'ideologically committed members' in 1984 put the number of PDPA devotees between 15,000 and 35,000.[86] The success of local party committees was similarly questionable. In areas where the PDPA already had some influence, this tended to continue. In regions where the PDPA had a limited pre-existing presence, the organization of new committees had little impact, beyond providing the regime with a statistic. Karmal admitted five years into his rule that 'party and state organs had "weak links with the inhabitants" of the tribal areas and decisions taken by the PDPA Central Committee and by the government affecting these regions "did not have much effect on the state of affairs"'. The NFF, at face value, indicated the PDPA's willingness to work with non-party members and to move gradually, using cooperation, towards the modernization of Afghanistan. Its actual incorporation of non-PDPA members into the government fold, however, was restricted. Most of the members of the NFF belonged to pre-existing organizations, most of which had been established, or greatly expanded, by the PDPA, including the Women's Democratic Council of Afghanistan, DOMA, and trade unions.[87]

As the Soviet presence in Afghanistan stretched into years, mission creep set in. Opportunities for shoring up the PDPA's vision of the state declined, overtaken by the civil war between government and resistance forces and the PDPA's own indolence. Despite the efforts of numerous Soviet ministries to bolster the Afghan economy and develop the government's infrastructures, their successes remained limited, and focus increasingly turned to maintaining an uncertain status quo. By the end of November 1984, delegates from the DRA's chamber of commerce and industry and representatives from the Afghan business community reported to I. T. Grishin, the Soviet deputy minister of foreign trade, that Afghanistan's public sector had 'grown and strengthened' but admitted the continued importance of private companies. This, Soviet and Afghan representatives agreed, was because the public sector had to focus on 'undermining the actions of the Afghan counter-revolution', while the private sector could work to develop Afghanistan's foreign trade and economic activities among the 'provincial population'.[88]

The permanent intergovernmental commission also had to expand its scope to account for the violence taking place alongside, and in reaction to, state-building. It put in place an agreement in April 1985 with the Soviet Ministry of Health to build a Centre for Prosthetics and Treatment of Persons with Disabilities in Kabul, which would have two hundred beds, an orthopaedic surgery wing, and a rehabilitation ward. This was only just preceded by the construction of two outpatient health clinics and a blood transfusion station; though agreed upon in March 1977, they were not completed until October 1985. Medical facilities gained new urgency, as the war increased in violence and size.[89]

While Politburo members initially might have believed that Afghans would come to accept the PDPA and its vision of socialism, or could be set on a pro-socialist trajectory, this failed to materialize. Instead, Soviet officials on the ground were increasingly forced to compromise, focusing on small-scale shifts and developments rather than nationwide political and social change. The war increasingly obstructed state-building, and hopes (PDPA or Soviet) for a modern socialist Afghanistan slowly leached away. Not only did the accompanying destruction force workers to undertake rebuilding and repairs, rather than new projects, but the war also limited the ways that existing infrastructures could be used. A Soviet reporter's interview with Ahmad Nabi, Chairman of the Kandahar Province Committee of the PDPA, revealed not only that resistance fighters targeted Soviet–Afghan building works but that any destruction had knock-on effects. 'The power transmission line that connects the city with a power station in neighboring Helmand Province was blown up by [insurgents], and we still haven't managed to repair it.' Nabi explained: 'Because of the shortage of electric power, the wool and textile factories are only operating on a single shift, and water cannot be pumped into the province's irrigation systems in sufficient quantities.' He went on to note: 'Small diesel generators are a help, but they are no solution to the problem, of course. They are inefficient and require a huge amount of expensive fuel, which is in short supply and whose delivery also entails considerable difficulties and costs under present conditions.'[90] A lack of power, combined with the increasing hardship workers faced in moving goods like fuel across the country, increasingly brought Afghanistan's state-run economies to a standstill.

And not only did Soviet representatives frequently find themselves tasked with rebuilding, thanks to the war, but they also faced huge personal risks. Soviet efforts to build a socialist Afghanistan increasingly rebounded onto Soviets on the ground, with devastating consequences. They were frequently targeted by resistance combatants. For example, Evgeni Okhrimiuk, a geologist working in Kabul, was kidnapped and held ransom by insurgents who demanded the government trade him for a political prisoner. Negotiations ultimately failed, and he was executed.[91] It is thus of little surprise that Soviet members of the intergovernmental commission demanded that the PDPA take more effective measures to 'create a safe working and living environment' for Soviets in Afghanistan. By 1984, deep into the civil war, the Soviet Union's members of the commission warned that they would continue to fulfil their obligations only 'depending on the implementation by the Afghan Party of security measures'.[92] But ultimately neither the safety of Soviet officials, nor their ability to build—and, increasingly, thanks to the war, rebuild—large infrastructure projects, was enough to ensure the success of joint Afghan–Soviet endeavours to develop a functioning state. The PDPA dream of a modern socialist Afghanistan, which was supposed to be the beneficiary of so much Soviet planning and work, succumbed not only to the ongoing war but also to shifts in Soviet thinking back in Moscow.

The growing realization among Soviet circles that their alliance with the Karmal regime and their extensive state-building activities were having little positive effect finally culminated in a decision to retrench and a regime change. Karmal was forced to step down, to be replaced by Mohammad Najibullah, the former head of KhAD with powerful friends in Moscow. That this change took more than five years to take place had less to do with the successes or failures of the PDPA and the Soviets working within Afghanistan than with the stagnancy and uncertainty of politics in Moscow. During the course of the first five years of Soviet occupation, the CPSU underwent a series of leadership changes. Brezhnev died in November 1982 and was replaced by Yuri Andropov, the former head of the KGB and one of the key architects of the Soviet Union's initial Afghan intervention. Andropov's health, however, proved no stronger than Brezhnev's, and he died at the age of 69 of renal failure in early February 1984, having been in power for less than sixteen months. His successor, Konstantin Chernenko, had an even briefer stint, dying in March 1985, little more than a year after coming to power. From within this morass of death and decay finally emerged a far more robust general secretary of the CPSU—one with ambitious plans for reforming not only the Soviet Union but its relations with the rest of the world.

Mikhail Gorbachev could hardly have been more different from his predecessors. By Politburo standards, he was a young man, taking the helm of the Soviet Union mere days after his fifty-fourth birthday (the youngest since Stalin). While he came from humble roots, he was the only member of the Politburo with a university education, a graduate of Moscow State University, and the first leader since Lenin to receive training in law. He had been active in the Komsomol and joined the CPSU in 1952. He became a member of the Central Committee in 1971, and joined the Politburo elite in 1978, in which he had responsibility for agriculture planning under the patronage of Andropov, who schemed to set him up as his successor (this was delayed by machinations that instead put in place the failing Chernenko).[93]

Upon coming to power, Gorbachev set in motion sweeping plans for change. The Soviet Union's economy was stagnant, its military bill sky-high. Gorbachev and his reformulated Politburo, which consisted of a younger generation of ambitious, equally reform-minded officials, sought to decrease spending on nuclear proliferation and competition with the US. Aspirations to reconfigure the Soviet approach to nuclear power would gain new urgency at the end of April 1986 when the disastrous explosion at Chernobyl revealed not only to Soviet officialdom but to the entire world the dangers of a nuclear meltdown.[94] Gorbachev's Politburo also sought economic reform and a shift away from state-led planning, as well as restrictions on Soviet military responsibilities abroad. As early as Chernenko's funeral in March 1985, Gorbachev informed East European leaders that the era of Soviet military interventions to shore up partner regimes abroad was over.[95] Gorbachev's reforms ultimately culminated in *glasnost* and *perestroika*: widespread social, economic, and political changes, the encouragement of more transparent decision-making processes, and, some would argue, ultimately the end of the Soviet Union.[96]

If Gorbachev wanted to reform the Soviet Union, refocusing on domestic issues and improving its image abroad, then being seen as an invading power was problematic, to say the least. Not only that, but the Soviet occupation of Afghanistan took needed resources away from *perestroika*. Soviet forces in Afghanistan were costly, tarnished the Soviet Union's reputation in Europe and across the non-Western world, and presented a clear point of conflict with the United States. Even while Gorbachev and his advisors maintained that the Soviet Union still had a role to play in the Third World—for example, providing support to the Sandinistas in Nicaragua as they faced a US trade embargo—they increasingly acknowledged that the Soviet–Afghan model had failed. Instead, Gorbachev's key advisors, particularly Anatoly Chernyaev, who came from the International Department and shared many of the views put forward in the late 1970s by Karen Brutents, argued for refocusing on limited support for socialist movements and parties abroad, ensuring that they did not become overly reliant on aid from the Soviets, and avoiding intervention.

In the broader context of Soviet foreign and domestic policy, then, Afghanistan was a sticking point. Gorbachev had a choice: to double down on earlier Soviet policy towards Afghanistan and make further attempts to reinforce the PDPA's legitimacy and lasting power or to acknowledge Soviet failure and pursue withdrawal. In the first year of his reign, Gorbachev's policies towards Afghanistan outwardly differed little from those of his predecessors. While he critiqued the Soviet thinking of the 1970s that argued underdeveloped non-Western countries could bypass the traditional stages of capitalist development that ultimately led to socialism, he made a final concerted effort to reinforce the PDPA. Gorbachev acknowledged and accepted the cost of an intensified military campaign in Afghanistan—in 1986, the CIA estimated that Soviet military costs had risen by more than 30 per cent—in the hopes that a victory that rooted out the resistance would create the circumstances for a Soviet withdrawal.[97]

Thus, in June 1985, Gorbachev began floating the idea of 'resolving the Afghan question', and, by October that year, he had gained Politburo approval to work towards a withdrawal of Soviet forces.[98] Chernyaev wrote approvingly in his meeting notes: 'Gorbachev should not delay this. I cannot imagine people in the USSR, who would be against it. Such an action would provide him with a moral and political platform, from which he could later move mountains.' He went so far as to add: 'It would be equivalent to Khrushchev's anti-Stalinist report at the [Twentieth] Congress. Not to mention the benefits the withdrawal would give us in foreign policy.'[99]

Discussions in 1985 and 1986 revealed some uncomfortable truths about the Soviet occupation of Afghanistan and its PDPA allies. Not only did the reinvigorated military campaign end in stalemate, but the PDPA and its Soviet collaborators had also failed to create the infrastructures needed to uphold the regime. At a 1986 meeting of the CPSU Politburo, Sergei Akhromeev, Chief of the General Staff, bemoaned the regime's fatal weaknesses. 'At the centre there is power, but in the provinces it is not there,' he complained. 'We control Kabul and the provincial centres, but we cannot establish authority in conquered areas.' He went on to declare dramatically: 'We have lost the struggle for the Afghan people.' Deputy Foreign Minister Yuli Vorontsov similarly pointed to PDPA officials who admitted that Afghanistan's rural population had benefited little from the revolution and estimated that the government controlled, at best, less than 30 per cent of Afghanistan's population, most of whom dwelled in the country's cities.[100] On 26 February 1986, Gorbachev famously acknowledged at the opening of the 27th CPSU party congress that 'counterrevolutionaries and imperialism have turned Afghanistan into a bleeding wound'. While he assured his audience that 'the USSR supports that country's efforts aimed at defending its sovereignty', he also bluntly declared the withdrawal of Soviet troops both necessary and imminent. All that was needed for this to occur, he said to applause, was a political settlement.[101]

A political settlement was not, in fact, the sole requirement. Gorbachev, with the support of his two key foreign-policy advisers, Eduard Shevardnadze and Chernyaev (neither of whom had extensive previous foreign-policy experience), had reached the conclusion that, within Afghanistan, Karmal was not the man for the job. If the Soviets wanted to achieve an orderly withdrawal that left some sort of ally in Kabul, they needed a sympathetic, and ideally effective, leader. Gorbachev's first meeting with Karmal in October 1985 had not gone well. Karmal, Gorbachev told the Politburo, had been 'dumbfounded' when Gorbachev told him a Soviet withdrawal must take place. 'He's been counting on us to stay there for a long time—if not forever.' Gorbachev told Karmal bluntly: 'We'll help you, but with arms only, not troops. And if you want to survive you'll have to broaden the base of the regime, forget socialism, make a deal with the truly influential forces, including the Mujahideen commanders and leaders of now-hostile organizations.' In a particularly damning assessment, Gorbachev informed Karmal he would need 'to revive Islam, respect traditions, and try to show the people some tangible benefits from the revolution'.[102] The PDPA, in Gorbachev's view, was incapable of following through with its earlier socialist visions and needed to backtrack. Karmal's response clearly did not inspire confidence, nor did the limited gains he had made in the preceding five years.

Gorbachev instead turned to Mohammad Najibullah. As a member of the Parcham faction, Najibullah initially had been invited to join Taraki's Revolutionary Council in 1978 before following his Parchamite comrades into exile during Taraki's and Amin's party purges (Najibullah spent the intervening years in Iran, then Yugoslavia). Upon Parcham's resurgence on the backs of the Soviet armed forces, Najibullah also returned to Kabul in December 1979, now at the head of KhAD.[103] According to J. N. Dixit, the Indian ambassador to Afghanistan, Najibullah 'conveyed the impression of being efficient, competent, assertive and alert'.[104] With KhAD, arguably the DRA's most functional department and the one that had the most to show from years of Soviet support, he seemed well placed to take charge and create the circumstances under which Soviet troops could exit, hopefully leaving behind a somewhat stable, Soviet-allied Afghanistan. He had practice working with non-party Afghans. As early as 1980, the KGB demanded that Afghan intelligence officers work with tribal and *qawm* leaders rather than trying to divest them of their local influence, as Taraki, Amin, and even Karmal had tried to do. Yet, while KhAD had experience working alongside existing leadership structures, Najibullah was never able to escape the stigma of having led the government's most brutal, violent department. Beneficence in power could not make up for years of arresting, torturing, and executing his and the PDPA's enemies or association with the invading Soviets. Moreover, his tendencies towards Pashtun nationalism were unlikely to appeal to Afghanistan's other ethnic populations.[105]

The precise nature of the debates in Moscow that led to Karmal's replacement by Najibullah remain unclear. What is apparent, however, is the speed with which Najibullah rose to the top of the PDPA. In November 1985, within a month of Gorbachev's meeting with Karmal, Najibullah was promoted to secretary of the PDPA Central Committee. By March 1986, Soviet leaders had informed Karmal that his 'poor health' and age required him to step down and make way for a younger, more virile leader. This became the official line—that Karmal would leave office owing to illness and frailty. Najibullah would later tell colleagues within the PDPA: 'We, his close comrades and friends, saw how the burden of many great responsibilities was worsening his health'.[106] A healthy Karmal's protests met with little sympathy in Moscow, and, in May 1986, at the 18th Plenum of the PDPA, Najibullah became chairman of the PDPA Politburo, pledging to 'realize the majestic and humane goals of the PDPA and the April revolution'.[107]

Gorbachev's initial conversations with Karmal had already made clear the direction the regime needed to take. Socialism, as it had been practised and understood

**Figure 3.3.** Mikhail Gorbachev and Mohammad Najibullah (SPUTNIK/Alamy Stock Photo)

by earlier PDPA leaders and supported by Soviet officials, was defunct. Echoing Gorbachev, Najibullah, in an early speech to the Kabul city party committee, emphasized: 'Criticism and self-criticism must become as necessary to us as the air.' He did not dispute statements made by Karmal in his final months, such as his calls to 'expand our influence on the masses and acquire new friends and political allies'.[108] Instead, he pinpointed what he saw as the key sticking point: 'our principle failing is precisely a lack of energetic action.' 'It is this gap between word and deed', he argued, 'that causes stagnation where there [ought] not to be any'.[109] As early as January 1986, state-sanctioned Soviet commentators began writing of 'national reconciliation' as the only solution for Afghanistan's future, arguing for 'certain compromises and an expansion of the social base of power'.[110] This trope was continued by Najibullah.

At the 20th plenum of the PDPA, held in November 1986, Najibullah laid out his vision for Afghanistan's future. He proved a master of metaphor, explaining to his audience: 'We build the edifice of the party and it depends on us to construct its walls straight or curved. We know how the repairing of a house or apartment is difficult,' he continued. 'The cause we have undertaken is millions of times more complicated than it. We want to reconstruct the society...' Thus, he argued: 'It is necessary for each of us to reconstruct ourselves and change our approach to the revolution.' The giant house that was Afghanistan needed a new foundation, and this foundation rested on the cooperation of the masses, which necessitated rethinking the regime's earlier policies.

Najibullah's statement walked a fine line between praising the earlier work of the PDPA and chastising its members for their shortcomings. He praised measures such as the National Fatherland Front and using *jirgas* as 'traditional' political structures that could be subsumed into the regime. But he demanded better implementation— 'the high schools and higher educational institutions should be turned into forts of revolution'—and increased flexibility—for example, the embrace of private, rather than state-led, production and non-party tribal and Islamic leaders. He finished by pointedly reminding his audience: 'we all, including leading cadres, should not forget that the PDPA is to serve the people.'[111]

The policy of national reconciliation, which came to define the key years of Najibullah's reign after it was announced in January 1987, took his November statements and amplified them. National reconciliation included a declared ceasefire in the fight against the resistance, a general amnesty of political prisoners and any Afghans who had 'perpetrated anti-DRA actions' prior to 15 January 1987, and plans to build a broader support base for the regime through new power-sharing mechanisms that included more non-PDPA members.[112] The policy, Najibullah indicated, needed to be 'comprehensive'. It required making contact with resistance leaders, 'enlisting tribal chiefs', and 'elections to local bodies of power'. He pledged to turn promises into action through the auspices of an 'extraordinary commission made up of authoritative people, elders, mullahs and representatives of party and state agencies and the neutral and opposing sides'.[113]

Upon first inspection, the reforms proposed under national reconciliation seemed ambitious and ranging. In the renamed Republic of Afghanistan (the 'Democratic' was dropped), a new constitution created a multi-party system and instated a *Loya Jirga*, or National Assembly, which met in November 1987. The ruling Revolutionary Council, whose membership had been decided by the PDPA, was disbanded by June 1988. Further constitutional amendments followed. In rural Afghanistan, reconciliation commissions had the power to convene 'peace *jirgas*', negotiate with local resistance commanders, and try to produce ceasefires, even, in some instances, allowing resistance leaders to assume local political power. The commissions could also suspend land reform (a process compounded by a new decree in mid-1987 that effectively did away with the upper limit on landownership, extending it to 100 jeribs from the 30 decreed by Karmal). In effect, national reconciliation revealed itself to be almost entirely focused on eliminating resistance to the regime by either rolling back earlier policies or wooing former enemies.

National reconciliation effectively signalled a volte-face in PDPA and Soviet ambitions for the Afghan state. 'Serving the people' meant diverting away from the socialist practices undertaken by first Taraki and Amin, then Karmal. It required recognizing where previous regimes had failed and trying to overcome their mistakes, what Gorbachev referred to as 'corrections' to local policy.[114] Soviet leaders also emphasized the need for Afghan self-reliance. The Afghan government must keep itself in power and find ways of making its state functional. No longer would Soviet leaders spend millions of roubles on infrastructure projects or combating insurgents. A political solution—one within Afghanistan, not just between Afghanistan and its neighbours—was necessary. The policy of national reconciliation indicated 'a shift from the conception of "pacification" as an auxiliary policy (the creation of a revolutionary social base remaining the final aim) to one where it was the means to gain a new legitimacy of the government'.[115] Not only that: it solidified and heightened the shift away from developing state structures begun by Afghan officials and supported, out of necessity, by the Soviets in preceding years. Now, the focus was on alliance-building. A modern socialist Afghanistan was no longer the end goal.

While Soviet leadership, unsurprisingly, approved of national reconciliation, what became increasingly clear from Politburo meetings was that the Kremlin had largely lost patience with the entire Afghan question. Gorbachev's observations on the situation in Afghanistan reflected Najibullah's own. 'The problem is not in the concept itself, but in its realization,' he mused in a November 1986 Politburo meeting. He concluded:

> We must operate more actively, and with this guide ourselves with two questions. First of all, in the course of two years effect the withdrawal of our troops from Afghanistan... Second of all, we must pursue a widening of the social base of the regime, taking into account the realistic arrangement of political forces.[116]

Soviet leadership clearly cared more about a Soviet troop withdrawal than the nature of Afghanistan's future governance.

Afghan requests for economic aid met with less sympathy than in previous years. Marshal Sokolov observed to the Politburo that Najibullah's regime was 'asking for three times more than they need. Yes, we ought to help. But'—and here we see the shift—'there must be a benefit. In 1981 we gave them 100 million [roubles] in free aid. And it all stayed with the elite. In the villages there is no kerosene, no matches, nothing.'[117] Economic aid had not achieved its aim of establishing a friendly, supportive Afghan public or functioning governing system, and national reconciliation ultimately proved no more successful than the policies pursued under Karmal. Instead, as contemporary scholars observed: 'The problem was that while conciliatory but symbolic changes did little to win over the Afghan opposition or reduce external hostility to the regime, they did serve to provoke hostility from within the PDPA.'[118] Gorbachev nevertheless concluded: 'We will not retreat once we have started.' He explained:

> When we went into Afghanistan we were wrapped up in the ideological aspects and calculated that we could jump over three stages right away: from feudalism to socialism. Now we can look at the situation openly and follow a realistic

policy... The comrades speak correctly: it is better to pay with money than with the lives of our people.[119]

The Politburo's observations spoke to an increasingly potent issue in the Soviet–Afghan War. More and more, discussions turned to the Soviet soldiers stuck in a hostile country and fighting an unwinnable war. Rather than the Kremlin's Afghan allies and the potential of Afghan socialism, these soldiers and growing discontent with the war within the Soviet Union occupied the Politburo's attention. The Soviet armed forces' failure to stamp out armed resistance reflected the broader Soviet failure to create a stable, enduring socialist Afghanistan. For Soviet audiences, particularly as *glasnost* provided opportunities for criticism of government policy, the dead, maimed, and shellshocked soldiers who returned from the Afghan battlefronts served to represent the disaster of the entire Soviet Afghanistan project.

Soviets serving in Afghanistan experienced a very different conflict from that debated by Politburo members in Moscow. For the Kremlin, the Soviet presence in Afghanistan was meant to reinforce the PDPA, build the Afghan state, and establish a legitimate, working government. The top levels of Soviet governance experienced the Afghan conflict as one of roubles and statistics, negotiations and talks, strategies and battlefield ploys. But, on the ground, the fear and insecurity of working in an increasingly hostile country—a country where determining friend from foe could be difficult and where enemy forces flitted in and out of reach, attacking Soviet forces then slipping back to rebel strongholds in Afghanistan's rugged mountain ranges or across the border into friendly Pakistan and Iran—shaped the thousands of Soviet soldiers and civilians. One soldier, Vladislav Tamirov, described the fear accompanying a Soviet-led ambush in his journal in August 1985:

We'd been going for several hours. A bright white moon lit up the valley with merciless light; we kept having to hide in the long shadows cast by the mountains. And the longer we walked, the higher the moon rose, the shorter the shadows became. In an hour, we'd have no place left to hide. In that cold light, we were easy targets. I never knew that night could be brighter than day. I wanted to fall down, hide, and wait for the sun to rise.[120]

Soviets on the ground witnessed first hand the failure of policy in Afghanistan. A fundamental question emerged—why were the Soviets there? What could they actually achieve? There is not space here to do justice to this question or to the experience of Soviets serving in both civilian and combat roles across Afghanistan, but I will draw briefly from Svetlana Alexievich's haunting book *Boys in Zinc* and the interviews she conducted with survivors. One military adviser perfectly summed up the Soviet conundrum: 'I...sincerely believed that a nomad's tent is worse than a five-storey house, that without a toilet bowl there is no culture. And we were going to swamp them with toilet bowls, and build them brick houses. Teach them to drive tractors.' But this failed. 'The peasants didn't want to take the land that we gave them.'

Not only did Afghan socialism fail, but soldiers faced widespread hostility. An artillery major recalled trying to save an injured Afghan girl.

I catch her, hold her close and stroke her. She bites and scratches, trembling all over. As if some wild animal has grabbed her, and not a human being. And suddenly I'm struck like lightning by the incredible thought that she doesn't believe I want to save her, she thinks I want to kill her. Russians can't do anything else, they only kill ...

He went on: 'We realized that out there: they didn't want this. And even if they did, what did we want it for?' One nurse recounted:

We went there to save, to help, to love. That's what we went for ... After some time went by, I caught myself thinking that I hated everything. I hated this soft, light sand that burned like fire. I hated these mountains ... I hated the occasional Afghan, carrying a basket of melons or standing beside his house. Who could tell where he had been last night and what he was doing?

In account after account, soldiers and civilians alike recalled the severity of the conflict, the high death count, the deep physical wounds and even deeper emotional damage, the turn of many troops to drugs and alcohol as a form of desperate, if only brief, escape. The sense of injury was made more profound by the lack of coverage in the Soviet Union of these combatants' experiences, a circumstance that changed only under Gorbachev. The same military advisor who saw his mission as one of modernizing with toilets, brick houses, and tractors was infuriated to discover when he visited Moscow in 1983: 'Here they were living and acting as if we didn't exist out there. As if there wasn't any war.' While Soviets on the ground fought to spread socialism abroad, at home, no one knew or cared.

The overwhelming consensus of Soviets returning home was a sense of loss—not just of comrades and friends, but of a sense of homeland and patriotism and a sense of self. 'I came back,' said one private. 'My mother undressed me like a little child and felt me all over: "Safe and unharmed, my little darling." Unharmed on the surface, but burning inside. Everything bothered me: bright sunlight bothered me, a cheerful song bothered me, someone laughing bothered me.' The war did not end in 1989. Another senior lieutenant recalled:

What do I dream about now? A long minefield. I'm filling out the record field. The number of mines, a drawing of the rows and reference-points for finding them. But my form has got lost ... In my dream I see children running about beside my minefield. They don't know that there are mines there. I have to shout to them: 'There are mines! Don't go that way!' I have to get there before them.[121]

Around fifteen thousand soldiers died, and another thirty-five thousand were wounded, as part of the Soviet effort to reinforce and rebuild a socialist state in

Afghanistan. 'In 1980, when I first arrived in Afghanistan, most of the soldiers were my age: they hadn't yet turned twenty,' wrote Artyom Borovik, a Russian journalist who, while working for the Moscow journal *Ogonyok*, reported alongside Soviet troops fighting in Afghanistan. 'But in 1989, on my last trip to Afghanistan, I noticed with horror that the army was ten years younger than I…One generation had entered Afghanistan. An entirely different generation was leaving it.'[122]

The pursuit of modernity is often violent. The PDPA demonstrated this, in the deaths of Daoud, Taraki, and Amin and in the regime's ready turn to coercion and physical threat to push through its reforms. The PDPA was ready to use force, if necessary, to create a modern socialist Afghanistan. The Soviet Union, by sending in armed forces to back up the PDPA, signalled that it not only approved but was willing to intensify the fight for Afghan socialism. But violence only begot more violence, rather than leading to victory. The lives of Soviet men and women were given to support the project of Afghan socialism, to create a modern Afghanistan in the image of the Soviet Union. The ultimate failings of this, the realization that many Afghans simply did not want this form of governance thrust upon them, brought into question the entire project of Soviet modernity and socialism. Soviet veterans returned home traumatized and disillusioned with the Soviet Union and its decades-long pledges to support Marxist regimes across the world. Were death and destruction really worth the cost of spreading socialism? Ultimately the experience of Soviet soldiers on the ground served as a gruesome metaphor for the failure of Soviet state-building and socialist visions of modernity.

Despite the surprise of the April 1978 coup and the dismay that Soviet leaders felt as they watched the PDPA succumb to infighting, once they chose to intervene, the Politburo's policy towards Afghanistan was far-reaching and ambitious. This was no mere military intervention. It was an attempt to take over and reinvigorate the processes of modernizing Afghanistan. The preceding decade had given Soviet leaders a (perhaps false) sense of strength in their Third World dealings, as they outmanoeuvred China and successfully intervened to shore up Marxism in places such as Angola and Ethiopia. Sending troops into Afghanistan in December 1979 followed the same rationale, of supporting a local vanguard party that seemed capable of leading the country's socialist transformation. But Politburo decision-making was short-sighted, as even lower-level Soviet officials tried to point out in the late 1970s. Afghanistan lacked the infrastructures or public support necessary for PDPA success, and, in many ways, the PDPA was its own worst enemy in its inability to build alliances with other Afghan political and social groups. The two years of PDPA rule that preceded the intervention created damage that a Soviet troop presence could not undo.

Nevertheless, the Politburo intended not only to prop up the PDPA under Karmal but to force through the infrastructures that would embed a socialist system in the country. Soviet leaders sought to create a functioning Afghan state where the PDPA stumbled, to follow through with the implementation of a socialist model of modernity that bore some resemblances to the Soviet Union. As such, the war in Afghanistan was largely conducted by Soviet state-builders, both civilian and military, tasked with reshaping every aspect of Afghan life, ranging from culture and education to economics and industry. Focusing too heavily on military battles and armed skirmishes of the 1980s obscures the real reasons for a Soviet intervention in the first place. This was a war not just to keep an ally in place but also to keep it within the socialist bloc and to demonstrate the prowess of Soviet policy in the Third World.

But, given that Soviet personnel entered a country already succumbing to civil war, the dream of a socialist Afghanistan could no more be realized by the Soviets than their PDPA allies. The fact that the Soviet and PDPA armed forces could not root out the resistance limited the possibilities to mould an Afghan population receptive to wide-ranging social, political, and economic change. So, too, did the nature of many of the political reforms, themselves. Gorbachev realized this in his examination of Afghanistan, and, upon coming to power, Najibullah increasingly found himself surrounded by hostile forces on all sides. But circumstances were exacerbated by developments not only within Afghanistan and the Soviet Union but also among Afghanistan's other neighbours. Leaders in Pakistan, Iran, China, and India had their own perspectives on the conflict engulfing Afghanistan, and they took advantage of the war between the PDPA and a widespread, growing resistance. In their own way, they, like the Soviet Union, tried to reshape Afghanistan and Afghans to suit their own interests. And this, much like the Soviet intervention, only served further to complicate Afghan political and social dynamics.

# 4

# Islamabad

In late January and early February 1980, a flurry of emergency meetings took place in Islamabad, Pakistan. The nation's capital is a sprawling city, with broad boulevards and massive government buildings. It had been the product of Pakistan's first military regime under Mohammad Ayub Khan, who, in the late 1950s, had decided that the country needed a dedicated capital city that represented his ambitions and modernization efforts. In contrast to the old capital, Karachi, with its haphazard mix of old and new, federal and provincial offices, Islamabad was a planned city with government buildings constructed to specification.[1] Now, in 1980, another military dictator sat in Ayub Khan's place, overseeing the civil administration working out of Islamabad and the military headquartered only miles away in Rawalpindi, an ancient city that had served as the biggest regional cantonment in the time of the Raj. General Mohammad Zia-ul-Haq awaited, first, the arrival of China's foreign minister, Huang Hua, then subsequent visits from Kurt Waldheim, secretary-general of the UN, and Zbigniew Brzezinski, President Carter's national security advisor. These one-to-one meetings were accompanied by an emergency summit of the Islamic Ministers of the Organization of the Islamic Conference (OIC), which brought together representatives from across the Muslim world, including Bangladesh, Iraq, Iran, Saudi Arabia, Somalia, Senegal, and Turkey. The same event had sparked all these meetings: the Soviet invasion of Afghanistan.

Each visitor expressed outrage at the Soviet Union's disregard for international norms and its willingness to enter a neighbouring country with military force. Huang was said to have pledged China's 'total material and moral support to Pakistan in this difficult hour', while Brzezinski awkwardly professed his admiration for Pakistan to Zia: 'you are a brave people and this is the quality which is not evenly distributed among the mankind.' He assured Pakistani officials: 'We are here to work with you together to overcome the difficulties and obstacles.' Waldheim, meanwhile, used the emergency talks to assess regional circumstances, acknowledging the situation was 'very tense'. The Islamic Ministers' meeting suspended Afghanistan's membership in the OIC, demanded an immediate withdrawal of Soviet troops, and asked all member states to halt any aid or assistance to the government of Afghanistan.[2]

Across these meetings, officials largely reached the same set of conclusions. First, they rejected Babrak Karmal's new government and denied its legitimacy. They accompanied this with accusations he was a mere Soviet puppet and did not truly represent the Afghan people. Secondly, they pledged their aid to Zia, the major general who had seized control of the Pakistan government in 1977. A chorus of support replaced recent criticisms of Zia's decision to execute the former president,

Zulfikar Ali Bhutto. Now, Zia was under threat as the leader of the country that shared the longest border with Afghanistan (its other lengthiest border, with the Soviet Union, clearly no longer mattered, or even existed). If the Soviet Union's push south and west was to be halted, Pakistan would need to stand firm. Pakistan presented the most useful and important front-line state. The Soviets could not be allowed to extend their influence into Pakistan, nor could Pakistan be allowed to succumb to internal disarray.

The PDPA's coup and the subsequent Soviet invasion took place at a unique historical juncture, one that ensured the crisis became regional and global and did not remain confined within Afghanistan. The rise of Nur Mohammad Taraki had coincided with unrest and regime change across Afghanistan's neighbours. Leaders such as Zia, Ayatollah Khomeini, and Deng Xiaoping sought to fortify their leadership domestically and internationally, not only cementing control over their populations but reasserting their states' sway in global politics. The eruption of civil war in Afghanistan, with Soviet involvement, provided opportunities for neighbouring leaders to assert the power of their own states (to the detriment of the PDPA) as well as to question Afghanistan's trajectory. These leaders used the Afghan crisis to settle old scores—for Pakistan, the Pashtunistan dispute, for China, preventing Soviet encirclement—while asserting their own power in regional and international relations.

Not only that, but the unexpected success of the PDPA also paralleled, and ultimately came into conflict with, the rise of Islamism as a potent international political force. This, in turn, shaped how Afghanistan's neighbours became involved in the civil war. Not only did they question Karmal's rise to power, but they provided support to Afghan Islamists as an alternative source of state leadership. While Khomeini had espoused a revolutionary Shi'ism from exile, Saudi Arabia's King Faisal had begun putting his vision of international Muslim unity into action from the late 1960s. The establishment of the Organization of the Islamic Conference in 1969 was one iteration of this new shared politicized Islam, which also found expression in widespread anti-American sentiment across the Muslim world following US support for Israel in the 1973 Arab–Israeli War and the 1978 Camp David Accords (the Soviets proved unable to capture this feeling for their own benefit). On 20 November 1979, Sunni extremists had stormed the Grand Mosque in Mecca and demanded the overthrow of the House of Saud, which in turn sparked protests across the world, including the storming of the American embassy in Islamabad. Across North Africa, the Middle East, and stretching into South Asia, many Muslims increasingly felt disgruntled and disempowered by international politics and particularly the Cold-War superpowers. Savvy state leaders like Zia spoke to this feeling and pledged to support an Islamization of politics. The Iranian revolution and, shortly after, opportunities to support a *jihad* against the Afghan socialists and their Soviet allies created a moment of global Islamic fervour, one that helped drive Afghanistan's own Islamists to the forefront of the resistance.[3]

While Pakistan and Iran approached the conflict with an eye to Islamization and their shared borders with Afghanistan, China became involved because of its suspicions regarding Soviet intentions, as well as its decades-old alliance with Pakistan. In response, sympathizing with the PDPA's aspirations and also deeply wary of the sudden international limelight (and almost unlimited foreign aid) thrust upon Pakistan as a front-line state in this new Islamic and Cold-War battlefield, India could not help but also become involved. What became clear as conflict played out in Afghanistan was that separating domestic events from regional and international affairs was increasingly difficult. The PDPA, with Soviet help, tried to assert the legitimacy of its state government, but, because the conflict spilled over Afghanistan's borders, most notably into Pakistan and Iran, its governing claims met with increasing disbelief. Instead, Afghanistan's neighbours used the conflict to try not only to reshape the Afghan nation state but also to reshape regional power dynamics. Pakistani, Iranian, and Chinese leaders all claimed that Afghanistan had ceased to exist as a country because of the Soviet invasion. They wanted to reaffirm Afghanistan's sovereignty and place in the international system—but in a way that benefited their own interests.

As such, the regional impact on the battle for Afghan modernity was manifold. Afghanistan's neighbours, headed by Pakistan, played a critical role in blunting the PDPA's attempts to revolutionize Afghanistan's political, social, and economic structures. In a regional and international climate where political Islam seemed like a real opportunity and a foreign invasion could not be tolerated, Afghanistan's neighbours led the international community in challenging Afghan socialism. Instead, by supporting the resistance groups and prioritizing the Islamists among them, they tried to reshape the Afghan nation state into one embedded in the Muslim world. This, in turn, increasingly created a binary between Afghan socialism and Islamism, both in the war and in its international framing. Regional engagement in the Afghan conflict nevertheless was shaped by each neighbour's own calculations and attempts to manipulate the war for its own ends. Not only that, but, even as Pakistan's and Iran's leaders claimed that the Islamists represented the future of the Afghan state, they did not persuade the United Nations' negotiators to recognize or engage with these non-state actors. Instead, talks would take place between the leaders of two neighbouring states: Afghanistan and Pakistan (Iran refused to be involved). Even while it attempted to reshape Afghanistan's future by creating opportunities for Islamist resistance leaders, Pakistan could not dislodge norms of international relations as overseen by the UN.

Islamabad became the centre of a regional attempt to halt Soviet expansion and subvert the PDPA within Afghanistan. Its proximity to the Afghan conflict, as well as the swelling number of refugees living around Peshawar, a little over 100 miles away, made Islamabad the perfect spot for planning a reaction against Soviet intrigues and for demanding an international solution to the crisis of Afghan politics. Pakistan was not alone in reacting to the growing war, and this chapter will make brief sojourns to Tehran, Beijing, and Delhi. The Soviet invasion of Afghanistan sparked a regional crisis, not just a domestic or international one. Collectively, Afghanistan's neighbours played a key role shaping the conflict in Afghanistan and the way that it was perceived across the world, making sure that a socialist Afghanistan could never fully materialize.

For a brief moment preceding the Soviet intervention, the rise of the PDPA seemed to present opportunities for improving Afghanistan's standing in regional relations. This almost immediately crumbled, thanks in part to the speed with which the PDPA's internal reforms imploded and in part to the competing concerns of the countries around Afghanistan. Ironically, of Afghanistan's near neighbours, the government of Pakistan initially expressed the least concern about the PDPA's socialist leanings. While the death of Daoud and the rise of Taraki were splashed across the front pages of national newspapers, Zia reacted mildly. The government of Pakistan officially recognized the new regime on 5 May, a little more than a week after the coup, and Zia's advisor on foreign affairs, Agha Shahi, declared political change in Afghanistan a purely internal affair.[4] Pakistani leaders seemed willing to accept Afghan socialism as just another in a long line of Afghan political shifts. Iranian leaders followed suit, though they worried about the PDPA's socialist predilections. According to sources in Tehran, the Shah 'intended to continue diplomatic relations', but, as allies of the United States, 'privately, Iranian leaders ridicule[d] statements by Mr Taraki that he will keep Afghanistan on a nonaligned course'.[5] In contrast, Indian leaders more actively welcomed the regime change. Daoud's 'tragedy', Ambassador S. K. Singh wrote back to Delhi, 'was that in his pronouncements, and perhaps in his thinking he was a radical reformist; but in his actions and deeds he was prince and a feudal lord'. Singh concluded: 'In retrospect, the years of Daoud's Status-quo Presidency…provided a necessary and required bridge between the centuries old monarchy in Afghanistan, and the Marxist-Leninist regime which [has] followed.'[6]

In Pakistan, Zia considered ways of taking advantage of the coup to advance his country's own international standing and direct Pakistanis' attention away from his increasingly despotic domestic reforms. While Zia initially had promised free, fair elections within ninety days of his own coup, he instead had extended martial law and amended the constitution to allow a military dictatorship. And, despite widespread protests and pressure from leaders across the world, he had also executed Zulfikar Ali Bhutto on trumped-up charges of conspiracy to murder a political opponent. Developments indicated Pakistan's political trajectory followed a very different course from that of Afghanistan. Reflecting his own religiosity, Zia introduced *shari'at* benches to determine whether Pakistan's laws aligned with Islam and enacted a number of conservative Islamic laws, which limited the rights of women and religious minorities.[7] Alongside Iran and Turkey, he took Pakistan out of the US-backed Central Treaty Organization (CENTO) and instead focused on the Islamic movements that had emerged across the 1970s. At the 1978 Asian Islamic Conference, held in Islamabad, he declared, 'we do not wish that Muslims may unite to seize the rights of any other country of the world', but promoted 'the Muslim "Ummah" becoming united and playing its due role in the world'.[8] While focusing on the Islamization of Pakistan politics, Zia hoped that the PDPA's rise might resolve two outstanding issues in Afghan–Pakistan relations: the thirty-year Durand Line border dispute and ongoing Afghan support for ethnonationalist autonomy movements among Pakistan's Pashtun and Baloch populations.

While a dormant issue in 1978, the Pashtunistan dispute had haunted Afghan–Pakistan relations ever since Pakistan's independence in 1947. It was not just the fact that consecutive Afghan regimes had refused to recognize the legality of the Durand Line. A fundamental fear within the government of Pakistan was that Pashtun ethnonationalism could lead to a bifurcation of the Pakistani state. Pakistan's political trajectory from 1947 was fundamentally shaped by the trauma of partition and the division of the subcontinent into two nation states. Not only had the government of Pakistan had to set up its national government almost from scratch while dealing with a massive refugee crisis, but its leaders had continuously struggled to reconcile aspirations to create a strong central government with recalcitrance from provinces that wanted more autonomy. The clash between Pakistan as a 'nation for Muslims' and one riven by ethnic and linguistic tensions came to a head with the 1971 war and the independence of Bangladesh (what had been East Pakistan). In the war's aftermath, Bhutto's government readily turned to Pakistan's armed forces to quash similar autonomy movements in Balochistan and the NWFP. Pakistan's leaders thus saw the Pashtunistan dispute as a threat to the Pakistani nation state and its very survival.[9]

Events in Afghanistan initially seemed to provide leverage for international support. While recognizing the new regime, Zia tried to take advantage of Western Cold-War fears that assumed that the rise of the PDPA was just the first step towards Soviet domination of South Asia and the Persian Gulf.[10] In talks with the American secretary of state, Agha Shahi dramatically declared 'the USSR is on Pakistan's borders' and requested 'a security guarantee as well as military and economic assistance'.[11] Such claims, however, fell on unsympathetic ears, thanks in part to Zia's continued pursuit of the 'Islamic bomb'. Zia's refusal to halt developing Pakistani nuclear capabilities—to symbolize Pakistani prestige and to deter India, which had exploded its first nuclear device in 1974—led to a rupture with the United States, which cut off development aid to Pakistan from April 1979 (even as US policymakers began diverting covert aid to the Afghan resistance movement via Pakistan that same summer).[12]

Pakistan's Chinese allies were more sympathetic. Chinese leaders feared that the rise of the PDPA signalled a Soviet move to contain China. Government-sponsored writers for the *Beijing Review* dramatically predicted the Soviet Union had 'started a large flanking move to encircle Western Europe with the main object of seizing sources of strategic materials vital to the West and controlling the major sea routes linking Western Europe and the United States and those linking the two with Africa and Asia'. They associated developments in Afghanistan with events in South-East Asia, claiming the Soviet Union was attempting to encircle Pakistan and Iran from its Afghan stronghold and sabotage Arab unity at the same time as it encouraged Vietnamese intransigence towards China. These were clearly signs, writers concluded, of the USSR's 'global counter-revolutionary strategy'.[13] 'The Soviet Union is attempting to build two positions of strength in the East and in the West linked by the sea,' Deng Xiaoping warned US President Jimmy Carter.[14] As early as August 1979, the Chinese official press likened the Soviet presence in Afghanistan to the United States' earlier catastrophic war in Vietnam. Much like the Americans in the 1960s, Chinese observers argued, the Soviets had two choices: 'to bring about a change of regime in Kabul or intervene directly in the conflict.'[15] This observation was prescient, and the PRC would be one of the first powers to contemplate supporting the Afghan resistance, working with its Pakistani allies to undermine a perceived Soviet spread.

Given the uncertainty about PDPA (and Soviet) intentions, and ongoing US–Pakistani tensions, Zia focused on more readily realizable regional issues. Initial meetings seemed to signify that leaders in both Pakistan and Afghanistan wanted decent relations, not a resurgence of earlier tensions. On the simmering Pashtunistan dispute and the Baloch autonomy movement that had plagued Islamabad throughout the 1970s, the PDPA's stance appeared similar to Daoud's. Taraki expressed verbal support for his Pashtun and Baloch brethren across the border but did not accompany statements with specific actions. In the UN General Assembly, Agha Shahi drew attention to the 'great deal of progress' made in talks between the two states rather than ongoing differences.[16] He also offered new negotiations to resolve 'outstanding differences', and a visit by Zia to Kabul followed in September 1978.[17] At this meeting, Zia focused on Pakistan and Afghanistan as Muslim countries, declaring, 'I believe in Islamic brotherhood' and pointing to the 'tremendous scope for co-operation', to which, ironically, Taraki agreed. The summit concluded with mutual expressions of goodwill and good neighbourliness. The leaders left unmentioned the PDPA's ambivalent approach to Islam within Afghanistan or Pakistan's ethnic politics.[18]

Relations, however, soon took a turn for the worst. As the PDPA's domestic shortcomings became evident, Taraki sought foreign scapegoats. His rhetoric on regional relations increasingly seesawed between the conciliatory and the inflammatory. At times, Radio Kabul portrayed Pakistan as the foe of the Afghan people, the territorial base for Afghanistan's enemies, and vowed Afghan support for Pashtun and Baloch self-determination. At others, broadcasts emphasized the DRA's hopes for good regional relations and argued that, if Pakistan treated its minorities more fairly, then nothing could hamper Pakistani–Afghan engagement.[19] The Durand Line separating Afghanistan and Pakistan again became a focus of tensions. But, in contrast to previous times, Afghan leaders did not focus solely on demands for Pashtun self-determination within Pakistan's borders. Instead, the fact that Afghans were leaving Afghanistan by crossing into Pakistan was a source of consternation for the PDPA, as was the growing resistance against the regime, which had bases in Pakistan and Iran, as well as in Afghanistan.

Pakistani sources tried to downplay the number of Afghan refugees flooding over the border, as well as the presence of resistance leaders around Peshawar. While Zia's visit to Kabul and the friendly state of bilateral relations were emphasized on the front page of newspapers like *Dawn*, major media barely mentioned the growing refugee crisis until late 1979. For example, on 25 September 1978, only a paragraph-long, back-page article in *Dawn* noted that 10,000 Afghans had entered Pakistan since the coup.[20] Even by mid-1979, when Pakistan resorted to approaching the UNHCR to support the Afghan refugees in Pakistan, the crisis received limited press. Zia maintained that Pakistan had no interest in Afghanistan's internal affairs and wanted only positive relations, arguing refugees were being accepted on humanitarian grounds and so long as they did not jeopardize relations between the two countries.[21] Similarly officials took pains to assert that the government of Pakistan was providing no support to Afghan 'hostiles', even while resistance leaders dwelled in Peshawar.[22] But, as the number of Afghans entering Pakistan grew, the topic could hardly be avoided.

Neither Afghan nor Soviet officials believed Zia's claims that Pakistan housed and fed Afghan refugees for purely humanitarian reasons. Media sources in both countries alleged that so-called refugees were actually coordinating hostilities against the PDPA. On 22 March 1979, the PDPA issued an official statement describing Afghans living in Pakistan as 'a group of traitors who have…found their interest endangered' and accused the government of Pakistan of enabling them. The Soviet ambassador in Islamabad also presented Zia with a note on 26 March protesting the 'counter-revolutionaries' who 'freely roamed up and down the Pak–Afghan border'.

At this early stage, both the PDPA and its Soviet backers began to frame Pakistan as the enemy of Afghan socialist modernity and a counter-revolutionary force. To all these accusations, the Pakistani government and press responded moderately. Pakistani officials lodged verbal protests with the opposing regimes and the United Nations. They publicly denied supporting any armed resistance and went so far as to make official pronouncements demanding that any Afghan hostiles 'appreciate the status of their stay in Pakistan and refrain from any activity which may put strains on the hospitality being offered to them'. The government also obstructed Pakistani politicians from speaking on the refugee crisis and banned refugee groups from holding press conferences.[23]

Matters changed when PDPA accusations began turning into border transgressions. On 13 March 1979, the government of Pakistan protested the shelling of a refugee camp about three to four kilometres inside Pakistani territory by Afghan artillery. American embassy officials became worried when Zia noted that 'he had "so far" ordered his forces not to shoot…but he said that the next DRA aircraft to violate Pak airspace "would be shot down"'. The PDPA responded in kind. On 7 April, the PDPA made counter-accusations, claiming that Pakistani troops disguised as Afghans had raided police posts in Paktia province.[24]

Formal complaints and accusations of illegal border crossings became a regular feature in bilateral relations and persisted and only grew in intensity during the 1980s. What became increasingly apparent was that the emergence of the PDPA would not resolve outstanding border issues and that the PDPA's attempts to assert legitimacy extended to its bilateral relations. Indeed, the growing civil war only exacerbated tensions over the Durand Line. Even while Afghan government officials adopted the historic argument that the line was a falsely imposed border and refused to recognize it, they could not help but be aware that, in reality, as soon as Afghans crossed over and entered Pakistan, they were beyond the reach of the Afghan state. And border transgressions did not help the PDPA's international standing, instead making the regime appear out of control and disobedient to the laws of international politics. Nevertheless, as the war within Afghanistan grew, matters only devolved into further violence.

At the same time that the PDPA antagonized the government of Pakistan, its relations with Iran also soured. As with Pakistan, the PDPA's relations with Iran were shaped by its blame game, as domestic unrest grew. The proximity of the March 1979 uprising in Herat to Afghanistan's border with Iran led the PDPA to accuse Khomeini of sending four thousand Iranian soldiers into Afghanistan to combat the government. The PDPA clearly did not want to acknowledge that Afghans, not foreigners, had fomented resistance to the government's reform efforts. Instead, Afghan media, such as the Kabul-based *Anis*, vilified both Islam and global imperialism, calling Khomeini and his compatriots 'the lackeys of imperialism in the guise of religion' and claiming 'the fanatic Muslims of Iran' had been sent to Herat to 'turn back the wheel of history'.[25] Impugning a foreign power was far easier than acknowledging the PDPA's own shortcomings, and such statements also increasingly highlighted a rift between socialist Afghanistan and its Islamist neighbours.

The Iranian government strongly protested these accusations and retaliated by claiming that, in fact, Afghan agents had tried to stir insurrection in the Iranian province of Sistan and Balochistan, linking back to Afghan support of Baloch ethnonationalism in Pakistan. According to a government spokesman: 'Agents of a foreign Government and anti-revolutionaries were plotting to launch a movement for separating Baluchistan from Iran.'[26] Accusations ran back and forth as each government accused the other of encouraging destabilization.

As with Pakistan, PDPA actions demonstrated to Iranian observers that Afghanistan was increasingly out of step with its neighbours. Tensions between Afghan socialist aspirations and Pakistani and Iranian interest in political Islam came to the surface. Zia's government welcomed the revolution in Iran as a symbol of promise in the Islamic world, overlooking any sectarian differences between Sunni and Shi'a Islam; as Ayatollah Khomeini, who had assumed power in February 1979, told Pakistan's foreign minister: 'The great Islamic solidarity which transcends all other considerations, should unite the Muslim nations so staunchly that no foreign Power would ever dream of dominating them.'[27] In contrast, Khomeini criticized the PDPA for its anti-Islamic policies and repression of 'religious people'.[28] Already the rationale for Pakistani and Iranian support for an Afghan resistance, particularly Afghan Islamists, was becoming clear.

During the first eighteen months of the PDPA's tenure, relations between Afghanistan and Pakistan and Iran worsened but did not descend into all-out conflict. While Pakistan and Iran both showed concern about their bilateral relations with Afghanistan, which became increasingly complicated as conflict within Afghanistan began to spill over, both states' leaders had other, more immediately pressing, problems. Zia and Khomeini were still in the process of cementing their leadership. (An American official snippily commented: 'Zia is clearly in over his head.'[29]) Khomeini also had to deal with the added pressure of tensions with Iran's other neighbour, Iraq, and the international crisis caused on 4 November 1979 when Iranian university students stormed the US embassy in Tehran, taking fifty-two American diplomats and citizens hostage.

Zia and Taraki held another round of talks in Havana during the conference of the Non-Aligned Movement (NAM) in early September 1979. Both leaders reaffirmed the need for political dialogue to ensure normal relations between their respective countries.[30] However, Taraki never followed up after his ill-fated attempt to assassinate Hafizullah Amin led to his own murder. Instead, Amin picked up the reins. Upon coming to power, Amin not only reissued an invitation for Zia to visit but also indicated that his government would no longer focus on the issue of Pashtun and Baloch autonomy in Pakistan. While having earlier touted an ethnic 'brotherhood' extending from the Oxus river in northern Afghanistan to the Attock, a river in Pakistani Punjab, in power Amin pragmatically recognized the need for good relations with Pakistan. He declared, 'history bore testimony that all past rulers of Afghanistan who had entered into "secret agreement" on the issue of Pakhtoons and Baluch had been discarded in "utter humiliation"', and offered to recognize the Durand Line.[31] But, before either Amin or Zia could act on this potential for improved relations, Amin himself was killed, replaced by Babrak Karmal as the Soviets swept into Afghanistan.

The movement of Soviet helicopters, armoured cars, tanks, and battalions across the border into Afghanistan at the end of December 1979 shattered any hopes or illusions of peace in the region. For the briefest moment, the government of Pakistan maintained its traditional line—that the coup bringing Karmal into power was an internal affair—as reporting seemed to indicate that the Soviet troop presence was limited and had arrived at the request of the new regime. However, within days, any existing doubts had vanished. There was little question in the mind of spectators not just in Pakistan but across the world that Soviet actions amounted to a takeover.

As information rushed into Islamabad, the government's tenor swiftly changed. Pakistani officials, alongside those in Iran, Saudi Arabia, China, and the United States, expressed the 'gravest concern' and decried the 'serious violation' of international norms by Soviet actions.[32] The government of Pakistan issued a statement. 'In less than two years there have been three bloody changes of regime in Afghanistan,' it noted. Pakistan had respected these changes as a country's right 'to order their internal affairs in accordance with their own wishes'. Now, however, the government concluded, the 'crisis in Afghanistan constitutes a serious aggravation of the situation and is bound to prolong the agony of the Afghan people, with whom Pakistan is linked by indissoluble ties of history, faith and culture'.[33]

For Pakistani observers, this was no longer a case of Afghan leaders pursuing their own vision of modernity within their political boundaries. Zia instructed

General Akhtar, head of Pakistan's Inter-Services Intelligence (ISI), to study and report on the implications of the Soviet invasion. Akhtar concluded that a continued Soviet push south-west through Pakistan to the Arabian Sea in pursuit of a warm-water port was both feasible and likely. The Soviets, Akhtar observed, could also collude with India to put additional pressure on Pakistan. Pakistan potentially faced a two-front war. Thus, Akhtar and Zia concluded, further Soviet expansionism had to be halted and Afghan independence returned.[34] The PDPA had demonstrated that socialism clearly did not work and had failed Afghanistan's own citizens by bowing to Soviet pressure. Afghanistan needed rescuing for its own sake and for the sake of the region.

The Soviet invasion of Afghanistan provided Pakistan with an unprecedented opportunity. Its location and its alliances made Pakistan the base for anti-Soviet activity and a regional fight against the shared PDPA–Soviet vision of a socialist Afghanistan. Sino-Pakistan relations had already been robust before the Soviet invasion, thanks to a series of treaties from the early 1960s and the completion of the Karakoram Highway jointly built by and linking the two countries. The Soviet intervention led Chinese leaders to reaffirm their relationship with Pakistan, pledge further support, and place additional pressure on the United States to resume aid. The CCP's official newspaper, the People's Daily, declared: 'The international community needs to enforce more rigorous sanctions, give greater support to the Afghan people's struggle and put the Soviet aggressors in an unbearable position. This alone will compel the Soviet Union...'.[35] During a visit to Islamabad, Vice-Defence Minister Xiao Ke declared, alongside criticisms of the Soviet presence in Afghanistan: 'The Chinese people and the People's Liberation Army firmly stand on the side of Pakistan which is under direct threat of Soviet aggression and expansion, and resolutely support the Pakistani people and army in their just struggle for safeguarding their state sovereignty and territorial integrity.'[36]

Vice-Premier Li Xiannian, in early March 1980, outlined three principles for a solution. Li demanded the unconditional withdrawal of Soviet troops; support for Afghan self-determination ('Let the Afghan people solve their own problems'); and, finally, international support for a resistance movement. 'It is completely justified for the people of the world to support the Afghan people in their just struggle against Soviet aggression,' he declared. 'This support cannot be regarded as interference in the internal affairs of Afghanistan.'[37] This declaration underpinned the Chinese decision to aid Afghan resistance fighters and refugees. Even as private discussions slowly improved Sino-Soviet relations in the realms of economics, science, and technology, Deng Xiaoping's regime continued publicly to maintain that relations would never be fully normalized until regional security issues, including an unconditional Soviet withdrawal from Afghanistan, had been resolved.[38]

The United States similarly reaffirmed its support for Pakistan. Pakistan became even more important in US strategy than in previous times. The total rupture of US–Iranian relations following the hostage crisis meant that Pakistan was effectively the only state in the region that shared a border with Afghanistan with which US officials could coordinate. A Chinese base, though the PRC worked in conjunction with the United States, made little sense, given the brevity of the Sino-Afghan border and other remaining tensions in relations between the two countries, most notably continued US recognition and support for Taiwan. Instead, President Carter, like Deng, pledged new aid and support for Pakistan, opting effectively to overlook Pakistan's continued pursuance of nuclear power in the name of US national security.

Zia recognized the opportunities created by the Soviet invasion and took advantage, proving that he was not, in fact, 'in over his head'. 'Frankly this is the best time for US–Pakistan cooperation,' he told Brzezinski and other American officials during meetings in Islamabad. 'You will find a neglected ally and you will build a dam against the Soviets.' Zia shrewdly negotiated for extra aid, playing on US fears. 'An antidote of the superpower is another superpower. The USSR is too much for us', he added, 'with or without Indian support'.[39] He famously rejected President Carter's first offer of $400 million, half of which would build up Pakistan's defence systems, as mere 'peanuts', seen widely as a dismissive reference to Carter's past as a peanut farmer.[40] He held out until the US provided a better offer. The Carter and Reagan administrations would ultimately provide more than $7.2 billion in funding, not only for the Afghan resistance but also for the Pakistani state to ensure it would not succumb to Soviet pressure.[41]

Equally importantly, the Soviet invasion of Afghanistan provided an opportunity for Zia to force Pakistanis to accept his regime. In the words of historian Ayesha Jalal: 'Turning *jihad* into an instrument of state policy, the Zia regime ensured its own longevity by deploying the state-controlled media to wage a vigorous campaign to purify Pakistani society.'[42] Given the previous few turbulent years—autonomy movements in its borderlands, political insecurity at the highest level, Bhutto's execution—Pakistan was hardly a united country. Moreover, various political groups throughout the country increasingly opposed Zia's autocratic turn and sought to work together to force elections. But the threat of Soviet encroachment gave Zia the backing of powerful allies, who would turn a blind eye if he chose repressive measures, as well as unlimited resources to pursue his policies. Foreign support provided Zia with the strength to crush any protest for the sake of national and regional security.[43] Zia's push for Islamization within Pakistan thus corresponded with his support for an Afghan Islamist movement.

Zia ruthlessly forced through domestic measures in the name of national unity and invoking the potential Soviet threat. His central government took advantage of the new cash flow, as well as fear of invasion, to engage more fully with Pakistan's frontier populations—those same Pashtuns and Baloch referred to by Afghan leaders, who historically had resisted social and political integration with the Pakistani centre and who were now on the front line of the conflict. Zia accelerated development efforts in Balochistan and the NWFP begun by his predecessor to further the state's reach in these provinces. He also encouraged religious leaders in local *madrassas*, particularly of the Deoband school, to recruit militias that were committed to supporting the Afghan resistance and upholding a militant Sunni vision of political Islam in the region.[44]

As Zia told a gathering in Peshawar shortly after the Soviet invasion: 'Every soldier of the country...is in a state of preparedness.' He also pointed to the numerous roots Pakistan had in the Islamic world. Pakistan 'is, by no means, alone and isolated. She has numerous friends in the comity of nations, particularly in the Islamic world who will not desert her.' The most important thing, he noted, 'is not foreign aid it is national unity which is based on the nation's profound faith in Islam'. He warned against 'certain elements in the country [who] had not reconciled themselves in its fundamental ideology'.[45] The foreign support pouring into Pakistan to aid an Afghan resistance went a long way towards reinforcing a certain vision of Pakistani statehood, one that relied on autocratic, centralized rule, increasingly drew on conservative religious elements, and used coercion forcibly to unite an ethnically fragmented country under the banner of Islam. In such rhetoric, Zia drew a clear binary between the evils of socialism prevalent in Afghanistan and the strengths of Islamization within Pakistan.

Iran's leaders were equally indignant at the Soviet invasion. At a press conference in Peshawar, Ayatollah Husain Noori, one of Khomeini's special representatives, said Iran refused to stand by during 'the troubles being faced by the Muslim country, Afghanistan', and pledged Iranian assistance to Afghanistan 'in letter and spirit'.[46] In late January, Iran deployed additional troops to its border with Afghanistan, reinforcing local garrisons, and, in early February, Iran's newly elected president, Abolhasan Bani-Sadr, declared in his inaugural address:

> Our revolution will not win unless it is exported. We are going to create a new order in which deprived people will not always be deprived. We Iranians, as long as our brothers in Palestine, Afghanistan, the Philippines and all over the world have not been liberated, will not put down our arms. We give our hand to deprived people all over the world.

This sentiment was affirmed by Khomeini's son as well.[47] As such, Iran, like Pakistan and China, pledged to take a proactive stance against the Soviet intervention and framed the fight in terms of global Islamic revolution. However, Khomeini's regime was limited in what it could do, especially given the ongoing American hostage crisis, which continued to dominate Iran's international relations and reporting on the country. The outbreak of the Iran–Iraq war, which lasted from 1980 to 1988, only served as an additional distraction.

While Pakistani, Iranian, and Chinese spokesmen were quick to condemn the Soviets and reject the claim that Babrak Karmal represented the will of the Afghan people, India was stuck in an uncomfortable position. Early in the PDPA's reign, Taraki had gone out of his way to woo India. In talks with Ambassador Singh, Taraki had emphasized the importance of Afghanistan's relations with India and assured him that the Indo-Afghan relationship was second only to the Soviet–Afghan one.[48] Indian leaders embraced this stance, even while they privately noted the regime's limitations. (Ambassador Singh had observed, 'the great strength of the Khalq Party, and its Government, lies in the weakness of their opponents and critics'.[49])

After visiting the Soviet Union in June 1979, at a time when resistance within Afghanistan was building, Indian Prime Minister Morarji Desai issued a joint statement with Brezhnev: 'While expressing themselves in favour of the aspirations of the people of Afghanistan and the preservation of their national independence, the two countries opposed any interference by outside forces in the internal affairs of Afghanistan.'[50] Even while voicing internal concerns about Taraki's and Amin's ready use of violence to wipe out their opponents, the Indian government pledged economic assistance to the Afghan state, including the provision of several turbines.[51] 'They seem to be somewhat unorthodox in their modes of behaviour', Prime Minister Desai wrote mildly to US President Carter, 'but I am sure that they will settle down as they gain more experience of affairs.'[52]

Clearly, the PDPA had not 'settled down'. Indian officials were disgruntled with the Soviet decision to go back on the earlier joint statement rejecting military intervention, but they sympathized far more with the Afghan vision of socialist anti-colonial modernity than with nearby Pakistani or Iranian Islamism. This was particularly true of Indira Gandhi, who emerged unexpectedly victorious in a nationwide election at the beginning of January 1980. As she moved forward with establishing a new government, she criticized armed intervention, but argued that the United States was largely responsible for destabilizing regional relations.[53] In an interview shortly after she returned as prime minister, she told Pakistani reporters:

India can never support one country sending its troops into another country. But at the same time, it must be kept in mind that the Cold War atmosphere which has been there for many years is again growing. Now if the Soviet Union feels that China and America together—and Pakistan has also aligned with them—are encircling her, she might put up a greater effort to consolidate and strengthen her position.[54]

The Indian government was clearly uncomfortable with the Soviets' armed intervention, but officials were equally wary of how the situation might tilt the regional balance of power away from India and towards its enemy neighbours, Pakistan and China. As pledges of support from China and the United States turned into weapons, military technology, and money for Pakistan, Indian officials expressed concern. The Indian embassy in Islamabad disapprovingly noted: 'Taking advantage of the Afghan situation, Pakistan held extensive discussions with USA and other Western and Islamic countries and China for procuring arms and it is learnt that China and USA have already agreed to give them the following arms...'.[55] The question, for Indian officials, was how Pakistan's newly improved relations with the United States, as well as its growing bonds with China, might affect India. Gandhi warned the US secretary of defense in February, just a month after the invasion, that 'any arms Pakistan acquired would induce a "dangerous state of mind"', while expressing confidence that Soviet forces would remain only 'until the government in Kabul is secure'.[56]

As always, the concern remained that Pakistani leaders would in fact use incoming aid to strengthen its position vis-a-vis India, not to defend itself against the

Soviets. Indian fears had to do less with the government in Afghanistan and more with the future of Indo-Pakistan relations. Pakistan might move closer to gaining military parity with India, or funding could be funnelled into Kashmir to support anti-Indian militants. Gandhi thus argued: 'I do not think there is any real danger to Pakistan.'[57] Moreover, Indian officials were further dismayed to see the NAM, to which India had committed so strongly as a force in world politics, slide into disarray. Members could not agree on a course of action on either the Soviet invasion of Afghanistan or ongoing tensions in South-East Asia (and the Iran–Iraq war would only further complicate relations within the NAM). Pakistan's entry into the NAM, which had seemed so promising in early 1979, served only to highlight that the movement was fracturing and that India, rather than leading in international politics, was increasingly out of step.[58]

As a result, India's response to the Soviet invasion of Afghanistan was far more confused and indecisive than that of Pakistan, Iran, or China, which coalesced around an alternative Islamist internationalism. While declaring the Soviet intervention unacceptable, Indian officials also protested against US, Chinese, and Pakistani support for Afghan resistance fighters, claiming this undermined Afghan politics.[59] India tried to walk a middle line that supported the PDPA's aspirations to modernize Afghanistan while remaining critical of foreign intervention. Circumstances, however, worked against this ambiguity. Pakistan, alongside Iran, China, the United States, and much of the international community, took the stance that the Soviet invasion had halted Afghan progress and eliminated Afghan political agency. As such, their job was to give support to the Afghans who 'truly' represented Afghanistan: the resistance parties and the refugees.

For the duration of the conflict, Pakistan, and to a lesser extent Iran, focused on undermining the PDPA and supporting an alternative Afghan leadership from among the resistance that shared an interest in Islamist modernity. Neighbouring state leaders and their backers brought into question the legitimacy of Babrak Karmal's regime and presented the resistance as the appropriate heads of a future Afghanistan. Pakistani support for the Islamist parties around Peshawar was undoubtedly self-serving: the government hoped to create a sympathetic government in Afghanistan whose goals corresponded with Pakistan's and which no longer focused on stirring ethnonationalist dissent. This nevertheless had widespread ramifications for Afghans, particularly those in residence in Pakistan.

Pakistani decision-making helped put Afghan Islamists at the forefront of the insurgency, in terms of aid, organizational assistance, and international attention. Even while the Afghan resistance played host to a wide array of political visions for Afghanistan's future—ranging from bringing back the exiled king, Zahir Shah, to liberal democratization using a national assembly, to a militant, exclusive, single-party state under the leadership of Hizb-i Islami—the Islamists rose to the top, thanks in large part to Pakistani assistance. Pakistan's response to the resistance ultimately took three forms: advocating a negotiated settlement of the conflict and the withdrawal of Soviet forces, direct engagement with the various Afghan resistance groups, and support for Afghan refugees.

We will return to the issue of negotiating the Soviet withdrawal in further detail in Chapter 8, as Pakistan, Iran, China, and even India, to an extent, turned to the leadership of the United Nations on this matter. However, one brief but fundamentally important point must be emphasized here. Regional reactions to the Soviet invasion played a critical role in shaping how much of the international community approached the Democratic Republic of Afghanistan after December 1979.

Pakistan, China, and Iran all refused to acknowledge Karmal's regime as the legitimate government of Afghanistan, instead arguing that, in fact, the Soviet Union was the power in charge, a stance adopted by many international powers. A government of Pakistan statement on 29 December 1979 made the point that the invasion was 'a serious violation of the norms of peaceful co-existence and the sacrosanct principles of the sovereignty of States and non-interference'. Officials argued: 'The change which took place two days ago is…qualitatively different [from previous coups] because of the factor of external military intervention.'[60] In China, a *Beijing Review* commentary similarly declared, 'From pulling the strings and using surrogates, their method has escalated to direct involvement with their own troops, armed occupation of a sovereign country and change of its government by violent means', while the *People's Daily* argued: 'Amin's sad end proved that the Soviet Union is the overlord in Afghanistan who not only dominates the country's internal, external and military affairs but actually decides who to be put in nominal power.'[61] The government of Iran also responded sceptically to Karmal's promise that his rule would 'be of infinite significance in the regaining of freedom and independent living of our people'. In an official protest note, Iranians wrote: 'If the present rulers of Afghanistan truly believe in their first statement and insist that its provisions be implemented, their call for the presence of the Soviet army in Afghanistan would not be essential at all.' The note went on: 'if they (the present rulers) are honest in what they say the first [thing] they should do is to ask the USSR troops to leave the Afghan territory.'[62]

These various statements, made in the international press, internal government memos, cross-government notes, and lodged with the UN, all served to emphasize Soviet, not Afghan, rule in Afghanistan. They questioned Karmal's legitimacy and argued that he had come to power—and thereafter remained in power—only at the whim of the Soviets. This was not entirely inaccurate. But the refusal of Afghanistan's main neighbours to recognize the most recent regime change as either a genuine expression of Afghan self-determination or a purely domestic matter complicated Afghanistan's standing in both regional and international politics. It thwarted PDPA-led negotiations for a Soviet withdrawal, since the other regional powers refused to speak directly with official Afghan representatives. Equally, the regional response brought into question who represented Afghans and the Afghan state. Equating the Karmal regime with the Soviets undermined the president's authority and standing in international politics, and it also forced conversations among political leaders across the world about who was truly 'Afghan' and who served the interests of the Afghan people.

India, meanwhile, held an uneasy middle course. While agreeing that a Soviet withdrawal needed to occur, Indira Gandhi's government continued to recognize Karmal's regime and advocate for negotiations that directly involved the PDPA. Relations between the two countries remained friendly, especially in comparison to the hostility emanating from Afghanistan's other neighbours. J. N. Dixit, who replaced Singh as Indian ambassador to Afghanistan, recalled in his diary a March 1982 conversation with Karmal, who noted Gandhi 'has the choice of either having a friendly progressive government like ours which respects and needs India, or she can have a number of Zia-ul Haqs and Khomeinis from Pakistan to Egypt'. Dixit, a clear-eyed diplomat who recognized the PDPA's weaknesses and overwhelming reliance on the Soviets, nevertheless concurred: 'To my mind, the choice was and is clear. No Zia-ul Haqs or cantankerous old religious zealots.'[63]

Indian leaders remained concerned that the armaments flooding into region, ostensibly on their way to Afghanistan, would be turned instead against India. Gandhi's government chose a three-pronged approach to the Afghan problem, advocating a peaceful withdrawal in the UN General Assembly, remaining friendly with Karmal's regime, and vociferously critiquing Pakistan, China, and the United States for supporting Afghan resistance fighters.[64] However, as the regional outlier and an indirect neighbour, India could not outweigh the criticisms issued by Pakistan, Iran, and China, and they, rather than India, led international discussions of the DRA, decrying the PDPA leaders as Soviet lackeys who did not represent the genuine desires of the Afghan people.

Indeed, the most important consequence of Afghanistan's neighbours' refusal to recognize Karmal's regime was the opportunity created for Afghan resistance groups to assert their influence internationally. While leaders in Pakistan, Iran, and China sought to turn Karmal and the PDPA into an international pariah, they did their best to advocate the interests of the Afghan resistance groups that had amassed as the PDPA consolidated power. Peshawar became a hive of Afghan exile activity and the centre for alternative political movements that sought to direct Afghanistan down a different path. Pakistan hosted the seven main political parties that came to represent much of the Afghan resistance, in the eyes of foreign observers, and Pakistani officials chose to work exclusively with these organizations in supporting an insurgency.

Regional leaders framed the Afghan resistance as an anti-colonial movement fighting against a Soviet empire to reinstate the will of the Afghan people. 'The people of Afghanistan are dauntless,' crowed one Chinese commentator. 'They had three times humbled imperialist Britain between 1838 and 1919. Today, the Soviet social-imperialism is running up against the same heroic resistance of the Afghan people to alien aggression.'[65] Agha Shahi, Zia's foreign affairs advisor, similarly told the UN General Assembly that widespread Afghan resistance expressed 'their rejection of an alien ideology to which they do not wish to submit' and 'their deep-rooted national tradition of uncompromising struggle against imperialism and colonialism'.[66]

In public statements Pakistan's leaders avoided acknowledging funding or accommodating the Afghan resistance, but Zia also pointedly warned against imperialist powers and their efforts 'to impose on the Muslim polity the anti-Islamic ideology'.[67] At the UN, Pakistan's representative declared that Afghan sovereignty and national independence had been 'compromised in favour of the export of ideology'.[68] By these logics, any resistance was not undermining the state of Afghanistan. The state of Afghanistan had ceased to exist and succumbed to Soviet imperial expansion. The Afghan resistance groups congregating across the border in Pakistan and Iran provided alternative leadership. And this exiled leadership had the potential to serve the interests of Afghanistan's neighbours, as well as to rebuild Afghanistan in new ways in the aftermath of the Soviet occupation.

The government of Pakistan saw joint Soviet–PDPA efforts in Afghanistan as evidence of socialist expansionism, not internally focused state-building. As such, Zia's government sought to provide enough support to the Afghan resistance to help them combat and drive back Soviet forces but not enough to aggravate the Soviets into launching serious attacks on Pakistan. The job of General Akhtar and the ISI, Zia informed him, was to make the Afghanistan conflict 'boil at the right temperature'.[69] ISI's Afghan bureau took control of the covert war against the Soviets and PDPA. While collaborating with the CIA, Akhtar and Zia strictly controlled the movement of US funding and weapons to the resistance: all foreign funding went through Pakistani hands first before reaching the Afghans. This gave ISI extensive powers to shape the resistance, the exiled political parties, the trajectory of the entire conflict, and thereby Afghanistan's future. (Officials within ISI also colluded with Afghan resistance leaders to sell US armaments on the black market, pocketing the profit.[70])

The government of Pakistan's support for seven main Afghan political parties around Peshawar was both strategic and practical. It simplified ISI's job, allowing Pakistani officials to identify a clear set of leaders with whom to interact and who could distribute Pakistani aid to their followers. As Mohammad Yousaf, a former operative who worked in ISI's Afghan bureau, later explained: 'It was through the Alliance political parties that Akhtar controlled the campaign effort. All Mujahideen commanders in the field were required to join a party. As it was only through the parties that arms were distributed, failure to join meant no weapons, which in turn led to loss of a following, prestige, and face.' This system of recognition gave the government of Pakistan additional means for overseeing and influencing the direction of the anti-Soviet, anti-PDPA resistance. ISI manipulated and played the parties off each other to serve Pakistani interests, since it held the budget strings. As Yousaf recalled:

The Afghan Bureau within ISI at first used to transport the arms forward by night, even closing down completely during daytime in the early days. Gradually more and more individual Mujahideen commanders and parties found their way onto the supply list, and the system got off the ground in a makeshift fashion. Such was the start of a 'pipeline' that was eventually to expand to a capacity of 1000 tons a week by 1986.[71]

Relying on the political parties streamlined Pakistani engagement with an otherwise disparate Afghan resistance and limited the bureaucratic burdens of hosting a large Afghan refugee population.

CIA observers noticed that ISI tended to ignore resistance leaders who had been tribal heads or had links with the old Musahiban ruling family. Akhtar claimed they were less effective in the battlefield.[72] Instead, ISI favoured political parties that couched their aims in religious and nationalist, not ethnic, terms. Several of the more moderate resistance party leaders sought to recover the Afghan territorial space, the erstwhile state of Afghanistan, and spoke of Afghan (not Pashtun, Tajik, Uzbek, or Hazara) nationalism and self-determination. For them, 'Afghan' had national connotations and referred to those who would live within the boundaries of an Afghanistan freed from Soviet dominion. The parties that ISI particularly preferred spoke more radically in religious terms, offering a new vision of the Afghan state that placed Islam at the forefront and proposing sweeping governing changes in line with the Quran and *shari'a*. ISI support for Islamist Afghan politics logically followed Zia's push for Islamization within Pakistan.[73] In turn, it helped turn the civil war in Afghanistan increasingly into one between socialist and Islamist visions of Afghanistan's future.

What was particularly significant overall was that the parties that received foreign aid, both moderate and Islamist, made little public mention of ethnicity—a sharp contrast from earlier generations of Afghan leaders whose pro-Pashtun policies had clashed with Pakistan's attempts to make Pashtuns 'Pakistani'. With the exception of one party with a large Tajik following, the other six Afghan resistance parties based in Peshawar were heavily dominated by ethnic Pashtuns. Yet they seldom turned publicly to Pashtun nationalism. This was due not only to each party's own stated aspirations but also increasingly to Pakistan's influence. As Hamid Gul, who replaced Akhtar as chief of the ISI in 1987, crowed: 'We are fighting a jihad and this is the first Islamic brigade in the modern era.'[74] For Pakistan, as with many of the Afghan Islamists, this was a fight united under the banner of Islam, not ethnicity.

The government of Pakistan's decision to support an Islamist Afghanistan—and not a return to the pre-PDPA status quo—grew from domestic, as well as regional, concerns. Pakistani leaders needed to prevent a resurgence of Pashtun nationalism and separatism. The influx of Afghans across the border into Pakistan, the vast majority of whom were also ethnically Pashtun, dramatically increased the number of Pashtuns in Pakistan. If they were not carefully managed, they had the potential to stir further anti-government sentiment among Pakistan's Pashtuns—and fuel a homegrown movement for an independent Pashtunistan.[75] By quashing any sign of Pashtun nationalism among Afghanistan's exiled political leaders, as well as curbing Pakistani Pashtun political activities in the NWFP or Balochistan, ISI limited the likelihood of the issue spreading further within Pakistan's borders. Not only that but discouraging Pashtun nationalism within the Afghan resistance also diminished the likelihood that it would disrupt future Afghan–Pakistan relations. The Pakistani demand for the PDPA to be replaced following a Soviet withdrawal created the opportunity for a new Afghan government filled with leaders moulded by ISI. Afghanistan's leaders, Pakistani officials hoped, would be absorbed by their Islamist and Afghan-wide agendas rather than focusing on their country's (and Pakistan's) ethnic parts.

The government of Pakistan's emphasis on an Islamist resistance gained additional impetus from both national and international actors. Leaders associated with two Pakistani political organizations (even though political parties were officially banned at the time) supported the Islamization of the resistance: *Jamaʿat-i Islami* and *Jamʿiyyat-i ʿUlamaʾ-i Islam*. Jamaʿat-i Islami, which had been founded by Mawdudi, the Islamist scholar whose writings also informed Afghan Islamism, helped train Afghan resistance leaders, including Gulbuddin Hekmatyar and Ahmad Shah Massoud. Jamʿiyyat-i ʿUlamaʾ-i Islam, meanwhile, took a leading role in developing the next generation of Afghan fighters through its *madrassas* based throughout the NWFP. The activities of these parties were augmented by local clerics, such as Abdul Haq, whose Haqqaniyya *madrassa* became a centre of pro-Zia sentiment, a crucial connection point between ISI officials and local militants, and a key training ground for many of the combatants who would later take a leading role in the Taliban. Zia's engagement with Saudi Arabia also reaped dividends. Pakistan's Saudi allies not only provided financial aid but also helped push (and finance) an international drive for Islamist fighters to travel to Pakistan and then Afghanistan to fight the Soviets and PDPA. These recruits included Osama bin Laden, future leader of al-Qaeda, and, more locally, Mullah Omar, future leader of the Taliban.[76]

Pakistan received ample support in its engagement with the Afghan resistance from China. As early as February 1980, a commentary in the *Beijing Review* declared: 'their struggle has become an important part of the anti-hegemonist cause of the people of the world. It is the unshakable duty of every peace-loving country to render its utmost support to shift struggle against foreign occupation.'[77] The PRC followed up such assertions with aid sent first to the government of Pakistan and then, through ISI, to members of the resistance. Between 1980 and 1985, China provided approximately $400 million in weaponry to the resistance, alongside foodstuffs and material supplies for Afghan refugees. In 1985, the PDPA complained that China had trained at least 30,000 'counter-revolutionaries' in camps across Pakistan and in China's own Xinjiang province.[78] Combatants' letters captured by PDPA forces spoke of 'advisors of friendly China' who 'crossed the border and entered three [to] four kilometers inside Afghanistan and inspected our internal fronts'. (Incensed Afghan officials pointed out Chinese hypocrisy, demanding: 'Could the Chinese leaders forget that it was the Soviet Union which once defended the revolution in China and gave broad military assistance to it in its struggle against Kuomintang's imperialist and reactionary aggression?'[79])

In aiding the Afghan rebels, Chinese officials chose to prioritize their relations with Pakistan over support for Afghan Maoists, who also actively fought the

PDPA. The *Sazman-i Javanan-i Mutaraqi* (Progressive Youth Organization, or PYO), had been established in Afghanistan in the mid-1960s, and it competed with the PDPA to attract followers. Other small Maoist organizations followed. The PYO had never been very strong, having struggled with decades of infighting and structural weaknesses, and it was hit hard by the 1978 coup. The PDPA, seeking ideological supremacy, captured and executed a number of PYO leaders, forcing many others into exile. While Afghan Maoists took part in the fight against the PDPA and its Soviet allies, they struggled to make inroads, lacking foreign aid. The disinterest of the PRC only made this more so.[80]

China's backing for the Pakistani-sponsored resistance groups made geostrategic sense. It also fit the broader move in Chinese foreign policy away from arming Maoist groups and towards championing nationalist movements, as in South-East Asia.[81] Pragmatically, Chinese contributions were more likely to be used efficiently if coupled with aid from other countries and directed to resistance leaders who had clear responsibilities and directives. In contrast to the increasingly regimented parties in Peshawar, the Afghan Maoists remained weak and based in small pockets across Afghanistan. They were neither easily reachable nor terribly well mobilized. Afghan Islamists, ironically, proved better at implementing Maoist insurgency strategies and tactics than Afghan Maoists, themselves.

Additionally, supporting Pakistan aligned with China's regional security needs. Chinese officials were clearly concerned about shoring up Pakistan as a means of restricting further Soviet seepage towards the Persian Gulf. In return for Chinese support on the question of the Soviet invasion, Zia publicly supported China's position on the crisis in South-East Asia, criticizing Vietnamese military aggression in Cambodia.[82] Thus, the strategic benefits of allying with Pakistan clearly outweighed any lingering ideological synergies between Afghanistan's Maoists and the PRC (and, given Deng's policy of modernization at the time, which itself was straying from Maoism, these ideological links were unravelling). Deng told Jimmy Carter shortly after the Soviet invasion: 'We must turn Afghanistan into a quagmire in which the Soviet Union is bogged down for a long time in a guerrilla warfare.' To do this, and to prevent further Soviet expansion, he concluded, 'there is no other way except giving aid to Pakistan'.[83]

Iran similarly supported the Afghan resistance, though its provisions of aid were restricted by Iran's own ongoing war with Iraq. Iran's leaders, after a brief flirtation with Gulbuddin Hekmatyar, largely focused aid on Afghanistan's Shi'as, many of whom shared religious and ethnic ties with parts of Iran. In an interesting turn of events, the Iranian government also attempted to turn the training of Afghan resistance fighters to their own benefit. The government not only established a number of centres where members of Shi'ite resistance organizations could gain military training but also then paid many of these trainees to fight on behalf of Iran in the Iran–Iraq war. After gaining experience on this battlefront, many returned to the war in Afghanistan, at times supported by Iranian nationals who were also sent by the government to fight in Afghanistan.[84] Iran and Pakistan coordinated resistance aid to an extent, though relations between the two states became somewhat strained when Pakistan opted to remain neutral in the Iran–Iraq war and as Sunni–Shi'a sectarianism grew.[85] Iran's leaders framed support for the Afghan resistance in terms of the insurgents' need to be represented in any settlement for the Soviet withdrawal. Given its own revolutionary practice of political Islam, Iran particularly pushed for the participation of Afghanistan's Islamists in any negotiations.

Regional imperatives thus helped push Afghan Islamists to the forefront of the resistance movement. Even as Afghan Islamists, themselves, remained divided between different political parties (and competing political visions), they became the most obvious representatives of the anti-PDPA movement, thanks to Pakistani and Iranian support. The resistance parties presented an alternative Afghan leadership that Pakistan, Iran, and, to a lesser extent, China could advocate for and support. Regional circumstances helped to reinforce an increasingly binary competition: Afghan socialism versus Afghan Islamism. The organization and mobilization of resistance fighters provided a key means for Afghanistan's neighbours to shape the ongoing conflict for their own benefit. This not only undermined the PDPA but also provided opportunities for officials in Afghanistan's neighbours to push for different political arrangements that served their own interests. Advocating a global Islamist revolution, preventing Soviet expansionism, and, more locally, suppressing ethnic nationalism among Pakistan's and Afghanistan's Pashtuns all overlapped and shaped political calculations. Supporting the resistance was largely self-serving for Afghanistan's neighbours, but it consequently pluralized the number of groups that claimed to lead Afghan politics. Wartime support for numerous resistance groups would inevitably complicate the Soviet withdrawal and any future settlement for a secure, independent Afghanistan.

Finally, alongside the political machinations that took place as Afghanistan's neighbours set up alternative leaders of a future Afghanistan, regional players also had to deal with a vast refugee crisis. Pakistan, Iran, and even India all hosted Afghans fleeing from the DRA. Pakistan accommodated many Afghan Pashtuns, especially from the eastern provinces, which shared a border with Pakistan. As the war progressed, the refugees diversified and included an increasing number of Afghanistan's different ethnic groups. All Afghans who arrived in Pakistan were expected to register with refugee camps organized jointly by the government of Pakistan and the United Nations High Commissioner for Refugees to receive support and housing. Not only that, but the Pakistan government used the Afghan political parties around Peshawar to organize and oversee the growing refugee population. This, in turn, gave additional influence to these parties, which gained oversight over hundreds of thousands of Afghans for the first time.

For Pakistan, the refugee crisis had other unexpected benefits. By accepting UNHCR aid from mid-1979, Zia's government in Pakistan gained not only financial and administrative backing for the Afghan refugees but also support for its own citizens. Most of the refugees opted to stay in Pakistan's border regions, in Balochistan and the NWFP. These were two of the poorer, less economically developed regions in Pakistan. The UNHCR mission to Pakistan recognized: 'No [refugee] program will have the slightest chance of success if it does not comply with the interests of the refugees and local alike.' Wary of antagonizing local populations, UN officials supported programmes that benefited Pakistani citizens alongside Afghan refugees: 'The development of the resources of the region would create indigenous wealth, hopefully to be shared among locals and refugees alike.'[86] With the support of organizations such as the League of Red Cross and Red Crescent Societies, the government built new medical facilities across the provinces to serve both populations. Similarly, NGOs paid for reforestation programmes and new infrastructures that supported both populations.[87] The provincial governments also were given extended powers, as they helped oversee the refugees alongside citizens.

Thus, the refugee crisis offered a means for the government of Pakistan not only to influence Afghan migrants but also to reassert its influence in its own border regions. The refugee influx provided Pakistan's central government with the opportunity and resources to cement its ties with Balochistan and the NWFP and emphasize their belonging within Pakistan, while more clearly divorcing them from neighbouring Afghanistan. Despite putting strain on Pakistan's resources, the refugee crisis thus provided Zia's regime with new opportunities to oversee Pakistani citizens whose ties to the state had been limited, fraught, or frequently shaped by transborder Pashtun and Baloch autonomy movements. The movement of refugees across the Durand Line actually helped to make the border between Afghanistan and Pakistan clearer. Not only did it mark where Afghan rule ended and Pakistani writ started, but it created the circumstances through which the government of Pakistan could champion and enforce its governance and oversight within these frontier provinces, differentiating them from neighbouring Afghanistan.

Alongside Pakistan, Iran and India also hosted refugees. Iran largely received Afghans from the western provinces and from among Afghanistan's Shi'a communities. These Afghans, predominantly ethnic Hazara, largely integrated into Iranian cities and towns, rather than settling in camps. Only a minority lived in established refugee camps (about 10 per cent by 1992), though the Iranian government sought UNHCR aid from 1983, pointing out that an estimated 1.5 million Afghans had settled at a time when Iran was facing its own problems with the Iran–Iraq war.[88]

India received fewer Afghan refugees. They tended to be intellectuals, wealthy businessmen, and former government officials who had opted to escape the PDPA's reign of terror. While some passed through Pakistan and made their way into India on foot, most flew from Kabul to Delhi. Only some of these envisioned a long stay in India, and many saw Delhi as a halfway point to resettling in countries outside the region, most notably the United States and Western Europe. The refugees seeking shelter in India slowly diversified as the war in Afghanistan progressed.[89] The government of India nevertheless maintained that 'Afghans in India were not refugees and that their visas are being and will be renewed according to immigration rules'. This stance meant that refugees would not complicate the state's relationship with

Afghanistan or the Soviet Union: framing Afghan arrivals as migrants seeking work was far more acceptable to all parties. However, this position also undermined local Afghans' ability to receive aid. The UNCHR's mission in India remained restricted, and it could offer only limited support in the form of small care and maintenance grants, medical treatment through a voluntary agency outpatient clinic, education support, and resettlement assistance.[90] This reflected India's own ambiguous relationship with the PDPA and again marked out its difference in the regional approach to the Afghan crisis. Unlike Pakistan and Iran, which used the refugee crisis and resistance to draw attention to Afghans who rejected the PDPA, the Indian government asserted its middling support for the PDPA by refusing to recognize a refugee crisis existed.

Without question, the Soviet invasion of Afghanistan created a regional crisis, one that largely moved through the halls of power in Islamabad. It embroiled Afghanistan's neighbours in the country's domestic affairs and shaped the course of the civil war. It therefore also gave them the opportunity to reshape ideas of Afghan modernity. Because Pakistan, Iran, and China, the other states besides the Soviet Union who shared borders with Afghanistan, refused to recognize Karmal's and later Najibullah's regimes, they forced a broader conversation about not only who governed Afghanistan but who had the right to do so. Indian sympathy for the PDPA, driven by its own security concerns, was drowned out by the fierce regional and international reaction to the Soviet intervention. International observers, led by Pakistan, China, and the United States, saw the entry of Soviet troops into Afghanistan as a sign of expansionist ambitions, not as the state-building and socialist-supporting mission envisioned by policy architects in Kabul and Moscow. As such, regardless of actual Soviet aims, Afghanistan's neighbours internationalized the conflict, expressing their own fears of Soviet imperialism and seeking to undermine the PDPA.

While each state was concerned about how events within Afghanistan might affect its own domestic politics, calculations also had to be made about regional balances of power and diplomacy. In this realm, older alliances and tensions came to the fore. The conflict strengthened relations between Pakistan and China, while it created new questions between India and Pakistan. Iran too was affected by the war, but its relations with its South and Central Asian neighbours were moderated by Khomeini's preoccupations with events in the Middle East.

Because of its location on the border with Afghanistan, its strategic alliances with China and the United States, and its Islamist aspirations and partnerships, Pakistan was the key site of the regional response. Pakistan ultimately sought to strengthen its regional position vis-a-vis both Afghanistan and India. The conflict provided Zia's government in Islamabad with an opportunity to quash the Pashtunistan debate while allowing the country to build up its resources and gain further parity with the Indian behemoth. By growing comparatively stronger, Pakistan, at least in theory, would be better placed in its relations with both Afghanistan and India and more able to negotiate ongoing regional issues like the Kashmir conflict.

The regional response to Afghanistan's turn to socialism and, subsequently, the Soviet invasion saw the intersection of many of the local, bilateral, and global undercurrents discussed in Chapter 1. The government of Pakistan's concerns about Soviet expansion became tied up with its desire to terminate Afghan irredentist claims on Pakistan's Pashtun population and to use the sudden glut of foreign aid to reinforce its domestic structures and develop its own defences against Indian as well as Soviet threats. For Iran, the war in Afghanistan was both an irritant and an opportunity to extend Khomeini's revolutionary message and model into a neighbouring country. China had less interest in the specific regional dynamics but gave aid to its Pakistani ally to halt perceived Soviet efforts to contain Chinese communism. India responded with consternation to these shifting sands, worried about its own regional and international position and the loss of a potential ally if the PDPA fell.

The most important consequence of the regional element to the Afghan conflict was the way it fractured Afghan political representation. It fundamentally undermined Karmal's attempts to continue building an Afghan socialist state, not only because countries such as China, Pakistan, and Iran refused to accept the PDPA as the leaders of Afghanistan after December 1979 but because they actively supported an armed resistance. By providing aid to a variety of Afghan resistance movements, these countries set up alternative leaders, each of whom had different visions for a post-withdrawal Afghanistan.

But the rise in the 1970s of global interest in political Islam ultimately favoured Afghan Islamists over other factions. It is interesting to consider how earlier regional leaders such as General Mohammad Ayub Khan or Mohammad Reza Pahlavi might have responded to the PDPA coup and Soviet intervention. Both were Muslim leaders, but certainly neither was Islamist: would they have supported the same political agenda? Or might they have favoured a return to Western-backed liberal modernization, thanks to their alliances with the United States and their own limited pursuit of political change? Yet, by the end of the 1970s, both Pakistan and Iran were governed by leaders who sought not only to embed Islamic practices within their states but to use Islam as a guiding political system. Thus, even while Pakistani and Iranian leaders supported an array of Afghan actors and political parties, intent on halting a Soviet spread, their particular interest in the Afghan Islamists gave these groups unprecedented power and influence. Afghan Islamists received extraordinary opportunities and resources to pursue a new form of politics in Afghanistan, and this, in turn, increasingly turned the civil war in Afghanistan into one between socialism and Islamism, muffling the voices of other groups across the political spectrum.

Nevertheless, leaders in Iran and Pakistan, supported by China, opted to back a host of Afghan political parties, not a single opposition group. As such, competition continued between different factions of Afghan Islamists, as well as between moderate and radical visionaries of Afghanistan's future. India remained aloof from this process, but its own equivocal stance on the future of Afghanistan—neither offering wholehearted support nor total condemnation—also helped to destabilize the situation further. The Democratic Republic of Afghanistan could not count on India as a reliable ally, which again limited its support in international politics.

As such, claimants to the leadership of Afghanistan multiplied, each with some modicum of support. The regional dynamics of the Afghan war halted the progress of Afghan socialism while creating the space for different conceptions of the Afghan state to progress. Support from neighbouring powers gave previously marginalized voices new opportunities and influence. By rejecting the PDPA's vision of Afghan modernity and supporting alternatives, Afghanistan's neighbours aggravated the fight over Afghanistan's future and the nature of its governance and furthered the accompanying violence. Most particularly, Pakistani and Iranian support brought the Afghan Islamists to the fore, presenting an Islamized Afghanistan as a real potential future. But, whether the Afghan resistance parties, themselves, were capable of turning this regional and international support into anything more concrete remained to be seen. The question that persisted was whether the Afghan leaders in exile could put the huge amounts of aid they received to use in creating an alternative to the PDPA. Could they be any more successful in establishing functioning components of an Afghan state? While the Afghan resistance, particularly the Islamist parties, had wildly ambitious aspirations for a future Afghanistan, they, like the PDPA, proved no more capable of creating a unified movement. The disparate nature of the regional response was reflected in the continued fragmentation of the Afghan resistance.

# 5

# Peshawar–Panjshir

> I am a socialist, Bolshevik my name.
> Socialism for me is merely, a game,
> To exploit the poor, make them fools,
> Young minds are my trusty fools,
>
> Red is the colour of my team.
> Bloodshed and violence my only dream.
> Democracy my enemy, religion I hate,
> Defeat and disgrace my eternal fate;
>
> ......
>
> I love all ideologies from the West,
> And discard those which are best,
> My own religion I hate and dread,
> Because it has not come from Stalingrad,
> Confession....................
> I am a socialist, a mod and a liar,
> Trying to deceive myself I never tire,
> My only hope for which I pray,
> Is socialism on the Judgement Day.[1]

In a small office, somewhere on the streets of Peshawar, the Cultural Committee of the Islamic Unity of the Afghan Mujahidin had set up a small publishing office. A coalition of several of the Afghan resistance parties operating from neighbouring Pakistan, Islamic Unity sought to disseminate its views and spur worldwide support for the rebellion against the Soviets and PDPA through its English-language publication the *Jihad Rays*. The poem just cited, entitled 'I am a Socialist', was included in the centrefold of its first issue for 1984. While the quality of the verse is debatable, the poem was certainly effective at one thing: positioning the Afghan resistance as the enemies of socialism, as embodied by the PDPA, and the defenders of the oppressed.

Over the course of the late 1970s and 1980s, Peshawar, the capital of Pakistan's NWFP, effectively became the substitute capital of an alternative Afghanistan. Peshawar was one of the most ancient cities in South and Central Asia, with ruins dating back more than two thousand years. It had been an important trading post during the Mughal period, in the sixteenth and seventeenth centuries, and it subsequently had served as the winter residence of the Durrani Empire, often seen as the precursor to the modern Afghan state. The establishment of the states of Afghanistan and Pakistan had not eliminated the historic ethnic and cultural ties between Pashtuns on either side of the border, as we have seen. Pashtuns comprised the major ethnic group across north-west Pakistan and south-east Afghanistan, and, in 1981, 68 per cent of households in the NWFP spoke Pashto, the language shared across the border.[2] The frontier between the two countries remained easily traversable, so locals could cross between states with ease, and many Pashtuns on either side embraced the *Pashtunwali* code of honour and conduct.[3] Thus it was of little surprise that Peshawar should become one of the key centres of the Afghan resistance, a city where Pakistan's ISI officers doled out aid and arms to the political parties put in charge of waging the war against the socialists, and from which Pakistani and NGO officials concentrated activities to support the millions of Afghan refugees who settled across the NWFP and neighbouring Balochistan. Thanks to foreign aid, Pakistani machinations, and internal developments, seven key organizations emerged, all of which sought to mobilize resistance and, after a future Soviet withdrawal, take over the governance of Afghanistan.

Afghan political exiles, particularly Afghan Islamists, had grouped around Peshawar since the early 1970s, as they sought to escape Daoud's rule and formulate their own visions of Afghanistan's future. Like the Afghan socialists, the Islamists coalescing in Pakistan had also opted to form political parties to bolster their structures and recruit supporters. The decision to create parties indicated the modern thinking of these groups: even if they began as haphazard organizations, they aspired to dominate, and fundamentally alter, Afghan politics and society. These structures reinforced the political nature of Afghan Islamism, not just its religious foundations. The two parties that pre-existed the 1978 coup, Jam'iyyat-i Islami, under Burhanuddin Rabbani, and Hizb-i Islami under Gulbuddin Hekmatyar, were soon followed by five more, as internal splits and the number of Afghans dwelling in Pakistan grew.

The seven political parties that emerged in exile in Peshawar, alongside others that mobilized in Iran and within Afghanistan, articulated varied visions for Afghanistan's future. Each party sought to represent the Afghan nation and to wrest control of the state back from the socialists. They sought to assert their legitimacy among the Afghans who rejected the PDPA and, as the poem at the beginning of this chapter indicates, to foreign, including English-speaking, audiences. They marshalled along ideological, political, nationalist, tribal, and ethnic lines. All the parties in Peshawar were undoubtedly Muslim. However, only some of them were 'Islamist'—that is to say, envisioning a revolutionized political system based around the key tenets of Islam and the Quran. Others were more interested in maintaining a certain status quo in Afghan politics, reasserting older political hierarchies, and reforming the Afghan nation. Some moderates sought the return of Zahir Shah from exile and a renewed Musahiban dynasty. Others derived leadership from among long-standing Sufi and tribal heads and suggested the resumption of a slower-paced liberalization and democratization.

Two hundred and twenty-five kilometres away, a different, but parallel, scene was emerging. The Panjshir Valley, deep in Afghanistan, at first glance seems like an odd location to become one of the key centres of the Afghan resistance. Panjshir was a backwater. In the twentieth century, it was perhaps best known for suffering a devastating earthquake in 1931. The land was dominated by a long, thin valley, and its inhabitants relied largely on farming tiny but fertile plots. The surrounding mountains were mined for lapis lazuli, a semi-precious stone. Unlike those living in much of Afghanistan, Panjshiris were overwhelmingly ethnic Tajiks, not Pashtun. Yet this remote valley turned into ground zero of the Afghan resistance, becoming the Achilles heel of the PDPA and its Soviet backers, thanks to the activities of a member of Jam'iyyat, Ahmad Shah Massoud.

Massoud would become one of the most iconic leaders of the Afghan resistance— Afghanistan's Che Guevara—and one of the most effective. He provides an interesting contrast to Gulbuddin Hekmatyar. The two shared the aspiration of an Islamist Afghanistan but differed drastically in how they pursued it. Massoud became a darling of the Western media for his ability to thwart the Soviets from within Afghanistan, but equally his efforts at wartime state-building deserve mention. Massoud accompanied insurgency with infrastructure and worked to make local populations receptive to his vision of an Islamist Afghanistan, which was shared by Burhanuddin Rabbani, the Peshawar-based leader of Jam'iyyat. Massoud also clashed violently with Hekmatyar, the most ruthless and unyielding of the Afghan political party leaders. Hizb-i Islami and Jam'iyyat-i Islami, and their respective leaders, disagreed on how and what form an Afghan Islamist state should take. While they all agreed that Islamism provided the best route for Afghanistan's political and social growth, they diverged on mechanisms: a single- or multi-party system, Islamism that was rigid and uncompromising or Islamism based on a gentler evolutionary process. This chapter thus explores two different paths that Afghan Islamism could (but ultimately did not) take.

Several contingencies helped launch the Afghan Islamists into the international spotlight to the detriment of more moderate forces. Like the PDPA, the Islamists' structures—ironically also derived in part from Maoist and Leninist organizational theories—placed them at an advantage when conflict broke out. The PDPA's coup also provided the Islamists with a clear enemy, a force to work against and from which they could clearly differentiate themselves (even as they frequently drew from the same political playbook, using violence against their Afghan enemies, trying to enforce political and social reforms, and seeking international approval). In other words, the PDPA's reforms made an Islamist Afghanistan a viable alternative, drawing Islamists from the political peripheries and centring them in debates about Afghanistan's future. The increasing pre-eminence of Afghan Islamists was also due, as we have seen, to a moment of expanding, globalized Islamism and the keen interest of Pakistan's and Iran's leaders in upholding and exporting political Islamization. Not only that, but, as the glut of foreign reporting drawn upon in this chapter shows, international, and particularly Western, audiences were drawn to a romanticized vision of the Muslim freedom fighter combating an evil Soviet empire. Together, global, regional, and national factors provided a unique opportunity for Islamists to claim Afghanistan's future.

The intersection between foreign intervention, regional dynamics, and internal political debates made Afghanistan's civil war in the 1980s radically different from earlier conflicts. Afghan political parties dominated the discussions of Afghanistan's future, while Zia's Islamist sympathies, alongside vast sums of money and material from foreign backers, provided opportunities for Afghanistan's Islamist parties to shift from marginal political exiles into the visionaries of an alternative Afghan modernism that fused politics and religion. This is not to say a single, unified Afghan resistance existed. In practice, it resembled a constellation of individuals and organizations dotted across the country and flitting over Afghanistan's borders into its neighbours. Within Afghanistan, anti-government action frequently developed organically, as local communities reacted to PDPA and Soviet policies and attempts to enact social, economic, and political changes.

Nevertheless, because of the ways they asserted their power among the Afghan refugee community, in relations with Pakistan's ISI, and in public pronouncements to the international community, Afghanistan's resistance parties, and particularly Hekmatyar's Hizb-i Islami and Rabbani's Jam'iyyat, rose to the fore. As such, this was no mere fight to overthrow the PDPA. It was a battle for the future of Afghanistan. Afghanistan's Islamists saw the war as an opportunity to realize their visions of Afghan politics and society. But, because of the numerous ruptures within the resistance, dividing Islamist from Islamist, party from party, and Afghan from Afghan, none of these visions would come to pass. The competing visions of Afghan Islamist modernity were simply incompatible—with each other and with the interests of other factions of Afghans who waged war on the PDPA and the Soviets for their own purposes.

By the time that the PDPA came to power, Hizb-i Islami under Hekmatyar and Jam'iyyat-i Islami under Rabbani were already established, if not particularly powerful. For a brief moment following the failed 1975 revolt, the Afghan Islamists in exile around Peshawar managed to paper over their differences, and Hekmatyar's and Rabbani's mutual dislike, and reunite into one movement under the banner of Hizb-i Islami. Demonstrating the Islamists' shared aspirations, the party, during this brief moment of unity, focused on strengthening its organization. It established a *shura*, or council, a manifesto and articles of association, and began publishing a newspaper. It focused on extending the work of Islamist cells still active within Afghanistan while seeking aid from sympathetic foreign powers. Rabbani, who spoke Arabic, travelled to Saudi Arabia and across the Middle East in pursuit of external support, while, more locally, the Islamists, and Hekmatyar in particular, received support from the Pakistani organization, Jama'at-i Islami. Briefly, Hizb-i Islami even offered to negotiate with Daoud, sensing his turn away from the socialists and an opportunity for the exiled Islamists to return. He never responded.[4]

However, tensions soon re-emerged, driven by internal weaknesses and ongoing mutual suspicions. Hekmatyar retained his belief that Rabbani had somehow been responsible for the failure of the 1975 revolt, an accusation he felt was justified after one of Rabbani's close associates, Jan Mohammad, admitted, after hours of torture, having spied for Daoud's government. Jan Mohammad's taped confession also mentioned one of Rabbani's young associates, a Tajik from Panjshir named Ahmad Shah Massoud. Massoud's father had served in the Afghan army but had sent him to Kabul University to study engineering, where he came into contact with the Muslim Youth during its early years. He was multilingual, speaking French, Dari, and Pashto, the product of early education at an Afghan lycée. He had participated in the abortive uprising against Daoud in 1975, fighting in Panjshir before fleeing to Pakistan. He blamed Hekmatyar for the deaths of the men he fought alongside; for his part, Hekmatyar painted Massoud and Rabbani with the same brush as Jan Mohammad—traitors to the Afghan Islamist cause.[5]

Alongside personal enmities, religious interpretations also came into conflict. Rabbani and Hekmatyar came to blows over the question of *takfir*, the 'act of declaring a certain Muslim to be a heretic'. Hekmatyar took the more militant line, arguing that a Muslim could be declared *takfir* based on political, not just religious, behaviour. Rabbani, in contrast, supported a more elastic definition that united Muslims regardless of political leanings. This theological debate highlighted the diverging political visions of the two leaders. While Rabbani demonstrated at this early stage a willingness to ally with more moderate political parties and Muslims (defined by religion, rather than politics), Hekmatyar took the more hard-line position where religion and politics completely fused, hinting at his later demands for a one-party system.

In the autumn of 1977, Hizb-i Islami split for good. Rabbani, after returning to Peshawar from a trip to Saudi Arabia, left Hizb-i Islami to restart and rebuild Jam'iyyat-i Islami, leaving Hekmatyar and his followers in charge of Hizb-i Islami. The differences in their names signalled their political variances: whereas *hizb* means 'party', *jam'iyyat* means 'association'. By its very title, Jam'iyyat demonstrated its greater willingness to compromise and be flexible, something that would stand it in great stead as civil war broke out in Afghanistan. On the other side, Hizb-i Islami's insistence on a strong party structure, based on the communist-party model, provided an alternative source of strength and a degree of cohesiveness not commonly found elsewhere in the Afghan resistance.[6] These two parties would continue to compete for supremacy, in both Pakistan and Afghanistan, once war broke out.

In the meantime, as the Afghan Islamists around Peshawar debated their structures, their aspirations, and their allegiances, the PDPA came to power, using the assassination of Mir Akbar Khyber to launch their 1978 coup. While Hizb-i Islami tried to take credit for Khyber's death—Hekmatyar claimed they 'had sent Khyber to hell'—Khyber's own relatives believed that members of the equally fractious PDPA were probably responsible.[7] Regardless, his death provided the necessary spark to ignite the PDPA's revolt and its manifold repercussions. The emergence of resistance to the PDPA has been hinted at and alluded to up to this point. Some of the broader causes of tensions have been discussed, including the pre-existing socialist–Islamist tensions, the PDPA's overly hasty attempts to reform and turn almost immediately to violence, and the additional provocation provided by the Soviet intervention and regional machinations. But that armed resistance against the government would ultimately take a different form from earlier social and political unrest was not immediately apparent.

Many Afghans' initial response to the April 1978 coup was middling. Indeed, some of the country's ethnic communities, including Hazara, Uzbeks, and Tajiks, initially welcomed the new government because it seemed to signal an end to Pashtun-majority rule. Afghanistan's ethnic tensions had been exacerbated by decades of rule by Pashtuns, whose leadership had been reinforced through familial and patrimonial networks (and at times through violence). Afghan leaders had prioritized these bonds and used them to strengthen the leadership of members of the Durrani confederation and particularly the Musahiban dynasty. In the late nineteenth century, Abdur Rahman effectively colonized what is now north-west Afghanistan by forcing Pashtun migration into the area. Pashtuns in this region became prosperous landowners to the detriment of local Turkmens and other groups. Likewise, Daoud had pushed pro-Pashtun policies during the 1970s, discouraging linguistic pluralism and attempting to ban ethnic surnames and ethnonyms.[8]

In contrast, Taraki announced a new 'nationality' programme shortly after the PDPA came to power, based on the Soviet Union's similar programme earlier in the twentieth century.[9] He pledged to promote multilingualism and to make Uzbek, Turkmen, Baloch, and Nuristani official state languages alongside Dari and Pashto. He promised to create institutions for their promulgation, including schooling in children's birth language, the publication of newspapers from Kabul in various dialects, and the inclusion of representatives of these linguistic–ethnic communities in the national government. The PDPA thus offered a distinct contrast to earlier Pashtun-focused regimes. Even ethnic communities like the Hazara, who were not recognized by the PDPA as a key linguistic group, briefly responded positively to the regime's proposed reforms, which promised to provide them with new opportunities and bring some parity between Afghanistan's ethnic and tribal groupings.

However, the PDPA's policies ultimately antagonized many Afghans, Pashtun and non-Pashtun alike. Afghans across the country questioned the regime's reforms to landownership and marriage practices, and many bemoaned the halt to liberal democratic (and monarchic) modernization. Even those who had initially welcomed the PDPA's proposed governing changes were frustrated by the government's inability to implement them adequately. Despite the PDPA's promises, the ruling elite remained overwhelmingly Pashtun, with only token members from other communities. Moreover, the regime's hostility towards local non-party leaders and tendency to turn quickly to violence to implement its policies and suppress resistance found few friends. The regime's harsh treatment of Hazara intellectuals and *ulama*, for example, led to revolt and the formation of the *Shura-yi Inqilab-i Ittifaq-i Islami-yi Afghanistan* (Revolutionary Council for the Islamic Unity of Afghanistan), a local council dominated by Shi'a clerics in the province of Hazarajat, which framed itself as a rejection of both the PDPA and Sunni dominance within Afghanistan. The Shura attempted to coordinate and oversee local resistance to the PDPA and Soviet forces, though it succumbed to infighting in the mid-1980s.[10]

Resistance to the PDPA thus crossed political, ethnic, tribal, and sectarian lines. Major outbreaks of violent anti-government activity erupted in the non-Pashtun areas of Nuristan and Herat—ironic, given the PDPA's attempts to woo Afghanistan's many ethnic groups—and smaller bursts of fighting in the Pashtun-dominated east were reported within months of the 1978 coup as well. Accounts emanating from Pakistan described clashes between local Pashtuns and PDPA forces in August and October 1978 around the provinces of Kandahar, Paktia, Ghazni, and Konar. Guerrilla forces claimed to have killed several hundred soldiers. The Afghan government, in turn, razed villages in the area, including Kamdesh in north Konar. PDPA retaliation only served further to antagonize resistance fighters, as their families fled to refugee shelters in neighbouring Pakistan.[11]

The first area where sustained violence erupted between locals and PDPA forces was in Manugi in Nuristan, north-east Afghanistan, in July 1978. There, at a government post, locals' queries about missing representatives in Kabul (unbeknownst to them, their relatives had been executed by the regime) devolved into a riot that spread into the valleys of Nuristan. The PDPA exacerbated matters by offering both weapons and money to local ethnic–tribal minorities to help combat the growing Nuristani revolt. This failed miserably, and a coalition of Nuristani tribes, with the support of other Afghans who travelled to the region to help fight government forces, soundly defeated a PDPA battalion.

The battles of Nuristan were followed by widespread revolts elsewhere. Fighting broke out in Hazarajat in December 1978, leading to the creation of the Shura and spreading across central Afghanistan. Inspired by the uprising in Herat in March 1979, most of western Afghanistan rebelled against the government. The summer of 1979 saw the outbreak of war in Panjshir and Takhar and the extension of resistance in Afghanistan's Pashtun-majority areas, where government efforts to buy local communities' loyalty failed. The extent to which this growing resistance threatened the security of the PDPA can be seen in Amin's decision to launch a full-scale military operation in Paktia province from September to October 1979. It, too, failed. By the time that the Soviets arrived in December 1979, three-quarters of the country was up in arms against its rulers.[12] At best, Afghanistan could be described as being in a state of civil war. The PDPA had failed spectacularly in implementing its reforms and cementing its power. The Soviet invasion only exacerbated matters further, bringing even more Afghans into the resistance.

As uprisings spread across Afghanistan, two distinct but interlinked developments unfolded. While many Afghans remained with their homes or temporarily sought shelter in nearby towns and cities, millions more fled, seeking refuge in Pakistan and Iran.[13] In Pakistan, they became embroiled in Afghan party politics, thanks to the organizational requirements of the refugee camps. Alongside this, many local leaders based within Afghanistan realized they needed additional supplies and support if they were to push out the socialists. They thus turned to transborder kinship networks and Afghans living in Pakistan and Iran for support. Collectively, these developments resulted in the exceptional rise of Afghan political parties in exile, fundamentally differentiating this civil war from previous Afghan conflicts and giving outsized influence to the Afghan Islamists based around Peshawar.

On 5 June 1978, only five weeks after the PDPA had come to power, Agence France-Presse reported that three hundred clergymen and army officers had sought refuge in Pakistan's tribal belt, fearing persecution by the new regime.[14] A steady stream followed. As the number of Afghan refugees overwhelmed the Pakistani government, it opted to use the exiled political parties to help register and organize arriving Afghans. To receive aid, Afghans had to become affiliated with one of the seven main Afghan political parties based out of Peshawar. After being screened by a party affiliate, refugees received party identity certificates, which they then had to present to Pakistani authorities to receive a passbook, which provided the basis for receiving supplies, food, and accommodation in a refugee camp.[15] This process helped alleviate some of the burden on Pakistan's overstretched resources, but also gave the Afghan political parties increasing influence within the refugee camps. Taken alongside ISI's decision to funnel all military support through the parties, rather than dealing with individuals or small groups of claimants, this meant that these exiled political organizations acquired huge influence and new opportunities to recruit supporters from within the camps and through negotiations with local commanders based in Afghanistan who needed resupplying. By early 1980, the government of Pakistan officially recognized six political parties as the representatives of the Afghan refugees and resistance as part of this process. A seventh was added to the list in 1981.[16]

Many Afghan exiles did not intend to remain out of their homeland but instead planned to reorganize, resupply, and return to Afghanistan to fight the PDPA. However, in mid-1978, before the US–Pakistani pipeline had started up, weapons were in short supply. Not only that, but the organizations that refugees encountered were disorganized and disunited. A number of refugee clerics, seeking better mobilization, hit on the idea of a new Islamic alliance, *Harakat-i Inqilab-i Islami-yi Afghanistan*, or the Revolutionary Islamic Movement, to reunite Hizb-i Islami and Jam'iyyat and draw in newly arrived Afghans. Mawlawi Mohammad Nabi Mohammadi, a well-known, respected cleric who had previously served in the Afghan parliament, was elected as the alliance's head in September 1978. The alliance, in a foretelling of a pattern that would become common throughout the 1980s, soon succumbed to infighting. Nabi was accused of providing inadequate support to a botched military uprising in Kandahar. He, in turn, claimed Hekmatyar and Rabbani were pursuing their own, rather than the alliance's, interests. Within months, Hekmatyar and Rabbani had re-established Hizb-i Islami and Jam'iyyat, respectively, while Nabi reframed Harakat-i Inqilab-i Islami as its own political party, one that largely received support from Afghan *ulama* and religious students (*taliban*) and with moderate political aims.

Hizb-i Islami underwent an additional split in 1979, dividing between followers of Hekmatyar and those of Mawlawi Yunis Khalis, an older cleric with long experience working with the Muslim Youth. A generational and interpretational divide separated the two groups, though each party stubbornly kept using the name Hizb-i Islami-yi Afghanistan. Hekmatyar led a younger, more militant Hizb-i Islami, while Khalis, like Rabbani, was supported by the generation of lecturers who had introduced Islamist thought to Kabul University students in the 1960s. His positions aligned more closely with Jam'iyyat's, but he felt that the name, Hizb-i Islami, and its party structures were too valuable to leave to Hekmatyar. Khalis, moreover, criticized Hekmatyar's understanding of Islam, calling him and his followers *kham*, or 'unripe'. Khalis, pointing to his own more advanced training, claimed his party wanted to lead a 'theological revolution'.[17]

Matters were further complicated by the emergence of two additional parties in late 1978 and 1979. *Jabhah-i Nijat-i Milli-yi Afghanistan*, the Afghanistan National Liberation Front, emerged under the leadership of Hazrat Sibghatullah Mujaddidi, who came from a politically influential family that had been involved in Afghan state politics since the nineteenth century. Many of his relatives had been murdered by the PDPA early in their reign, owing to the family's potential to draw anti-government followers, which only added to his sense of significance. *Mahaz-i Milli-yi Islami-yi Afghanistan*, the National Islamic Front, was founded by Pir Sayyid Ahmad Gailani, who came from a family of renowned Sufi *pirs* and was known to have strong ties with the former king of Afghanistan, Zahir Shah. A seventh major party would join the scene in Pakistan in 1981 under the leadership of Abdur Rasul Sayyaf. Like Rabbani, he had attended al-Azhar University in Cairo, where he encountered the Muslim Brotherhood. He had been imprisoned by Daoud and was not released until Karmal's general amnesty in 1980. Also like Rabbani, Sayyaf spoke fluent Arabic, adding to his appeal to interested Arab sponsors. His party, *Ittihad-i Islami Bara-yi Azadi-yi Afghanistan*, Islamic Union for the Freedom of Afghanistan, became known for its Arab-funded wealth and backing, as well as its ties to Saudi Wahabbism and radically anti-Shi'a politics.[18]

The war against the PDPA took the broad form of three phases. The first broke out immediately following the April 1978 coup and lasted until the Soviet invasion in December 1979. The second occurred from roughly 1980 to 1985, while the third endured from 1986 to the Soviet withdrawal in February 1989. (Of course, fighting did not stop then.) The first phase, as already described, was marked by disorganization, lacked coordination, and resulted from resistance breaking out locally in response to PDPA reforms. The second was a period of shifting alliances, during which the parties vied for power around Peshawar, among the refugees, and within Afghanistan. Many of the political parties had pockets of support dotted across Afghanistan that depended on pre-existing political and social (tribal, kinship, patronage, ethnic, and religious) networks. Much of the fighting remained regional, as party leaders depended on local allies to take action in areas where they had influence. Small groups of resistance fighters took part in raids and ambushes against

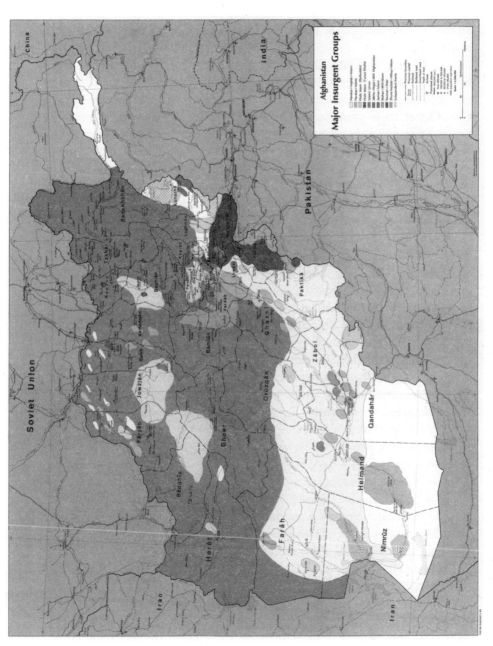

**Map 6.** Historical map of major resistance groups, c.1985 (Library of Congress, Geography and Map Division)

Soviet and PDPA forces. Some received weaponry and supplies from the political parties in Pakistan and Iran. Others relied on pre-owned guns or firearms gleaned from the battlefield. Overall, however, the Afghan resistance was outgunned and out-supplied by the Soviets. Helicopters proved a boon for the Soviets, as they safely shuttled Soviet and PDPA troops between locations, free from the threat of ground attack.

From 1986, as the Soviet decision to withdraw from Afghanistan became apparent, the war shifted. The Soviet army became less interested in large offensives to root out the resistance and instead took a more defensive role. Not only that, but the United States began providing Stinger missiles. These surface-to-air rockets, alongside growing Soviet disillusionment, helped to equalize the battle to some extent (though the Soviets correspondingly changed tactics).[19] Various commanders across Afghanistan, flush with newly imported modern weapons, took a bolder approach and went on the offensive. By the end of 1987, much of north-east Afghanistan was under resistance command. From May 1988, as Soviet troops began leaving the country, resistance fighters began taking control of former Soviet bases, and occupied the first provincial capitals of Bamyan, Takhar, and (briefly) Kunduz in August 1988. By the time the Soviet troop withdrawal had finished in February 1989, the country was in a military stalemate where Najibullah's regime retained control of important centres and major cities such as Kabul, Khost, and Jalalabad (and a retaken Kunduz), but the resistance had large rural strongholds across the country.[20]

The fortunes of the seven political parties based in Pakistan waxed and waned throughout the 1980s, and inter-party alliances came and went. For the duration of the war, support for Gailani's and Mujaddidi's parties remained limited but stable. Their combatants, whose alliances with either party relied overwhelmingly on tribal and kinship networks, were largely active in the Pashtun-dominated eastern and southern regions of Afghanistan. Immediately following the Soviet invasion, Nabi's Harakat-i Inqilab-i Islami emerged as one of the PDPA's strongest opponents, thanks to its nationwide network of clergy at non-government *madrassas*. However, it declined in strength from 1981, as many Dari-speakers and non-Pashtuns (Tajik and Uzbeks) switched their allegiances to Jam'iyyat, which increasingly became known as a Tajik party. Harakat-i Inqilab-i Islami retained influence in the Helmand Valley, though its allied warlords in the region acted largely independently of the party head in Peshawar. Khalis's Hizb-i Islami relied on Islamist and tribal networks for support, particularly among Ghilzai Pashtuns and Pashtuns residing in eastern Afghanistan. His commanders were particularly active in and around Kabul, where they maintained an insurgency in the city, as well as in Paktia province. In contrast to these parties, Sayyaf's Ittihad-i Islami had few existing network links running throughout Afghanistan. Ittihad-i Islami's strength derived from its wealth, its ability to create new networks by providing supplies to willing allies, and its oversight of many of the foreign fighters who travelled from across the Middle East and the world to come and wage war in Afghanistan.[21]

An initial alliance of five parties (Jam'iyyat, Mahaz-i Milli-yi Islami, Jabhah-i Nijat-i Milli, Harakat-i Inqilab-i Islami, and Khalis's Hizb-i Islami) was announced on 19 March 1980 under the leadership of Sayyaf, but it quickly foundered, as Sayyaf took the alliance, Ittihad-i Islami Bara-yi Azadi-yi Afghanistan, and turned it into his own political party with Saudi backing. A second coalition of the seven main Peshawar parties, the *Ittihad-i Islami-yi Mujahidin-i Afghanistan* (Islamic Union of Mujahidin of Afghanistan), emerged in August 1981, but lasted only a matter of months before several of the parties withdrew. The three more moderate parties under Gailani, Mujaddidi, and Nabi created their own smaller alliance, using the same name. Alongside this persisted a very loose alliance between the two Hizb-i Islamis, Jam'iyyat, Ittihad-i Islami, and splinter factions from Harakat-i Inqilab-i Islami and Jabhah-i Nijat-i Milli. Party alliances remained largely unchanged until 1985, when a more lasting, but equally ineffective, alliance emerged, owing to additional pressure from Pakistan, Saudi Arabia, and the United States—again under the name Ittihad-i Islami-yi Mujahidin-i Afghanistan.[22]

The split in 1980 of the main Afghan political parties into two factions indicated a broader ideological and political division within the resistance. While Jam'iyyat, both Hizb-i Islami parties, and Ittihad-i Islami espoused political Islam and envisioned an Islamist Afghanistan, the other parties were less radical. They largely sought to return Afghan modernity to its earlier path of liberal constitutionalism, headed by either a monarch or elected leader(s), rather than fundamentally rethinking Afghanistan's political trajectory.

The 'traditionalist' parties under Gailani, Mujaddidi, and Nabi sought ways to avert their country from the path towards socialism and ensure their own continued significance within their communities. By and large, the leaders in these parties had held positions of power in pre-coup Afghanistan, and included important *khans*, former allies of the royal family, Sufi *pirs*, and some *ulama* and *mullahs*. They largely did not see the rise of the PDPA and Soviet intervention as an opportunity to reappraise erstwhile social and political establishments within Afghanistan. Instead, they sought, in many ways, to return to and continue the more moderate modernization processes begun under the Afghan royal family. Gailani was suspected of representing and wanting to bring back Zahir Shah as Afghanistan's ruler. Other traditionalists, while not desiring the return of the king, nevertheless identified Afghanistan's Western-educated non-socialist elites as the country's future leaders. Jabhah-i Nijat-i Milli and Harakat-i Inqilab-i Islami, which included more orthodox Muslims and *ulama* uninterested in the politicization of Islam, had little plan for a post-Soviet, post-PDPA, Afghanistan but nevertheless asserted their intention 'to defend our national traditions' and, vaguely, 'the establishment of an Islamic society in which all the political, economic and social affairs [will] be founded on the teachings of Islam'.[23]

The traditionalist parties were wary of what Western observers increasingly described as the 'fundamentalist' parties. Moderate leaders like Gailani decried Hizb-i Islami and Jam'iyyat as 'radicals' with 'extremist ideology' and warned foreign funders that 'Afghans might conclude they would be better off under the Soviets than these extremists'.[24] While this argument was a clear ploy by Gailani to increase the aid provided to his own party, he was not wrong to call the vision of leaders like

Hekmatyar radical. Indeed, these parties, much like the PDPA, sought their own revolution in Afghanistan.

Rabbani, Khalis, and particularly Hekmatyar and Sayyaf, the two most extreme party leaders, envisioned a new Afghanistan where Islam and politics were inseparable. For all of these parties, Islamism did not mean a return to the past. Instead, it required using Islam to practise modern politics. As Rabbani expounded:

> When we say we want a government on the model of the early Islamic pattern, many people think we want to move history backward and have a living situation exactly as 14 centuries ago... But the issue is not as simple as they think. We do not see any difficulty in implementing the principles and values which prevailed in the time of Prophet Mohammad (Peace be upon Him) in our society.

He went on to explain:

> Islam enjoins that the leader of the Muslim Umma should be chosen from among the people. This was done in the case of the righteous Caliphs. And today election of the ruler is the most advanced form of government. Shoora [council] is an Islamic principle. It is the order of the Holy Qoran to Muslims to decide their affairs on the basis of consultation. This is almost the same thing you have as a parliament today.

Rabbani pointed to governing principles evident in contemporaneous political models and drew parallels in Islamic thinking: 'Islam enjoins on its followers to have good and friendly relations with all the people until Islamic ideology is not suppressed, so that Islam has the freedom to present its ideology to all the people. And this is the right of freedom of speech, and no one can object to it today.'[25] Islam provided the key to Afghan political and social modernity, not through a return to the past but through a reconfiguration of Afghanistan's future. And it provided an alternative to either the socialist or the capitalist models, instead locating modern governing structures in the strictures of Islamic thought and teaching.

This is not to say that the political parties disagreed on all matters. In sweeping terms, the Afghan groups based around Peshawar agreed on six basic points:

- They opposed the Soviet intervention.
- They opposed the Soviet Union, more broadly.
- They opposed Marxism and atheism.
- They advocated national liberation and self-determination.
- They advocated an independent Afghan state.
- They advocated an Islamic state (with varying interpretations).

The parties broadly shared the same goals: the forced withdrawal of Soviet troops, affirmation of Afghanistan as a state in the international system, and a political shift

**Figure 5.1.** Resistance-party political cartoon: A *mujahid* hand tries to dam communism and prevent it flooding Afghanistan. The slogan at the top references the renowned Persian poet Sa'adi's text, *Golistan*: 'The source of a fountain may [here replaced with 'should'] be stopped with a bodkin [arrowhead], but when it is full, it cannot be crossed on an elephant' (Afghanistan Centre at Kabul University)

away from Marxism that would reaffirm not only Afghanistan's independence but its adherence to Islam.

But disagreements persisted, compounding frictions within the resistance. On a political level, party leaders could not come to terms on specifics:

- What was Afghanistan's place in the international community to be?
- Who were the 'enemies' of the resistance?
- What entailed an 'Islamic' Afghanistan?
- How would Afghanistan reconcile its ethnic, tribal, and social diversity?
- What role would resistance commanders play in a post-withdrawal Afghanistan?[26]

The traditionalists and Islamists had fundamentally different visions of Afghanistan's future political hierarchy. The Islamists positioned religious figures as political, as well as spiritual, leaders in a post-withdrawal Afghanistan, a position that moved far beyond Islam as merely 'uniting a country that was historically divided by ethnic, tribal, linguistic, and regional differences', the view taken by traditionalists.[27] How could party leaders reconcile this vision of Afghanistan with one that reinstated older forms of political leadership in Afghanistan? It looked impossible, especially as time passed and different parties hardened their attitudes. Hekmatyar's Hizb-i Islami, in particular, became increasingly hostile to both the traditionalists and more moderate Islamists and focused on single-party rule.

Personality clashes between party leaders also persisted and prevented cooperation, most notably between Gulbuddin Hekmatyar and just about every other leader. These increasingly manifested in inter-party, as well as interpersonal, competition, further aggravated by increasingly uneven funding, as Western observers acknowledged, however reluctantly, Hizb-i Islami's 'superior organization' even while criticizing its 'ruthlessness and uncompromising stance'.[28] Hekmatyar not only did not get along with his co-Islamist Rabbani but also dismissed traditionalist leaders like Gailani as the 'epitome of decadent, superstition-ridden and self-seeking men' who had no place in the future Afghanistan.[29]

Circumstances converged to allow an Islamist movement, which might otherwise have remained on the fringes of Afghan society, to come to the fore of the Afghan resistance. As David Edwards wrote, reflecting on his anthropology fieldwork in Peshawar in the 1980s: 'I found the profusion of [Islamist] parties puzzling, particularly since Islam had seemed such a taken-for-granted but politically insignificant part of Afghan society a decade earlier.'[30] Indeed, Islamists such as Hekmatyar and Rabbani had been allowed to settle in Peshawar only because of the antagonistic relationship between Pakistan and Afghanistan in the mid-1970s, while the Islamist movement, itself, had been largely excluded from Afghan politics. But support for these groups—among Afghans, regional powers, and international players—skyrocketed because the Soviet invasion of Afghanistan turned the crisis from a local to a global one. Zia's sympathies created new links between Pakistani and Afghan Islamists through the auspices of ISI, Jama'at-i Islami, and Jam'iyyat-i 'Ulama'-i Islam. And, significantly, the American decision to expand its financial and military support for the Pakistan-based Afghan resistance compounded with the government of Pakistan's decision to use the Afghan parties to distribute this aid, reworking the conflict to the benefit of the parties.

This was particularly true of the Islamist parties, which proved to be better organized and more effective in combat. By 1987, an officer in Pakistan's ISI estimated that Hekmatyar's Hizb-i Islami received 18–20 per cent of foreign aid, with Rabbani's Jam'iyyat close behind at 18–19 per cent and the Islamists collectively receiving almost three-quarters of all foreign funding.[31] A British Foreign and Commonwealth Office official, dismissing reports that the former king, Zahir Shah, might be capable of uniting the fractured resistance, concluded: 'The clock cannot simply be put back.'[32] The rise of the Afghan political parties around Peshawar, and their backing from Pakistani and US state leaders, as well as the Muslim world, fundamentally changed the stakes of the Afghan civil war. This was not merely a revolt or demand for regime change. More radical party leaders aspired to use victory in the war to reshape Afghan politics and society.

This is not to say that the Afghan Islamists or the seven main political parties had a monopoly over the Afghan resistance.[33] Indeed, the fact that the Islamist parties, whether Hizb-i Islami, Jam'iyyat, or Ittihad-i Islami, never managed to dominate the resistance and create a single, unified movement was one of the reasons that civil war persisted after the Soviet withdrawal. Many combatants resented the attention paid to the Pakistan-based parties when their continued bickering threatened to undermine the movement against the Soviets. In 1980 and again in 1981, groups of *mullahs* and tribal leaders outside the main parties pushed for the establishment of a representative *Loya Jirga* (Grand Assembly) to lead and unite the resistance. *Loya Jirga* advocates accused the Peshawar parties of not being 'capable of leading freedom fighters and Afghan society', of being 'the main cause of disunity' and 'hegemonist leaders' unable to unite Afghanistan. They also ominously, though presciently, warned that 'house to house fighting and bloodshed among muslim brothers are the real anxiety that [the] Nation foresee [*sic*] after the liberation of Afghanistan'.[34] Nevertheless, because the government of Pakistan refused to support resistance political activities conducted outside the main parties, such initiatives by non-party groups fell flat, bereft of funding and restricted in their ability to act on either Afghan or Pakistani soil. The parties, themselves, also saw attempts to form a *Loya Jirga* as an attack on their influence—each party would have had only a limited number of representatives in the assembly—and, if nothing else united them, they agreed that they were, and should remain, the true leaders of the resistance.[35]

Moreover, the parties in Peshawar did not represent the ethnic diversity of the resistance within Afghanistan. With the exception of Jam'iyyat, and its Tajik leader, Rabbani, the Peshawar parties were overwhelmingly dominated by ethnic Pashtuns. In contrast, multi-ethnic alliances were common within Afghanistan as the most practical means of defeating government forces.[36] How, then, were the exiled parties to represent all Afghans in a post-withdrawal state? Could they even be said to be representative? Whether they would lead a change in nationwide politics, or instead re-embrace Pashtun dominance and Pashtun nationalism, to the detriment of Afghanistan's other communities, was a matter of concern. In this regard, one contemporary observer noted that the Islamists potentially had the upper hand because they could offer a 'resolution of age old political problems in Afghanistan: the reworking of ethnic animosities, the integration of non-Pushtun elements into an Afghan identity, the submergence of the need for revenge for past ethnic injustices and, finally, the integration of a new national identity along Afghan or even broader lines'.[37] Islamism placed religion ahead of ethnicity in nationalizing and governing politics, in theory if not necessarily in practice.

Another sign of the divisions within the resistance, in terms of religion, politics, and ethnicity, was the development of a number of Shi'a resistance organizations, many of which received support from Iran. Shi'a resistance emerged among Afghanistan's Hazara population, which not only shared ethnic and religious ties with Iranian Hazara but had also faced long-term political discrimination and violence from Afghanistan's Pashtun ruling elite. Many Hazara saw the revolt against the PDPA as an opportunity to liberate Hazarajat from the oppression of the Afghan state, whether Pashtun or socialist. Educated Hazara nationalists gravitated towards Shi'a Islamist thinkers such as Khomeini and Ali Shariati, while others embraced communism (including Sultan Ali Keshtmand, who became prime minister under Karmal). While some Hazara students had initially been involved in the Muslim Youth at Kabul University in the 1960s, they had broken ties owing to ideological differences. Many Shi'a Islamists also agreed with the significance of restoring *shari'a*, but a number of them embraced the Iranian model of a cleric-led revolution. Tensions nevertheless emerged between Hazara nationalists and Islamists early in the war with the creation of the Shura in Hazarajat. A number of Hazara nationalists chose to flee the Shura's conservative religious leadership, while some Iranian observers decried the Shura's exploitation of local peasants.

Tensions persisted between nationalists who sought to protect local Hazara, traditional *ulama* who had no interest in a revolutionary Islamist state, and the more radical followers of Khomeini. While Iran briefly supported Hekmatyar's Hizb-i Islami, seeing clear parallels between his political aspirations and Khomeini's Islamist vision, the country's leaders increasingly focused on Shi'a groups. Radical Shi'a groups embraced Khomeini's dictum 'Neither East nor West but Islam', and participated in the Iran–Iraq war on the Iranian side. As was the case among Afghan exiles in Pakistan, the number of Shi'a political organizations based in Afghanistan as well as in Iran (and also in Pakistan) flourished. They included, among others, *Harakat-i Islami-yi Afghanistan* (Islamic Movement), *Sazman-i Nasr-i Inqilab-i Islami-yi Afghanistan* (Victory Organization for Islamic Revolution), *Pasdaran-i Jihad-i Islami-yi Afghanistan* (Guardians of the Islamic Jihad), *Hizbullah* (Party of God), *Sazman-i Mujahidin-i Mustaza'fin* (Organization of Warriors of the Dispossessed), and *Hizb-i Radd-i Islami* (Islamic Thunder). As with the parties based in Pakistan, divisions existed. While Hizbullah, Sazman-i Nasr, and Pasdaran were pro-Khomeini and supported his religious and political interpretations, others, such as the Sazman-i Mujahidin, the Shura in Hazarajat, and *Shura-yi Farhangi-yi Islami-yi Afghanistan* (Islamic Cultural Council of Afghanistan), based out of Quetta, Pakistan, remained largely independent of Iranian influence. In 1987, Iran managed to broker a coalition between eight of the Shi'a Islamist groups, creating the *Shura-yi I'tilaf-i Islami-yi Afghanistan* (Council of Islamic Alliance of Afghanistan), which was renamed *Hizb-i Vahdat-i Islami-yi Afghanistan* (Islamic Unity Party of Afghanistan) in June 1990.[38]

The development of resistance parties with backing from both Pakistan and Iran fundamentally distinguished the civil war of the 1980s from earlier anti-government revolts and rebellions. While various pre-existing social networks remained significant for uniting insurgents and in the waging of local battles, regional and international impetuses meant that, if combatants within Afghanistan needed supplies or weapons, then they often had to look to the political parties in exile for support. The government of Pakistan's decision to funnel foreign aid through the political parties gave them new, disproportionate influence, and Zia's partiality for the Islamists pushed them to the fore. Moreover, the fact that Hekmatyar's Hizb-i Islami and Jam'iyyat had already established party-like structures in Peshawar before the PDPA came to power meant that other Afghan exiles arriving in Pakistan had to follow suit if they wanted to assert their parity. While the emergence of so many different

Afghan organizations in, or with support from, Pakistan and Iran highlighted divisions within the resistance and the emergence of competing visions for Afghanistan, the fact remained that the war in Afghanistan was one in which political parties took on a key role. In turn, for some party leaders, the war in Afghanistan was not merely intended to overthrow the PDPA. It offered an opportunity to reshape Afghan politics and society.

The belief that political Islam could potentially overcome historical divides and truly unite an Afghan nation was potent. For Afghan Islamists, as for the PDPA, the conflict was a necessary step in Afghanistan's evolution and in its path to political and social revolution. But, just as the PDPA struggled with its own internal divides between the Khalq and Parcham factions, the Afghan Islamist movement remained disunited. This resulted in part from ideological differences, such as between Hekmatyar's uncompromising Hizb-i Islami and Rabbani's more conciliatory Jam'iyyat. But it also was due to the very different organizational structures that parties such as Hizb-i Islami and Jam'iyyat adopted in their fight against the socialists. In constructing 'modern' political organizations, Hizb-i Islami and Jam'iyyat took

**Figure 5.2.** Resistance-group political cartoon of a group of Afghan men planting the green flag of *jihad* on top of a mountain. The image mirrors the famous photograph of American Marines raising Old Glory at the Battle of Iwo Jima during the Second World War (Afghanistan Center at Kabul University)

very different routes. While at times these two organizations overlapped in the ways they sought to assert their legitimacy, overall, because they approached the war and the spread of Afghan Islamism in different ways, they could never unite to support a single vision of Afghan Islamist modernity.

The Afghan Islamists, like their Marxist counterparts, attempted to assert their visions of a modern Afghanistan, as well as their fitness to rule the country. And, like the socialists, they ran into various stumbling blocks. Early PDPA leaders, especially Taraki and Amin, had clear ideas of how they wanted to change Afghanistan and pursued these ruthlessly through government decrees. But, while the PDPA had a clear rationale for their policies, they failed in their short-sighted implementation practices. In contrast, the Afghan exile parties succeeded exceptionally in undertaking an armed resistance, but to what end? What remained unclear was how victories on the battlefield would translate into a governing system. Examining Hekmatyar's Hizb-i Islami and Rabbani's Jam'iyyat highlights two competing models of Afghan Islamist state-building. While Hekmatyar focused on mobilization in and around the refugee camps in Pakistan, Rabbani and his allies, most notably Massoud, attempted to create functioning governing systems *within* war-torn Afghanistan. Comparing the two reveals a number of key issues. A general model of an Islamist Afghanistan did not exist, and Hizb-i Islami and Jam'iyyat promoted competing archetypes. Nevertheless, both parties recognized the significance of gaining supporters among Afghans *and* in the international community in order to assert their legitimacy. Thus, each party shared a two-pronged approach meant to appeal to domestic and foreign audiences. Finally, personality was key. Both Hekmatyar and Massoud were charismatic and effective. This brought additional attention, and consequently support and funding, to their parties and also helped push them to the fore of discussions about a post-Soviet Afghanistan.

As residents in Pakistan, Afghan Islamists had to navigate the troubled waters of regional relations. The exiled parties, based as they were around Peshawar, could not afford to alienate their Pakistani hosts. The government of Pakistan's decision-making had given the parties extended power and influence and created a system of relations that would persist throughout the war and even after the Soviet withdrawal. But, within these mechanisms, Pakistan's ISI still had the power to choose *which* party it wanted to favour. Foreign aid was not distributed evenly.[39] More supplies, weapons, and money found their way to the parties that were most sympathetic to the Pakistani cause and whose own aims aligned with those of Zia. Zia's regime was hostile to parties that prioritized Pashtun ethnonationalism but supportive of the Islamists who complemented his own Islamization policies and served as potential allies.

Hekmatyar's Hizb-i Islami proved the most successful in navigating this relationship, despite its overwhelmingly Pashtun membership. Pakistani support for Hizb-i Islami goes some way to explaining Hekmatyar's extensive influence in and around Peshawar. ISI openly preferred Hekmatyar's party and sent disproportionate amounts of aid in its direction. Brigadier Mohammad Yousaf, head of ISI's Afghan bureau, described Hekmatyar as 'the toughest and most vigorous of all the Alliance Leaders', and explained: 'By giving them the weapons you were sure that the weapons will not be sold in Pakistan because he [Hekmatyar] was strict to the extent of being ruthless.'[40]

Hekmatyar's party also found a ready local ally in Jama'at-i Islami, the Pakistani Islamist political party originally founded by Mawdudi. Hekmatyar maintained strong relations with Jama'at-i Islami, whose leaders, in turn, ensured his party remained well supplied. As a contemporary reporter explained:

The reason for Jamaat's preference is a mix of ideology and pragmatism, because Gulbaddin espouses the cause of Islamic reformism—an international resurgence which aims to establish a purist Islamic order in Kabul. His following is also disciplined and was at one time considered to be the most effective instrument for overthrowing pro-Soviet administrations in Afghanistan.

The reporter went on:

Hezb-i-Islami is also primarily Pakhtoon. Central power in Afghanistan, however tenuous, has traditionally been the preserve of the Pakhtoon tribes and therefore for Pakistan's security and foreign policy interests, it is the crescent of Pakhtoons living along the border and stretching from Kunar to Kandahar which must be the first concern of both the authorities in Peshawar and Jamaat-i-Islami Pakistan.[41]

But good relations with ISI and Jama'at-i Islami did not, alone, give Hekmatyar such outstanding influence. His internal party structures ensured loyalty. Of all the resistance parties, Hizb-i Islami undoubtedly was the most tightly organized. Hekmatyar's insistence on a strong party structure had been evident since the mid-1970s, during the first botched alliance between Hizb-i Islami and Rabbani's Jam'iyyat. Hizb-i Islami from the mid- to late 1970s onwards was strictly managed and heavily reliant on a central leader. Hekmatyar, and his carefully chosen subordinates, oversaw every aspect of party action. He established a party newspaper, *Shahadat*, translated as 'martyrdom' and 'witness' in Dari, Pashto, and Arabic, as well as additional broadsides specifically targeting female audiences. With Pakistani agreement, he rented land on the outskirts of Peshawar to house party members, which became known as *Nasrat Mina*, or Victory Quarter. Hizb-i Islami opened at least two schools in Peshawar, where students learned Dari, Pashto, and English while receiving religious instruction. Initially, the party indicated that women, too, had the right to education so long as this took place in separate institutions.[42]

Hizb-i Islami issued a manual of 'personal and professional standards' to members, which outlined how to be not only devout Islamist soldiers—'Always be thinking about jihad and martyrdom in the way of God. Make yourself completely ready'— but also responsible party members—'Defend the decisions of the party with full power'. Behind this lay a highly organized party structure, comprised of various committees with specific responsibilities. Alongside these, Hekmatyar's Hizb-i Islami retained its influence around Peshawar through its deadly security service, *Sakhar*, the Organization for the Service of Islam. Sakhar monitored the activities of Afghan leftists and Islamists alike, including, most likely, Hizb-i Islami's own members. As Brigadier Yousaf commented: 'Once you join his party it was difficult to leave.'[43]

Hizb-i Islami's charter, which was widely circulated in 1988, laid out an expansive yet somewhat vague vision of a future Afghanistan. It emphasized the primacy of *shari'a* while promising further regulations to ban 'adultery, drunkenness, gambling, obscenity, and moral corruption'. Likewise, the party identified *madrassas* and *darul hufaz* (schools for memorizing the Quran) as the key sources of Afghan education and pointed out the need for 'spiritual and ethical training' to accompany any occupational development (notably, military training would also be compulsory across educational institutions). Fascinatingly, many of Hizb-i Islami's economic and political vows, even while undertaking to uphold 'Islamic order', mirrored the PDPA's. Hizb-i Islami, too, pledged to provide better wages for teachers and workers, to establish a better standard of living, to create 'healthy institutions comprised of religious, responsible and competent officials', to root out corruption, and to reform the military and prisons. In the realm of economics, the party also prioritized land redistribution and state oversight of industry. In one particularly notable declaration (and sounding remarkably like the PDPA), Hizb-i Islami promised: 'In the course of activities exerted for the industrialization of the country, priority will be given to the principles of "labor" and "need" and not that of "capital".'

But the party also pointedly pledged not to emulate the PDPA's failures. The charter vowed to provide agricultural tools, seeds, and fertilizers and not to 'misappropriate' agriculture or pasture for 'industrial purposes', a move away from PDPA–Soviet focus on widespread industrialization. In an Islamist turn, it pledged to reform banking, introduce *zakat*, a compulsory tax for Muslims, and to outlaw investment in 'illegal fields'. Not only that, but the charter promised to uphold strict gender divides, banning men and women from working together and outlawing co-education. Finally, while pledging to establish good relations with 'all countries of the world' and to uphold world peace and security, Hizb-i Islami (like the PDPA) condemned colonialism and exploitation and also pledged 'equal struggle against East or West imperialism'.[44] Clearly, the party drew in part from the same modernizing toolbox as the PDPA when looking to economic and administrative reform, even while it divined further shifts from the Quran and Islamic teachings. Hizb-i Islami's charter demonstrated that, like the PDPA, Hekmatyar had no intention of returning to a pre-1978 status quo but instead aimed to initiate nationwide political, social, and economic change.

In wartime, many of these aspirations, which derived in part from earlier discussions among Afghan Islamists in the 1960s, did not play out in practice. Hekmatyar focused on personal and party gain and a mixture of legitimate and illicit trade. The party purchased a factory to manufacture water pumps and invested in properties around Peshawar. It was also reported that Hekmatyar controlled 150 rickshaws in

Peshawar and siphoned off medicine, clothing, and food intended for refugees and resold them. Hizb-i Islami commanders also engaged in the growing narcotics trade and reportedly ran heroin laboratories and refineries across both Pakistan and Afghanistan.[45]

Moreover, echoing Hekmatyar's personal pre-1978 history, Hizb-i Islami was the most militant of the resistance parties. This demonstrated itself in the war against the Soviets *and* in Hekmatyar's ongoing conflicts with the other Afghan parties. From an early stage, Hizb-i Islami activated underground cells to launch anti-government protests in and around Kabul, and combatants took part in fighting in Nangarhar and Kunar provinces. However, Hizb-i Islami avoided extensive direct conflict with the Soviets, focusing on building up bases of power once they were liberated rather than expanding the fight. Later in the 1980s, the party ran training camps in Pakistan not only for party members but also for 'Afghan Arabs', the fighters from across the Islamic world who responded to the call to arms issued by Abdallah Azzam, the Palestinian Islamist who first taught at the International Islamic University in Islamabad then settled in Peshawar to establish the *Maktab al-Khidamat*, or Services Bureau, to mobilize and organize foreign fighters to take part in the Afghan *jihad*.[46]

Hizb-i Islami 'regarded the Islamic revolution as being more important than the war and thought that the struggle against the Soviets could only be successfully carried out when the party had gained control over the resistance movement'. Hekmatyar's party, like Sayyaf's Ittihad-i Islami, differed from the other groups in that it did not rely on existing social networks to spread its influence. After gaining control of a region within Afghanistan, Hizb-i Islami ignored extant political structures and installed party members as local leaders. These leaders were 'visionaries, dogmatic, and living their whole life for the party and devoted to Hekmatyar' and thus had few links with locals.[47] While this spoke to these fighters' ideological commitment to Hizb-i Islami, it did not appeal to many of the Afghans who were subjected to this new authority. It instead highlighted Hekmatyar's envisioned mode of politics: single-party rule where locals were subordinated to party members. As such, Hekmatyar's party drastically differed in its organization and political models from governing precedents within Afghanistan.

This single-minded focus on its own authority did not provide space for cooperation between Hizb-i Islami and other resistance groups. Hekmatyar's combatants refused to allow other resistance parties to function in areas of Afghanistan that they had liberated. And, while Hizb-i Islami took part in a number of the failed coalitions during the war, Hekmatyar was by far the least trusted participant, since he demonstrated he had few qualms with using violence against his personal and political enemies. UNHCR officials, while overseeing refugees, received numerous reports about Afghans who had simply 'disappeared' in the NWFP alongside reports that Hekmatyar's Hizb-i Islami had begun an 'elimination campaign', which had already led to the 'liquidation' of more than a hundred people since the beginning of 1981.[48] One of those who disappeared early was Dr Abdul Samat Durrani. Durrani was a member of *Fedayoun*, a small political party that, according to the Islamist parties, was 'leftist' (what the UNHCR concluded was 'a designation difficult to assess since it includes anybody who is not strictly in their line'). He had been working alongside other exiled Afghan doctors to collect medical goods from private donors to ship into war-torn Afghanistan. On 28 May 1982, he was apparently kidnapped in front of his office in Peshawar, never to be seen again. His colleagues immediately accused Hizb-i Islami of masterminding the abduction, something Hekmatyar decried as '"Russians" trying to discredit his party and himself'. While unable to prove Hekmatyar's guilt, the UNHCR warned that 'an increasing feeling of unrest and anxiety is spreading among those Afghans who are not Gulbuddin's followers and a growing number of them are considering going underground'.[49]

As the war progressed, Hekmatyar went even further, ordering Hizb-i Islami's resistance fighters to eliminate other resistance combatants, even though they ostensibly all shared the same goal of defeating the Soviets. Additional high-profile assassinations followed, including a prominent writer and journalist, Aziz-ur-Rahman Ulfat, in 1984 and Sayyid Bahauddin Majrooh in 1988. Majrooh headed the non-party Afghan Information Centre, which in 1987 released a survey of 1,787 refugees, the vast majority of whom demanded the return of the exiled king, Zahir Shah, following a Soviet withdrawal and indicated a desire for party cooperation, not one-party rule, as envisioned by Hizb-i Islami. Majrooh's murder was largely seen as retaliation for this veiled criticism of Hekmatyar's party politics.[50] Throughout the 1980s, reports also intensified of attacks by Hekmatyar's forces on other resistance groups. In line with his ideological inflexibility, which, if anything, became even less accommodating as the war progressed, Hekmatyar sought to eliminate all enemies. For Hekmatyar, there was little opportunity for compromise.

As such, while Hekmatyar basked in widespread praise from inside and outside the resistance early on, his ruthless competition with the other Afghan political parties, his ready turn to violence against his fellow combatants, and his criticism of his Western backers meant that his reputation declined from 1981.[51] Nevertheless, Hekmatyar had so embedded Hizb-i Islami into the network of foreign aid, refugee support, and resistance supplies, as well as turning party members into an effective, if ruthless, fighting machine, that Hizb-i Islami would remain one of the most recognizable of the parties. Like the PDPA, Hekmatyar continued to rely on his reign of terror and strong party structures to remain at the forefront of the war.

While many observers initially saw Hizb-i Islami as a leading resistance party, by the early to mid-1980s Jam'iyyat's activities in Afghanistan were increasingly described as the future of the Afghan resistance.[52] Rabbani and Jam'iyyat worked quite differently. Unlike Hizb-i Islami and its strict party organization, Jam'iyyat functioned as a 'dominant party which had renounced its quintessential character to absorb people who were not ideologically committed from the very beginning'.[53] Jam'iyyat, in other words, allowed other Afghan Muslims to join the party as the conflict progressed and as different insurgents saw the appeal of Jam'iyyat's message and organization. This spoke to the earlier rupture between Hizb-i Islami and Jam'iyyat

**Figure 5.3.** Burhanuddin Rabbani (left) (Internet Archive, The Afghan Media Resource Center/Najibullah Seddiqi)

over defining *takfir*. In wartime, Jam'iyyat proved willing to accommodate members with the aim of developing their support for the Islamist message, rather than forcing them to accept it. This flexibility and gradualism were reflected in Jam'iyyat's structures as well. Where Hekmatyar and Hizb-i Islami focused on building up and regulating party composition around Peshawar, where its power centre resided, Jam'iyyat developed a broader network of followers who were more active within Afghanistan.

Jam'iyyat, like Hizb-i Islami and the other major political parties, also produced a charter outlining its aspirations, but it was rather vague. While it was forward-looking, the declaration also drew on the longer history of Islam in Afghanistan to prove its legitimacy. Like Hizb-i Islami, Jam'iyyat decried the ruination wrought on Afghanistan by foreign actors, claiming 'filthy networks of imperialism' had removed 'the genuine teachings of Islam from the lives of the people'. In contrast, Jam'iyyat was the 'sincere custodian of the shining teachings of Islam and the hardline defender of the deprived classes', and the charter pointedly emphasized Jam'iyyat's pre-1978 opposition to the government as a sign of its devotion to the Afghan nation. Jam'iyyat, too, promised to root out corruption and provide for citizens' rights and needs ('through the application of the noble system of Islam'). The party sought a more egalitarian economic system, including land redistribution, and improved living standards across the country, but the charter made virtually no mention of what sort of political system the party envisioned.

Jam'iyyat was noticeably inclusive in its demands for a future Afghanistan. The charter made a point of rejecting 'linguistic, family and regional discriminations', demanded equality for 'all ethnical groups and tribes', a stark riposte to decades of Pashtun domination, and also promised to defend Islamic minorities. It further pledged women would 'enjoy all the rights and privileges granted to them by the shining teachings of Islam', though without specifying what these rights and privileges might entail. The charter ended with a call for unity across Afghan society to end the war, 'the continuation of which will destroy our history and culture, traditions, sanctities and all other values'.

While making clear the prominence and necessity of Islam for guiding Afghanistan's trajectory, Jam'iyyat highlighted as well how Islam served as a means of fusing Afghanistan's past and future. The Islamization of Afghan politics and society, Jam'iyyat argued, would 'lead our society towards its path of progress', a process that had been disrupted by previous 'treacherous leaders'.[54] Jam'iyyat's Islamism would correct Afghanistan's political path, respecting Afghanistan's culture and past while embedding the tenets of the Quran and *sharia*. Jam'iyyat's charter read more nebulously and less stridently than Hizb-i Islami's (it was also much shorter), and it shared fewer parallels with the PDPA. As such, while Jam'iyyat clearly intended to reshape Afghan society, it appeared less militant and more cooperative in its approach.

Jam'iyyat gained prominence through its success at mobilizing different social networks, drawing supporters from among Sufis, *mawlawi*, or religious scholars, and numerous ethnic groups, as well as Islamists. But, equally importantly, Jam'iyyat's local commanders demonstrated political, as well as military, savvy. In zones that Jam'iyyat liberated, local commanders, such as Ismael Khan around Herat, Zabiullah at Mazar-e Sharif, and Massoud in Panjshir, used their military successes to create structures that blended military and political mobilization and that drew locals into party participation. In comparison to those of Hizb-i Islami, Jam'iyyat's command structures were far more accommodating. Where Hizb-i Islami revolved around Hekmatyar, his closest allies, and his decision-making, Rabbani indicated willingness to engage in partnerships that allowed local resistance leaders extensive independence and influence. He remained open to power-sharing, both with other resistance parties and within Jam'iyyat, where he encouraged the rise of leaders within Afghanistan like Ahmad Shah Massoud.[55]

Massoud's victories most obviously highlighted the successes of Jam'iyyat's policy. As the 'lion of Panjshir', he became the international face of the Afghan resistance, alongside leaders like Safiullah Afzali in Herat. Massoud returned to Panjshir from Pakistan in 1979 to foment resistance against the Soviets, and his military successes brought him and Jam'iyyat international prominence.[56] But his attempts to create a functioning administration in the Panjshir Valley are equally interesting. Massoud's efforts to introduce political and social stability, alongside fighting a war against the PDPA and Soviets, give a taste of what a Jam'iyyat Islamist state might have looked like if civil war had not persisted after the Soviet withdrawal.

At just 80 kilometres from Kabul, lying close to the Bagram airfield, the Soviets' main air base, and near the Salang tunnel, the key thoroughfare connecting Kabul to Afghanistan's northern cities, and hence Soviet supplies to Afghanistan's administrative centre, the Panjshir Valley was a military prize. Controlling Panjshir was strategically important for both government and resistance forces because of the

**Figure 5.4.** Ahmad Shah Massoud (centre) and resistance fighters (Internet Archive, The Afghan Media Resource Center)

potential threat to transport lines. But geography complicated strategy. Surrounded by craggy, steep mountains, the valley was extremely difficult to attack, and caves running through the mountains also provided insurgents and civilians ready hiding places during armed offensives. Under Massoud's command, Afghan resistance fighters managed to fend off Soviet army offensives against Panjshir nine times between 1980 and 1985. The valley thus became a model of resistance success.

Afghan resistance leaders from across the country travelled there to learn how Massoud had managed to defeat the technologically superior Soviet–PDPA forces. They also began exporting the Panjshir model to other resistance strongholds. In the Panjshir Valley, Massoud and his commanders established five different governing bodies, including a military committee, responsible for recruiting combatants and providing fighters with weapons, clothing, and supplies, and an economic committee to oversee goods coming into the valley and levy taxes on transportation and commerce, including the mining of lapis lazuli. The committee's responsibilities later expanded to include taxation of Panjshiris living outside the valley, particularly in Kabul. He also organized a culture and propaganda committee, which distributed materials provided by Jam'iyyat headquarters in Peshawar; an intelligence committee, which monitored and developed spy networks to support the resistance; and a judicial committee, which administered justice for both locals and prisoners of war.[57]

Massoud's mobilization clearly went beyond that of a mere insurgency, and his focus extended past beating Soviet armed forces. This was emphasized by Jam'iyyat representatives in their propaganda. As Mohammad Es'haq, a Jam'iyyat political officer, told international audiences: 'Mujahideen have made achievements in the civil organisation field which is necessary to keep the people interested in the cause.

The people choose their leaders who run their affairs. For the first time in the history of our country a type of real and popular election is taking place.'[58] Massoud sought to build public support for the resistance and to establish governing practices that could outlast the war. This required focusing not only on combat tactics but protecting and supporting the civilians caught in the crossfire. One of his aides recalled: 'Massoud said about the Resistance, "Without the support of the people you cannot do anything." Support of people can exist because the people are *against* the occupation, but you cannot keep those emotions unless you do something *for* people so they can survive and move forward—hope that they can have, hope for the future.'[59]

In contrast to Hizb-i Islami's strategy of installing party members as local commanders, Massoud actively involved pre-existing community leaders. His command structures were layered, bringing together representatives from local villages and communities, wider districts, and finally an area-wide organization under himself. 'He did not leave his organization just at the village, district, ethnic, clan, or tribal level. From the beginning, he created unity among three dimensions: in the village, on the road, and at the group level,' noted Humayun Tandar, Jam'iyyat's representative in France.[60] In January 1985, Massoud brought together Jam'iyyat commanders from across five north-eastern provinces to create a coordinating council, what would become the Supervisory Council of the North.[61]

In this way, Massoud and Hekmatyar functioned similarly, as their activities disrupted pre-existing social and political networks. But, where Hekmatyar just ignored these networks, Massoud overcame local divisions and the potential hostility of the valley's extant leaders by instead incorporating them in Jam'iyyat's more flexible structures. Notably as well, Massoud did not force locals to join the resistance. He made this clear in a 1981 interview with a French journalist where he explained why he was so selective in recruiting resistance fighters. 'First, we have not got enough weapons,' he admitted. 'Second, we have to ensure that enough people are available to run the economy, the farms, and the administration. There is a role for everyone.' However, he warned, 'if it really comes to the crunch, then everyone will be ready to fight. During the last Russian offensives,' he pointed out, 'we had women firing guns at the enemy'.[62]

Massoud adopted a wartime strategy that focused on slowly developing Jam'iyyat converts, not enforcing party rule (though he was not immune to interparty competition, which would grow increasingly violent in the 1990s). He demonstrated Jam'iyyat's beneficence, encouraging the development of a local economy in Panjshir and building new schools and hospitals. In areas that Massoud and his allies controlled, they emphasized the significance of law and order. In the village of Sabz Dara, in Badakshan, Masood Khalili, one of Massoud's political officers, was told the story of a woman's affair with her brother-in-law, which ended in her lover murdering her husband with an axe. Woman and lover were arrested by Massoud's allies, but, rather than pass judgment himself, the local commander ordered a trial before a judge. While the lover was sentenced to death, the woman was found not guilty after denying three times that she had been involved. The local resistance leaders, Khalili was informed, did not agree with the judgment, but they nevertheless abided by the judge's ruling. Khalili reflected in a letter to his wife: 'It is very promising. I hope, one day we can expand on it because I do not think that in most other areas controlled by the resistance we have the same model. It impressed me a lot.'[63] Safiullah Afzali, who headed Jam'iyyat's operations in Herat until his assassination in July 1987, took a similar approach. Afzali explained:

> We inform the people about the Islamic Government. Cultural committees have been founded among the government staff, people and workers. Women's organ-izations have been established in the cities, and primary schools have been estab-lished in the liberated regions to give children Islamic education. In the mosques, the Holy Quran and principles of Islam are being taught to educate the people about the Islamic Government.[64]

Thus, Jam'iyyat's initiatives, led by men like Massoud and Afzali as well as Rabbani, provided a prototype for what could have been an Afghan Islamist state that took advantage of and embedded older Afghan political, social, and ethnic networks. Es'haq lauded Massoud in *AFGHANews* in 1987:

> He is thinking in terms of self-sufficiency in economic fields in the liberated areas. According to him Mujahideen have to do something for the benefit of the people. The people should not see only bombs and bullets from a Revolution. He con-siders development projects a useful way of helping the people.

Crucially, Es'haq noted, 'some of these ideas come into conflict with the traditional way of life of the people'. But, he went on to claim, Massoud's 'skill is in encouraging the most conservative elements of the society to support his program. In all his important decisions he seeks the consent of commanders, Ulema (religious scholars) and public as a whole.'[65]

Starstruck reports from foreign journalists also pointed to another of Massoud's strengths: his ability to engage with international audiences. Massoud became famous by hosting foreign reporters, who then told Western audiences about his exploits. Massoud's media engagement was canny. He used contacts with international media outlets to seek direct foreign support when Panjshir was on the brink of famine owing to continued war.[66] This produced material aid, as NGOs sent in medical teams and supplies. His pronouncements also reached Afghans living abroad and inspired them to commit to the resistance. Daoud Mir, at the time a young university student in France, travelled to Panjshir after watching 'A Valley against an Empire', a documentary made by French filmmakers. He subsequently returned to France as Jam'iyyat's official representative.[67]

Massoud was not alone in looking abroad to gain support for the Afghan resistance. Much as the PDPA drew parallels between its reforms and those taking place in other socialist states and framed its aspirations in terms of global anti-colonialism, leaders within the Islamist and traditionalist parties were aware of the need to foster international sympathy for the resistance's position and to pressure the Soviets to withdraw (and ideally to take their PDPA lackeys with them). Consequently, the various Islamist parties, Jam'iyyat and Hizb-i Islami especially, undertook their own international marketing campaigns. Gailani, leader of Mahaz-i Milli-yi Islami, jealously admitted to British Foreign Office officials: 'The propaganda of these groups had made a considerable impact abroad.'[68]

Jam'iyyat and Hizb-i Islami opened their own offices in places such as London and Los Angeles and also published and circulated worldwide a number of English-, Arabic-, Dari-, and Pashto-language newsletters to advocate and explain their actions to foreign observers. Jam'iyyat, for example, published two different bi-monthly newsletters for Western audiences, *Mirror of Jehad: The Voice of Afghan Mujahideen* and *AFGHANews*, which provided reports on fighting and negotiations and editorials on events in Afghanistan (and, as we have seen, lavishly praised commanders like Massoud). Hizb-i Islami under Hekmatyar published *The Mujahideen Monthly* with a similar mix of opinion and analysis pieces (see Figure 5.5). Party leaders used these publications to demonstrate the global significance of the war in Afghanistan, cultivate further support, and begin discussing different models of Islamic political organization.[69]

In these publications, resistance writers framed their political aspirations in terms familiar to foreign audiences. Aware of their Western backers, in English-language publications they squarely placed blame for most international crises on 'Russian social imperialism' (a term, itself, rooted in Maoist thought, showing how Maoism had percolated into the anti-Soviet war and insurgency tenets).[70] At the same time, they made little critique of American foreign policy. They also framed their opinions in terms of anti-colonialism and imperial greed. For example, Jam'iyyat writers claimed, somewhat dubiously, that 'bloody manoeuvres of the Russian social imperialists encouraged Zionists to push out Palestinians from their fatherland' and that 'the war between the Muslim nations of Iran and Iraq is a clear example which has been caused by expansionists, specially by the conspiracies of the Russian social imperialism'.[71] Even though Hizb-i Islami was more openly anti-Western in its policies, *Mujahideen Monthly* initially made few antagonistic statements regarding the United States or its allies. Instead, it, too, focused on critiques of the Soviet Union, coupled with photos of Hekmatyar with groups of resistance fighters and emotive images of young, wounded Afghan children with captions like 'Have you seen my parents?'[72] Such news items spoke to foreign interest in providing both military and humanitarian assistance to Afghans. *Mujahideen Monthly*, alongside Hizb-i Islami's other Dari and Pashto publications, also provided the party with the opportunity to connect with Muslims across the world. A letters section allowed foreign Muslims to write in and have their messages, in which they offered support to the resistance, published.[73]

Both parties also used such publications to explain their aims in the Afghan war. The first page of the *Mujahideen Monthly*, for example, began with a summary of Hizb-i Islami's goals. Early issues showed an extended quote from Hekmatyar:

**Figure 5.5.** Gulbuddin Hekmatyar on the cover of *Mujahideen Monthly*, January 1986 (Afghanistan Center at Kabul University)

- We want to establish an independent, non-aligned and stable Islamic government in Afghanistan.

- The future government of free Afghanistan will maintain friendly relations with all States except those acting against the faith, independence and territorial integrity of our homeland.

- We will make independent judgements on all international issues, supporting the rights and condemning the wrong.

- Our internal and external policies will be based on the Quran and Sunnah.

- The rights of all Afghan nationals would be duly protected by the Islamic State of Afghanistan.

- The Islamic State will take all possible measures for the promotion of science and technology and for the reconstruction and development of Afghanistan in order to make it a self-reliant and selfsufficient [sic] State.[74]

This articulation of Hekmatyar's aims is striking. Thinking back to statements by the PDPA's Nur Mohammad Taraki and Babrak Karmal, several similarities emerge. Like the Afghan socialists, Hizb-i Islami emphasized the importance of non-alignment, Afghan independence in international relations, and the rights of all Afghans. Hizb-i Islami, too, pledged to accept many of the norms of international politics—state sovereignty, peaceful relations with other states, protection of its own citizens. The difference with the PDPA emerged with Hizb-i Islami's promise to base governance on the Quran and Sunnah, though the statement lacked an explanation of what this precisely entailed. Hekmatyar's party framed its aspirations in terms that would be familiar and acceptable to other state leaders while rooting them in Islam. Hizb-i Islami demonstrated a clear ability to use the language of modern international politics—'territorial integrity', 'rights', 'promotion of science and technology', 'self-reliant and self-sufficient state'.

Jam'iyyat used *Mirror of Jehad* for similar purposes. One newsletter explained:

> The ultimate goal of Afghan people like their Jehad will be completely based on the Islamic principles and order. The political, social and economic life of Afghan nation will be built on the basis of high Islamic values whose final goal and aim is humanism, peace-philanthropism, peaceful co-existence, benevolence, tolerance and sympathy with all mankind.

Much like Hizb-i Islami, this statement spoke to high-minded, universalist political aspirations—peaceful coexistence, tolerance, human rights—while hinting at specific Islamic underpinnings of these issues.[75] Es'haq reiterated such ideas as he toured the world to gain support for his party. At a seminar at the Institute of Foreign Affairs of Sweden in Stockholm, in early December 1985, he explained that Jam'iyyat's 'aim is to liberate Afghanistan, and to let the people decide their future according to their cultural heritage and religious beliefs'. He also emphasized the resistance's international significance, explaining to the Afghan American Action Federation in Washington, DC: 'If we fail no small country in the world can feel safe and world peace will become even more fragile.'[76] Clearly such statements and publications were intended to encourage international sympathy for the Islamists' cause and to reinforce the legitimacy of their claims.

Jam'iyyat, Hizb-i Islami, and the loose alliances of Afghan resistance parties also adopted the language of Western humanitarianism to assert themselves as the representatives of the Afghan refugee community. Party leaders took advantage of the uncertainty of camp life to embed their organizations among exiled Afghans. They stepped into a leadership void created through a twofold process. For many local communities, traditional leadership structures no longer sufficed. The deaths of many religious and political leaders frequently had precipitated the flight of families and whole communities into Pakistan and Iran. As such, many Afghan refugees arrived without pre-existing authority figures. Those leaders who made it across the border were confronted with a host of new problems, which they were not necessarily equipped to address. They needed to navigate the relationship between camp authority and refugee. Many simply could not, lacking the skills, linguistic or diplomatic, to engage with NGO and government representatives.

The exiled political parties took advantage of community leaders' shortcomings and the global community's focus on the refugee crisis and manipulated the images and rhetoric of suffering employed by international agencies to better their own circumstances (see Figure 5.6). One of the Hizb-i Islami parties wrote directly to the UNHCR office in Islamabad requesting the provision of additional tents for refugee families. Party representatives pointedly noted: 'The place they are living is very wet and not suitable for living. In every family most of the children and women are sick. They need a better place for living.'[77] Mohammad Nasim Azidi, President (Refugee Affairs) for Gailani's moderate Mahaz-i Milli-yi Islami, wrote even more dramatically to the government of Pakistan and UNHCR demanding aid for 'the helpless 405 families of Afghan refugees along with 20 orphan families [who] are still awaiting merciful consideration to their gigantic problems'. He emphasized: 'the victimised masses are facing constant trouble and hindrance in passing their hard days very terribly.'[78]

An organization that called itself Afghan Refugees Humanitarian Islamic Unity similarly corresponded with Pakistan's Commissioner for Afghan Refugees, offering its support in providing 'speedy action in favour of those refugee families (including women, children, and old unhealthy peoples), who, in this cold weather, are without shelter and assistance...'.[79] The UNHCR could hardly ignore such pleas, which

**Figure 5.6.** Resistance-group political cartoon. The Farsi script reads 'Unmanly Crimes of Russia', a reference to the military campaign waged by the Soviets in Afghanistan and its civilian victims (Afghanistan Center at Kabul University)

highlighted the plight of the Afghan refugee. By embracing a rhetoric of suffering and the image of the refugee that publics across the world could recognize, Afghan leaders created additional opportunities to receive aid, as well as to publicize their anguish. This, alongside the Pakistani decision to use the political parties to register Afghan refugees, created exceptional opportunities for the parties to gain new recruits, and thus to push forward their various visions of Afghanistan's future.

Hizb-i Islami participated alongside Jam'iyyat and the other more moderate political parties in using the refugee camps as recruiting grounds and taking advantage of the huge amounts of international aid to strengthen its own position among the refugees. But, from an early stage, Hizb-i Islami publications and statements made clear that the party's focus was its own political supremacy in a post-withdrawal Afghanistan with Hekmatyar at its head. The party developed a cult of personality that placed Hekmatyar front and centre, much more than leaders in other parties. *Mujahideen Monthly* showcased 'Amir Hekmatyar' on almost every page and contained countless photos of him posing with groups of combatants. The January 1986 issue even included details of a general amnesty that he had issued, as part of the re-formed Ittihad-i Islami-yi Mujahidin-i Afghanistan, to 'all those Afghans who served in the lower echelons of the enemy, collaborated for short durations, unknowingly or under compulsion' and invited them to 'join the ranks of the Muslim nation of Afghanistan'. The framing implied that Hekmatyar alone had undertaken this step rather than, in reality, as part of a broader coalition of resistance groups.[80] While he embraced the role of a *shura*, a consultative body that would oversee lawmaking, as another means of centralizing the power of Hizb-i Islami in post-war Afghanistan, the *shura*, itself, would be vetted by Hekmatyar and his closest allies.[81] Proposals for Afghanistan's future re-emphasized Hekmatyar's key role.

Hekmatyar's influence was thus built around his charisma, the strength of his personality, his ideological fervour, and his refusal to compromise. Initially, Hizb-i Islami's rigidity, in its political stance and the strict training of members, appealed to foreign-aid providers, as well as the party's Pakistani hosts. However, this same inflexibility also began to hinder the party's spread. By the late 1980s, Hekmatyar was articulating a vision of a post-withdrawal Afghanistan that was governed by a single party—Hizb-i Islami—and excluded political rivals. A party constitution published in 1987 pledged to implement a system where 'only pious religious people could run the administration with honesty and effectively' and the state could punish any manner of transgressions. As with earlier statements, how the government would function was not entirely clear—'national representation' in some sort of assembly was hinted at, as was the prominence of Islamic law, but leadership remained unnamed or titled.[82]

Hekmatyar became increasingly outspoken in his critique of the West (even as he continued to accept US covert aid) and publicly supported Islamists like Khomeini, Libya's Muammar al-Gaddafi, the Palestinian Liberation Organization, and the Muslim Brotherhood. Hizb-i Islami's charter claimed: 'All the nations of the West and East are undermining the newly established systems, and for these reasons they fight with every nation.'[83] A Pakistani official bemoaned Hekmatyar's decision in 1985

to refuse a meeting with President Ronald Reagan as 'a grave error in judgment...
confirming the US in its view that such men in power in Kabul would be as dangerous as the communists'.[84] Nevertheless, there were never any doubts that Hekmatyar
was one of the main resistance leaders. He, like Rabbani, appeared time and again in
reporting on the conflict, and he increasingly undertook trips abroad to represent
both Hizb-i Islami and the broader Afghan resistance. Even as foreign powers and
Afghans alike questioned his refusal to cooperate for any stretch with the other parties, as splits emerged within his party, and as some fighters baulked at Hizb-i Islami's
policies, Hekmatyar remained a key figure in the Afghan resistance.[85]

Hekmatyar saw Jam'iyyat, Rabbani, and particularly Massoud as threats to Hizb-i
Islami's victory. Tensions between the two groups that had pre-existed the PDPA
coup boiled over in wartime. Massoud, his international reputation, and his successes on the ground clearly posed a menace to Hizb-i Islami domination. Hekmatyar
was particularly incensed by Massoud's decision to negotiate a truce with the Soviets
in 1983. Not only did this indicate that foreign powers like the Soviets took Massoud
seriously as a leader within the resistance, but Massoud used the truce to seize control of Andarab, a district neighbouring Panjshir that had been under the control of
a Hizb-i Islami ally, Juma Khan. Hizb-i Islami fighters cut off the trails that linked
Massoud's command centres to Pakistan-based weapon and aid supply chains, trying to weaken Jam'iyyat's war effort. In 1984, clashes broke out between Jam'iyyat
and Hizb-i Islami combatants after the death of several Jam'iyyat commanders in a
firefight with Hizb-i Islami militants.[86] Soviet observers looked on with delight.
They, too, saw Massoud's state-building efforts as a threat. A report in *Mirror of the
Jehad* detailing the fifth offensive on Panjshir in 1982 noted that Soviet forces focused
on attacking civilian locations. This was intended to deflate morale, lose Jam'iyyat
followers, and destroy Panjshiris' homes and livelihoods. The Soviets 'had done a lot
of propaganda about the defeat and annihilation of Mujahideen and restoration of
the so-called law and order in the Valley', the publication reported. Most significantly, Soviets then 'declared that they were busy with voluntary developmental
works in the inauguration of schools, distribution of consumption material among
the people etc.'.[87] Ironically, the Soviets replicated Jam'iyyat's work to prove their
own support for the Afghan people.

Hekmatyar's actions failed to undermine Massoud's reputation, which continued
to compete with Hekmatyar's own. Massoud presented Jam'iyyat as a clear, viable
alternative to Hizb-i Islami, one that awed international audiences took seriously. In
an interview released as part of the French documentary 'A Valley against an Empire',
Massoud explained:

I think there are four reasons [for the resistance's success]. The first reason is that
my combat troops like to wage war against an enemy in order to attain *Jannad*; if
we die we attain or *Jannad*.

Interviewer: Jehad?

Massoud: Jannad.

Interviewer: You mean the Holy War?

Massoud: Jannad, Jannad, the Garden of God... Yes, you know what I am talking about?

Interviewer: You mean that the *mujahidin* who die reach the Garden of God?

Massoud: They reach *Jannad* and because of that they are not afraid to die. The first thing is the help of God. The second thing is that the *mujahidin* are all very courageous and now for the war they are complete, how do you say it, complete?

Interviewer: They are prepared.

Massoud: They are prepared to begin the war, to continue the war. The third thing is the structure of the valley, the mountains and rivers; for us it is an advantage, but not for the enemy. The fourth thing is that the enemy doesn't know us, he doesn't know the way and doesn't know the mountains and other things.

What is striking in Massoud's interview is not only his focus on victory but his contrast with Hekmatyar. He credited his fighters and geography for his success rather than self-aggrandising. The documentary breathlessly concluded: 'Neither rebels nor outlaws nor wild mountaineers, we discovered in the Panshir Valley an organized people's resistance being developed. It has already won a battle over despair, disorder and fanaticism.'[88] However, the resistance's ongoing battles—with the Soviets and PDPA and within itself between parties such as Hizb-i Islami and Jam'iyyat—demonstrated that this was far from the truth. Instead, a war persisted between competing Islamist visions of Afghanistan's future alongside a war against socialist aggression.

Jam'iyyat and Hekmatyar's Hizb-i Islami came closest to putting some of their ideas into practice during the 1980s, though all of their efforts, too, were limited by the need to prioritize the war against the PDPA and the Soviets. Nevertheless, their range of non-military activities gives some idea of how they envisioned their leadership in a socialist-free Afghanistan. Much like the PDPA, Jam'iyyat and Hizb-i Islami engaged with international audiences at the same time that they appealed to Afghans inside and outside Afghanistan. They also interacted with their regional hosts, mobilized Afghan exiles, worked with refugees in Pakistan, and coordinated with resistance fighters who continued to be based in Afghanistan. But they differed in their political structures, their willingness to work with non-party members, and, ultimately, in the ways they envisioned a functioning Islamist Afghanistan. While Hekmatyar and his party, much like the PDPA, tended towards an authoritarian view where Hizb-i Islami enjoyed single-party rule, Rabbani, Massoud, and their partnership with each other and other resistance commanders illustrated more moderate, inclusive methods that gradually melded local political and social dynamics into Jam'iyyat practices. Comparing Jam'iyyat and Hizb-i Islami demonstrates two different routes that an Islamist Afghanistan could have taken.

But the fact remained that, despite the prominent spotlight placed on the political parties and leaders such as Hekmatyar or Massoud, they neither controlled nor were fully representative of the Afghan resistance. Their planning and activities took place against the backdrop of a widescale insurgency. Discrepancies emerged between the Peshawar-based resistance and militants who remained within Afghanistan. While the resistance parties in Pakistan were the recipients and distributors of foreign funding, many remained reliant on commanders and combatants located predominantly within Afghanistan to undertake the war against the Soviets and PDPA. This convoluted power dynamics, as party leaders depended on local commanders to combat their enemies, even as they had the benefit of international attention, money, and supplies. In order to spread their influence, the Peshawar parties had to make agreements and alliances with commanders based in Afghanistan. Because 'these parties had a limited number of activists in their ranks, the only viable option was to recruit existing strongmen and warlords inside Afghanistan [who] would be attracted by the offer of weapons and other supplies'.[89] While internal recruits became party members in name, they did not necessarily share the same ideological motivations. Accepting party membership in return for provisions was a pragmatic choice.

As the war progressed, the role of the exiled political parties remained unclear, in large part because of the sheer number of competing factions. Some Afghan-based warlords became increasingly independent. Famed commanders like Massoud could reach out directly to international supporters while also taking advantage of party links, but others manipulated local circumstances for their own benefit. Resistance leaders in Helmand, for example, took advantage of local opium production. In Musa Qala, in northern Helmand, Nasim Akhundzada, while affiliated with the moderate Harakat-i Inqilab-i Islami party, became largely self-sufficient by taxing poppy growth, opening an office in Zahidan, Iran, to oversee opium export and accepting additional funding from KhAD, the government secret service, which feared the spread of Hizb-i Islami's influence and was willing to pay other resistance fighters to restrict party growth.[90]

Political party activities also had unintended consequences. While Hekmatyar's Hizb-i Islami, Jam'iyyat, and increasingly the Saudi-favoured Ittihad-i Islami, under Sayyaf's leadership, received the majority of ISI aid, other parties developed their own networks and activities. Khalis's Hizb-i Islami and Harakat-i Inqilab-i Islami coordinated with Jam'iyyat-i 'Ulama'-i Islam, Pakistan's Deoband political party, and Jalaluddin Haqqani, an Islamic scholar from the Afghan–Pakistan borderlands who had developed a strong sense of traditionalist 'Pashtun Islamism' rooted in local tribal mobilization. This coalition pursued the establishment of new seminaries along the Afghan–Pakistan border, welcoming young Afghan refugees and targeting their transformation into *mujahidin*. They succeeded in creating a network of *madrassas* and mechanisms for recruiting and training new followers. Not only did this serve as the basis for the future Haqqani network, with Haqqani, himself, taking an active role in mobilizing Afghan Arabs, but many young Afghan *taliban*, or students, were attracted to Deobandi Islam and found leadership within its *madrassas*.[91]

One such young man, Abdul Salam Zaeef, whose family had fled Afghanistan in 1979, was inspired by elders in his refugee camp affiliated with Harakat-i Inqilab-i Islami and Ittihad-i Islami to join the resistance in 1983 at the age of 15. He quickly became disillusioned with 'carrying out mundane tasks for other people', according to his memoir, and he 'decided to go to Nelgham to join the *Taliban*', by which he meant the religious students largely affiliated with Harakat-i Inqilab-i Islami. He explained: 'A group of religious scholars and students with different backgrounds...They were fighting out of their deep religious belief in *jihad* and the faith in God...unlike many other *mujahedeen* who fought for money or land.'[92] It was from this milieu that the Taliban movement of the 1990s would emerge as a source of opposition to the Afghan resistance parties, and Zaeef would go on to become a key Taliban leader.

From the mid- to late 1980s, the growing number of Afghan Arabs, the foreign fighters from across the world who came to take part in a *jihad*, also began changing the tenor of the conflict. Another Afghan resistance fighter, Massood Farivar, recollected in his memoir:

> While we called our struggle a jihad, a holy war, we were fighting first and foremost to liberate our country. The Arabs, who saw us as lesser Muslims, were seeking heavenly rewards. The more politically minded of these fighters declared, with a fierce conviction I could never understand, that 'jihad will go on until the green flag of Islam flutters over Moscow and Washington'—an ominous utterance we shrugged off as the rhetorical ejaculation of misguided men.[93]

The war against the Soviets accrued new, different meanings as foreign fighters became involved not to liberate Afghanistan but for their own purposes.

The Soviet–Afghan war, which coincided and intersected with growing interest in party politics and alternative senses of Afghanistan's future, wrought huge changes to the politics of resistance in Afghanistan. What had begun as localized conflicts in response to direct PDPA and Soviet interventions developed into a different war, one in which, for the first time, political parties undertook an active role in forming and directing a rebellion. In this sense, the war against the Soviets served as a potential catalyst and a modernizing force that could undermine both socialist and pre-socialist structures in Afghanistan. It created influential roles for political parties, bodies that previously had little clout in Afghanistan, and it brought political Islam to the fore, a new vision of Islam that fused religious and political practices and did not just rely on the age-old slogan of 'Islam in danger' to mobilize support.

In turn, the parties brought forward a host of ideas concerning the future of Afghanistan. Circumstances increasingly placed international attention on Afghan Islamists while downplaying other parties' pleas for moderate liberalization, a return to a constitutional monarchy, or parliamentarianism. Afghan Islamists benefited from what regional and international leaders increasingly perceived as a competition between Islamism and socialism, which in turn became fact in the way that aid was provided to the resistance. Thus, some parties, Jam'iyyat and Hizb-i Islami at the forefront, began considering and implementing the structures that could carry through from war-torn battlefield to post-conflict state-building. And, like the PDPA, Jam'iyyat and Hizb-i Islami sought to reshape Afghan politics in fundamentally new ways.

Despite their intertwined histories, Hizb-i Islami's and Jam'iyyat's activities from 1980 onwards provided two starkly different models of Afghan Islamist modernity.

Jamʿiyyat's was more accommodating and envisioned an evolving Afghan polity that became increasingly Islamist and ideologically tied to Jamʿiyyat through the careful political wrangling of its commanders and the party's willingness to integrate existing local political and social structures. Hizb-i Islami, in contrast, much more closely resembled the early PDPA: intent on single-party rule, rigidly and hierarchically organized, and intolerant of alternative viewpoints. It is perhaps interesting to note that, while the PDPA became more and more yielding as the war progressed, Hizb-i Islami became even more stubbornly inflexible. This allowed Hekmatyar to build a cult of personality and to position his party as the sole arbiter of Afghan modernity, but, equally, it undermined chances for cooperation across the resistance. As a united whole, the problem remained that the parties lacked a clear consensus or authority to implement ideas for a future, post-conflict Afghanistan.

A final issue particularly limited the influence of the Peshawar-based parties: their exclusion from the UN-led talks on the Soviet occupation. The parties' claims to legitimacy and leadership were unsurprisingly undermined by their absence from the negotiations that would ultimately lead to the Soviet withdrawal. As much as resistance party leaders claimed to represent Afghanistan, UN observers saw them as non-state actors—or state claimants rather than state leaders. The fact that the parties were largely active outside of Afghan territory undermined their declarations of sovereign power. Resistance leaders continued to lobby the UN for inclusion in the peace talks but with little success. In October 1985, for example, Hekmatyar sent a heated letter to Javier Perez de Cuellar, secretary-general of the UN, declaring: 'it appears to us to be the height of hypocrisy for the United Nations Organization to repeatedly condemn Soviet intervention in Afghanistan while at the same time recognizing the representative of the regime installed by the Soviet Union as the legitimate representative of the Afghan people.'[94] Jamʿiyyat leaders similarly attacked the Geneva Accords through which the Soviets agreed to withdraw their troops.

However, such protests fell on deaf ears. Resistance leaders remained helpless bystanders, watching as Afghanistan's future was negotiated without their input. Consequently, the parties had only a limited ability to shape talks through their Pakistani and American allies and also were given almost no say on how a withdrawal should progress—or what it should lead to. They, much like the PDPA, remained constrained by the major international powers of the time. While the Soviets oversaw the PDPA, increasingly the United States took a key role in shaping the international community's approach to the Soviet–Afghan war. In a fundamental irony and tragedy of the conflict, American policymakers did not recognize how the resistance political parties represented an alternative vision of Afghan modernity. Instead, they returned to colonial-era tropes of Afghans as backward, feudal, and tribal to understand the Soviet–Afghan war and determine the US role in it. Because the United States refused to identify an opportunity for new, alternative forms of Afghan politics, the resistance itself also came to be limited in implementing such visions of a revolutionized Afghan polity.

# 6
# Washington

On 10 March 1982, a televised special ceremony took place in the East Room of the White House. Upon the podium sat President Ronald Reagan; members of his administration, including Vice-President George H. W. Bush; and a young Afghan refugee living on the west coast of the United States, Nahid Mojadidi. Mojadidi stepped up to the podium, where she haltingly spoke 'on behalf of the future generation of Afghans who hope to live in a free and independent Afghanistan' about her experiences of the Soviet war. She declared: 'We will continue our fight, our war,' before presenting President Reagan with an Afghan flag. Amid loud applause, Reagan and Mojadidi embraced before Reagan himself turned to the microphone (see Figure 6.1).[1]

'Today, we recognize a nation of unsung heroes whose courageous struggle is one of the epics of our time. The Afghan people have matched their heroism against the most terrifying weapons of modern warfare in the Soviet arsenal.' Reagan went on, 'We cannot and will not turn our backs on this struggle. Few acts of international aggression have been so universally condemned.' He told his audience and viewers at home that 21 March (not incidentally Nowruz, the Persian New Year, celebrated by Afghans) would be observed as Afghanistan Day: 'a true celebration, and not just for freedom in Afghanistan, but, for freedom wherever it is threatened or suppressed the world over.'[2]

In his speech, the president emphasized the United States' humanitarian contributions to the desperate Afghan refugee crisis, pointing to $200 million in support over the past two years as well as a further pledge of $21.3 million in food aid. In contrast, no mention was made of the extensive covert aid funnelled via America's CIA to Pakistan's ISI and thereafter to Afghan resistance fighters. This military and financial backing, not humanitarian aid, comprised the bulk of US support in the Afghan war. By 1987, the United States was providing an annual $700 million in military assistance to the Afghan resistance, and covert aid cost American taxpayers more than $3 billion over the course of the 1980s.[3]

For the United States, the Soviet invasion of Afghanistan created an international crisis, one that could not be separated from the global Cold War. In a worldwide conflict between East and West, and capitalist and communist models of modernity, the Soviet Union could not be allowed to extend its influence. Fears of Soviet expansion had precipitated American international operations ever since the end of the Second World War—all-out war in Korea and Vietnam, anti-Soviet, pro-American propaganda campaigns across the world, domestic and foreign political manipulation, and the extension of American power through forms of economic and political aid or

**Figure 6.1.** Ronald Reagan meeting Nahid Mojadidi (Ronald Reagan Presidential Library)

cultural diplomacy. While great power tensions had temporarily cooled during the era of detente (roughly 1969–74), they threatened to resume as the Soviets intervened first in Angola and then in the Horn of Africa to shore up Marxist regimes. Zbigniew Brzezinski, Jimmy Carter's national security advisor, warned during the crisis in the Horn that the Soviets 'must understand that there are consequences in their behavior. If we do not react, we are destroying our own posture.'[4] While the immediate consequences in east Africa remained limited, this would not be the case in Afghanistan. The scale of the Soviet intervention, coming, as it did, on the heels of the Kremlin's meddling in Africa and alongside the Iranian revolution, made Afghanistan the site of an American stand against Soviet expansionism.

In the eyes of the Carter administration, the coup in Afghanistan, alongside events in Iran, signalled that all was not well for American regional, or global, interests. Officials saw the People's Democratic Party of Afghanistan and its leader, Nur Mohammad Taraki, as 'a pro-Soviet Communist organization', which increasingly relied on the Soviet Union for aid. The overthrow of Iran's Shah in early 1979 and his replacement with the militantly anti-American Ayatollah Khomeini left US policymakers bereft of one of their key regional allies and oil suppliers. Almost immediately after the Soviet invasion of Afghanistan, President Carter declared in his State of the Union address that an arc of crisis existed in South-West Asia—a threat to 'all those who rely on oil from the Middle East and who are concerned with global peace and stability'. In what came to be known as the Carter doctrine, and which would be further developed under Reagan, US national security policy placed a premium on

ring-fencing Soviet influence and reinforcing the security of Afghanistan's neighbours. Soviet influence could not be allowed to spread any further.[5]

The ongoing civil war in Afghanistan provided a critical opportunity for US officials to pursue this doctrine. Covert aid to the widespread Afghan resistance became
central to the policies of containing and rolling back Soviet influence in South-West
Asia, while widely publicized humanitarian aid underpinned American claims to be
upholding Afghan 'freedom'. Yet US policymakers had little interest in the future of
Afghanistan. As Marshall Shulman, special advisor on Soviet affairs to Carter's secretary of state, recalled in the mid-1990s: 'It was not the strategic importance of the
area that concerned me, but I felt that we had to respond to the use of force on a
large scale across the border in a way that might set a precedent.' American leaders
felt the need to respond to Soviet aggression and prevent the spread of Soviet strategic interests, not to intervene on behalf of Afghans who protested socialist rule.
While Soviet policymakers were driven by concerns about the PDPA's stability and
ideological strength, US officials concentrated on the 'Soviet overhang' in the Persian
Gulf.[6] As such, they did not recognize Soviet focus on reinforcing Afghan socialism
and, later on, keeping the PDPA in power. Instead, they deliberated how to make the
best possible use of resistance to keep both Soviets and the PDPA embroiled in war
within Afghanistan.

American thinking regarding the Afghan resistance thus ultimately undermined
both socialist and Islamist efforts to modernize Afghanistan and gave little consideration to Afghan experiences on the ground. US engagement with resistance fighters, even while filtered through Pakistan's ISI, was coloured by American reliance on
British colonial-era images of Afghans as backward, feudal, and tribal. Officials recognized neither the PDPA's nor the resistance leaders' visions of Afghan modernity,
nor did they take seriously either's attempts to reshape Afghan politics and society.
In American eyes, the PDPA were mere Soviet lackeys, especially after December
1979, while resistance heads, traditionalist and Islamist alike, were dismissed as a
ragtag collection of parochial leaders with little political capability. For US officials,
this did not matter. While American rhetoric focused on the Afghan freedom
struggle, little actual planning went into what a 'free' Afghan state should look like.
Reagan did not conflate freedom with democracy, and his officials gave minimal
thought to the present or future of the Afghans they aided or to what the Afghan
state should become. Their focus on halting and undermining Soviet expansionism
did not require a united resistance that agreed on a vision for a post-withdrawal
Afghanistan. Over the course of the 1980s, the billions of American dollars pumped
into Afghanistan, whether as arms and weapons or blankets and tents, did little more
than encourage divisions, ongoing violence, and displacement.

In April 1978, Afghanistan was not the United States' main concern. Jimmy Carter
was far more interested in brokering peace talks in the Middle East, which would
result later that year in the Camp David Accords, continuing talks on strategic arms
limitations, and pursuing his human-rights agenda. Negotiations on SALT II inched

forward, but detente had been seriously rattled by the crises in Africa, particularly Soviet military supplies to Ethiopia's revolutionary Marxist regime, as well as ongoing trials of Soviet dissidents that clashed with Carter's support for human rights. As Shulman recollected:

> This was the closing phase of decolonization. What this meant...was that there was a new fluidity in international politics. It opened up new opportunities for competition and conflict in places such as Angola, Mozambique, and Ethiopia. This upset the definition of detente as it had been understood in the Nixon–Kissinger era.

Carter warned that Soviet actions undermined good relations between the super-powers, and delayed SALT talks. Circumstances were further complicated by the unrest faced by the United States' staunch ally, the Shah of Iran. Against the backdrop of myriad international concerns and uncertainty about the future of Soviet–American relations, the PDPA's sudden rise to power came as a shock.[7]

American interest in Daoud's regime had been limited, though officials kept an eye on how Afghan poppy production might shape the United States' declared 'War on Drugs'. Counter-narcotics, however, did not prepare officials for the abrupt emergence of the socialist regime. Instead, as Bruce Flatin, a career diplomat who served in Afghanistan in 1977–9, put it, the PDPA-led coup

> was our first look at the Afghan communist party. As we said at the time, it was like watching the Loch Ness monster rising out of the water. We were able to see the nature of this large and well-organized movement for the first time. What had been as often described in rumors was at last out in the open.

While the coup came as a shock, officials in the Department of State dismissed rumours that the Soviets had been behind the PDPA. 'Although they had probably become somewhat disillusioned with President Daoud, we do not think they would have tried to take over this important non-aligned country,' they wrote to President Carter.[8]

Yet both the American press and government officials were quick to label the PDPA 'communist', despite Taraki's careful efforts to present the party and the DRA as politically non-aligned. Embassy officers were critical of Taraki's early public statements, expressing 'surprise that the Communists have taken over complete power openly' and presciently warning: 'The devout traditionalist majority of this society hardly seems ready to accept the leadership of what is, relatively speaking, a minuscule Communist elite'. While Taraki sought formal recognition from the United States and assured embassy officials that the PDPA's focus was a strong, independent Afghanistan, President Carter told the American media: 'The question is not one of recognition, but of whether diplomatic relations should continue'. Nevertheless, the United States extended recognition to the DRA on 6 May.[9]

One of the great ironies of the PDPA coup was that both Nur Mohammad Taraki and Hafizullah Amin were well known to US officials. Frank Schmelzer, a career foreign service officer, remembered encountering Taraki first as a translator for the Afghan embassy in India and later as a press attaché with the embassy in Washington. 'I knew he hated the royal family. I knew he had socialist leanings and wanted Afghanistan to advance in one hell of a hurry. But I did not know that he was forming the Communist Party of Afghanistan. Apparently no one else did either.' Taraki had even worked as a translator for the US Information Service in the US embassy. Richard Ross, a cultural affairs officer in Kabul from 1977–9, remembered: 'They said, "It couldn't have been Taraki! Why that mild-mannered man with those thick glasses, who sat there and read the Persian language press then told the political officer what it said? He, he, he…it's not him!" Oh, but oh, yes it was!' Meanwhile, Amin had attended Columbia University's teachers' college as either a Fulbright student or a USAID recipient (accounts differ). Officers familiar with Amin agreed that he had struggled in the programme and 'came away from that experience with a great deal of anti-Americanism. It festered over the years and eventually obviously showed up.'[10]

In the immediate aftermath of the coup, Ambassador Theodore Eliot dramatically wrote to the State Department: '[What] the British fought to prevent for over one hundred years—and what the Shah has regarded as one of his worst nightmares— has finally occurred. Direct Russian influence appears to have moved south of the Oxus and the Hindu Kush.' He went on to admit: 'We do not yet know with any degree of certitude the degree of Soviet orientation of Afghanistan's new communist regime. Are we dealing with a Bulgaria, a Yugoslavia—or, perhaps, with an eventual Afghan SSR?' Another report, in contrast, suggested the Soviets had little do with the coup. 'Although the Soviets are probably not displeased with events, they may be cautious about exerting overt and conspicuous influence in order not to unduly alarm Afghanistan's neighbors.'[11] Clearly the US embassy was unsure of the direction that the new Afghan regime intended to take, but fear of Soviet manipulation was rampant. Was Afghanistan to be subsumed into the Union of Soviet Socialist Republics? Would it maintain a degree of independence? Matters on the ground were murky.

What remained obvious, however, was that the PDPA's coup threatened to disrupt the region. American officials worried about the coup's impact on neighbouring Pakistan and Iran, fears that were exacerbated by correspondence with local leaders. Pakistan's General Zia dramatically spelled out the United States' own anxieties: 'We know that the Afghan barrier has been breached and our country lies directly in the path of the flood which rolled out of Czarist Russia in the last century and is now flowing in full force towards the Indian Ocean and the Persian Gulf.' It was not just a matter of Soviet expansionism, though this was the major concern. Ambassador Eliot went on to muse: 'Now that the communists have revealed the true nature of the coup regime, will effective opposition arise? Many observers here think that eventuality is highly probable in devout, traditionalist Afghanistan.' Eliot pointed out the PDPA's major flaw—that its ambitions did not match those of most Afghans, particularly those living outside of Kabul. In this regard, US analysis was perceptive in predicting the quick rise of countrywide resistance to the PDPA. And the United States would ultimately take advantage of this potential for resistance in order to prevent Soviet advancement.[12]

Initial US engagement with the PDPA reflected the uncertainty expressed by Eliot in the immediate aftermath of the coup. US development aid haltingly continued, and a series of American officials met Taraki and his colleagues. But the upsurge in Soviet economic funding and the increasingly visible presence of Soviet advisors seemed to indicate Afghanistan's Marxist turn. Eliot soon left his post to be replaced by Ambassador Adolph 'Spike' Dubs. Before he departed, Eliot met Taraki one last time in June 1978. The prime minister asked the ambassador to pass on several messages to 'Comrade' Carter. Taraki sought to assure the president that 'Afghanistan remains independent and will never be a satellite of any country', and he followed up these promises with a request for additional economic aid—more than $100 million— to provide Afghans with 'food, clothing, and shelter'. Eliot noted discouragingly: 'his approach to meeting these needs was clearly via infrastructure and heavy industry projects [as modelled by the Soviet Union throughout the twentieth century]. Our poor majority focus, with its emphasis on agriculture, education and health did not excite him.'

Eliot also went on the offensive during the meeting. He questioned Taraki's claim that Afghanistan acted independently, pointing out that 'the international positions his government had so far expressed in Havana and New York, and in the Kabul press, ranging from African to disarmament projects, suggested that Afghan foreign policy was no different from that of the Soviet Union'. He went on to warn: 'If this identity of policies persisted, the American people would inevitably raise questions about Afghanistan's independence and nonalignment.' Eliot subsequently confided to the State Department: 'I came away ever more convinced that relations between our two governments will never be close, and that rocky times may lie ahead.'[13]

The fate of Ambassador Dubs sealed the American conviction that Afghanistan's trajectory did not align with the United States. Dubs was a veteran of the Second World War and a career diplomat, the son of German immigrants from Russia, who spoke numerous languages and rose to be one of the State Department's top Kremlinologists. His university friends had nicknamed him 'Spike', since he shared a first name with Hitler, a nickname that stuck with him in the foreign service. Upon arriving in Kabul, Dubs was initially cautious. In an early statement of US policy towards Afghanistan, he argued: 'Although the Democratic Republic of Afghanistan (DRA) has leftist antecedents, we believe it premature to attempt to characterize it with some degree of accuracy or to attach a specific label to it. The signals are mixed.' He noted Afghan officials' efforts to distinguish their country from the Soviet Union and argued that options needed to be left open. James Taylor, a political officer in the US embassy in Kabul at the time, described Dubs's approach as 'yes these guys are pretty bad, but they are in control…If we don't work with them we might as well go home.'[14] Had Dubs remained in control in Kabul, perhaps US policy towards the PDPA might have remained more moderate and the decision to provide covert aid to the Afghan resistance taken less quickly. But this was not to be. On the morning of 14 February 1979, Dubs's armoured car was pulled over on his way to work, and the ambassador was taken hostage. Within a matter of hours, he was dead.

The death of Spike Dubs remains a contested event. What is known is that, shortly before 9 a.m., a man dressed in an Afghan police uniform flagged down Dubs's car. After asking the driver to roll down the car's windows, the man put a gun to the driver's head and demanded the car doors be unlocked, at which point three other men jumped into the car. They directed the driver at gunpoint to the Kabul Hotel, one of the capital's most popular hotels, especially among foreigners and tourists. The men hustled Dubs into a hotel room several floors up, while the driver, who was allowed to leave, promptly reported what had happened to the US embassy.

Bruce Flatin immediately rushed to the hotel, leading a team of ten from the embassy, where he encountered Afghan police and military men and Soviet embassy officials. They told him that 'terrorists' had seized Dubs and were demanding the release of several anti-regime Afghan leaders before they would free the ambassador. American officials in the hotel and the embassy tried to persuade the Afghan government not to take precipitous action to secure Dubs by force. 'I was assured by the Afghans and the Soviets that they would not endanger the Ambassador. I was assured they were going to do their best to negotiate,' remembered Flatin. 'But later in the morning…it was clear they had received an order to hit the room…At a certain point there was a loud shot and then a gun fight lasted exactly 40 seconds…The floor just shook with the gun fire coming from the hallway where I was standing and from the bank building across the street into the room.' Upon entering the room, Flatin and the other Americans saw that the room had flooded, owing to a radiator burst in the gunfight. 'When the whole thing was over there could not have been one cubic centimeter in that room that didn't have a bullet pass through it. A gnat flying in that room would have been hit.' Of the three suspected terrorists, one was dead, one was heavily wounded, and one was being held captive, a paper bag over his head. Dubs was slumped over in a chair. He had suffered multiple gunshot wounds.

Who killed Dubs and why remains unknown, though speculation has persisted that the PDPA was behind his death. What is clear, however, is that the ambassador's death had immediate ramifications for the United States' relations with Afghanistan. As a consequence of his assassination, and anger with the Afghan government's decision to storm the hotel room where he was being held, US–Afghan relations soured. US officials terminated aid operations in the country, removed Peace Corps volunteers, and halted economic support. The American embassy presence was scaled back, as lower-level officials were redeployed outside the country. 'We just had essentially a listening post,' remembered Taylor, a point reflected in the decrease in official reporting.[15] By the summer of 1979, US–DRA interactions were minimal.

This is not to say that the United States had lost interest in Afghanistan and its future. Concerns about deepening Soviet relations with the regime in Kabul ran alongside increasing awareness of the anti-government resistance growing across the country. As early as 14 July 1978, the CIA had reported that 'anti-government groups may be able to organize resistance and may attempt counterrevolution', noting growing military and civilian discontent with the PDPA. Indeed, combatants had approached J. Bruce Amstutz, an embassy official, in June seeking support for a counter-coup. Less than five months after the 'Saur Revolution', a National Security Council aide and South Asia specialist, Tom Thornton, wrote to Brzezinski: 'As you are probably aware, things in Afghanistan are deteriorating rapidly: the regime is devouring its children with amazing speeds; its base of support is narrowing; Soviet influence is probably growing; and there appears to be quite a bit of spontaneous opposition outside of Kabul.' While Thornton made no policy recommendations, he desired 'to make sure you are keeping this unfortunate situation in mind'.[16]

As the DRA fell increasingly into disarray with infighting among members of the PDPA, growing numbers of Soviet civilian and military advisors on the ground, and violent resistance breaking out in areas across the country, Thornton was right to point out a deteriorating situation. Zbigniew Brzezinski, effectively the architect of much of Carter's foreign policy, clearly agreed. Brzezinski, the son of Polish diplomats who had chosen to remain in Canada rather than return to Soviet-controlled Poland, had obtained his doctorate from Harvard and taught at Columbia University, beginning to work with the State Department in the mid-1960s. He was militantly anti-Soviet, though he flip-flopped in his policy positions, beginning as a staunch supporter of the American war in French Indochina/Vietnam but later protesting against President Johnson's decision to extend the US war effort. He was ruthless and outspoken, to the extent that Carter's secretary of state, Cyrus Vance, ultimately resigned rather than work with him. The overriding belief driving Brzezinski was that Soviet expansion must be stopped at all costs. As such, his position on Afghanistan was unsurprising.[17]

The death of Dubs precipitated a new request by Brzezinski for a 'coherent and systematic plan for Afghanistan', which led to governmental discussions about providing covert aid to Afghan rebels, though no clear consensus emerged for or against. The March 1979 Herat revolt stimulated fresh interest in the resistance, much as it aggravated Soviet concerns about the PDPA's reign. While the Soviets subsequently increased their aid to the PDPA, even while refusing to send in armed forces, the US State and Defense Departments, alongside the CIA, debated the merits of engaging with the resistance. A special meeting of top government officials on 6 April 1979 directed the CIA to begin exploratory talks with Pakistan's ISI about potential financial, training, and material support for insurgent groups. On 3 July, President Jimmy Carter authorized limited financial support for the growing number of Afghan resistance fighters. Aid was distributed by America's Pakistani allies, even though relations between the two states remained frigid at this stage thanks to Zia's continuing quest for nuclear power.

Later on, in a 1998 interview, Brzezinski would gloatingly claim that America's intention was to give 'the USSR their own Vietnam'. This overstated matters.

If anything, the subsequent Soviet intervention more closely mirrored the United States' 1965 invasion of the Dominican Republic, where American troops were similarly deployed to ensure political stability and avoid the appearance of being soft on communism in America's own backyard (the main difference was that US engagement in the DR did not turn into a decade-long quagmire). In reality, the initial amount provided to the Afghan resistance was small, about $500,000, and intended to provide non-military support. Of course, it would grow as the situation became more serious, but the original provision was certainly inadequate to force a Soviet armed intervention. Instead it adhered to broader US practices of providing limited covert support to anti-communist forces worldwide.[18]

Covert operations had been key to US foreign policy throughout the Second World War, and the growing tensions between the United States and Soviet Union in the aftermath of conflict had led to the establishment of the CIA in 1947 under President Harry Truman. From then, the CIA had played a key role in US Cold-War strategy, providing opportunities for the government surreptitiously to promote American interests abroad, obstruct Soviet policy, support allies across the world, and undermine, even topple, perceived enemies of the United States. As the Cold War became global, CIA operations correspondingly expanded. CIA operatives orchestrated the 1953 coup that ousted Iran's prime minister, Mohammad Mossadegh, and worked with mercenaries to overthrow the newly independent government of Patrice Lumumba in the Congo in the early 1960s. This is not to say that US covert operations were always successful. The Bay of Pigs fiasco, in which the CIA spectacularly failed to launch a counter-revolution against Fidel Castro, brought renewed scrutiny to American covert operations, as well as international embarrassment to the Kennedy administration. In the 1970s, CIA agents also failed to install a friendly regime in Angola, despite spending $32 million in 1975 alone. Covert operations and aid nevertheless remained a hallmark of US foreign policy. As Stansfield Turner, director of the CIA under Carter, recalled: 'I always felt that my responsibility when there was a major development in foreign policy was to ask the Agency people whether there was something we could contribute in a covert way.' US officials under Ronald Reagan would provide covert support for the right-wing anti-Marxist contras in Nicaragua, alongside the extensive funds that the CIA funnelled to Afghan resistance movements.[19]

US concerns in Afghanistan were regional and global, rather than focused on, or interested in, specific local dynamics. Unrest in Iran was a far more pressing concern, but one that linked to potential developments in Afghanistan. As Gary Sick, who served on Carter's National Security Council, later explained:

> in terms of US objectives, there was a very strong perception of a strategy in collapse. Because of Mozambique, Ethiopia, South Yemen, and certainly the events in Iran, there was in the United States a perception that, regardless of whether there was a Soviet 'grand design' or not, our strategic position was collapsing.

Within the Carter administration, some officials feared that the Soviets had a hand in the Iranian Revolution. Taken alongside Afghanistan's turn to socialism, the United States, according to Sick, had 'to apply a tourniquet to stop the flow of blood...it had less to do with any Soviet design, or the lack of a design, than it did with simply perceiving that US interests in the region were being severely harmed and something had to be done'.[20]

This provided the rationale for the United States to support the Afghan resistance— a verdict that predated the Soviet decision to intervene. Indeed, in the autumn of 1979, embassy officials in Kabul sent anxious reports to Washington about the increased stationing of Soviet airborne troops 'just north of the Oxus', and, in a memorandum to President Carter on 4 October 1979, Brzezinski pointed to the visit of General Ivan Pavlovskii, chief of Soviet ground forces, as a clear sign of deteriorating circumstances in Afghanistan and a corresponding swell in Soviet influence. 'Pavlovskii's presence suggests we are unlikely to see a sudden Soviet military intervention, instead', he wrote dramatically, 'the intervention is now in progress with a slow buildup of advisers and security forces'. He ominously warned: 'By the time the Pavlovskii mission is complete, a *de facto* Soviet military intervention may well be the case'. An advisor to the secretary of state pithily pointed out:

> In the beginning, we simply talked about 'Soviet military intervention'; *however*, with a $275 million military assistance program in process and 3,000 or more advisors in the country, this has already occurred. Subsequently, we talked about 'the introduction of Soviet combat units'; *however*, with the introduction in June 1979 of a security force of 400 Soviet troops at Bagram airbase, this has already occurred. Lately, we have talked about 'large scale Soviet intervention'; *however*, with an earlier report of 3,600 Soviet military personnel in Kabul and a more recent report of 500–1,000 Soviet advisors arriving at two Afghan armored divisions nearby, this may also have occurred or be in progress.[21]

The significance of all of this was that, when the actual Soviet invasion did take place in December, the United States already had in place the mechanisms for expanding covert aid into what would become a war against the Soviet Union, not just a counter-insurgency against an unpopular Afghan regime.

The Soviet invasion destroyed the need for caution. As one National Security Council (NSC) staff member wrote almost immediately, 'The speciousness and bald-faced arrogance of the Soviet action can hardly be exaggerated...We need a clear, sharp and unequivocal response, which should be given full play by all our communications media'. It not only brought into question the future of the Afghan state but aggravated fears about the security of the Persian Gulf. President Carter issued a sharp rebuke to Brezhnev, telling him:

> My Government can in no way accept the Soviet Government's explanation...that Soviet military forces were sent in Afghanistan at the request of the leadership of

that country. The facts of the matter clearly show that these same Soviet forces were employed to overthrow the established government of Afghanistan and to impose a new government.[22]

If there was a silver lining, however, the intervention placed the United States on the 'right' side of history. The Soviet invasion of Afghanistan was highly publicized and met with widespread criticism. Debates in the UN General Assembly accused the Soviets of undermining another nation state's independence and taking unlawful action. Brzezinski at once pointed out: 'There are already 300,000 refugees from Afghanistan in Pakistan, and we will be in a position to indict the Soviets for causing massive human suffering.' At this stage, the clear choice for President Carter was to associate the United States with the Afghans resisting Soviet expansion, and thereby to increase US provisions to the resistance. As Brzezinski warned Carter a day after the intervention: 'the Soviets might be able to assert themselves effectively, and in world politics nothings succeeds like success, whatever the moral aspects.' Consequently, he believed: 'It is essential that Afghanistani [*sic*] resistance continues. This means more money as well as arms shipments to the rebels, and some technical advice.'[23]

In the immediate aftermath of the invasion, Brzezinski outlined what he saw to be the key driving factors in US policy towards Afghanistan and the Soviet Union. 'Our response', he concluded, 'has to be a *sustained one and a regional one*'. While he noted that US–Soviet dialogue could continue, he cautioned that, 'whatever we do in the region, *it will be costly*. The more we can do with our allies, the better, but the major initiative will have to come from us.' Thus, we see one of the key reasons that Pakistan became the centre of anti-Soviet and anti-PDPA activities (despite the attack on the American embassy in Islamabad in November 1979, in which a marine was killed). Brzezinski linked the security of Afghanistan to US interests across the Middle East and South Asia, warning: 'if we do not respond in a timely fashion, the consequences of an inadequate response will be even more horrendous.'[24]

Carter confirmed this view in his State of the Union address, thereby signalling a drastic shift in his foreign policy away from global political cooperation and economic interdependence.[25] In the public broadcast, the president hawkishly placed events in Afghanistan in a broader context of turmoil across the region. He warned against

the steady growth and increased projection of Soviet military power beyond its own borders; the overwhelming dependence of the Western democracies on oil supplies from the Middle East; and the press of social and religious and economic and political change in the many nations of the developing world, exemplified by the revolution in Iran.

He argued: 'All must be faced together, squarely and courageously' and emphasized that the United States would combat Soviet expansionism not only in Afghanistan but across the world. He sought the support of America's allies. Referring specifically to Afghanistan, he called on countries to place economic sanctions on the Soviet

Union and to boycott the 1980 Moscow Olympics. In what became the defining feature of the Carter doctrine, the president asserted:

This situation demands careful thought, steady nerves, and resolute action, not only for this year but for many years to come. It demands collective efforts to meet this new threat to security in the Persian Gulf and in Southwest Asia…And it demands consultation and close cooperation with countries in the area which might be threatened.[26]

The future of Afghanistan was thus central to the future of a much broader region, one that had huge economic and political significance to the United States and the rest of the world. The Soviets could not be allowed to expand their influence any further.

Carter had little chance to act on these declarations. He had other, more pressing concerns. In the region of South-West Asia, Afghanistan had less emotional claim than the unfolding crisis in Iran, including both the revolution and the hostage crisis. On 24 April 1980, a US military operation failed in its rescue mission and only exacerbated US–Iranian tensions. Moreover, the crisis unfolded in an election year. Taken alongside many Americans' concerns about the state of the economy following the 1970s oil crisis, Carter's bungling of the hostage situation helped lead to his downfall. In November, Carter was defeated by the Republican nominee, Ronald Reagan, a former actor who had served as governor of California and ran on a platform of economic growth and curtailing Soviet expansion. Republicans excoriated the Carter administration because 'it neither understands totalitarianism nor appreciates the way tyrants take advantage of weakness'. They warned: 'The brutal invasion of Afghanistan promises to be only the forerunner of much more serious threats to the West—and to world peace—should the Carter Administration somehow cling to power.'[27] Immediately after Reagan had taken office, the hostages were released and returned to the United States. This seemed to augur well for Reagan, as he pledged to uphold his electoral promises.

Despite campaign assurances that seemed to place Reagan at odds with Carter, in fact his policy towards Afghanistan did not differ drastically. The Reagan doctrine, which developed between 1980 and 1983, logically extended from the Carter doctrine. Where Carter had declared that Soviet expansion must be stopped, Reagan argued for a further step. In fact, Soviet influence needed to be rolled back. Not only could it not extend beyond countries like Afghanistan; it also needed to be reduced and forced back within the Soviet Union's own borders. For Reagan, Afghanistan thus was a clear battleground in a Cold War where hopes of detente were all but gone, and he criticized media outlets that described Afghan resistance fighters as 'rebels'. During his presidential campaign, days after the Soviet invasion, he declared: 'I feel we ought to be funnelling weapons through [Pakistan] that can be delivered to those freedom fighters in Afghanistan to fight for their own freedom.' He went on: 'I think there's nothing wrong with giving weapons to a free people to defend their freedom.'[28] Reagan's embrace of the resistance as 'freedom fighters' would percolate into Western popular culture during the 1980s. Both Rambo and James Bond ventured to Afghanistan in the 1980s as they battled corrupt, evil Soviet spies and officers.[29] Notably, US focus remained on these fighters and far less on the Afghan civilians bearing the brunt of the war.

Within two months of taking office, Reagan's national security advisors had begun developing further political and military policies for South-West Asia, asked Congress for an increased defence budget for regional strategy, and connected further with local allies to help pursue the United States' regional strategy. Like Brzezinski before them, Reagan's NSC advisors emphasized the importance of regional powers in containing Soviet expansion. Pakistan was the obvious choice, given the loss of Iran, Indian ambivalence, the shared border with Afghanistan, and the fact that US foreign policy towards Pakistan and Afghanistan had been intertwined for decades. 'Because of its geographic location and its large well-trained armed forces,' they argued, 'a strong, independent, anti-Soviet Pakistan that is willing to cooperate with the US can play a key role in our overall regional strategy'. The US–Pakistani relationship remained at a premium, as Reagan's administration continued to funnel covert aid to the resistance via Pakistan's ISI. Support for anti-communist movements like the Afghan resistance fell under the remit of 'security assistance', as promoted in Reagan's National Security Decision Directive (NSDD) 32 of May 1982. Continued aid was reaffirmed by NSDD 75 in 1983, which declared: 'The US objective is to keep maximum pressure on Moscow for withdrawal and to ensure that the Soviets' political, military, and other costs remain high while the occupation continues'. This would finally result, in 1986, in the provision of Stinger missiles to the resistance fighters.[30]

This is not to say that the United States' approach to Afghanistan was plain sailing. At the end of July 1981, Secretary of State Alexander Haig reported that a recent Soviet propaganda drive had succeeded in undermining the United States' international position through its implication that the US was 'unwilling to negotiate about questions of international concern'. In fact, he informed embassies across the world, the United States was intent on political solutions to all matter of issues, pointing out that the SALT talks were about to resume with the USSR. Nevertheless, Haig emphasized that 'Afghanistan is simultaneously the most pressing problem and could provide the greatest improvement in the international situation'. As such, he indicated that the Reagan administration wanted a political solution to the Soviet occupation of Afghanistan, and the secretary of state requested embassy officials across the world to 'direct maximum energy and initiative to mount a sustained offensive against the Soviet occupation of Afghanistan, and Soviet intransigence on a negotiated withdrawal from the country'. He noted this would be a 'long-term campaign with your host government, local media, and other contact, aimed at increasing international pressure for a free Afghanistan'. He concluded: 'The Soviet occupation and puppet government are failures—with continued Afghan resistance and sufficient international pressure the Soviets can be persuaded to agree to a political solution and to withdraw.'[31]

**Figure 6.2.** Ronald Reagan with resistance fighters, 1983 (Ronald Reagan Presidential Library)

The United Nations' negotiators ultimately pushed forward talks between the United States, the Soviet Union, and their respective Pakistani and Afghan allies, leading finally to the Geneva Accords in 1988 and the Soviet withdrawal in February 1989. But, for the majority of the decade, humanitarian and covert aid defined American approaches to the Soviet occupation. Support for Afghan refugees provided the public face of US activities, a clear alternative to the Soviet-caused 'massive human suffering' that Brzezinski had pointed to, while the CIA sought ways to undermine the Soviet presence in Afghanistan at every turn.

On 25 February 1985, a little more than five years after the Soviet invasion, members of the congressional task force on Afghanistan, analysts, journalists, and NGO representatives came together to discuss the imminence of famine in war-torn Afghanistan. In opening statements, Congressman Donald Ritter, a Pennsylvanian Republican, declared: 'In Afghanistan…nature, although the terrain is rough, although supply links have always been limited, nature is not at fault. What is at fault is a conscious and premeditated policy at work which is bringing famine to that country.' Decrying what he called the Soviets' 'scorched-earth policy', Congressman Ritter declared to applause that 'we have, as Americans, a moral duty to respond to these humanitarian needs of these struggling people'.[32]

A broader sense of moral responsibility resulted in the procurement of vast amounts of money and supplies to address not only the issue of hunger but also the other needs of the war-torn Afghan community. The humanitarian response to the

Soviet intervention was extensive. It largely revolved around the needs of the Afghan refugees living in Pakistan (and, to a lesser extent, Iran), as many NGOs struggled to gain entrance into Afghanistan, where, unsurprisingly, the PDPA rejected the notion that a humanitarian crisis might exist. Numerous international organizations came to these refugees' aid, chief among them the United Nations High Commissioner for Refugees. These were accompanied by nationally based committees from countries across Europe, South Asia, the Middle East, and North America.

Prior to the Soviet invasion, the US government hesitated to participate openly in UNHCR support for the Afghan refugees rushing into Pakistan. As the few remaining officials in the American embassy in Kabul cautioned: 'Although this embassy endorses the idea of UNHCR support for the expensive refugee-relief program in Pakistan, we recommend that, if possible, the USG not be seen as playing an active role in stimulating UNHCR involvement.' Bruce Amstutz explained: 'This would only constitute further "proof" of what the DRA regards as hostile USG intent against the Khalqi regime.'[33] This stance changed with the events of December 1979.

On 11 January 1980, two weeks after the Soviet invasion, President Carter announced the United States would finance one-third of the UNHCR–World Food Program refugee relief programme. Reagan's subsequent statements concerning Afghanistan Day in 1982 obviously built on this. Assisting the refugees based just in Pakistan cost about $400 million a year. That meant that, by January 1990, humanitarian relief for Afghans had easily cost the United States $1.3 billion, and this did not account for the independent actions of American NGOs that worked in parallel to the government. Under both the Carter and the Reagan administrations, assistance to the Afghan refugee population largely moved through the UNHCR, the Word Bank, and the World Food Program. Aid took the form of wheat imports, financial and material support for UNHCR-run refugee camps, transport trucks, and sometimes the sending of experts from the Centers for Disease Control to examine refugee patients. Alongside this, NGOs such as the Afghan Relief Committee assembled to raise money, support the building of hospitals, collect desperately needed supplies such as tents and blankets, and write to Congress to demand additional US support for both the refugees and the resistance.[34]

Nevertheless, American support for Afghan refugees was not purely altruistic. As the scholar Michael Barnett has pointed out: 'Humanitarian governance may have its heart in the right place, but it is still a form of governance, and governance always includes power.' Indeed, humanitarian aid provided the beneficent public face of the United States' huge, largely covert involvement in Afghanistan. Where the morality and legality of covert aid could be disputed, humanitarian aid placed the US on the side of righteousness. Not only did humanitarian aid make the United States look good, but it gave US officials additional leverage. Power dynamics—in terms of the United States' place in the international community, its relationship with Pakistan and Afghanistan, and the relationship between the presidential administration and the elected congressmen—shaped US humanitarian aid to suffering Afghans. US officials found the political aspect of US humanitarian aid appealing. Frank Loy, an American diplomat in Pakistan, explained that, by working with the UNHCR, he 'believe[d] we can get substantial visibility and an understanding of the US origin of contributions…Most of these can be marked with some US identification and can be contributed with some fanfare.'[35]

In the light of Loy's intimations, the performance of giving was as important as what was given. In this instance, the State Department located 117,000 blankets with 'American markings' to warm fleeing Afghans. By literally marking humanitarian aid as American, such donations showcased the generosity of the United States and the American people. It put the United States on the side of the helpless refugees, in direct contrast to the Soviet Union and its bristling military presence in Afghanistan. Additionally, properly marketed US aid had the potential of shoring up domestic and international support for the presidential administration (more successfully for Reagan than for Carter). To this end, Carter proclaimed the week of 21–27 July 1980 Afghanistan Relief Week and called upon all Americans to contribute to humanitarian relief efforts. US humanitarianism not only provided needed aid to Afghans but also broadcast the image of a benevolent, generous, moral superpower to the international community and the American people.[36]

The US government's concerns about the refugees, themselves, were not always comprehensive. The idea of blanketing refugees with American markings had obvious visual and propaganda appeal. But US aid at times could be middling. Humanitarian aid provided US officials with additional means to improve relations with the Pakistani government. This became increasingly clear through the course of the Afghan war, when time and again US officials noted but did not act on the fact that only a fraction of the food and material supplies delivered from the United States via the UNHCR actually reached the refugees (as with weapons, Pakistani intermediaries and Afghan party leaders frequently took a cut). In another example, after meeting Brigadier Saeed Azhar, Pakistan's chief commissioner for Afghan refugees, US embassy officials suggested providing US-made trucks to deliver relief goods to refugees located across the NWFP. The American embassy in Islamabad supported importing US trucks rather than purchasing local vehicles, not only because it was a 'better choice than paying unverifiable and, in most cases, exorbitant trucker fees' but also because it provided a 'good opportunity to enhance US image among refugees' and was 'certain to benefit US business.'[37]

In fact, the trucks were far less successful than anticipated, as a review undertaken in November 1983 made clear. During the negotiations that led to the donation of the American trucks, US and Pakistani officials opted for models with moderate suspension, assuming vehicles would travel on Pakistan's paved roads to deliver supplies. In reality, the trucks rumbled across rough, rocky, frequently roadless terrain to bring supplies to refugee settlements. Because the trucks were not designed for such conditions, they could not carry full loads, sparking complaints from local officials, who did not receive the expected amount of provisions and thus could not fully support local Afghans. The situation would have been farcical if its consequences were not potentially lethal. Half-empty trucks that left refugees bereft of needed supplies were hardly fulfilling their humanitarian purpose, and they were unlikely to 'enhance US image' locally. Nevertheless, the State Department objected to paying for modifications enabling the trucks to carry larger loads, instead blaming Pakistan's National Logistics Cell.[38] The situation devolved into squabbling about who was to blame, rather than how best to support Afghans. Clearly State Department officials' interest in humanitarian aid was limited. Local Afghans' opinions mattered less than people who wielded real power, whether voters at home, the international community, or foreign government representatives.

Moreover, the publicity associated with such humanitarian projects placed additional pressures—and to an extent, accountability—on the American government. While the Department of State in March 1984 praised the work of the World Food Program, members also urged the need for closer scrutiny to ensure that assistance levels matched refugee numbers (determining who was, in fact, a refugee rather than a local Pakistani or a member of the resistance proved almost impossible for the duration of the conflict). They warned: 'The Afghan refugee program is highly visible. Any major irregularities that might arise would be known immediately…This could ultimately bring about loss of donor support.'[39] In this regard, keeping a close eye on the ways that humanitarian aid was distributed was critical not only as a matter of pride but also because the United States balked at providing unnecessary supplies at extensive cost. But it also became an additional price of the conflict, requiring US officials to monitor the support provided by themselves and their allies. The question became the extent to which humanitarian aid benefited the United States' global image versus how much it just created additional work.

This is not to say that all US humanitarian aid during the conflict was so calculated. A number of US embassy and consulate officials who travelled through the NWFP and Balochistan expressed real concerns about the needs of refugees—their health, diets, shelters, and education—and made recommendations for refugees' uplift through the auspices of the UNHCR, and ultimately the United States. Certainly, the work of the Afghan Relief Committee, for example, which collected money for a small hospital near the Khyber Pass, was focused less on propaganda than on ameliorating suffering.[40] Yet, as an organization based largely on the goodwill and support of citizen fundraisers, it did not have the structural or financial underpinning to provide support on the same scale as the US government. Instead, aid from local American NGOs remained secondary to that supplied by the US government. And, equally, US government responses to the humanitarian needs of the Afghan refugees remained secondary to broader strategic calculations related to the global Cold War. While the requirements of the Afghan refugees and the ways that US money and goods could fulfil them occupied extensive correspondence between US representatives in Islamabad, Peshawar, and Washington, humanitarian provisions were arguably of lesser interest to many officials than the other critical facet of US involvement in the Afghan war: covert aid.

While the United States' public-facing humanitarian activities largely emanated from downtown Washington, American policy towards Afghanistan was predominantly driven by the vast amount of intelligence data collected and collated in nearby Langley, Virginia. Eight miles west of Washington, the headquarters of the Central Intelligence Agency was a large, 1950s-era building, envisioned by former Director for Central Intelligence Allen Dulles as a university campus-like space for intelligence officers—close enough to Washington to be useful to policymakers, far enough away to be secure and secluded.[41] There, the Directorate of Intelligence gathered information from more than a dozen analysis centres that drove American conceptions of Afghanistan and Afghans. Analysts with the Office of Near Eastern and South Asian Affairs, mostly nameless in the archives, thanks to redactions, played a particularly important role, generating thousands of pages of data on the Soviet invasion, Afghanistan's political, social, and ethnic dynamics, and the growing resistance.

Given that the majority of US assistance to Afghanistan was provided under the auspices of the CIA, it is worth asking how its analysts understood the conflict and those involved in it. Several overriding themes appeared in intelligence reports. The most prominent harked back to embassy officials' reliance on British colonial tropes, comparison between Afghans and American Indians, and focus on the general backwardness of the country. For the CIA, Afghan 'tribes' were the main arbiter and category of politics and society, driven by a traditionalism that rejected state structures and Soviet manipulation. Without question, tribal leadership and networks were significant, both in the resistance and in influencing whether Afghans chose to leave their homeland or stay. As we have seen, the KBG-backed KhAD tried to broker deals with local tribal leaders and their followers to ensure their support for the PDPA, while, conversely, moderate resistance parties such as Mujaddidi's Jabhah-i Nijat-i Milli and Gailani's Mahaz-i Milli-yi Islami used tribal networks to spread the civil war. But it was less these individuals and networks that interested analysts and more the idea of the tribe as a specific type of political unit that could be mobilized in full against the Soviets.

Officials had little conception of Afghanistan as a modern state. They echoed the US Information Service (USIS) officer Kenneth Yates, who said: 'Afghanistan has always been infected with factional fighting. The Afghans do things differently from other nation states.' CIA analysts, like their State Department counterparts, emphasized Afghanistan's lack of political and economic development, as well as its ostensible tribal social and political divisions. Stanfield Turner recollected that, initially, 'I felt that our supplying weapons to the rebels would be asking them to commit suicide…As I went through this dilemma with the CIA analysts on Afghanistan, they persuaded me that the rebels were going to fight regardless of what weapons they had. Such was their nature.'[42] Afghans' traditional, tribal 'nature', intelligence officers argued, created local resistance to the governing changes driven by the PDPA.

As such, US policymakers overlooked the Afghan political party model that developed around Peshawar. They ignored the fact that party leaders, particularly Islamists such as Hekmatyar and Rabbani, did not see themselves as backward, traditional, or tribal but rather as fundamentally modern. They disregarded or failed adequately to acknowledge the ways that some of the parties undermined and tried to replace older social and political networks. Instead, emphasis on traditionalism led the CIA and other governmental departments to embrace factionalism within the resistance as a necessary component of combatting the Soviets. Little effort was made to encourage unification within the resistance or to consider how a widespread, disparate insurgency might transition to state-building in a post-withdrawal Afghanistan. Instead of framing the war in Afghanistan in terms of modernity, as the Afghan Islamists, socialists, and even, to an extent, Soviets did, American policymakers assumed that Afghanistan's *lack* of modernity fuelled the resistance.

Shortly after the Soviet invasion in December 1979, the CIA's Office of Scientific Intelligence predicted a prolonged, widespread resistance to the PDPA. Officials weighed local Afghan political and social expectations against the actions of the socialist regime. They noted: 'Communist revolutionaries have tried to overturn tradition rather than adapt to it, to eliminate local autonomy, to destroy the elite class by confiscating its land, and to undermine the authority of the Muslim religious establishment.' These actions, officials believed, were repugnant to much of Afghanistan's rural population. Western media reports seemed to support this interpretation. In one *New York Times* article, a guerrilla fighter, interviewed on the outskirts of a bombed-out village, was quoted: 'They wanted to send everybody to their classes, even the old men and the women with 10 children, so we killed the teacher, who was a Communist, and fled.' Another fighter, a former major general in the Afghan air force, reportedly stated: 'This is the way we have lived for 20 centuries. It is a good way.'[43]

Much like other government officials in Washington and at outposts in Kabul or Islamabad, CIA analysts turned to Afghan history as they interpreted it. They emphasized that, 'for thousands of years, the topography and Afghan cultural mores mitigated against the formation of a strong central government and even against a strong union of the tribes themselves'. They concluded: 'tribal society is responding to a modern, well-organized threat in traditional terms. The tribes are fighting as they have fought for centuries: independently, locally, and with a minimum of leadership.'[44] In these officials' understanding, for many, especially rural Afghans, the PDPA's policies represented a clear threat to their communities' social and political structures. Where the past had encouraged a fragmented state in which local forms of government and tribal organization had been paramount, the PDPA wanted a strong, central government. In CIA eyes, Afghan resistance members were employing historical tactics to prevent seismic political change. Above all else, tribal dynamics needed to be preserved.

The CIA's Southwest Asia Analytic Center's Office of Political Analysis wrote in September 1980: 'To the extent that the tribesmen have an ideology it is a belief that a combination of Islam and even older tribal traditions is the proper guide for action.' They further explained: 'Tradition also tends to sanctify everything from rules governing property ownership to ways of treating illness. Any change in the traditional way of life is considered wrong, and modern ideas—whether Communist or Western—are seen as a threat.' In one of the CIA's regular 'Afghanistan Situation

Reports' from late November 1986, analysts maintained the same view, despite almost eight years of fighting, concluding:

Pashtun tribal groups under traditional leaders have fought against the regime and the Soviets in many areas for several years, but their capacity to increase pressure on the regime is limited. They usually participate in the fighting only if it suits their own tribal objectives and tend not to fight in areas outside their tribal region. They resist being organized into units led by nontribal members and generally resist military training from nontribal people.[45]

The CIA's emphasis on Afghans' history as independent, local, and with minimum leadership led analysts to conclude that Afghanistan's tribe-based resistance could not defeat the Soviets. Their political and social traditions limited their ability to unify and cooperate and prevented them from seeking an alternative government to the Afghan socialists. However, these conclusions did not lead to discussions either within the CIA or across other government departments about how to overcome these fissures. Instead, officials showed little interest in either uniting or directing the insurgency. A 1987 NSDD on Afghanistan, nine years after the PDPA's coup, offered only a single, vague sentence alluding to the need to 'encourage a more effective resistance political front'.[46] The rest of the five-page document focused on support for Pakistan and putting as much pressure on the Soviets as possible. The fact of the matter was that US officials cared little about the future of Afghanistan so long as the conflict embroiled the Soviets.

Moreover, while emphasizing Afghanistan's tribal, traditional nature, CIA analysts largely dismissed Islam as a critical political or social factor within the Afghan resistance. They vaguely acknowledged its general importance in Afghan society and as an increasing source of resistance to the atheist Soviet regime, but they downplayed its potential political significance. When CIA analysts did mention Islam, it was inevitably intertwined with tribal identity. During the early years of the Soviet occupation, religion was rarely spoken of as a source of motivation independent of tribal and social traditions. The resistance, according to the Office of Near Eastern and South Asian Analysis, was 'fighting to preserve Islam and tradition from outside interference, just as Afghan rebels have done for centuries'.[47]

Analysts argued that Afghans were just as backward in their understanding of Islam as they were in their reliance on tribal structures. The Office of Scientific Intelligence pointed out that Afghanistan had not produced any 'profound religious philosophers' and dismissed local *mullahs*' religious training as 'haphazard' and approaching Islam 'in simple ways'. According to the CIA, while most Afghan insurgents claimed to be fighting in the name of Islam, their religious interpretations varied widely and had weak theological roots. Another analyst noted: 'In many talks with newsmen ... in Afghanistan, insurgents in the field have usually said they are fighting to defend Islam, but their definition of Islam appears to include all traditional ways including the Pashtun code of revenge and other customs that are not Islamic.'[48] Of course, part of the reason for this divergence within the resistance lay in the ambiguities of political Islam as asserted by resistance party leaders. But the implication for American observers was that, while the *mujahidin* would unite to fight in the name of Allah, they could not agree on what this actually meant. In this reading, Islam was intrinsic to most Afghans' daily lives, but it had less impact than other tribal practices. They did not take into account how Afghans' practice and understanding of Islam could, and did, change as a result of the war.

In reality, Islam was an important motivating factor for many resistance fighters, moderate and Islamist alike, just as it served as a source of coordination within and across some of the major political parties hosted in Peshawar. The CIA's view of Islam was at odds with that of the Afghan Islamists, who did not see their religious–political practices as a return to the past but rather as a new model for the future. Taking a closer look at political Islam, or 'fundamentalist Islam', as many American officials came to call it, would have revealed the essentially modern aspirations of parties such as Hizb-i Islami and Jam'iyyat. Moreover, religion was critical in shaping many Afghan refugees' experiences in neighbouring Pakistan. CIA reporting nevertheless reveals broader American (mis)understanding of Afghanistan and its inhabitants' political, social, and religious dynamics as fundamentally reactionary.

Five years into the war, CIA analysts continued to predict:

> Islam will dictate the language but not the content of the conflict between the Soviet-controlled Babrak regime and the resistance. The fratricidal discord among the resistance groups may decrease over time, but, even if the Soviet occupiers should decide to withdraw from Afghanistan, fundamentalists, moderates, and secular rivals would continue to compete for a role in any future government.

Some analysts even began to see Islam as a limiting factor. One report criticized: 'Although strong belief in a just cause and the ultimate trust in God helps sustain morale, in a guerrilla war this fatalism also works against developing strategy and tactics and against the acceptance of proper training. Many Afghans believe that faith is enough to drive out the Soviets, and they need only to put themselves in God's hands to win the war.'[49]

Notably, Afghanistan was not alone in being described by the CIA as illiberal and outdated. The 1979 revolution in Iran that brought in Ayatollah Khomeini forced Americans to reflect on the regional 'resurgence of Islam'. Analysts in the Directorate of Intelligence's Office of Regional and Political Analysis briefly expressed concern in February 1979 that Islam might be a 'militant and potentially destabilizing political force', but they concluded that 'the vitality of Islam has been a cyclical thing'. They identified Islam as a 'destabilizing impact' rather than a potential force for revolutionary social and political change. Further analysis in March 1981 that reflected collectively on the Afghan resistance, the Iranian revolution, and other instances of increasing Islamic politicization in the Middle East—and concurrent outbreaks of anti-American sentiment—argued:

> The root cause for the intense expressions of anti-US feelings is the dissatisfaction and humiliation the Muslim peoples are experiencing in their collective lives. As the traditional social order breaks down, the answers drawn from the past are insufficient for coping with the complexity of the modern world; the structure provided by Islam cannot contain the anger and frustration of the Muslim people uprooted from their traditional milieu.[50]

In effect, Islam was the problem, not the solution.

Much as officials described Afghanistan's tribal organization as outdated, they assumed Islam was pre-modern and linked directly to a 'traditional social order'. They argued that Islam appealed to populations in South-West Asia, including Iran, Afghanistan, and, to an extent, Pakistan, because it provided an alternative to both the 'Christian West' and 'atheist Soviet Marxism' and could serve as a 'vehicle to spread separatist unrest to other regions.'[51] According to such analysis, locals used Islam to channel other regional interests and movements rather than embracing it as a motivational end in itself. This belied the very real changes taking place across the region. Islam clearly had political force and significance, as could be seen not only in Iran and among the Afghan resistance but in Zia's developing Islamist policies within Pakistan and the rise of militant Wahabbi groups in Saudi Arabia.

In conversations in the 1990s, American policymakers acknowledged that they had fundamentally misunderstood Islam's political and social power. Gary Sick recalled: 'We had no deep understanding of Islamic fundamentalism, or of where it might lead. And, I think, we were surprised—as I believe the Soviets were surprised—at the way it played out.' Turner agreed: 'we did not understand Islamic fundamentalism; we really were totally in the cold here when this phenomenon overtook us in Iran.'[52] This myopia clearly persisted in the United States' dealings with Afghanistan. Regardless of matters on the ground, the CIA dismissed Islam as a potentially transformational force across the region. This indifference continued even as the exiled political parties in Peshawar became increasingly enmeshed in the insurgency.

In June 1986, a number of Afghan resistance leaders visited Washington. They had a packed schedule. On 18 June alone, they had an 8 a.m. radio discussion, taped an interview with Dan Rather for 'The CBS Evening News', met Vice President George H. W. Bush, attended a lunch in their honour at the State Department, and then conducted a series of press interviews. That afternoon, Burhanuddin Rabbani criticized American coverage of the Soviet occupation. 'Some of you American press are calling us "rebels," as if we were fighting a legal government,' he complained via an interpreter. 'We are fighting against invaders...And a free press must call us by the name we really are. Mujahedeen: Freedom Fighters.'[53]

Such ambiguity in the American press was hardly surprising. The media's public rhetoric matched the same uncertainty, even ambivalence, expressed by the Reagan administration. Certainly, for the CIA and the NSC, the Afghan resistance's significance lay in its power to absorb Soviet men and money. Reagan embraced the semantics of Afghan 'freedom', but this did not transition into policy decisions. The president may have praised the Afghan resistance as freedom fighters, but his emphasis was that 'those are people fighting for their own country and not wanting to become a satellite state of the Soviet Union'.[54] Freedom meant independence from the Soviet Union, not American support for a total re-envisioning of Afghan nationhood.

Even as a negotiated Soviet withdrawal began to seem increasingly possible, American attitudes were slow to shift. CIA analysts began paying closer attention to the seven exiled political parties in Peshawar, but to little end. Among the seven main parties that had emerged in Peshawar, CIA analysts noted increasing polarization between the 'fundamentalist' and 'moderate' factions from the beginning of 1981. Reporting focused on this division, rather than seeking further nuances or differentiations within each group. CIA reporting relied on sweeping generalizations. The fundamentalists were described as opposing a return of the Afghan monarchy and desiring a 'revolutionary Islamic state'. The moderates, in contrast, were understood to seek a return to the pre-socialist days with a secular democratic state.[55] An increasing difference between the two was the moderates' willingness to negotiate with the Soviets, while the fundamentalists, according to CIA reports, largely rejected anything but a total Soviet withdrawal. Analysts spent little time detailing the government that either faction might institute, should a Soviet retreat occur. Instead, unsurprisingly, the CIA focused largely on identifying which of these factions would better uphold US interests in the region.

Rather than delving into each faction's religious and political underpinnings, officials focused on which was more 'pro-Western'. Officials believed fundamentalists were 'suspicious of the West' (Hekmatyar's refusal to meet Reagan did not refute this). In contrast, the moderates appeared more sympathetic, particularly because of their support from Afghan exile communities in Europe. Their stated preference for a democratic system also probably appealed to US officials. However, CIA observers criticized the moderates' general disorganization. According to one report:

> They have overlapping command structures that seem to frustrate rather than facilitate decision making. They favor friends and relatives for leadership positions rather than effective leaders. They make no effort to coordinate their fighting in Afghanistan, and the leaders themselves seem more concerned with their religious standing than with running effective guerrilla operations. Many potential followers undoubtedly become exasperated with the chaos.[56]

US officials nevertheless briefly mobilized, alongside their Saudi and Pakistani allies, to force an uneasy alliance between the seven parties in 1985.

If analysts considered the future of Afghanistan, neither moderates nor Islamists seemed to offer a favourable outcome. Four years after first discussing the fundamentalist–moderate divide, analysts still wrote that the fundamentalists, without differentiating between different parties or leaders, wanted a 'theocratic state, modelled on Iran', while moderates desired 'a secular government vaguely based on Islamic tenets'. This belied the very different models of Islamism emerging within the Afghan resistance, as well as their alternatives. The fundamentalists, analysts believed, were unlikely to support US interests in the regions ideologically, while, tactically, the moderates were weaker. Instead, analysts' major conclusion was that the 'majority' of insurgents wanted 'considerable autonomy for their region or ethnic group and favor[ed] a minimum of interference in local affairs from Kabul'. In other words, resistance fighters sought the same diffuse, tribal, reactionary society that American analysts linked to earlier times. Combatants rejected a modern Afghanistan, analysts believed, and as a consequence, American officials did not recognize the potential for change that a decade of war had created. Nor did they suggest how any 'pro-Western' government might overcome Afghanistan's supposed backwardness and tribal divides. As UN-led talks in Geneva began to accelerate, analysts in the Afghanistan Branch of the Office of Near Eastern and South Asian Analysis predicted that 'differences among the resistance leaders will likely prevent them from achieving a unified position on the negotiations. The fundamentalists and traditionalists do not share the same vision of a post-Soviet Afghanistan; attempting to define a new regime would risk splitting the alliance and forcing its collapse.'[57] The future of the Afghan state, it seemed, would be left to chance.

Ultimately, a paradox emerged in US policy towards Afghanistan. American leaders from Carter and Reagan down through the ranks supported the Afghan resistance movement. Soviet expansionism had to be halted; its forces could not be allowed to move further south-west, potentially threatening the entire Persian Gulf region. Thus, while couching policy towards Afghanistan in terms of Afghan freedom, American officials were far more concerned about the global Cold War. A 'free' Afghanistan was not necessarily a modern nation state along the lines of other members of the international political system. Rolling back the Soviets remained the Reagan administration's key focus, not post-conflict state-building in Afghanistan.

In many respects, this set of priorities should not be surprising. For Americans, the Cold War, after all, was premised first and foremost on the security of the United States and its major allies. Afghan combatants were bit players, in comparison. 'Freedom' did not necessarily mean 'democracy', as had been demonstrated, for example, by ongoing US support for authoritarian allies in Iran and South Korea and willingness to turn a blind eye to human rights abuses in Indonesia and Cambodia.[58] Moreover, numerous American governments had avoided the financial costs and political difficulties that accompanied post-war redevelopment for decades. Following the lengthy rebuilding of war-wrecked Japan and Germany in the 1940s and 1950s, American policymakers dodged similar protracted situations in countries where they intervened militarily. As one scholar has observed, 'US interventions in such places as the Dominican Republic, Lebanon, Grenada and Panama were undertaken to overthrow unfriendly regimes and reinstall friendly ones, rather than bring about fundamental societal transformations'.[59] Why should Afghanistan be any different? US support for the resistance was intended to destroy the Afghan socialist experiment, not promote a specific form of governance. If anything, state-building in Afghanistan seemed an even more daunting task if we take at face value American perceptions that Afghanistan was particularly divided and backward. How much of a state was there to rebuild?

As a consequence, despite the lines of enquiry pursued by congressional committees—not only on famine but also on humanitarian conditions more broadly—which decried the Soviet Union as having 'brought Afghanistan human misery of all descriptions', realpolitik meant that officials in the Reagan administration, the CIA, and the State Department did little to pursue policies that might ameliorate conditions within Afghanistan or create the foundations of a new Afghan government. While there remained the visible US contribution to humanitarian aid among the Afghan refugees, covert aid intended to bog down Soviet forces was far more crucial and expansive. It was also fundamentally violent and left far more Afghan than Soviet bodies in its wake. The Cold-War context of US aid to both the Afghan refugees and resistance meant that competition with—and superiority to—the Soviet Union mattered far more than matters on the ground. While American officials publicly equivocated about their support for the resistance and used Pakistan's intelligence service as a cover, they were ready to claim and mark their support for the Afghan refugees, who were under the spotlight of international attention.

The results of these actions were that, much like the regional powers that became involved in the Soviet–Afghan war, American policy helped to destabilize Afghanistan. But, in contrast to the other involved players, US officials focused on Afghanistan's past rather than competing alternatives for Afghanistan's future. Like their regional allies, US policymakers rejected the idea that the PDPA regime in Afghanistan legitimately represented the Afghan people. Instead, they opted to support Afghans largely located outside of Afghanistan: resistance fighters and refugees. Yet American leaders showed less interest than their regional allies in the future of these borderless Afghans. Where Pakistan and Iran created opportunities for Afghan Islamists to rise to the fore of the resistance and espouse their visions of a future Afghanistan, American leaders neither chose key resistance parties to support, nor did they really seek any sort of functioning party coalition. They did not take seriously the visions of parties such as Hizb-i Islami and Jam'iyyat. Instead, reports emanating from the CIA reinforced the idea that, perhaps, a modern Afghan state could not exist. Unlike the other factions and powers involved in the Afghan conflict, US observers disregarded the accompanying war over Afghan modernity. Instead, in American eyes, the powers of tribal factionalism and tradition were just too strong.

American conceptions of Afghanistan and Afghan identity did not correspond with matters on the ground. They did not take into account the very modern visions that Afghan ideologues, whether Islamist or Marxist (or other), had for their country but instead assumed such models were impossible in an Afghan context. Despite American assumptions, the battle remained for the future of Afghanistan—a state, a nation, of Afghans. But American observers seemed unable to move beyond the idea that Afghanistan was the Wild West: brutal and ungovernable.

What, then, would happen once a Soviet withdrawal began? Who would take the lead? Who best served American interests? Reagan's policies left more questions than answers, and developments in the 1980s did not set a precedent for long-term American engagement with local Afghans. Whether the United States would remain as invested in Afghanistan if the Soviet Union was no longer a threat seemed doubtful. We will return to the US role in later chapters. For now, we will turn to the victims of the competing visions of modernity: the millions of Afghan refugees who chose exile rather than remaining in their homeland.

# 7
# Nasir Bagh

In 1981, the Afghan Refugees Commissionerate (established by the government of Pakistan in 1979) published a series of English-language pamphlets. Printed in colour, the front of one showed a collection of several hundred dull, brown canvas tents rising out of a dusty plain on the banks of a canal, shaded by leafy green trees. Another revealed children playing in a waterway, watched over by adults standing along its bank. On a third, a group of men posed in front of a battered Mercedes van. Another pamphlet displayed a sign stuck haphazardly into a small knoll, which proudly read: 'Religious School and Islamic Society of Afghanistan for Refugees'. Each pamphlet contained numerous photographs. Images showed grazing cows and goats and cohorts of men and children sitting in or near tents and listening to lessons from teachers and clerics. Another showed a slight breeze causing a white flag with a red crescent to flutter above a tent marked as the local hospital. Sadly, many more photos showed Afghans—young and old, male and female—with missing limbs, bandaged wounds, or receiving some form of medical treatment.

Nasir Bagh, which the first pamphlet publicized, was one of the dozens of refugee camps built across Pakistan's NWFP and Balochistan in the late 1970s and early 1980s. It was located only 10 kilometres north-west of Peshawar and lay alongside the Warsak Canal, which provided it with a ready source of water. Already, by 30 September 1981, its administrators had registered 12,322 residents, comprised of Pashtuns from Nangarhar and Kabul provinces, as well as Hazara, Tajiks, and Uzbeks. The camp's pamphlet detailed the amenities provided to refugees in Nasir Bagh by the government of Pakistan and the UNHCR: not only shelters but food provisions, clothing and bedding, medical centres, schools, and mosques. The author commented: 'The Political, Social, Cultural and religious Suppression coupled with ruthless attitude of Kabul Administration and the Alien forces created [an] atmosphere of complete insecurity and general scare and it became impossible for them to stay in their homeland.'[1] Nasir Bagh would become one of the largest refugee camps of the 1980s, remaining a semi-permanent settlement, and the home of exiled Afghans, until 2002.[2]

War turned Afghanistan into a country on the move. In discussing the Soviet invasion of Afghanistan, the policies pursued by the PDPA, the rise of a countrywide resistance, and the subterfuge of the United States, it can be easy to forget the war's deadly and very real human costs. But the violent conflict in Afghanistan created one of the largest, most prolonged refugee crises the modern world has ever known. At its peak, between 1985 and 1990, the UNHCR estimated that 6.2 million Afghans were living in neighbouring Pakistan and Iran. Tens of thousands more managed to resettle in Europe and North America. 'At the height of displacement, the Afghan refugees constituted up to 60 per cent of the entire world refugee population.'[3] Additionally, thousands of other Afghans faced a crisis of internal displacement, escaping homes in rebel strongholds for the safety of government-held cities, or, conversely, government-ruled regions for resistance bases. Increasingly, urban centres proved as treacherous as the countryside, wracked with guerrilla activity. Over the course of the 1980s, Kabul became bloated and overstretched, swelling from 913,000 inhabitants in 1979 to 1,287,000 by 1986 and closer to 2,000,000 by 1991.[4]

A huge proportion of Afghanistan's population decided, over the course of the 1980s, that the uncertainty of exile was preferable to remaining at home, whether this meant fleeing to Afghanistan's cities or escaping the rule of a Marxist regime. As one refugee told an American reporter in anguish: 'Afghanistan is finished. Finished for good.'[5] With the expanding war, personal safety could no longer be assured by either the Afghan government or rebel leaders. The war threatened Afghan lives in numerous ways—destroying property, shelter, food sources, and local economies and taking limbs and lives. Afghans sought to escape bombing, forced conscription into the government's armed forces, or pressure to join local socialist cadres.[6] Violence was committed on both sides, by government and resistance forces alike. Civilians suffered the consequences, getting caught in skirmishes or discovering that a village had become a battlefield. Even in Afghanistan's urban centres, many of which were ostensibly controlled by the PDPA, explosions, assassination attempts, and protests with the potential to turn violent threatened daily life.

Afghan civilians found themselves trapped in the crossfire between the Marxists' and Islamists' competing visions of modernity. They were both the subjects and envisioned supporters of state-led modernization, whether in terms of the PDPA's economic and social reforms or the Islamists' political–religious mobilization. As such, they were simultaneously the targets and the victims of the violent struggle between Marxism and Islamism and their respective Soviet and US supporters. This was the case both within Afghanistan and in the refugee camps in neighbouring Pakistan and Iran (though the focus of this chapter will remain in Pakistan). Because of ISI's reliance on the seven main political parties around Peshawar in dealing with resistance fighters and refugees alike, the moderate and Islamist parties both accrued new influence among Afghan exiles—especially as refugee families had to join one of these parties if they wanted to receive any government- or UNHCR-sanctioned aid.

The refugee crisis thus posed not just a humanitarian crisis but a fundamental challenge to the Afghan nation state. By fleeing their homeland, Afghans brought into question the legitimacy of the PDPA, as well as the issue of who constituted Afghan citizens and where Afghanistan was located. While an ostensibly Afghan territory existed on maps of the world, almost half of its population had fled these boundaries rather than live under its current rulers. So did an Afghan nation exist within these international borders, or were, perhaps, refugee camps the new site of Afghan nationhood? Camps increasingly functioned as 'nations in exile'.[7] The very presence of millions of Afghans living outside their country's perimeters symbolized the failure of the PDPA truly to capture and assert control over Afghanistan as a nation state. Instead, refugees sought alternative governing arrangements and living spaces, and, because camp life disrupted pre-existing leadership structures, it also forced many to reckon with their identity and sense of belonging to an Afghan nation.

Afghan refugees not only had to navigate the growing socialist–Islamist and moderate–Islamist binaries. The decision to leave Afghanistan and flee to neighbouring Pakistan also entangled Afghan civilians with an additional modernizing force: the UNHCR and its affiliated NGOs. While the Afghan–Pakistan borderlands had, for decades, even centuries, been the site of regular migration, the sheer number of Afghans who flooded into Pakistan shared no historical precedent.[8] Local Pashtun communities across the NWFP and Balochistan, who in previous times could be counted on to extend hospitality (*malmastia*) and sanctuary (*nanawati*) to individuals, families, and communities in need, simply could not host and accommodate millions of Afghans, some of whom shared kinship and tribal networks with Pakistan's Pashtuns and some of whom did not. The government of Pakistan was forced to turn to the UNHCR for help managing this overflowing population.

The UNHCR, with decades of experience, took charge of the refugee crisis and thereby introduced Afghans to an entirely new set of governing and oversight mechanisms. By creating organized camps, requiring refugees to register, and implementing plans for Afghans' social and economic uplift, UNHCR officials introduced Afghans to the practical realities of a modern governing force. Somewhat ironically, where Afghan Marxists and Islamists aspired to and discussed ways to revolutionize Afghan politics and society but found only limited means to do so, the UNHCR, with the help of its Pakistani and NGO backers, fundamentally reworked many Afghans' daily lives, even as this branch of the United Nations offered only limited visions of what a modern Afghan society should look like. The UNHCR's imperatives among Afghan refugees reinforced the fact that the war of the 1980s was a war for the soul of Afghan society and politics. Afghan refugees became enmeshed in three different, competing visions of modernity—those of the Marxists, those of the Islamists, and those of the international community, represented by the UNHCR and (as Chapter 8 will show) the UN General Assembly. In turn, this forced a reckoning for many Afghans as they sought to define their own experiences of exile, accepting (at least reluctantly) the idea of being victims but also drawing strength from alternative religious and ethnic networks.

As millions of Afghans experienced the 1980s outside their homeland, refugee camps became important spaces for renegotiating Afghan politics and societal norms. The exodus of so many Afghans, cutting across gender, age, class, political, tribal, and ethnic divides, profoundly affected every facet of Afghan society. While it reinforced the prominence of the resistance parties based in Peshawar, it also introduced refugees to additional models of social, economic, and political practice supported by international donors. And this, itself, had numerous, unintended consequences. The experience of exile led many Afghans to rethink their own identity and their relationship with an Afghan homeland. None came out unscathed, and what instead emerged were numerous iterations of what it meant to be Afghan, when one could no longer live in Afghanistan.

In the late twentieth century, several waves of migrants fled Afghanistan. The first, comprising Afghan Islamists and dissidents, began in the early 1970s as a result of the upheaval caused by Mohammad Daoud Khan's 1973 coup. The second wave, and the focus here, resulted from the rise of the PDPA and subsequent Soviet invasion, and would endure from the late 1970s to the late 1980s, when a number of Afghans attempted to return home following the Soviet withdrawal. However, a third wave of refugees began almost immediately, as civil war continued to embroil the country, and a fourth wave commenced after the victories of the Taliban in the mid-1990s.[9]

Afghans began entering neighbouring Pakistan and Iran soon after Taraki's April 1978 takeover. Supporters of Daoud's regime were followed by Afghans who grew increasingly wary of the governing changes taking place under first Taraki, then Amin, and then Karmal. Some Afghans reacted hostilely to the PDPA's promotion of co-education, and many questioned land reform. The PDPA's open embrace of Marxism in late 1978 and its antagonism towards Islam further exacerbated matters, as did the regime's increasing reliance on its armed forces to carry out its writ. Afghans from across the country, from a range of educational and social backgrounds, increasingly saw escape as the better alternative to remaining under the control of the new government.

While much public rhetoric focused on the shortcomings of the new regime and its stance on Islam, violence and the threat of violence most immediately informed

**Figure 7.1.** Newcomer refugees at Nasir Bagh camp (Internet Archive, The Afghan Media Resource Center/Muhammad Rahim)

Afghans' decisions to depart from their homeland. Rahim Uddin, from Zabul province, and Umara Khan, from Kunar province, both told sympathetic American reporters that they and their families had fled to escape the PDPA's ideas as well as its increasingly violent policies. In Uddin's village, local *mullahs* who critiqued the PDPA had disappeared, probably thanks to the secret police, and were never seen again. Inhabitants of both Uddin's and Khan's villages fled to the mountains when reports emerged of government and Soviet troops moving into their areas. Their settlements were razed to the ground by state forces. 'The next day', Khan recalled, 'they sent a group to the hills to talk to us. They told us that if we accepted the government, we would get help to rebuild our homes. We told them we had our Koran.' While many of the men subsequently sought out and joined local resistance forces, others helped guide their villages' women, children, and elders over the border and into exile. Uddin, his family, and other villagers hid in the mountains for four days before finally crossing into Pakistan. By February 1980, he and seven family members were sharing an 8-foot × 12-foot tent in a refugee camp of eleven thousand.[10]

Masood Farivar, who fought with the resistance, also experienced the violence of the PDPA state. He recounted visiting Kabul's infamous Pul-i Charkhi prison after Karmal came to power and announced a general amnesty to prisoners who had been arrested under Taraki and Amin. Hoping that his uncle had been released, Farivar and his family waited for hours as other former prisoners streamed out of the prison. 'The prisoners released that day, far from being hardcore counterrevolutionaries,' he recounted, 'were mostly ordinary people who had been picked up by the previous regime's secret police for small offenses against the state'. Farivar's uncle, Ghulam Ali, never appeared. 'Deep in their hearts Mother and Grandma knew Uncle Kamkay was dead.'[11] It is hardly surprising that, not long after this, Farivar's family, too, fled to Pakistan.

If civilians did not escape, they bore the brunt of the civil war. This was made horrifyingly clear in the spring of 1979, in what one survivor called the 'war of Kerala'. Kerala was a village of about five thousand people located in Kunar province, east of Kabul. Its inhabitants were known to be sympathetic to local rebels, and resistance forces had taken to sheltering there on occasion. On the morning of 20 April, thirty-two rebels had holed up in a local compound when Afghan government forces (potentially with some Soviet soldiers—accounts differ) entered Kerala to root out 'troublemakers'.

Fighting erupted, and the army chose to take drastic measures. According to one witness: 'They forced all the men to line up in crouching positions in the field just outside the town and then opened up with their machine guns from behind.' One survivor, 16-year-old Mohammad Ashoq, recalled: 'My father told me to get up and run. But a soldier stopped me. Again my father told me to run away, and I ran to the mosque. Behind me I heard the sound of gunfire. From the mosque, I saw soldiers take more men to another field and shoot them after an Afghan officer shouted, "Fire!"'. At least 640 men were killed, though some reported the figure as closer to 1,000. The village's women, who had also sought shelter in the mosque, were largely spared but subsequently forced to leave. Some men managed to escape among the women by dressing in *chadors*, women's veils. By February 1980, only about twenty or thirty people reportedly remained in the once-thriving village. The rest had fled to Pakistan, while some headed to rebel-controlled strongholds in Afghanistan's mountains. Soviet personnel disputed claims made in the Western press about events at Kerala, claiming the massacre was fictional, but in many respects whether this specific incident was real or not did not matter. It remained symbolic of the prevailing violence that destroyed local communities and sent many Afghans abroad.[12]

Initially, Afghans settled in Pakistan among predominantly Pashtun local communities in the NWFP and Balochistan. They were hosted by and integrated into local villages and communities, in accordance with the principles of Pashtuns' shared code of honour and conduct, *Pashtunwali*. Within *Pashtunwali, melmastia* 'demands that guests be welcomed without question and be given the best of whatever the host has to offer', while *nanawati* 'is a right to seek protection, request pardon or demand help from a more powerful person or kin group by a weaker one'.[13] However, as the number of Afghans grew, local communities simply could not handle the influx. The frontier provinces lacked the infrastructures or means to handle a huge swell in their populations. Moreover, as the case of Nasir Bagh demonstrated, many of Afghanistan's ethnic groups increasingly sought refuge in Pakistan, despite lacking the tribal and familial ties that bound Afghanistan's Pashtuns to those in Pakistan.

Pakistan initially tried to tackle the growing refugee crisis on its own, wary of antagonizing relations with Afghanistan. The central government, working with provincial officials in the NWFP and Balochistan, organized three regional centres for fleeing Afghans, where they could be registered and provided with immediate assistance. One was located in Balochistan, one in Peshawar, and one in Chitral. Refugee commissioners were appointed at the provincial level in the NWFP and at district levels in Balochistan. By December 1978, about six thousand Afghans were living in these centres, while another six thousand were scattered among local communities.[14] By January 1980, the number of Afghans in Pakistan had grown to six hundred thousand, and by June 1980, it had breached one million.

As relations between Zia and the PDPA soured, the congregations of Afghans along the Durand Line posed a number of problems for Pakistan. They not only placed a disproportionate burden on local communities and their resources but also were far from Pakistan's bureaucratic centres, making aid and administrative provisions exceedingly difficult. The NWFP, Balochistan, and their inhabitants lacked the means to accommodate and feed so many bodies. Officials also worried that Afghan migrants' location so near the border would precipitate retaliation from the PDPA and their Soviet allies. While Zia claimed that Pakistan hosted Afghans purely on humanitarian grounds, the PDPA continued to claim that the Afghans in Pakistan were combatants and enemies of the revolution, not refugees. There was some truth to this claim, which only further complicated the Pakistani position and made organizing and overseeing Afghan asylum-seekers that much more critical. By the spring of 1979, months before the Soviet invasion, the scale of the crisis had forced the government of Pakistan to seek international support.

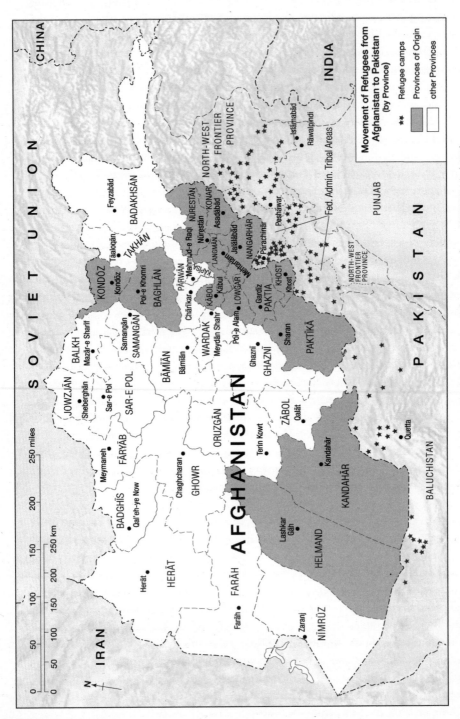

**Map 7.** Map of refugee camps in Pakistan, by province, c.1989 (drawn using information from UNHCR and CIA)

In a May 1979 memorandum to the UNHCR, Pakistan's Economic Affairs Division outlined the government's concerns. 'These refugees come from all sectors of Afghan society and include teachers, religious leaders, doctors, engineers, etc. As most of them were in a pitiable condition at the time of entry in Pakistan, the government felt it necessary on purely humanitarian grounds, to give them food and shelter.' The government emphasized: 'Abrupt and sudden as all refugee influxes are, Pakistan could do no more than take the emergent and ad hoc measures to meet the situation and make the most of whatever resources it had at its disposal in these far-flung and difficult areas.' The consequences were huge. Refugees were being housed wherever space could be found: camps of tents and huts were hastily constructed, private rooms requisitioned, 'even rest-houses, under-construction schools and hospitals and other departmental buildings have been put into commission for this purpose causing total dislocation to the functions of these institutions'.

The influx of Afghan arrivals had already overwhelmed the recently appointed refugee commissioners in the NWFP and Balochistan. Report authors pointed out that, mere days before the memorandum had been finalized, an additional twenty thousand refugees had reportedly reached Zhob district in Balochistan. For the financial year ending 30 June 1979, the government had spent Rs 4,09,12,000 (approximately $4.1 million) on the assumption that the country would receive forty-seven thousand refugees. 'Since this number has already been far exceeded,' officials concluded, 'the above budgeted amount would have to be supplemented during the current financial year'. The government of Pakistan thus desperately wrote: 'In view of the continued deterioration of the internal situation in Afghanistan, the present refugee problem has already assumed grave proportions far beyond our limited resources. Pakistan Government would, therefore, welcome any international assistance to meet this grave situation.'[15]

The UNHCR could hardly refuse to act in this obvious humanitarian crisis. Its Geneva headquarters quickly dispatched two of its officials to Pakistan to observe the situation, where they, alongside local officials, visited the Afghan border to see the refugee areas for themselves. The most pressing matter, in the view of both the UNHCR and the government of Pakistan, was to 'shift refugee locations away from the border, in orderly established camps administered by the authorities'.[16] Both Pakistan and the UNHCR wanted to discourage the continued movement of Afghans across the border, concerned about the potential for border transgressions by PDPA forces and seeking to avoid DRA claims that the Afghans settled in Pakistan were insurgents, not refugees. Together, the government of Pakistan and the UNHCR identified the camp as the nexus of Afghan refugee life. By August 1979, five large refugee camps had been established in the NWFP at Warsaw, Gandaf, Miranshah, Datta Khel, and Chitral, containing, in total, 15,030 residents. In Balochistan, six camps—at Quetta, Panjpai, and Pishin—housed 9,970 refugees, while another twenty-nine smaller establishments held an estimated total population of close to 26,595. Roughly another 118,022 Afghans still lived among locals in the NWFP and needed to be relocated.[17]

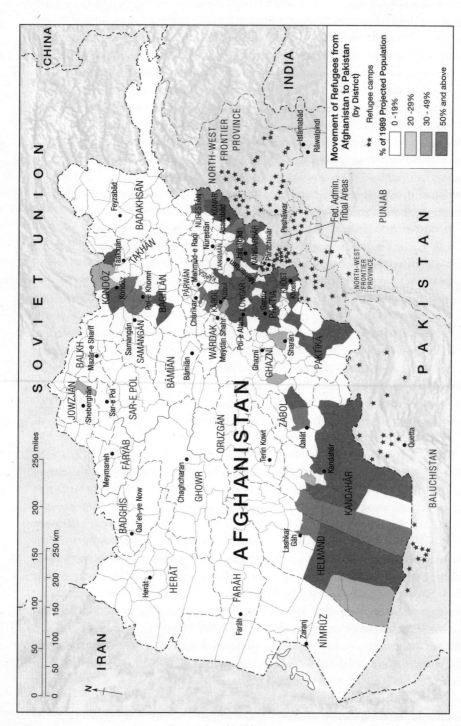

**Map 8.** Map of refugee camps in Pakistan, by district, c.1989 (drawn using information from UNHCR and CIA)

The number of camps only grew, as more refugees arrived in the country and officials continued shifting Afghans from local villages into camps. By late 1981, the government of Pakistan reported 240 Refugee Tentage Villages (RTVs) across sixteen districts in the NWFP and Balochistan and two million registered refugees. By July 1983, the number of RTVs had grown to 330. By the end of 1991, according to Pakistani sources, 3.2 million Afghan refugees were living in 345 camps. The decision of the government of Pakistan and UNHCR to focus support efforts through camp structures differentiated the Afghans living in Pakistan from earlier generations of migrants, making them the object of foreign attention and, for the first time, 'refugees', as understood by the international community.[18]

'Refugee' is a loaded term, one that international institutions have spent decades refining. At a basic level, a refugee can be defined using the 1951 Geneva Convention Relating to the Status of Refugees:

> the term 'refugee' shall apply to any person who ... owing to well-founded fear of being persecuted for reasons of race, religion, nationality, membership of a particular social group or political opinion, is outside the country of his [or her] nationality and is unable or, owing to such fear, is unwilling to avail himself of the protection of that country; or who, not having a nationality and being outside the country of his former habitual residence as a result of such events, is unable or, owing to such fear, is unwilling to return to it.[19]

Of course, refugees clearly preceded this definition: people have fled their homelands and the threat of persecution, seeking sanctuary elsewhere, for centuries, even millennia. In the modern world, refugees have become easier to identify as state borders have hardened. Passports, immigration controls, and border posts have allowed state leaders to monitor and regulate flows of people, to identify which people are fleeing or seeking refuge, as well as why. The demarcation and monitoring of borders, especially in the twentieth century, paralleled the growing consensus that states needed to work together to prevent crises that threatened humanity across state lines. Thus, in 1921, the League of Nations, with the support of the International Red Cross and Red Crescent societies, established a high commissioner for refugees, which was intended to deal with Russians fleeing from the Bolshevik Revolution.[20] In 1950, the UNHCR was established to oversee the repatriation and rehoming of Europeans displaced by the Second World War. The 1951 Convention thus was a response to the vast movements of Europeans. It was also symbolic of a new age of international politics that emphasized the importance of global governance through the auspices of the United Nations, a theme we will return to in Chapter 8.[21]

Yet, the early UNHCR refused to account for global refugee crises. The 1947 partition of South Asia, in one of the most violent episodes of the subcontinent's history, had led to the mass movement of millions of Hindus, Muslims, and Sikhs across the newly created borders separating independent India and Pakistan. The UN did not acknowledge this refugee crisis or provide any support to the fledgling governments, as they struggled to establish camps, settle their new citizens, and deal with widespread atrocities and sexual violence. Similarly, the UNHCR took no interest in the millions displaced by the Second World War in Asia, or those fleeing across state boundaries as the Chinese Civil War raged and imperial powers such as Britain and France violently reasserted their control over colonies such as Malaya and Indochina.[22] In both practice and definition, the refugee of the 1950s was European. Thus, in an unsurprising turn of events, countries such as Pakistan and India refused to sign the 1951 Geneva Convention when their citizens were so clearly excluded, a decision that would inform both states' approaches to the Afghans and limit the UNHCR's remit in these countries. Even a 1967 Protocol Relating to the Status of Refugees went only so far in eliminating the Eurocentrism of the earlier definition. While it expanded the geographical scope of refugee crises, it did not eliminate the inherent Westernism of much humanitarian aid to refugees.

Crises in the late 1950s in Europe and North Africa—the 1956 Hungarian uprising and the Algerian war for independence—slowly expanded the UNHCR's remit. As Hungarians fled the Soviet crackdown, neighbouring Austria and later Yugoslavia sought UN support. For the first time, the UNHCR assumed full responsibility for coordinating and running a refugee relief programme. It soon became the go-to lead agency for refugee relief, as state and UN leaders realized the benefits of working with one organization, rather than many, to manage a refugee crisis. The war in Algeria, meanwhile, played a crucial role in expanding the UNHCR's activities outside Europe. As more than two hundred thousand Algerians fled to Tunisia and Morocco, the UN General Assembly chose to expand the UNHCR's autonomy, no longer requiring the organization to consult the General Assembly each time it wanted to take action. By the end of the 1950s, the UNHCR could function largely independently and was broadly recognized as the key instrument for dealing with refugee crises across the world.[23]

UN member states insisted that the UNHCR was a humanitarian agency, not a political one.[24] It could not take a political 'side'—its responsibility was to all humanity. Initially it was intended only to provide legal aid to refugees, helping to identify them and provide guidance to state leaders. But, in a context of worldwide Cold War and expanding responsibilities, avoiding politics was virtually impossible. One side's refugees were another side's dissidents. Many of the UNHCR's early activities in Europe revolved around people escaping the Soviet-controlled East and socialist modernizing projects for the capitalist West, which did not encourage the Soviet Union to embrace the agency. While Western Europeans saw fleeing Hungarians as refugees, Eastern Europeans called them rebels and claimed they had little reason to flee (a similar argument would play out regarding Afghans). The United States' support for the UNHCR, meanwhile, was largely strategic. As a 1961 State Department memorandum noted: 'We believe that the spread of unrest in Africa and southeast Asia attaches growing importance to the High Commissioner's good offices function...Our national interest dictates that we should continue our leading role in support of the High Commissioner.'[25] Realpolitik dictated that the US back the UNHCR to combat the spread of Soviet influence across the globe.

The rapid expansion of decolonization in the late 1950s and 1960s, and its intersection with the Cold War, correspondingly led to the movement of people, some forced and some by choice. In areas where empire ended violently, such as the Congo, Algeria, Malaya, Nigeria, or Vietnam, thousands were forced on the move to escape war, to avoid punishment for choosing the losing side, or to seek new livelihoods. By the end of the twentieth century, refugees were perceived to be a crisis rooted in the non-Western world, with 97 per cent of the world's refugees located in the Third World.[26] The UNHCR took the leading role in dealing with these displaced persons. As the high commissioner for refugees noted in a 1960s report on decolonization in Africa:

> In response to the drama of hundreds of thousands of men, women, and children fleeing their villages and their homelands, the international community has entrusted my Office with the task of helping these uprooted people, first to survive and then to create a new existence if it is clear there is no hope of their being able to return voluntarily to the homes they have left behind.[27]

UNHCR engagement with refugees, particularly in the Global South, proved that politics could not be disentangled from flight. 'Refugeeness allowed Western "nonpolitical" intervention through the UNHCR and NGOs in these regions where "political" interference would have been impossible, first through emergency refugee

**Figure 7.2.** UNHCR tent for teacher and children in a refugee camp in Miranshah, Waziristan, Pakistan (Internet Archive, The Afghan Media Resource Center/ Manzoor Shah)

aid, and then additional programs of refugee development.' Even as refugees, themselves, questioned, undermined, and engaged in myriad ways with UNHCR activities intended to support displaced persons, the fact remained that the UNHCR and its supporters were solution driven. In other words, they focused on the mechanisms, infrastructures, and technologies that would best allow them to oversee, categorize, and care for refugees, which, intentionally or not, reshaped refugees themselves. 'The inhabitants of refugee camps, analogous to those residing in prisons and asylums, were not assumed to be liberal citizens capable of exercising choice. A well-administered camp promised to bring them into line with the requirements of such citizenship.'[28] Refugee camps thus, in some ways, served as state microcosms where residents could be shaped and influenced to act in certain ways: made 'modern', as defined by the UNHCR and its Western backers. Indeed, in Pakistan's refugee camps, the UNHCR competed with Afghan leaders to reshape Afghan livelihoods and social practices in ways not dissimilar to the PDPA, Hizb-i Islami, or Jam'iyyat.

Despite the government of Pakistan's uneasy relationship with the UNHCR—not only had it not signed the 1951 Convention; it also had a history of tensions with the UN and UNHCR, thanks to the ongoing Kashmir dispute and the UNHCR's role helping Bengali refugees escaping Pakistan during and after the 1971 war—Pakistani officials had little choice but to engage with UNHCR officials, given the scale of the Afghan crisis.[29] Nevertheless, the one major stipulation that Pakistani leaders made was that foreign aid had to be provided through the auspices of the Pakistani authorities, limiting the UNHCR's remit in the country—and ultimately allowing the Afghan resistance parties, with ISI support, to undermine UNHCR attempts to keep the camps apolitical.[30] While the UNHCR could establish and run refugee camps, they could do so only with Pakistani agreement and oversight.

Following their first visit to Pakistan in June 1979, UNHCR officials recommended a division of responsibilities between the international organization and government of Pakistan. UNHCR-led humanitarian assistance programmes would provide care and maintenance, establish functioning camps, and create 'self-sufficiency projects' for refugees. Pakistani officials, in turn, would identify and register arriving refugees, provide appropriate land for camps, create an administrative oversight system, waive customs duties and taxes on all aid goods, and collaborate with NGO representatives.[31] Based on these recommendations, the UNHCR officially agreed to an aid programme in Pakistan to

> include provision for care and maintenance of the refugees during an initial period, establishment of settlements away from the border, shelter, food, household goods, building of dispensaries (including equipment and medical supplies), transport facilities and measures to promote the self-sufficiency of the refugees.[32]

A major shared concern was the fact that the UNHCR's traditional strategies for dealing with refugee crises looked unfeasible for Afghan refugees. In past cases, the

UNHCR's first priority was voluntary repatriation: refugees should return home once circumstances had settled. Yet no end was in sight for the war in Afghanistan, particularly after December 1979. The second option involved encouraging third-country resettlement in other, perhaps non-neighbouring, countries. Again, issues emerged: many Afghans preferred to stay close to Afghanistan, and their cultural and social ties with Pakistan (and Iran) meant that leaving was unappealing. Additionally, many Western countries, still busy settling refugees from South-East Asia's decolonization wars, resisted accepting large numbers of Afghans. The UNHCR's third preferred alternative was to encourage refugees to integrate into their host country. However, the scale of the Afghan refugee crisis eliminated this possibility: too many Afghans had arrived for ready assimilation.[33]

In discussing the future of Afghan refugees, the closest comparison that UNHCR officials could make was with the case of the Palestinians. Since the mid-twentieth century, thousands of Palestinians had been housed for decades in originally temporary camps and thus largely remained stateless, serving as a warning for leaders across the world. Fears grew that exiled Afghans could become similarly permanently displaced.[34] The UNHCR high commissioner pointed out resignedly: 'Unfortunately, none of the three classical durable solutions to a given refugee problem can apply in the case of Afghans in Pakistan.' He concluded: 'This sadly makes the fate of Afghans in Pakistan dramatic, and possibly unique compared to other refugee situations, where, however distant, a solution lies somewhere on the horizon.'[35]

Officials, both within the government of Pakistan and at the UNHCR, were staggered by the sheer number of fleeing Afghans. A UNHCR briefing noted: 'At EXCOM of 1979, an annual budget of some US$10.3 million was approved for a caseload of 228,000. In less than 2 years, this budget has grown tenfold, as has the number of refugees. Yet we are today basically working with the same tools as when the programme began.' For 1981, a joint review by the UNHCR and the government of Pakistan estimated that nearly $1 billion was needed for refugees' non-food and supplementary food requirements. Basic food supplies, meanwhile, comprised 310,250 tons of wheat, 18,615 tons of edible oil, and 18,615 tons of powdered milk, costing $119.75 million. When health and housing provisions were added into the mix, officials estimated $218 million were required to take care of Afghan refugees for the year 1981—and this excluded support that had already been provided.[36]

With Pakistan's decision to open its borders to the UNHCR, the Afghan refugee crisis became a global issue. The Soviet invasion in December 1979 only made it more so, providing a Cold-War impetus for citizens worldwide to show their support to Afghans forced to flee invading socialist forces. Representatives of the UN Development Programme, UNICEF, World Food Programme (WFP), International Committee of the Red Cross, and League of Red Cross and Red Crescent Societies became involved in various aspects of caring for the refugees in late 1979. These were assisted and supported by benevolent societies from across the world. Some, like the Salvation Army, sent employees to Pakistan to work in camps. Others fundraised and collected goods to deliver to impoverished Afghans. Church World

Services, an NGO based in New York, chartered a jet to fly 90,000 lb of blankets, clothing, and medicine to Pakistan.[37] Much of the aid sent to the country was welcomed, but some was met with bemusement. A 1980 article in the *New York Times* began:

> Sardines in tomato sauce, high-heeled shoes, brassieres, briefcases and weight-reducing powder are among the donations shipped from around the world for the million Afghan refugees estimated to be in Pakistan. 'I am sure it was done with the best of intentions,' a perplexed relief worker said, 'but much of it is totally useless'.[38]

Fortunately, the majority of aid sent to Pakistan had more value.

The UNHCR's mandate in Pakistan was to organize and coordinate the international and regional response to the Afghan refugee crisis. In order to do so, this required 'translat[ing] complex, illegible and multiple local claims into standard categories that can be recorded, compared and used'.[39] In other words, the UNHCR first needed to identify and record *who* was an Afghan refugee. This placed emphasis on being Afghan, an identity that eschewed ethnic, tribal, or *qawm* affiliations for a national one, as well as being a refugee in line with the 1951 and 1967 UN protocols. Thus, much like those of the PDPA and Islamists, UNHCR officials' identification processes brought into question extant social and political networks and instead relied on units more familiar to Western audiences—families and nationalities. This was accompanied by the creation of appropriate local infrastructures to address refugees' needs. Even while the UNHCR's overarching structures were weak and reliant on local partnerships, particularly with the government of Pakistan, the way that this played out within the refugee camps was to reorder Afghan social, economic, and political dynamics.

To understand how and why the UNHCR's activities had such a fundamental impact on Afghans' daily lives, the sheer scale of the structures underpinning refugee settlements needs to be appreciated. Refugee management was a joint UNHCR–Pakistani endeavour. The government of Pakistan established a chief commissioner for Afghan refugees at the federal level, who coordinated with the UN, private voluntary organizations, state directors of relief operations, and deputy directors responsible for stores and transportation, medical services, and public relations. Alongside these were regional deputy directors covering both the NWFP and Balochistan. At the provincial level, refugee commissioners oversaw additional officials for relief operations, security, and administration, while collaborating with local UNHCR and NGO representatives. Below the provincial level were district commissioners, political agents, and district refugee administrators; area administrators, each of whom had responsibility for five RTVs; and then, finally, RTV administrators. RTV administrators worked most closely with refugees, overseeing the distribution of food and relief goods and managing disbursement and accounts, registration, health, infrastructure, and security issues. By mid-1981, 6,648 personnel were employed purely for refugee management, excluding specialized services such as medical and educational staff.[40]

Camp personnel had expansive responsibilities. Officials tried to register and organize refugees and provide for their needs. Upon arrival, each family was given a passbook issued by the chief commissionerate for Afghan refugees. A passport-sized booklet with all instructions written in English and Urdu, the passbook recorded crucial information about Afghan arrivals and allowed officials to monitor them in the camps. It included information about the passbook holders and their families, date and point of entry, accompanying belongings, and numerous pages dedicated to the minutiae of camp living: a record of the basic goods provided to each arrival, pages to record monthly rations of foodstuffs and maintenance allowances, and medical records, where camp doctors would note inspections and provision of various injections. Its final instructions warned recipients that the passbook would be withdrawn if the holder left Pakistan and that 'Citizenship of Pakistan cannot be claimed with this Pass Book'.[41] The passbook clearly indicated that UNHCR option three—local assimilation—was not on the cards, while also trying to discourage continued border crossings.

UNHCR officials worried about corruption as an inevitable partner to the registration process. While the government of Pakistan, by September 1981, had officially registered 2.3 million Afghan refugees, local UNHCR and WFP representatives agreed on an estimate closer to 1.7 million.[42] Some refugees managed to register more than once, thereby increasing their rations. Other registered refugees did not actually exist, and their collected goods were sold on the black market. UNHCR officials fretted about the potential impact of refugees on nearby Pakistani communities, including the potential for black-market trading to undermine local economies and stir resentment.[43] They also expressed reservations about the government of Pakistan's decision to use the exiled Afghan political parties as registration intermediaries. One UNHCR official reported: 'there are instances where some refugees who do not wish to associate themselves with any political party consequently face difficulties obtaining the Identity Certificates and the Registration Card, and are thus not eligible for material assistance.'[44] As many Afghan family heads became party members out of necessity—the parties demanded affiliation as the cost of receiving a passbook—resistance politics seeped into the camps, with widespread consequences.

The UNHCR and government of Pakistan tried to limit each RTV to 5,000 members, or about 700–800 families. Some of the bigger refugee settlements were thus subdivided into multiple RTVs. Each RTV had its own medical dispensary, with medicines and equipment; a primary school, with two teachers and supplies; and a religious instructor and mosque. Officials ensured that RTVs had a readily accessible water supply, building pipelines to bring in water if necessary, as well as vocational centres to promote economic self-reliance and space for livestock. RTVs also provided direct assistance to refugee families, providing shelter, usually a tent, bedding, basic food rations, clothing, and utensils. The government of Pakistan allotted a regular cash allowance for each refugee ($5.05, or 50 rupees), with a maximum of $50.50 (500 rupees) per family. For 1981, the government estimated that each refugee's immediate needs cost about $15, totalling $360 million for all registered refugees.[45]

Once camps were up and running, officials did not just leave resident Afghans to their own devices. Instead, Afghan refugees' health, education, and employability were all closely monitored within the camps (see Figure 7.3). The UNHCR, working with the Red Cross and Red Crescent Societies, took numerous steps to improve camp dwellers' physical wellbeing. Alongside each RTV's dispensary, health clinics and small hospitals were established at the district and provincial levels, and Health Mobile Units, staffed with male and female doctors and technical operators, visited each RTV three times a week to treat patients.[46] Additionally, more specialized procedures were made available. For example, the Pakistan Red Crescent Society, working with the Swiss Red Cross, established an eye clinic for Afghan refugees and local Pakistanis that could complete surgical procedures to treat curable blindness and provide medications to deal with various eye diseases.[47] Officials also prioritized education and encouraged families to send their children to the camps' primary schools. Nasir Bagh Camp had four primary schools to educate 436 students.[48] Officials likewise sought increased female education schemes, though with uneven success. Where some Afghan communities embraced a more active role for women outside the home, others rejected these and instead re-emphasized the social practice of *purdah*.[49]

International organizations also touted 'self-reliance' to develop refugees' skills and to fend off idleness. At the end of August 1979, an inter-agency mission of

**Figure 7.3.** Afghan refugee boys studying in a school (Internet Archive, The Afghan Media Resource Center/Shair Ali)

representatives from the UNHCR, WFP, and UNICEF visited Pakistan to assess the needs of refugees. In their findings, they emphasized the importance of self-sufficiency. 'Generally speaking,' they reported,

> the refugees appear receptive to the idea of starting productive activities, though their primary objective remains to return as soon as possible to their country of origin. Some reluctance exists, however, due to the belief that such schemes may lead to permanent settlement in the country of asylum.

They concluded: 'Wherever this misconception emerges, a considerable persuasion effort would have to be undertaken by the local authorities in order to place the objective into proper perspective.' 'Productive activities', the mission insisted, were important for refugees returning to their homeland, not just during their tenure abroad. The mission thus proposed agricultural and handicraft activities 'to utilize the refugees' traditional skills'.[50]

In this realm, the modernizing impetuses of Western-led humanitarianism became especially apparent and, to some extent, paralleled Soviet activities within Afghan territory. Self-reliance schemes walked a fine line between trying to reshape Afghan social and economic practices while respecting pre-existing community hierarchies. Notably, camp observers seized on opportunities to influence all Afghans. The refugee camp, as a confined setting, was a far cry from Afghanistan, where historical governing initiatives (with and without foreign aid) had been exercised unevenly and had targeted some tribal and ethnic groups and regions more than others.

To an extent, it is unsurprising that international institutions and NGOs funnelling millions of dollars into aid expected refugees to work. Indeed, Michael Day-Thompson, a British consultant to the UNHCR, argued that Afghan refugees were 'being turned remorselessly into beggars with palms extended upwards'. He warned: 'It may be that history will show that we and the other sources of aid in Pakistan have done more damage to the natural independence and self-respect of the Afghan than the Russians themselves.'[51] Self-reliance, by this logic, would give refugees a focus for their energies, while also helping them to develop and hone important, lifelong skills.

However, at the same time, NGOs from Europe and North America had historically tried to implement Western versions of modernization in non-Western communities, regardless of their fit. Indeed, many NGOs emerged from the Western empires that had colonized so much of the world under the justification of 'modernizing' or 'civilizing' those under their rule.[52] Refugee camps offered the perfect opportunity to try to adjust community practices, even as foreign workers aimed to respect what they perceived to be 'traditional' customs. This tension can be seen with a mission from the International Labour Organization (ILO), which visited a number of refugee camps in November 1982. In their subsequent report, organizers explained: 'greater self-reliance is generally interpreted to mean that a larger proportion of the needs of refugees for maintenance and care be met through their own efforts, and that the proportionate contributions from the host country and the international community decline over time.' They emphasized that one 'major consideration underlying our approach has been to ground our proposals in the social and cultural context of the refugees'. This had led them to 'obtain some understanding of the role and leadership style of "maliks" and "jam" leaders, and of the part they might play in the initiation and management of projects suggested by us'.

Officials used their interactions with local leaders to conclude that 'the role and position of women and the division of work in the household among the different Afghan tribes, have defined the limits of what is feasible and acceptable for schemes for women refugees'. The mission used such knowledge to propose a number of different programmes, including training 'to upgrade the basic traditional skills of the refugees as well as to introduce newer modern skills'; a plan for refugees to gain construction skills; the development of kitchen gardens and poultry-raising; promotion of handicraft export; and modernization of Afghan households and healthcare practices by educating women.[53] To demonstrate their cultural sensitivity, officials opted to channel aid through what they perceived to be traditional community structures.[54]

Such plans demonstrated that international organizations, much like the PDPA, Hizb-i Islami, or Jam'iyyat, also tried to reshape, or 'upgrade', Afghan social and political relations. Organizations like the ILO undertook steps not only further to develop Afghan refugees' employability but to show them how to live in a specific way. Yet the belief that Afghans needed to be taught how to tend gardens or raise

**Figure 7.4.** An Afghan refugee woman sewing clothes (Internet Archive, The Afghan Media Resource Center/IRC (International Rescue Committee))

chickens, or how to heat food more efficiently, or about appropriate family hygiene was potentially patronizing and, to an extent, paralleled US (and some Soviet) assumptions about Afghanistan's supposedly backward nature. It assumed that Afghan refugees were incapable of developing opportunities or guiding their own lives without outside help. (It also overlooked the agrarian backgrounds of many Afghans who had fled to Pakistan and who probably had experience in both gardening and poultry-raising.) In one sense, ILO concerns were justified. Given their location in a foreign country, Afghans clearly did not have the same opportunities as they would have had at home. But the fact remained that many ILO members were not, themselves, Afghan. The refugee crisis provided foreign agents with the opportunity to re-educate and remould Afghans' lives and livelihoods, to make them modern, as they thought appropriate.

Afghans who chose to leave their homes and flee to Pakistan thus confronted a massive apparatus that sought to oversee and manage their lives within the camps. Refugee camp activities reveal a deep irony to the Afghan refugee experience. Millions had fled Afghanistan because they rejected the PDPA's efforts to intervene in their daily lives. They did not trust government policy and were reluctant to change their lifestyles. But the decision to flee did not, in fact, ensure that Afghan lives and livelihoods remained unchanged. Instead, Afghans exchanged one form of government oversight for another—one that was just as, perhaps even more, invasive. Reports like the ILO's revealed officials' intent to interfere in Afghan daily life in a way that most Afghans had never experienced. Life in exile boiled down to the fact that, if refugees wanted any sort of assistance, they needed to register and become, at least officially, camp residents. The war in Afghanistan brought tens, if not hundreds, of thousands of Afghans into contact with administrative oversight through the auspices of the refugee camp. But this unintentionally provided opportunities for Afghan party leaders to take advantage of these new living dynamics to extend their influence at the same time that Afghan self-identifications also began to shift.

The refugee crisis and the grouping of thousands of Afghans into camps dotted across the NWFP and Balochistan had consequences for Afghan leadership structures as well as for notions of *Afghaniyat* or 'Afghanness'. UNHCR and Pakistani efforts to bureaucratize camps exacerbated political crises produced by the killing of political, religious, and social leaders by the PDPA and the inability of some local leaders to adjust to the new circumstances of refugee life.

Initially, local Afghan leaders asserted their influence within camps and tried to intermediate between camp officials and Afghans. Within the camps, Afghans from the same families, ethnic groups, villages, and regions—the same *qawm*—tended to stick together. As such, surviving village elders still had the opportunity to represent their communities within the camps. Early on, *qawm* leaders served as 'ration *maliks*', as they came to be known, liaising with officials to acquire and distribute aid to other refugees. They would present a list of those they represented and collect each families' allotted rations. 'The ration maliki system allowed refugees to equate the camp context with the village administration system that traditionally existed in Afghanistan,' the anthropologist David Edwards observed. 'In both situations, the point of contact with the government could be limited and tribal leaders were able to function as the primary representatives of the government to the people.'[55]

This system, however, could not last in extant form. As refugee camps became more organized and additional external administrators became responsible for different aspects of camp life, officials refused to keep working with these same community leaders. The system was seen as a source of potential corruption. What was to stop a ration *malik* from claiming that he was collecting rations for a community of 200 when, in fact, he led a community of 20? One UNHCR observer disapprovingly noted: 'rations have been delivered to the leaders of non-resident groups, who were under no obligation to prove the existence of their followers. I understand that one man has in the past collected rations for 17,000 alleged members of his group.'[56] Officials tried to use the nuclear family instead, as seen by the passbook. This would make family heads responsible for collecting their family's rations, while allowing administrators to ensure more closely that refugees were receiving appropriate aid. This directive undermined the authority of *qawm* leaders. Because administrators were uncertain about the size of community that the *maliks* who were requesting rations actually represented, they chose not to accept their legitimacy and instead prioritized a unit with which they were more familiar—the family. In contrast to circumstances within Afghanistan, community leaders in the camps had to prove their legitimacy—not so much within their own *qawm* but to outsiders.

Yet there were simply too many families inhabiting each refugee camp for administrators to address them individually. As such, officials still sought representation from among the refugees, but they opted to work with Afghans who shared the same language of humanitarianism and needs. While *maliks* and local *mullahs* remained important resources within their communities, they increasingly ran into competition. For many camp communities, the ration *malik* changed from being a traditional leader—someone who would also have had a role of authority within Afghanistan— to a new generation of leadership. A sociologist who visited camps in Chagai district reported to the UNHCR: 'The majority of maliks [in these camps] became maliks in Pakistan. The people selected them to receive their food supplies.'[57] These representatives were frequently younger men who had spent time abroad and spoke foreign languages. Because they could interact with foreign officials, they became invested with a different sort of authority—authority recognized by foreign actors that then placed them in a position of power within local communities. These new ration *maliks* existed side-by-side with extant *qawm* and political party leaders, and each played a critical role.[58] Much as the PDPA and Islamist parties tried to disrupt long-standing hierarchies and provided opportunities for individuals from humble origins, like Taraki, to achieve prominence, so did camp administrators create a space for competing leaders to emerge.

We have already discussed the ways in which political party leaders took advantage of the opportunities provided by Pakistan's ISI and adopted the language of Western humanitarianism—the image of the suffering refugee—to integrate and absorb Afghan refugees into the political party system. Indeed, the Afghan resistance parties were not alone in taking advantage of camp structures for their own benefit. The South West Africa People's Organization (SWAPO), for example, similarly took advantage of (and established its own) camps of exiles and used them as bases for national liberation struggles and to reconfigure Namibian politics and society. Though SWAPO camps did not rely on support from organizations like the UNHCR (instead receiving aid from sympathetic regional partners), similar reconfigurations of politics and identity took place.[59]

Equally, it is important to recognize that many Afghans also joined a political party for the opportunities it offered, not just economic or nutritional necessity. The political parties took a leading political and social role within the camps. They participated in RTV committees to help address conflicts between refugees.[60] The parties built their own schools and *madrassas* and acted as an additional source of leadership. The moderate alliance of Gailani, Mujaddidi, and Nabi, for example, claimed to have established 180 primary schools, 10 secondary schools, and 4 high schools for refugees by October 1983. It also established medical and theological institutes in Peshawar. In taking a leading role in refugees' educations, parties lobbied the UNHCR to provide foreign scholarships. 'One of our great problems with the refugees', one party representative noted, 'is that a great number of school graduates as well as University Degree Holders…are now in refugee camps. Job opportunity and pursuance of higher studies is rare.'[61] The parties thus engaged and competed with the UNHCR and NGOs to provide refugees with opportunities for education, socialization, and political mobilization.

The resistance parties created prospects for Afghans who had chosen exile but were now forced to stay in camps, waiting to see what would happen next. The parties offered men the chance to do something in the war against the PDPA, as well as escape from a life of uncertainty within the camps. Self-reliance schemes simply could not fill this void. For many Afghans, such programmes bore little resemblance to their old working lives. Rural men could not continue farming and agricultural pursuits: the NWFP and Balochistan lacked enough arable fields, and Afghan workers would have to compete not only with each other but with local Pakistanis for these precious plots of land. Refugee camps also provided the ideal recruiting grounds for new cohorts of resistance fighters. They were packed with men, young and old, who suddenly lacked their typical daily activities. 'Traditionally', according to one observer, 'most rural boys would be occupied in learning to farm and herd, but now they seek any activities, no matter how inappropriate, to fill idle time provided by less than adequate education and vocational training.'[62]

The resistance parties looked to Afghanistan's future in many ways. Not only did they recruit combatants from among the refugees, but they also sought to develop the next generation of Afghan intellectuals and bureaucrats. One group of engineers educated at Kabul University wrote to the UNHCR:

> We don't want to be helped by 500 or 700 Pakistani rupees and be given a tent in the refugee's camp, sitting idle and our hands under our chins, waiting for the future. Our worries are our mental and physical potentialities, our natural creativities and talents, our maturities and youngnesses [*sic*] that should not be kept idle and useless. Why is it not possible to be directed to a productive channel of engineering services?[63]

Party leaders encouraged educated Afghans to seek additional experiences abroad. The young engineers explained: 'Our Afghan fighters do not let us to joine [*sic*] them in their fighting, instead they encourage us to use this opportunity for gaining as much knowledge of technology as we can, to be the technological assets of future peacefull [*sic*] Afghanistan.'[64] The parties, these young engineers believed, were preparing them not just for war but for its aftermath.

The refugee crisis also reshaped how many Afghans thought of themselves and their relationship with an Afghan nation. Not all Afghans experienced exile in the same ways. In their fieldwork among Afghan refugees in Pakistan during the 1980s, the anthropologists Pierre Centlivres and Micheline Centlivres-Demont identified the fracturing of Afghan identity along three general lines, which I will expand upon here. The first of these involved renewed emphasis on Afghans' tribal (and ethnic) affiliations. The second was an affirmation of Afghans' adherence to Islam and their

**Figure 7.5** Demonstration of Afghan refugees against the PDPA in Peshawar, Pakistan (Internet Archive, The Afghan Media Resource Center/Shafiqullah)

embrace of themselves as *mohajirin*. The final was self-identification as 'refugees' in line with the 1951 Convention discussed previously.

For Afghan Pashtuns who chose to move to Pakistan, *Pashtunwali* and its tenets of *nanawati, malmastia,* and *badal* (revenge) played a critical role in their choice to flee to and stay in Pakistan, their acceptance among Pakistani Pashtuns, and the decision of many to take up arms against the PDPA. Reaffirming *Pashtunwali* made fleeing Afghanistan an honourable choice. For Pashtuns, 'seeking asylum (*panah*) is an entirely acceptable avenue for those whose integrity is compromised or who are in danger from the government or a local enemy'.[65] Embracing *Pashtunwali* as a significant social and political determinant took away any shame that might otherwise be affiliated with flight or leaving the scene of battle. It also offered ethnic and tribal affiliations among Pashtuns as alternative structures to the DRA's radical political and social policies.

This reaffirmation of tribal or ethnic affiliation was not unique to Afghanistan's Pashtuns. Ethnic divisions in Afghanistan were a point of contention for both the PDPA and resistance organizations, and ethnic and religious ties similarly influenced the trajectory of Afghan refugees. Groups that arrived in Pakistan tended to cluster together in refugee camps and re-form communities based along ethnic lines, such as Tajiks and Turkmans.[66] Afghanistan's Hazara predominantly chose to settle in Iran, though a sizeable contingent also gathered around Quetta. Much like Pashtuns who fled Pakistan, Hazara shared ethnic and religious ties with their Iranian hosts, and their movement mirrored historical migration patterns. For generations, Hazara had travelled between Afghanistan and Iran in pursuit of economic opportunities. In the early 1970s, several hundred thousand already resided in Iran as migrant workers. After the events of 1978, many Hazara chose to move semi-permanently to Iran, where they were granted refugee status by the Iranian government, registered, and issued with 'blue cards'. In contrast to Pakistan, Afghan Hazara were more fully integrated into Iranian society and provided with various social benefits and employment.[67] Refugee camps remained fewer and far between, in part because the UNHCR (and its major American funders) provided far less aid to Iran than to Pakistan. The polarization of Afghanistan's ethnic communities only re-emphasized pre-existing tensions between the country's different ethnic groups. But reaffirmation of ethnic and tribal community in exile was hardly surprising, as it provided a source of continuity against the backdrop of so much change.

Secondly, Islam offered another key source of identity and meaning among Afghans. Many Afghans perceived the PDPA and their Soviet allies as un-Islamic, even anti-Islamic. In contrast, Islamist thought became a major source of inspiration for some of the most powerful resistance groups and helped thousands of Afghan men to style themselves as *mujahidin* conducting *jihad* against the Soviets and PDPA. For refugees, rumours that Soviet and PDPA forces were burning Qurans or forcing Afghans to give up Islam—as well as the very real killings of clerics and Muslim political–religious community leaders—had led many to flee. As Ghanam Rang, an elder in the Matasangar refugee camp, explained to Western reporters: 'We ourselves started fighting for the glory of Islam. We are believers in God, and these people wanted us to leave our faith. Tell me, how can I renounce my religion?'[68]

The *mohajir* was the flip side of the *mujahid*, or holy warrior. In Arabic, *mohajir* translates as refugee, but, in usage, it frequently has specifically religious connotations. 'A *mohajer* is one who voluntarily goes into exile, and who has severed the ties with his own people and his possessions to take refuge in a land of Islam.'[69] In Islamic history, the first *mohajirin* were the followers of the Prophet Mohammad who fled alongside him from Mecca to Medina in AD 622 to flee persecution, the *hijrat*.[70] Much like faithfully observing Pashtunwali, self-identifying as *mohajirin* provided both a rationale and a sense of dignity to Afghan exiles. They fled 'persecution by non-believers.

This identifier also linked Afghan refugees to the rest of the Islamic world. Circassians fleeing the North Caucasus in the nineteenth century had sought refuge across the Ottoman Empire as *mohajirin* escaping religious and ethnic discrimination and widespread massacres in the Russian Empire. Likewise, the *mohajir* had a weighty history within Pakistan, where Muslims who had migrated to Pakistan during the 1947 partition had framed their decision to resettle from India to Pakistan in religious terms.[71] This Islamic framework appealed particularly to a Pakistani officialdom wary of how the influx of Afghans might exacerbate ethnic tensions within Pakistan while also focused on its own political Islamization. Thus, the government of Pakistan, like many Afghans, embraced the terminology of the *mohajir*. In Urdu, 'refugee' can be defined simply as one seeking refuge or shelter (پناه گزینوں, *panah gzinon*) or as *mohajir* (مهاجر). In registering refugees, the government officially termed them 'افغان مهاجرین' (Afghan *mohajirin*)—Afghan Islamic exiles, not merely people seeking shelter—a small but significant difference that re-emphasized Afghans' and Pakistanis' shared religion, the PDPA's shortcomings, and older, broader Muslim histories of suffering for faith.[72]

In contrast, accepting the UNHCR definition of refugees diverged from pre-existing identifiers of tribe, ethnicity, and Islam and lacked roots in Afghan society and history. This reconceptualization of Afghans accompanied UNHCR oversight of camp life and desire to identify and organize Afghans along lines familiar to foreign bureaucrats and officials. It thus was a concept applied by outside actors and implied the acceptance of certain stereotypes. The refugee, as understood in popular global culture, is usually 'a victim of circumstances over which he has no control, condemned to poverty and dependence, and having a right to humanitarian relief; he must be given refuge, protected, nourished, and cared for—in other words taken charge of'.[73] This view was exemplified by another English-language pamphlet published in Islamabad in the early 1980s, entitled *Afghan Refugees in Pakistan*. The refugees on the front of the pamphlet included three tired, but stern-looking Afghan men staring directly at the photographer's lens. Around them huddled a woman and eight children, some of whom perched on rough sacks, presumably filled with their belongings. Inside the booklet were additional photos of barefoot, unsmiling children and bewildered old men. The text included statements like: 'Old and infirm, maimed and mutilated, male and female, with sucking babies, tiny toddlers and infants, three million of them!'[74]

This image is striking in how it differs from that of the *mohajir* or adherent to *Pashtunwali*. The latter two emphasized Afghans' dignity, the honour in their choice to reject the PDPA and instead adhere loyally to Islam and their local community or ethnic group, even if that meant leaving their homeland. The Afghan refugee that the UNHCR understood and portrayed, in contrast, was 'poor, ill-educated, and undernourished…pathetic individuals, their children and a few belongings on their backs, fleeing with fear and bewilderment in their eye'.[75] This conception of the Afghan refugee undermined the sense of agency and strength embedded in other identities, as well as providing the justification for foreigners' 'self-reliance' schemes. In the interpretation put forward by international observers, including the UNHCR, Afghans *had* to flee. They had no choice but to escape, and now they needed to be cared *for*. And this was an image that Afghans, to an extent, had grudgingly to accept if they wanted to receive aid and accommodation while abroad. The resistance parties took advantage of this identifier to insert themselves into discussions of Afghan identity and to provide a further alternative to this image of Afghan as victim: Afghan party member.

Without question, many Afghans—individuals and communities alike—had experienced horrific violence and faced little alternative but flight, but it is simplistic and reductive merely to consider Afghan refugees as helpless and bewildered. It ignores other local framings of Afghan migration and the ways that various Afghans wrestled with their experience of displacement. Nevertheless, put most simply, Afghans had little choice but to accept international conceptions of refugeeness if they wanted to receive aid.

The experience of fleeing and being forced to resettle within a regulated camp framework was one that produced uncertainty in all aspects of Afghan life. It involved massive upheaval and insecurity, and, as days became weeks, weeks months, and months years, the question increasingly became *if*, not when, exile would end. Would refugees ever be able to return home to Afghanistan?

It is worth pausing briefly to consider the huge emotional costs of flight and exile, of the civil war's violence, something that has been explored by scholars who have conducted more recent research among Afghan forced migrants. Many Afghans chose to flee in the hopes that they would escape the terrors of the PDPA regime, but one form of fear was frequently replaced by another. Not only could many Afghans not forget what they had experienced at the hands of the PDPA, but the potential impossibility of returning home also haunted many. One Afghan woman, who ultimately settled in California, described her family's experiences:

My father was put in prison many times. He was a leader of Mujahideen, so they hit him a lot, they gave him electric shocks and very painful punishment. During these times my mother was almost mute; she didn't eat, she didn't sleep, she was crying too much. Another year, my uncle was put in jail. When my father took him food and clothes, the jail officer said, 'Don't bother to bring anything for him because they took him very far from here.' This meant that they killed him. For about a year my family was crying. There was nothing we could do for him, we lost him forever. But we never forgot his handsome young face. When they caught my father again—and we knew that if they took him to jail, he would never come out alive—we escaped. Now my father is mentally sick; he is always crying, upset. He doesn't sleep, and nobody can talk with him.[76]

While Afghans, like this family, could leave the location where they had experienced huge pain, they could not escape their experiences or memories. Survivors' guilt and grief for family members who had been killed haunted many. Another young man remembered his brother's death at the hands of a boy whom they thought was a friend but who was, in fact, spying for the PDPA.

His friend pretended his gun was not loaded and, in front of all the others, he shot my brother in the heart. After two days they brought this handsome young boy's dead body to his mother. She didn't want to come here [outside Afghanistan]. She said, 'How can I leave the soul of my son alone over there?' We believe she is mentally sick; she talks with her son always, I mean with herself. She lost weight and she forgot to eat; she doesn't sleep.[77]

For many, the experience of travelling from Afghanistan to Pakistan or Iran only exacerbated their anguish. The trip was harrowing. One elderly woman remembered:

In Jalalabad we hired someone to take us to Peshawar...It was the worst nightmare in my entire life. The gunship helicopters and fear of punishment by communists made it more treacherous. These days I have bad dreams, like walking on dead bodies because there was no other way. Among the dead is my husband who curses me for doing so.[78]

The journey was never easy, and many Afghans continued to carry the terrors of the experience with them into camp life.

For many, experiences in Afghanistan stimulated anger and a determination to fight back. Thus, refugee camps became bases for resistance fighters who moved back and forth across the border as part of their efforts to combat the PDPA and the Soviets. But, for others, camps became a place of refuge. Much has been made of the limitations that camp life placed on Afghan women. Women were disproportionately affected by the Afghan war. The majority of camp inhabitants were women and children. By the end of the 1980s, the UNHCR estimated that 48 per cent of refugees were children under the age of 15, while 28 per cent were women.[79] The men officially registered in RTVs were mobile. Some came in and out of camps on a daily basis, going to jobs across the NWFP and Balochistan. Many, of course, left for longer periods of time, crossing the border to fight with the resistance and returning to resupply or have wounds treated. Women, in contrast, were more static, remaining in camps, often in family compounds. The practice of *purdah*, or segregation of men and women, was highly visible and largely accepted in many camps.

Many Western observers at the time, including those attached to the UNHCR and other NGOs, were highly critical of this perceived restriction on women's rights and autonomy within camps. A report for Save the Children Sweden bemoaned as late as 1994 that women's 'ability to participate in training programs, community based activities and mobility within and outside the camps is controled [*sic*] by these institutions dominated by men'. The author concluded: 'The members of these peer groups need to be gender sensitized so that they could better appreciate, acknowledge and recognize the contributions of the "silent female labour force".'[80] A female doctor in Mir Alizai camp told a UNHCR group that, while many women would use the camp's medical clinics only for treatments, 'perhaps a few also come because the clinic provides a meeting place where women can share amongst themselves their many preoccupations of daily existence under camp conditions. Such a place of meeting', she concluded, 'is badly needed for women, many of whom are isolated behind their mud compounds'.[81] They certainly had a point. In Afghanistan, women had more mobility. In rural communities, women actively took part in agriculture and stock-raising. In Afghanistan's cities, women frequently led less cloistered lives and embraced various aspects of Western-modelled and state-induced modernization. This mobility was severely restricted in a camp setting.

However, two points arise. First, not all women had the same experience of exile. Even while some of the Islamist Afghan political parties used their growing influence to encourage *purdah* and gender segregation for religious purity, organizations like the Revolutionary Association of the Women of Afghanistan (RAWA) actively worked alongside them to represent women and protest against reactionary policies. Founded in 1977 by Meena (typically known only by her first name), RAWA had been active in Afghanistan, organizing women's literacy campaigns and marches protesting against the PDPA. It continued its educational activities from exile in 1981, setting up handicraft centres and girls' schools, publishing a feminist political magazine, *Payam-i Zan*, and even organizing women to accompany resistance fighters back into Afghanistan to re-establish schools for locals. The Afghan Women's Network similarly tried to ensure that women received representation in the ongoing Geneva peace talks. More affluent, educated Afghan women had at least some opportunities to use their forced migration for political and social mobilization.[82] Other women actively embraced and took advantage of education opportunities for themselves and their children in the refugee camps.[83]

Unsurprisingly, party leaders, particularly the more radical Islamists, saw RAWA and other feminist activities as a threat to their own supremacy. In 1986, Meena's husband was captured and killed by members of Hekmatyar's Hizb-i Islami, and, less than four months later, Meena was assassinated. Her followers also blamed Hekmatyar. Meena became another in the line of political targets that Hizb-i Islami eliminated in its quest for power.[84] RAWA, however, responded by accelerating its activities among refugees, including educational activities, the building of orphanages, and provision of health and humanitarian support. Members also began organizing public demonstrations, including a protest to coincide with the anniversary of the Soviet invasion in December 1987. As one RAWA member subsequently explained in an interview:

> If we had a public face and could make ourselves more known, we could scare the enemy... We learned from the history of our country's situation and our acquaintance with the enemy that the more we remained silent, the wilder the fundamentalists would react and the more we would be their victims.[85]

RAWA's activities point to some of the growing divides within the resistance and further indicate the sense of uncertainty among Afghans that accompanied a potential Soviet withdrawal. Not only that, but Hizb-i Islami's attacks on RAWA reinforce the fact that refugee camps also remained sites of potential violence, where parties like Hizb-i Islami would go to great measures to assert their own power and influence among Afghan civilians.

The second point is that, for some women, *purdah* was not something imposed but rather something they welcomed. Amid the chaos of resettlement and the numerous changes that camp life inevitably forced on Afghan families—the destruction of living patterns, the dearth of employment opportunities, the loss of family members to the war—'inward-oriented residences provide psychological as well as physical protection while the refugees are largely dependent on outside for survival', as Nancy Hatch Dupree observed during camp visits in Pakistan.[86] Family homes within the camps became safe spaces for refugee women, where they could take at least limited control of family matters and try to provide some semblance of stability. While Afghan men may have turned to *purdah* to deal with their own feelings of political and economic insecurity—enforcing *purdah* allowed them to assert their control over their wives and families—'many women become more inclined to conform to traditional ideals governing their behavior when crises threaten. For them, stricter seclusion provides both physical and psychological shelter.'[87] This is neither to promote nor to condemn the practice of *purdah* and the restrictions placed on many Afghan women within refugee society, but it is necessary to recognize that at least some women embraced the practice as a means of providing themselves with safety and comfort in an otherwise fraught time.

For many Afghans, the experience of exile resulted in a longing for home, or *vatan*, and an idealization of what life had been like in Afghanistan. One inhabitant of Nasir Bagh summed up this sentiment: 'Life was good there. Nights were good. One's own country is always beautiful. Have you not heard the Pashto couplet that nobody leaves his/her country with their own consent, but either because they have become poor or out of grief for the beloved?'[88] Another woman, who arrived in Pakistan during the civil war that followed the Soviet withdrawal, noted: 'We had a good life in Afghanistan when there was still peace. We had property and everything. Most importantly we had relatives. Now we have no one.'[89] *Landays*, two-line verses of song frequently improvised by women, similarly expressed longing for home:

> My beloved, my sun, rise above the horizon and obliterate my nights of exile.
> The darkness of solitude cloaks me from all sides.
>
> Living in this land of exile is ravaging my heart,
> May God let me return to the foot of my tall mountains!
>
> The woman in exile never stops dying,
> Turn her face, then, toward her native land so that she may breathe her last.[90]

*Vatan* was so important, not only for being a territorial homeland but also for its associated sense of familiarity and family bonds. One Afghan woman, who still lived in Iran in 2004, reflected: 'With a degree in electronic engineering I taught at Kabul University and then got married with the man I loved, a university teacher. We had to leave our beautiful home after the USSR invasion. My husband was injured and became disabled. In Iran, I became the head of the family.' Wistfully, she said: 'I hope that when we go back to Afghanistan, my children who are educated in Iran will be able to work in their own profession.'[91] The hope that the war would end and Afghans could return to Afghanistan and resume their lives persisted.

But the fact remained that Afghans who could return to Afghanistan would have undergone experiences that profoundly reshaped their sense of self, community, and nation. While navigating a course between the PDPA, the resistance political parties, and camp administrators, thousands of Afghan civilians experienced competing visions of modernity, each of which sought to reshape the individual's relationship with politics and broader Afghan society. The UNHCR and its Pakistan-sanctioned activities, just as much as the Afghan Marxists and Islamists, intervened, or attempted to intervene, in everyday Afghan living practices. The UNHCR introduced a model of modern personhood based on the organization's experiences in war-ravaged societies as well as the United Nations' rootedness in older Western imperial structures. UNHCR and NGO representatives working within the camps tried to respect local social and political practices but nevertheless remained focused on developing Afghans who adopted social and economic norms imported from abroad.

Yet camp administrators could never be fully successful in reshaping Afghans to fit this image. This was in part due to Afghans' own experiences before and during the process of fleeing their homeland. As has been similarly observed in the case of Africa's Great Lakes region: 'Because refugees bring with them into exile the social, economic, and political contexts of their prior lives and subjectivities, refugee encounters can greatly influence the tenor and pace of nationalism.'[92] Afghans' own perspectives of their selves, their nation, and their future shaped their approaches to life in exile. Alongside this, camps offered new spaces for Afghan political party activity. Thanks to Pakistan's oversight of the UNHCR mission and decision to use the parties to help register refugees, refugee camps became another site of competition over Afghan modernity, a contest between UNHCR-led models that prioritized Afghans' 'refugeeness' and party models, particularly Islamist, that attempted to shape active citizens in a future, politically stable Afghanistan.

The crisis of displacement sparked by the rise of the PDPA and the subsequent Soviet intervention had unintended consequences for millions of Afghans who fled their homeland. While they rejected a state under a Marxist regime and backed by a foreign power, this did not mean they rejected the Afghan nation. Instead, arguably, an alternative Afghan nation began to emerge within refugee camps, as previously marginal political parties came to represent refugees to UNHCR and Pakistani representatives and replaced many community leaders. Refugee camps created opportunities for new forms of politics to emerge in exile that asserted their own nationalist visions and state practices. The refugee crisis thus brought into question the nature of Afghan governance and its future as a nation state. How could a legitimate Afghanistan continue to exist if so many of its own citizens rejected its government and instead chose to live abroad?

The UNHCR was not the only international organization invested in the future of Afghans and Afghan modernity. Its parent organization, the United Nations, became equally involved in negotiating the future of Afghanistan. But, where the UNHCR's remit focused on individual Afghans and *qawms* residing within the camps, for the UN, its General Assembly, and secretary-general, the stakes were the nature of Afghan sovereignty and the state of Afghanistan. While the UNHCR looked to the well-being of Afghans on the ground, the UN took the lead in determining who represented Afghanistan in the international arena and what form its politics should ultimately take. Even as talks progressed abroad at the United Nations, the question remained whether a negotiated Soviet withdrawal would allow Afghans to return home. The Geneva Accords did not make this a sure thing.

# 8
# Geneva

At 3.45 p.m., on the sunny, cold afternoon of 10 January 1980 in New York City, a host of international delegates entered the General Assembly of the United Nations (UNGA). When everyone had entered and found their seats, Salim Ahmed Salim, president of the UNGA (and permanent representative of Tanzania), called the room to order. After holding a minute of silence for prayer and meditation, he quickly ran through a handful of administrative issues before turning to the matter that had brought the assembly together that day.

Salim presided over only the sixth emergency session of the General Assembly to have taken place since the United Nations' founding on 24 October 1945. The previous five emergency sessions had similarly dealt with crises in international politics: the British and French attempt to take over the Suez Canal and the Soviet invasion of Hungary, both in 1956; the civil war in Lebanon in 1958; the 1960 Congo crisis; and the 1967 Arab–Israeli War. The sixth was no different. The Soviet invasion of Afghanistan posed a fundamental question about international law and relations between sovereign, independent states. Salim made no opening remarks, but immediately turned the floor over to Shah Mohammad Dost, Afghanistan's foreign minister. And with that, all hell broke loose.

It was the polite, strained hell of most diplomatic conferences: few raised voices or interruptions, no loud outbursts of fury, and no physical violence. Instead, there were terse, tense speeches and polite, yet no-less-eviscerating, verbal attacks. But what nonetheless became obvious from the outset was that this was an all-out fight. Beginning the conversation, Dost immediately declared: 'The convening of a special session of the General Assembly on this issue constitutes an open and flagrant interference in the internal affairs of the Democratic Republic of Afghanistan.' He went on: 'The attempts to drag the United Nations into a debate on matters which are entirely within the competence and jurisdiction of the Afghan people and the Government of the Democratic Republic of Afghanistan merely severely undermine the prestige and discredit the authority of this body.'

Matters only worsened from there, as debates progressed through the rest of the 10th and continued through 11 and 12 January. The General Assembly largely divided along Cold-War lines. Dost argued:

It is obvious that those who initiated this campaign of slander—the United States and China—have not given up their attempts to use the United Nations to cover up their own imperialistic and hegemonist plans concerning Afghanistan and are attempting to create the atmosphere of the cold war in this international forum.

He was backed up by other Soviet allies, such as Henryk Jaroszek, representing Poland, who not only pledged his country's 'solidarity with Afghanistan in its persistent struggle in the defence of its political independence and territorial integrity' but went on to accuse the UN of serving as 'a smoke-screen to cover the aggressive designs of the most reactionary circles of imperialism'. Oleg Alexandrovich Troyanovsky, the career diplomat representing the Soviet Union, similarly maintained: 'Those who have created the unsavoury agitation about the Afghanistan question deliberately seek to conceal, behind a screen of misinformation and slander, the real purport and true picture of events occurring in Afghanistan.'

On the other side were the countries we have already seen opposing the Soviet invasion, as well as dozens of member states that were former colonies. Chen Chu, from China, blasted Afghan and Soviet claims. 'Upon whose invitation did Soviet troops invade Afghanistan and how was the invitation extended?' he demanded to know. 'Was it extended by Mr Amin? Obviously, Mr Amin was not that stupid. Then, was it extended by Mr Karmal? But at that time Mr Karmal was somewhere in Eastern Europe and, by the way, he was not then the leader of the Afghan Government.' He derisively concluded: 'There is only one answer, namely, that it was the Soviet Government itself that "invited" Soviet troops to invade Afghanistan.'

Agha Shahi, Pakistan's foreign minister, led a withering attack on both Afghanistan and the Soviet Union, pointing to the global threat and citing the same strategic concerns that animated US policymakers:

> The presence of foreign troops in Afghanistan is not a bilateral matter; it is a matter of grave international concern. The armed intervention in Afghanistan on the grounds that the Soviet Union could not have allowed that country to become a 'beach-head' for aggression against itself constitutes a most alarming precedent.

He re-emphasized that, because of Soviet actions, 'even the most exemplary of nonaligned nations, could become a victim of armed intervention by a more powerful neighbour'. He potently demanded (and slyly took a dig at India's NAM leadership):

> What confidence can be placed by the non-aligned world in assurances by great Powers to respect their sovereignty, national independence and territorial integrity and to eschew aggression, military invasion and armed intervention in the pursuit of their competition and rivalry for spheres of influence and strategic gains?

Later on, Donald McHenry, the United States' permanent representative, spoke only briefly, simply stating: 'Today we are faced with a challenge to the principles of the Charter as grave as any that necessitated our meeting during previous crises. We need no long oration, no extensive remarks, to remind us why we are gathered here.'

Despite Afghan and Soviet protests, the assembly overwhelmingly passed a resolution on 14 January condemning the invasion and calling for 'the immediate, unconditional and total withdrawal of the foreign troops'.[1] One hundred and four countries voted in favour of the resolution, eighteen voted against, and eighteen abstained.

The sixth emergency session of the UNGA marked the beginning of the heated discussions about Afghanistan's future that took place in the offices, halls, and chambers of the United Nations. Throughout the Soviet occupation of Afghanistan, the UNGA at its meetings in New York passed resolution after resolution demanding the departure of Soviet troops. Meanwhile, halfway across the world, a parallel conversation was taking place in Geneva, Switzerland. There, on the banks of Lake Geneva, sits the majestic Palais des Nations, a complex of beautiful, ivory-coloured, neoclassical buildings set amidst verdant parkland. The Palais des Nations was built during the interwar years to house the League of Nations, the first attempt by world powers to pursue global governance in the aftermath of the First World War's carnage. The League, by the end of the 1930s, had failed in its mandate to prevent conflict between nations, but officials across the world still aspired to a forum of international politics where all states could be represented, a space for diplomacy and negotiations that would prevent violence across the world.[2] Thus it was logical that the Palais des Nations, following the end of the Second World War, would become the United Nations Office, second only in significance to the complex built for purpose in New York City.

The Soviet invasion of Afghanistan posed a global crisis, not merely a national or regional one. It was not just a matter of the Cold War and superpower ideological and political competition. The entry of Soviet troops into an ostensibly independent country brought into question the very nature of political independence and the precious idea of self-determination. Leaders from across the world debated who had the right to decide Afghanistan's way forward, and who was holding the reins of power—the Soviets or the Afghans. The PDPA claimed legitimacy, but the continued outflow of refugees into Afghanistan's neighbouring countries, as well as the scepticism expressed by the vast majority of UN member states, spoke otherwise.

The crisis in Afghanistan highlighted a key issue in late-twentieth-century politics, the close interrelationship between the national and the international. The PDPA's claims that its pursuits were purely focused within Afghanistan and on Afghanistan's relations with the rest of the world clashed with its enemies' claims that the Soviet presence in Afghanistan posed a threat to international norms and laws, as well as to the Afghan nation state itself. Debates about who governed Afghanistan, and how, forced discussions not only about states' rule within their own borders but also about how an international system of states functions when one member's independence seems under threat. Because these questions were fundamental to international politics, the United Nations became deeply embroiled in the Afghan crisis.

The Soviet intervention launched a broader conversation about the nature of modern international politics, a modernity expressed through the sanctity of statehood, sovereignty, and self-determination. It threatened both Afghanistan's sovereignty and the international system of state-led politics. As Amoakon-Edjampan Thiemele, the representative from the Côte d'Ivoire, pointed out at the January 1980 emergency session:

> While most of us, for decades, had our very physical, cultural and social existence flouted, some of the founders of the United Nations have never known foreign subjugation, the denial of their very being or the situation of the dominated with no other right than that of submission...The issue before us today, in its brutality, seems to us to be shaking the foundations of our present-day civilization.[3]

For international observers, local debates about Afghan politics and the struggle between Afghan socialism and Islamism were part of a broader conundrum. They worried whether the Soviet intervention encouraged a precedent in international affairs that justified superpower occupation and allowed foreign leaders to dictate an occupied state's journey towards externally shaped visions of modernity.

The UNGA gave its secretary-general the mandate to determine who represented the Afghan nation and what constituted a sovereign Afghan state. Even while reluctantly recognizing Karmal's regime as the official government of Afghanistan, the UN, through its talks with the PDPA's Pakistani and American opponents, also brought into question the PDPA's right to rule as well as its claims to represent all Afghans. The fact that the Afghan refugee crisis became a major sticking point in discussions demonstrated that UN officials were concerned not only with Afghans' humanitarian needs but also with the political models that would allow them to return home and resume their status quo as citizens, rather than refugees.

Throughout the 1980s, the Palais des Nations hosted a series of talks regarding the 'Afghanistan question'. Special representatives and foreign ministers from Afghanistan and Pakistan, and sometimes the Soviet Union and the United States, shuttled in and out of Geneva to sit down with UN representatives. They all sought to resolve a political quandary. Was the presence of Soviet troops in Afghanistan merely the result of bilateral treaty arrangements? Or did it signify an armed takeover of another sovereign state? What conditions were needed for Soviet troops to be removed? UN officials tried to find common ground on these questions, particularly between leaders in Afghanistan—who argued that they led a truly independent, free country—and Pakistan—the PDPA's most vocal critic and host to more than one million Afghan refugees. UN negotiators pursued a political agreement that would lead simultaneously to the withdrawal of foreign troops from Afghan soil and the opportunity for refugees to return safely to their homes. This proved an almost impossible task. The Geneva Accords, a four-part agreement signed on 14 April 1988, took almost seven years to negotiate, and, even then, it left many matters almost entirely unsettled.

Even before the Soviet invasion had taken place in December 1979, the United Nations offered an important arena for Afghan politics. Leaders from the Musahiban dynasty had taken their quarrels with Pakistan over their shared Pashtun population to the General Assembly, though with little success, and the PDPA used correspondence with Kurt Waldheim, then-UN secretary-general, as well as statements in the General Assembly to assert the political legitimacy of the new regime and justify its vision of Afghan modernity.[4] In one of his first communications with Waldheim, Nur Mohammad Taraki declared:

> The Democratic Republic of Afghanistan, as an active member of the non-aligned movement, loyally abides by the lofty principles of the United Nations Charter; adopts as its slogan the combat against all kinds of discrimination, *apartheid*, old and neo-colonialism; confirms the right of self-determination of nations and peoples based on their free will and devoid of foreign intervention; continues its relentless efforts for the establishment and consolidation of a real and lasting peace, realization of general and complete disarmament and the further strengthening of the United Nations.[5]

In such statements, Taraki and other leaders of the PDPA referred to norms of international governance that were enshrined in the UN order. But what was global governance? How did states and their leaders persuade other nations to accept them in the international arena? The United Nations had provided a key forum for discussions on these topics ever since its formation, and it fundamentally shaped the discussions that took place in international arenas about the Soviet intervention.

The United Nations, at its birth, was both universal and highly exclusionary. It was meant to be an international forum open to all independent nation states. But its main architects were also the world's most powerful, some of whom possessed numerous overseas colonies that, in fact, prevented a majority of the world's population from pursuing political independence. The preamble to the UN charter, written in 1945, highlighted many of the UN's key aspirations. It pledged to uphold equal rights, to respect the sovereignty of nations, to promote good relations between countries.[6] Yet the preamble was also drafted by Jan Christiaan Smuts, a South African statesman whose advocacy for colonial rule had helped fashion the British commonwealth system and who, perhaps most ironically, advocated racial segregation between Black and white South Africans. While the UN was framed in terms of universal rights and equality, in reality, its key promoters saw the organization as a means for maintaining their own influence in international politics.[7]

Western imperial powers had previously used the League of Nations to reaffirm governance over their colonies, and initially saw the UN as little different. The UN Security Council served as a clear mechanism of this: permanent members of the Security Council, with their power of veto, included the UK and France, two imperial powers that had little interest in divesting themselves of their empires. Alongside them were the main Cold-War rivals, the US and USSR. (China, the fifth permanent member, provided an entirely different conundrum, as a result of the Chinese Civil War. Only in 1971 was the PRC recognized as a member of the Security Council. Until this point, the Guomindang in Taiwan, a staunch ally of the

West, held the seat representing China.) The power imbalances evident in the Security Council also initially played out in the General Assembly. When a number of African and Asian states banded together in September 1955 to force a discussion of the Algerian war for independence on the UNGA agenda, French representatives walked out of the assembly rather than discuss their colonial possession.[8]

The advent of decolonization, as the debate over Algeria would show, nevertheless forced the UN to change. The 1955 conference in Bandung signalled a moment of Afro-Asian solidarity, bringing together representatives from newly independent states such as India and Indonesia and soon-to-be-liberated colonies like the Gold Coast (Ghana), who articulated a shared vision of global governance that celebrated national independence, self-determination, and world peace. The conference's attendees asserted the power and promise of political, cultural, and economic exchange emanating from the Third World and an international system comprised of nations from across the globe, not just Europe and North America. Afghan leaders took part alongside their Afro-Asian counterparts, celebrating Afghanistan's even longer history of anti-colonialism and pointing to its practice of bi-tarafi—'without sides'—in international relations. The Non-Aligned Movement (NAM) would build on many of Bandung's foundations, seeking a path in international relations that evaded Cold-War politicking and focused on reasserting the rights of individual states in international politics.[9]

As countries emerged from colonial rule and became independent nation states, they sought admittance into the UNGA. Between 1945 and 1965 alone, the number of UN member states more than doubled from 51 to 117. Once admitted, these new countries seized the opportunity to change the UN's political agenda and make it more universally representative. Anti-colonial leaders forced a rethinking of the UN's remit and principles. Political self-determination became the answer to the evils of empire and imperial domination. New nations needed to assert their right to govern themselves, as well as their recognition of their neighbours' rights to do the same. This, in turn, made the UN increasingly responsible for the twin activities of defending the nation state, which came to embody national self-determination, and defending the individual, human rights. Activists across the world used the universalist language of the UN to force discussions about racism, not only in former colonies but in countries like the United States, with its tortured history of slavery, discrimination, and segregation. But groups in the decolonizing world, such as the Nagas in north-east India and the West Irians in West Papua, who demanded forms of self-determination that came up against the political models adopted by newly independent states, were silenced.[10]

Many of these discussions culminated in, and were further spurred by, the General Assembly's 94th plenary meeting on 14 December 1960, where member states passed the 'Declaration on the Granting of Independence to Colonial Countries and Peoples'. The resolution acknowledged 'the need for the creation of conditions of stability and well-being and peaceful and friendly relations based on respect for the principles of equal rights and self-determination of all peoples', while emphasizing that 'the process of liberation is irresistible and irreversible', 'an end must be put to colonialism', and 'all peoples have the right to self-determination; by virtue of that right they freely determine their political status and freely pursue their economic, social and cultural development'.[11] By the 1970s, the less nimble nation state had replaced many of the mobile, transnational anti-colonial movements that had fired the independence of states like Algeria.[12] The UN was the arena of more static independent nation states, and membership implied widespread recognition and legitimacy in international relations.

The UN's preamble and the 1960 declaration on decolonization collectively presented several key aspects of international politics:

- Self-determination: The right of people and states to choose their own form of governance.
- International peace and security: The need for different states not to intervene in the affairs of other sovereign countries and to settle disputes peacefully.
- Equal rights: The protection of both peoples and states from forms of oppression and subjugation.

PDPA leaders like Taraki asserted their right to govern by pointing to norms of international law. The PDPA's modern Afghanistan relied not only on domestic reform but on international recognition. The April 1978 coup was thus framed in the universalist terms of self-determination and political independence. Taraki explained: 'The people of Afghanistan brought about a revolution based on real democracy, in other words actual sovereignty of the people.' The revolution, in his mind, represented 'the will of the people'.

Perhaps equally notably, Taraki pointed to other issues of international governance in his correspondence with Secretary-General Waldheim. By critiquing systems of inequality like apartheid—the UN had recently posed sanctions against the South African government—and affirming Afghan support for international peace, Taraki aligned his regime with the rest of the UN's member states. He indicated his government's support for the UN's remit as well as insisting that his regime was adequately functional to concern itself with foreign policy and international crises, not just domestic issues. Taraki similarly drew renewed attention to the issue of self-determination worldwide, repledging Afghan support for ethnic Pashtun and Baloch self-governance in Pakistan, though this was a complicated ploy. Given that Afghanistan did not recognize its eastern border, its own sovereignty remained ambiguous. He nevertheless promised: 'The Democratic Republic of Afghanistan will continue its efforts through negotiations and peaceful talks with Pakistan for the solution of the national issue of the Pashtun and Baloch people, based on their own will and historical background.'[13]

Waldheim, in turn, accepted these assurances that the PDPA represented Afghan self-determination and intentions to uphold the international order. 'I very much welcome your expression of support for the work and objectives of the world

Organization', he wrote to Taraki, 'and wish to assure you that the United Nations, for its part, stands ready to lend every assistance to the Democratic Republic of Afghanistan in its endeavours towards economic and social development'.[14] At this early stage in the PDPA's rise, UN leaders, like Afghanistan's neighbours, signalled a willingness to accept the PDPA as the new rulers of Afghanistan. Taraki's was just one in a line of coups, a largely domestic affair.

Matters were upended by the Soviet intervention, as well as the spread of Afghan refugees. The entry of Soviet troops brought into question the same issues of international governance that the PDPA had touted. Was Babrak Karmal's 'invitation' for Soviet troops another manifestation of Afghan political self-determination? Or did a military presence indicate a breach of international peace and security? Alongside this, the UN had to wrestle with a vast humanitarian crisis that threatened to destabilize the entire region of South-Central Asia, not just empty Afghanistan of its population.

Karmal, in initial pronouncements, reiterated: 'The foundation of the basic power of the DRA is constituted by the people and it belongs to the people.' In correspondence with Waldheim, he praised 'the Treaty of Friendship and Cooperation of December 5, 1978 with the Soviet Union, the great country of peace, which by nature guarantees permanent peace and security in the region', and he asserted that Afghanistan and the Soviet Union would 'expand on a higher plane, in a new manner and in all dimensions, their unbeatable fraternal friendship which is a manifestation of the independent will and patriotism of the people of Afghanistan during the past 60 years after the nation's independence'. The joint Soviet–Afghan action against Hafizullah Amin, he explained, made Afghan independence 'a basic principle of an appropriate national tradition with complete honesty, emanating from our national progressive Afghan character'. Karmal claimed Soviet aid had allowed his government to right the wrongs committed by his predecessors and return Afghanistan to the path, the 'higher plane', of modern representative politics.[15]

The Politburo similarly ordered Soviet representatives at the UN to assert that 'in accordance with Article 51 of the UN Charter the Democratic Republic of Afghanistan has the internationally recognized right to turn to the Soviet Union with a request for aid and assistance in repelling aggression and the Soviet Union [has the right] to grant such aid and assistance'. They argued that the need for Soviet support resulted from outside interference in Afghan domestic affairs—most immediately, foreign aid to a dangerous resistance movement—as well as extant treaty arrangements. Soviet representatives were additionally instructed to impress upon audiences that 'the Soviet Union again stresses that, as before, its sole wish regarding Afghanistan is to see this state be independent and sovereign, conducting a policy of good-neighborliness and peace, firmly respecting and carrying out its international obligations, including those according to the UN Charter'.[16]

As such, the PDPA and their Soviet allies framed the military intervention in terms of international norms: the right of Afghans to choose and embrace a Marxist regime and the legality of bilateral treaties that allowed one state to provide another with armed assistance. The Soviets, both argued, had merely responded to an Afghan request made in line with their 1978 treaty. Soviet troops thus fulfilled that country's obligations under this agreement. While this logic might have stood at first glance, with subsequent analysis, the matter became rather blurry. The fact that the Soviet military manoeuvres accompanied the assassination of Afghanistan's erstwhile leader, Amin, and his replacement by Karmal, who had been in exile in Czechoslovakia, undermined Soviet claims to be working with the Afghan 'government'. Moreover, whether troops were meant to prevent foreign intervention, as the Soviet government claimed, or to uphold and support Afghan self-determination, as asserted by Karmal, was unclear. (And, while PDPA and Soviet representatives pointed to defending Afghan sovereignty, they still refused to recognize the border with Pakistan that would have circumscribed part of the Afghan state.) In some respects, these issues centred on protecting the state from both domestic and foreign threats. But the line between invited intervention and armed invasion wavered.

The UN played host to all manner of arguments about the legality and rationale for a Soviet presence in Afghanistan. Many of these debates were not new. As early as the interwar League of Nations, members had debated the nature of political sovereignty in states like Iraq, which remained a 'quasi-state' that was ostensibly independent but had clear ties to the British Empire.[17] When Soviet interventions in Hungary (1956) and Czechoslovakia (1968) provoked international outcry and debates in the UN, Soviet leaders framed their actions as responding to local government requests for 'help' to get rid of 'counter-revolutionary forces'.[18] While the UNGA condemned the Soviet use of force in Hungary, the Security Council never acted on the General Assembly's resolution, owing to the inevitability of a Soviet veto (and the parallel Suez Crisis, a conflict on which Soviet and US policymakers, for once, agreed). Likewise, during the 1960 Congo crisis, discussions of Congolese self-determination played out against the clash between Soviet and American competition for the Third World. (Discussions of Syrian and Israeli interventions in Lebanon in 1976 and 1982, in contrast, were hardly mentioned and dismissed as part of the 'Middle East Situation', though the UN sent a peacekeeping force in 1978.[19]) In these earlier cases, the UN had proved largely helpless, restricted by the US and Soviet veto powers, other distracting international events, and a clear lack of international consensus. With Afghanistan, however, the vast majority of member states all lined up against the Soviet Union and their PDPA puppets. This was not just a Cold-War rupture. It reopened a wound for all countries that had struggled against the chains of imperialism to emerge finally free. One of their own—not only that, but one of the earliest to achieve political independence in the twentieth century—could not be allowed to re-succumb to empire.

Pakistani, Iranian, Chinese, and American leaders all framed the entry of Soviet troops as the rupturing of international law. Alongside their statements at the Emergency Session of the UNGA, the PRC additionally released an announcement as soon as news of the invasion broke, declaring: 'This armed intervention wantonly violates all norms of international relations.' Chinese officials pointed out: 'It not only encroaches upon the sovereignty and independence of Afghanistan but poses a grave threat to peace and security in Asia and the whole world.' They drew direct parallels between Afghanistan and Kampuchea (Cambodia), decrying the puppet regimes that had come to power thanks to 'foreign aggressor troops'. But in the South-East Asian case, dogged Chinese (and American) support allowed the exiled genocidal Pol Pot regime to retain Cambodia's seat at the UN. Afghan resistance leaders would have no such opportunity.[20]

The government of Iran issued a particularly blistering attack:

> The excuse that other foreign countries have directly intervened in Afghanistan is totally unacceptable, because the Afghani nation had risen up against the previous governments, which the present regime regards as traitors. If those (the previous) governments were non-Islamic and anti-national, the revolt of the people of Afghanistan was therefore right, and there was no need for the intervention of the Soviet army.

Afghans alone, in other words, should have been left to fight out who would next rule Afghanistan.

The Iranian protest note left Soviet and PDPA claims in tatters. Iranian representatives demanded to know: 'If the past governments of Afghanistan were honest, how [is it] the Soviet government considers them incompetent?' They insisted on an explanation why and 'how the present government, which has launched a coup d'état against the former regime, [then] suddenly, after a few hours, admits an army it had already agreed should assemble on the borders, into Afghanistan'. The base logic of Afghan and Soviet statements, Iranian representatives argued, simply did not make sense. As such, they harshly condemned Soviet action as 'an act which is in contrast with all the values that guarantee the equality and fraternity of human beings in the world'.[21] There was little question in these powers' minds that, in fact, Soviet actions broke with all norms of international relations. This was no bilateral action but a government takeover by hostile external forces, the forced implementation of an unwanted socialist model reliant on Soviet soldiers and weapons. They, alongside the majority of the UNGA, refused to see the events of December 1979 as either domestic or bilateral, but instead as a threat to international relations and politics.

Before reaching the UNGA as the topic of the sixth emergency session, the Soviet invasion of Afghanistan was first discussed by the UN Security Council between 5 and 9 January 1980. Discussions devolved into finger-pointing across Cold-War divisions. The USSR used its veto power to abort a resolution demanding the immediate withdrawal of troops. However, the fact that only the Soviet Union and its East German ally voted against the resolution meant that the issue was subsequently referred to the General Assembly: of fifteen Security Council members, twelve voted for it, while Zambia abstained.[22] The General Assembly, in turn, overwhelmingly passed its own resolution demanding the total, immediate, and unconditional withdrawal of Soviet troops from Afghan soil. Specifically, the UNGA's final resolution posed the following. The General Assembly:

1. Reaffirm[ed] that respect for the sovereignty, territorial integrity and political independence of every State is a fundamental principle of the Charter of the United Nations, any violation of which on any pretext whatsoever is contrary to its aims and purposes;

2. Strongly deplore[d] the recent armed intervention in Afghanistan, which is inconsistent with that principle;

3. Appeal[ed] to all States to respect the sovereignty, territorial integrity, political independence and nonaligned character of Afghanistan and to refrain from any interference in the internal affairs of that country;

4. Call[ed] for the immediate, unconditional and total withdrawal of the foreign troops from Afghanistan in order to enable its people to determine their own form of government and choose their economic, political and social systems free from outside intervention, subversion, coercion or constraint of any kind whatsoever;

5. Urge[d] all parties concerned to assist in bringing about, speedily and in accordance with the purposes and principles of the Charter, conditions necessary for the voluntary return of the Afghan refugees to their homes;

6. Appeal[ed] to all States and national and international organizations to extend humanitarian relief assistance with a view to alleviating the hardship of the Afghan refugees in co-ordination with the United Nations High Commissioner for Refugees;

7. Request[ed] the Secretary-General to keep Member States and the Security Council promptly and concurrently informed on the progress towards the implementation of the present resolution;

8. Call[ed] upon the Security Council to consider ways and means which could assist in the implementation of the present resolution.[23]

The UN's members demanded not only the end of the Soviet presence in Afghanistan but also reaffirmation of the principles of international politics. They sought to reassert the political independence of member states and to limit more powerful countries' ability to interfere in the affairs of others. They brought into question whether the PDPA represented a form of modern Afghan politics that had the support of the country's citizens and whether socialist modernism was being implemented by Afghans, themselves, or Soviets. The secretary-general thus received a directive to follow up and encourage the Soviets, and their Afghan allies, to obey this resolution.

The United Nations was not merely an important arena in which state leaders wrestled with the meanings of twentieth-century governance and the interplay between states, their neighbours, and the international community. UN officials, themselves, also attempted to shape these discussions, alongside the nature of state-building across the world. We have already seen this in the case of the UNHCR, which crafted understanding of and policy towards refugees. Other UN organizations, such as the Economic and Social Council, Development Programme, UNICEF, even its peacekeeping operations, also sought to shape political and social dynamics within and between states.[24] In the case of negotiating a Soviet withdrawal from Afghanistan, first Kurt Waldheim and then his successor, Javier Perez de Cuellar, were tasked with pushing for some sort of resolution. UN officials faced the tricky job of trying to bring peace back to the region while navigating between two opposing members of the Security Council, the US and USSR, either of whom could, and did, wield their veto power in response to UNGA resolutions. UN negotiators sought to create the means for a Soviet withdrawal but to avoid conversations about what an Afghan state should specifically look like. Their remit, they believed, was to restore international relations to the status quo, not to interfere in internal Afghan affairs.

The UN position was further complicated by the attempts of other international forums to address the crisis. The Organization of the Islamic Conference (OIC), for example, categorically condemned the Soviet invasion as an attack on the world's *ummah* and demanded the withdrawal of troops. Most significantly, it decided to suspend Afghan membership in the OIC and called on all member states 'to withhold recognition of the illegal regime in Afghanistan and sever diplomatic relations with that country until the complete withdrawal of Soviet troops from Afghanistan'.[25] This stance would fundamentally shape how UN negotiators could tackle the crisis. The OIC also briefly considered holding additional conferences on the issue but subsequently decided to leave most diplomatic measures to the UN.

The NAM similarly wrestled with the crisis, though with less success, as members could not agree on a course of action. Yugoslavia immediately demanded a resolution on 'non-interference in internal affairs', while Cuba stubbornly supported the Soviet Union. Pakistan, with the backing of the OIC, demanded an immediate troop withdrawal, while Iran went even further, suggesting Afghanistan be expelled from the movement. Afghan leaders unsurprisingly denounced all NAM interference. India, one of the NAM's historic key leaders, found itself sidelined in its middling critique of the Soviet invasion of Afghanistan, which sharply contrasted with its harsh condemnation of China's activities in Cambodia (and earlier support for Vietnam's Cambodian ventures). At the NAM Foreign Ministers' conference in early 1981, hosted in Delhi, Indian representatives tried unsuccessfully to toe a middle line. A final resolution at the conference papered over these cracks, calling for a political settlement 'on the basis of the withdrawal of foreign troops' and reaffirming the 'territorial integrity and non-aligned status of Afghanistan and strict observance of the principles of non-intervention and non-interference'. But discussions showed that members could not fully agree on how to achieve this—or on who determined whether Afghanistan's territorial integrity and non-alignment remained intact.[26] This was a trend that would also play out during the UN-led negotiations. The NAM, meanwhile, facing the additional eruption of the Iraq–Iran war, largely succumbed to internal disputes and 'staged a self-harming theater of the absurd'.[27]

The European Economic Community (EEC) proposed an additional conference on the crisis that would force a Soviet withdrawal while providing international guarantees for Afghan independence. PDPA representatives, however, would not be invited to take part until the second stage of talks after guarantee agreements had already been put in place.[28] While there was some initial enthusiasm for the EEC proposal, eventually state leaders agreed to leave the situation to the auspices of the UN. Even though political officeholders across the world questioned the legitimacy of the Afghan regime, they reluctantly accepted that the PDPA needed some sort of involvement in negotiating a Soviet departure.

The UNGA reaffirmed its stance on Afghanistan at its November 1980 sessions, where members passed a resolution on the 20th calling for the secretary-general to appoint a special representative to seek a political resolution, a move that the DRA and Soviet representatives vigorously protested. (India, wavering in its feelings towards both Afghanistan and the Soviet Union, expressed concerns that a special representative would only 'aggravate' matters.) The UNGA's final resolution repeated almost verbatim Pakistan's four requirements for a political settlement of the Afghan crisis: 'the preservation of the sovereignty, territorial integrity, political independence and non-aligned character of Afghanistan'; 'the right of the Afghan people to determine their own form of government and to choose their economic, political and social system free from outside intervention, subversion, coercion or constraint of any kind whatsoever'; 'the immediate withdrawal of the foreign troops from Afghanistan'; and 'a political solution and the creation of the necessary conditions which would enable the Afghan refugees to return voluntarily to their homes in safety and honour'.[29]

Based on this resolution, Secretary-General Waldheim appointed Javier Perez de Cuellar as his special representative on the Afghan issue. Perez de Cuellar was a career diplomat, born in Lima, Peru, in 1920. He had served in the Peruvian Ministry of Foreign Affairs since the 1940s. Indeed, as a young diplomat, he had been a member of Peru's delegation to the first session of the UNGA, which took place in London before it became housed in New York. After serving in various Peruvian embassies across the world, he became the country's permanent representative to the UN in 1970, subsequently serving as Waldheim's special representative on Cyprus (1976–7) and under-secretary-general for special political affairs in 1980–1, before taking up the post of special representative on Afghanistan.

At the UN, Perez de Cuellar was known for his moderation rather than for grandstanding. He was disciplined and professional.

His brand of intimacy was measured and delicate: sitting next to a visitor on the couch facing his UN desk, he would emphasize a point by tapping his fingers, ever so lightly and for a fleeting moment, on the back of his visitor's hand. At close quarters, in dealing with individual leaders and diplomats, he inspired confidence and trust, and, as a UN official, he soon became known for possessing the coveted but elusive and indefinable gift of a 'safe pair of hands'.[30]

Perez de Cuellar thus seemed the right man for the job—well-respected and clearly capable of engaging with a number of states, none of whom agreed on Afghan politics or Afghanistan's future.

Perez de Cuellar almost immediately set about trying to arrange talks between the warring sides. From the outside, this looked like an almost impossible task. A fundamental difference existed in how Afghan and Pakistani leaders approached the crisis. Whereas Pakistani officials framed the Soviet presence in Afghanistan as a test of international relations and global politics, Afghan leaders stubbornly insisted on the need for negotiations on specifically local issues: improving regional relations, halting the transgression of Afghanistan's borders by resistance bodies, and organizing the return of refugees. They wanted to limit the scope of any talks and to conduct them on a country-by-country basis. Thus, where Pakistani leaders sought to use talks to undermine the PDPA's leadership, Afghan leaders sought to reassert their own legitimacy. The regional debate over Afghan modernity went global, using the rhetoric of self-determination and independence.

As early as May 1980, the DRA issued a statement welcoming a general 'political settlement' through which 'the question of withdrawal of the Soviet limited military contingents from Afghanistan should be resolved'. Referring to the armed resistance, the PDPA pointedly noted: 'The cessation and guaranteed non-recurrence of military invasions and any other forms of interference into the internal affairs of Afghanistan would be eliminated.' In order to achieve this, M. Farid Zarif, Afghanistan's permanent representative to the UN, argued that Afghanistan's outstanding issues needed discussion through bilateral talks between Afghanistan and its neighbours, Iran and Pakistan. This, he claimed, could resolve what the DRA saw as the two key problems for its political security: the return of Afghan refugees and the cessation of Pakistani- and Iranian-backed resistance movements. 'Such agreements', Zarif suggested, 'would contain generally acceptable principles concerning mutual respect for sovereignty, readiness to develop relations on the basis of principles of good neighbourliness and non-interference in the internal affairs'.[31] He then proposed that the Soviet Union and United States act as international guarantors for these bilateral agreements.

Zarif's proposal made important points but overlooked a key issue. The governments of Pakistan and Iran had no interest in bilateral talks. More than that, both governments refused even to consider bilateral talks, thanks in large part to the OIC resolutions from the end of January. As members of the OIC, both states had agreed to uphold the decision withholding recognition of Karmal's regime. Because Pakistani and Iranian officials rejected the political legitimacy of the PDPA, talks could not progress between officials from Afghanistan and Pakistan or Iran. Afghanistan's neighbours argued that members of the PDPA did not truly represent the Afghan people.

Agha Shahi made this very clear at the UNGA's Plenary Session on 17 November 1980. He explained: 'Pakistan's non-recognition of the present regime in Kabul stems from its principled opposition to foreign military intervention, no matter where it occurs.' Citing the international politics that also underpinned the Sino-Pakistani relationship, he pointed out: 'It is this same position of principle which precludes Pakistan's recognition of the Heng Samrin regime in Kampuchea [Cambodia]. Pakistan will have no hesitation in extending recognition to any government in power in Kabul, once the foreign forces are completely withdrawn from Afghanistan.'

He also dismissed Afghan suggestions that this was merely a regional dispute. 'The Afghanistan question…concerns', he argued, 'the fundamental principles of non-use of force, non-intervention and non-interference, all of which have been violated in the case of the non-aligned Islamic State of Afghanistan.'[32] For Agha Shahi and the government of Pakistan—who calculated their stance based on fears of further Soviet expansion, the appeal of the foreign aid flooding into the country, and the chance to put to rest long-standing tensions with Afghanistan—the issue at hand was not just a matter of refugees flooding into Pakistan or of encouraging resistance against the PDPA. Norms of international political practice were at stake.

Agha Shahi bluntly repeated the point he had made at the UNGA emergency session. Framing the conflict in Cold-War terms, he noted: 'The military intervention has set back the process of detente, reversed the trend towards relaxation of international tensions and darkened the prospects for disarmament. It has opened an ominous new chapter in the history of super power rivalry and contention for spheres of influence and hegemony.' He emphasized: 'The climate of mutual trust and confidence among the major powers, built over more than a decade on the basis of the principles of peaceful co-existence and detente, reflected in the Helsinki accords and the SALT negotiations, has been vitiated by the armed intervention in Afghanistan.' Therefore, he concluded, returning to the tenets of international law,

> two basic facts lie at the heart of the Afghanistan tragedy. First, an attempt was made to determine the outcome of purely internal political differences amongst the Afghan people, by the induction of a large foreign military force. Second, no effort was made to arrive at a peaceful political settlement even when it became manifest that the people of Afghanistan would not acquiesce in the imposition of a regime by foreign military occupation.[33]

If we look at their public statements in and out of the General Assembly, Afghan and Pakistani officials, the two most outspoken, seemed to agree on hardly anything. Pakistan had scored a political victory in having its resolution passed by the UNGA in November 1980. The Afghan foreign minister responded furiously, saying that, in fact, Pakistan, not Afghanistan, disregarded international norms by supporting resistance fighters, and he accused the General Assembly of hypocrisy and of refusing to accept Afghan (PDPA) self-determination. The UN, he fumed, 'sought to tell the Afghan people what kind of socio-economic system and government it should have'. He concluded that the General Assembly was a 'waste of time' and pointedly declared that 'no committee, conference or international gathering, under whatever label, could serve to normalize the situation in and around Afghanistan.'[34]

However, once Perez de Cuellar had initiated confidential conversations with Pakistani and Afghan representatives, what became evident was that neither side was as intransigent as its public pronouncements indicated. In fact, both sides showed willingness to find common ground in order to ease the regional situation. As President Zia told Waldheim: 'In his opinion, the Soviet Union was not as yet prepared to withdraw from Afghanistan but, he did not wish Moscow to have any pretext to attack Pakistan.' As fears receded that the Soviets meant to use Afghanistan as a launch site for a further push towards the Persian Gulf, Agha Shahi privately indicated to Perez de Cuellar that Pakistan was willing to negotiate with Afghan 'authorities', while abstaining from referring to them as government representatives. Instead, Pakistan officials would accept them as envoys of the PDPA.

Pakistani officials further intimated they would consider trilateral talks involving Afghan, Pakistani, and Iranian representatives, though they continued to baulk at bilateral negotiations, given that they saw events in Afghanistan as a global crisis. They also agreed that talks did not need to take place explicitly within the framework established by the November 1980 UNGA resolution, thus taking a step back from the intense international scrutiny demanded in that text. Perhaps most importantly and consequentially, Pakistani officials told the secretary-general and Perez de Cuellar that they were not invested in having Afghan resistance parties involved in the talks, a point that would undoubtedly have further complicated the potential negotiations. While they anticipated that resistance leaders would be consulted at some stage before talks finished, the government of Pakistan sought to steer the conversation, much as it manipulated the resistance parties, for its own purposes.[35]

On the Afghan side, Foreign Minister Dost maintained that his government still sought bilateral talks, but both he and the Soviet ambassador, Richard Ovinnikov, told Perez de Cuellar that they were ready to accept a UN 'representative' at such talks, 'though they would not like to see him as a full participant to, or organiser, of the meeting'.[36] Perez de Cuellar assured them that his role was only 'to maintain the dialogue alive; at times, in order to preserve the very existence of the dialogue, he could present conciliatory formulas'. As such, the Afghans and Soviets accepted a representative of the international community, so long as his role was not one of handing out edicts. Dost also indicated he was willing to negotiate with Pakistan as either a government representative or a member of the Central Committee of the PDPA. 'What mattered', he said, 'was the negotiations were to be conducted on an equal footing'.[37]

Between trips to Kabul, Islamabad, Tehran, New York, and Geneva, progress slowly inched forward. Both Perez de Cuellar and Waldheim met extensively with the foreign ministers of Pakistan and Afghanistan, while the secretary-general also travelled to Moscow, where he discussed the potential talks with Soviet representatives. By January 1981, Soviet leaders had dropped their earlier demand that Pakistan and Iran recognize Karmal's regime and had acknowledged the uses of UN-led negotiations.[38] Soviet leaders instead saw the PDPA's participation as its own means of asserting the regime's legitimacy and demonstrating that it accepted the norms of international governance. From 1982, the Politburo, under the failing Brezhnev, also recognized the UN's potential to help the Soviets get out of Afghanistan while keeping the PDPA in place. As early as 27 November 1982, Foreign Minister Andrei Gromyko ordered Politburo members to begin making plans for a Soviet withdrawal. From this perspective, the UN's participation ideally would provide an opportunity for a Soviet retreat while leaving the Karmal regime in power: the UN created an opportunity to continue Afghan socialist modernism but back in the hands of the PDPA.[39]

Meanwhile, President Carter, and subsequently Reagan, indicated that the United States would back a special representative from the UN and serve as a joint guarantor of Afghan neutrality. Carter wrote personally to Secretary-General Waldheim to emphasize the strength of feeling in the UNGA about the demand for a special representative. In talks with Soviet representatives, Reagan's secretary of state, George P. Shultz, continued to fence with Gromyko about the nature of the Soviet troop presence, pointedly noting the need for 'a government freely chosen by the Afghan people'. But both sides expressed their hopes for 'progress in Geneva' and embraced UN-led talks as a means of overcoming the impasse between the two sides' fundamentally different interpretations of local events. The UN provided the auspices for a diplomatic solution through which neither power lost face. Nevertheless, both American and Soviet officials also made clear that talks predominantly needed to take place between Afghanistan and its neighbours.[40]

While Afghan and Pakistani officials largely accepted these changes, Iranian leaders were less flexible. Jamal Shemirani, chargé d'affaires with Iran's permanent mission to the UN, told Perez de Cuellar that Iran refused to take part in any negotiations before Soviet troops had withdrawn, and, unlike Pakistan, demanded that talks officially involve representatives of the resistance. Moreover, he bluntly stated, 'Iran rejected the suggestion for any bilateral negotiation with Afghanistan'. He explained: 'This would imply that Iran was part of the Afghan crisis when in fact the crisis was simply the result of actions which did not depend on Iran.'[41] The Afghans and Soviets, he implied, needed to clean up their own mess. The Iranian government consequently kept aloof of Perez de Cuellar's talks with Pakistan and Afghanistan. Given that Iran was six months into a war with its other neighbour, Iraq, which would embroil the two countries until 1988 and cost Iran hundreds of thousands of lives, Afghanistan was not Iranian officials' main concern.

By 26 September 1981, officials from Pakistan and Afghanistan had formally expressed their willingness to take part in 'substantive talks'. A month earlier, the DRA had issued a statement laying out what it desired from either bilateral or trilateral talks (Afghan officials evidently had been brought around to Pakistan's earlier suggestion of Iranian participation, though this did not come to pass). The DRA desired mutual respect and non-interference, mechanisms to allow refugees to return, international guarantors for any agreements, and the cessation of armed interference from abroad. These ideas aligned well with the demands previously made by Agha Shahi in the UNGA and demonstrated that common ground for talks did indeed exist. Thus, from the end of September, Perez de Cuellar began preparing for the next stage of negotiations, collating background information that would inform subsequent discussions.[42]

The next substantive talks, however, did not begin until mid-1982. This delay largely resulted from dynamics internal to the UN, rather than events in the region. Kurt Waldheim had come to the end of his second term as secretary-general of the United Nations, a post that was appointed by the Security Council. He attempted to run for an unprecedented third term, but this ended in impasse. China vetoed his candidacy, wanting a non-Western representative, and his only opponent, Salim Ahmed Salim from Tanzania, was correspondingly rejected by the United States. The future of the secretary-general was left in limbo for six weeks, deadlocked by a Security Council that would not accept either proffered candidate.

In the end, both candidates withdrew from the race, and, in their stead, Javier Perez de Cuellar, the same special representative who had been handling the Afghanistan situation, was selected as the next secretary-general of the United Nations. Upon coming to office, Perez de Cuellar pointedly emphasized:

> In the present state of international affairs, the Security Council is often unable to adopt a resolution because of division among its Permanent Members. Equally often, it makes a recommendation which is rejected by one of the parties, or it adopts a resolution which is not supported, or is perceived as not being supported, by some important states directly or indirectly involved. In all such cases, the Secretary-General has to act as the main intermediary between parties, and to help pave the way if he can for an eventual accommodation between them.[43]

The impasse interrupted negotiations regarding Afghanistan. Not only was who would be helming the UN briefly unclear, but Perez de Cuellar's promotion necessitated the appointment of a new special representative to handle the negotiations. Perez de Cuellar ultimately chose Diego Cordovez, an Ecuadorian career diplomat with the United Nations. From 1981 to 1988, Cordovez served as its under-secretary for special political affairs, and, in this capacity, he led the negotiations that finally led to the withdrawal of Soviet troops from Afghanistan. So proud was Cordovez of the role he played in ending the Afghan conflict that, upon retirement from the UN, he persuaded the Ecuadorian government to rename the street on which he lived in Quito 'Afghanistan Street' and chose to live in house no. 88—commemorating the 1988 Geneva Accords.[44]

The Economist once referred to Cordovez as 'the most patient man in the world'.[45] He spent seven years negotiating a settlement that would withdraw Soviet troops from Afghanistan. Talks resumed in June 1982 at the Palais des Nations in Geneva, where Cordovez met Pakistani and Afghan delegations. Following these talks, he travelled to Islamabad, Kabul, and Tehran in late January 1983 for a round of consultations before two more sets of talks took place in Geneva, the second in April and the third in June 1983. The first three sets of talks in Geneva were complicated and prolonged by Pakistan's continued refusal to hold direct talks with Afghan representatives. The very mechanisms of the talks were time-consuming. As Cordovez later recalled: 'Each delegation would come to the Palais des Nations separately, one in the morning and the other in the afternoon, taking turns throughout the week so that each delegation would come roughly the same number of times in the morning and in the afternoon. The two delegations', he noted, 'were never to be in the building at the same time'.[46]

The next round of talks in Geneva did not take place until August 1984, following another visit by Cordovez to South and Central Asia in April of that year. At that stage, matters became slightly easier when both sides accepted the idea of 'proximity talks'. Representatives from both countries were now willing to be in the Palais des Nations at the same time, albeit in different rooms. This did not, however, accelerate negotiations, nor did Gorbachev's signalling, from 1985, that the Soviets were more interested than ever in a diplomatic solution.[47] Another seven rounds of proximity talks took place between 1985 and 1988, the final round occurring on 8 April 1988. During this time, Cordovez travelled to Islamabad and Kabul another four times. Finally, on 14 April 1988, the Geneva Accords were signed, going into effect on 15 May. The Accords included four different agreements:

- A Bilateral Agreement between the Republic of Afghanistan and the Islamic Republic of Pakistan on the Principles of Mutual Relations, in particular on Non-interference and Non-intervention
- A Bilateral Agreement between the Republic of Afghanistan and the Islamic Republic of Pakistan on the Voluntary Return of Refugees
- A Declaration of International Guarantees
- An Agreement on the Interrelationships for the Settlement of the Situation Relating to Afghanistan.[48]

In sum, these agreements were intended to deal with all the most complicated aspects of the Afghan situation, creating the means for a Soviet troop withdrawal, the resumption of friendly regional relations, the return of Afghan refugees, and affirmation of Afghan self-determination. They spoke, at least in name, to the tenets of international law and the resumption of good interstate relations. But the texts of each agreement were deceptively simple, belying the number of years, the countless hours of meetings that went into making such agreements possible—and the fact that they still had little underpinning in the violent realities of the Afghan civil war.

That the Geneva Accords took so long to negotiate was due in part to external circumstances and in part to the substance of the agreements, themselves. The PDPA under Karmal still focused on embedding its position within Afghanistan and enforcing obedience from the general population, with the help of its Soviet allies. The failings of these projects, however, led to regime change and Karmal's replacement with Mohammad Najibullah. Najibullah, in turn, pushed forward with his policy of national reconciliation, an attempt to expand support for the party and extend cooperation with opposition groups. Nevertheless, widespread violence against the government continued, supported by the exiled political parties around Peshawar, as well as resistance groups based in Afghanistan.

Alongside the developments taking place within Afghanistan was the rise of Gorbachev. His commitment to withdrawing Soviet troops as soon as possible also shaped the negotiations and, from late 1985, made the Soviets more willing to push through an agreement. No longer would he stand for the 'bleeding wound'. Gorbachev not only forced Karmal's replacement with Najibullah but also reached out to the United States. In October 1985, Ronald Reagan had laid out his vision for a regional peace process during a speech at the United Nations. Referring to the crisis in Afghanistan, as well as Cambodia, he demanded talks between warring factions in each state, new Soviet–US discussions, and the reintegration of these states into the world economy. 'This will be', he declared, 'a clear step forward to help people choose their future more freely'. This indication of US willingness to negotiate, alongside improving relations elsewhere, symbolized by the signing of a new treaty on intermediate-range nuclear force, led to a new series of US–Soviet parlays regarding the Afghanistan question. Foreign Minister Shevardnadze assured Secretary of State Shultz in September 1987, 'we will leave Afghanistan. It may be in five months or a year, but it is not a question of it happening in the remote future.' For the Soviets, there was little reason to prolong talks at the United Nations any further. Instead, their focus turned to pressuring their Afghan allies to accept a settlement.[49]

Meanwhile Pakistani leaders were increasingly preoccupied with their domestic political situation as well. Mohammad Zia-ul-Haq had reluctantly lifted martial rule at the end of 1985, though he had done everything within his powers (which were wide-ranging) to limit the reach of the newly elected national assembly. Yet even his extensive sway could not prevent the widespread protests that erupted, demanding the end of his rule. Violence was on the rise in many areas of Pakistan, as firearms meant for the Afghan resistance instead found their way into the black market, increasingly militant groups of Pakistani Islamists emerged thanks to Zia's ruthless push for Islamization, and new tensions erupted between Pakistan's different ethno-linguistic groups.

Against this backdrop, Zia baulked at signing the Geneva Accords, but he soon found he had little choice. He faced pressure from his American allies, who had responded positively to Gorbachev's overtures, while the civilian prime minister, Mohammad Khan Junejo, with the backing of members of the national assembly, demanded that the government follow through on its promises to both the international community and Afghans languishing in Pakistan to create a way for refugees to return home to a peaceful Afghanistan. Zia reluctantly agreed, though he deeply resented Junejo's interference. The final four months of Zia's reign would be dominated by a growing feud between the military junta and Pakistan's civilian leaders, particularly Junejo. This was abruptly terminated by the sudden death of Zia and most of Pakistan's high-ranking military officers in a suspicious plane crash on 17 August 1988.[50]

The processes leading to the Geneva Accords suffered not only from this political wrangling within and between the states involved in various aspects of the UN-led negotiations but also from the way that the deadly conflict continued playing out on the ground. There was no escaping the ongoing violence tearing Afghanistan apart. Afghan and Pakistani negotiators took starkly different stances on the meaning and workings of non-intervention and disputed the character of the Afghan refugees, two issues that directly informed the UN discussions.

Two of the main parts of the Geneva Accords dealt with non-interference and 'inter-relationships', or the ways that different states engaged with each other. Pakistani and Afghan representatives agreed in theory that no state should intervene in the affairs of another and that interstate relations should play out peacefully, in accordance with the principles of the UN charter. In practice, the ongoing civil war prevented either party from signing this bilateral agreement until the late 1980s. Continued Pakistani (and Iranian, Chinese, Saudi, and American) aid to Afghan resistance fighters blatantly demonstrated that Afghanistan's neighbours had little interest in pursuing policies of non-interference and non-intervention. Instead, despite public claims to the contrary, they flagrantly supported Afghan resistance combatants crossing the Durand Line to fight against the PDPA. The Afghan–Pakistan borderlands consequently became the site of frequent armed skirmishing and the source of extensive finger-pointing.

The continued activities of the resistance unsurprisingly incensed Afghan leaders, who, alongside their Soviet allies, did their best militarily to halt this transborder movement. Afghanistan's permanent representative complained to Perez de Cuellar that Pakistan had become 'a springboard of aggression and training base for the Afghan counter-revolutionary elements in order to carry out aggression against the territory of the DRA'.[51] But PDPA efforts to outmanoeuvre and defeat combatants frequently led Afghan and Soviet forces to violate the border with Pakistan in pursuit of insurgents. Consequently, throughout the 1980s, Afghan and Pakistani representatives sent first Waldheim, then Perez de Cuellar, scores of letters protesting against the actions of the other.

These complaints largely revolved around violations of the neighbouring country's air space and accompanying cross-border strafing and bombings. Time and again, Afghan representatives argued that Pakistani authorities were 'infringing upon the sovereignty and territorial integrity of Afghanistan', and listed specific incidents, including dates, type of attack, property damages, and casualties. Pakistani officials responded in kind, while making defiant, chest-beating threats that Pakistan would safeguard its independence and territory, with force if necessary. Unsurprisingly, each state vehemently denied the other's accusations. Pakistani or Afghan claims were always 'false and baseless' or 'slanderous propaganda', depending on who was responding to the complaint.[52]

These mutual accusations became a source of public political point-scoring, through which Afghan and Pakistani officials tried to undermine their neighbour while promoting themselves, continuing a decades-old enmity. In a particularly biting protest, Afghanistan's M. Farid Zarif snidely declared:

Pakistan's brief history has proven that whenever the regime in that country was challenged by a powerful internal resistance and protest of the Pakistani people, it always resorted to fabricating slanderous accusations against its neighbouring countries and flared up a propaganda war against them in an attempt to divert the public opinion of Pakistan and that of the world from the crucial political, social and economic problems confronting the regime.

He went on bitterly to decry the 'smokescreen', which hid the fact that 'Pakistan has turned into an imperialist springboard of aggression for launching an undeclared war against the Democratic Republic of Afghanistan'.[53]

Pakistani officials, in turn, argued that continued Afghan transgressions revealed the true brutality of the PDPA's regime. They pointed to ongoing Soviet and Afghan bombings across the Pakistani border. Defenceless Afghans 'who have left their homes to escape persecution and reprisals are not being spared from murderous attacks even in the refugee camps'.[54] Sahabzada Yaqub Khan, Pakistan's foreign minister, rather sanctimoniously (and falsely) claimed that Pakistan had 'exercised restraint and patience in the face of these frequent attacks in the hope that Pakistan's warnings and the expression of international concern about Kabul's aggressive acts would serve to restrain the Kabul authorities from pursuing this dangerous course'.[55]

Each side accused the other of intentionally launching military attacks to slow the progress of the Geneva Accords. In the same letter to Perez de Cuellar, Yaqub Khan claimed: 'The fact that the Kabul authorities have chosen to escalate acts of aggression on the eve of the talks in Geneva raises doubts about the sincerity with which they are approaching the search for a just and comprehensive settlement.' As late as February 1987, Pakistan's Prime Minister Junejo declared that Afghan air raids were 'nothing but an attempt to sabotage the Geneva Talks'.[56]

The 1988 bilateral agreements signed by the governments of Pakistan and Afghanistan on non-interference and non-intervention bound each country 'to respect the sovereignty, political independence, territorial integrity, national unity, security and non-alignment' of the other, as well as each country's 'national identity and cultural heritage'. Both parties also agreed not to allow their countries to be 'used in any manner which would violate the sovereignty [and] political independence' of the other.[57] In other words, the PDPA agreed to halt the regular air- and ground-attacks on Pakistani soil, while the government of Pakistan ostensibly pledged to stop aiding Afghan resistance groups. Both sides agreed to respect their countries' shared border—even though the legality of the Durand Line remained under dispute—and to use peaceful means, rather than force, in settling quarrels. In reality, these agreements did not put a halt to fighting and served more as a publicity stunt that allowed each participant in the UN-led talks to claim that it was acting according to international law.

Negotiations in Geneva could not paper over the fact that, on the ground, neither country acknowledged nor upheld its neighbour's sovereignty. While ongoing skirmishing, both verbal and military, undermined talks on the issues of non-interference and non-intervention, the future of the Afghan refugees additionally shaped international perspectives on the crisis. The refugee problem was a thorn in the PDPA's side, a source of international embarrassment that the PDPA tried not to acknowledge. Because the PDPA denied that a refugee crisis existed, UN and state representatives had to jump through any number of rhetorical hoops to create an agreement that recognized that Afghans (refugees or not) needed to be able to live within Afghanistan rather than abroad.

The government of Pakistan, alongside the UN's representatives, was keen to establish the circumstances under which those who had fled Afghanistan could safely return. While willing to play host to the Afghan refugees for a limited duration, Pakistan's leaders did not want to integrate Afghans into Pakistani society in the long term. Equally, the presence of so many Afghan refugees in Pakistan's frontier provinces placed a huge burden on the government's infrastructures and local populations. Pakistani representatives consequently made the return of Afghan refugees a key point of negotiation. As Agha Shahi told the secretary-general: 'Pakistan could not afford to become the permanent home of so many refugees. Because of that, at the later stage, they would have to become part of a political solution.'[58] The government of Iran concurred, though, as with other aspects of the negotiations, it largely refrained from discussions.

The government of Afghanistan faced a complicated position. The PDPA claimed to represent the will of the Afghan people, but to what extent could a government really assert its legitimacy when so many Afghans opted for life abroad rather than embracing the regime? Upon coming to power, Karmal and his government clearly knew that a refugee crisis existed, even if they baulked at acknowledging it. Instead, the PDPA focused on the claim that the refugee camps harboured resistance fighters, an accusation steeped in truth. Delineating between the two was often difficult. The UNHCR had likewise struggled to separate one from the other, while the government of Pakistan and representatives of the exiled Afghan political parties intentionally embraced ambiguous identities—Afghans in Pakistan could be both refugees *and* resistance members. Framing Afghan refugees as insurgents allowed the PDPA to make the argument that Afghans in neighbouring Pakistan and Iran were combatants intent on the destruction of the Afghan state, rather than accepting that millions of Afghans rejected the PDPA's vision of modernity.

In truth, the mere presence of countless Afghans in neighbouring Pakistan and Iran undercut PDPA claims to speak for the Afghan people. Their presence beyond Afghanistan's borders—but so tantalizingly close!—meant that they lay outside the state's purview and rule of law. They provided an alternative Afghan interest group, one in which the international community clearly invested time, money, and reporting. The fact that the political parties around Peshawar (alongside resistance leaders in Iran and groups within Afghanistan) asserted their own leadership in part by building alternative modes of Afghan politics among the refugees further infuriated and threatened the PDPA. The blurring of lines between refugee and resistance meant that the PDPA could not easily identify an opposing force. They struggled to distinguish resistance fighters and their families from those individuals who merely sought to flee persecution and violence.

Karmal initially asked refugees to return home and declared that a general amnesty would take place. He blamed Amin for causing so many Afghans to leave and pleaded in a radio broadcast for them to come back: 'They should deliver to their national revolutionary government the arms they have received from the enemy, end fratricide and voluntarily return to the country its tranquility and security'. He asked them instead to pick up arms to defend their fatherland.[59] In a subsequent statement, his government further asserted: 'The Government of the Democratic Republic of Afghanistan expects all those Afghans, once deceived by the propaganda of the enemies of the Revolution, to realize the changes of the situation.'[60] Thus, Karmal initially indicated that Afghan refugees *might* exist—but only because of Amin, who had derailed the government's efforts and veered off the rightful path of change. The government stressed that the only '*genuine refugees* with bona-fide[s] are those who left the country because of the atmosphere of oppression and fear, created by the fascist Government of Amin on the instigation of the enemies of Afghanistan before December 27th, 1979'.[61] Karmal went so far as to describe Amin as 'anti-party, anti-government, anti-revolutionary and anti-human'.[62]

Karmal's subsequent claims that a 'number of patriotic forces' had returned to Afghanistan clearly stretched the truth. The refugee exodus actually intensified. Consequently, the DRA had to seek new justifications for the ongoing presence of so many Afghans outside Afghanistan's borders while still touting the political power of the PDPA regime. State representatives maintained, in talks with UN officials, that refugees, if they did exist, needed to return to Afghanistan, but they also issued a number of statements that hopelessly contradicted each other.

One government tactic included arguing that a refugee crisis simply did not exist. PDPA representatives claimed that those 'Afghans' in Pakistan were actually migratory populations whom Pakistani officials prevented from following their traditional seasonal migration patterns. Zarif told Perez de Cuellar: 'In his view, it was impossible to distinguish between Afghans and Pakistanis because they share the same costumes and the same language. The majority of them belong to the Pashtun tribe which lived in both countries. Furthermore, this was the season when the nomads would migrate from Afghanistan into Pakistan.'[63] Similarly, in a statement to the UNGA on 23 November 1983, Zarif pointed to a UNHCR article on

> the Powindas, most of whom are nomadic Pathans but include other tribes, cut across the main tribal and linguistic groupings. These herdsmen, traders and itinerant labourers, have traditionally gone south in winter, often travelling as far as the Punjab and Sind provinces [in Pakistan], before returning to Afghanistan during the hot summer months...Now their migratory pattern has been upset, and many thousands of them swell the ranks of the refugees.[64]

Zarif also gleefully pointed out UNHCR concerns about the double registration of refugees at different camps as another indication that, again, there was hardly a refugee crisis of the scale claimed by Pakistan and other international observers.[65] Afghan officials used such material to argue that Afghans living in Pakistan did not qualify as refugees. Instead, Pakistan, Afghan leaders argued, had created an artificial refugee crisis. As such, Afghanistan's foreign minister told Kurt Waldheim that he 'rejected the Pakistani definition that all Afghans in Pakistani territory were refugees. In his view many were nomads, a few were *bona fide* refugees and the others were rebels and counter-revolutionaries'.[66]

But Afghan officials could not fully explain away refugees by arguing they were nomads or Pakistani Pashtuns. Afghans dwelling in camps received far too much international attention, and many of them had the same thing to say: they had fled Afghanistan to protect themselves and their families, to escape the threat of socialism and state violence, and to uphold their faith. As a consequence, Afghan government officials sought to emphasize Pakistani intransigence. At an early stage, Shah Mohammad Dost angrily told the secretary-general: 'The Government of Pakistan has converted the so-called Afghan refugee camps in that country to a tourist attraction and...an integral part of the sight-seeing programme for foreign dignatories [sic].'[67] The camps, DRA representatives argued, trained 'counter-revolutionaries' and 'rebels'. The foreign minister and other DRA representatives decried 'mercenaries' living in the camps who represented other states' interests against 'the Afghan people'.[68]

Those refugees who might exist, the foreign minister asserted, 'were completely manipulated by the counter-revolutionaries and represented the reserve for the terrorist activities of the gang leaders'.[69] Zarif also claimed that the government of Pakistan was intentionally withholding information and DRA statements from refugees, something Pakistani officials refuted, publicly offering to let neutral observers tour the camps.[70] Later in the conflict, Afghan representatives claimed that the governments of Pakistan and Iran actively prevented refugees from returning home. Pakistani officials disagreed and instead pointed to ongoing border skirmishes and the Afghan bombing of refugee camps on Pakistani territory as 'a brutal reminder of the callous attitude of the Kabul regime towards the refugees', as well as 'the farcical nature of Kabul's much bruited pleas for their return'.[71]

Afghan state representatives did their best to differentiate between 'real' or 'bona fide' refugees and 'those who are engaged in provocations, subversive activities and armed aggressions'.[72] This involved an attempt to disaggregate refugees from combatants and a strategy to delegitimize Afghan resistance forces. PDPA leaders admitted that 'there were also *bona fide* refugees who were the victims of the interference in the internal affairs of Afghanistan'.[73] But, they claimed, these refugees were actually fleeing fighting conducted by resistance fighters—what they framed as Pakistani interference in Afghan affairs—not the PDPA's reforms.

Thus, the official Afghan position on the return of refugees knew no single logic. On one hand, PDPA leaders desired refugees to return to Afghanistan and support the government. This would reinforce the regime's authority and recentre Afghan politics within Afghanistan's borders. On the other hand, leaders did not want to acknowledge the scale of the crisis and could not help but be wary of returning Afghans. Were they returning to their homes, or did they form part of an armed resistance? In pronouncements made about national reconciliation in early 1987, the Afghan government did not mention refugees at all, declaring only: 'We are ready to forgive the deceived persons and to warmly embrace them.' Instead, Najibullah placed emphasis on 'free Afghanistan' as the common homeland of all Afghans and the source of popular politics.[74]

International attention on the Afghan civil war forced conversations about the future of the Afghan refugee populations, but the inability of PDPA leaders to decide on a clear approach to the refugee crisis undermined efforts to reach an agreement at the UN. While all parties involved in negotiations agreed that Afghans needed to return to Afghanistan, Afghan state officials could not allow foreign representatives to place too much emphasis on a refugee crisis for fear of undermining their own claims to represent Afghanistan. For their part, UN officials tried to gauge how Afghan refugees might respond to the eventual accords. Working with the government of Pakistan and the UNHCR, they attempted to talk to refugees. This was not purely a humanitarian matter. In fact, despite the UN's official stance against negotiating with non-state representatives and UNHCR attempts to provide only non-political aid within the camps, the ambiguities of the refugee-resistance fighter identity actually provided UN negotiators with opportunities to suss out local perspectives. As Perez de Cuellar explained to the foreign minister of Iran: 'The Babrak Karmal Government legally represented Afghanistan in the UN, and no country objected to their credentials. Therefore, the Secretary-General could not deal directly with the guerrillas.' However, he added, 'through the refugees with whom consultations would be held, the UN would ascertain the views of the Mujahideen.'[75] The UN could thus surreptitiously find out the resistance's perspectives on negotiations, even if they refused to involve them directly.

Afghan refugees became central to the UN-led negotiations because their presence, in the millions, outside Afghanistan's borders indicated to international observers that many Afghans did not accept the PDPA's claims to represent Afghan self-determination. The intersection between a humanitarian crisis and a debate about who did, or should, decide Afghanistan's political future forced the refugee question to become a key focus of UN-led talks. The refugees posed a fundamental problem that the PDPA had to address, even as it tried to claim that Afghans embraced PDPA governance. The complicated, contradictory PDPA position on Afghan refugees, alongside the ongoing disputes regarding non-intervention and non-interference, slowed talks in Geneva. The question was not merely the safe, voluntary return of refugees, nor the potential for resistance fighters to disguise themselves as refugees and thus re-enter Afghanistan and cause further disruption: it boiled down to who represented Afghanistan. Nevertheless, by the end of negotiations, both Pakistan and Afghanistan had signed an agreement to allow the free return of refugees to Afghanistan, to uphold their 'free choice of domicile and freedom of movement', as well as their civic and working rights and the right to 'participate on an equal basis in the civic affairs of the Republic of Afghanistan'. Pakistan, for its part, agreed to 'facilitate the voluntary, orderly and peaceful repatriation of all Afghan refugees'.[76] At least on the face of it, the refugee matter had been resolved.

Upon the signing of the Geneva Accords, Diego Cordovez issued a public statement. He began: 'Some of you have been with me throughout the almost six years of these negotiations and have witnessed some of the frustrations that we have suffered. But at the same time, it has of course been for me a very rewarding, indeed an unforgettable experience.' He went on to say:

I am absolutely convinced that all concerned have been trying to work out not just *any* agreement but in fact the *best* possible agreement. What we have tried during these long years is to draft—with great care, with great caution and with great persistence—an agreement which will effectively serve the purpose of assisting the Afghan people to bring about an end to their suffering.

He acknowledged: 'It is not a perfect settlement, because it was worked out by human beings. Precisely for that reason, however, I believe that it is a settlement which reflects the reality of the situation.' He then noted: 'The fact that we were able to overcome such enormous difficulties make[s] me quite hopeful that the problems that will be undoubtedly encountered in the implementation of this settlement will also be overcome.'[77]

Cordovez's statement spoke to the hope of the accords while acknowledging their imperfections. On paper, the Geneva Accords had addressed the main issues raised eight years earlier in the UNGA. They ensured the timetabled withdrawal of Soviet troops. They established guarantees for the peaceful return of refugees to their homeland. And they set out the conditions for peaceful regional and international relations. However, as Cordovez also noted, the settlement was not perfect, nor could it ever have been so. The nature of talks on non-interference and the refugee crisis had demonstrated that parties involved in the talks would never fully agree on a single interpretation or policy. The fact that they had even managed an agreement that everyone was willing to sign was a major achievement.

But, given the discord surrounding the talks, it is hardly surprising that the Geneva Accords left a number of issues unresolved. The most outstanding problem was implementation: how were the accords to be put into practice? The agreements included a memorandum of understanding that established a UN deputy to the representative of the secretary-general and two inspection teams, one based in Kabul, the other in Islamabad, to monitor implementation of the accords. However, the deputy's role was that of an observer who would relay complaints from one side to the other. UN influence thus relied almost entirely on the goodwill of the governments of Pakistan and Afghanistan and their willingness to follow through on any issues brought up by the deputy.[78]

Another issue with implementation related to the international guarantors. American and Soviet officials touted the signing of the Geneva Accords as a huge success. Reagan declared: 'We take great pride in having assisted the Afghan people in this triumph, and they can count on our continued support.'[79] For his part, Gorbachev told Najibullah: 'The signing of the Accords could create a framework so that events do not take on extremely acute forms.' He pointed out:

'When there are obligations of parties there are opportunities to put pressure on those who shirk them.'[80]

While both the Soviet Union and the United States publicly celebrated the accords, they proved less than forthcoming in their roles as international guarantors. In the final months of talks, Gorbachev had suggested to Reagan that 'the Soviet Union would name a specific date for the withdrawal of its troops, and the United States would obligate itself to halt aid to known Afghan forces. That is, we would act synchronously.' Reagan and Secretary of State Shultz baulked at this, instead suggesting that the United States would halt aid sixty days after the Soviet withdrawal had begun. When the Soviets, in turn, rejected this idea, US officials proposed a three-month moratorium on all military aid from both sides, suggesting it 'would allow the dust to settle.'

Soviet officials again rejected this idea, and by the time that the accords had been signed, agreement still had not been reached on halting foreign aid either to government or to resistance forces. The final US stance, according to Under-Secretary for State Michael Armacost, remained that 'the United States retains the right, consistent with its obligations as a guarantor, to provide military assistance to parties in Afghanistan. Should the Soviet Union exercise restraint in providing military assistance, the US similarly will exercise restraint.' Secretary of State Shultz similarly warned, as he signed the accords in Geneva, that 'it is our right to provide military aid to the resistance…but we are prepared to meet the restraint with restraint'. On the Soviet side, Gorbachev assured Najibullah of ongoing support, even as Soviet troops began departing from the country in May 1988, promising to provide military aid 'in all cases when there are attacks on our troops. If necessary powerful strikes need to be launched on the rebel bands…In a word, both the carrot and the stick need to be employed.' Thus, even while acting as 'guarantors', neither the Soviet Union nor the United States was willing to take the first step in restricting continued warfare.[81] Instead, each took a tit-for-tat approach. Clearly neither international signatory was particularly worried about ensuring the halt of military conflict after the signing of the accords.

The inability of the Geneva Accords to prevent fighting on the ground correspondingly became clear almost immediately. Less than two months after the agreements went into effect, the UN secretary-general received yet further protests from the government of Afghanistan about ongoing Pakistani interference and disregard for the accords' agreements. 'The other side is acting as if the Geneva Accords are signed solely for the return of the limited contingent of the Soviet troops,' Shah Mohammad Dost complained. He argued: 'they are committing a blatant violation of all thirteen paragraphs of the second article of the first instrument.'[82] Pakistani officials responded in kind, bringing further violations of Pakistani territory by Afghan armed forces to the attention of the UN and warning that 'if such attacks did not cease the entire responsibility for the serious consequences would rest on [Afghanistan]'.[83] Collectively, these protests lodged with the UN demonstrate that, despite signed agreements regarding non-interference and non-intervention, fighting persisted across the Durand Line.

A final pressing issue outlasted the negotiation of the Geneva Accords: the future of the government in Afghanistan. While Najibullah's representatives had signed the accords, Pakistani and American officials still maintained that his government did not represent the will of the Afghan people. Pakistani leaders, in particular, demanded the establishment of an interim government that included representatives from the resistance groups and refugees, alongside those from the PDPA. However, the accords notably made no mention of the future Afghan government. Soviet and American leaders had concluded they both wanted a 'neutral, non-aligned Afghanistan', but they differed in how to achieve this. Gorbachev urged the continuation of the national reconciliation process begun under Najibullah, warning against 'the creation of a fundamentalist, Moslem government'. Reagan and his administration resisted. Richard Solomon, from the Department of State, pointed out that 'abstract principles', like national reconciliation, 'would be of little help...What was needed were concrete steps, and there were serious disagreements on the specifics'.

Gorbachev and Shevardnadze, eager to withdraw Soviet troops, ultimately backed off, acknowledging that attempts to create a functioning interim government would impede a Soviet exit. As Shevardnadze told Shultz shortly before the accords were signed: 'In some villages, counter-revolutionary forces reigned; in others, the Kabul regime held sway. But they lived as neighbours. That was the Afghan way. It had taken the Soviets time to understand this.' In other words, no clear solution lay in sight. Thus, as Cordovez explained in a January 1988 press briefing, 'that question had not been included in the negotiations. That was for the Afghans themselves to decide. It would be impertinent for anyone outside to be involved in that process.' Instead, he pointed to that other key UN responsibility: 'The principle of self-determination should be respected.'[84]

Najibullah tried to make the argument that his government had already taken adequate steps to become representative. 'The proclamation of the policy of national reconciliation', he argued, 'greatly helped the acceleration of the peaceful solution of the situation around Afghanistan to put forward a concrete proposal on the formation of a coalition government, including the opposition armed groups and the forces confronting the Afghan State'.[85] Najibullah believed he had already begun the process of establishing a coalition government. The government of Pakistan rejected this view and demanded that representatives of the exile parties in Peshawar be consulted.

However, Pakistan's earlier agreement that the resistance parties would not be actively involved in the negotiations leading to the Geneva Accords undermined these demands.[86] Yaqub Khan, Pakistan's foreign minister, suggested an advisory group comprised of representatives of the opposition groups, refugees, and the PDPA to come up with a governing solution, a proposal that increasingly appealed to Soviet representatives when it became clear that fighting was not going to stop, even as Soviet troops withdrew.[87] Rabbani's Jam'iyyat, alongside the other Peshawar-based parties, was incensed. An editorial in Jam'iyyat's *AFGHANews* argued: 'A broad-based government, for the Mujahideen and people who fought for over ten years to defeat the enemy, does not mean [a] coalition with the puppet regime or joining hands with the PDPA. People started their fight against the PDPA in order to remove it and not to make a coalition.'[88]

Unsurprisingly, no one could agree who should take part in a coalition government. Nor was it clear how a regime comprising two sides that had been at war for a decade could function. Were cooperation and collaboration between Najibullah, the remnants of the PDPA, and resistance leaders really feasible? Moreover, which resistance leaders would take part? Leaders of the seven parties in Peshawar took very different stances on the future of Afghan governance, ranging from Hekmatyar's insistence on one-party rule under Hizb-i Islami, to Rabbani's and Massoud's more moderate, cooperative approach, to Gailani's suggestion to bring back the exiled king. Additionally, these leaders did not represent the entirety of the Afghan resistance. What about leaders who had remained within Afghanistan? Where did they fit in? With no mechanisms in place for the creation of an interim government, a clear path forward remained illusory. Thus, while the Geneva Accords held to the letter of international law and political independence, they did not speak to the true spirit of self-determination. The United Nations asserted that Afghans should determine their own form of political modernity, but its officials did nothing to facilitate this. Instead, as in so many other instances, the idea of Afghan self-determination, or Afghan-identified modernity, trumped its implementation.

The United Nations became involved in Afghanistan because the Soviet invasion and accompanying civil war not only threatened regional and international relations but also undermined the very tenets of global governance and the system of law and order upon which state leaders relied. It brought into question a system of modern international relations that relied on respect for state sovereignty and the much more ambiguous idea that state populations should determine their own governance. Soviet decision-making forced a reckoning about the nature of political authority and the right of a people to rule themselves. It also necessitated reconsideration of the balance of power between states large and small, influential and ineffectual.

Events in Afghanistan revealed imperialism's pernicious afterlives—now in the name of Cold-War competition—despite the hard-fought years by dozens of states to overturn such power dynamics. The United Nations had provided the space in which newly independent leaders had pursued 'an anti-imperial project that...demand[ed] an expansive vision of an egalitarian world order'. But, equally, former colonies had ultimately chosen the nation state as the main unit of this world order, and, as such, subnational liberation movements, like the Afghan Islamists, struggled to have a voice in international politics.[89] Thus, in the 1980s, member states demanded that the UN take action to uphold this vision of global governance—a vision where small, weak states like Afghanistan had just as much right to independence and political decision-making as their more powerful neighbours. But, because only one group could officially represent the Afghan nation—the PDPA, holding forth in the UNGA— resistance groups ultimately struggled to propose and receive adequate support for an alternative.

The Geneva Accords ostensibly created an opportunity for Afghans to take back control of their political destiny. But the accords revealed the problems that had hampered UN-led negotiations all along: they simply were not representative. While they brought together members of the PDPA and regional and international actors such as Pakistan, the Soviet Union, and the United States, they did not involve those other Afghans fundamentally impacted by the conflict, the refugees or resistance groups. While Afghan refugees were clearly a target of the talks, their views on Afghan self-determination or nationhood were largely remarkable for their absence. The same went for the excluded resistance leaders. The exigencies of UN-led talks meant that, while Pakistani leaders supported Afghan Islamism on the ground, they did not help it gain the same legitimacy in international circles. Likewise, US officials like Reagan, while keen to welcome 'freedom fighters' to Washington, did not advocate for their political legitimacy in governing arenas. The UN's emphasis on interstate relations, not the demands of non-state representatives, meant that the resistance parties did not get a place at the negotiating table, which in turn meant that the future of Afghan politics and the nature of Afghan modernity remained undetermined. International observers promised an Afghan nation state would exist, but how was uncertain.

By May 1988, when the accords went into effect, questions still outpaced answers. UN negotiators had worked tirelessly for more than seven years to bring together representatives of Afghanistan, Pakistan, the Soviet Union, and the United States and to broker a withdrawal of Soviet troops. In this remit, they had succeeded. But what would happen next? Even as Soviet troops were airlifted and driven out of Afghanistan, future steps remained hazy. On paper, everyone agreed that the Afghan refugees should return, that Pakistan would no longer support Afghan resistance fighters against the PDPA, and that Afghanistan would stop bombing the Pakistani borderlands. But, even weeks after the accords had gone into force, none of these things had occurred. Violence and fighting persisted, and there was little immediate sign of a mass return of Afghans from abroad. Meanwhile, Soviet and American guarantors threatened to continue funding violence if the other side also did.

The most fundamental lingering question—for Afghans, as well as for regional and international observers—was that of Afghanistan's political future. Who represented the Afghan people, who would lead a post-withdrawal Afghan state, and what this state would look like remained far from settled. Najibullah indicated that he foresaw the PDPA remaining in power. Afghan resistance leaders and their international backers did not. The government of Iran derided the Geneva agreements for excluding Afghan resistance representatives. Iran's Ministry of Foreign Affairs bitterly hit out: 'Unfortunately, the international organisations have always failed to ensure the interests of the Muslim and Third World nations.' The OIC, while cautiously welcoming the agreements, nevertheless reiterated that it 'supported and recognized the role of the Afghan Mujahideen Alliance for the restoration of the Islamic independent and non-aligned status of Afghanistan'.[90]

The future of the Afghan state and people remained contested but also ultimately beyond the scope of UN-led talks, revealing the limits of international institutions and their influence. The issue of Afghan self-determination revealed a sad irony: the United Nations, while an international political arbiter and arena for debates on sovereignty and statehood, chose to leave the issue of Afghan self-determination within Afghanistan, but without assistance or oversight. Afghans themselves, Cordovez argued, should fashion their own government. But, with the continued involvement of so many foreign powers—UN observers, Soviet advisors, US funders, Pakistani officials—how could Afghan self-determination occur truly independently of outside interference? And how was the will of the people to be either ascertained or enforced?

While the United Nations succeeded in creating the circumstances through which the Soviet Union would withdraw its troops, its negotiators failed to establish a regional peace. This had little to do with the abilities of negotiators such as Javier Perez de Cuellar and Diego Cordovez, who put countless hours and exceptional diplomatic skill into negotiations. Instead, the real problem lay with the fact that the talks in Geneva simply did not reflect events on the ground in Afghanistan and Pakistan. While talks took place among the Swiss Alps or the skyscrapers of New York, bombs kept falling and people kept dying in the mountains and plains of Afghanistan. How likely was this to change when the Soviet troops had left? As we know, not at all. As conflict persisted, hopes for alternative Afghan modernities receded into the past.

# 9

# Back to Kabul

On the face of it, little changed on the ground when the last Soviet troops crossed the Amu Darya river and retreated to Soviet Uzbekistan on 15 February 1989 (see Figure 9.1). Fighting continued between government and resistance forces within Afghanistan and along its southern borders. Refugees in their millions continued to live abroad. Soviet and American leaders kept a vague eye on the conflict, even as they increasingly focused on other domestic and international developments. Officials with the UNHCR and the UN Good Offices Mission in Afghanistan and Pakistan (UNGOMAP) were kept busy documenting ongoing skirmishing as well as mapping out a potential return for Afghans living abroad. The future of Afghanistan remained uncertain. Who would govern, and how, continued to be contested.

At the same time, everything was different. UNHCR officials, trying to gauge whether refugees could return home, produced province-by-province reports, all of which came to the same conclusion: the Afghanistan of 1989 could not support returnees. Roads across the country had been sewn with anti-tank mines. Warehouses, schools, and hospitals that pre-existed the 1978 coup had been destroyed. Provinces frequently lacked the medical infrastructures to support a healthy population, and major repairs were needed to canals and fields to make agriculture viable.

Political circumstances across the country remained uncertain and diverse. In Hesa-i-Awal Behsud, Wardak province, a *shura*, or council, comprising an alliance of Shi'a resistance leaders oversaw local populations. In Chamkani in Paktia, power was divided between two *shuras*, one of resistance commanders and one of local tribal leaders. In districts across Nangarhar province, various resistance parties vied with each other for local control. In Surkh Rud district, for example, UNHCR observers reported: 'Pir Gailani's home is in Sawati village, Surkh Rud. Despite this fact, he does not have a significant following in this area. HIG [Hekmatyar's Hizb-i Islami] used to be influential, but they created many problems for the people, and consequently lost much support to HIK [Khalis's Hizb-i Islami].'[1]

At the time of the Soviet withdrawal, neither government nor resistance forces had a clear upper hand. One thing became increasingly apparent, however: this was no longer a battle for Afghan modernity. It was a fight for power and influence, whatever form that might take. In February 1989, as the final Soviet troops left, Najibullah remained in state in Kabul, but his grasp on power was weak. He faced renewed party infighting between members of the Khalq and Parcham factions, which had never been fully reconciled, while turning the PDPA's focus away from socialism. He renamed the party *Hizb-i Vatan*, or Homeland Party, and pledged to pursue democracy and a market-based economy. The Soviet newspaper *Izvestia*

**Figure 9.1.** Red Army soldiers cross the Amu Darya river at the Soviet–Afghan border in Termez, 15 February 1989 (VITALY ARMAND/AFP via Gerry Images)

approvingly remarked in August 1988 that the party was 'ridding itself of the mistakes of the past and overcoming the effects of pseudoleftist excesses'.[2] Afghan socialism was increasingly a thing of the past.

However, attempts to expand Najibullah's base of support amounted to little. The Afghan army continued to face high rates of desertion, the economy remained in a shambles, Afghans living under government protection relied heavily on Soviet-provided foodstuffs to survive, and the government depended on continued Soviet military supplies to fight the resistance. Yet Najibullah managed to remain in power until March 1992, surviving a coup attempt in March 1990. While continued Soviet support provided one reason Najibullah clung to power, the infighting within the Afghan resistance created another.[3]

The inter-party competition that had prevented any serious resistance alliance from taking shape in the early to mid-1980s persisted and in many ways only worsened. US, Pakistani, and Saudi officials made a brief attempt in January 1989 to force together an Interim Islamic Government of Afghanistan (IIG) comprised of representatives of the seven main parties based around Peshawar. The IIG, however, excluded representatives from the PDPA and Afghan Shi'a groups, as well as most commanders based within Afghanistan, and members of the new government were overwhelmingly Ghilzai Pashtuns. Alongside this, Pakistan's ISI continued to distribute aid to the individual parties, not the IIG. Quarrels quickly emerged about which party leaders should be given which positions in this new 'government'.[4]

With encouragement from ISI, the IIG launched an attack on the city of Jalalabad, a government stronghold, in March 1989. If successful, the venture would have reinforced the legitimacy of the IIG and given it a firm base of power within Afghanistan, rather than Pakistan. Instead, resistance forces proved incapable of breaking through heavily fortified town defences, suffered from air and Scud missile attacks, and managed only to antagonize local civilians, who suffered heavy casualties.[5] The IIG's defeat, in turn, led to finger-pointing, as members of the disparate political parties blamed each other. Long-time tensions erupted (again) in violence. When Massoud and his Supervisory Council of the North, which had a string of military successes across north-eastern Afghanistan, suggested an alternative military strategy for reclaiming Afghanistan, Hekmatyar's Hizb-i Islami responded in July 1989 by massacring a number of his commanders, bringing the long-standing feud between Hekmatyar and Massoud, and Hizb-i Islami and Jam'iyyat, into the open. The interim government succumbed to infighting, providing the shell, rather than the core, of a government. Meanwhile, local commanders in Afghanistan increasingly made their own arrangements and alliances to gain necessary supplies, demonstrating their independence from much of the political wrangling taking place among the Pakistan-based parties. Any strategic gains made by party combatants were gradually being undermined, as *qawm*, ethnic, and tribal leaders re-emerged at the fore of provincial and district politics.[6]

Regional circumstances also began to shift, further complicating matters. The government of Iran, finally freed of its war with Iraq, turned to Afghanistan with renewed interest. In 1990, the government helped organize an alliance between the major Shi'a resistance parties under the name *Hizb-i Vahdat* (Unity Party). Hizb-i Vahdat sought an understanding with Rabbani's Jam'iyyat and some of the moderate nationalist parties based out of Pakistan. Pakistan, which was facing bitter internal divides between its new civilian prime minister, Benazir Bhutto (daughter of the executed Zulfikar Ali Bhutto), and the military establishment, was increasingly divided in its policy towards the Afghan resistance. Army and ISI leaders remained firmly attached to the Afghan Islamists, particularly Hekmatyar, while Bhutto expressed more interest in wresting power back from the Pakistan army.[7] Hekmatyar and Sayyaf (of Ittihad-i Islami) also managed to alienate regional backers by opposing the US entry into the Gulf War on behalf of Saudi Arabia. These more militant Islamists decried Western intervention in Islamic affairs (or in affairs between Islamic countries), bringing their parties into dispute with the Americans, the Saudis, who halted funding, and the government (though not the military) in Pakistan.

Meanwhile, even while both the United States and the Soviet Union claimed to adhere to the Geneva Accords, neither side halted the provision of aid to their Afghan allies. Soviet leaders continued to provide Najibullah's government with an estimated $250 million–$300 million in military and economic aid per month.[8] Ronald Reagan faced pressure from members of the US Senate not to 'cease, suspend, diminish or otherwise restrict assistance to the Afghan resistance...until it is absolutely clear that the Soviets have terminated their military position'.[9] But Reagan, who was coming to the end of his presidential term, had little else to do with Afghanistan, and instead the future of US–Afghan and US–Soviet relations was left in the hands of his former vice president, George H. W. Bush. As president from 1989, Bush continued to provide arms to the resistance, though increasing tensions with the government of Pakistan and concerns about 'sidelining extremists' made the US administration increasingly unwilling to rely purely on ISI and its party of choice, Hekmatyar's Hizb-i Islami.[10]

Both Bush and Gorbachev realized the impasse in Afghanistan could not endure. Neither the United States nor the Soviet Union wanted to remain bogged down in Afghanistan forever. Nor was this really an option, particularly for the crumbling Soviet Union. Communism had largely collapsed in Eastern Europe in 1989, and widespread social and political reforms, even revolutions, were taking place through-out the former Soviet bloc. Gorbachev survived an attempted coup in August 1991, but he almost immediately stepped down as general secretary of the CPSU. Gorbachev ended his presidency on 25 December that year, marking the end, as well, of the Soviet Union and Soviet superpower competition with the United States.[11] Meanwhile, US attentions in the region turned increasingly towards the Persian Gulf, where Iraq's invasion of Kuwait precipitated an armed US intervention, Operation Desert Storm, from August 1990 to February 1991 to bolster the Saudi Arabian position in the region (and protect US access to Saudi oilfields).[12] Neither power, increasingly, had time, money, or interest to expend on Afghanistan.

In a sort of irony, American and Soviet leaders turned back to the United Nations to help facilitate an exit from the ongoing quagmire. The two powers that had reluc-tantly participated in UN-led negotiations in the 1980s and truculently refused to stop funding the Afghan civil war at last recognized the futility of their positions and the need to find a way out of the conflict. This had the additional irony that it forced the United States, as well as the United Nations, to take a more active interest in the future of Afghan politics. As one member of the Department of State acknowledged to a UN negotiator in October 1989, American policy 'was one of political settlement'.[13]

Officials with UNGOMAP wrote to the secretary-general in August 1989 insisting that the UN help settle Afghanistan's political future, not just rely on self-determination to take its natural course. UN observers argued a political process in Afghanistan was 'unrealistic' 'without the cooperation of all those countries who, throughout the years, have supported politically and practically one or the other of the Afghan groups'. A global war required a global solution. They called for an initiative by the secretary-general to achieve a 'basic consensus' internationally on Afghanistan's political future and establish 'incentives...to encourage the Afghans to focus on a political solution', as well as 'disincentives which would possibly be used should the Afghans fail to achieve a political solution'.[14] As such, UN, US, and Soviet negotiators all recognized by September 1989 the need for some sort of broad-based government that could, ideally, end the civil war and reunite Afghanistan.

High-level talks between US and Soviet representatives continued through 1990, as the two sides debated how best to underpin a new Afghan government. While US officials insisted that Najibullah had to go and promoted an interim arrangement, their Soviet counterparts maintained that an election could take place under the auspices of Najibullah or an independent commission. By December 1990, both sides agreed that the UN should oversee and sponsor some sort of transition mechanism to replace the existing government (including Najibullah), though the US and Soviet sides failed to agree to a specific date for 'negative symmetry'—when both countries would halt the provision of weapons and aid to their respective sides. Nevertheless, in May 1991, Secretary-General Javier Perez de Cuellar was able to announce an 'international consensus' for a political settlement in Afghanistan, with support from not just the United States and the Soviet Union but also Pakistan and Saudi Arabia, whose aid to the resistance had been dimmed by circumstances relating to the Gulf War. An interim authority would organize 'free and fair elections, in accordance with Afghan traditions', while participants in the civil war would adopt a ceasefire and their foreign backers would stop aid.[15] On 13 September 1991, Soviet Foreign Minister Boris Pankin and US Secretary of State James Baker signed an agreement that pledged to end all aid to Afghan forces by 1 January 1992 and support an 'independent authority' to oversee an Afghan election.

With international backing, UN officials set to creating this independent authority. It ended in failure. The mechanism proposed by the UN was unwieldy. Boutros Boutros-Ghali, who replaced Perez de Cuellar as secretary-general, announced in January 1992 a plan for an 'Afghan gathering' constituting 150 representatives selected by different Afghan interest groups, who, in turn, would elect a committee of 35 to oversee consultations leading, later on, to a 'nationwide meeting to decide on an interim government and the holding of elections'.[16] Afghan participation, however, proved uneven. While the moderate Pakistan-based parties and the Hizb-i Vahdat Shi'a alliance submitted lists of proposed participants, the Islamist parties, including Jam'iyyat, did not, nor did Najibullah or Zahir Shah, the former Afghan king whom so many refugees had indicated they would support.

Finally, under pressure from the US, Pakistan, and the UN, and now bereft of Soviet support, Najibullah was induced to provide a list of government representatives to take part in the UN mechanisms—and to accept his own resignation. In a radio broadcast on 18 March 1992, Najibullah announced: 'I agree that once an understanding is reached through the United Nations process for the establishment of an interim government in Kabul, all powers and executive authority will be transferred to the interim government.'[17] Najibullah's announcement indicated the end of an era: not an abrupt, sudden end, but rather one in the making ever since national reconciliation had been announced in 1987, if not longer. Afghan socialist modernism had failed. It lacked supporters in the international community, and it lacked supporters at home. Afghanistan's political future, everyone acknowledged, would not be a socialist one.

Najibullah's resignation, however, did not smooth the path towards an Afghan government. While party leaders across the political spectrum gave into pressure to sign onto the UN plan, many continued to question the shape of the interim government. These included not only resistance leaders like Rabbani but also former followers of Najibullah. As Najibullah handed in his resignation on 15 April 1992 and prepared to leave Afghanistan, his exit was blocked by former Parchamites. Najibullah would spend the remaining years of his life in hiding in the UN's Kabul office. He never left Afghanistan, and his exit from the UN compound only took place by force under the new Taliban government on 26 September 1996. Najibullah was tortured and executed by the new regime, his body pulled through the streets of Kabul and then hung in front of the old palace. Thus ended the PDPA's hopes for a socialist Afghanistan.

Even with Najibullah out of the way, the competition for control of Afghanistan remained divided, factional, and extremely messy and came no nearer to a consensus. While many local commanders continued to mobilize to protect and strengthen their communities' interests, ignoring party politics, four main bodies vied for power at the Afghan centre. The Shi'a Hizb-i Vahdat, with its stronghold in Hazarajat and Iranian backing, sought to mobilize Afghan Shi'as. Hekmatyar continued recruiting Hizb-i Islami members from Pakistan's refugee camps, mobilizing an overwhelmingly ethnic Pashtun following and benefiting from foreign support from more radical Pakistani and Arab Islamist groups. However, he struggled to retain a strong foothold or local alliances within Afghanistan, unsurprisingly given Hizb-i Islami's inability to work very successfully with local allies throughout the 1980s. Jam'iyyat, meanwhile, retained its stronghold in north-east Afghanistan, taking advantage of strong Tajik backing, Massoud's experiences in the Panjshir Valley during the 1980s, and infrastructures put in place by the Supervisory Council of the North, including the first *mujahidin* bank established in the city of Taliqan in 1991. Finally, a former Afghan army commander, Abdul Rashid Dostum, established a citadel in Mazar-e Sharif in northern Afghanistan, from which he led Uzbeks from former government militias as well as other non-Pashtun northerners and former PDPA members, including Babrak Karmal.[18]

Alliances came and went between these four groups (and within these groups and with other factions), and their membership and composition correspondingly fluctuated. Who was fighting whom was not always clear. Conflict was even exacerbated, as resistance party leaders ostensibly came together (again) to form an interim government. Negotiations in April 1992 resulted in what became known as the Peshawar Accords. While Hekmatyar was excluded from talks—a joint military effort by Massoud and Dostum had just expelled Hizb-i Islami forces from Kabul—the other leaders agreed to an interim government with a rotating leadership. Mujaddidi, moderate leader of Jabhah-i Nijat-i Milli, would serve as president for the first two months, followed by Rabbani for the next four. After this six-month period, participants agreed, a *shura* would establish a government that would remain in power for eighteen months until nationwide elections took place.

Ongoing fighting around Kabul provided a rationale for Rabbani's presidency to be extended by an additional forty-five days, and, after this delay, the *shura* that took place in December 1992 elected Rabbani president and was boycotted by the other parties who saw clear signs of Jam'iyyat manipulation. This, in turn, provided part of the impetus for Hizb-i Vahdat and Dostum to turn on Rabbani and Massoud, whom they increasingly suspected of wanting power for themselves, not a united Afghanistan. Further Saudi- and Pakistani-backed talks in March 1993 created yet another new agreement, one that brought Hekmatyar back into the fold and made him prime minister under President Rabbani. Massoud was ousted as the government's defence minister. UN negotiators made a final attempt in 1994 to negotiate a ceasefire and create a national government, but these were still bogged down in political impasses by the end of that year.[19]

In a great irony, Rabbani increasingly appeared like Hekmatyar in his quest for power and influence. While not demanding single-party rule, Rabbani clearly expected and supported his own leadership, rather than the more encompassing system Jam'iyyat had espoused in the 1980s. Rabbani's decision-making fundamentally undermined the opportunities his party had created for itself in the war against the PDPA and the Soviets, with ensuing violence. His obvious unwillingness to give up power undercut Jam'iyyat claims to represent an Afghan nation. Not only that: his focus on retaining the presidency soured relations between Jam'iyyat and the other resistance forces. Massoud and his soldiers also became the targets (and instigators) of attacks, although they continued to hold their own in military confrontations and retained control in much of the north-east.

At this stage, the country was so divided that any hopes of exporting the Panjshir model that Massoud had developed in wartime were gone. All the parties focused largely on combat, not state-building. Much like Afghan socialism, Rabbani's, Massoud's, and Hekmatyar's visions of an Islamist Afghanistan also dwindled, overtaken by the interpersonal and inter-party conflicts that had rumbled throughout the 1980s and resurged with a vengeance following the Soviet withdrawal. With Afghan Islamists fighting other Islamists and nationalists, an Islamist Afghanistan was impossible. Neither Jam'iyyat nor Hizb-i Islami had the opportunity to test their models of Islamist statehood, too embroiled in fighting each other, too focused on gaining power, and ultimately exhibiting less interest in the Afghan civilians caught in the crossfire.

Instead, a completely different, largely unexpected Islamic force came to dominate within Afghanistan. In October 1994, Benazir Bhutto's government, looking to extend trade links with the newly independent Central Asian republics, dispatched a Pakistani convoy through Afghanistan to Turkmenistan and Uzbekistan. While Bhutto had arranged the trucks' transit with two of the local commanders, Dostum and Ismail Khan, the Jam'iyyat-allied commander who controlled the Herat *shura*, the convoy was nevertheless stopped by local armed groups in Kandahar province. Five days later, the trucks were freed and sent on their way—but their liberators were not Afghan resistance leaders. Instead, they were several hundred religious students who called themselves the Taliban and responded to widespread frustrations with the lack of law and order in Afghanistan and the neighbouring Pakistan borderlands.

The Taliban emerged from the *madrassas* of the NWFP and Balochistan, which had multiplied during the Soviet–Afghan war. Pakistan's Jam'iyyat-i 'Ulama'-i Islam had helped establish dozens of new seminaries during the conflict, which educated Afghan refugees and local Pakistanis alike. Jam'iyyat-i 'Ulama'-i Islam had links with several of the resistance groups, most prominently Khalis's Hizb-i Islami and Harakat-i Inqilab-i Islami, and students from Jam'iyyat-i 'Ulama'-i Islam's *madrassas* took an active part in the fight against the Soviets. One such Jam'iyyat-i 'Ulama'-i Islam-affiliated participant who emerged in the fighting was a religious teacher, Mullah Mohammad Omar Mujahed. Mullah Omar, as he came to be known, was a Durrani Pashtun who became a Harakat-i Inqilab-i Islami commander in Arghestan district, Kandahar. After the Soviet withdrawal, he had retired from combat, becoming the head of a local *madrassa*. However, disgusted with the ongoing power struggles between the resistance party leaders and the accompanying descent of many areas of Afghanistan into lawlessness, Mullah Omar and his Jam'iyyat-i 'Ulama'-i Islam-trained compatriots pledged to restore order, root out corruption, and create a new national government.

By October 1994, the Taliban had secured control over Kandahar, denounced resistance leaders, begun collecting weapons from the local population, and destroyed checkpoints used to extort money from locals. They had also taken over the province's governance. As one of the Taliban's leaders, Abdul Salam Zaeef, recalled in his memoir: 'The *shari'a* would be our guiding law and would be implemented by us. We would prosecute vice and foster virtue, and would stop those who were bleeding the land.'[20] In contrast to visions of Islamic governance espoused by the likes of Jam'iyyat, the Taliban's politics relied on a strict interpretation of Islamic law and the rejection of many extant social and political components, most notably (and in stark contrast to the PDPA and the resistance) party organizations. The Taliban focused heavily on individual morality. They not only shuttered girls' schools and enforced *purdah* but also destroyed televisions, forbade sports and recreational activities, and demanded men grow long beards.[21] Public punishments, like flogging and stoning, would later follow.

The Taliban, in many ways, was no less radical than Hizb-i Islami or the PDPA. The organization rooted politics in *shari'a*, with *ulama* the key political authorities as interpreters of Islamic law. Mullah Omar's initial ten-man *shura* would expand to thirty-five after the taking of Kabul and become the main source of government, supported by other local councils across the country, which were often headed by local *mullahs* (to the exclusion of influential landowners and the educated class). In a sharp rupture with the past, the Taliban insisted on regularly rotating officials to prevent regional divisions within Afghanistan. And, in April 1996, Mullah Omar would be declared 'commander of the faithful' (*amir al-mu'minin*), a title previously reserved for the caliphs serving as Muhammad's successors, in a ceremony intended to indicate that 'the *amir* was regarded as God-sent rather than elected in the usual sense'. Clearly, the Taliban interpreted Islam's political intent in very different ways from Hizb-i Islami, Jam'iyyat, and other Islamist resistance parties and also rejected the moderates' interests in democratization and constitutionalism. Instead, they pursued an alternative governing agenda that would likewise reshape Afghan politics and society.[22]

In comparison to the disorganization of the resistance groups fighting the civil war, the Taliban demonstrated themselves to be strictly regimented and structured. Not only did the Taliban begin to accrue support from locals relieved to have a pause in the fighting and corruption, but the movement also gained backing from the government of Pakistan. Even ISI had grown increasingly disillusioned with Hekmatyar and sceptical of his chances of political success. The Taliban provided a means of bringing security and order back to Afghanistan and paving the way for Pakistan to engage, across Afghanistan, with the post-Soviet Central Asian republics (and their bountiful natural resources). By February 1995, the Taliban had accrued new followers and taken control of Wardak province. By the 14th of that month, they had overrun Hekmatyar's base in Charasyab, Logar province (Hekmatyar was forced to flee). Within three months of having captured Kandahar, the Taliban controlled twelve of Afghanistan's thirty-one provinces. In March, they reached the outskirts of Kabul and asked government leaders to surrender but were repulsed.[23]

Even as the Taliban faced temporary setbacks, their political significance received an additional boost from meetings with the UN mediator, who made a last-ditch attempt to create a national government. Taliban representatives told the mediator an interim government could consist only of 'good Muslims'—followers of the Taliban's militantly conservative line—a position rejected by both the UN and Rabbani.[24] The Taliban, meanwhile, focused on strengthening their strategic position, succeeding in capturing Herat in September 1995; its famous resistance leader, Ismail Khan, was forced to retreat to Iran. Through this move, the Taliban surrounded Kabul on its southern and western sides.

The strength of the Taliban position forced the resistance party leaders to reconsider their mutual antagonisms. In January and February 1996, Rabbani initiated new talks with Hekmatyar, Dostum, and Hizb-i Vahdat, and power-sharing was mooted. Foreign powers also began to take an increasing interest, but, while Rabbani and his allies received aid from Iran, the Taliban thrived on supplies from the governments of Pakistan and Saudi Arabia. American interest in Afghanistan revived enough for the US to propose an international arms embargo at the UN Security Council in April 1996, but the Clinton administration remained ambivalent in its approaches to both the Rabbani government and the Taliban. It was suspicious of Iranian support for Rabbani and doubtful of the Taliban's plans to take over Kabul. Meanwhile, Taliban forces continued to launch rocket attacks on Kabul and made further battle plans. In August, they took Jalalabad, and by mid-September had also captured Nangarhar, Laghman, and Kunar provinces. Having surrounded Kabul on three sides, the Taliban swept into the capital on 26 September 1996. While the Taliban focused on executing Najibullah, Rabbani and other members of his regime fled the city.

In the aftermath, Massoud and Dostum, among others, established the Northern Alliance, the last bastion against a Taliban takeover of the entirety of Afghanistan.

It suffered defeats in February and May 1997, owing to Taliban successes and intra-alliance fighting. But, even as the Taliban wrested control of 90 per cent of the country, the Northern Alliance held firm in its resistance. Rabbani continued to lead a small government in exile in the lands held by the Northern Alliance, one recognized by many international governments but lacking the military and political strength to confront the Taliban. The Taliban, meanwhile, though recognized as legitimate heads of state by Pakistan, Saudi Arabia, and the United Arab Emirates, remained a pariah within an international community horrified by what effectively amounted to an ethnic-cleansing campaign against the Hazara during the 1998 Taliban capture of Mazar-e Sharif, the destruction of the ancient Buddha statues near Bamyan, and the Taliban's repressive political and social policies, particularly towards women.[25]

The Taliban's decision to host other Islamic extremists—individuals and groups who focused on Islam as the response to American hegemony and sought a global *jihad*—also led to its disavowal by many Western countries. In May 1996, the Taliban welcomed Osama bin Laden, one of the Wahabbist 'Afghan Arabs' who had fought in Afghanistan on the side of the resistance in the 1980s and who had taken over as the head of al-Qaeda after the death of Abdullah Azam in 1989. Like the Taliban, bin Laden had been disillusioned with the resistance's infighting and had returned to Saudi Arabia, later travelling to Sudan to take part in another Islamic revolution. Upon being asked to leave by Sudanese authorities (under Saudi and US pressure), bin Laden returned to Afghanistan, living first in Jalalabad and then in Kandahar. Al-Qaeda's successful bombings of US embassies in Kenya and Tanzania heightened global focus on bin Laden and his Taliban backers, as the Clinton administration launched worldwide initiatives to find and arrest bin Laden and his followers.[26]

As the Taliban continued in its efforts to destroy the Northern Alliance, install its socially conservative reign, and back the global Islamic fight against the West, a new exodus of Afghans took place. The civil war among the resistance parties had swelled the ranks of Afghans living abroad and led to continuing displacement of populations within Afghanistan as they sought to evade fighting. Another wave of refugees emerged in response to the Taliban's harsh rule and joined generations of Afghans raised abroad who had little experience of living in an Afghan homeland. The UNHCR's hopes of a widescale return of Afghan refugees faded against the realities of ongoing violence and repression.[27]

Ahmad Shah Massoud again became the face of an Afghan resistance. While Hekmatyar languished in exile in Iran from 1996 and Rabbani struggled to hold together a government in the lands under the Northern Alliance, Massoud remained in the international spotlight owing to his abilities to keep warding off Taliban attacks. A November 1999 profile in the *New York Times*, entitled 'An Afghan "Lion" Wages War on Taliban with Rifles and Fax Machine', praised 'the Lion's mystique for cunning'. Its author proclaimed: 'He is a man who wanted to be an architect in a nation that was once starting to prosper, and instead he became a military tactician in a woebegone country whose cities are in ruins.'[28] A similar profile ran in January 2001, striking an even more pessimistic note: 'About the only glimmer of hope for the coalition's long-term survival is the promise of a United Nations arms embargo against the Taliban for its refusal to hand over the Saudi terrorist leader Osama bin Laden.'[29]

Massoud, in such reporting, represented both the hopes and the futilities of Afghan modernism. On the one hand, Western profiles of Massoud highlighted the precariousness of his position, his stoicism in the face of overwhelming forces. On the other, they demonstrated that many still saw him as a viable alternative to the Taliban, a potential leader of a future Afghanistan. Despite his influence in only a small region of Afghanistan, Massoud continued to offer an alternative leadership for Afghanistan, an alternative vision that contrasted with the Taliban's. Clearly the Taliban and their al-Qaeda allies saw him as such. On 9 September 2001, Ahmad Shah Massoud was assassinated by two Arab suicide bombers posing as reporters. They were suspected of being agents of al-Qaeda, though this has never been definitively proven. Two days later, Osama bin Laden launched his attacks on the United States. Less than a month after, on 7 October 2001, US President George W. Bush launched Operation Enduring Freedom, sending US troops onto Afghan soil to overthrow the Taliban. Another twenty years of foreign occupation would follow, though American troops replaced Soviets.

With the death of Massoud and Operation Enduring Freedom, opportunities for Afghan Islamist modernism, of the type espoused in the 1980s, also breathed their last. The visions of Afghan modernity put forward by socialists and Islamists alike had been left on the field of battle. What remained was a war-torn country, millions of refugees, and an international community that struggled to understand Afghanistan outside the bounds of national and international security. Whether, or how, anyone might contemplate Afghan modernities remained a test for the future rather than a means of reflecting on the past.

The Afghanistan that emerged after 1989, following a socialist 'revolution' and ten years of civil war, was fundamentally different from the Afghanistan that had existed in 1978. But it was not the Afghanistan hoped for or envisioned by many of the individuals, groups, and organizations that had been embroiled in the conflict. If events in and around Afghanistan in the 1990s revealed anything, it was Afghanistan's lost futures. Afghan socialism had failed. So had the competing visions of Afghan Islamism espoused by Gulbuddin Hekmatyar's Hizb-i Islami and Burhanuddin Rabbani's Jam'iyyat-i Islami. Moderate liberal constitutionalists and monarchists such as Sayyid Ahmad Gailani or the former king, Zahir Shah, remained in exile or bogged down in civil war. Afghan refugees' desire for *vatan*, or homeland, remained a distant hope for millions unable to return to a war-torn country lacking the infrastructures for rebuilding. International observers from the UN and UNHCR looked on helplessly, finding themselves no more able to broker a new government in the 1990s than in the 1980s. Meanwhile, a growing air of disinterest overhung US and Russian policy. Russian leaders no longer desired worldwide socialist revolution and just wanted to be rid of the Afghan burden. In turn, satisfied that they had emerged victorious in a global Cold War, US leaders pivoted from the threat of worldwide communism and, for a brief moment, luxuriated in a sense of unmatched global power.

What took place over the course of the late 1970s and the 1980s was a war over the nature of Afghanistan's politics, society, and economy, a war over the meaning of Afghan citizenship and statehood—a war for Afghanistan's future that was ultimately lost. It was a conflict driven by ideas and aspirations that receded into the background, and into the past, with renewed fighting in the 1990s that fractured Afghans into numerous interest groups divided by politics, ethnicity, ideology, location, and alliance. Before 1989, even though internal divisions appeared quite clearly, whether between the PDPA's Khalq and Parcham factions or among the seven resistance parties based around Peshawar, these groups sought to reshape Afghanistan, not merely control it. They sought to institute their visions of Afghan modernity, to create an Afghanistan united by a statewide vision of politics and a nationwide consensus on what it meant to be an active Afghan citizen. The opportunities to institute such visions were gone by the mid-1990s, and instead the war had become one of survival.

This failure of Afghan politics was not preordained and was a messy, protracted affair. Afghanistan's descent into civil war resulted from the tangled intersection between domestic, regional, and international affairs and a moment of broader global change. For decades, Afghan elites and intellectuals had debated the nature of Afghan politics, citing the merits of different models of economic, social, and political participation and exploring ways to fuse local practices with forms of modernization rooted in the Muslim, anti-colonial, and Western (North Atlantic and Soviet) worlds. Indeed, the regime changes that had taken place throughout the twentieth century highlighted the aspirations of numerous Afghan elites to evolve Afghan politics, with particular emphasis on constitutionalism, representative government, and a strong head of state. Not only that but the modernity that Afghan leaders sought took place in international as well as domestic realms. In an era when the nation state became the chief building block of international relations, Afghans asserted their legitimacy and their governing visions to foreign, as well as local, audiences. This meant, among other things, participating in the United Nations, the 1955 Afro-Asian Conference, and the Non-Aligned Movement; engaging with the Soviet Union and United States and Cold-War politics; and disputing Pakistan's political borders and shedding light on issues of ethnonationalism and self-determination.

The emergence of Afghan socialism and Islamism was a direct consequence of earlier decades of political reform and change, and the fact that the PDPA, Hizb-i Islami, and Jam'iyyat all assumed the form of political parties attests to earlier quests for different models of political modernity. These parties strove to reframe Afghan politics and drew on extensive global networks for ideas, allies, and support. They shared similarities ranging from their organizational structures to their focus on anti-imperialism and Afghan self-determination. And, even while they framed themselves as fundamentally different from other Afghan modernizers, they drew on precedents established by earlier Afghan liberals, such as the demand for *bi-tarafi*, or non-alignment, in international politics, increased participation from across Afghan society, and a more representative, inclusive government. They all also relied on long-standing links between Afghanistan and the rest of the world, whether with the country's northern Soviet neighbours or with states across the Global South with whom Afghans shared cultural, educational, economic, and political links.

These strands of Afghan political thought—socialism and Islamism—were far from dominant in mid-century Afghanistan, yet they emerged as the two most prominent camps during the Afghan civil war of the 1980s. Indeed, the creation of an increasingly clear binary between Afghan socialism and Afghan Islamism had far more to do with regional and international circumstances than with these visions and models, themselves. Their rise proved contingent on the Cold-War system of alliances and the upsurge in interest in the late 1960s and 1970s in Islamism as a compelling political force.

The PDPA proved able to take advantage of domestic ambivalences and frustrations with Mohammad Daoud Khan's stilted reforms to launch a military coup that toppled the Musahiban dynasty for good. That the party managed to remain in power relied in part on its Soviet allies and in part on the ongoing fractures within the resistance. The PDPA's political vision shared many commonalities with other socialist parties across the non-Western world, and Nur Mohammad Taraki, Hafizullah Amin, and Babrak Karmal drew parallels between reforms in Afghanistan and those taking place in countries such as Ethiopia and Vietnam. But, where the PDPA's ideas had promise, its implementations did not. The PDPA opted for speed over stamina, hastily pushing through land reform and new marriage laws without adequately considering how such changes would be received or how to embed them into Afghan politics and society.

From Moscow, Soviet leaders looked on in dismay as the PDPA's socialist aspirations turned into a civil war. Even while the Soviets neither anticipated nor fully supported the 'Saur Revolution', they could not let a struggling socialist ally succumb to infighting. 'It was a people's democratic movement,' remembered Soviet General Valentin Varennikov. 'And that is exactly why the Soviet Union, naturally, supported this movement.'[30] Brezhnev and the Politburo took the decision in December 1979 to send in soldiers and state-builders to secure the gains of the revolution, to ensure that the PDPA (under a new leader) remained in power, and, if possible, to keep Afghanistan part of the socialist bloc. Politburo decision-making drew on the Soviet Union's successes in backing socialist movements in Africa and South-East Asia earlier in the 1970s, but circumstances in Afghanistan proved far more challenging. Not only did the decision to send in thousands of troops undermine the Soviet Union's international reputation, but what quickly became obvious was that Afghanistan lacked the local officials to implement the PDPA's socialist vision, which the Soviets supported, however ambivalently. Over the course of the 1980s, Soviet officials concluded that modernization undertaken by foreigners and not Afghans had failed to win local (or international) support or legitimize the PDPA. Instead, it had only led to the deaths and maiming of thousands of Soviets.

The Soviet decision to intervene sparked a much larger chain of events. The emergence of the PDPA and its Soviet backing took place alongside a resurgence in Islam as a powerful force. Political Islam served as a means of guaranteeing the independence and rights of Muslims across the world, and, like pan-Asianism, Afro-Asian solidarity movements, and tricontinentalism, it framed global politics beyond Cold-War divisions and placed emphasis on the power and sovereignty of states across the Global South. Afghanistan's neighbours, Pakistan and Iran, and to a lesser extent India and China, brought such impetuses to the war in Afghanistan. Events in Iran demonstrated that an Islamist revolution was possible. Pakistan's leaders, likewise interested in the Islamization of their country's domestic and foreign policies, opted to support the Afghan Islamists (as did Iran) as an alternative to Afghan socialism and earlier regimes' focus on ethnic Pashtun nationalism. This, in itself, gave unprecedented power and opportunity to Afghanistan's Islamists, allowing them not only to compete with but even to surpass more moderate resistance groups thanks to the huge amounts of foreign aid and international attention they received. Afghanistan's neighbours played a crucial role in internationalizing the civil war and creating unexpected opportunities for Afghan Islamism to become a dynamic power against the PDPA.

The rise of Afghan Islamism was further aided in part by the United States, where President Jimmy Carter's administration saw the movement of Soviet soldiers not as an effort to shore up a struggling ally and neighbour but as a calculated move to expand Soviet influence all the way to the Persian Gulf. In turn, he and his advisors turned to their regional ally, Pakistan, and its contacts with the growing Afghan resistance, and issued orders for millions of dollars in aid to be sent to Afghan rebels to bog down Soviet troops. Yet, for Carter and Reagan after him, the battle was not one for Afghanistan's future. Neither president had much interest in either Afghan Islamism or the more moderate political parties. They focused, rather, on the idea that Afghan tribal 'freedom fighters' could undermine Soviet expansionism rather than rebuild Afghanistan. For the United States, this was a war of containment that relied on the assumption that Afghanistan was not, and could not be, a modern state.

Despite the huge opportunities provided by the sudden wave of funding, weapons, and foreign support, Afghan Islamist groups proved hardly more successful than the PDPA in pursuing their visions of political modernity. As with the PDPA, this had little to do with the available resources and largely resulted from internal shortcomings. Groups such as Hizb-i Islami and Jam'iyyat could not agree on a single, shared vision of Afghan Islamism, and instead they pursued competing models of what an Islamist Afghanistan might look like. While Hekmatyar focused on single-party rule and mobilizing supporters among the refugees, Rabbani's Jam'iyyat was more active across Afghanistan and Pakistan and proved adept at integrating existing resistance groups and community leaders into the party fold. Ultimately the disunity within the Afghan resistance—between Islamists and among moderate and

Islamist parties alike—meant that, while resistance fighters successfully pinned down PDPA forces, they failed to create a viable state alternative.

If events from the late 1970s into the 1990s demonstrated the failure of different competing visions of Afghan modernity, they also highlighted the shortcomings of international politics and global governance. On the one hand, many foreign powers insisted that an Afghan state should exist and participate in an international system of nation states. They saw the Soviet invasion not only as an attack on Afghanistan's sovereignty but as an affront to international law and the status quo of interstate politics. On the other hand, much like Afghan elites, themselves, foreign observers proved incapable of agreeing on what Afghan modernity within the international system looked like—or if it was even possible. American analysts remained intent on colonial-era ideas of Afghanistan as backward and tribal, incapable of long-term political change. Soviet policymakers attempted to shore up the PDPA without succeeding in implementing socialism. Regional actors sought to embed Afghanistan into growing Islamist networks. The United Nations, meanwhile, tried to moderate between these different factions, but, while its negotiators managed to facilitate a withdrawal of Soviet troops, they avoided making space for one vision of Afghanistan's future over another. While UN officials advocated for Afghan self-determination, they, too, struggled with issues of application, particularly because so few Afghans actually took part in the negotiations that led to a Soviet retreat. With only a handful of PDPA representatives involved in the UN-led talks alongside Pakistani, American, and Soviet leaders, the question remained: which Afghans would determine their political future? And how? Different alternatives for Afghan politics, which often involved only a limited number of Afghan interest groups, proved incompatible.

More than anything else, the refugee crisis that accompanied and outlasted the Afghan civil war demonstrated the failure of the Afghan nation-state project and the international system. The fact that millions of Afghans chose to leave the country rather than accept PDPA rule demonstrated the new regime's lack of legitimacy. Yet, even with extensive help from the international community, Afghan resistance parties, whether Islamist or more moderate, proved incapable of creating the circumstances under which Afghans could return home. The refugee crisis posed a fundamental question for Afghanistan and the international community, one that has been replicated in recent years with continued forced migration and refugee crises across South Asia, Africa, and the Middle East: can a state really be said to exist and to be part of the international community when so many of the people who are ostensibly its citizens refuse to live there? What happens to a state and the international system when people choose statelessness over a homeland? The circumstances that force such choices, in themselves, highlight a sense of political crisis. Equally, the fact that so many refugees increasingly are stuck in camps and cannot benefit from the UNHCR's older strategies of repatriation or assimilation—much like the millions of Afghans in the 1980s and 1990s—is telling.

The war of the 1980s demonstrated that neither Afghan nor international actors, alone, could determine political legitimacy in Afghanistan. The visions of an Afghan state touted by the Islamists, socialists, or moderates fused global and local conceptions of politics and the social contract, thanks in large part to the anti-colonial networks that helped circulate ideas of nationalism, democratization, constitutionalism, Marxism, and Islamism. An earlier 'Afghan' form of political legitimacy where 'whoever gained power and could hold it was deemed legitimate as long as he could provide security and fend off rivals' no longer existed.[31] Events forced a reconceptualization of power, not just because of the ideas and actions of Afghan party leaders but also thanks to the experiences of displacement that disrupted so many communities' hierarchies and social practices. While the deployment of a foreign troop body clearly undermined the PDPA's legitimacy, it did not mean that Afghans rejected international engagement. The strength of Afghan attachment to the UN, and the concerted effort of resistance leaders (and refugees) to engage with international audiences, demonstrated that political legitimacy resided in a delicate balance between citizen, nation, and internationalism, and between security and recognition, that no Afghan political party managed to achieve. A return to pre-1978 forms of political legitimacy was impossible.

Ultimately, the story of the Afghan civil war of the 1970s, 1980s, and 1990s was one of violence. Part of this, of course, was the violence of the battlefield, the military encounters between PDPA and resistance forces, the campaigns undertaken by Soviet soldiers to crush a nationwide rebellion, the US decision to fund a covert war. But to focus purely on military hostilities in the Afghan war is simply inadequate and

**Figure 9.2.** Destroyed Kabul, 1996 (Jenny Matthews/Alamy Stock Photo)

belies the more pervasive, widespread nature of the war's cruelty: the fundamental violence of modernity. Modernizing, for the PDPA, meant not only torturing and executing enemies of the state but ruthlessly pushing through intensive, life-altering reforms with little consideration for their immediate repercussions for Afghan individuals, families, and communities. Violence, or the threat of violence, became a key tool of governance in socialist Afghanistan. In turn, the brutality of the PDPA begot further bloodshed. Groups resisting the regime likewise turned to armed force to retaliate against the PDPA and its supporters, creating a civil war out of a political dispute. Not only that, but, as groups like Hekmatyar's Hizb-i Islami accrued increasing arms and influence, they also resorted to hostilities against competing interest groups within the resistance. Physical (and emotional) assaults became a key tool of the resistance—not only in combating the PDPA but in asserting hierarchies of power among the anti-PDPA groups.

Violence, in other words, became systematized and normalized in political and social interactions, between resistance members and socialists, Islamists and moderates, Islamists and Islamists, or parties and refugees. It became a factor of daily life to be used or feared and a tool for legitimization and de-legitimization, in equal parts. In turn, violence added to the sense of uncertainty and precariousness experienced by millions of Afghans living in refugee camps or remaining within Afghanistan. Afghan civilians not only faced the horror of losing family members, having their homes destroyed, or their own bodies maimed and impaired: they also experienced the deep-seated fear and trauma of war and, for many, the insecurity of exile. As UNHCR officials observed time and again, the length and brutality of the war only increased uncertainty about when, or even if, Afghans could return home and resume some form of normalcy. The violence of the conflict, whether physical or psychological, meant that, in fact, a return was not possible because a new normal would have to be created. The country simply could not resume a pre-1978 status quo. Afghan civilians thus faced fundamental political, social, and cultural changes owing to the militarized and systemic violence of the conflict.

The civil war also highlighted how deeply embedded violence had become in international relations. The Soviet Union's reliance on its armed forces to shore up the PDPA's state-building visions and the United States' ready turn to guerrilla warfare revealed the decay in the international system wrought by the global Cold War. The prompt use of covert and overt military tactics by both superpowers indicated their limited respect for the sovereignty and independence of other nations. Instead, both turned to violence as an easy remedy for asserting their own power and influence with little thought for ramifications on the ground. Likewise, the ease with which regional actors such as Pakistan, Iran, Saudi Arabia, and China turned to supporting an armed resistance in a foreign country spoke to fundamental problems in the states system. How could international politics rely on peaceful interstate relations when the United States and Soviet Union or regional players so easily flouted international law? The moment of the early 1960s, when so many postcolonial leaders embraced statehood and state-led politics as a key symbol of their independence from empire, with the United Nations serving as a crucial arena, was gone. Instead, it had given way to circumstances in which leaders across the world quickly and readily turned to violence as a means of improving the standing of their own countries while undermining others. The ready encouragement of violence in the Afghan civil war by foreign actors was a symptom of a greater sickness in the international system that was not localized to Afghanistan. Instead, Afghanistan was a site, a battlefield, in a much broader and equally brutal conflict over the nature of international relations.

The violence of the civil war in Afghanistan and the ready willingness of foreign, as well as local, actors to employ brutal methods to support certain visions of Afghan and international modernity led to a breakdown in local, regional, and international systems rather than opportunities for Afghanistan to rebuild and rejoin global politics as a functioning (Islamist, constitutionalist, socialist, or monarchist) nation state. Instead, the violence of the encounter lived on, not only in the brutal tactics used by the Taliban but in the ways that foreign powers would continue to deal with Afghanistan and Afghans. The stage was already set for the wars, and the failed state-building, of the twenty-first century—not only in Afghanistan but across the world.

# Epilogue

After 2001, many of the central figures of *Afghan Crucible* again became involved in Afghan politics. Former members of the resistance took part in political negotiations and the 2004 presidential elections. Burhanuddin Rabbani backed the US-led invasion and served as interim president before Hamid Karzai, himself a former resistance fighter, was selected as president at the Bonn Conference. (Rabbani was assassinated by the Taliban in 2011.) Karzai's other supporters included Sayyid Ahmed Gailani and the former king, Zahir Shah, who returned to Afghanistan in 2002. Gulbuddin Hekmatyar opposed the US intervention and remained in exile in Pakistan until his pardon in 2016, when he re-entered Afghan politics. As in the 1980s, the government of Pakistan became a key US partner in the region, though in the twenty-first century it was often Taliban fighters who took advantage of the porousness of the Durand Line to seek shelter from attack. Neither the US nor Pakistan proved successful in rooting out these forces, though the turn to drone attacks has had terrible consequences for local inhabitants. Russia supported the US invasion, also wary of terrorist threats, though in recent years Russian leaders have looked to some resurgent Taliban leaders as a means of countering the growing influence of Islamic State (and as US–Russian tensions have grown). The United Nations, for its part, echoed the US and Russian positions. In the aftermath of the September 11 attacks, the UN Security Council passed resolutions justifying armed intervention in Afghanistan in the name of international security and asserting the need to create a new Afghanistan.[1]

While foreign forces and domestic elites turned to state- and nation-building within Afghanistan, they did so with the intention of preserving national and international security. Securitization and the threat of international terrorism, not visions of modernity, served as the impetus for a collective effort to construct functioning institutions and development projects across Afghanistan, to support the creation of a constitution and representative government. Stabilizing Afghan politics and society, international observers calculated, would likewise undermine the threat of terrorists and other non-state actors. This, in turn, reinforced the narrative of Afghanistan as a 'failed' or 'rogue' state whose very lack of state institutions threatened the world order. Foreign actors became involved to rectify what they increasingly framed as Afghanistan's own shortcomings.

International approaches to Afghanistan in the twenty-first century have had their roots in the Afghan civil war of the 1980s in ways that are both tragic and ironic. Institutions like the United Nations and countries like the United States, in the twenty-first century, chose to participate actively in Afghan state-building in ways that they had not in the late twentieth. Not only that, but these international actors became involved in Afghan affairs in the 2000s because of the failings of their policies in the 1980s. Then, US officials had taken little interest in Afghanistan's political trajectory and had done little more than ensure a Soviet withdrawal. The UN had neither offered a clear means of gauging Afghan political aspirations nor helped encourage the institutions that would allow Afghans to determine their political futures or embed them in society. While both the US and the UN had expressed limited interest in some of these processes in the 1990s, by then it was already too late, as the civil war had intensified, political impasses persisted, and millions of Afghans remained abroad.

Perhaps most telling and significant was the way that American interpretations of the nature of Afghanistan, its people, and its history increasingly dominated narratives. The more nuanced, positivist visions of Afghanistan's future espoused in the late twentieth century by Afghans and foreign actors alike, who were interested in socialist, Islamist, constitutionalist, democratic, or monarchist possibilities, were swept away and replaced overwhelmingly by public narratives focusing on Afghanistan's supposedly backward, tribal, feudal, and fragmented nature. In other words, American focus on Afghanistan's lack of modernity—a viewpoint rejected by most actors in the 1980s—went mainstream in the 2000s.[2] This, in consequence, has often served to mute the voices of Afghans and other groups who still assert the country's potential modernities. The dominance of this US-led narrative regarding Afghanistan has, itself, undermined the historical and present agency of Afghans who not only engaged in debates about their country's politics and society but also actively participated in the international community.

In more recent times, the United States continued to dominate and in ways that hinted its leaders had not necessarily learned the lessons of the past. When direct negotiations between the US government and the Taliban began in July 2018, representatives of the Afghan government were excluded (at the Taliban's behest). Discussions revolved around a 'framework' for national reconciliation (a familiar term), one that would allow American troops to withdraw and prevent the return of al-Qaeda-type terrorist groups to Afghanistan. The Agreement for Bringing Peace to Afghanistan, signed on 29 February 2020, additionally stipulated 'intra-Afghan negotiations' about the country's political future (though the standing government could only agree to take part through a 'Joint Declaration between the Islamic Republic of Afghanistan and the United States of America for Bringing Peace to Afghanistan', thanks to continued Taliban rejection of direct contact). In terms of Afghan politics, the agreement only pledged 'the new government to be inclusive and reflect the aspirations of all Afghans'. The restricted nature of the agreement and its ambiguity regarding Afghanistan's future, in many ways, were a clear echo of the UN-led talks of the 1980s: limited in their participation and opaque in their outcomes.

While intra-Afghan talks, indeed, began in September 2020, the first round consisted of eighty-two days of haggling over procedural matters before government and Taliban representatives exchanged proposed agendas. The agendas revealed various stark contrasts. The Afghan government proposed to discuss a 'roadmap for political participation' while the Taliban demanded an 'Islamic government' and talks about the 'type of future Islamic government'. Again, discussions turned to the type of regime that best suited Afghanistan (and the international community), but clear tensions existed between the two sides' ideas, as well as between potential modes of implementation. Not only that but fears persisted about how a Taliban regime might treat Afghanistan's religious and ethnic diversity. The Taliban's earlier repression and mass killing of Hazara have not been forgotten.[3]

By mid-2021, intra-Afghan talks had continued in fits and starts but without making any real progress. Instead, the headlines that dominated international media cycles focused on President Joe Biden's decision to begin a final withdrawal of US troops for completion by 11 September 2021, the twentieth anniversary of the 9/11 attacks. While American leaders justified the need to reorient the United States' national security priorities to a public tired of foreign intervention, vague promises of 'diplomatic support' for the Afghan government carried much the same ambiguity as assurances in the 1990s to back 'Afghan self-determination'. As the United States withdrew, regional actors stepped up, recognizing the severity of the ongoing crisis and its potential to surge across national borders and sensing an opportunity to rebalance regional relations. In another whisper of the past, Pakistani, Iranian, and Chinese officials met Afghan delegations and hosted a series of conferences in the hopes of negotiating Afghanistan's future. Even these diplomatic manoeuvres became largely meaningless after a stunning series of Taliban military successes swept the sitting Afghan government out and the Taliban back into power, creating fresh uncertainty about the future of Afghan politics and society.[4]

What has remained clear is that the cycle of violence precipitated by the 1978 PDPA coup has not ended. In an even more tragic repeat of the past, peace, itself, did not accompany peace talks. A surge in violence paralleled the start of intra-Afghan negotiations, with a 60 per cent increase in civilian casualties. Targeted killings of Afghan doctors, educators, reporters, civil servants, and community leaders increased. In a merging of past and present, Nargis Noorzai Faizan told the *New York Times* about the assassination of her military prosecutor husband, Pamir Faizan, by gunmen in Kabul: 'I was a 4-year-old when my father got killed by mujahedeen insurgents. He was an officer in the army and thought that he didn't make trouble for anyone, so he won't be targeted. He was assassinated. Now I am 30, and I lost my husband to another insurgency.'[5]

Following the announcement of the US withdrawal, bloodshed skyrocketed. The UNHCR issued a warning in June 2021 of an imminent humanitarian crisis, reporting that an estimated 270,000 Afghans had been displaced from their homes since January 2021, adding to an uprooted population of more than 3.5 million, while civilian casualties had risen 29 per cent. Human Rights Watch likewise reported on Taliban-led atrocities against civilians and officials with connections to the government and security forces, and images of desperately fleeing Afghans briefly dominated international media, as Taliban forces entered Kabul. Meanwhile, calls for a 'second resistance' began emerging in some of Afghanistan's northern provinces, as local non-state groups mobilized against the Taliban onslaught and state security forces crumbled, recalling echoes of the 1980s and 1990s.[6]

We cannot draw direct or absolute parallels between the current war in Afghanistan and that of the 1980s. This would obscure the huge changes that have taken place within Afghanistan and in the international community in the intervening decades. If the past years have taught us anything, it should be that the ready willingness of Western policymakers and pundits to make simple comparisons between British colonial experiences on the Indo-Afghan frontier and twenty-first century NATO forces in Afghanistan, or to assume the primacy of Afghan 'traditionalism' and 'tribalism', leaves international actors ill-prepared to encourage real, dynamic political change and masks a much more complicated reality. It also fails to recognize the ways in which young Afghans, who hope to be at the heart of Afghan state- and nation-building, seek to change the narrative and actively imagine and debate different futures for their country.[7]

It is difficult to know what Afghanistan's future holds. In *Afghan Crucible*, I have tried to offer an opportunity for more critical and careful reflection on what lessons can be taken from the past—the history of Afghanistan, its region, and the international community—to rupture the cycle of violence. That violence has persisted into the twenty-first century is as much a consequence of the global nature of the war that took place in the 1980s as it is more recent circumstances. Afghanistan's wars have often been global, even if not in ways that the international community chooses to claim. The Afghan civil war demonstrated how interconnected, by the end of the twentieth century, local, regional, and international political dynamics had become. The history of the Afghan civil war, then, is also that of the international community, and it offers us the chance to reflect on Afghanistan's alternative pasts as well as the possibilities and pitfalls of Afghanistan's potential futures.

# Chart of Major Resistance Parties and Organizations

| Party | Leader | Ideology | Leadership base |
|---|---|---|---|
| *Mahaz-i Milli-yi Islami-yi Afghanistan* (National Islamic Front of Afghanistan) | Pir Sayyid Ahmad Gailani | Traditionalist, nationalist, royalist | Peshawar |
| *Jabhah-i Nijat-i Milli-yi Afghanistan* (Afghanistan National Liberation Front) | Sibghatullah Mujaddidi | Traditionalist, nationalist | Peshawar |
| *Harakat-i Inqilab-i Islami-yi Afghanistan* (Movement of the Islamic Revolution) | Mawlawi Muhammad Nabi Muhammadi | Islamic traditionalist | Peshawar |
| *Hizb-i Islami-yi Afghanistan, Hikmatyar* (Islamic Party of Afghanistan, Hikmatyar) | Gulbuddin Hikmatyar | Radical Islamist | Peshawar |
| *Hizb-i Islami-yi Afghanistan, Khalis* (Islamic Party of Afghanistan, Khalis) | Mawlawi Khalis | Sunni Islamist, anti-Shi'a | Peshawar |
| *Jam'iyyat-i Islami-yi Afghanistan* (Islamic Society of Afghanistan) | Burhanuddin Rabbani | Moderate Islamist, alliance focused | Peshawar |
| *Ittihad-i Islami Bara-yi Azadi-yi Afghanistan* (Islamic Union for the Freedom of Afghanistan) | Abd al-Rabb al-Rasul Sayyaf | Radical Islamist, Salafi, anti-Shi'a, key Saudi ties | Peshawar |
| *Shura-yi Inqilab-i Ittifaq-i Islami-yi Afghanistan* (Council of Islamic Union) | Sayed Ali Behishti | Shi'a traditionalist, Afghan nationalist | Hazarajat, Afghanistan |

| Party | Leader | Ideology | Leadership base |
|---|---|---|---|
| *Sazman-i Nasr-i Inqilab-i Islami-yi Afghanistan* (Victory Organization for Islamic Revolution) | Muhammad Hussain Sadiqi and central council | Shi'ite, pro-Khomeini Islamist | Iran |
| *Pasdaran-i Jihad-i Islami-yi Afghanistan* (Guardians of the Islamic Jihad) | Ali Jan Zahedi and central council | Shi'ite, pro-Khomeini Islamist | Iran |
| *Hizbullah* (Party of God) | Sheikh Wusuqi and Qari Ali Ahmed Darwazi | Shi'ite, pro-Khomeini Islamist | Iran |

*Source*: Barnett R. Rubin, *The Fragmentation of Afghanistan: State Formation and Collapse in the International System* (1995; New Haven: Yale University Press, 2002), 208–9; Hafizullah Emadi, 'Exporting Iran's Revolution: The Radicalization of the Shiite Movement in Afghanistan', *Middle Eastern Studies*, 31/1 (1995), 1–12, at 9. See also Niamatullah Ibrahimi, 'At the Sources of Factionalism and Civil War in Hazarajat', Crisis States Working Papers Series no. 2, working paper no. 41 (2009); Olivier Roy, *Islam and Resistance in Afghanistan* (Cambridge: Cambridge University Press, 1990 edn), chs 7, 8, 9.

# Note on Sources

Researching and writing a new history of the war in Afghanistan have been both invigorating and challenging. I have been privileged in this project not only by the extensive scholarship that precedes and underpins my own work but also by the opportunities I have had to travel to archives across the world to research this text. Nevertheless, all historical projects have limitations, and this book is no exception.

A lot of different factors come into play while researching a historical project: time, funding, university responsibilities, teaching duties, archival access, language skills, and, in this case, security and personal safety concerns (both for myself and for any potential Afghan interlocutors). Unfortunately, I was unable to travel to Afghanistan in preparing this book. Likewise, financial and time constraints led me to prioritize learning and using Russian over Pashto or Dari. These choices have inevitably shaped what is written here. I cannot, and this book does not, represent an Afghan perspective on the conflict. While it seeks to explore and contextualize Afghan decision-making and ways in which large swathes of the country's population responded hostilely to PDPA government reforms, it tries not to make assertions about how or why individual Afghans responded to socialist, Islamist, or other visions of modernity in different ways. In other words, this is not an on-the-ground history of the Soviet invasion. Instead, this book has been animated by my own training as a global historian and my interest in forefronting Afghanistan into our understanding of international politics in the twentieth century.

As an event that brought in so many historical actors from across the world, the Afghan civil war has left a global paper trail, though not necessarily an even one. *Afghan Crucible* draws on state, institutional, and private archives from across North America, Europe, and South Asia. The actors involved in the civil war have left behind materials that vary in their depth, focus, and accessibility. The UN and UNHCR, which were so involved with the Afghan refugees and refugee camps, the negotiations that led to the Soviet withdrawal, and the PDPA's quest for international legitimation (and other countries' attempts to undermine it), have provided particularly rich materials. The Reagan and Carter administrations likewise left large amounts of reporting and data, which can be found across a number of archives and libraries. In contrast, I have followed the Soviet Union's state-building initiatives within Afghanistan, revealed at the State Archive of the Russian Federation, rather than focusing as strictly on top-level decision-making in Moscow, the papers for which remain largely classified at the Russian State Archive of Contemporary History. In exploring the regional ramifications of the civil war, I have depended heavily on newspapers, publicly available government statements, and memoirs, rather than state archives. Much of the material from regional actors remains classified or difficult to access (and, as experience researching my first book demonstrated, material gained in Pakistani archives can swiftly be taken away).

Afghan voices and perspectives can be found in all of these materials. Both PDPA and resistance party leaders corresponded with foreign leaders, lobbied the international community, or engaged in regional debates. They translated their manifestos into other languages. While many paper sources from before and during the civil war were destroyed in the course of fighting in Kabul in the 1990s, Afghan materials have been made available to scholars worldwide via the Afghanistan Digital Collections, a joint project of the University of Arizona and Kabul University, and the University of Nebraska's online collections. I have taken advantage of these online repositories, many of which showcase Afghans' internationalist thinking and outreach. The collection of resistance party publications in Pashto and Dari at Stanford's Hoover Institution and the Islamic Fundamentalist Audio Recordings Collection at Yale University remain source bases that I wish I had been able to use but could not, lacking the time and resources.

Archives and collections used for this manuscript include:

Afghanistan Center at Kabul University Digital Collections
Arthur Paul Afghanistan Collection at the University of Nebraska-Omaha
Cold War International History Project, Wilson Center (Washington, DC)
Jimmy Carter Presidential Library (Atlanta, GA)
Marxists Internet Archive
National Archives of India (New Delhi)
National Security Archive (Washington, DC)
Ronald Reagan Presidential Library (Simi Valley, CA)
Russian State Archive of the Economy (Moscow)
State Archive for Contemporary History (Moscow)
State Archive of the Russian Federation (Moscow)
Sterling Library, Yale University (New Haven, CT)
The National Archives (Kew, United Kingdom)
United Nations Archives (New York)
United Nations High Commissioner for Refugees Archives (Geneva)
United States National Archives II (College Park, MD)

# Further Reading

The Soviet intervention spawned a huge body of literature by contemporary academics in the 1980s and early 1990s. These works set many of the parameters for later studies, exploring the rise of Afghan socialism and Islamism, detailing the failures of both movements to effect real change, and framing the conflict as part of a Cold-War struggle. Failures, scholars argued, were largely rooted in Cold-War machinations, the parties' own shortcomings, and pre-existing weaknesses in Afghan state and society, its internal divisions along ethnic and tribal lines, and earlier regimes' failures to extend state control effectively into Afghanistan's provinces. Key works include:

Amstutz, J. Bruce, *Afghanistan: The First Five Years of Occupation* (Washington: National Defense University, 1986)

Arnold, Anthony, *Afghanistan's Two-Party Communism: Parcham and Khalq* (Stanford: Hoover Institution Press, 1983)

Halliday, Fred, 'The War and Revolution in Afghanistan', *New Left Review*, 119 (1980), 20–41.

Hammond, Thomas, *Red Flag over Afghanistan: The Communist Coup, the Soviet Invasion, and the Consequences* (Epping: Bowker, 1984)

Hyman, Anthony, *Afghanistan under Soviet Domination 1964–91* (Basingstoke: Macmillan, 1992)

Kakar, M. Hassan, *Afghanistan: The Soviet Invasion and the Afghan Response, 1979–1982* (Berkeley and Los Angeles: University of California Press, 1995)

Roy, Olivier, *Islam and Resistance in Afghanistan* (Cambridge: Cambridge University Press, 1990 edn)

Rubin, Barnett R., *The Fragmentation of Afghanistan: State Formation and Collapse in the International System* (1995; New Haven: Yale University Press, 2002)

Rubin, Barnett R., *The Search for Peace in Afghanistan: From Buffer State to Failed State* (New Haven: Yale University Press, 1995)

Shahrani, M. Nazif, and Canfield, Robert L. (eds), *Revolutions and Rebellions in Afghanistan: Anthropological Perspectives* (Berkeley and Los Angeles: University of California Press, 1984)

Another wave came out in the early 2000s that provided further nuance to these studies, including:

Dorronsoro, Gilles, *Revolution Unending: Afghanistan 1979 to the Present* (London: Hurst & Co., 2005)

Edwards, David B., *Before Taliban: Genealogies of the Afghan Jihad* (Berkeley and Los Angeles: University of California Press, 2002)

Giustozzi, Antonio, *War, Politics and Society in Afghanistan, 1978–1992* (London: Hurst & Co., 2000)

Goodson, Larry P., *Afghanistan's Endless War: State Failure, Regional Politics, and the Rise of the Taliban* (Seattle: University of Washington Press, 2001)

Monsutti, Alessandro, *War and Migration: Social Networks and Economic Strategies of the Hazaras of Afghanistan*, trans. Patrick Camiller (London: Routledge, 2005)

Following the September 11, 2001, attacks and the US-led NATO intervention, many journalists, scholars, and policy analysts continued to publish studies of the Soviet invasion while also turning to longer histories of foreign military involvement in Afghanistan not only to understand the roots of the twenty-first-century conflict but also in an attempt to avoid the mistakes of history and chart a more favourable path of regime change and state-building. Military histories of Afghanistan particularly flourished, as did studies of contemporary developments. The number of books is simply too vast to outline here, but ones that I have drawn on include:

Bashir, Shahzad, and Crews, Robert D. (eds), *Under the Drones: Modern Lives in the Afghanistan–Pakistan Borderlands* (Cambridge, MA: Harvard University Press, 2012)

Braithwaite, Rodric, *Afgantsy: The Russians in Afghanistan, 1979–89* (London: Profile, 2012)

Coll, Steve, *Ghost Wars: The Secret History of the CIA, Afghanistan, and Bin Laden, from the Soviet Invasion to September 10, 2001* (London: Penguin Books, 2005)

Crile, George, *Charlie Wilson's War: The Extraordinary Story of the Cover Operation that Changed the History of our Times* (London: Atlantic Books, 2007)

Feifer, Gregory, *The Great Gamble: The Soviet War in Afghanistan* (New York: HarperCollins, 2009)

Marsden, Magnus, and Hopkins, Benjamin D. (eds), *Beyond Swat: History, Society and Economy along the Afghanistan–Pakistan Frontier* (London: Hurst & Co., 2013)

Tomsen, Peter, *The Wars of Afghanistan: Messianic Terrorism, Tribal Conflicts, and the Failures of Great Powers* (New York: PublicAffairs, 2011)

Alongside studies focusing on the Soviet invasion, three other bodies of literature have served to emphasize Afghanistan's global significance. First is the growing body of scholarship that has recognized Afghanistan's global connections across the nineteenth and twentieth centuries, breaking away from older narratives focusing on Afghanistan's supposed insularity and backwardness. Historians, anthropologists, and social scientists have shown that we cannot think of Afghanistan's political trajectory either as fully implemented by foreign actors or as emerging from purely domestic initiatives. Instead, Western conceptualizations of Afghanistan emerged from complicated interactions between Afghans and foreigners. So, too, did the Afghan state:

Barfield, Thomas J., *Afghanistan: A Cultural and Political History* (Princeton: Princeton University Press, 2010)

Bayly, Martin J., *Taming the Imperial Imagination: Colonial Knowledge, International Relations, and the Anglo-Afghan Encounter, 1808–1878* (Cambridge: Cambridge University Press, 2016)

Hanifi, Shah Mahmoud, *Connecting Histories in Afghanistan: Market Relations and State Formation on a Colonial Frontier* (Stanford, CA: Stanford University Press, 2011)

Hopkins, B. D., *The Making of Modern Afghanistan* (Basingstoke: Palgrave Macmillan, 2008)

Manchanda, Nivi, *Imagining Afghanistan: The History and Politics of Imperial Knowledge* (Cambridge: Cambridge University Press, 2020)

Marsden, Magnus, and Hopkins, Benjamin D., *Fragments of the Afghan Frontier* (London: Hurst & Co., 2012)

Monsutti, Alessandro, *Homo Itinerans: Towards a Global Ethnography of Afghanistan* (New York: Bergahn Books, 2021)

Likewise, over the past two decades, historians have produced crucial work that demonstrates that Afghanistan and its social, cultural, economic, and political histories are fundamentally global. These texts have further disrupted the trope of Afghanistan as inward-looking:

Ahmed, Faiz, *Afghanistan Rising: Islamic Law and Statecraft between the Ottoman and British Empires* (Cambridge, MA: Harvard University Press, 2017)

Caron, James M., *A History of Pashto Literature: Or, Pashto Histories of the World* (London: Hurst & Co., 2017)

Crews, Robert D., *Afghan Modern: The History of a Global Nation* (Cambridge, MA: Belknap Press of Harvard University Press, 2015)

Green, Nile, 'The Trans-Border Traffic of Afghan Modernism: Afghanistan and the Indian "Urdusphere"', *Comparative Studies in Society and History*, 53/3 (2011), 479–508

Green, Nile (ed.), *Afghanistan's Islam: From Conversion to the Taliban* (Berkeley and Los Angeles: University of California Press, 2017)

Green, Nile, and Arbabzadah, Nushin (eds), *Afghanistan in Ink: Literature between Diaspora and Nation* (London: Hurst & Company, 2013)

Green, Nile, et al., 'Roundtable: The Future of Afghan History', *International Journal of Middle East Studies*, 45/1 (2013), 127–48

Secondly, scholarship on the global Cold War, starting with the work of Odd Arne Westad, has demonstrated that the war in Afghanistan fit into a broader trend of twentieth-century confrontation in the Third World. This took the forms of violence as well as development. On Afghanistan in the Cold War, see:

Cullather, Nick, 'Damming Afghanistan: Modernization in a Buffer State', *Journal of American History*, 89/2 (2002), 512–37

Giustozzi, Antonio, and Kalinovsky, Artemy M., *Missionaries of Modernity: Advisory Missions and the Struggle for Hegemony in Afghanistan and Beyond* (London: Hurst & Co., 2016)

Kalinovsky, Artemy M., *A Long Goodbye: The Soviet Withdrawal from Afghanistan* (Cambridge, MA: Harvard University Press, 2011)

Nunan, Timothy, *Humanitarian Invasion: Global Development in Cold War Afghanistan* (New York: Cambridge University Press, 2016)

Additional key works on the Cold War in the Third World include:

Brazinsky, Gregg, *Winning the Third World: Sino-American Rivalry during the Cold War* (Chapel Hill: University of North Carolina, 2017)

Chamberlin, Paul Thomas, *The Cold War's Killing Fields: Rethinking the Long Peace* (New York: HarperCollins, 2018)

Connelly, Matthew, *A Diplomatic Revolution: Algeria's Fight for Independence and the Origins of the Post-Cold War Era* (Oxford: Oxford University Press, 2002)

Friedman, Jeremy, *Shadow Cold War: The Sino-Soviet Competition for the Third World* (Chapel Hill: University of North Carolina Press, 2015)

Lüthi, Lorenz M., *Cold Wars: Asia, the Middle East, Europe* (Cambridge: Cambridge University Press, 2020)

Parker, Jason C., *Hearts, Minds, Voices: US Cold War Public Diplomacy and the Formation of the Third World* (New York: Oxford University Press, 2016)

Westad, Odd Arne, *The Cold War: A World History* (London: Allen Lane, 2017)

Westad, Odd Arne, *The Global Cold War: Third World Interventions and the Making of our Times* (Cambridge: Cambridge University Press, 2007)

Finally, this book would not have been possible without scholarship that has emphasized the global significance of anti-colonialism and decolonization, which both paralleled and inter-sected with the Cold War. Afghan actors actively embraced the ethos of anti-colonialism to rethink Afghanistan's domestic politics and place in the world. We can follow both the ideas and the networks that linked Afghans to communities across the world that likewise sought to rethink their political futures in new, potentially radical ways. These texts reveal the universalism of many Afghans' political and social aspirations as well as parallels across the world:

Aydin, Cemil, *The Politics of Anti-Westernism in Asia: Visions of World Order in Pan-Islamic and Pan-Asian Thought* (New York: Columbia University Press, 2007)

Aydin, Cemil, *The Idea of the Muslim World: A Global Intellectual History* (Cambridge, MA: Harvard University Press, 2017)

Bayly, Christopher, and Harper, Tim, *Forgotten Wars: The End of Britain's Asian Empire* (London: Allen Lane, 2007)

Byrne, Jeffrey James, *Mecca of Revolution: Algeria, Decolonization, and the Third World Order* (New York: Oxford University Press, 2016)

Cooper, Frederick, *Colonialism in Question: Theory, Knowledge, History* (Berkeley and Los Angeles: University of California Press, 2005)

Getachew, Adom, *Worldmaking after Empire: The Rise and Fall of Self-Determination* (Princeton: Princeton University Press, 2019)

Lee, Christopher J. (ed.), *Making a World after Empire: The Bandung Movement and its Political Afterlives* (Athens, OH: Ohio University Press, 2010)

Manela, Erez, *The Wilsonian Moment: Self-Determination and the International Origins of Anticolonial Nationalism* (New York: Oxford University Press, 2009)

Prashad, Vijay, *The Darker Nations: A People's History of the Third World* (New York: New Press, 2007)

Wilder, Gary, *Freedom Time: Negritude, Decolonization, and the Future of the World* (Durham, NC: Duke University Press, 2015)

# Notes

## Abbreviations

| | |
|---|---|
| AAD | Access to Archival Databases |
| AAN | Afghanistan Analysts Network |
| ACKU | Afghanistan Center at Kabul University |
| ADST | Association for Diplomatic Studies Oral History Collection |
| APP | American Presidency Project |
| APRF | Archive of the President of the Russian Federation |
| *CDSP* | *Current Digest of the Soviet Press* |
| CREST | CIA Records Search Tool |
| CWIHP | Cold War International History Project |
| DNSA | Digital National Security Archive |
| FBIS | Foreign Broadcast Information Service |
| *FRUS* | *Foreign Relations of the United States* |
| GARF | State Archive of the Russian Federation |
| JCPL | Jimmy Carter Presidential Library |
| JPCP | Javier Perez de Cuellar Papers, Manuscripts and Archives, Yale University |
| IRAP | International Research and Advisory Panel |
| NAI | National Archives of India |
| NSC | National Security Council |
| RGAE | Russian State Archive of the Economy |
| RGANI | Russian State Archive of Contemporary History |
| RGASPI | Russian State Archive of Social and Political History |
| RRPL | Ronald Reagan Presidential Library |
| TNA | The National Archives, United Kingdom |
| UN ARMS | United Nations Archives and Records Management System |
| UNHCR | United Nations High Commissioner for Refugee |
| USGPO | US Government Printing Office |

# Prologue

1. ' "Our Lives Changed": Afghans Remember the Coming of the Soviet Troops', 27 December 2019, AAN, https://www.afghanistan-analysts.org/en/reports/war-and-peace/when-our-lives-changed-afghans-remember-the-coming-of-the-soviet-troops/ (accessed 21 July 2020).
2. William Borders, 'Coup is Reported in Afghanistan: Rebels Say they Killed President', *New York Times*, 28 April 1978, p. 1.
3. The interviews were kept anonymous.

4. The idea of Afghanistan as the graveyard of empires was particularly popularized by Seth Jones, *In the Graveyard of Empires: America's War in Afghanistan* (New York: W. W. Norton & Co., 2009).

5. Barnett R. Rubin, *The Fragmentation of Afghanistan: State Formation and Collapse in the International System* (1995; New Haven: Yale University Press, 2002).

## Introduction

1. Paul Thomas Chamberlin, *The Cold War's Killing Fields: Rethinking the Long Peace* (New York: HarperCollins, 2018), ch. 16.

2. Lorenz M. Lüthi, *Cold Wars: Asia, the Middle East, Europe* (Cambridge: Cambridge University Press, 2020), pp. 1–3, ch. 20. See also Odd Arne Westad, *The Global Cold War: Third World Interventions and the Making of our Times* (Cambridge: Cambridge University Press, 2007), ch. 8. In the text, I use the terms 'Third World' and 'Global South' somewhat interchangeably to delineate the non-Western world. But the text also subscribes to the idea that the 'Third World signified an alternative to the discredited philosophies of Western and communist civilization…Anticolonialism, world peace, and global economic equality were the dominant themes of this transformative impulse' (Jeffrey James Byrne, *Mecca of Revolution: Algeria, Decolonization, and the Third World Order* (New York: Oxford University Press, 2016), 5).

3. Like Lorenz Lüthi's recent work, this book demonstrates 'we need to change the focus—or better adopt multiple foci—in order to decenter the Cold War in a systematic fashion, to move structural developments into the foreground, to restore middle powers and smaller actors to visibility, and to link events horizontally to each other (and not only vertically to the great powers)' (Lüthi, *Cold Wars*, 3).

4. In conceptualizing empire, I draw on Ann Stoler's idea of 'imperial formations', which provides a more expansive definition of imperialism that denotes 'gradated forms of sovereignty' and highlights the 'ongoing quality of processes of decimation, displacement, and reclamation' (Ann Laura Stoler, 'Imperial Debris: Reflections on Ruins and Ruination', *Cultural Anthropology*, 23/2 (2008), 191–219, at 193).

5. On the imperialism of the Soviet Union, see Westad, *Global Cold War*, ch. 2; Vladislav Zubok and Constantine Pleshakov, *Inside the Kremlin's Cold War: From Stalin to Khrushchev* (Cambridge, MA: Harvard University Press, 1996), 3.

6. The term *qawm* is complicated and could encompass a person's village or equally a broader kinship, ethnic, or tribal group. See Thomas Barfield, *Afghanistan: A Cultural and Political History* (Princeton: Princeton University Press, 2010), 18. The meaning and implications of being 'tribal' are likewise complicated and explored in further depth in Chapter 1.

7. Barnett R. Rubin, *The Fragmentation of Afghanistan: State Formation and Collapse in the International System* (1995; New Haven.: Yale University Press, 2002), 15. Rubin also expands on these themes, as well as providing policy recommendations, in *Afghanistan from the Cold War through the War on Terror* (Oxford: Oxford University Press, 2013).

8. Faiz Ahmed, *Afghanistan Rising: Islamic Law and Statecraft between the Ottoman and British Empires* (Cambridge, MA: Harvard University Press, 2017), 277.

9. This contrasts pervasive narratives focusing on Afghan exceptionalism as the graveyard of empires and an arena of failed state-building. On some of the many ways that Afghanistan has been understood or imagined as exceptional, see Martin Bayly, *Taming the Imperial Imagination: Colonial Knowledge, International Relations, and the Anglo-Afghan Encounter, 1808–1878* (Cambridge: Cambridge University Press, 2016), 6–10.

10. Because of the primacy of aspiration in this study, I focus on modernity and the ways that historical actors attempted to implement their interpretations of modernity, rather than speaking in terms of less idealistic and more process-focused development. Frederick Cooper, *Colonialism in Question Theory, Knowledge, History* (Berkeley and Los Angeles: University of California Press, 2005), 115–17; David Scott, *Conscripts of Modernity: The Tragedy of Colonial Enlightenment* (Durham, NC: Duke University Press, 2004), 106. See also Michael E. Latham, 'Introduction', in *Staging Growth: Modernization, Development, and the Global Cold War* (Amherst, MA: University of Massachusetts Press, 2003), 1–23.

11. Empire was premised on a notion of liberalism that rationalized European expansion through its promises to 'civilize' colonised lands and peoples. In other words, imperialists sought to 'modernize' their subjects by citing contemporary theories of progress that envisioned the linear evolution of societies from undeveloped (not European) to developed (European). In order to place colonial subjects in this evolutionary process, European officials also sought to study and categorize indigenous communities. Thus, concepts such as 'tribe' and 'caste' became fundamental for interpreting local populations' social practices, differentiating them from Europeans, and justifying why they needed to be governed externally—and, by that logic, brought up to the same level as Europeans. Empire, then, was about producing knowledge and knowledge-systems as well as modern citizens. Such practices thus reshaped dynamics within many colonies—both those formally integrated into empire and those under informal economic and political pressure—as imperialists intervened in the local social, political, and economic order. See Karuna Mantena, *Alibis of Empire: Henry Maine and the Ends of Liberal Imperialism* (Princeton: Princeton University Press, 2010); Uday Mehta, *Liberalism and Empire: A Study in Nineteenth-Century British Liberal Thought* (Chicago: University of Chicago Press, 1999); Jennifer Pitts, *A Turn to Empire: The Rise of Imperial Liberalism in Britain and France* (Princeton: Princeton University Press, 2005); Nicholas B. Dirks, *Castes of Mind Colonialism and the Making of Modern India* (Princeton: Princeton University Press, 2001). On critiques of empire's preoccupation with modernity and civilization, see Cooper, *Colonialism in Question*, ch. 5; Dipesh Chakrabarty, *Provincializing Europe: Postcolonial Thought and Historical Difference* (Princeton: Princeton University Press, 2000).

12. As Artemy M. Kalinovsky explains, 'communism and its Soviet variant Marxism-Leninism were ideologies of development: history proceeded through stages, from feudalism to capitalism to socialism and finally to communism, and it was up to a vanguard to hurry it along to that final stage' (*Laboratory of Socialist Development: Cold War Politics and Decolonization in Soviet Tajikistan* (Ithaca, NY: Cornell University Press, 2018), 7). The scholarship on modernization, modernization theory, and development in the Cold War has become vast. Some of the texts I have drawn on in thinking about the meaning of modernity and its relationship to modernization and development in the Cold-War context

include: Nick Cullather, *The Hungry World: America's Cold War Battle against Poverty in Asia* (Cambridge, MA: Harvard University Press, 2010); David Engerman and Corinna Unger, 'Towards a Global History of Modernization', *Diplomatic History*, 33/3 (2009), 375–85; David Ekbladh, *The Great American Mission: Modernization and the Construction of an American World Order* (Princeton: Princeton University Press, 2010); Joseph Hodge, 'Writing the History of Development (The First Wave)', *Humanity*, 6/3 (2015), 429–63; Joseph Hodge, 'Writing the History of Development (Part 2: Longer, Deeper, Wider)', *Humanity*, 7/1 (2016), 125–74; Alessandro Iandolo, 'The Rise and Fall of the Soviet Model of Development', *Cold War History*, 12/4 (2012), 683–704; Michael E. Latham, *The Right Kind of Revolution: Modernization, Development, and US Foreign Policy from the Cold War to the Present* (Ithaca, NY: Cornell University Press, 2011). On its anti-colonial critiques, see Frederick Cooper, 'Writing the History of Development', *Journal of Modern European History*, 8/1 (2010), 5–23; Frederick Cooper, 'Modernising Bureaucrats, Backward Africans and the Development Concept', in F. Cooper and R. Packard (eds), *International Development and the Social Sciences* (Berkeley and Los Angeles: University of California Press, 1997), 64–92; Arturo Escobar, *Encountering Development: The Making and Unmaking of the Third World* (Princeton: Princeton University Press, 2011); James Ferguson, *The Anti-Politics Machine: Development, Depoliticization, and Bureaucratic Power in Lesotho* (Cambridge: Cambridge University Press, 1990); James C. Scott, *Seeing like a State: How Certain Schemes to Improve the Human Condition Have Failed* (New Haven: Yale University Press, 1999).

13. In thinking about how events of the late 1970s and early 1980s saw the entanglement and clash of multiple Afghan modernities, I have drawn on S. N. Eisenstadt, 'Multiple Modernities', *Daedalus*, 129/1 (2000), 1–29; also Sudipta Kaviraj, 'Modernity and Politics in India', *Daedalus*, 129/1 (2000), 137–62.

## Chapter 1

1. Natalia Tsvetkova, 'Americanisation, Sovietisation, and Resistance at Kabul University: Limits of the Educational Reforms', *History of Education*, 46/3 (2017), 343–65, at 350; Louis Dupree, *Afghanistan* (Princeton: Princeton University Press, 1980 edn), 599.

2. See Faridullah Bezhan, 'Kabul University and Political Dynamics in Afghanistan, 1964–73', *South Asia Research*, 34/3 (2014), 225–39.

3. Robert D. Crews, *Afghan Modern: The History of a Global Nation* (Cambridge, MA: Belknap Press of Harvard University Press, 2015), ch. 4 (Tarzi quotation from p. 117); Vartan Gregorian, 'Mahmud Tarzi and Saraj-ol-Akhbar: Ideology of Nationalism and Modernization in Afghanistan', *Middle East Journal*, 21/3 (1967), 345–68; Senzil Nawad, 'The State, the Clergy, and British Imperial Policy in Afghanistan during the 19th and Early 20th Centuries', *International Journal of Middle East Studies*, 29/4 (1997), 581–605, at 598. See also Thomas Barfield, *Afghanistan: A Cultural and Political History* (Princeton: Princeton University Press, 2010), ch. 4.

4. Chris Sands and Fazelminallah Qazizai, *Night Letters: Gulbuddin Hekmatyar and the Afghan Islamists who Changed the World* (London: Hurst & Co., 2019), 226–8.

5. Faiz Ahmed, 'In the Name of a Law: Islamic Legal Modernism and the Making of Afghanistan's 1923 Constitution', *International Journal of Middle East Studies*, 48 (2016), 655–77, at 660.

6. Huma Ahmed-Ghosh, 'A History of Women in Afghanistan: Lessons Learnt for the Future or Yesterdays and Tomorrow: Women in Afghanistan', *Journal of International Women's Studies*, 4/3 (2003), 1–14, at 4; Barfield, *Afghanistan*, ch. 4; Crews, *Afghan Modern*, chs 3, 4; Dupree, *Afghanistan*, ch. 20; Asta Olesen, *Islam and Politics in Afghanistan* (Richmond, Surrey: Curzon Press, 1995), ch. 5.

7. Hafizullah Emadi, 'Radical Political Movements in Afghanistan and their Politics of Peoples' Empowerment and Liberation', *Central Asian Survey*, 20/4 (2001), 427–50, at 430.

8. Elisabeth Leake, *The Defiant Border: The Afghan–Pakistan Borderlands in the Era of Decolonization, 1936–65* (Cambridge: Cambridge University Press, 2017), ch. 5.

9. See Emadi, 'Radical Political Movements', 428, 436.

10. Elisabeth Leake, 'Afghan Internationalism and the Question of Afghanistan's Political Legitimacy', *Afghanistan*, 1/1 (2018), 68–94.

11. Thomas Ruttig, 'How It All Began: A Short Look at the Pre-1979 Origins of Afghanistan's Conflicts', AAN, 19 January 2013, http://www.afghanistan-analysts.org/wp-content/uploads/downloads/2013/02/20130111Ruttig-How_It_All_Began_FINAL.pdf (accessed 16 August 2018).

12. Odd Arne Westad, *The Global Cold War: Third World Interventions and the Making of our Times* (Cambridge: Cambridge University Press, 2007), chs 2, 3.

13. See Jeremy Friedman, *Shadow Cold War: The Sino-Soviet Competition for the Third World* (Chapel Hill: University of North Carolina Press, 2015), ch. 3; Niamatullah Ibrahimi, 'Ideology without Leadership: The Rise and Decline of Maoism in Afghanistan', 31 August 2012, AAN, https://www.afghanistan-analysts.org/wp-content/uploads/downloads/2012/09/NIbr-Maoists-final.pdf (accessed 21 December 2020).

14. Barnett R. Rubin, *The Fragmentation of Afghanistan: State Formation and Collapse in the International System* (1995; New Haven: Yale University Press, 2002), 85.

15. Olivier Roy, 'The Origins of the Afghan Communist Party', *Central Asian Survey*, 7/2–3 (1988), 41–57, at 46.

16. Louis Dupree, 'Leftist Movements in Afghanistan: Part 1: Red Flag over the Hindu Kush', American Universities Field Staff Reports, 1979, p. 6; Ludwig Adamec, *First Supplement to the Who's Who of Afghanistan* (Graz, Austria: Akademische Druck-u. Verlagsanstalt, 1979), 15–16.

17. Dupree, 'Leftist Movements in Afghanistan', 6.

18. 'Background of Hafizullah Amin', from A. A Lyakhovskii, *Plamya Afghana* (Moscow: Iskon, 1999), CWIHP.

19. M. Hassan Kakar, *Afghanistan: The Soviet Invasion and the Afghan Response, 1979–1982* (Berkeley and Los Angeles: University of California Press, 1995), 65, 308.

20. Kakar, *Afghanistan*, 312–13; Adamec, *Who's Who*, 12; Nancy Hatch Dupree, *Najibullah* (Peshawar, 1990), ACKU Digital Collection, http://www.afghandata.org:8080/xmlui/handle/azu/3257 (accessed 17 September 2021).

21. Anthony Arnold, *Afghanistan's Two-Party Communism: Parcham and Khalq* (Stanford: Hoover Institution Press, 1983), app. A.

22. Ibid., app. A.

23. Ibid. 25. See Geoffrey Wheeler, 'Islam and the Soviet Union', *Middle Eastern Studies*, 13/1 (1977), 40–9. For a more nuanced reflection on Soviet relations with Central Asia and Muslims, see Steven Sabol, 'The Creation of Soviet Central Asia: The 1924 National Delimitation', *Central Asian Survey*, 14/2 (1995), 225–41; Galina M. Yemelianova, *Russia and Islam: A Historical Survey* (Basingstoke: Palgrave, 2002), ch. 4.

24. See Lowell Dittmer, 'The Structural Evolution of "Criticism and Self-Criticism"', *China Quarterly*, 53 (1973), 708–29. See also Westad, *Global Cold War*, ch. 2.

25. Arnold, *Afghanistan's Two-Party Communism*, app. B.

26. Ibid. 30; Fred Halliday, 'Revolution in Afghanistan', *New Left Review*, 112 (1978), 3–44, at 40.

27. Roy, 'Origins of the Afghan Communist Party', 44.

28. Arnold, *Afghanistan's Two-Party Communism*, 35–6.

29. Halliday, 'Revolution in Afghanistan', 25–6.

30. David B. Edwards, *Before Taliban: Genealogies of the Afghan Jihad* (Berkeley and Los Angeles: University of California Press, 2002), 47.

31. Muslims were not alone in turning to religion to inform political development. Much of European history revolved around the intimate relationship between Christianity, the divine right of kings, and negotiating power dynamics between church and state. In colonial and postcolonial India, Hinduism has also been politicized and increasingly informs state governance. See Glenn Burgess, 'The Divine Right of Kings Reconsidered', *English Historical Review*, 107/425 (1992), 837–61; Christophe Jaffrelot (ed.), *Hindu Nationalism: A Reader* (Princeton: Princeton University Press, 2007).

32. Carrie Rosefsky Wickham, *The Muslim Brotherhood: Evolution of an Islamist Movement* (Princeton: Princeton University Press, 2013 edn), 23, 20. See also Cemil Aydin, *The Idea of the Muslim World: A Global Intellectual History* (Cambridge, MA: Harvard University Press, 2017); Cemil Aydin, *The Politics of Anti-Westernism in Asia: Visions of World Order in Pan-Islamic and Pan-Asian Thought* (New York: Columbia University Press, 2007), esp. chs 5, 6; Richard P. Mitchell, *The Society of the Muslim Brothers* (New York: Oxford University Press, 1993); Gail Minault, *The Khilafat Movement: Religious Symbolism and Political Mobilization in India* (Oxford: Oxford University Press, 1982); Faridah Zaman, 'Revolutionary History and the Post-Colonial Muslim: Re-Writing the "Silk Letters Conspiracy" of 1916', *South Asia: Journal of South Asian Studies*, 39/3 (2016), 626–43.

33. Heather Campbell, 'Lessons to be Learnt? The Third Anglo-Afghan War', *RUSI Journal*, 160/2 (2015), 76–85; Sultan-I-Rome, 'The North-West Frontier Province in the Khilafat and Hijrat Movements', *Islamic Studies*, 43/1 (2004), 51–78. For longer histories of Islam's intersections with politics in this region, see also Sana Haroon, *Frontier of Faith: Islam in the Indo-Afghan Borderland* (London: Hurst & Co., 2007).

34. Niamatullah Ibrahimi, *The Hazaras and the Afghan State: Rebellion, Exclusion and the Struggle for Recognition* (London: Hurst & Co., 2017), 110–11; Hafizullah Emadi, *Dynamics of Political Development in Afghanistan: The British, Russian, and American Invasions* (New York: Palgrave Macmillan, 2010), 130.

35. Sana Haroon, 'The Rise of Deobandi Islam in the North-West Frontier Province and its Implications in Colonial India and Pakistan 1914–1996', *Journal of the Royal Asiatic Society*, 18/1 (2008), 47–70, at 66–9; Olesen, *Islam and Politics in Afghanistan*, 188. See also Faiz Ahmed, *Afghanistan Rising: Islamic Law and Statecraft between the Ottoman and British Empires* (Cambridge, MA: Harvard University Press, 2017).

36. Hafizullah Emadi, 'Exporting Iran's Revolution: The Radicalization of the Shiite Movement in Afghanistan', *Middle Eastern Studies*, 31/1 (1995), 1–12; Kakar, *Afghanistan*, 81. For a broader discussion and comparison of these thinkers' ideas, see Gilles Kepel, *Jihad: The Trail of Political Islam* (London: I. B. Tauris, 2006 edn); Jan-Peter Hartung, *A*

*System of Life: Mawdudi and the Ideologisation of Islam* (London: Hurst & Co., 2013), esp. ch. 5.

37. Yoginder Sikand, 'Sayyed Abul Hasan 'Ali Nadwi and Contemporary Islamic Thought in India', in *The Blackwell Companion to Contemporary Islamic Thought*, ed. Ibrahim M. Abu-Rabi' (Oxford: Blackwell Publishing, 2006), 88–104; Hartung, *A System of Life*, 194.

38. Cited in Kakar, *Afghanistan*, 82.

39. Cited in Seyyed Vali Reza Nasr, *Mawdudi and the Making of Islamic Revivalism* (Oxford: Oxford University Press, 1996), 51.

40. Joas Wagemakers, 'Salafism', *Oxford Research Encyclopaedia of Religion* (Oxford: Oxford University Press, 2016) https://oxfordre.com/religion/view/10.1093/acrefore/97801993 40378.001.0001/acrefore-9780199340378-e-255 (accessed 21 December 2020).

41. Nasr, *Mawdudi*, 51.

42. James Toth, *Sayyid Qutb: The Life and Legacy of a Radical Islamic Intellectual* (New York: Oxford University Press, 2013), 6–7.

43. Faisal Devji, *Landscapes of the Jihad: Militancy, Morality, Modernity* (London: Hurst & Co., 2005), 30.

44. Olivier Roy, *Islam and Resistance in Afghanistan* (Cambridge: Cambridge University Press, 1990 edn), 69.

45. See Nasr, *Mawdudi*, ch. 5.

46. Toth, *Sayyid Qutb*, 192, also ch. 10; S. Khatab, 'Hakimiyyah and Jahiliyyah in the Thought of Sayyid Qutb', *Middle Eastern Studies*, 38/3 (2002), 145–70.

47. Toth, *Sayyid Qutb*, 211.

48. Ibid. 212.

49. Kakar, *Afghanistan*, 83–4.

50. On the use of such terms, see, e.g., Edwards, *Before Taliban*; Kakar, *Afghanistan*; Roy, *Islam and Resistance*; Rubin, *Fragmentation of Afghanistan*.

51. See Keppel, *Jihad*, ch. 2; Devji, *Landscapes of the Jihad*.

52. Kakar, *Afghanistan*, 89.

53. Edwards, *Before Taliban*, 204.

54. Ibid. 216; Sands and Qazizai, *Night Letters*, 68–9.

55. Barnett R. Rubin, 'Political Elites in Afghanistan: Rentier State Building, Rentier State Wrecking', *International Journal of Middle East Studies*, 24/1 (1992), 77–99, at 81; Kakar, *Afghanistan*, 86.

56. Edwards, *Before Taliban*, 228, 214–17.

57. Roy, *Islam and Resistance*, 71–2.

58. Cited in Kakar, *Afghanistan*, 86.

59. Rubin, 'Political Elites', 81.

60. Mohammad Es'haq, 'Evolution of the Islamic Movement in Afghanistan, Part 2', *AFGHANews*, 5/2, 15 January 1989.

61. Kakar, *Afghanistan*, 89–90; also Sands and Qazizai, *Night Letters*, ch. 4.

62. Mohammad Es'haq, 'Evolution of the Islamic Movement in Afghanistan, Part 3', *AFGHANews*, 5/3, 1 February 1989.

63. Edwards, *Before Taliban*, 235–6.

64. Ibid. 236–8, 249; Kakar, *Afghanistan*, 88–92.

65. Tahir Amin, 'Afghan Resistance: Past, Present, and Future', *Asian Survey*, 24/4 (1984), 373–99, at 382.

66. Faridullah Bezhan, 'The Pashtunistan Issue and Politics in Afghanistan, 1947–1952', *Middle East Journal*, 68/2 (2014), 197–209, at 199; Anthony Hyman, *Afghanistan under Soviet Domination, 1964–91* (Basingstoke: Macmillan, 1992), 70; see also Anthony Hyman, 'Nationalism in Afghanistan', *International Journal of Middle East Studies*, 34/2 (2002), 299–315.

67. See Leake, *The Defiant Border*; Leake, 'At the Nation-State's Edge: Centre–Periphery Relations in Post-1947 South Asia', *Historical Journal*, 59/2 (2016), 509–39; 'Speech by the Afghan President Mohammad Daoud at the Civic Reception Given in his Honour at the Shalimar Gardens, Lahore, 7 March 1978', in Mehrunissa Ali (ed.), *Pak–Afghan Discord: A Historical Perspective: Documents, 1855–1979* (Karachi: Pakistan Study Centre, 1990), 384–7.

68. Arnold, *Afghanistan's Two-Party Communism*, app. A.

69. Emadi, 'Exporting Iran's Revolution', 4.

70. See Lorenz M. Lüthi, *The Sino-Soviet Split: Cold War in the Communist World* (Princeton: Princeton University Press, 2008); Chen Jian, *Mao's China and the Cold War* (Chapel Hill: University of North Carolina Press, 2001).

71. Hyman, *Afghanistan under Soviet Domination*, 50.

72. See Odd Arne Westad and Sophie Quinn-Judge (eds), *The Third Indochina War: Conflict between China, Vietnam and Cambodia, 1972–79* (London: Routledge, 2006), especially the chapters by Lien-Hang T. Nguyen, Ben Kiernan, and Quinn-Judge.

73. 'New Hanoi Hoax', *Peking Review*, 21/50, 15 December 1978, pp. 21–2.

74. Leake, *The Defiant Border*, 232–4; Avinash Paliwal, *My Enemy's Enemy: India in Afghanistan from the Soviet Invasion to the US Withdrawal* (London: Hurst & Co., 2017), 32–3.

75. Paliwal, *My Enemy's Enemy*, 37; also David Engerman, *The Price of Aid: The Economic Cold War in India* (Cambridge, MA: Harvard University Press, 2018); Antonio Giustozzi and Artemy M. Kalinovsky, *Missionaries of Modernity: Advisory Missions and the Struggle for Hegemony in Afghanistan and Beyond* (New York: Oxford University Press, 2016); Paul Robinson and Jay Dixon, 'Soviet Development Theory and Economic and Technical Assistance to Afghanistan, 1954–1991', *Historian*, 72/3 (2010), 599–623.

76. Ayesha Jalal, *The Struggle for Pakistan: A Muslim Homeland and Global Politics* (Cambridge, MA: Belknap Press of Harvard University Press, 2014), ch. 6; Shahid Javed Burki, *Pakistan under Bhutto, 1971–1977* (London: Macmillan, 1980). Two earlier military coups had put in place Generals Mohammad Ayub Khan and Agha Mohammad Yahya Khan as the country's leaders.

77. Shahid Javed Burki, 'Pakistan under Zia, 1977–1988', *Asian Survey*, 28/10 (1988), 1082–100, at 1084.

78. Ibid. 1085.

79. Jalal, *Struggle for Pakistan*, ch. 7.

80. Debate persists as to whether Zia was assassinated and, if so, by whom. See, e.g., Naziha Syed Ali, 'Dawn Investigations: Mystery Still Surrounds Gen Zia's Death, 30 Years On', *Dawn*, 12 March 2019, https://www.dawn.com/news/1427540 (accessed 21 December 2020).

81. See Ramachandra Guha, *India after Gandhi: The History of the World's Largest Democracy* (London: Pan, 2008), chs 22, 23, 24; also Gyan Prakash, *Emergency Chronicles: Indira Gandhi and Democracy's Turning Point* (Princeton: Princeton University Press, 2019).

82. Rana Mitter, *A Bitter Revolution: China's Struggle with the Modern World* (Oxford: Oxford University Press, 2004), chs 6, 7; Ezra Vogel, *Deng Xiaoping and the Transformation of*

*China* (Cambridge, MA: Belknap Press of Harvard University Press, 2011), ch. 7; Sergey Radchenko, *Unwanted Visionaries: The Soviet Failure in Asia at the End of the Cold War* (Oxford: Oxford University Press, 2014), 26–7.

83. Shahrough Akhavi, 'The Ideology and Praxis of Shi'ism in the Iranian Revolution', *Comparative Studies in Society and History*, 25/2 (1983), 195–221; Said Amir Arjomand, *The Turban for the Crown: The Islamic Revolution in Iran* (Oxford: Oxford University Press, 1989); Charles Kurzman, 'Structural Opportunity and Perceived Opportunity in Social-Movement Theory: The Iranian Revolution of 1979', *American Sociological Review*, 61/1 (1996), 153–70; Theda Skocpol, 'Rentier State and Shi'a Islam in the Iranian Revolution', *Theory and Society*, 11/3 (1982), 265–83. On the Shah's relationship with the United States, see also Roham Alvandi, *Nixon, Kissinger, and the Shah: The United States and Iran in the Cold War* (New York: Oxford University Press, 2014).

84. Hyman, *Afghanistan under Soviet Domination*, 42; Alam Payind, 'Soviet–Afghan Relations from Cooperation to Occupation', *International Journal of Middle East Studies*, 21/1 (1989), 107–28, at 108–9.

85. See Paul M. McGarr, *The Cold War in South Asia: Britain, the United States and the Indian Subcontinent* (Cambridge: Cambridge University Press, 2013); Robert J. McMahon, *The Cold War on the Periphery: The United States, India, and Pakistan* (New York: Columbia University Press, 1994); Gary J. Bass, *The Blood Telegram: Nixon, Kissinger, and a Forgotten Genocide* (New York: Alfred A. Knopf, 2013); Srinath Raghavan, *1971: A Global History of the Creation of Bangladesh* (Cambridge, MA: Harvard University Press, 2013).

86. Nick Cullather, 'Damming Afghanistan: Modernization in a Buffer State', *Journal of American History*, 89/2 (2002), 512–37; Leake, *The Defiant Border*, ch. 5.

87. Christopher R. W. Dietrich, *Oil Revolution: Anticolonial Elites, Sovereign Rights, and the Economic Culture of Decolonization* (New York: Cambridge University Press, 2017); Daniel Yergin, *The Price: The Epic Quest for Oil, Money, and Power* (New York: Simon & Schuster, 1990).

88. See, e.g., Olaf Caroe, *Wells of Power: The Oilfield of South-Western Asia: A Regional and Global Study* (London: Macmillan, 1951); also Peter John Probst, *The Future of the Great Game: Sir Olaf Caroe, India's Independence, and the Defense of Asia* (Akron, OH: University of Akron Press, 2010).

89. See Aleksandr Fursenko and Timothy Naftali, *Khrushchev's Cold War: The Inside Story of an American Adversary* (New York: W. W. Norton & Co., 2006), ch. 3.

90. Halliday, 'Revolution in Afghanistan', 22.

91. Nikolai A. Bulganin and Nikita S. Khrushchev, *Visit of Friendship to India, Burma and Afghanistan: Speeches and Official Documents* (Moscow, 1956), 221; Timothy Nunan, 'The Soviet Elphinstone: Colonial Histories, Post-Colonial Presents, and Socialist Futures in the Soviet Reception of British Orientalism', in Shah Mahmoud Hanifi (ed.), *Mountstuart Elphinstone in South Asia: Pioneer of British Colonial Rule* (New York: Oxford University Press, 2019), 275–98, at 284.

92. Memorandum of conversation, 2 June 1960, in Madeline Chi et al. (eds), *FRUS, 1958–1960*, 15 (Washington: USGPO, 1992), no. 388.

93. Timothy Nunan, *Humanitarian Invasion: Global Development in Cold War Afghanistan* (New York: Cambridge University Press, 2016), 92–106, 102; Hyman, *Afghanistan under Soviet Domination*, 28–9.

94. Kh. K. Karimov, 'A Short Report on the Work of the "People's Education in Soviet Tajikistan (Kabul, November 20–December 2 1965)" Exhibition', 1 December 1965, RGANI, fo. 5., op 35, d. 225, ll. 5–10, CWIHP.

95. Cited in Nunan, *Humanitarian Invasion*, 81; Nobel Symposium, 'The Intervention in Afghanistan and the Fall of Detente', trans. Svetlana Savranskaya, ed. David A. Welch and Odd Arne Westad, Lysebu, Norway, 17–20 September 1995 (Oslo: Norwegian Nobel Institute, 1996), 10.

96. 'Top Secret Attachment, by KGB cipher Kabul', 2 June 1974, CWIHP.

97. Martin Bayly, *Taming the Imperial Imagination: Colonial Knowledge, International Relations, and the Anglo-Afghan Encounter, 1808–1878* (Cambridge: Cambridge University Press, 2016), 3. See also Mukulika Banerjee, *The Pathan Unarmed* (Karachi: Oxford University Press, 2000); Crews, *Afghan Modern*, ch. 2; B. D. Hopkins, *The Making of Modern Afghanistan* (Basingstoke: Palgrave Macmillan, 2008); Benjamin Hopkins, *Ruling the Savage Periphery: Frontier Governance and the Making of the Modern State* (Cambridge, MA: Harvard University Press, 2020); Charles Lindholm, 'Images of the Pathan: The Usefulness of Colonial Ethnography', *European Journal of Sociology*, 21/2 (1980), 350–61.

98. Nunan, 'The Soviet Elphinstone', 285.

99. Ibid. 283–90.

100. See Alessandro Monsutti, 'Anthropologizing Afghanistan: Colonial and Postcolonial Encounters', *Annual Review of Anthropology*, 42 (2013), 269–85.

101. Ambassador Theodore L. Eliot, Jr, interviewed by Robert Martens, 24 April 1992, ADST.

102. James W. Spain, *The Pathan Borderland* (The Hague: Mouton & Co., 1963), 76; John P. Harrod, interviewed by Charles Stuart Kennedy, 1 March 1999, ADST. See also Elisabeth Leake, 'Elphinstone and the Afghan–Pathan Elision: Comparative British and American Approaches in the Twentieth Century', in Hanifi (ed.), *Mountstuart Elphinstone in South Asia*, 299–317.

103. Dupree, *Afghanistan*, 659.

## Chapter 2

1. Kate Clark, 'An April Day that Changed Afghanistan 2: Afghans Remember the "Saur Revolution"', AAN, 27 April 2018, https://www.afghanistan-analysts.org/en/reports/context-culture/an-april-day-that-changed-afghanistan-2-afghans-remember-the-saur-revolution/ (accessed 25 February 2020).

2. Rodric Braithwaite, *Afgantsy: The Russians in Afghanistan 1979–89* (London: Profile Books, 2012), 39–41; Odd Arne Westad, *The Global Cold War: Third World Interventions and the Making of our Times* (Cambridge: Cambridge University Press, 2007), 302.

3. David B. Edwards, *Before Taliban: Genealogies of the Afghan Jihad* (Berkeley and Los Angeles: University of California Press, 2002), 28.

4. William Borders, 'Coup is Reported in Afghanistan: Rebels Say They Killed President', *New York Times*, 28 April 1978, p. 1.

5. William Borders, 'New Afghan Leader Begins Selecting his Top Aides: Bulgaria Recognizes…', *New York Times*, 2 May 1978, p. 5.

6. Cited in Edwards, *Before Taliban*, 30.

7. Gilles Dorronsoro, *Revolution Unending: Afghanistan 1979 to the Present* (London: Hurst & Co., 2005), 94.

8. As George Lawson has pointed out, many revolutionary situations 'do not lead to revolutionary outcomes' (*Anatomies of Revolution* (Cambridge: Cambridge University Press, 2019), 6).

9. Text of statement of Nur Mohammad Taraki, Chairman of the Revolutionary Council and Prime Minister, broadcasted over Radio Afghanistan on 10 May 1978, ACKU Digital Collection, http://www.afghandata.org:8080/xmlui/handle/azu/17796 (accessed 25 May 2018).

10. 'Reasons for Coup in Afghanistan Explained by President, PM Daoud in Press Conference', *Kabul Times*, 25 July 1973, p. 1.

11. Text of statement of Nur Mohammad Taraki.

12. 'Political Letter from USSR Ambassador to Afghanistan A. Puzanov to Soviet Foreign Ministry, "About the Domestic Political Situation in the DRA," (notes)', 31 May 1978, RGANI, fo. 5, op. 75, d. 1179, pp. 2–17, CWIHP.

13. 'Amin Speech Marks Great October Revolution Anniversary', Kabul, 1 December 1978, FBIS MEA-78-232.

14. Louis Dupree, 'Afghanistan under the Khalq', *Problems of Communism* (July–August 1979), 34–50, at 40.

15. Ministry of Information and Culture, *Aryana (Democratic Republic of Afghanistan)*, October–November 1978.

16. '23 Royal Family Members Stripped of Citizenship', *Kabul Times*, 14 June 1978, pp. 1, 4.

17. ' "The Resort to Arms was the Final Mistake": Interview with an Afghan Marxist Source', *MERIP Reports*, 89 (1980), 20–4, at 23.

18. Edwards, *Before Taliban*, 34.

19. 'Great Leader Taraki's Biography', *Kabul Times,* 30 October 1978, pp. 1–4.

20. Fred Halliday, 'Revolution in Afghanistan', *New Left Review*, 112 (1978), 3–44, at 25–6, 40.

21. See almost daily articles in *Kabul Times* between May and June 1978; Edwards, *Before Taliban*, 65.

22. 'Kabul Reports on Revolutionary Council Session', Kabul Domestic Service, 12 July 1978, FBIS MEA-78-143.

23. 'A Fresh Look at Traditional Farming in Asia', *Kabul Times*, 14 June 1978, p. 3.

24. 'Taraki Interviewed on Country's Course', Hamburg *Die Zeit*, 9 June 1978, FBIS MEA-78-112.

25. 'Taraki States Principles of Afghan Revolution', Kabul Domestic Service, 27 July 1978, FBIS MEA-78-157.

26. 'Land Distributed to 158 Families in Helmand Province', Kabul, 12 August 1978, FBIS MEA-78-157.

27. M. Nazif Shahrani, 'Introduction: Marxist "Revolution" and Islamic Resistance in Afghanistan', in M. Nazif Shahrani and Robert Canfield (eds), *Revolutions and Rebellions in Afghanistan: Anthropological Perspectives* (Berkeley and Los Angeles: University of California Press, 1984), 3–57, at 15.

28. 'Decree No. 8 of the Revolutionary Council', *Kabul Times*, 2 December 1978, pp. 2–3; see also 'Crisis over Afghanistan', *Strategic Survey*, 80/1 (1979), 48–55.

29. Franklin Obeng-Odoom, 'Understanding Land Reform in Ghana: A Critical Postcolonial Institutional Approach', *Review of Radical Political Economics*, 48/4 (2016), 661–80; Donald C. Williams, 'Measuring the Impact of Land Reform Policy in Nigeria', *Journal of Modern African Studies*, 30/4 (1992), 587–608; Alain de Janvry and Lynn Ground, 'Types and Consequences of Land Reform in Latin America', *Latin American Perspectives*, 5/4 (1978), 90–112; Edwin E. Moise, 'Land Reform and Land Reform Errors in North Vietnam', *Pacific Affairs*, 49/1 (1976), 70–92; Madhav Joshi and T. David Mason, 'Land Tenure, Democracy, and Insurgency in Nepal: Peasant Support for Insurgency Versus Democracy', *Asian Survey*, 47/ 3 (2007), 393–414, at 403; Arild

Engelsen Ruud, 'Land and Power: The Marxist Conquest of Rural Bengal', *Modern Asian Studies*, 28/2 (1994), 357–80.

30. 'Information about the Visit of the Afghan Party and State Delegation, Headed by Prime Minister of the Democratic Republic of Afghanistan Nur Mohamed Tarakhi to the USSR', 4 December 1978, Diplomatic Archive, Sofia, F. 335, Op. 35, CWIHP; Timothy Nunan, 'From Land Reform to Veterinarians without Borders in Cold War Afghanistan', *Comparativ*, 27 (2017), 98–114, at 105–8.

31. Paul Brietzke, 'Land Reform in Revolutionary Ethiopia', *Journal of Modern African Studies*, 14/4 (1976), 637–60, at 637.

32. Editorial, *Kabul Times*, 2 December 1978, p. 3.

33. 'Over 100 Killed in Government, Rightist Clashes', Agence France Presse, 28 August 1978, FBIS MEA-78-168.

34. 'Kabul Garrison Command Emphasizes Curfew Requirements', Kabul Domestic Service, 23 July 1978, FBIS MEA-78-151.

35. Halliday, 'Revolution in Afghanistan', 41; M. Hassan Kakar, *Afghanistan: The Soviet Invasion and the Afghan Response, 1979–1982* (Berkeley and Los Angeles: University of California Press, 1995), 61–4.

36. Frud Bezhan and Petr Kubalek, 'The Afghan President (To Be) who Lived a Secret Life in a Czechoslovak Forest', Radio Free Europe, 3 November 2019, https://www.rferl.org/a/that-time-an-afghan-president-(to-be)-was-secretly-hiding-in-a-czechoslovak-forest/30250494.html (accessed 19 June 2020).

37. 'Information from CC CPSU to GDR Leader Erich Honecker', 13 October 1978, Stiftung Archiv der Partaien und Massenorganisationen der DDR im Bundesarchiv, Berlin, J 2/202, A. 575, CWIHP.

38. Nobel Symposium, 'The Intervention in Afghanistan and the Fall of Detente', trans. Svetlana Savranskaya, ed. David A. Welch and Odd Arne Westad, Lysebu, Norway, 17–20 September 1995 (Oslo: Norwegian Nobel Institute, 1996), 10–11.

39. See *Kabul Times*; Edwards, *Before Taliban*, 66–8; Fred Halliday, 'The War and Revolution in Afghanistan', *New Left Review*, 119 (1980), 20–41, at 34.

40. 'Taraki Interviewed on Country's Course'.

41. Halliday, 'War and Revolution', 24.

42. 'Government Affirms Respect for Private Property', Kabul Domestic Service, 30 July 1978, FBIS MEA-78-157.

43. 'Memo on Protocol #149 of the Politburo, "Our future policy in connection with the situation in Afghanistan"', 1 April 1979, RGANI, fo. 89, op. 14, d. 27, p. 11, CWIHP; Nunan, 'From Land Reform', 108–9.

44. Feroz Ahmed and Jim Paul, '"The Khalq Failed to Comprehend the Contradictions of the Rural Sector": Interview with Feroz Ahmed', *MERIP Reports*, 89 (1980), 13–20, at 13.

45. 'Crisis over Afghanistan'; Halliday, 'War and Revolution', 39.

46. 'Decree Number Seven Issued', *Kabul Times*, 18 October 1978, p. 1.

47. See Timothy Nunan, *Humanitarian Invasion: Global Development in Cold War Afghanistan* (New York: Cambridge University Press, 2016), p. 182 and ch. 5.

48. Cited in Nancy Tapper, 'Causes and Consequences of the Abolition of Brideprice in Afghanistan', in *Revolutions and Rebellions in Afghanistan*, 291–305, at 295.

49. See Parwin Ali Majrooh, 'Afghan Women between Marxism and Islamic Fundamentalism', *Central Asian Survey*, 8/3 (1989), 87–98, esp. 88.

50. Nancy Hatch Dupree, 'Revolutionary Rhetoric and Afghan Women', Afghanistan Council occasional paper 23 (January 1981), 10.
51. Tapper, 'Causes and Consequences', 297.
52. Ibid. 298.
53. Ibid. 292.
54. Dupree, 'Revolutionary Rhetoric', 11.
55. Ibid. 12.
56. Ibid. 5–6.
57. See biographical note in Kakar, *Afghanistan*, 314–15.
58. Olga Smirnova, 'The Soviet Feminist Army', BBC World Service, 1 September 2020, https://www.bbc.co.uk/sounds/play/w3ct0x2g (accessed 22 December 2020).
59. Cited in Dupree, 'Revolutionary Rhetoric', 4, 5.
60. 'Abortion Can Never Be the Lesser Evil', *Kabul Times*, 31 May 1978, p. 3; 'A Plea for Tolerance', *Kabul Times*, 31 May 1978, p. 3.
61. Dupree, 'Revolutionary Rhetoric', 7.
62. Ibid. 12.
63. See Sana Haroon, *Frontier of Faith: A History of Religious Mobilization in the Pakhtun Tribal Areas c.1890–1950* (Karachi: Oxford University Press, 2011), 85, 117–24; also Leon B. Poullada, *Reform and Rebellion in Afghanistan, 1919–1929: King Amanullah's Failure to Modernize a Tribal Society* (Ithaca, NY: Cornell University Press, 1973); Nile Green, 'The Faqir and the Subalterns: Mapping the Holy Man in Colonial South Asia', *Journal of Asian History*, 41/1 (2007), 57–84.
64. See Barnett R. Rubin, *The Fragmentation of Afghanistan: State Formation and Collapse in the International System* (1995; New Haven: Yale University Press, 2002), 84–5; Halliday, 'War and Revolution', 25.
65. Eren Tasar, 'Soviet Policies toward Islam: Domestic and International Considerations', in Philip E. Muehlenbeck (ed.), *Religion and the Cold War: A Global Perspective* (Nashville: Vanderbilt University Press, 2012), 158–81, at 167–70; Jeremy Friedman, *Shadow Cold War: The Sino-Soviet Competition for the Third World* (Chapel Hill: University of North Carolina Press, 2015), 110–11.
66. 'Taraki Interviewed on Country's Course'.
67. 'We are Sons of Muslims and Respect Principles of Holy Islam: Taraki', *Kabul Times*, 13 June 1978, p. 1.
68. 'President Taraki Addresses Nation on 'Id Al-Fitr', Kabul, 4 September 1978, FBIS MEA-78-173.
69. Rubin, *Fragmentation of Afghanistan*, 115.
70. 'Great Leader Speaks to Youth', *Kabul Times*, 27 November 1978, p. 4.
71. 'Ikhwanis Serve Alien Interests', *Kabul Times*, 28 November 1978, p. 2.
72. 'Amin Speech Marks Great October Revolution Anniversary'.
73. 'Memo on Protocol #149 of the Politburo'.
74. Roy, *Islam and Resistance*, 96–7.
75. Ahmed and Paul, 'Khalq Failed', 14.
76. Edwards, *Before Taliban*, 82.
77. 'Memo on Protocol #149 of the Politburo'.
78. 'Reports on Fighting at Herat in West', Agence France Presse, 20 Marcy 1979, FBIS MEA-79-056.

79. Edwards, *Before Taliban*, 256; Halliday, 'War and Revolution', 30.

80. Kakar, *Afghanistan*, 34.

81. Rubin, *Fragmentation of Afghanistan*, 115.

82. Clark, 'An April Day that Changed Afghanistan 2'.

83. Edwards, *Before Taliban*, 83; Halliday, 'War and Revolution', 28.

84. 'Kabul Carries Message from Muslims of USSR', Kabul, 30 March 1979, FBIS MEA-79-065.

85. 'Amin: Arms Aid Welcomed; No Need for Foreign Troops', Kabul, 12 May 1979, MEA-79-095.

86. 'Polish Newspaper Interviews Amin on Revolution's Program', Warsaw Polska Agencja Prasaowa, 4 June 1979, FBIS MEA-79-111.

87. 'People's Representatives Respond to Taraki Speech', Kabul, 23 July 1979, FBIS MEA-79-144; 'Text of Islamic Scholars' Declaration on Khalqi State', Kabul, 12 August 1979, FBIS MEA-79-157.

88. Edwards, *Before Taliban*, 88–90; Kakar, *Afghanistan*, 34–6.

89. Arnold, *Afghanistan's Two-Party Communism*, 94–5; Halliday, 'War and Revolution', 34–6.

90. Bismellah Sahak to Kurt Waldheim, Policy Statement of the Democratic Republic of Afghanistan, 10 January 1980, S-0442-0330-7, UN ARMS.

91. Fred Halliday and Zahir Tanin, 'The Communist Regime in Afghanistan 1978–1992: Institutions and Conflicts', *Europe-Asia Studies*, 50/8 (1998), 1357–80, at 1364, 1366.

92. Ibid. 1367.

## Chapter 3

1. K. Rashidov, 'Report from Afghanistan: Return', *Izvestia*, 8 March 1980, in *CDSP*, 32/10.

2. Artemy M. Kalinovksy, 'The Blind Leading the Blind: Soviet Advisors, Counter-Insurgency and Nation-Building in Afghanistan', CWIHP Working Paper 60 (January 2010), 2–3.

3. Leonid Bhreznev, 'The Brezhnev Doctrine', *Pravda*, 25 September 1968, https://source-books.fordham.edu/mod/1968brezhnev.asp (accessed 23 December 2020).

4. Jeremy Friedman, *Shadow Cold War: The Sino-Soviet Competition for the Third World* (Chapel Hill: University of North Carolina Press, 2015), 160–1, 189–90.

5. Odd Arne Westad, *The Global Cold War: Third World Interventions and the Making of our Times* (Cambridge: Cambridge University Press, 2007), 205, 202–6; Vladislav Zubok, 'The Soviet Union and Detente of the 1970s', *Cold War History*, 8/4 (2008), 427–47.

6. Both quotations taken from Westad, *Global Cold War*, 277, 282.

7. Westad, *Global Cold War*, chs 6, 7; Friedman, *Shadow Cold War*, ch. 5, esp. pp. 203–10.

8. Odd Arne Westad, 'Prelude to Invasion: The Soviet Union and the Afghan Communists, 1978–1979', *International History Review*, 16/1 (1994), 49–69, at 51; see also Westad, *Global Cold War*, ch. 8.

9. Nobel Symposium, 'The Intervention in Afghanistan and the Fall of Detente', trans. Svetlana Savranskaya, ed. David A. Welch and Odd Arne Westad, Lysebu, Norway, 17–20 September 1995 (Oslo: Norwegian Nobel Institute, 1996), 7.

10. 'Record of Conversation, Soviet Ambassador A. M. Puzanov and Taraki', 18 June 1978, RGANI, fo. 5, op. 75, d. 1181, ll. 22–27, CWIHP.

11.  Westad, 'Prelude to Invasion', 56–7.
12.  'Information about the Visit of the Afghan Party and State Delegation, headed by Prime Minister of the Democratic Republic of Afghanistan Nur Mohamed Tarakhi to the USSR', 4 December 1978, Diplomatic Archive, Sofia, Bulgaria, fo. 335, op. 35, CWIHP.
13.  'Meeting of Kosygin, Gromyko, Ustinov, and Ponomarev with Taraki in Moscow', 20 March 1979, RGANI, fo. 89, per. 14, d. 26, CWIHP.
14.  Ibid.
15.  'Soviet Communication to the Hungarian Leadership on the Situation in Afghanistan', 28 March 1979, National Archives of Hungary, M-KS 288, fo. 11/4380.o.e., CWIHP; 'Soviet Allegation of Conspiracy to Overthrow Afghan Government', 29 March 1979, DNSA, CIA Covert Operations.
16.  A. A. Liakhovskii, *Tragediya i doblest afgana* (Moscow: Iskon, 1995), 76. Liakhovskii notes that the recommendations made in this document were approved during the CC CPSU Politburo meeting of 28 June 1979, in Resolution No. P, 156/XI. See CWIHP Bulletin no. 8/9 (1996/7), 152–3, and the included article by Odd Arne Westad, 'Concerning the Situation in "A": New Russian Evidence on the Soviet Intervention in Afghanistan', 128–32.
17.  'Report on the Situation in Afghanistan, Gromyko, Andropov, Ustinov, and Ponomarev to CPSU CC', 29 November 1979, APRF, fo. 3, op. 82, d. 173, pp. 118–27, CWIHP.
18.  Telegram from Chief Soviet Military Adviser, 'Report from Kabul', 2 December 1979, from Lyakhovskii, *Tragediya i doblest afgana*, CWIHP; Telegram from Chief Soviet Military Adviser, 'Report from Kabul', 4 December 1979, from Lyakhovskii, *Tragediya i doblest afgana,* CWIHP.
19.  'Personal Memorandum Andropov to Brezhnev', 1 December 1979, APRF, CWIHP.
20.  Vladislav M. Zubok, *A Failed Empire: The Soviet Union in the Cold War* (Chapel Hill: University of North Carolina Press, 2007), 263. See also Stephanie Freeman, 'The Making of an Accidental Crisis: The United States and the NATO Dual-Track Decision of 1979', *Diplomacy & Statecraft*, 25/2 (2014), 331–55.
21.  Lyakhovskii, *Tragediya i doblest afgana*, ch. 2, sect. 7; 'Directive No. 312/12/001 of 24 December 1979 Signed by Ustinov and Ogarkov', 24 December 1979, in A. A. Lyakhovskii, *Plamya afgana* (Moscow: Iskon, 1999), CWIHP.
22.  Stephen Tanner, *Afghanistan: A Military History from Alexander the Great to the War against the Taliban* (Philadelphia: Da Capo Press, 2009 edn), 235–6. For more on the military side of the war, see also Gregory Feifer, *The Great Gamble: The Soviet War in Afghanistan* (New York: HarperCollins, 2009).
23.  Westad, 'Prelude to Invasion', 64.
24.  Jiri Valenta, 'From Prague to Kabul: The Soviet Style of Invasion', *International Security*, 5/2 (1980), 114–41.
25.  Friedman, *Shadow Cold War*, 213.
26.  Symposium, 'Intervention in Afghanistan', 8.
27.  'Meeting of Kosygin, Gromyko, Ustinov, and Ponomarev with Taraki in Moscow'.
28.  Rodric Braithwaite, *Afgantsy: The Russians in Afghanistan 1979–89* (London: Profile Books, 2012), ch. 4.
29.  Thomas T. Hammond, *Red Flag over Afghanistan: The Communist Coup, the Soviet Invasion, and the Consequences* (Epping: Bowker, 1984), 149.

30. Artemy M. Kalinovsky, 'Decision-Making and the Soviet War in Afghanistan: From Intervention to Withdrawal', *Journal of Cold War Studies*, 11/4 (2009), 46–73, at 52.

31. 'Rancor High among Afghans', *New York Times*, 15 January 1980, p. 1.

32. The Russian General Staff, *The Soviet–Afghan War: How a Superpower Fought and Lost*, trans. and ed. Lester W. Grau and Michael A. Gress (Lawrence: University Press of Kansas, 2002), 306. See also Lester W. Grau, *The Bear Went over the Mountain: Soviet Combat Tactics in Afghanistan* (London: Frank Cass, 1998), and Ali Ahmad Jalali and Lester W. Grau, *The Other Side of the Mountain: Mujahideen Tactics in the Soviet–Afghan War* (Middlewich: Express, 2010 edn).

33. 'Politburo Decision on Soviet Policy on Afghanistan, with Report on Proposal by Fidel Castro to Mediate between Afghanistan and Pakistan, and Approved Letter from L. I. Brezhnev to Fidel Castro', 10 March 1980, RGANI, fo. 89, per. 34, d. 5, CWIHP.

34. On this longer pre-history, see Antonio Giustozzi and Artemy M. Kalinovsky, *Missionaries of Modernity: Advisory Missions and the Struggle for Hegemony in Afghanistan and Beyond* (London: Hurst & Co., 2016); Artemy M. Kalinovsky and Antonio Giustozzi, 'The Professional Middle Class in Afghanistan: From Pivot of Development to Political Marginality', *Humanity*, 8/2 (2017), 355–78; Timothy Nunan, 'From Land Reform to Veterinarians without Borders in Cold War Afghanistan', *Comparativ*, 27 (2017), 98–114.

35. Westad, 'Prelude to Invasion', 67.

36. Paul Robinson and Jay Dixon, *Aiding Afghanistan: A History of Soviet Assistance to a Developing Country* (New York: Columbia University Press, 2013), 95–6.

37. Ibid. 96.

38. Memo on Protocol no. 149 of the Politburo, 'Our Future Policy in Connection with the Situation in Afghanistan', 1 April 1979, RGANI, fo. 89, per. 14, d. 28, CWIHP.

39. Nunan, 'From Land Reform to Veterinarians', 110.

40. Kalinovsky, 'Blind Leading the Blind', 4–5. See also Alessandro Iandolo, 'The Rise and Fall of the "Soviet Model of Development" in West Africa, 1957–64', *Cold War History*, 12/4 (2012), 683–704.

41. Robinson and Dixon, *Aiding Afghanistan*, 94.

42. Artemy M. Kalinovsky, 'Central Asian Soldiers and the Soviet War in Afghanistan: An Introduction', in Marlene Laruelle (ed.), *The Central Asia–Afghanistan Relationship: From Soviet Intervention to the Silk Road Initiatives* (London: Lexington Press, 2017), 3–20; Kalinovsky, *Laboratory of Socialist Development*, 214–17. On earlier Soviet state-building, see Francine Hirsch, *Empire of Nations: Ethnographic Knowledge & the Making of the Soviet Union* (Ithaca, NY: Cornell University Press, 2005); Francine Hirsch, 'Toward an Empire of Nations: Border-Making and the Formation of Soviet National Identities', *Russian Review*, 59 (2000), 201–26; Orlando Figes, 'The Red Army and Mass Mobilization during the Russian Civil War 1918–1920', *Past & Present*, 129 (1990), 168–211.

43. 'Statement of the Soviet Union and the Democratic Republic of Afghanistan', *Pravda*, 20 October 1980, in *CDSP* 32/42.

44. Hammond, *Red Flag over Afghanistan*, 149.

45. 'The 26th Congress of the Communist Party of the Soviet Union: The Report of the CPSU Central Committee to the 26th Congress of the Communist Party of the Soviet Union and the Party's Immediate Tasks in the Fields of Domestic and Foreign Policy—Delivered by Comrade L. I. Brezhnev, General Secretary of the CPSU Central Committee, on Feb. 23, 1981', *Pravda* and *Izvestia*, 24 February 1981, in *CDSP* 33/8.

46. 'Defending the Interests of the Working People.—The National Conference of the People's Democratic Party of Afghanistan Opens', *Pravda*, 15 March 1982, in *CDSP* 34/11.

47. Antonio Giustozzi, *War, Politics and Society in Afghanistan, 1978–1992* (London: Hurst & Co., 2000), 25–6.

48. Timothy Nunan, *Humanitarian Invasion: Global Development in Cold War Afghanistan* (New York: Cambridge University Press, 2016), 161.

49. 'Defending the Interests of the Working People.—The National Conference of the People's Democratic Party of Afghanistan Opens', *Pravda*, 15 March 1982, in *CDSP* 34/11.

50. 'Election Meetings of Working People: Unshakable Policy of Peace.—Voters Meet with P. N. Ponomarev', *Pravda*, 5 February 1980, in *CDSP* 32/5.

51. Cited in Hammond, *Red Flag over Afghanistan*, 152.

52. Artemy M. Kalinovsky, *A Long Goodbye: The Soviet Withdrawal from Afghanistan* (Cambridge, MA: Harvard University Press, 2011), 237.

53. Cited in ibid. 101.

54. Braithwaite, *Afgantsy*, 148.

55. Robinson and Dixon, *Aiding Afghanistan*, 99.

56. 'Cooperation Expands and Grows Stronger', *Izvestia*, 9 March 1984, in *CDSP* 36/10.

57. B. A. Runov to Yu. F. Chubarov, 12 December 1983, GARF, fo. P5446, op. 144, d. 1552, pp. 3–4.

58. 'Protokol: chetvertogo zasedaniia postoiannoi mezhpravitel'stvennoi Sovetsko-Afghanskoi komissii po ekonomicheskomu sotrudnichestvu', 13 September 1984, GARF, fo. P5446, op. 144, d. 1551, pp. 1–24.

59. Ibid.

60. 'O Sovetsko-Afganskom sotrudnichestve v oblasti avtomobil'nogo transporta', 12 December 1983, GARF, fo. P5446, op. 144, d. 1552, pp. 8–17; 'O sotrudnichestve s DRA v oblasti stroitel'stva transportnykh ob'ektov', 16 July 1985, GARF, fo. P5446, op. 145, d. 1613, pp. 68–71.

61. 'Route of Peace and Cooperation' *Pravda*, 13 May 1982, in *CDSP* 34/19.

62. See, e.g., Protokol no. 1 zasedaniia Sovetskoi chasti komissii, 14 February 1986, GARF, fo. P5446, op. 147, d. 1673, pp. 1–8; also 'O Sovetsko-Afganskom sotrudnichestve v oblasti dobychi gaza', 1985, GARF, fo. P5446, op. 145, d. 1614, pp. 8–17.

63. 'O dosrochnom zavershenii stroitel'stva ustanovki po pererabotke gazovogo kontsentrata v motornoe toplivo v DRA', 18 November 1986, GARF, fo. P5446, op. 147, d. 1561, pp. 28–9.

64. Kalinovsky, 'Blind Leading the Blind', 10.

65. Barnett R. Rubin, *The Fragmentation of Afghanistan* (1995; New Haven: Yale University Press, 2002), 130.

66. V. N. Sozutov, 'Zapis' besedy: zamestitelia ministra vneshnei torgovli SSSR t. Grishina I.T. s poslom Demokraticheskoi Respubliki Afghanistan v SSSR Kh. Mangalom, sostoiavsheisia 14 oktiabria 1982 g.', 27 October 1982, RGAE, fo. 412, op. 32, d. 2214, p. 10.

67. Iu. V. Zimin, 'Zapis' besedy: nachal'nika upravleniia torgovli so stranami azii kiseleva m.a. s torgpredom DRA v sss saekom, sostaiavsheisia 23 iiunia 1982 goda', 8 June 1982, RGAE, fo. 412, op. 32, d. 2214, pp. 6–7.

68. Sozutov, 'Zapis' besedy: zamestitelia ministra vneshnei torgovli SSSR t. Grishina I.T. s poslom Demokraticheskoi Respubliki Afghanistan v SSSR Kh. Mangalom, sostoiavsheisia 14 oktiabria 1982 g'.

69. V. N. Sozutov, 'Zapis' besedy: nachal'nika upravlenia torgovli so stranami azii t. Kiseleva M.A. s zamestitelem ministra torgovli DRA t Abdul Salamom, sostoiavsheisia

22 marta 1982 goda v MVT s 12.00 Do 13.15', 6 April 1982, RGAE, fo. 412, op. 32, d. 2214, pp. 1–3.

70. 'CPSU CC Politburo Decision on Afghanistan, with Report by Gromyko, Andropov, Ustinov, and Zagladin, 7 April 1980', 10 April 1980, APRF, fo. 3, op. 82, d. 176, ll. 9–17, CWIHP.

71. See Giustozzi, *War, Politics and Society*, 36–7, 253, and ch. 3 for further detail.

72. Yu. V. Irkhin, 'Behind the Decisions of the 26th CPSU Congress: Vanguard Revolutionary Parties of the Working People in Newly Independent Countries', *Voprosy Istorii* (April 1982), in *CDSP* 34/27.

73. Rubin, *Fragmentation of Afghanistan*, 128.

74. See J. Bruce Amstutz, *Afghanistan: The First Five Years of Occupation* (Washington: National Defense University, 1986), 298–314; GARF, fo. P5446, op. 144, d. 1550, pp. 29–34; fo. P5446, op. 144, d. 1552, pp. 120–5; fo. P5446, op. 145, d. 1613, pp. 21–5.

75. Fred Halliday and Tahir Zanin, 'The Communist Regime in Afghanistan 1978–1992: Institutions and Conflicts', *Europe–Asia Studies*, 50/8 (1998), 1357–80, at 1363.

76. Giustozzi, *War, Politics and Society*, 137–42.

77. Ivan Shchedrov, 'Commentator's Column: Important Landmark', *Pravda*, 18 June 1981, in *CDSP* 33/24.

78. O. Kitsenko, 'Patriotic Mission—the Role of the National Patriotic Front in the Life of the Democratic Republic of Afghanistan', *Pravda*, 16 January 1983, in *CDSP* 35/3.

79. 'Postanovlenie: sekretariata tsk kommunisticheskoi partii sovetskogo soyuza', 18 July 1980, in Pierre Allan et al. (eds), *Sowjetische Geheimdokumente zum Afghanistankrieg (1978–1991)* (Zurich: Vdf, Hochschulverlag AG an Der ETH Zurich, 1995), 386; RGANI, fo. 89, op. 46, d. 73, pp. 1–24.

80. Robert Hornsby, 'The Post-Stalin Komsomol and the Soviet Fight for Third World Youth', *Cold War History*, 16/1 (2016), 83–100, at 86.

81. Ibid. 91.

82. See RGASPI, fo. 3, op. 13, d. 4, pp. 20–5; RGASPI, fo. 3, op. 13., d. 8, pp. 1–14.

83. Hornsby, 'Post-Stalin Komsomol', 91.

84. RGASPI, fo. M-3, op. 13, d. 17, pp. 1–9.

85. Vasiliy Mitrokhin, 'The KGB in Afghanistan', CWIHP Working Paper 40 (July 2002; updated July 2009), 135; Halliday and Zanin, 'Communist Regime in Afghanistan', 1364.

86. Giustozzi, *War, Politics and Society*, 34; see also tables 6–13 in ibid. 253–7.

87. Ibid. 37, 142–5.

88. A. A. Gagarin, 'Zapis' besedy: zamestitelia ministra vneshnei torgovli SSSR tov. Grishina I.T. s delegatsiei trr DRA i Afganskikh delovykh krugov, sosteiavsheisia 22 noiabria 1984 goda', 4 January 1985, RGAE, fo. 412, op. 32, d. 3569, pp. 1–4.

89. 'Ob okazanii sodeistviia Afganistanu v sozdanii dvukh ob'ektov zdravookhraneniia', 25 February 1986, GARF, fo. P5446, op. 147, d. 1677, pp. 37–8; 'O khode yypolneniia zadaniia po proektirovaniiu tsentra po protezirovaniiu i lecheniiu invalidov v g.Kabule', 21 April 1986, GARF, fo. P5446, op. 147, d. 1677, p. 63.

90. D. Meshchaninov, 'Letter from Afghanistan: Kandahar's Troubled Days', *Izvestia*, 20 March 1987, in *CDSP* 39/12.

91. Braithwaite, *Afgantsy*, 160–1.

92. 'Protokol: chetvertogo zasedaniia postoiannoi mezhpravitel'stvennoi Sovetsko-Afghanskoi komissii po ekonomicheskomu sotrudnichestvu', 13 September 1984, GARF, fo. P5446, op. 144, d. 1551, pp. 1–24.

93. Stephen Kotkin, *Armageddon Averted: The Soviet Collapse, 1970–2000* (Oxford: Oxford University Press, 2001), ch. 2.

94. See Zubok, *Failed Empire*, ch. 9.

95. Archie Brown, 'Perestroika and the End of the Cold War', *Cold War History*, 7/1 (2007), 1–17, at 3.

96. Sylvia Woodby and Alfred Evans (eds), *Restructuring Soviet Ideology: Gorbachev's New Thinking* (New York: Routledge, 1991); Archie Brown, 'Gorbachev, Lenin, and the Break with Leninism', *Demokratizatsiya*, 15/2 (2007), 230–44.

97. Westad, *Global Cold War*, ch. 10.

98. Kalinovsky, 'Decision-Making', 61.

99. Anatoly S. Chernyaev Diary, 4 April 1985, DNSA, Soviet–US Relations, 1985–91.

100. Halliday and Zanin, 'Communist Regime in Afghanistan', 1367.

101. 'The Kremlin, February 25', *Pravda* and *Izvestia*, 26 February 1986, in *CDSP* 38/8.

102. 'President Gorbachev's Decision to End Afghan War', 17 October 1985, DNSA, Terrorism and US Policy, 1968–2002.

103. Ludwig Adamec, *First Supplement to the Who's Who of Afghanistan* (Graz, Austria: Akademische Druck-u. Verlagsanstalt, 1979), 12; Kalinovsky, *Long Goodbye*, 95.

104. Cited in Kalinovsky, *Long Goodbye*, 96.

105. Mitrokhin, 'The KGB in Afghanistan', 141; Kalinovsky, *Long Goodbye*, 96.

106. 'Speech of Comrade Najib General Secretary of PDPA CC on Organisational Questions at the 20th Plenum of the PDPA CC', in Ḥizb-i Dimūkrātīk-i Khalq-i Afghānistān and Najib (ed.), *20th Plenum of PDPA CC: Documents* (Kabul: State Printing House, 1986).

107. Kalinovsky, *Long Goodbye*, 96–7; 'Plenary Session of the PDPA Central Committee', *Pravda*, 5 May 1986, in *CDSP* 38/18.

108. '(Editorial)—For the Expansion of the Afghan Revolution's Social Base', *Pravda*, 21 December 1985, in *CDSP* 37/51.

109. 'Strengthening the Revolution—Speech by Comrade Najibullah at the Plenary Session of the Kabul City Party Committee', *Pravda*, 15 May 1986, in *CDSP* 38/20.

110. Pavel Demchenko, 'Commentator's Column: Base Expands', *Pravda*, 3 January 1986, in *CDSP* 38/1.

111. 'The Main Speech of Comrade Najib, General Secretary of the PDPA CC at 20th Plenum of PDPA CC on the Implementation of the Resolutions of the 16th Plenum of the PDPA CC and Other Undelayable Tasks of the Party', in *20th Plenum of PDPA CC: Documents*.

112. Rubin, *Fragmentation of Afghanistan*, 146–7; Shah Mohammad Dost to Javier Perez de Cuellar, 'Decree on the General Amnesty on the Occasion of the Declaration of National Reconciliation', 29 January 1987, UN ARMS, S-1024-2-2.

113. 'The Goal is National Reconciliation—Najib's Report to the PDPA Central Committee', *Pravda*, 2 January 1987, in *CDSP* 39/1.

114. Westad, *Global Cold War*, 366.

115. Giustozzi, *War, Politics and Society*, 170. See ibid., ch. 13, for further detail on national reconciliation; also Halliday and Zanin, 'Communist Regime in Afghanistan', 1365–9.

116. 'CPSU CC Politburo Meeting Minutes (excerpt)', 13 November 1986, RGANI, fo. 89, per. 42, d. 16, CWIHP.

117. 'Notes from Politburo Meeting, 21–22 January 1987 (Excerpt)', 22 January 1987, Gorbachev Foundation, Moscow, CWIHP.

118. Halliday and Zanin, 'Communist Regime in Afghanistan', 1368.

119. 'Notes from Politburo Meeting, 21–22 January 1987 (Excerpt)'.

120. Vladislav Tamarov, *Afghanistan: A Russian Soldier's Story* (Berkeley: Ten Speed Press, 2001 edn), 30.

121. Svetlana Alexievich, *Boys in Zinc*, trans. Andrew Bromfield (London: Penguin, 2017), 47, 115, 117, 34, 46, 163, 128–9.

122. Artyom Borovik, *The Hidden War: The True Story of War in Afghanistan* (London: Faber and Faber, 2001), 13.

## Chapter 4

1. See Markus Daechsel, *Islamabad and the Politics of International Development in Pakistan* (Cambridge: Cambridge University Press, 2015).

2. 'Full Unanimity in Assessment of Afghan Situation', *Dawn*, 22 January 1980, p. 1; '"Talks Useful and Constructive", Says Zia', *Dawn*, 3 February 1980, pp. 1, 4; 'Whole International Situation Very Tense—Waldheim', *Dawn*, 24 January 1980, p. 1; 'First Extraordinary Sessions of the ICFM Islamabad (27–29 January, 1980)', in Sa'ad S. Khan (ed.), *Friends Indeed: Review & Reference on Pakistan–OIC Relations* (Islamabad: National Institute of Historical and Cultural Research, 2004), 33–44.

3. See Cemil Aydin, *The Idea of the Muslim World: A Global Intellectual History* (Cambridge, MA: Harvard University Press, 2017), ch. 6.

4. 'Respect of State Sovereignty', *Dawn*, 8 June 1978, p. 1.

5. Nicholas Gage, 'Iran Fears Threat from Afghans to its Oil Passage Route in Gulf', *New York Times*, 20 May 1978, p. 4.

6. S. K. Singh, Ambassador, Indian Embassy, Kabul, 'Annual Political Report for 1978', 1 March 1979, NAI, EA HI/1011/13/79-I.

7. Ayesha Jalal, *The Struggle for Pakistan: A Muslim Homeland and Global Politics* (Cambridge, MA: Belknap Press of Harvard University Press, 2014), 223–4.

8. 'Zia's Call for Unity of Muslim States', *Dawn*, 7 July 1978, p. 1.

9. See Sarah Ansari and William Gould, *Boundaries of Belonging: Localities, Citizenship and Rights in India and Pakistan* (Cambridge: Cambridge University Press, 2019); Elisabeth Leake, 'At the Nation-State's Edge: Centre–Periphery Relations in Post-1947 South Asia', *Historical Journal*, 59/2 (2016), 509–39.

10. See, e.g., Gage, 'Iran Fears'; Jonathan C. Randal, 'Iran, Fearful of Soviets, Seeks Calm in Pakistan', *Washington Post*, 19 May 1978, p. A26; Near East–South Asia Division, Office of Political Analysis, 'Afghanistan's Relations with its Neighbors (U)' (June 1979), CREST, CIA-RDP80T00942A001100120001-9.

11. Telegram from the Department of State to the Embassy in Pakistan, 29 May 1978, in Seth A. Rotramel (ed.), *FRUS, 1977–1980*, 19 (Washington: USGPO, 2019), no. 281.

12. See Malcolm M. Craig, 'United States, Britain, Pakistan, and the "Islamic Bomb", 1977–80', *International History Review*, 38/5 (2016), 857–79.

13. 'Social–Imperialist Strategy in Asia', *Beijing Review*, 22/3, 19 January 1979, pp. 13–16. This was a common line taken throughout the end of the 1970s and into the early 1980s by the Chinese press, and numerous similar articles appeared in later issues of the *Beijing Review*. See also Lorenz M. Lüthi, *Cold Wars: Asia, the Middle East, Europe* (Cambridge: Cambridge University Press, 2020), 531.

14. Memorandum of Conversation, 29 January 1979, in David P. Nickles (ed.), *FRUS, 1977–1980*, 8 (Washington: USGPO, 2013), no. 202.

15. 'Afghanistan Soviet Vietnam, Says China', *Dawn*, 24 August 1979, p. 1.

16. 'Statement by the Adviser on Foreign Affairs, Mr Agha Shahi, in the UN General Assembly in Exercise of the Right of Reply to the Statement Made by the Leader of the Afghan Delegation', 3 October 1978, in Mehrunissa Ali (ed.), *Pak–Afghan Discord: A Historical Perspective: Documents, 1855–1979* (Karachi: Pakistan Study Centre, 1990), 394–5.

17. 'Respect of State Sovereignty', *Dawn*, 8 June 1978, p. 1.

18. 'Kabul Promises on Border', *Dawn*, 10 September 1978, p. 1.

19. This same trend was apparent in the *Kabul Times* throughout 1978 and 1979 and was commented on in Pakistani publications like *Dawn*.

20. '10,000 Afghans Entered Pakistan since April Coup', *Dawn*, 25 September 1978, p. 10.

21. 'No Interference in Kabul's Affairs: Zia', *Dawn*, 20 March 1979, p. 1.

22. US Embassy, Pakistan, to State Department, 12 March 1979, DNSA, Afghanistan.

23. 'Reported Version of the Statement by a Pakistan Foreign Office Spokesman on Allegations Made by the Soviet Press, 29 March 1979', in Ali, *Pak–Afghan Discord*, 400–1; 'Statement Issued by the Government of Afghanistan Accusing Pakistan of Training Afghan Refugees for Subversive Activities in Afghanistan, 22 March 1979', in ibid. 401–2; 'Statement Issued by the Government of Pakistan Regarding the Activities of Afghan Refugees in Pakistan, 24 March 1979', in ibid. 403; also 'Soviet Charges "Unjustified": No Training to Afghan Refugees in Pakistan', *Dawn*, 4 June 1979, p. 1; Telegram from the Embassy in Pakistan to the Department of State, 28 March 1979, in *FRUS, 1977–1980*, 19, no. 332.

24. Telegram from the Embassy in Pakistan to the Department of State; 'Strong Protest to Afghanistan', *Dawn*, 26 March 1979, p. 1; 'Kabul's Charge of Raid False, Baseless', *Dawn*, 10 April 1979, p. 1.

25. Quoted in 'A Glance at Kabul Press', *Kabul Times*, 1 April 1979, p. 3.

26. 'Iran to Protest to Kabul', *Dawn*, 11 April 1979, p. 1.

27. 'Ties with Pakistan Based on Islam', *Dawn*, 11 April 1979, p. 1.

28. Telegram from the Embassy in Pakistan to the Department of State.

29. Thomas Thornton, Memorandum for Zbigniew Brzezinski, 18 January 1979, DNSA, CIA Covert Operations.

30. 'Zia, Tarahki [*sic*] Meet Again in Havana', *Dawn*, 9 September 1979, p. 1.

31. Hafizullah Emadi, *Dynamics of Political Development in Afghanistan: The British, Russian, and American Invasions* (New York: Palgrave Macmillan, 2010), 115; 'Amin Invites Zia', *Dawn*, 18 September 1979, p. 1.

32. See, among numerous other articles, 'Pakistan's Grave Concern at Kabul Development', *Dawn*, 30 December 1979, p. 1; 'US Demands Pullout of Soviet Troops', ibid.; 'Iran, S. Arabia Slate Soviet Action', ibid.

33. 'Statement Issued by the Government of Pakistan Concerning the Developments in Afghanistan, 29 December 1979', in Ali, *Pak–Afghan Discord*, 422–3.

34. Bruce Riedel, *What We Won: America's Secret War in Afghanistan, 1979–89* (Washington: Brookings Institution Press, 2014), 60–1; Arshad Ali and Robert G. Atman, 'The Evolution of the National Security State in Pakistan: 1947–1989', *Democracy and Security*, 15/4 (2019), 301–27, at 318.

35. 'Conditional Troop Withdrawal Means Refusal to Withdraw', reproduced in *Beijing Review*, 23/10, 10 March 1980, pp. 25–6.

36. 'Chinese Envoys Abroad', *Beijing Review*, 23/13, 31 March 1980, pp. 7–8.

37. 'Three Principles for Solution to Afghan Issue', *Beijing Review*, 23/11, 17 March 1980, p. 3.

38. See Sergey Radchenko, *Unwanted Visionaries: The Soviet Failure in Asia at the End of the Cold War* (Oxford: Oxford University Press, 2014).

39. 'Summary Record of Talks', 2–3 February 1980, in *FRUS, 1977–1980*, 19, no. 423.

40. W. Eric Gustafson and William L. Richter, 'Pakistan in 1980: Weathering the Storm', *Asian Survey*, 21/2 (1981), 162–71, at 163.

41. Jalal, *Struggle for Pakistan*, 233.

42. Ibid. 234.

43. Ibid. 235–8. See also Saadia Toor, *The State of Islam: Culture and Cold War Politics in Pakistan* (London: Pluto Press, 2011), 137–58.

44. Sana Haroon, 'The Rise of Deobandi Islam in the North-West Frontier Province and its Implications in Colonial India and Pakistan 1914–1996', *Journal of the Royal Asiatic Society*, 18/1 (2008), 47–70, at 66–9.

45. 'Pakistan Ready to Meet Any Challenge—Zia', *Dawn*, 14 January 1980, p. 1.

46. 'Iran to Aid Afghans in Letter and Spirit—Ayatollah Noori', *Dawn*, 7 January 1980, p. 10.

47. 'Iran Troops on Afghan Border', *Dawn*, 21 January 1980, p. 1; CIA Office of Political Analysis Intelligence Memorandum, 'Iran: Bani-Sadr's Foreign Policy views', 5 February 1980, CREST, CIA-RDP81B00401R000500100012-5.

48. S. K. Singh, Ambassador, Indian Embassy, Kabul, 'Annual Political Report for 1978', 1 March 1979, NAI, EA HI/1011/13/79-I.

49. Ibid.

50. R. C. Joshi, First Secretary, Indian Embassy, Kabul, 'Monthly Record of Events—June, 1979', 17 July 1979, NAI, EA HI/1012/1/79.

51. J. S. Teja, Ambassador, Indian Embassy, Kabul, 'Annual Political Report—1979', 1 March 1980, NAI, EA HI/1011/13/80-I; Avinash Paliwal, *My Enemy's Enemy: India in Afghanistan from the Soviet Invasion to the US Withdrawal* (London: Hurst & Co., 2017), 43.

52. Letter from Indian Prime Minister Desai to President Carter, 10 February 1979, in *FRUS, 1977–1980*, 19, no. 126.

53. 'India Blames USSR & US', *Dawn*, 9 January 1980, p. 1.

54. 'Indira Wants Asian States' Dialogue', *Dawn*, 21 January 1980, pp. 1, 5.

55. S. K. Lambah, Counsellor, Indian Embassy, Islamabad, 'Monthly Record of Events for the Month of January 1980', 3 February 1980, NAI, EA HI/1012/25/80.

56. Telegram from the Embassy in India to the Department of State, 1 February 1980, in *FRUS, 1977–1980*, 19, no. 169.

57. 'Indira Wants Asian States' Dialogue'.

58. Lüthi, *Cold Wars*, 531–5.

59. See Paliwal, *My Enemy's Enemy*, ch. 3.

60. 'Pakistan's Grave Concern at Kabul Development', *Dawn*, 30 December 1979, p. 1.

61. 'China Condemns Soviet Military Invasion of Afghanistan', *Beijing Review*, 23/1, 7 January 1980, p. 3; *People's Daily*, cited in 'US Demands Pullout of Soviet Troops', 4.

62. 'Iran Protests Soviet Intervention in Afghanistan', December 1979, UN ARMS, S-0904-1-4; Bismellah Sahak to Kurt Waldheim, Policy Statement of the Democratic Republic of Afghanistan, 10 January 1980, UN ARMS, S-0442-0330-7.

63. J. N. Dixit, *An Afghan Diary: Zahir Shah to Taliban* (New Delhi: Konark Publishers, 2000), 70.

64. Paliwal, *Enemy's Enemy*, 49.

65. 'Afghans Resist Invaders', *Beijing Review*, 23/6, 11 February 1980, p. 10.

66. Second Plenary Meeting, 10.55 a.m., 11 January 1980, UN General Assembly Sixth Emergency Special Session Official Records.

67. 'Zia Urges Islamic States to Condemn Intervention by Force', *Dawn*, 9 January 1980, p. 1, back page.

68. Second Plenary Meeting, 10.55 a.m., 11 January 1980.

69. Cited in Riedel, *What We Won*, 62.

70. Steve Coll, *Ghost Wars: The Secret History of the CIA, Afghanistan, and bin Laden, from the Soviet Invasion to September 10, 2001* (London: Penguin Books, 2005), ch. 3; Zahid Hussain, *Frontline Pakistan: The Struggle with Militant Islam* (London: I. B. Tauris, 2007), 16–18.

71. Mohammad Yousaf, *Silent Soldier: The Man behind the Afghan Jehad General Akhtar Abdur Rahman Shaheed* (Lahore: Jang Publishers, 1991), 47, 66.

72. Coll, *Ghost Wars*, 68.

73. Stephen Philip Cohen, *The Idea of Pakistan* (Washington: Brookings Institution Press, 2004), ch. 5, esp. pp. 170–96.

74. Cited in Christophe Jaffrelot, *The Pakistan Paradox: Instability and Resilience* (Oxford: Oxford University Press, 2015), 502.

75. Coll, *Ghost Wars*, 62.

76. Jaffrelot, *Pakistan Paradox*, 502–5; Haroon, 'Rise of Deobandi Islam', 66–9; Coll, *Ghost Wars*, ch. 4; see also Mustafa Hamid and Leah Farrall, *The Arabs at War in Afghanistan* (London: Hurst & Co., 2015).

77. 'Lessons to Be Drawn from Afghanistan', *Beijing Review*, 23/5, 4 February 1980, pp. 9–12.

78. Hafizullah Emadi, 'Radical Political Movements in Afghanistan and their Politics of Peoples' Empowerment and Liberation', *Central Asian Survey*, 20/4 (2001), 427–50, at 443–4.

79. DRA Ministry of Foreign Affairs Information and Press Department, *White Book: China's Interference in the Internal Affairs of the Democratic Republic of Afghanistan* (Kabul: DRA Ministry of Foreign Affairs Information and Press Department, 1985), 39, 22.

80. See Niamatullah Ibrahimi, 'Ideology without Leadership: The Rise and Decline of Maoism in Afghanistan', 31 August 2012, AAN, https://www.afghanistan-analysts.org/wp-content/uploads/downloads/2012/09/NIbr-Maoists-final.pdf (accessed 21 December 2020).

81. Julia Lovell, *Maoism: A Global History* (London: Bodley Head, 2019), 227.

82. A. Z. Hilali, 'China's Response to the Soviet Invasion of Afghanistan', *Central Asian Survey*, 20/3 (2001), 323–51, at 335.

83. Memorandum of Conversation, 8 January 1980, in *FRUS, 1977–1980*, 8, no. 292.

84. Hafizullah Emadi, 'Exporting Iran's Revolution: The Radicalization of the Shiite Movement in Afghanistan', *Middle Eastern Studies*, 31/1 (1995), 1–12, at 8–10.

85. Jaffrelot, *Pakistan Paradox*, 485–9.

86. Brief of the High Commissioner, UNHCR Operation in Pakistan, n.d., UNHCR, Fonds 13, Sub-fonds 2, Series 2, Box 39.

87. See, e.g., League of Red Cross Societies, 'Afghan Refugees in Pakistan', 28 February 1980, UNHCR, Fonds 11, Series 2, Box 764. For more on the ways that the refugee crisis could potentially shape local dynamics, see Akbar S. Ahmed, 'The Impact of the Afghan Refugees on Ethnicity and Politics in Baluchistan (Pakistan)', *Central Asian Survey*, 9/3 (1990), 43–56.

88. See Fariba Adelkhah and Zuzanna Olszewska, 'The Iranian Afghans', *Iranian Studies*, 40/2 (2007), 137–65; Alessandro Monsutti, 'Migration as a Rite of Passage: Young Afghans Building Masculinity and Adulthood in Iran', *Iranian Studies*, 40/2 (2007), 167–85; also UNHCR, Fonds 11, Series 2, Box 104.

89. S. Bari, 'Mission Report (New Delhi, India—27 October–1 November 1980)', 26 November 1980, UNHCR, Fonds 11, Series 2, Box 96; Candida Toscani, 'Mission Report (New Delhi, India—5 January to 27 February 1981)', 12 March 1981, UNHCR, Fonds 11, Series 2, Box 96.

90. S. Bari, 'Mission Report (New Delhi, India—27 October–1 November 1980)'; 'Report on Mission to New Delhi, India from 4–11 December 1982 by Messrs A. J. F. Simmance and G. A. Everts', 31 January 1983, UNHCR, Fonds 11, Series 2, Box 97.

## Chapter 5

1. 'I Am a Socialist', *Jihad Rays*, 3/1–2 (1984).

2. *1981 Census Report of the North West Frontier Province* (Islamabad: Population Census Organisation, Statistics Division, Government of Pakistan, December 1984).

3. Thomas Barfield, 'Afghan Customary Law and its Relationship to Formal Judicial Institutions', United States Institute for Peace, June 2003, https://www.usip.org/sites/default/files/file/barfield2.pdf (accessed 8 July 2019).

4. David B. Edwards, *Before Taliban: Genealogies of the Afghan Jihad* (Berkeley and Los Angeles: University of California Press, 2002), 240–1; Chris Sands and Fazelminallah Qazizai, *Night Letters: Gulbuddin Hekmatyar and the Afghan Islamists who Changed the World* (London: Hurst & Co., 2019), 95.

5. Sands and Qazizai, *Night Letters*, 100–5.

6. Olivier Roy, 'The Origins of the Islamist Movement in Afghanistan', *Central Asian Survey*, 3/2 (1984), 117–27, at 125–6; Edwards, *Before Taliban*, 241.

7. Sands and Qazizai, *Night Letters*, 110.

8. Amin Saikal, *Modern Afghanistan: A History of Struggle and Survival* (London: I. B. Tauris, 2004), ch. 1; Nancy Tapper, 'The Advent of Pashtun "Maldars" in North-Western Afghanistan', *Bulletin of the School of Oriental and African Studies, University of London*, 36/1 (1973), 55–79; Pierre Centlivres and Micheline Centlivres-Demont, 'State, National Awareness and Levels of Identity in Afghanistan from Monarchy to Islamic State', *Central Asian Survey*, 19/3–4 (2000), 419–28, at 421.

9. See Terry Martin, *The Affirmative Action Empire: Nations and Nationalism in the Soviet Union, 1923–1939* (Ithaca, NY: Cornell University Press, 2001).

10. Niamatullah Ibrahimi, *The Hazaras and the Afghan State: Rebellion, Exclusion and the Struggle for Recognition* (London: Hurst, 2017), 118; Eden Naby, 'The Ethnic Factor in Soviet–Afghan Relations', *Asian Survey*, 20/3 (1980), 237–56; Niamatullah Ibrahimi, 'The Failure of a Clerical Proto-State: Hazarajat, 1979–1984', Crisis States Working Papers Series no. 2, working paper no. 6 (2006).

11. 'Over 100 Killed in Government, Rights Clashes', Agence France Presse, 28 August 1978, FBIS MEA-78-168; 'Pathan Guerrillas Claim to Have Killed 100 Afghan Soldiers', Agence France Presse, 29 October 1978, FBIS MEA-78-212.

12. Olivier Roy, *Islam and Resistance in Afghanistan* (Cambridge: Cambridge University Press, 1990 edn), 99–102.

13. Ibid. 165–71.

14. 'Moslem Clergymen, Army Officers Flee Country', Agence France Presse, 5 June 1978, FBIS MEA-78-109.

15. Brief of the High Commissioner, 'Protection Issues in Pakistan', n.d., UNHCR, Fonds 13, Sub-fonds 2, Series 2, Box 39; Rüdiger Schoch, 'Afghan Refugees in Pakistan during the 1980s: Cold War Politics and Registration Practice', New Issues in Refugee Research, UNHCR (June 2008), 8–9.

16. Barnett Rubin, *The Fragmentation of Afghanistan: State Formation and Collapse in the International System* (1995; New Haven: Yale University Press, 2002), 198.

17. Edwards, *Before Taliban*, 248–9.

18. For further specifics on the rise of the Afghan political parties, see Rubin, *Fragmentation of Afghanistan*, ch. 9; Edwards, *Before Taliban*, ch. 7; Gilles Dorronsoro, *Revolution Unending: Afghanistan 1979 to the Present* (London: Hurst & Co., 2005), ch. 4.

19. Steven Tanner, *Afghanistan: A Military History from Alexander the Great to the War against the Taliban* (Philadelphia: Da Capo Books, 2009 edn), ch. 10; Alan J. Kuperman, 'The Stinger Missile and US Intervention in Afghanistan', *Political Science Quarterly*, 114/2 (1999), 219–63; Nobel Symposium, 'The Intervention in Afghanistan and the Fall of Detente', trans. Svetlana Savranskaya, ed. David A. Welch and Odd Arne Westad, Lysebu, Norway, 17–20 September 1995 (Oslo: Norwegian Nobel Institute, 1996), 169.

20. Roy, *Islam and Resistance*, chs 8, 13; also Dorronsoro, *Revolution Unending*, chs 3, 6.

21. Rubin, *Fragmentation of Afghanistan*, 203–21; Roy, *Islam and Resistance*, ch. 8.

22. Edwards, *Before Taliban*, 266–8; Rubin, *Fragmentation of Afghanistan*, 224; Roy, *Islam and Resistance*, 122–4.

23. Rubin, *Fragmentation of Afghanistan*, 203–13, 211.

24. 'Summary Record of a Call on the Minister of State for Foreign and Commonwealth Affairs, the Hon. Douglas Hurd CBE MP, by the Leader of the National Islamic Front of Afghanistan, Sayed Ahmad Gailani, at the Foreign and Commonwealth Office at 3.30 pm on 12 November', 12 November 1980, TNA, FCO 37/2217.

25. Cited in Eden Naby, 'The Changing Role of Islam as a Unifying Force in Afghanistan', in Ali Banuazizi and Myron Weiner (eds), *The State, Religion, and Ethnic Politics: Afghanistan, Iran, and Pakistan* (Syracuse: Syracuse University Press, 1986), 124–54, at 147–9.

26. These points are taken from figures 2 and 3 in Allen E. Dorn, 'Countering the Revolution: The Mujahideen Counterrevolution', Afghanistan Forum occasional paper 28 (February 1989), 23–4.

27. Shah M. Tarzi, 'Politics of the Afghan Resistance Movement: Cleavages, Disunity, and Fragmentation', *Asian Survey*, 31/6 (1991), 479–95, at 482.

28. D. R. Gallwey, Chargé d'Affaires, UK Embassy Islamabad, to D. J. Gowan, SAD, 'Afghan Resistance Politics', 10 May 1981, TNA, FCO 37/2384.

29. Cited in Dorn, 'Countering the Revolution', 6.

30. Edwards, *Before Taliban*, 226.

31. Mohammad Yousaf and Mark Adkin, *Afghanistan: The Bear Trap: The Defeat of a Superpower* (Havertown, PA: Casemate, 2001 edn), 105.

32. R. A. Longmire to Mr Featherstone, 'King Zahir Shah: Your Minute to Dr Hoare of 27 April 1981', 12 May 1981, TNA, FCO 37/2384.

33. This speaks to Gilles Dorronsoro's arguments, who has described the war using three 'reference points'—a tribal revolt, an ethnic war, or a 'blend of religion and politics'— none of which are wholly explanatory (*Revolution Unending*, 8–18).

34. Vakeel Dost Mohammad Gorgaij Baloch to UK Ambassador, Islamabad, 'Resolution of the United Tribes of Afghanistan', 22 July 1981, TNA, FCO 37/2384.

35. Edwards, *Before Taliban*, 261.

36. Tarzi, 'Politics of the Afghan Resistance', 486, 488.

37. Eden Naby, 'Islam within the Afghan Resistance', *Third World Quarterly*, 10/2 (1988), 787–805, at 794.

38. Hafizullah Emadi, 'Exporting Iran's Revolution: The Radicalization of the Shiite Movement in Afghanistan', *Middle Eastern Studies*, 31/1 (1995), 1–12, at 8–10; Hafizullah Emadi, *Dynamics of Political Development in Afghanistan: The British, Russian, and American Invasions* (New York: Palgrave Macmillan, 2010), 131–2, 140–4; Roy, *Islam and Resistance*, ch. 9; Ibrahimi, *Hazaras and the Afghan State*, chs 4, 5.

39. See Mohammad Yousaf, *Silent Soldier: The Man behind the Afghan Jehad General Akhtar Abdur Rahman Shaheed* (Lahore: Jang Publishers, 1991).

40. Yousaf, *The Bear Trap*, 40; cited in Steve Coll, *Ghost Wars: The Secret History of the CIA, Afghanistan, and bin Laden, from the Soviet Invasion to September 10, 2001* (London: Penguin Books, 2005), 119.

41. John Fullerton, 'A Rift among Rebels', *Afghanistan Forum*, 11/1 (January 1983), 9–10.

42. Sands and Qazizai, *Night Letters*, 162–5; Nancy Hatch Dupree, 'Revolutionary Rhetoric and Afghan Women', Afghanistan Council occasional paper 23 (January 1981), 16.

43. Sands and Qazizai, *Night Letters*, 190, 199–200; Fullerton, 'A Rift among Rebels'; Coll, *Ghost Wars*, 119.

44. 'Charter of Hezb-e-Islami Afghanistan (Hekmatyar)', printed in *Afghan Jehad: Quarterly Magazine of the Cultural Council of Afghanistan Resistance*, 1/3 (1988), 59–70.

45. David B. Edwards, 'Summoning Muslims: Print, Politics, and Religious Ideology in Afghanistan', *Journal of Asian Studies*, 52/3 (1993), 609–28, at 619–20; Sands and Qazizai, *Night Letters*, 198–9; 'Dossiers of Alliance—7 Rebel Leaders', in A. A Lyakhovskii, *Plamya afghana* (Moscow: Iskon, 1999), CWIHP; Salman Hussain, 'Looking for "Tribals" without Politics, "Warlords" without History: The Drug Economy, Development and Political Power in Afghanistan', *Identities*, 19/3 (2012), 249–67, at 260.

46. Sands and Qazizai, *Night Letters*, 181, 205–7; Robert D. Crews, *Afghan Modern: The History of a Global Nation* (Cambridge, MA: Belknap Press of Harvard University Press, 2015), 258–60. See also Thomas Hegghammer, *The Caravan: Abdallah Azzam and the Rise of Global Jihad* (Cambridge: Cambridge University Press, 2020).

47. Roy, *Islam and Resistance*, 133.

48. I. Khan to P. M. Moussalli, 'Disappearance of Afghan Refugees in Pakistan', 2 July 1982, UNHCR, Fonds 11, Series 2, Box 154.

49. G. Walzer to T. Barnes, 'Dr Abdul Samat Durrani', 22 June 1982, UNHCR, Fonds 11, Series 2, Box 154.

50. Sands and Qazizai, *Night Letters*, 226–8; Roy, *Islam and Resistance*, 134.

51. Sands and Qazizai, *Night Letters*, 226–8.

52. See, e.g., US Department of State, Bureau of Intelligence and Research, 'The Afghan Resistance Movement', 16 March 1982, DNSA, Afghanistan.

53. Roy, *Islam and Resistance*, 120.

54. 'Charter of Jamiat-e-Islami Afghanistan', printed in *Afghan Jehad: Quarterly Magazine of the Cultural Council of Afghanistan Resistance*, 1/3 (1988), 75–9.

55. Roy, *Islam and Resistance*, 130–3; Rubin, *Fragmentation of Afghanistan*, 218–20.

56. Crews, *Afghan Modern*, 272–3.

57. Jerome Bony and Christophe de Ponfilly, 'A Valley against an Empire', *Central Asian Survey*, 1/4 (1983), 133–47, at 137–8; also 'Resistance in Afghanistan: The Panjshir Model', *Spotlight on Regional Affairs*, 4/3 (March 1985), 20.

58. Mohammad Es'haq, *Afghan Resistance: Achievements & Problems* (Pakistan: Jami'at-i-Islami Afghanistan, 1986), 6.

59. Marcela Grad, *Massoud: An Intimate Portrait of the Legendary Afghan Leader* (St Louis, MO: Webster University Press, 2009), 70.

60. Ibid. 77.

61. Rubin, *Fragmentation of Afghanistan*, 236.

62. Edward Girardet, 'With the Resistance in Afghanistan', *Christian Science Monitor* (1981), 21.

63. Masood Khalili, *Whispers of War: An Afghan Freedom Fighter's Account of the Soviet Invasion*, trans. Mahmud Khalili (New Delhi: Sage, 2017), 193–7.

64. 'Interview with Mujahid Brother Safiullah, Commander of the Herat Front', *Mirror of Jehad: The Voice of Afghan Mujahideen*, 1/4 (July–August 1982), 28.

65. Mohammad Es'haq, 'From the Diary of Jehad (Part IV)', *AFGHANews*, 3/24, 15 December 1987, p. 7.

66. See 'Panjshir Famine', *Afghanistan Forum Newsletter*, 11/2 (March 1983), 11.

67. Grad, *Massoud*, 41.

68. 'Summary Record of a Call on the Minister of State for Foreign and Commonwealth Affairs, the Hon Douglas Hurd CBE MP, by the Leader of the National Islamic Front of Afghanistan, Sayed Ahmad Gailani'.

69. See Simon Wolfgang Fuchs, 'Glossy Global Leadership: Unpacking the Multilingual Religious Thought of the Jihad', in Nile Green (ed.), *Afghanistan's Islam: From Conversion to the Taliban* (Berkeley and Los Angeles: University of California Press, 2017), 189–206.

70. Chen Jian, *Mao's China and the Cold War* (Chapel Hill: University of North Carolina Press, 2001), 243.

71. 'Tragic Blows on Islam and the Indifference of Muslims', *Mirror of Jehad: The Voice of Afghan Mujahideen*, 1/4 (July–August 1982), 7–9.

72. *Mujahideen Monthly*, 3 (March 1986).

73. Crews, *Afghan Modern*, 265–6.

74. *Mujahideen Monthly*, 1 (January 1986); *Mujahideen Monthly*, 3 (March 1986).

75. 'Problems in the Issue of Afghanistan', *Mirror of Jehad: The Voice of Afghan Mujahideen*, 1/4 (July–August 1982), 40.

76. Es'haq, *Afghan Resistance*, 1, 12.

77. 'Aminullah, Secretary, Political Committee, Hezb-i-Islami Afghanistan to Mr Hashim, Refugees Relief Committee, UN, Islamabad', 29 November 1979, UNHCR, Fonds 11, Series 2, Box 153.

78. Mohammad Nasim Azidi, President (Refugees Affairs), National Islamic Front of Afghanistan, to Commissioner, Afghan Refugees, NWFP, 'Request for Issuing Registration Order to the Camp Commander, Jamrud Refugees Camp: Refugees of Dag Behsood who Shifted to Jamrud as per Your Kind Instructions', 26 September 1981, UNHCR, Fonds 11, Series 2, Box 154; Mohammad Nasim Azidi, President (Refugees Affairs), National Islamic Front of Afghanistan, to Commissioner, Afghan Refugees, NWFP, 'Merciful Condition of Helpless Families of Afghan Refugees of Narola Refugees Camp: District Bannu', September 1981, UNHCR, Fonds 11, Series 2, Box 154.

79. 'Afghan Refugees Humanitarian Islamic Unity to Shamsher Khan, Commissioner for Afghan Refugees, Peshawar', 6 November 1979, UNHCR, Fonds 11, Series 2, Box 153.

80. 'Declaration of General Amnesty: Hekmatyar', *Mujahideen Monthly*, 1/1 (January 1986), 8.

81. Fuchs, 'Glossy Global Leadership', 203.

82. *Charter of Islamic Party of Afghanistan* (Pakistan: Shahadat Press, 1987).

83. Ibid.

84. Sands and Qazizai, *Night Letters*, 212; Yousaf, *The Bear Trap*, 41.

85. Roy, *Islam and Resistance*, 134.

86. Rubin, *Fragmentation of Afghanistan*, 158; Sands and Qazizai, *Night Letters*, 230–4.

87. 'The Fifth Crushing Defeat of Russians in Panjshir', *Mirror of Jehad: The Voice of Afghan Mujahideen*, 1/4 (July–August 1982), 21–2.

88. Bony and de Ponfilly, 'A Valley against an Empire', 141–2, 147.

89. Antonio Giustozzi, 'The Missing Ingredient: Non-Ideological Insurgency and State Collapse in Western Afghanistan, 1979-1992', Crisis States Working Papers series no. 2, working paper no. 11 (2007), 4; Dorronsoro, *Revolution Unending*, 162–9.

90. Mike Martin, *An Intimate War: An Oral History of the Helmand Conflict* (London: Hurst & Co., 2014), 45–6, 52–6.

91. Vahid Brown and Don Rassler, *Fountainhead of Jihad: The Haqqani Nexus, 1973–2012* (New York: Columbia University Press, 2013), ch. 2; Neamatollah Nojumi, *The Rise of the Taliban in Afghanistan: Mass Mobilization, Civil War, and the Future of the Region* (New York: Palgrave, 2002), ch. 7; Sana Haroon, 'The Rise of Deobandi Islam in the North-West Frontier Province and its Implications in Colonial India and Pakistan 1914–1996', *Journal of the Royal Asiatic Society*, 18/1 (2008), 47–70.

92. Abdul Salam Zaeef, *My Life with the Taliban*, ed. Alex Strick van Linschoten and Felix Kuehn (London: Hurst & Co., 2010), 22.

93. Masood Farivar, *Confessions of a Mullah Warrior* (New York: Atlantic Monthly Press, 2009), 5.

94. 'Letter to the United Nations', *Mujahideen Monthly*, 1/1 (January 1986), 9.

## Chapter 6

1. 'March 10, 1982. President Reagan Speech on Afghanistan Day Proclamation. East Room', Master Tape 40, RRPL, Records of the White House Television Office. I have kept the spelling of 'Mojadidi' as it was reported and used in archives.

2. Ronald Reagan, 'Remarks on Signing the Afghanistan Day Proclamation', 10 March 1982, APP, https://www.presidency.ucsb.edu/documents/remarks-signing-the-afghanistan-day-proclamation-1 (accessed 18 June 2019).

3. Andrew Hartman, '"The Red Template": US Policy in Soviet-Occupied Afghanistan', *Third World Quarterly*, 23/3 (2002), 467–89, at 476.

4. Cited in Odd Arne Westad, *The Global Cold War: Third World Interventions and the Making of our Times* (Cambridge: Cambridge University Press, 2007), 282.

5. Graham Hovey, 'Afghan Coup was Surprise to US: Policies Not Yet Clear', *New York Times*, 2 May 1978, p. 4; Jimmy Carter, 'The State of the Union Address Delivered before a Joint Session of the Congress', 23 January 1980, APP, https://www.presidency.ucsb.edu/documents/the-state-the-union-address-delivered-before-joint-session-the-congress (accessed 18 June 2019).

6. Nobel Symposium, 'The Intervention in Afghanistan and the Fall of Detente', trans. Svetlana Savranskaya, ed. David A. Welch and Odd Arne Westad, Lysebu, Norway, 17–20 September 1995 (Oslo: Norwegian Nobel Institute, 1996), 140, 149.

7. Nobel Symposium, 'Intervention in Afghanistan', 134. See Melvyn P. Leffler, *For the Soul of Mankind: The United States, the Soviet Union, and the Cold War* (New York: Hill & Wang, 2007), ch. 4; Daniel J. Sargent, *A Superpower Transformed: The Remaking of American Foreign Relations in the 1970s* (New York: Oxford University Press, 2015), 267–73.

8. Bruce A. Flatin, interviewed by Charles Stuart Kennedy, 27 January 1993, ADST; Paper Prepared in the Department of State, 29 April 1978, in David Zierler (ed.), *FRUS, 1977–1980*, 12 (Washington: USGPO, 2018), no. 8. On the War on Drugs, see James Tharin Bradford, *Poppies, Politics, and Power: Afghanistan and the Global History of Drugs and Diplomacy* (Ithaca, NY: Cornell University Press, 2019) ch. 5.

9. Telegram from the Embassy in Afghanistan to the Departments of State and Defense, the National Security Agency, and the United States Pacific Command, 30 April 1978, *FRUS, 1977–1980*, 12, no. 10; Hovey, 'Afghan Coup was Surprise to U.S.'; Conor Tobin, 'The Myth of the "Afghan Trap": Zbigniew Brzezinski and Afghanistan, 1978–1979', *Diplomatic History*, dhz065, https://doi.org/10.1093/dh/dhz065, p. 4.

10. Frank E. Schmelzer, interviewed by Mike Springmann, 1 December 1992, ADST; Richard Fenton Ross, interviewed by Charles Stuart Kennedy, 19 June 2003, ADST; Louis Taylor, interviewed by Charles Stuart Kennedy, 19 January 2001, ADST.

11. Theodore Eliot to Secretary of State, 'Some Further Thoughts on Afghanistan's Communist Revolution', 1 May 1978, AAD; Memorandum for Dr Zbigniew Brzezinski, 'Afghanistan Coup', from Peter Tarnoff, 29 April 1978, JCPL, National Security Affairs, Brzezinski Country Files, Box 1, Folder Afghanistan: 1/77–3/79.

12. Letter from Pakistani General Zia to President Carter, 9 May 1978, in *FRUS, 1977–1980*, 12, no. 16; Eliot, 'Some Further Thoughts'.

13. Theodore Eliot to State Department, 'My Farewell Call on Premier Taraki', Telegram 4752, 12 June 1978, AAD.

14. Adolph Dubs to State Department, 'US Policy toward the Democratic Republic of Afghanistan', Telegram 5981, 24 July 1978, AAD; James E. Taylor, interviewed by Charles Kennedy, 5 December 1995, ADST.

15. Flatin interview, ADST; Taylor interview, ADST.

16. Thomas Thornton to Zbigniew Brzezinski and David Aaron, 'Opposition in Afghanistan', 14 July 1978, JCPL, National Security Affairs, Brzezinski Country Files, Box 1, Folder Afghanistan: 1/77–3/79; Editorial Note, in *FRUS, 1977–1980*, 12, no. 25; Thomas Thornton to Zbigniew Brzezinski, 'Afghanistan', 11 September 1978, JCPL, National Security Affairs, Brzezinski Country Files, Box 1, Folder Afghanistan: 1/77–3/79.

17. 'Zbigniew Brzezinski, National Security Adviser to Jimmy Carter, Dies at 89', *New York Times*, 26 May 2017, https://www.nytimes.com/2017/05/26/us/zbigniew-brzezinski-dead-national-security-adviser-to-carter.html (accessed 18 June 2019). See also Justin Vaïsse, *Zbigniew Brzezinski: America's Grand Strategist* (Cambridge, MA: Harvard University Press, 2018).

18. Cited in Tobin, 'The Myth of the "Afghan Trap"', 7; Minutes of a Special Coordination Committee Meeting, 6 April 1979, in *FRUS, 1977–1980*, 12, no. 48; Robert M. Gates, *From the Shadows: The Ultimate Insider's Story of Five Presidents and how they Won the Cold War* (New York: Simon & Schuster, 1996), 146. See Alan J. Kuperman, 'The Stinger Missile and US Intervention in Afghanistan', *Political Science Quarterly*, 114/2 (1999),

219–63, at 221; H. Sidky, 'War, Changing Patterns of Warfare, State Collapse, and Transnational Violence in Afghanistan: 1978–2001', *Modern Asian Studies*, 41/4 (2007), 849–88. On the US intervention in the Dominican Republic, see Jesse Hoffnung-Garskof, '"Yankee, Go Home…and Take Me with You!": Imperialism and International Migration into Santo Domingo, Dominican Republic, 1961–1966', *Canadian Journal of Latin American and Caribbean Studies*, 29/57–8 (2004), 39–65, at 48–9; Piero Gleijeses, *The Dominican Crisis: The 1965 Constitutionalist Revolt and American Intervention*, trans. Lawrence Lipson (Baltimore: Johns Hopkins University Press, 1979).

19. Nobel Symposium, 'Intervention in Afghanistan', 143. On US covert operations, see James Callahan, *Covert Action in the Cold War: US Policy, Intelligence and CIA Operations* (London: I. B. Tauris, 2009); Douglas Little, 'Mission Impossible: The CIA and the Cult of Covert Action in the Middle East', *Diplomatic History*, 28/5 (2004), 663–701; James M. Scott, 'Interbranch Rivalry and the Reagan Doctrine in Nicaragua', *Political Science Quarterly*, 112/2 (1997), 237–60; Klaas Voß, 'Plausibly Deniable: Mercenaries in US Covert Interventions during the Cold War, 1964–1987', *Cold War History*, 16/1 (2016), 37–60; Stephen R. Weissman, 'CIA Covert Action in Zaire and Angola: Patterns and Consequences', *Political Science Quarterly*, 94/2 (1979), 263–86, at 284.

20. Nobel Symposium, 'Intervention in Afghanistan', 37.

21. Telegram from the Embassy in Afghanistan to the Department of State, 4 October 1979, in *FRUS, 1977–1980*, 12, no. 72; Zbigniew Brzezinski to Jimmy Carter, 'Daily Report', 4 October 1979, JCPL, CREST, NLC-1-12-6-12-8; Memorandum from the Secretary of State's Special Adviser on Soviet Affairs (Shulman) to Secretary of State Vance, 3 October 1979, in *FRUS, 1977–1980*, 12, no. 70.

22. Memorandum from Marshall Brement of the National Security Council Staff to the President's Assistant for National Security Affairs (Brzezinski) and the President's Deputy Assistant for National Security Affairs (Aaron), 28 December 1979, ibid., no. 112; Hotline Message from President Carter to General Secretary Brezhnev, 28 December 1979, ibid., no. 113.

23. Zbigniew Brzezinski, 'Reflections on Soviet Intervention in Afghanistan', 26 December 1979, JCPL, National Security Affairs, Brzezinski Country Files, Box 1, Folder Afghanistan, 4–12/79.

24. Zbigniew Brzezinski to Jimmy Carter, 'A Long-Term Strategy for Coping with the Consequences of the Soviet Action in Afghanistan', 9 January 1980, JCPL, Zbigniew Brzezinski Collection, Geographic Files, Box 17, Folder Southwest Asia/Persian Gulf—Minutes of meetings (1/79–1/80). For more on the embassy attack, see Steve Coll, *Ghost Wars: The Secret History of the CIA, Afghanistan, and bin Laden, from the Soviet Invasion to September 10, 2001* (London: Penguin Books, 2005), ch. 1.

25. Sargent, *Superpower Transformed*, 261–2. For more on Carter's earlier foreign policy, see *Superpower Transformed*, ch. 8.

26. Carter, 'State of the Union'.

27. Republican Party Platform of 1980, 15 July 1980, APP, https://www.presidency.ucsb.edu/documents/republican-party-platform-1980 (accessed 18 June 2019); Memorandum for Mr Richard V. Allen, The White House, 'Checklist on US Responses to Afghanistan Invasion', 24 March 1981, RRPL, Executive Secretariat, NSC: Country Files, Box 34, Folder Afghanistan 13/6/81–5/19/81.

28. Robert Lindsey, 'Reagan Urges Bases in Mideast and Missiles for Afghan Rebels', *New York Times*, 10 January 1980, p. B8.

29. See *Rambo III* (1988) and *The Living Daylights* (1987).

30. Study Memorandum, 'Pakistan', 6 March 1981, RRPL, NSC: Records, Near East and South Asian Affairs Directorate, Box 91134, Folder IG on Pakistan, March 6, 1981; NSDD 32, 'US National Security Strategy', 20 May 1982, RRPL, https://www.reaganlibrary.gov/sites/default/files/archives/reference/scanned-nsdds/nsdd32.pdf (accessed 18 June 2019); NSDD 75, 'US Relations with the USSR', 17 January 1983, RRPL, https://www.reaganlibrary.gov/sites/default/files/archives/reference/scanned-nsdds/nsdd75.pdf (accessed 18 June 2019). For more on the negotiations leading to this sale, see Kuperman, 'The Stinger Missile'. For more on the Reagan Doctrine, see James M. Scott, 'Reagan's Doctrine? The Formulation of an American Foreign Policy Strategy', *Presidential Studies Quarterly*, 26/4 (1996), 1047–61.

31. Secretary of State to All Diplomatic Posts, 29 July 1981, RRPL, Executive Secretariat, NSC: Country Files, Box 34, Folder Afghanistan 7/14/81–12/26/81.

32. US Congressional Task Force on Afghanistan, Hearing on Famine, 25 February 1985, DNSA, Afghanistan. I make the same argument as in this section in abbreviated form in Elisabeth Leake, 'The United States and Afghanistan: Ambiguity and Impasse, 1945–2015', in Christopher R. Dietrich (ed.), *A Companion to US Foreign Relations: Colonial Era to the Present*, ii (Hoboken, NJ: Wiley Blackwell, 2020), 1005–26, at 1018.

33. US Embassy, Afghanistan, to State Department, 'Afghan Refugee Situation in Pakistan', 25 August 1979, DNSA, Afghanistan.

34. Secretary of State to Frank Loy, Department of State Briefing Memorandum, 11 January 1980, DNSA, Afghanistan; Helga Baitenmann, 'NGOs and the Afghan War: The Politicisation of Humanitarian Aid', *Third World Quarterly*, 12/1 (1990), 62–85, at 64.

35. Michael Barnett, *Empire of Humanity: A History of Humanitarianism* (Ithaca, NY: Cornell University Press, 2011), 12; Frank Loy to Mr Christopher, 'Assistance to Afghan Refugees in Pakistan', 25 January 1980, DNSA, Afghanistan.

36. Department of State to all Near Eastern and South Asian outposts, 'Presidential Proclamation on Afghanistan Relief Week', 1 July 1980, DNSA, Afghanistan. Carter's Secretary of State had argued: 'The current Congressional perception is that the United States is once again slow to respond to an emerging refugee assistance effort. It also hurts us on the Hill if we are viewed as being too late with our efforts' (Secretary of State to Frank Loy, Department of State briefing memorandum, 11 January 1980, DNSA, Afghanistan). See also Barbara Keys, *Reclaiming American Virtue: The Human Rights Revolution of the 1970s* (Cambridge, MA: Harvard University Press, 2014).

37. US Embassy, Islamabad, to Department of State, 'Afghan Refugee Relief: Transportation Assistance', 19 June 1981, DNSA, Afghanistan; US Ambassador Hummel to Department of State, 'Afghan Refugee Relief', 19 June 1981, DNSA, Afghanistan.

38. Department of State to US Embassy, Islamabad, 'US-Donated Refugee Relief Trucks', 21 November 1983, DNSA, Afghanistan.

39. See Department of State telegram, 'WFP and Afghan Refugees', 8 March 1984, DNSA, Afghanistan.

40. Department of State telegram, 'Afghanistan Relief Committee', 13 October 1980, DNSA, Afghanistan.

41. 'About CIA', Central Intelligence Agency, https://www.cia.gov/about-cia/headquarters-tour/headquarters-photo-tour (accessed 18 May 2018). I expand on many of the arguments made in this section in 'Spooks, Tribes, and Holy Men: The Central Intelligence Agency and the Soviet Invasion of Afghanistan', *Journal of Contemporary History*, 53/1 (2018), 240–62.

42. Kenneth Yates, interviewed by Charles Stuart Kennedy, 20 March 1997, ADST; Nobel Symposium, 'Intervention in Afghanistan', 143–4.

43. Office of Scientific Intelligence, 'Tribalism versus Communism in Afghanistan: The Cultural Roots of Instability (An Intelligence Assessment)', January 1980, CREST, CIA-RDP81B00401R000600170006-5; John Kifner, 'Guerrillas' Request: Guns', *New York Times*, 8 January 1980, p. 1.

44. Office of Scientific Intelligence, 'Tribalism versus Communism'.

45. Southwest Asia Analytic Center, Office of Political Analysis, 'The Soviets and the Tribes of Southwest Asia', 23 September 1980, CREST, CIA-RDP85T00287R000102180001-1; 'Afghanistan Situation Report', 25 November 1986, CREST, CIA-RDP86T01017R000303240001-8. See also 'Afghanistan Situation Report', 9 July 1985, CREST, CIA-RDP85T01058R000406580001-3.

46. NSDD 270, 'Afghanistan', 1 May 1987, RRPL, https://www.reaganlibrary.gov/sites/default/files/archives/reference/scanned-nsdds/nsdd270.pdf (accessed 28 June 2019).

47. Pakistan–Afghanistan–Bangladesh Branch, South Asia Division, Office of Near Eastern and South Asian Analysis, 'Afghanistan: The Politics of the Resistance Movement. An Intelligence Assessment', October 1981, CREST, CIA-RDP06T00412R000200520001-1.

48. Office of Scientific Intelligence, 'Tribalism versus Communism'; 'Afghanistan: Goals and Prospects for the Insurgents', May 1983, CREST, CIA-RDP84S00556R000200080004-3.

49. Office of Near Eastern and South Asian Analysis, 'Islam and Politics: A Compendium', April 1984, CREST, CIA-RDP84S00927R000300110003-7; 'Afghanistan Situation Report', 25 November 1986, CREST, CIA-RDP86T01017R000303240001-8.

50. National Foreign Assessment Center, 'The Resurgence of Islam,' March 1979, JCPL, CREST, NLC-6-52-1-2-5; Office of Political Analysis, 'Resurgent Islamic Nationalism in the Middle East. An Intelligence Assessment', March 1981, CREST, CIA-RDP06T00412R000200170001-0.

51. International Issues Division, Office of Political Analysis, 'Effects of the Southwest Asian Crises on Key Global Issues (An Intelligence Assessment)', May 1980, CREST, CIA-RDP81B00401R000600200004-3.

52. Nobel Symposium, 'Intervention in Afghanistan', 44, 47.

53. Bernard Gwertzman, 'Afghans Put Case before All Forums', *New York Times*, 19 June 1986, p. B8.

54. Howell Raines, 'Reagan Hinting at Arms for Afghan Rebels', *New York Times*, 10 March 1981, p A3.

55. Pakistan-Afghanistan-Bangladesh Branch, 'Afghanistan: The Politics of the Resistance Movement'.

56. 'Afghanistan: Goals and Prospects for the Insurgents', May 1983, CREST, CIA-RDP84S00556R000200080004-3; 'Near East and South Asia Review', 29 March 1985, CREST, CIA-RDP85T01184R000301390002-9; 'Afghanistan Situation Report', 27 November 1984, CREST, CIA-RDP85T00287R00130235001-9.

57. Insurgency Branch, Office of Global Issues, 'Insurgency: 1985 in Review (An Intelligence Assessment)', April 1986, CREST, CIA-RDP97R00694R000600020001-2; Afghanistan Branch, South Asia Division, Office of Near Eastern and South Asian Analysis, 'Afghanistan: Resistance Views of Peace Negotiations', 18 April 1986, CREST, CIA-RDP86T01017R000202240001-0.

58. Sargent, *Superpower Transformed*, 257–60.

59. James F. Dobbins, 'America's Role in Nation-Building: From Germany to Iraq', *Survival*, 45/4 (2003), 87–110, at 88.

# Chapter 7

1.  Ahmed Zeb Khan (ed.), *Nasir Bagh Refugee Camp* (Peshawar: Afghan Refugees Commissionerate, 1981). Other pamphlets in the same 1981 'Afghan Refugees in Pakistan' series included *Gandaf Refugees Camp: The Oldest Camp, Jalozai Refugees Camp, Bara Kai Refugees Camp*, and *Azakhel Refugees Camp*.

2.  Rupert Colville, 'Famous Pakistan Camp Closes as Last Convoy Heads Home', UNHCR, 21 May 2002, https://www.unhcr.org/news/latest/2002/5/3cea5f544/famous-pakistan-camp-closes-convoy-heads-home.html (accessed 11 April 2019).

3.  Susanne Schmeidl, '(Human) Security Dilemmas: Long-Term Implications of the Afghan Refugee Crisis', *Third World Quarterly*, 23/1 (2002), 7–29, at 10.

4.  Pierre Centlivres, 'A State of the Art Review of Research on Internally Displaced, Refugees and Returnees from and in Afghanistan', report prepared for the Planning Committee of the Fourth IRAP Conference on Forced Migration (London: 1994), 37.

5.  William Borders, 'Afghan Refugees Vow to Go Back to Press Fight with Soviet Forces', *New York Times*, 5 January 1980, p. 1.

6.  Centlivres, 'State of the Art Review', 9–10.

7.  For more on this concept, see Liisa H. Malkki, *Purity and Exile: Violence, Memory and National Cosmology among Hutu Refugees in Tanzania* (Chicago: University of Chicago Press, 1995).

8.  See Louis Dupree, 'Settlement and Migration Patterns in Afghanistan: A Tentative Statement', *Modern Asian Studies*, 9/3 (1975), 397–413; Sultan-I-Rome, 'The North-West Frontier Province in the Khilafat and Hijrat Movements', *Islamic Studies*, 43/1 (2004), 51–78.

9.  On waves of Afghan migration, see Mir Hekmatullah Sadat, 'Hyphenating Afghaniyat (Afghanness) in the Afghan Diaspora', *Journal of Muslim Minority Affairs*, 28/3 (2006), 329–42.

10. 'Afghan Refugee Says he Fled from Communism', *New York Times*, 17 February 1980, p. 10; Michael T. Kaufman, 'Afghan Refugees Tell why they Fled Taraki's Regime: One Man's History…', *New York Times*, 15 August 1979, p. A2.

11. Masood Farivar, *Confessions of a Mullah Warrior* (Berkeley: Atlantic Monthly Press, 2009), 57.

12. 'Massacre Described by Afghan Refugees: They Tell of Surviving Army', *New York Times*, 17 February 1980, p. 10; 'The Kerala Massacre', *Washington Post*, 6 February 1980, p. A18; 'Foul Concoction', *Pravda*, 6 February 1980, in *CDSP* 32/5.

13. Thomas Barfield, 'Afghan Customary Law and its Relationship to Formal Judicial Institutions', United States Institute for Peace, June 2003, https://www.usip.org/sites/default/files/file/barfield2.pdf (accessed 8 July 2019).

14. H. C. von Sponeck, Deputy Resident Representative, 'Note for File, Meeting with Mr Amir Usman, Director General (AIT), Ministry of Foreign Affairs, Government of Pakistan, 6 December 1978', UNHCR, Fonds 11, Series 2, Box 153; Government of Pakistan, Economic Affairs, 'Memorandum on Assistance from UNHCR for Afghan Refugees in Pakistan', May 1979, UNHCR, Fonds 11, Series 2, Box 153.

15. Government of Pakistan, 'Memorandum on Assistance'.

16. H. Utkan, 'Assistance to Refugees in Pakistan', 22 June 1979, UNHCR, Fonds 11, Series 2, Box 153.

17. Government of Pakistan, States and Frontier Regions Division, 'Supplementary Memorandum on Assistance from the UNHCR for Afghan Refugees in Pakistan', August 1979, UNHCR, Fonds 11, Series 2, Box 153.

18. Syed Shabbir Hussain, *Afghan Refugees in Pakistan* (Islamabad: Barqsons Printers Limited, *c.*1981), 9; 'Brief of the High Commissioner, UNHCR Operation in Pakistan'; League of Red Cross Societies, 'Pakistan: Afghan Refugees, Appeal', 5 July 1983, UNHCR, Fonds 11, Series 2, Box 764; Centlivres, 'State of the Art Review', 14.

19. Liissa H. Malkki, 'Refugees and Exile: From "Refugee Studies" to the National Order of Things', *Annual Review of Anthropology*, 24 (1995), 495–523, at 501.

20. Randy Lippert, 'Governing Refugees: The Relevance of Governmentality to Understanding the International Refugee Regime', *Alternatives: Global, Local, Political*, 24/3 (1999), 295–328, at 300.

21. See Peter Gatrell, *The Making of the Modern Refugee* (Oxford: Oxford University Press, 2013); also Mira Siegelberg, *Statelessness: A Modern History* (Cambridge, MA: Harvard University Press, 2020).

22. See Glen Peterson, 'Sovereignty, International Law, and the Uneven Development of the International Refugee Regime', *Modern Asian Studies*, 49/2 (2015), 439–68.

23. Gil Loescher, *The UNHCR and World Politics: A Perilous Path* (Oxford: Oxford University Press, 2001), ch. 4.

24. Michael Barnett, *Empire of Humanity: A History of Humanitarianism* (Ithaca, NY: Cornell University Press, 2011), 140.

25. Cited in Loescher, *UNHCR and World Politics*, 91.

26. Ibid.

27. Cited in Lippert, 'Governing Refugees', 306.

28. Lippert, 'Governing Refugees', 305, 309. On ways that refugees could undermine camp governmentality, see Carolina Moulin and Peter Nyers, '"We Live in a Country of UNHCR"—Refugee Protests and Global Political Society', *International Political Sociology*, 1 (2007): 356–72.

29. See Loescher, *UNHCR and World Politics*, 155–60; also Pia Oberoi, *Exile and Belonging: Refugees and State Policy in South Asia* (New Delhi: Oxford University Press, 2006), ch. 5.

30. Rüdiger Schoch, 'Afghan Refugees in Pakistan during the 1980s: Cold War Politics and Registration Practice', New Issues in Refugee Research, UNHCR (June 2008), 5. See also Sarah Kenyon Lischer, *Dangerous Sanctuaries: Refugee Camps, Civil Wars, and the Dilemmas of Humanitarian Aid* (Ithaca, NY: Cornell University Press, 2006), ch. 3; Gatrell, *Making of the Modern Refugee*, 255–9.

31. H. Utkan, 'Assistance to Refugees in Pakistan', 22 June 1979, UNHCR, Fonds 11, Series 2, Box 153.

32. 'Assistance to Afghan Refugees in Pakistan', n.d., UNHCR, Fonds 11, Series 2, Box 153.

33. See Rüdiger Schoch, 'UNHCR and the Afghan Refugees in the Early 1980s: Between Humanitarian Action and Cold War Politics', *Refugee Survey Quarterly*, 27/1 (2008), 45–57, at 50–1.

34. UNHCR officials made direct comparisons between the two communities. See 'Brief of the High Commissioner, UNHCR Operation in Pakistan', n.d., UNHCR, Fonds 13, Sub-fonds 2, Series 2, Box 39. Palestinian refugees have been a major focus of academic work, though some scholars have pointed to their absence from refugee studies (see Khaled Furani and Dan Rabinowitz, 'The Ethnographic Arriving of Palestine', *Annual Review of Anthropology*, 40 (2011), 475–91). Work that does reflect on Palestinian refugees includes the special issue of *Refugee Survey Quarterly*, 'UNRWA and the Palestinian Refugees 60 Years Later', 28/2–3 (2009); Robert Bowker, *Palestinian Refugees: Mythology, Identity, and*

*the Search for Peace* (Boulder, CO: Lynne Rienner, 2003); Ilana Feldman, 'The Humanitarian Condition: Palestinian Refugees and the Politics of Living', *Humanity: An International Journal of Human Rights, Humanitarianism, and Development*, 3/2 (2012), 155–72; Rosemary Sayigh, 'Sources of Palestinian Nationalism: A Study of a Palestinian Camp in Lebanon', *Journal of Palestine Studies*, 6/4 (1977), 17–40; as well as other articles in the *Journal of Palestine Studies*.

35. Brief of the High Commissioner, 'UNHCR Operation in Pakistan', n.d., UNHCR, Fonds 13, Sub-fonds 2, Series 2, Box 39.

36. Aide-Memoire, 'Humanitarian Assistance to Refugees in Pakistan', n.d., UNHCR, Fonds 13, Sub-fonds 2, Series 2, Box 39.

37. 'Church Unit Airlifts Supplies to Afghanistan Refugees', *Washington Post*, 20 January 1980, p. D36.

38. 'Pakistan's Afghan Refugees Get Some Useless Aid: Energies into Wrong Channels', *New York Times*, 26 October 1980, p. 8.

39. Joel Glasman, 'Seeing like a Refugee Agency: A Short History of UNHCR Classifications in Central Africa (1961–2015)', *Journal of Refugee Studies*, 30/2 (2017), 337–62, at 340.

40. Hussain, *Afghan Refugees in Pakistan*, 9.

41. Copy of a Pass Book, n.d., UNHCR, Fonds 13, Sub-fonds 2, Series 2, Box 39.

42. N. de Keller, 'Note for the File: Re-Registration of Afghan Refugees in Pakistan', 7 September 1981, UNHCR, Fonds 13, Sub-fonds 2, Series 2, Box 39.

43. Ibid.

44. Brief of the High Commissioner, 'Protection Issues in Pakistan', n.d., UNHCR, Fonds 13, Sub-fonds 2, Series 2, Box 39.

45. Hussain, *Afghan Refugees in Pakistan*; 'Brief of the High Commissioner, UNHCR Operation in Pakistan'.

46. Hussain, *Afghan Refugees in Pakistan*.

47. League of Red Cross and Red Crescent Societies, 'Pakistan: Afghan Refugees, Situation Report', 23 July 1984, UNHCR, Fonds 11, Series 2, Box 764.

48. Khan, *Nasir Bagh Refugee Camp*.

49. See Kerry M. Connor, 'Skill Inventory of Afghan Women Refugees in the North West Frontier and Baluchistan Provinces', report for UNICEF, 20 December 1988.

50. 'Inter-Agency Mission Report', n.d., UNHCR, Fonds 11, Series 2, Box 153.

51. 'A Summary of the Main Points Made by Michael Day-Thompson during the De-Briefing at Centre William Frappard on 15th July, 1981', n.d., UNHCR, Fonds 13, Sub-fonds 2, Series 2, Box 39.

52. See Barnett, *Empire of Humanity*; Neta C. Crawford, *Argument and Change in World Politics: Ethics, Decolonization, and Humanitarian Intervention* (Cambridge: Cambridge University Press, 2004).

53. International Labour Organization, UNHCR, *Tradition and Dynamism among Afghan Refugees* (Geneva, 1983).

54. Ayesha Khan, 'Afghan Refugee Women's Experience of Conflict and Disintegration', *Meridians*, 3/1 (2002), 89–121, at 96.

55. David B. Edwards, 'Marginality and Migration: Cultural Dimensions of the Afghan Refugee Problem', *International Migration Review*, 20/2 (1986), 313–25, at 319.

56. 'Mission Report, Pakistan (6–12 June 1981)', n.d., UNHCR, Fonds 13, Sub-fonds 2, Series 2, Box 39.

57. Surriya Kasi, 'Visit with Sociologist to Chagai District 3.9.1982–18.6.1982', n.d., UNHCR, Fonds 11, Series 2, Box 154.

58. See Pierre Centlivres and Micheline Centlivres-Demont, 'The Afghan Refugees in Pakistan: A Nation in Exile', *Current Sociology*, 36/2 (1988), 71–92, at 86–7; Louis Dupree, 'Cultural Changes and the Mujahidin and Muhajerin', in Bo Huldt and Erland Jansson (eds), *The Tragedy of Afghanistan: The Social, Cultural and Political Impact of the Soviet Invasion* (New York: Croom Helm, 1988), 20–37, at 33.

59. See Christian A. Williams, *National Liberation in Postcolonial Southern Africa: A Historical Ethnography of SWAPO's Exile Camps* (Cambridge: Cambridge University Press, 2015).

60. Centlivres, 'State of the Art Review', 28.

61. M. Yaqub Roshan, Islamic Unity of Afghanistan Mujahideen, to UNHCR, 15 October 1983, UNHCR, Fonds 11, Series 2, Box 154.

62. Nancy Hatch Dupree, 'The Afghan Refugee Family Abroad: A Focus on Pakistan', *Afghanistan Studies Journal*, 1 (1988), 29–47, at 41. The UNHCR was troubled by the fact that the political parties were clearly taking advantage of the refugee camps for blatantly political recruitment purposes. As one official stressed: 'UNHCR aid cannot be seen as supporting active combatants in a resistance movement in a neighbouring country' (T. J. Barnes to G. Walzer, 'Distancing Refugees from the Border', 29 February 1984, UNHCR, Fonds 11, Series 2, Box 154). But the UNHCR's choices were limited. By the mid-1980s, NGO officials were firmly entrenched in Pakistan and had their hands full with a refugee crisis that refused to die down. Moreover, the UNHCR remained at the mercy of the government of Pakistan, which could always decide to eject UNHCR officials, even though they were desperately needed. Thus, despite UNHCR disquiet, the refugee camps became a hub of activity for the resistance.

63. Letters from Afghan Refugees, 28 January 1983, UNHCR, Fonds 11, Series 2, Box 154.

64. Ibid.

65. Edwards, 'Marginality and Migration', 316.

66. Centlivres, 'State of the Art Review', 16.

67. See UNHCR, Fonds 11, Series 2, Box 104; Fariba Adelkhah and Zuzanna Olszewska, 'The Iranian Afghans', *Iranian Studies*, 40/2 (2007), 137–65; Alessandro Monsutti, 'Migration as a Rite of Passage: Young Afghans Building Masculinity and Adulthood in Iran', *Iranian Studies*, 40/2 (2007), 167–85.

68. William Branigin, 'Afghan Refugees Stay Close to Border: They Ask for Weapons to Carry…', *Washington Post*, 30 January 1980, p. A20.

69. Pierre Centlivres and Micheline Centlivres-Demont, 'The Afghan Refugee in Pakistan: An Ambiguous Identity', *Journal of Refugee Studies*, 1/2 (1988), 141–52, at 145. See also Pierre Centlivres, 'Les Trois Poles de l'identité Afghane au Pakistan', *L'Homme*, 108 (1988), 134–46.

70. Edwards, 'Marginality and Migration', 316.

71. Vladimir Hamed-Troyansky, 'Circassian Refugees and the Making of Amman, 1878–1914', *International Journal of Middle East Studies*, 49/4 (2017), 605–23; Sarah Ansari, 'Partition, Migration and Refugees: Responses to the Arrival of *Muhajirs* in Sind during 1947–48', *South Asia: Journal of South Asian Studies*, 18, special issue (1995), 95–108.

72. Copy of a Pass Book, n.d., UNHCR, Fonds 13, Sub-fonds 2, Series 2, Box 39.

73. Centlivres and Centlivres-Demont, 'Afghan Refugee in Pakistan', 143–4.

74. Hussain, *Afghan Refugees in Pakistan*.

75. F. D'Souza, cited in Centlivres and Centlivres-Demont, 'Afghan Refugee in Pakistan', 144.

76. Juliene G. Lipson, 'Afghan Refugees in California: Mental Health Issues', *Issues in Mental Health Nursing*, 14/4 (1993), 411–23, at 417.

77. Ibid. 417.

78. Ibid. 418.

79. Centlivres, 'State of the Art Review', 24, 26.

80. Shirin Persson, 'A Case Study of Selected Afghan Refugee Camps in the North West Frontier Province, Pakistan', report prepared for Rädda Barnen (Save the Children Sweden) (April 1994), 1.

81. International Labour Organization, *Tradition and Dynamism*, 159.

82. Khan, 'Afghan Refugee Women's Experience', 97.

83. See Connor, 'Skill Inventory of Afghan Women Refugees in the North West Frontier and Baluchistan Provinces'.

84. Anne E. Brodsky, *With All Our Strength: The Revolutionary Association of the Women of Afghanistan* (New York: Routledge, 2004), esp. ch. 3.

85. Cited in ibid. 98.

86. Dupree, 'Afghan Refugee Family', 32; Centlivres and Centlivres-Demont, 'Afghan Refugees in Pakistan', 80.

87. Dupree, 'Afghan Refugee Family', 38. On Afghan women's experiences, see also Nancy Hatch Dupree, 'Women in Afghanistan: A Preliminary Needs Assessment', UNIFEM occasional paper no. 9 (1989); Nancy Hatch Dupree, 'The Role of Afghan Women after Repatriation', paper presented at conference sponsored by Afghanistan–Nothilfe E.V. (1988).

88. Khan, 'Afghan Refugee Women's Experience', 99.

89. Ibid. 102.

90. Said Bahodine Majrouh (ed.), *Songs of Love and War: Afghan Women's Poetry* (New York: Other Press, 2003 translation), 43, 49.

91. Elaheh Rostami-Povey, 'Gender, Agency and Identity: The Case of Afghan Women in Afghanistan, Pakistan and Iran', *Journal of Development Studies*, 43/2 (2007), 294–311, at 301.

92. Jill Rosenthal, 'From "Migrants" to "Refugees": Identity, Aid, and Decolonization in Ngara District, Tanzania', *Journal of African History*, 56 (2015), 261–79, at 267.

## Chapter 8

1. First plenary meeting, 3.45 p.m., 10 January 1980, UN General Assembly Sixth Emergency Special Session Official Records; Second plenary meeting, 10.55 a.m., 11 January 1980, UN General Assembly Sixth Emergency Special Session Official Records; Third plenary meeting, 3.30 p.m., 11 January 1980, UN General Assembly Sixth Emergency Special Session Official Records; Fourth plenary meeting, 11.05 a.m., 12 January 1980, UN General Assembly Sixth Emergency Special Session Official Records; Fifth plenary meeting, 3.20 p.m., 12 January 1980, UN General Assembly Sixth Emergency Special Session Official Records; ES-6/2, 'The Situation in Afghanistan and its Implications for International Peace and Security', UN General Assembly Sixth Emergency Resolutions.

2. For more on the League of Nations, see Susan Pedersen, 'Back to the League of Nations', *American Historical Review*, 112/4 (2007), 1091–117.

3. Third plenary meeting, 3.30 p.m., 11 January 1980, UN General Assembly Sixth Emergency Special Session Official Records.

4. Elisabeth Leake, 'Afghan Internationalism and the Question of Afghanistan's Political Legitimacy', *Afghanistan*, 1/1 (2018), 68–94.

5. Nur Mohammad Taraki to Kurt Waldheim (Unofficial Translation), June 1978, UN ARMS, S-0904-72-10.

6. United Nations Charter: Preamble, Purposes and Principles, 26 June 1945, http://www.un-documents.net/ch-ppp.htm (accessed 25 July 2019).

7. Mark Mazower, *No Enchanted Palace: The End of Empire and the Ideological Origins of the United Nations* (Princeton: Princeton University Press, 2009). On the League of Nations precedents for the UN, see Susan Pedersen, *The Guardians: The League of Nations and the Crisis of Empire* (Oxford: Oxford University Press, 2015).

8. David L. Bosco, *Five to Rule Them All: The UN Security Council and the Making of the Modern World* (New York: Oxford University Press, 2009); Matthew Connelly, 'Taking Off the Cold War Lens: Visions of North–South Conflict during the Algerian War for Independence', *American Historical Review*, 105/3 (2000), 739–69, at 756. See also Alanna O'Malley, *The Diplomacy of Decolonisation: America, Britain and the United Nations during the Congo Crisis 1960–64* (Manchester: Manchester University Press, 2018).

9. See Christopher J. Lee (ed.), *Making a World after Empire: The Bandung Moment and its Political Afterlives* (Athens, OH: Ohio University Press, 2010); Vijay Prashad, *The Darker Nations: A People's History of the Third World* (New York: New Press, 2007); Nataša Mišković, Harald Fischer-Tiné, and Nada Boškovska (eds), *The Non-Aligned Movement and the Cold War: Delhi—Bandung—Belgrade* (New York: Routledge, 2014).

10. Histories of the UN and its relationship with rights, race, and the nation state have grown extensively in recent years. See, e.g., Adom Getachew, *Worldmaking after Empire: The Rise and Fall of Self-Determination* (Princeton: Princeton University Press, 2019), esp. ch. 3; Carole Anderson, *Eyes off the Price: The United Nations and the African American Struggle for Human Rights, 1944–1955* (Cambridge: Cambridge University Press, 2003); also Sunil Amrith and Glenda Sluga, 'New Histories of the United Nations', *Journal of World History*, 19/3 (2008), 251–74; Eva-Maria Muschik, 'Managing the World: The United Nations, Decolonization, and the Strange Triumph of State Sovereignty in the 1950s and 1960s', *Journal of Global History*, 13/1 (2018), 121–44; John D. Kelly and Martha Kaplan, 'My Ambition is Much Higher than Independence: US Power, the UN World, the Nation-State, and their Critics', in Prasenjit Duara (ed.), *Decolonization: Perspectives Now and Then* (London: Routledge, 2003), 131–51; Lydia Walker, 'Decolonization in the 1960s: On Legitimate and Illegitimate Nationalist Claims-Making', *Past and Present*, 242 (2019), 227–64; Emma Kluge, 'West Papua and the International History of Decolonization, 1961–69', *International History Review*, 42/6 (2020), 1155–72.

11. 'Declaration on the Granting of Independence to Colonial Countries and Peoples', UN General Assembly, 94th plenary meeting, 14 December 1960.

12. Jeffrey James Byrne, *Mecca of Revolution: Algeria, Decolonization and the Third World Order* (New York: Oxford University Press, 2016), 175.

13. Nur Mohammad Taraki to Kurt Waldheim.

14. Kurt Waldheim to Nur Mohammad Taraki, 12 June 1978, UN ARMS, S-0904-72-10.

15. Bismellah Sahak to Kurt Waldheim, 'Policy Statement of the Democratic Republic of Afghanistan', 10 January 1980, UN ARMS, S-0442-0330-7.

16. 'Cable to the Soviet Representative at the UN on the Development of the Situation in Afghanistan', 27 December 1979, from Boris Gromov, *Ogranichennyy Kontingent* (Moscow: Progress, 1994), CWIHP.

17. Susan Pedersen, 'Getting out of Iraq—in 1932: The League of Nations and the Road to Normative Statehood', *American Historical Review*, 115/4 (2010), 975–1000.

18. Andras Nagy, 'Shattered Hopes amid Violent Repression: The Hungarian Revolution and the United Nations (Part 1)', *Journal of Cold War Studies*, 19/4 (2017), 42–73, at 55.

19. O'Malley, *Diplomacy of Decolonization*; Alessandro Iandolo, 'Imbalance of Power: The Soviet Union and the Congo Crisis, 1960–1961', *Journal of Cold War Studies*, 16/2 (2014), 32–55; Alexandra Novosseloff, 'United Nations Interim Force in Lebanon (UNIFIL I)', in Joachim A. Koops et al., *The Oxford Handbook of United Nations Peacekeeping Operations* (Oxford: Oxford University Press, 2015), 248–56; see also UNGA resolutions A/RES/31/61, A/RES/37/123 A-F, and A/RES/37/123E.

20. Statement of the Government of the People's Republic of China, 30 December 1979, UN ARMS, S-0442-0330-7; First plenary meeting, 3.45 p.m., 10 January 1980, UN General Assembly Sixth Emergency Special Session Official Records; Daniel J. Sargent, *A Superpower Transformed: The Remaking of American Foreign Relations in the 1970s* (New York: Oxford University Press, 2015), 271.

21. 'Iran Protests Soviet Intervention in Afghanistan', undated, UN ARMS, S-0904-1-4.

22. UN Security Council Resolution 462, 'International Peace and Security', 9 January 1980, http://unscr.com/en/resolutions/doc/462 (accessed 24 July 2019).

23. 'Resolutions and Decisions Adopted by the General Assembly during Its Sixth Emergency Special Session, 10-14 January 1980', Official Records: Sixth Emergency Special Session Supplement no. 1 (A/ES-6/7), June 1980, UN ARMS, S-0904-89-5.

24. For an overview of UN activities, see Eva-Maria Muschik, 'Introduction: Towards a Global History in International Organizations and Decolonization' (forthcoming); also Amy L. Sayward, *The United Nations in International History* (London: Bloomsbury Academic, 2017); Paul Kennedy, *The Parliament of Man: The United Nations and the Quest for World Government* (London: Allen Lane, 2006).

25. Niaz A. Naik to Kurt Waldheim, 'Final Declaration of the Extraordinary Session of the Islamic Conference of Foreign Ministers, Islamabad—Pakistan', 11 February 1980, UN ARMS, S-0442-0330-7.

26. Cited in M. S. Rajan, 'The Non-Aligned Movement: The New Delhi Conference and After', *Southeast Asian Affairs* (1982), 60–72, at 63–4.

27. 'Soviet Briefing on the Need to Counter-Balance Yugoslav Endeavors Concerning the Afghan Question in the Non-Aligned Countries', 1980, National Archives of Hungary, M-KS 288 f. 11, CWIHP; Yasmin Qureshi, 'Non-Aligned Foreign Ministers' Conference: Delhi 1981', *Pakistan Horizon*, 34/2 (1981), 78–101; Lorenz M. Lüthi, *Cold Wars: Asia, the Middle East, Europe* (Cambridge: Cambridge University Press, 2020), 531–5, 535.

28. Department of Political and Security Council Affairs, Political Affairs Division, 'The European Community's Initiative on Afghanistan', 9 July 1981, UN ARMS, S-1067-1-6.

29. Note for the File, 1 December 1980, UN ARMS, S-0904-89-5; UNGA Resolution 35/37, 'The Situation in Afghanistan and Its Implications for International Peace and Security', 20 November 1980; 'Statement by His Excellency Mr Agha Shahi, Minister for Foreign Affairs of the Islamic Republic of Pakistan, on Agenda Item 116: The Situation in Afghanistan and its Implications for International Peace and Security in the Plenary

Meeting of the General Assembly on November 17, 1980', 17 November 1980, UN ARMS, S-0904-1-5.

30. Manuel Frohlich and Abiodun Williams, *The UN Secretary-General and the Security Council: A Dynamic Relationship* (Oxford: Oxford University Press, 2018), 117.

31. M. Farid Zarif to Kurt Waldheim, 'Statement of the Government of the Democratic Republic of Afghanistan', 15 May 1980, UN ARMS, S-0442-0330-7.

32. 'Statement by His Excellency Mr Agha Shahi, Minister for Foreign Affairs of the Islamic Republic of Pakistan, on Agenda Item 116'.

33. Ibid.

34. Press Briefing by Foreign Minister of Afghanistan, 21 November 1980, UN ARMS, S-1067-1-4.

35. Summary Notes on the Secretary-General's Meeting with the President of Pakistan, 2 February 1981, UN ARMS, S-1067-1-3; Note for the Secretary-General, 16 January 1981, UN ARMS, S-1067-1-1; Notes on the Meeting with the Chargé d'Affaires of the Permanent Mission of Iran, 24 March 1981, UN ARMS, S-1067-1-3; 'Notes on Meeting with the Representative of the United States, Held at UN Headquarters on 13 January 1981 at 11.00 Hours', 15 January 1981, UN ARMS, S-0904-89-5.

36. Note for the Secretary-General, 16 January 1981.

37. Notes on a Meeting with the Secretary-General and Foreign Minister of Afghanistan, 11 February 1981, UN ARMS, S-1067-1-3.

38. 'Dispute on Afghanistan', *Washington Post*, 7 January 1981, p. A20.

39. Artemy M. Kalinovsky, *A Long Goodbye: The Soviet Withdrawal from Afghanistan* (Cambridge, MA: Harvard University Press, 2011), 67–9.

40. 'Afghanistan File, GP/NI', undated, UN ARMS, S-1067-1-1; Telegram from the Department of State to the Mission to the United Nations, 8 December 1980, in David Zierler (ed.), *FRUS, 1977–1980*, 12 (Washington: USGPO, 2018), no. 337; 'Memorandum of Conversation', 4 October 1982, in James Graham Wilson (ed.), *FRUS, 1981–1988*, 3 (Washington: USGPO, 2016), no. 221.

41. Notes on the Meeting with the Chargé d'Affaires of the Permanent Mission of Iran, 24 March 1981, UN ARMS, S-1067-1-3.

42. Notes on the Secretary-General's Meeting with the Foreign Minister of Afghanistan, 26 September 1981, UN ARMS, S-1067-1-3.

43. Frohlich and Williams, *The UN Secretary-General*, 131–2.

44. William Neuman, 'Diego Cordovez, U.N. Envoy and Conflict Mediator, Dies at 78', *New York Times*, 29 May 2014, https://www.nytimes.com/2014/05/30/world/americas/diego-cordovez-envoy-and-conflict-mediator-dies-at-78.html (accessed 12 June 2018).

45. Ibid.

46. Diego Cordovez and Selig S. Harrison, *Out of Afghanistan: The Inside Story of the Soviet Withdrawal* (New York: Oxford University Press, 1995), 84.

47. Kalinovsky, *Long Goodbye*, 108.

48. Informal and Unofficial Background Note, 'The Geneva Negotiations on the Situation Relating to Afghanistan', undated, UN ARMS, S-1024-2-3.

49. Artemy M. Kalinovsky, 'Decision-Making and the Soviet War in Afghanistan: From Intervention to Withdrawal', *Journal of Cold War Studies*, 11/4 (2009), 46–73, at 60–2; Ronald Reagan, 'Address to the 40th Session of the United Nations General Assembly in New York, New York', 24 October 1985, https://www.reaganlibrary.gov/research/

speeches/102485a (accessed 14 April 2020); Shevardnadze, cited in Artemy M. Kalinovsky, 'Old Politics, New Diplomacy: The Geneva Accords and the Soviet Withdrawal from Afghanistan', *Cold War History*, 8/3 (2008), 381–404, at 387.

50. Ayesha Jalal, *The Struggle for Pakistan: A Muslim Homeland and Global Politics* (Cambridge, MA: Belknap Press of Harvard University Press, 2014), 244–58.

51. M. Farid Zarif to Javier Perez de Cuellar, 6 September 1984, UN ARMS, S-1024-2-6.

52. M. Farid Zarif to Kurt Waldheim, 'The Acts of Aerial Aggression and Other Intrusions of Pakistan into the Territory of the Democratic Republic of Afghanistan', 17 November 1980, UN ARMS, S-0904-1-5; Sahabzada Yaqub Khan to Javier Perez de Cuellar, 23 August 1984, UN ARMS, S-1024-74-5; S. Shah Nawaz to Javier Perez de Cuellar, 12 December 1984, UN ARMS, S-1024-2-1; M. Farid Zarif to Javier Perez de Cuellar, 6 September 1984, UN ARMS, S-1024-2-6.

53. M. Farid Zarif to Javier Perez de Cuellar, 13 October 1983, UN ARMS, S-1024-2-1.

54. Mohammad Nasser Mian to Javier Perez de Cuellar, 21 May 1987, UN ARMS, S-1024-2-2.

55. Sahabzada Yaqub Khan to Javier Perez de Cuellar, 23 August 1984.

56. Excerpts from the comments of the Prime Minister of Pakistan on 26 and 27 February 1987, sent by Aneesuddin Ahmed to Javier Perez de Cuellar, 2 March 1987, UN ARMS, S-1024-2-2.

57. 'Bilateral Agreement between the Republic of Afghanistan and the Islamic Republic of Pakistan on the Principles of Mutual Relations, in Particular on Non-Interference and Non-Intervention', 14 April 1988, UN ARMS, S-1024-2-3.

58. Notes on the Meeting with the Foreign Minister of Pakistan, 29 April 1981, UN ARMS, S-1067-1-3.

59. Bismellah Sahak to Kurt Waldheim, 'Policy Statement of the Democratic Republic of Afghanistan'.

60. Bismellah Sahak to Kurt Waldheim, 'Statement of the Government of the Democratic Republic of Afghanistan on the so-Called Afghan Refugees Problem', 24 March 1980, UN ARMS, S-0904-1-6.

61. Ibid.

62. Bismellah Sahak to Waldheim, 'Policy Statement of the Democratic Republic of Afghanistan'.

63. Notes on the Meeting with the Permanent Representative of Afghanistan, 30 September 1981, UN ARMS, S-1067-1-3.

64. Permanent Representative of Afghanistan to the UN to President of General Assembly, 'The Situation in Afghanistan and its Implications for International Peace and Security', 7 December 1983, UN ARMS, S-1043-12-1.

65. Ibid.

66. Notes on the Secretary-General's Meeting with the Foreign Minister of Afghanistan, 26 September 1981, UN ARMS, S-1067-1-3.

67. Shah Mohammad Dost to Kurt Waldheim, 24 February 1980, UN ARMS, S-0904-1-6.

68. See Note on the Meeting with the President of the Revolutionary Council of Afghanistan, 16 April 1981, UN ARMS, S-1067-1-3; M. Farid Zarif to Kurt Waldheim, 12 November 1981, UN ARMS, S-0904-1-4.

69. Notes on the Secretary-General's Meeting with the Minister for Foreign Affairs of Afghanistan, 23 November 1983, JPCP, Box 8, Folder 88.

70. M. Farid Zarif to Javier Perez de Cuellar, 8 February 1982, UN ARMS, S-1024-99-1; S. Shah Nawaz to Javier Perez de Cuellar, 3 September 1982, UN ARMS, S-0442-0331-2.

71. Abdul Wakil to Javier Perez de Cuellar (via Shah Mohammad Dost), 2 February 1987, UN ARMS, S-1024-2-2; Aneesuddin Ahmed to Javier Perez de Cuellar, 2 March 1987; Abdul Wakil to Javier Perez de Cuellar (via Shah Mohammad Dost), 26 March 1987, UN ARMS, S-1024-2-2.

72. Sahak to Waldheim, 'Statement of the Government of the Democratic Republic of Afghanistan on the so-Called Afghan Refugees Problem'.

73. Notes on a Meeting with the Foreign Minister of Afghanistan, 29 September 1981, UN ARMS, S-1067-1-3.

74. M. Farid Zarif to Javier Perez de Cuellar, 'Declaration on National Reconciliation', 6 January 1987, UN ARMS, S-1024-3-3.

75. 'Record Note on Meeting of the Secretary-General and Mr Palme with the Foreign Minister of Iran', 30 September 1983, JPCP, Box 5, Folder 63.

76. 'Bilateral Agreement between the Republic of Afghanistan and the Islamic Republic of Pakistan on the Voluntary Return of Refugees', 14 April 1988, UN ARMS, S-1024-2-3.

77. 'Statement Made by Under-Secretary-General Diego Cordovez at the Conclusion of the Negotiations on the Situation Relating to Afghanistan', 8 April 1988, UN ARMS, S-1024-2-3.

78. See 'Implementation of the Agreements on the Settlement of the Situation Relating to Afghanistan: Progress Report by the Representative of the Secretary-General', 26 July 1988, UN ARMS, S-1024-2-4.

79. 'President Reagan, Apr. 11, 1988', Department of State *Bulletin* (June 1988), 54.

80. 'Record of a Conversation of M. S. Gorbachev with President of Afghanistan, General Secretary of the CC PDPA Najibullah, Tashkent', 7 April 1988, Gorbachev Foundation, CWIHP.

81. 'Conversation between M. S. Gorbachev and Ronald Reagan on Afghanistan (Excerpt)', 10 December 1987, Gorbachev Foundation, CWIHP; J. P. Kavanagh, 'Note to File', 25 March 1988, UN ARMS, S-1024-2-3; 'Testimony for Michael Armacost before the Senate Foreign Relations Committee', 23 June 1988, RRPL, Shirin Tahir-Kheli Files, Box 91911, Chronology June–December 1988 [6/1/1988–6/28/1988]; 'Secretary Shultz, Geneva, Apr. 14, 1988', Department of State *Bulletin* (June 1988), 55; 'Record of a Conversation of M. S. Gorbachev with President of Afghanistan, General Secretary of the CC PDPA Najibullah', 13 June 1988, Gorbachev Foundation, CWIHP.

82. Shah Mohammad Dost to Javier Perez de Cuellar, 'Statement of Mr Abdul Wakil, Minister of Foreign Affairs of Afghanistan, to the Joint Session of the Afghan Parliament on 27 June 1988', 7 July 1988, UN ARMS, S-1024-2-4.

83  S. Shah Nawaz to Javier Perez de Cuellar, 25 May 1988, UN ARMS, S-1024-2-4.

84. Memorandum of Conversation, 9 December 1987, in *FRUS, 1981–1988*, 6, no. 111; Memorandum of Conversation, 21 March 1988, in ibid. 6/32; Memorandum of Conversation, 21 April 1988, in ibid. 6/145; Memorandum of Conversation, 1 June 1988, in ibid. 6/162; Press Briefing by Under-Secretary-General Cordovez, 18 January 1988, UN ARMS, S-1024-2-3.

85. Shah Mohammad Dost to Javier Perez de Cuellar, 'Statement by Najibullah, President of the Republic of Afghanistan, February 8, 1988', 10 February 1988, UN ARMS, S-1024-2-3.

86. The United States similarly did not push for resistance member participation. This undoubtedly resulted in part from the Carter and Reagan administrations' ambivalence towards the Afghan resistance, but also in part because the US had refused to back a UN resolution in the 1970s that recognized the Palestine Liberation Organization (PLO) as the official representatives of a state of Palestine. Support for an Afghan resistance party to represent the Afghan state at the UN would have followed a similar rationale, and thus was deemed impossible (see Paul Chamberlin, 'The Struggle against Oppression Everywhere: The Global Politics of Palestinian Liberation', *Middle Eastern Studies*, 47/1 (2011), 25–41). The Soviets also tried to use the US position on the PLO to point out the shortcomings of UN-led talks on Afghanistan. Early on, one Soviet official noted that 'UN resolutions are not always appropriate bases for negotiations, and the US implicitly recognized this when it refused to implement the UNGA resolution on the recognition of the PLO as the exclusive representative of the Palestinian people' ('Telegram from the Department of State to Secretary of State Haig's Delegation', 5 May 1981, in *FRUS 1981–1988*, 3, no. 49).

87. Notes on the Secretary-General's Meeting with the Permanent Representative of the USSR, 23 December 1988, JPCP, Box 10, Folder 103.

88. Editorial, 'Cordovez's Proposal Seems Impractical', *AFGHANews* 4/15 (1 August 1988), 4.

89. Getachew, *Worldmaking After Empire*, 74. See Lydia Walker, *States-in-Waiting: Twentieth-Century Decolonization and Its Discontents* (forthcoming).

90. Mohammad Ja'afar Mahallati to Javier Perez de Cuellar, 13 April 1988, JPCP, Box 8, Folder 88; Final Communiqué of the 17th Islamic Conference of Foreign Ministers (21–25 March 1988), 3 September 1988, https://www.oic-oci.org/docdown/?docID=4346&refID=1220 (accessed 14 April 2020).

# Chapter 9

1. UNHCR Background Report 'Nangarhar Province', 1 September 1989 (Data Collection for Afghan Repatriation Project). By September 1989, UNHCR Background Reports had been completed for Baghlan, Farah, Ghazni, Helmand, Herat, Kandahar, Laghman, Logar, Nangarhar, Nimroz, Paktia, Paktika, and Zabul provinces.

2. A. Bovin, 'Afghanistan: The Counterrevolution Resists', *Izvestia*, 14 July 1988, p. 5, *CDSP* 4/28, 10 August 1988.

3. Barnett Rubin, 'Post-Cold War State Disintegration: The Failure of International Conflict Resolution in Afghanistan', *Journal of International Affairs*, 46/2 (1993), 469–92, at 479–80; 'Note on the Meeting with the Secretary-General and the President of the Republic of Afghanistan', 4 September 1990, JPCP, Box 8, Folder 88.

4. Barnet Rubin, *The Fragmentation of Afghanistan* (1995; New Haven: Yale University Press, 2002), 250–1.

5. Theodore L. Eliot, Jr, 'Afghanistan in 1989: Stalemate', *Asian Survey*, 30/2 (1990), 158–66, at 159.

6. Barnett Rubin, *The Search for Peace in Afghanistan* (New Haven: Yale University Press, 1995), 118–19. See also Olivier Roy, 'Afghanistan: Back to Tribalism or on to Lebanon?', *Third World Quarterly*, 11/4 (1989), 70–82; Olivier Roy, 'Afghanistan: Le retour des vieux demons', *Esprit*, 10/155 (1989), 108–14; Nazif M. Shahrani, 'War, Factionalism, and the State in Afghanistan', *American Anthropologist*, 104/3 (2002), 715–22.

7. Rubin, *Fragmentation of Afghanistan*, 252–5; Rubin, *Search for Peace*, 113.

8. Larry P. Goodson, *Afghanistan's Endless War: State Failure, Regional Politics, and the Rise of the Taliban* (Seattle: University of Washington Press, 2001), 70–3.

9. Richard P. Cronin, 'Afghanistan in 1988: Year of Decision', *Asian Survey*, 29/2 (1989), 207–15, at 211.

10. Eliot, 'Afghanistan in 1989', 164; Rubin, 'Post-Cold War State Disintegration', 481.

11. Vladislav M. Zubok, *A Failed Empire: The Soviet Union in the Cold War* (Chapel Hill: University of North Carolina Press, 2007), ch. 10.

12. See Jeffrey A. Engel (ed.), *Into the Desert: Reflections on the Gulf War* (New York: Oxford University Press, 2013); Jeffrey A. Engel, *When the World Seemed New: George H. W. Bush and the End of the Cold War* (New York: Houghton Mifflin Harcourt, 2017).

13. Notes on Mr Picco's Meeting with the Staff in Charge of Afghanistan at the State Department, 6 October 1989, UN ARMS, S-1024-3-4.

14. Unsigned, 'The Secretary-General's Initiative in Afghanistan', undated, JPCP, Box 8, Folder 88.

15. Rubin, 'Post-Cold War State Disintegration', 482–4; Javier Perez de Cuellar, 'Statement by the Secretary-General on Afghanistan', undated, JPCP, Box 8, Folder 88.

16. Rubin, *Search for Peace*, 127.

17. Cited in Rubin, 'Post-Cold War State Disintegration', 469.

18. Rubin, *Fragmentation of Afghanistan*, 259; Rubin, *Search for Peace*, 129; Goodson, *Afghanistan's Endless War*, 73–6. On the complexities of Afghan leadership, see also Olivier Roy, 'Afghanistan: Internal Politics and Socio-Economic Dynamics and Groupings', WRITENET paper no. 14/2002 (March 2003).

19. Rubin, *Search for Peace*, 128–35.

20. Abdul Salam Zaeef, *My Life with the Taliban* (London: Hurst & Co., 2010), 65.

21. Ahmed Rashid, *Taliban: Islam, Oil and the New Great Game in Central Asia* (London: I. B. Tauris, 2001 edn), 29; Olivier Roy, 'Changing Patterns among Radical Islamist Movements', *Brown Journal of World Affairs*, 6/1 (1999), 109–20, at 119; Gilles Kepel, *Jihad: The Trail of Political Islam* (London: I. B. Tauris, 2006 edn), 228–36; Nazif M. Shahrani, 'The Taliban Enigma: Person-Centred Politics & Extremism in Afghanistan', *ISIM Newsletter*, 6 (2000), 20–1.

22. Gilles Dorronsoro, *Revolution Unending: Afghanistan 1979 to the Present* (London: Hurst & Co., 2005), ch. 9 (quotation from p. 280); Faisal Devji, *Landscapes of the Jihad: Militancy, Morality, Modernity* (London: Hurst & Co., 2005), 22–3. For more on the modernism of the Taliban and also al-Qaeda, see Devji, *Landscapes of the Jihad*, and Faisal Devji, *The Terrorist in Search of Humanity: Militant Islam and Global Politics* (London: Hurst & Co., 2008).

23. Rashid, *Taliban*, 30; Neamotullah Nojumi, *The Rise of the Taliban in Afghanistan: Mass Mobilization, Civil War, and the Future of the Region* (New York: Palgrave, 2002), 136.

24. Rashid, *Taliban*, 35.

25. See Zalmay Khalilzad, 'Anarchy in Afghanistan', *Journal of International Affairs*, 51/1 (1997), 37–56; Ahmed Rashid, 'Back with a Vengeance: Proxy War in Afghanistan', *World Today*, 52/3 (1996), 60–3.

26. Rashid, *Taliban*, ch. 10; Thomas Hegghammer, *The Caravan: Abdallah Azzam and the Rise of Global Jihad* (Cambridge: Cambridge University Press, 2020); Don Rassler, 'Al-Qaida and the Pakistani Harakat Movement: Reflections and Questions about the Pre-2001 Period', *Perspectives on Terrorism*, 11/6 (2017), 38–54.

# Index

Leabharlanna Poiblí Chathair Baile Átha Cliath

Dublin City Public Libraries